A Documentary History of Slavery in North America

Winfred Sandler

A
Documentary History
of
Slavery in North America

Edited with Commentary by

Willie Lee Rose
The Johns Hopkins University

New York
Oxford University Press
London   1976   Toronto

for my husband William George Rose who cheered me on

Contents

SIX: THE SLAVE'S PROTEST: RESISTANCE SHORT OF REBELLION

Contents

NINE: MEN, WOMEN, AND CHILDREN

TEN: AFTER HOURS . . . BELIEFS AND AMUSEMENTS

Contents

Acknowledgments

I owe many debts to those who have made general and specific suggestions, although I can hardly hope to give thanks to all. My colleagues and graduate students at the University of Virginia and at The Johns Hopkins University, and abroad in the profession, have offered countless opportunities for conversation and the exploration of ideas. Nevertheless, many of the documents were found at the end of a long chase for a particular item that would make a particular point; therefore Peyton McCrary, Charles Cheape, Holt Merchant, and James T. Currie, who served one after another as research assistants at the University of Virginia, are especially to be thanked for doing so much of the chasing. They often provided helpful suggestions as well as the legwork in the libraries.

Individual items of special importance were suggested for inclusion by Miss Fredrika Teute, an editor on the Madison Papers publication project at the University of Virginia, by Professor Charles Dew of the University of Missouri at Columbia, by Professor Robert Dawidoff of the Claremont Graduate School, by Professor W. W. Freehling of The Johns Hopkins University, and Mr. Philip Leonard, then of the Virginia State Archives. Mr. Leonard, over the years, has offered numerous suggestions, and I am deeply grateful for all of them. Mr. Nicholas Oldsberg of the South Carolina Department of Archives and History gave me important help in pinpointing the submission of an undated petition. For permission to use manuscripts from the John Hartwell Cocke Papers at the University of Virginia, I thank Messrs Joseph F. Johnston and John Page Elliott. For permission to take an excerpt from Dr. Adolf Benson's translation of *Peter Kalm's Travels,* I thank Mrs. Sarah N. Tyler and Miss Emma Nichukon.

Presses and libraries granting me permission to reproduce works still under copyright, or restricted in some way, are named when the documents appear; their generous cooperation has made my work much easier. I want also to thank my colleague Professor John Baldwin particularly for his kind assistance in translating the quotations from the Latin that appear in documents 37 and 39. Mrs. Maria Stewart has done most of the typing, which was exacting and in many cases tedious. She performed nobly.

To Professor Alfred Young of the University of Northern Illinois are due special thanks for the consistent interest he has shown in this work over more years than I like to recall. He has read the entire manuscript several times, and made numerous helpful suggestions on style and content.

Acknowledgments

Though he is not to be held responsible for errors of fact or interpretation that may remain, his expert knowledge of the Colonial and early national periods came to my aid on many occasions, especially in the earlier chapters. Having discovered the unhappy truth that it is actually more difficult to convey a fair and balanced impression of truth through a selection of raw documents than with the full range of language and interpretation that the usual history affords, I would have given up the task more than once without Professor Young's enthusiasm for this project. I hope the volume may in some degree vindicate his faith and optimism.

My husband, William George Rose, is an honest and compassionate critic who has also given me the benefit of a careful reading of the entire manuscript. His comments I value especially, as coming from that rare and much-to-be-treasured being, the "educated lay reader" who tolerates no obscure or pedantic language. Only he knows how long this task has taken me, its real costs, and how many "holidays" were not holidays for either of us because of this book. For his patience and good humor I am deeply grateful, and it is therefore to him that I dedicate this volume.

W. L. R.

Baltimore
October 1, 1975

Introduction

There is an inherent frustration in assembling a book of documents—a frustration that develops slowly in the editor attempting the task for the first time. Like the child who has arranged his building blocks several ways, the editor may reach the conclusion at last, if he is a resolute realist, that he hasn't got a house. The documents will not speak for themselves, and the editor hasn't unlimited license to do it for them. To build a house one needs mortar, a little paint, a builder's permit, and responsibility. Therefore this particular editor must ruefully confess that the book the reader now has in hand will not be a history of slavery, but rather a book that may help the reader to *think* about the history of slavery, which is just what the editor has done in putting it together.

The effort began with the modest ambition to print a few significant documents that came to my attention in the course of research on a related topic. But as the collection grew, the idea evolved to make the documents illustrate the historical development of slavery in this country, to fit the pieces into a loose chronology that would suggest some of the paradoxes of our dark experience with bondage and mastership in a democratic republic. How slavery grew in the English colonies of North America in a particularly severe legal form at a time when free workers were among the freest and best-paid in the world raises questions as yet unanswered. How the Founding Fathers contented themselves with words against slavery and took no action, at the very time when opposition to what Judge St. George Tucker called *political* slavery grew strong enough to raise a revolution against England, is not, even after close attention by brilliant scholars, entirely clear. How slavery itself became milder in practice and harsher in statute and more restrictive of personal liberty during that very period when democratic and humanitarian influences were expanding poses a question that would in the answering, no doubt, resolve many another thorny question. It is not, however, the legitimate assignment of a documentary history to resolve such problems, but rather to illustrate them.

I have ventured also to indicate the remarkable variety of sources available to the study of the "peculiar institution," making the collection a sample case of travelers' accounts, fugitive slave narratives, songs and riddles, newspaper advertisements, legal cases, criminal trials, statutes, petitions, planters' diaries and inventories. Included are several examples of a most elusive kind of evidence—letters of slaves themselves. If including a few of every breed reminds the reader too much of Noah's incredible ark, I hope he will understand and sympathize at least, with my struggle to balance the load. Occasionally an interesting white elephant had to be left behind because two just like him were already aboard; sometimes a startlingly tiny creature, a mere snippet, was included because it represented some unique aspect of slavery, or some crucial moment in the development of slavery. Some of the documents were introduced primarily to demonstrate the value of the uncalculated offhand observation for the close scholar who distrusts set-piece adversary performances as mirrors of truth.

But beyond suggesting historical paradoxes, and demonstrating the variety that exists among the sources, I have hoped that the documents would also offer the reader an opportunity to see for himself some of the problems created for the historian by the shortcomings of the sources. Many readers will require no prompting from the editor to recognize the problems associated with the interpretation of these documents. The most intractable questions connected with American Negro slavery are still intractable because of the nature of the sources. For the early colonial period, especially the seventeenth century, the record is fragmentary, and limited—more than the historian would like it to be—to court records and statutes. Understanding these is often complicated by ambiguities of language, the change in the meaning of certain words over time, and further by the age-old difficulty of determining whether a given law reflects majority opinion and practice as it existed at some remote and particular moment in time, or an effort to change common habits of the common people. For instance, we may ask whether colonial statutes punishing miscegenation indicate that this practice was regarded by the lawmakers with special aversion, or that it was so common as to appear menacing to white society. (See document 2.) The implications about race prejudice in practice among the colonists would be exactly opposite. All we can say with perfect safety and confidence is that some citizens practiced miscegenation, and that others, for some reason, either economic, social, or religious, did not approve.

A slightly different problem is posed by the barbarous punishments meted out to slaves in the seventeenth and eighteenth centuries. How, in a period when free white offenders were for some crimes punished by branding and mutilation, when the heads of victims of the law rotted in full view of the public at the Tower of London, can we determine how much of the brutality experienced by slaves in the colonies was owing to their legal condition, built on racial slavery, and how much to the pervasive callousness and indifference of the society at large to human suffering? One thing is certain: historians should be most careful to pick their illustrations from the particular period they are studying, for the meaning of these punishments as an indication of social attitudes was much changed over time. What would have been shocking in the mid-nineteenth century would have been little more than a vague disturbance in ruder, cruder times, even though the victim's pain and humiliation were certainly as great.

With the advance of the eighteenth century, evidence of all kinds increases in volume, but it only reaches satisfactory proportions in the nineteenth century, when slavery began to be recognized as anachronistic, and as an acute moral and political dilemma. From the third decade of the nineteenth century the problem is no longer a problem of skimpiness—for reams were written about slavery—but one of credibility.

In one of his finer ironies, Jakob Burckhardt once wrote that "Ill deeds should, as far as possible, be committed naïvely, for the aesthetic effect of legal justifications and recriminations on both sides is deplorable." [1] Burckhardt, the great Swiss historian of the Italian Renaissance, had international exploitation and shabby conquests in mind, but the reader of many abolition attacks and certainly of the larger portion of the proslavery defense will understand the application. Slavery was not "committed" naïvely. Americans North and South, defenders and attackers in both sections, recognized that slavery was at variance with the principles of the Declaration of Independence, and the particular aesthetic effects of defending the institution in those circumstances were indeed deplorable.

Aside from the problem of aesthetics, however, the historian is left with the disagreeable fact that much of what he must regard as "primary evidence," and patiently consult as "the record," is in fact either polemical or defensive, and directly or indirectly influenced by the slavery debate. Because few thoughtful men of the nineteenth century were indifferent to the moral question—for which we must be grateful—few of our sources are morally indifferent. The historian is much in the position of a conscientious juror in a difficult murder trial. He must anticipate that the truthfulness of all important witnesses will sooner or later come under attack; yet in the end he must make up his own mind. He will be fortunate if his own integrity is not assailed by fellow jurors who have been persuaded to a different view.

It is fortunate that documents do not have to be truthful or accurate in every detail in order to be useful to scholars. With regard to the sources for slavery studies this becomes increasingly the case, because the questions that now interest the historian and the modern reader are no longer

1. Jakob Christoph Burckhardt, *Force and Freedom: Reflections on History*, ed. James Hastings Nichols (New York: Pantheon Books, 1943), p. 116.

quite the same as those of the century-old slavery debate. At least they certainly ought not to be the same. Thére is no longer the need to demonstrate that slavery was a destructive, immoral, and unjust social institution, but rather to discover in what ways it was destructive, the degree to which it was recognized as immoral, and the effects of its injustices on both the enslaved and the enslavers. Thus it is possible to find collateral uses for evidence that might once have been laughed out of court.

The utility of the source depends upon what sort of question has been raised. Even if the historian dismisses altogether the writings of abolitionists and the arguments of the pro-slavery writers—and this would in each case be an unnecessary handicap—he still has such unintentional evidence as plantation manuals and account books. He has also planters' letters, travelers' accounts, and narratives of fugitive slaves, and other self-conscious evidence that may be of great value if used with close attention to motive and interest—economic and ideological, overt and covert. But however much the historian may question some of the evidence he must use, he has to be glad that there is so much of it, because he has to sift it so carefully, and check it against other pieces of verifiable data. Too often the author must depend upon his own instinct to tell him when he has struck an important clue, and trust that the instinct is soundly based on a good understanding of his particular traveler, his particular fugitive slave, the circumstances of the slave's revelations, or his particular planter, and the circumstances of *his* revelations. It is, if anything, more dangerous to quote outside an understood context in the study of slavery than it is in almost any other topic in our history.

It is significant to know, for instance, that Austin Steward, who recounts (in document 57) an almost unbelievable instance of slave resistance in the late eighteenth century, that he was a responsible citizen who wrote his own book, who had held important offices in a community of organized fugitives in Canada, and that his autobiography is concerned with many subjects beyond the slavery debate. Of John Hartwell Cocke's report (document 91) on the morals and morale of his Alabama estate, it helps to know that he put private funds into the colonization of his own freed slaves in Liberia. About George Featherstonhaugh's report of the Creole father counting his children (document 86), one recalls that it is, after all, hearsay, however charming and witty in the telling. Of the Rose and Rufus story (document 88) there are further pros and cons to be borne in mind. Rose told her story long after the event, to someone else, who took it down. That person could possibly have influenced the form the story took. But would she have told that kind of story, about a forced mating, to a person who seemed unsympathetic? And if Rose had been aiming at sensationalism herself, would she have dealt so charitably with her former master, his grotesque requirement of her notwithstanding? Alas, the story bears the evidence of truth. It is good to know that Lucy McKim Garrison, who had the larger part in gathering the slave music of documents 98 and 101, was a very well-trained musician for her day. Even Nat Turner's account of the Southampton insurrection has to be read with the fact in mind that it was taken down by Dr. Thomas R. Gray, who was white, and not free of the passionate feelings then raging in his county.

In the explanatory headnotes I have attempted to sketch in enough of the context of each document to permit the reader to make his own discount for the prejudice of the author, and to judge the value of the "evidence." I have not attempted to snatch that obligation from the reader. I must assume responsibility for the choices, however, and to the extent that these reflect my own ideas of what is interesting about slavery as it existed in the United States, there is a built-in bias. The reader has a right to know about that.

Most of the documents reflect a preference for what might be called the "interior" aspects of the "peculiar institution," for the bits of evidence, sometimes most casually and indirectly offered, about the personal and psychological consequences of slavery for the persons of both colors who lived in its thrall, a taste for the human response that glimmers just beyond the tangible facts of work in the field, tedium, and hard discipline. Such evidence is elusive, and much of the best of it is not suitable for inclusion in a documentary history, for it is unself-consciously rendered, often buried as a casual aside in something wordy on some altogether different subject. But I have included such of this material of suitable length as I could find, trusting that the reader will understand why it is there.

With a few exceptions, writings specifically identifiable as contributions to the anti-slavery or pro-slavery arguments have been avoided. But certain aspects of the slavery debate are so thoroughly woven into the internal workings of slavery as to be indispensable. A slave-owning planter's defensiveness may be of the kind that protests too much, that searches Scripture too feverishly for holy sanction, that always prefers the word "servant" to the word "slave," or even "Negro." When such passages seemed to speak loudly about the man as master, they are included. Sometimes one is able to make a calculated guess about whether the planter had suppressed feelings of guilt, and if he had, whether those surfaced as aggression against his slaves, or a private life of personal torment, or some further complicated form of masochism. The witness of a slave master who criticizes others of his class for bad treatment of slaves is about the most persuasive condemnation of slavery readily available. It also reveals some sense of the fitness of things as understood in the planter's community, and is therefore valuable because it does so.

Fugitive slave narratives have also been included in a number of instances, even when the author was also a prominent abolitionist, as was Frederick Douglass. What Douglass had to say seemed relevant to the interior theme: it seemed to explain some difficult psychological points for the comprehension of moderns living relatively free lives in the mid-twentieth century. Certain things only a slave could know, and only a fugitive had an opportunity to describe. Aside from the songs and stories, the riddles, and other cultural survivals from slavery, there is no other way to resurrect the underside of slavery than through the recollections of survivors themselves.

But to say that the emphasis of the present volume is on what might be called the "interior" aspects of slavery is to do no more than fix an angle of vision. Actually many of the most lively and tightly-argued controversies in the scholarship of this subject hinge upon still unresolved enigmas of this interior view. A number of questions would yield to analysis more readily if we had a clearer idea of what life was like from day to day on certain given kinds of plantations, in certain given periods of time, in definable regions. We would then know better how to interpret actions of masters and slaves, and would be better able to determine whether some actions of slaves are called more properly accommodation or resistance. What *is* resistance in a slave society? Were some slave groups more militant in their resistance than others because of the tradition they came from, or the life they entered in the New World? and can we distinguish between a consciously adopted role of servile obedience and the role as it was internalized in "Sambo"?

So much for the first general area of debate. A second that would profit also from a closer view of the inner workings of slavery has to do with the role of law in the evolution of slavery as an institution in this country, and the significance of the statutory law as governor and indicator of personal relations under the slave regime. Was race prejudice, or the need for labor in good supply, the stronger force in the seventeenth-century beginnings of slavery? To what extent did religion and nineteenth-century "sensibility" soften the harsh face of the law? What role did racial fears and tensions play in the retention of slavery?

Above all, it must be recognized that only through an "interior" view is it possible to reach a sensible conclusion concerning the nearly exhausted subject of the personality of slaves, the degree to which slaves were able to maintain a sense of individuality in the face of a regime designed to obliterate individual urgings. The same may be said of the other face of the "personality" question: what were the effects of owning slaves on the slave-owning class? Like the opposite poles of a magnetic field, slave and master held one another in suspension. They were what they were because of each other, and each, in no fanciful sense, created the role of the other.

The master's power was so nearly absolute that his effectiveness in this process is easier to recognize than the slave's. This was not because the statues failed to define the wanton killing of a slave as murder, for they did; or because cruel and unusual punishments were not forbidden, for they were; but because the slave himself had no procedural means of redress worthy of the name. His testimony could not be accepted in court against his master, even if his case got that far. Whipping was not regarded in any case as being out of the ordinary unless conducted with great viciousness, and calculated to kill, which was a very difficult matter to prove. Given this situation, the slave's role as an exploited agricultural laborer was laid out for him by every sanction of society, and society expected the master to keep his slaves from offending other white people by word or deed, if not by thought.

But when we observe families discussing what to do about child abuse, (as one does in document 79), and when we come upon "Box" Brown relating his own condition as a slave to the Christian religion professed by himself as well as his owner (document 56), when we find slaves making decisions for themselves and for their owners (as in documents 77 and 61) we know that this is no easy question to answer, and that it is necessary to look behind the laws to discover the practice of slavery in individual communities and on individual plantations. Only then can a satisfactory generalization arise, one that covers the full variety of response on the part of the master and the slave.

Because men are not animals, even slaves were dealt with best by the provision of some human incentives; and so we discover, in the case of a master whose slaves are about to be hired for work in an iron foundry, a certain reservation about sending them where they do not want to go (document 65). They could run away, and it is therefore the task of the employer to outwit the slaves, if he can, and somehow show the owner that he will not suffer a disadvantage. The diverse occupations slaves were put to indicates more than specialized training for special tasks; it often indicates as well the necessity of the slave's assuming responsibility for choices. To a much larger degree than has been supposed, slave "drivers" made decisions about farming operations as well as the morale of the workers. They were often "broken" by their masters for failure in the second responsibility, and being "driver" was in that way not altogether unlike appointment to political office.

It must also be said, however, that not every master regarded force as a failure of diplomacy, but rather took force as a first recourse. Triumphant manifestations of the human personality had difficulty surviving on plantations owned by such men. The master made the difference, and some there were too avaricious to care for the feelings of their slaves or their neighbors, too sick of mind to notice either, or too stupid to consult their own best interests.

Such questions as those suggested above do not yield to statistical analysis. Even if one chose some arbitrary indicator that could be counted—for instance, the numbers of uprisings, the numbers of runnings-away, or the numbers of slaves who had their own economic enterprises apart from their masters—the incidents themselves could not be read correctly without a close study of the context of each incident. Unlike housing and mortality statistics, or rates of morbidity, psychological attitudes yield to individual analysis only. Only one measure comes to mind as a partial aid. The numbers of freedmen who took the initiative for their own fate in 1865 indicates that the majority of slaves had gained a respect for education and understood the value of independently owned farm property for a man who must make his living on farming. And of course others were for some time bewildered by the challenges of freedom appearing so suddenly. At the other end of the spectrum were those who offered violent resistance to the slave system, but when resistance was undertaken impulsively and individually, the action was usually self-destructive. Most slaves learned how to channel their opposition more effectively.

The survival of individuality among slaves is owing not exclusively to the master's perception of the wiser course in dealing with his chattels, but as much to the slave's knowledge of the psychological needs of his master, and the slave's competence in deploying subtly his tenuous advantages as a "dependent." By this means the slave had a hand in creating the master's role. By working assiduously for his master's interests, by strictly subordinating his own will (or appearing to do so), the slave could win for himself some room for maneuver. By excessive gratefulness, by flattery, by praising his master to others (who might tell the master), a certain kind of slave could, in a manner of speaking, put a certain kind of master on his best behavior. Conversely, a foresighted slave might add to his quiver of rewards a few poison arrows: the tendency to break, lose, or destroy equipment, extreme puzzlement over simple instructions, or abuse of livestock. These were, of course, very dangerous weapons if not judiciously employed, and could easily backfire. Whether they are properly called "resistance" is a matter of controversy, one that depends on how much political organization and intent a given historian requires for a definition of "resistance." But surely psychological manipulation gained the slave the opportunity to score occasionally in the battle of wills.

There is a certain kind of strength that goes with weakness, and a certain weakness that goes with strength, as the diaries of courtesans will demonstrate, and as children have always known. This is because power likes approval, and there are means that power dislikes to employ. The slave who learned to exploit these techniques for survival on the precarious raft of another man's good will has been called "Sambo," an inglorious sobriquet indeed, with cowardly connotations. But it is presumptuous in posterity to dismiss contemptuously the methods that enabled generations of slaves to endure their harsh lot in life, and to snatch from it a few human satisfactions.

At the end of the Civil War, Mary Boykin Chesnut described her father-in-law, whom she considered to be representative, at ninety-three, blind and deaf, of the best of his class: "Partly patriarch, partly *grand seigneur*, this old man is of a species that we will see no more; the last of the lordly planters who ruled this Southern world. His manners are unequalled still, but underneath this smooth exterior lies the grip of a tyrant whose will has never been crossed." [2] From masters with elegant manners to those with the worst, all shared a common attribution of uncommon power. Slavery, under these circumstances, did not have to be the most profitable institution available for investment, but merely a viable one. There were so many other gratifications. The self-image of the patriarch was agreeable, as William Byrd wrote the Earl of Orrery, early in the eighteenth century:

> Besides the advantage of a pure Air, we abound in all kinds of Provisions without expence (I mean we who have Plantations). I have a large Family of my own, and my doors are open to Every Body yet I have no Bills to pay, and half-a-Crown will rest undisturbed in my pocket for many Moons together. Like one of the Patriarchs, I have my Flocks and my Herds, my Bond-men and

2. *A Diary from Dixie*, ed. Ben Ames Williams (Boston: Houghton Mifflin, Sentry edition, 1949), p. 534.

Bond-women, and every Soart [sort] of Trade amongst my own Servants, so that I live in a kind of Independence on every one but Providence. However this Soart of Life is without expence, yet it is attended with a great deal of trouble. I must take care to keep all my people to their Duty, to set all the Springs in motion and to make every one draw his equal Share to carry the Machine forward. But then 'tis an amusement in this silent Country and a continual exercise of our Patience and Economy.[3]

"Independence" is the key word, for Byrd and for those who followed him. Studying their behavior, and the behavior of those who lived under, with, around, behind, and beyond the little autocracies the planters built has provided me with many hours of reflection about the nature of freedom and bondage. In the slave era these conditions were nearly absolute, though those who lived in the two respective conditions lived in close proximity. In more recent times the conditions have lost much of their sharpness, and there are few who would say that they are absolutely free, but rather under some bonds to a distant and intangible economic force, a political authority, a human failing of their own, or even a tyrannical idea. The bonds are various and harder to identify. If these hundred-odd fragments from the record of human slavery reflect some incidental light on the significance of freedom, and the art of living a free life, the editor will be well satisfied.

3. July 5, 1726, in *Virginia Magazine of History and Biography* 32 (December 1924):27.

ONE
Slavery in the English Colonies of North America

1. The First Blacks Arrive in Virginia

Very little is known about the real status and ultimate destiny of the first black people brought to Virginia in 1619. From the limited evidence available, however, it is possible to establish a few facts. These persons were undoubtedly picked up in the Spanish West Indies by a Dutch privateer in the course of what was otherwise an unprofitable plundering expedition. The Dutch vessel sailed northward for the Virginia capes in the company of the *Treasurer,* an English privateer that had been in the West Indies on the same business, and with no better luck. Both ships were in need of supplies. The *Treasurer,* arriving a few days after the Dutch ship, and also carrying Negroes, was not permitted to trade with the colony, because the King objected to the colonists' encouraging English vessels in their marauding of the Spaniards. For this reason the colonial leaders may have minimized the number of blacks they accepted in exchange for provisions with the Dutch ship.

Though the evidence suggests that the Governor himself, and the Cape merchant, bought the blacks, we know little or nothing about the blacks' status. There were then no statutes establishing slavery, and at least some of the blacks brought into the colony in 1619 became free men within a few years. But why? Because they may have been Christian converts? Because they were emancipated by their masters? Or because the institution of slavery had not evolved out of the widely practiced indenture system that covered servants coming from England? In any case, that these first comers were "bought" does not prove slavery, because the same word was used to describe the employment of indentured white servants. Even prospective wives were "bought."

Here, in a letter to Sir Edwin Sandys, John Rolfe, then Secretary and Recorder of the Virginia colony, quietly sets down the beginning of the history of blacks in British North America.

John Rolfe to Sir Edwin Sandys, January? 1619/20.

About the latter end of August, a Dutch man of Warr of the burden of a 160 tuñes arriued at Point-Comfort, the Commando^rs name Capt Jope, his Pilott for the West Indies one Mr Marmaduke an Englishman. They mett wth the Trẽr in the West Indyes, and deter-

Source: Susan Myra Kingsbury, ed., *The Records of the Virginia Company of London,* 4 vols. (Washington, D.C.: U.S. Government Printing Office, 1933), 3:243.

myned to hold consort shipp hether-
ward, but in their passage lost one the
other. He brought not any thing but
20. and odd Negroes, wch the Governo^r
and Cape Marchant bought for vic-
tualle (whereof he was in greate need

as he p[re]tended) at the best and ea-
syest rate they could. He hadd a lardge
and ample Comÿssion from his Ex-
cellency to range and to take purchase
in the West Indyes.

2. Slavery Becomes a Legal Fact in Virginia

Historians who disagree about the original status of the Negro "servants"
of 1619 have no problem in agreeing that, whatever the earliest practice,
the colonial statutes of Virginia did not acknowledge slavery until 1661.
Virginia was the third colony to make legal recognition of the condition
that had evolved out of indentured servitude. During the forty years following the arrival of the Dutch man-of-war in 1619, slavery developed as a
legal institution. It is therefore with considerable interest that the historian examines the first appearance of separate forms of punishment for
Negro servants. If he has some idea that color prejudice may have preceded slavery rather than the other way around, the historian will examine
the early occasions of the punishment of fornication between white and
black persons most closely. At what point did the runaway servant, black,
become subject to different and more degrading punishments than the
runaway servant, white? and why? It is plain that whether the laws were
endorsements of current practice, or designed to change practice, they
were ever more heavily marking the line between white and black, servant
and slave.

The following documents are taken from the Virginia laws. The first two
are decisions made by the Governor and his Council sitting as a court. The

Source: William Waller Hening, ed., *The Statutes at Large: Being a Collection of All the Laws of Virginia, from the First Session of the Legislature in the Year 1619*, 13 vols. (Richmond, 1809–23). Hereafter cited as *Statutes.*

other items are statutes of the Assembly. In each case the year of the decision or Act is enclosed in brackets.

[1630]

September 17th, 1630. Hugh Davis to be soundly whipped, before an assembly of Negroes and others for abusing himself to the dishonor of God and shame of Christians, by defiling his body in lying with a negro; which fault he is to acknowledge next Sabbath day.
Statutes 1:146

[1640]

Robert Sweet to do penance in church according to laws of England, for getting a negroe woman with child and the woman whipt.
Statutes 1:552

[1659–60]
Act XIV.
An Act for repealing an Act for Irish Servants.

Whereas the act for Irish servants comeing in without indentures enjoyning them to serve six yeeres, carried with it both rigour and inconvenience, many by the length of time they have to serve discouraged from comeing into the country, And by that meanes the peopling of the country retarded, And these inconveniencies augmented by the addition of the last clause in that act, That all aliens should be included, *Bee it therefore enacted and confirmed,* That the whole act be repealed

and made void and null, And that for the future no servant comeing into the country without indentures, of what christian nation soever, shall serve longer then those of our own country, of the like age: *And it is further enacted,* That what alien soever arrive here before that clause was inserted and that hath been by vertue of that last clause inforced to serve any time longer then the custom of the countrey did oblige them to shall be allowed competent wages by their severall masters for the time they have overserved, Any act, order of court or judgment to the contrary notwithstanding, *Provided alwaies* that all such aliens as came in servants during the time that the said clause was in force shall serve according to the tenor of that act.
Statutes 1:538–39

[1659–60]
Act XVI.
An Act for the Dutch and all other Strangers for Tradeing to this Place.

Whereas the restriction of trade hath appeared to be the greatest impediment to the advance of the estimation and value of our present only commodity tobacco, *Bee it enacted and confirmed,* That the Dutch and all strangers of what Xtian nation soever in amity with the people of England shall have free liberty to trade with vs, for all allowable comodities, And receive protection from vs to our vtmost powers

[17]

while they are in our jurisdiction, and shall have equall right and justice with our own nation in all courts of judicature, *Provided* they give bond and pay the impost of tenn shillings per hogshead laid vpon all tobacco exported to any fforreigne dominions and give bond according to act, *Alwaies provided,* That if the said Dutch or other forreiners shall import any negro slaves, They the said Dutch or others shall, for the tobacco really produced by the sale of the said negro, pay only the impost of two shillings per hogshead, the like being paid by our owne nation.
Statutes 1:540

[1660–61]
Act XXII.
English running away with negroes.

Bee itt enacted That in case any English servant shall run away in company with any negroes who are incapable of makeing satisfaction by addition of time, *Bee it enacted* that the English so running away in company with them shall serve for the time of the said negroes absence as they are to do for their owne by a former act.
Statutes 2:26

[1661–62]
Act CII.
Run-aways.

Whereas there are diverse loytering runaways in this country who very often absent themselves from their masters service and sometimes in a long time cannot be found, the losse of the time and the charge in the seeking

them often exceeding the value of their labor: *Bee it therefore enacted* that all runaways that shall absent themselves from their said masters service, shalbe lyable to make satisfaction by service after the times by custome or indenture is expired (vizt.) double their times of service soe neglected, and if the time of their running away was in the crop or the charge of recovering them extraordinary the court shall lymitt a longer time of service proportionable to the damage the master shall make appeare he hath susteyned, and because the adjudging the time they should serve is often referred untill the time by indenture is expired, when the proofe of what is due is very uncertaine, *it is enacted* that the master of any runaway that intends to take the benefitt of this act, shall as soone as he hath recovered him carry him to the next commissioner and there declare and prove the time of his absence, and the charge he hath bin at in his recovery, which commissioner thereupon shall grant his certificate, and the court on that certificate passe judgment for the time he shall serve for his absence; and in case any English servant shall run away in company of any negroes who are incapable of making satisfaction by addition of a time, *it is enacted* that the English soe running away in the company with them shall at the time of service to their owne masters expired, serve the masters of the said negroes for thier absence soe long as they should have done by this act if they had not beene slaves, every christian in company serving his proportion; and if the negroes be lost or dye in such time of their being run away, the christian servants in company with

them shall by proportion among them, either pay fower thousand five hundred pounds of tobacco and caske or fower yeares service for every negro soe lost or dead.
Statutes 2:116–17

[1662]
Act XII.
Negro womens children to serve according to the condition of the mother.

Whereas some doubts have arrisen whether children got by any Englishman upon a negro woman should be slave or ffree, *Be it therefore enacted and declared by this present grand assembly,* that all children borne in this country shalbe held bond or free only according to the condition of the mother, *And* that if any christian shall committ ffornication with a negro man or woman, hee or shee soe offending shall pay double the ffines imposed by the former act.
Statutes 2:170

[1667]
Act III.
An act declaring that baptisme of slaves doth not exempt them from bondage.

Whereas some doubts have risen whether children that are slaves by birth, and by the charity and piety of their owners made pertakers of the blessed sacrament of baptisme, should by vertue of their baptisme be made ffree; *It is enacted and declared by this grand assembly, and the authority thereof,* that the conferring of baptisme doth not alter the condition of the person as to his bondage or ffreedome; that diverse masters, ffreed from this doubt, may more carefully endeavor the propagation of christianity by permitting children, though slaves, or those of greater growth if capable to be admitted to that sacrament.
Statutes 2:260

[1670]
Act V.
Noe Negroes nor Indians to buy christian servants.

Whereas it hath beene questioned whither Indians or negroes manumited, or otherwise free, could be capable of purchasing christian servants, *It is enacted* that noe negro or Indian though baptised and enjoyned their owne ffreedome shall be capable of any such purchase of christians, but yet not debarred from buying any of their owne nation.
Statutes 2:280–81

[1670]
Act XII.
What tyme Indians to serve.

Whereas some dispute have arisen whither Indians taken in warr by any other nation, and by that nation that taketh them sold to the English, are servants for life or terme of yeares, *It is resolved and enacted* that all servants not being christians imported into this colony by shipping shalbe slaves for their lives; but what shall come by land shall serve, if boyes or girles, un-

till thirty yeares of age, if men or women twelve yeares and no longer.
Statutes 2:283

[1680]
Act X.
An act for preventing Negroes Insurrections.

Whereas the frequent meeting of considerable numbers of negroe slaves under pretence of feasts and burialls is judged of dangerous consequence; for prevention whereof for the future, *Bee it enacted by the kings most excellent majestie by and with the consent of the generall assembly, and it is hereby enacted by the authority aforesaid,* that from and after the publication of this law, it shall not be lawfull for any negroe or other slave to carry or arme himselfe with any club, staffe, gunn, sword or any other weapon of defence or offence, nor to goe or depart from of his masters ground without a certificate from his master, mistris or overseer, and such permission not to be granted but upon perticuler and necessary occasions; and every negroe or slave soe offending not haveing a certificate as aforesaid shalbe sent to the next constable, who is hereby enjoyned and required to give the said negroe twenty lashes on his bare back well layd on, and soe sent home to his said master, mistris or overseer. *And it is further enacted by the authority aforesaid* that if any negroe or other slave shall presume to lift up his hand in opposition against any christian, shall for every such offence, upon due proofe made thereof by the oath of the party before a magistrate, have and receive

thirty lashes on his bare back well laid on. *And it is hereby further enacted by the authority aforesaid* that if any negroe or other slave shall absent himself from his masters service and lye hid and lurking in obscure places, comitting injuries to the inhabitants, and shall resist any person or persons that shalby any lawfull authority be imployed to apprehend and take the said negroe, that then in case of such resistance, it shalbe lawfull for such person or persons to kill the said negroe or slave soe lying out and resisting, and that this law be once every six months published at the respective county courts and parish churches within this colony.
Statutes 2:481–82

[1691]
Act XVI.
An act for suppressing outlying Slaves.

Whereas many times negroes, mulattoes, and other slaves unlawfully absent themselves from their masters and mistresses service, and lie hid and lurk in obscure places killing hoggs and committing other injuries to the inhabitants of this dominion, for remedy whereof for the future, *Be it enacted by their majesties lieutenant governour, councell and burgesses of this present generall assembly and the authoritie thereof, and it is hereby enacted,* that in all such cases upon intelligence of any such negroes, mulattoes, or other slaves lying out, two of their majesties justices of the peace of that county, whereof one to be of the quorum, where such negroes, mulattoes or other slave shall be, shall be impowered and commanded, and are hereby impowered and commanded to issue out their warrants directed to the sherrife of the same county to apprehend such negroes, mulattoes, and other slaves, which said sherriffe is hereby likewise required upon all such occasions to raise such and soe many forces from time to time as he shall think convenient and necessary for the effectuall apprehending such negroes, mulattoes and other slaves, and in case any negroes, mulattoes or other slave or slaves lying out as aforesaid shall resist, runaway, or refuse to deliver and surrender him or themselves to any person or persons that shall be by lawfull authority employed to apprehend and take such negroes, mulattoes or other slaves that in such cases it shall and may be lawfull for such person and persons to kill and distroy such negroes, mulattoes, and other slave or slaves by gunn or any otherwaise whatsoever.

Provided that where any negroe or mulattoe slave or slaves shall be killed in pursuance of this act, the owner or owners of such negro or mulatto slave shall be paid for such negro or mulatto slave four thousand pounds of tobacco by the publique. And for prevention of that abominable mixture and spurious issue which hereafter may encrease in this dominion, as well by negroes, mulattoes, and Indians intermarrying with English, or other white women, as by their unlawfull accompanying with one another, *Be it enacted by the authoritie aforesaid, and it is hereby enacted,* that for the time to come, whatsoever English or other white man or women being free shall intermarry with a negroe, mulatto, or Indian man or woman bond or free, shall within three months after such marriage be banished and removed from this dominion forever, and that the justices of each respective countie within this dominion make it their perticular care, that this act be put in effectuall execution. *And be it further enacted by the authoritie aforesaid, and it is hereby enacted,* That if any English woman being free shall have a bastard child by any negro or mulatto, she pay the sume of fifteen pounds sterling, within one moneth after such bastard child shall be born, to the Church wardens of the parish where she shall be delivered of such child, and in default of such payment she shall be taken into the possession *[of]* the said Church wardens and disposed of for five yeares, and the said fine of fifteen pounds, or whatever the woman shall be disposed of for, shall be paid, one third part to their majesties for and towards the support of the government and the contingent charges thereof, and the other third part to the use of the parish where the offence is committed, and the other third part to the informer, and that such bastard child be bound out as a servant by the said Church wardens untill he or she shall attaine the age of thirty yeares, and in case such English woman that shall have such bastard child be a servant, she shall be sold by the said Church wardens, (after her time is expired that she ought by law to serve her master) for five yeares, and the money she shall be sold for divided as is before appointed, and the child to serve as aforesaid.

And forasmuch as great inconveniences may happen to this country by the setting of negroes and mulattoes free, by their either entertaining negro slaves from their masters service, or receiveing stolen goods, or being grown old bringing a charge upon the country; for prevention thereof, *Be it enacted by the authority aforesaid, and it is hereby enacted,* That no negro or mulatto be after the end of this present session of assembly set free by any person or persons whatsoever, unless such person or persons, their heires, executors or administrators pay for the transportation of such negro or negroes out of the countrey within six moneths after such setting them free, upon penalty of paying of tenn pounds sterling to the Church wardens of the parish where such person shall dwell with, which money, or so much thereof as shall be necessary, the said Church wardens are to cause the said negro or mulatto to be transported out of the countrey, and the remainder of the said money to imploy to the use of the poor of the parish.

Statutes 3:86–88

---

3. Virginia Discriminates in the Punishment of Runaways

The Council and the General Court had occasion in the summer of 1640 to punish two groups of servants who had run away from Virginia masters. In each group there was one Negro, and in each case the Negro received a significantly different punishment from that of his white companions. There are multiple ambiguities in the law, making interpretation of motive and intent difficult, but it seems probable that both these black men, John Punch and Emanuel, served for the rest of their lives. That is the probable reason they were punished not by the addition of time but by being whipped.

9th OF JULY 1640.
Whereas Hugh Gwyn hath by order from this Board Brought back from *Maryland* three servants formerly run away from the said *Gwyn, the court doth therefore order* that the said three

Source: Henry R. McIlwaine, ed., *Minutes of the Council and General Court of Colonial Virginia 1622–1632, 1670–1676. With Notes and Excerpts from Original Council and General Court Records, into 1683, Now Lost* (Richmond: Virginia State Library, 1924), pp. 466–67.

servants shall receive the punishment of whipping and to have thirty stripes apiece one called *Victor, a dutchman,* the other a *Scotchman* called *James Gregory,* shall first serve out their times with their master according to their Indentures, and one whole year apiece after the time of their service is Expired. By their said Indentures in recompense of his Loss sustained by their absence and after that service to their said master is Expired to serve the colony for three whole years apiece, and that the third being a negro named *John Punch* shall serve his said master or his assigns for the time of his natural Life here or elsewhere.

JULY 22, 1640.

Whereas complaint has been made to this Board by Capt *Wm Pierce* Esqr that six of his servants and a negro of Mr *Reginolds* has plotted to run away unto the *Dutch* plantation from their said masters and did assay to put the same in Execution upon *Saturday* night being the 18th day *July* 1640 as appeared to the Board by the Examinations of *Andrew Noxe, Richd Hill, Richd Cookeson* and *John Williams* and likewise by the confession of *Christopher Miller, Peter Wilcocke,* and *Emanuel* the foresaid Negro who had at the fore said time, taken the skiff of the said Capt *Wm Pierce* their master, and corn powder and shot and guns, to accomplish their said purposes, which said p[er]sons sailed down in the said skiff to *Elizabeth* river where they were

taken and brought back again, the Court taking the same into consideration, as a dangerous p[re]cident for the future time (if unpunished) did order that *Christopher Miller* a *dutchman* (a prince agent in the business) should receive the punishment of whipping and to have thirty stripes, and to be burnt in the cheek with the letter R and to work with a shakle on his legg for one whole year, and longer if said master shall see cause and after his full time of service is Expired with his said master to serve the colony for seven whole years, and the said *Peter Wilcocke* to receive thirty stripes and to be Burnt in the cheek with the letter R and, after his term of service is Expired with his said master to serve the colony for three years and the said *Richd Cookson* after his full time expired with his master to serve the colony for two years and a half, and the said *Richd Hill* to remain upon his good behaviour until the next offence and the said *Andrew Noxe* to receive thirty stripes, and the said *John Williams* a *dutchman* and a Chirugeon after his full time of service is Expired with his master to serve the colony for seven years, and *Emanuel* the Negro to receive thirty stripes and to be burnt in the cheek with the letter R. and to work in shakle one year or more as his master shall fee cause, and all those who are condemned to serve the colony after their times are expired with their masters, then their said masters are required hereby to p[re]sent to this board their said servants so condemned to the colony.

4. Maryland Establishes Slavery for Life

In a Maryland statute of 1664 the fateful phrase *durante vita* appeared, stipulating "service for life." At the same time the condition of children of slaves was fixed after that of their fathers. The intention of the law was, apparently, to discourage the mating of white women with Negro slaves, for in this case the children of these white women would be slaves. But the policy of following the paternal line was soon dropped, because by its terms the free mulatto population developed at the same rate that white men impregnated slave women. Thus rapidly did an important fundamental of English law give way before the combined forces of racial antipathy, sexual license, and the need of an exploitable labor force in the new plantation country.

An Act Concerning Negroes & other Slaues.

Bee itt Enacted by the Right Honble the Lord Proprietary by the aduice and Consent of the upper and lower house of this present Generall Assembly That all Negroes or other slaues already within the Prouince And all Negroes and other slaues to bee hereafter imported into the Prouince shall serue Durante Vita[.] And all Children born of any Negro or other slaue shall be Slaues as their ffathers were for the terme of their liues[.] And forasmuch as divers freeborne English women forgettfull of their free Condicōn and to the disgrace of our Nation doe inter-marry with Negro Slaues by which alsoe diuers suites may arise touching the Issue of such woemen and a great damage doth befall the Masters of such Negroes for preuention whereof for deterring such freeborne women from such shamefull Matches Bee itt further Enacted by the Authority advice and Consent aforesaid That whatsoever free borne woman shall inter marry with any slaue from and after the Last day of this present Assembly shall Serue the master of such slaue dureing the life of her husband And that all the Issue of such freeborne woemen soe marryed shall be Slaues as their fathers were[.] And Bee itt further Enacted that all the Issues of English or other freeborne woemen that haue already marryed Negroes shall serve the Masters of their Parents till they be Thirty yeares of age and noe longer.

Source: William Hand Browne, ed., *Archives of Maryland: Proceedings and Acts of the General Assembly of Maryland, January, 1637/8–September, 1664* (Baltimore: Maryland Historical Society, 1883), pp. 533–34.

5. Robert Beverley Distinguishes between Servants and Slaves

Whatever confusion may have existed about the slave status of black persons in the early decades following 1620, by the beginning of the eighteenth century the legal distinctions between black and white, slave and indentured servant, were generally understood. In 1703 Robert Beverley, a young Virginian traveling in England, was asked to read a manuscript by John Oldmixon about the Virginia colony. Beverley found the account to be so full of error that he could not begin to set the author straight, and so determined to write a book of his own about Virginia. This he did in 1705.

In the selection below, drawn from a second revised edition completed in 1722, Beverley describes the condition of slaves and servants, explaining the differences between the labor assigned to the women of the two groups, and the legal position of indentured servants. Beverley's emphasis on the favorable position of servants is undoubtedly owing to a desire to encourage the immigration to Virginia of white labor. While he may have exaggerated the happiness of those in indentures, in his description of their legal defenses he clearly tells, by omission, of defenses that the slaves did *not* have.

OF THE SERVANTS AND SLAVES
IN VIRGINIA.

§ 50. Their servants they distinguish by the names of slaves for life, and servants for a time.

Slaves are the negroes and their posterity, following the condition of the mother, according to the maxim, *partus frequitur ventrem.* They are called slaves, in respect of the time of their servitude, because it is for life.

Servants, are those which serve only for a few years, according to the time of their indenture, or the custom of the country. The custom of the country takes place upon such as have no indentures. The law in this case is, that if such servants be under nineteen years of age, they must be brought into court to have their age adjudged; and from the age they are judged to be of, they must serve until they reach four and twenty; but if they be adjudged upwards of nineteen, they are then only to be servants for the term of five years.

Source: Robert Beverley, *The History of Virginia, in Four Parts.* Reprinted from the Author's Second Revised Edition, London, 1722 (Richmond: J. W. Randolph, 1855), pp. 219-22.

§ 51. The male servants, and slaves of both sexes, are employed together in tilling and manuring the ground, in sowing and planting tobacco, corn, &c. Some distinction indeed is made between them in their clothes, and food; but the work of both is no other than what the overseers, the freemen, and the planters themselves do.

Sufficient distinction is also made between the female servants, and slaves; for a white woman is rarely or never put to work in the ground, if she be good for anything else; and to discourage all planters from using any women so, their law makes female servants working in the ground tithables, while it suffers all other white women to be absolutely exempted; whereas, on the other hand, it is a common thing to work a woman slave out of doors, nor does the law make any distinction in her taxes, whether her work be abroad or at home.

§ 52. Because I have heard how strangely cruel and severe the service of this country is represented in some parts of England, I can't forbear affirming, that the work of their servants and slaves is no other than what every common freeman does; neither is any servant required to do more in a day than his overseer; and I can assure you, with great truth, that generally their slaves are not worked near so hard, nor so many hours in a day, as the husbandmen, and day laborers in England. An overseer is a man, that having served his time, has acquired the skill and character of an experienced planter, and is therefore entrusted with the direction of the servants and slaves.

But to complete this account of servants, I shall give you a short relation of the care their laws take, that they be used as tenderly as possible:

BY THE LAWS OF THEIR COUNTRY,

1. All servants whatsoever have their complaints heard without fee or reward; but if the master be found faulty, the charge of the complaint is cast upon him, otherwise the business is done *ex officio*.

2. Any justice of the peace may receive the complaint of a servant, and order everything relating thereto, till the next county court, where it will be finally determined.

3. All masters are under the correction and censure of the county courts, to provide for their servants good and wholesome diet, clothing and lodging.

4. They are always to appear upon the first notice given of the complaint of their servants, otherwise to forfeit the service of them until they do appear.

5. All servants' complaints are to be received at any time in court, without process, and shall not be delayed for want of form; but the merits of the complaint must be immediately enquired into by the justices; and if the master cause any delay therein, the court may remove such servants, if they see cause, until the master will come to trial.

6. If a master shall at any time disobey an order of court, made upon any complaint of a servant, the court is empowered to remove such servant forthwith to another master who will be kinder, giving to the former master the produce only, (after fees deducted,) of

what such servants shall be sold for by public outcry.

7. If a master should be so cruel, as to use his servant ill, that is fallen sick or lame in his service, and thereby rendered unfit for labor, he must be removed by the church wardens out of the way of such cruelty, and boarded in some good planter's house, till the time of his freedom, the charge of which must be laid before the next county court, which has power to levy the same, from time to time, upon the goods and chattels of the master, after which, the charge of such boarding is to come upon the parish in general.

8. All hired servants are entitled to these privileges.

9. No master of a servant can make a new bargain for service, or other matter with his servant, without the privity and consent of the county court, to prevent the masters overreaching, or scaring such servant into an unreasonable compliance.

10. The property of all money and goods sent over thither to servants, or carried in with them, is reserved to themselves, and remains entirely at their disposal.

11. Each servant at his freedom receives of his master ten bushels of corn, (which is sufficient for almost a year,) two new suits of clothes, both linen and woolen, and a gun, twenty shillings value, and then becomes as free in all respects, and as much entitled to the liberties and privileges of the country, as any of the inhabitants or natives are, if such servants were not aliens.

12. Each servant has then also a right to take up fifty acres of land, where he can find any unpatented.

This is what the laws prescribe in favor of servants, by which you may find, that the cruelties and severities imputed to that country, are an unjust reflection. For no people more abhor the thoughts of such usage, than the Virginians, nor take more precaution to prevent it now, whatever it was in former days.

---

6. The Reverend Le Jau Proselytizes Slaves on the Carolina Frontier

---

The colonial frontier of South Carolina moved out from Charleston in two directions—both toward the interior and toward the ocean—over the rich marshlands that extended to the north and the southwest of the little

Source: Francis Le Jau, *The Carolina Chronicle of Dr. Francis Le Jau, 1706–1717*, ed. Frank W. Klingberg (Berkeley: University of California Press, 1956), pp. 60–137 *passim*. Reprinted by permission of the Regents of the University of California.

town. Early in the eighteenth century the Society for the Propagation of the Gospel sent out missionaries from England to encourage the practice of the official Anglican faith in the Carolinas. The Reverend Francis Le Jau was a particularly happy choice for South Carolina, because he was a converted Huguenot Calvinist, and approximately one-sixth of the population in the colony were French refugees of that faith whom the Anglicans wished to bring into their fold.

Dr. Le Jau arrived in Charleston in 1706, and shortly went out to St. James's Parish on Goose Creek, where he struggled to organize a congregation, to convert the Indians and baptize the slaves, and to do his best to soften the manners of their powerful owners. The reluctance of the owners to consent to the baptism of their slaves is rooted in the earliest of justifications of slavery—that the Africans were heathen. Although the legal question involved as to whether baptism effected emancipation had already been settled in the negative, Negroes were slow to abandon that hope, and Dr. Le Jau, moreover, suspected that some owners disliked the obligations of Christian brotherhood toward their slaves, which would require them to be more lenient in discipline and more generous as providers.

Although careful to work through the planters rather than against them, Le Jau was nevertheless a sympathetic observer of the habits and customs of the Indians and slaves who suffered under the severities of white rule. Serving in South Carolina until his death in 1717, at the age of fifty-two, Le Jau left an amazing record of a particularly turbulent frontier community, where political threats from the Spanish in Florida were matched by the dread of Indian raids and the fear of servile insurrection among the rapidly increasing slave community. These were hardly worse than the fevers of the region, which yearly carried away many slaves and citizens, Indians and Negroes.

From letters of the Reverend Francis Le Jau to the Secretary of the Society for the Propagation of the Gospel.

[October 20, 1709]— . . . As for the Spiritual State of my Parish this is the Account I can give of it for the present.

The extent of it is 20 Miles in length, and from 7 to 14 in breadth. Number of families 80. of the Church of England. Dissenting families 7, if so many, I find but 4 very strict. Baptised this half year past a Marryed Woman and 17 Children. Actual Communicants in all about 50: Constant Communicants every two Months near 30, among whom are two Negroes.

Since I came I baptised in all 2 Adults & 47 Children. Our Congregation is generally of about 100 Persons, sometimes more, several that were inclinable to some of the dissenting partys shew themselves pritty constant among us, and I do what possible to edify them and give them satisfaction in their doubts. On Sunday next I design God willing to baptise two very sensible and honest Negro Men whom I have kept upon tryal these two Years. Several others have spoken to me also; I do nothing too hastily in that respect. I instruct them and must have the consent of their Masters with a good Testimony and proof of their honest life and sober Conversation. Some Masters in my parish are very well satisfyed with my Proceedings in that respect: others do not seem to be so; yet they have given over opposing my design openly; it is to be hoped the good Example of the one will have an influence over the others. I must do the Justice to my Parishioners that tho' many Young Gentlemen are Masters of Great Estates, they and almost all the heads of all our Neighbouring families are an Example of Sobriety, honest[y] & Zeal for the Service of the Church to all the province.

To remove all pretence from the Adult Slaves I shall baptise of their being free upon that Account, I have thought fit to require first their consent to this following declaration *You declare in the Presence of God and before this Congregation that you do not ask for the holy baptism out of any design to ffree yourself from the Duty and Obedience you owe to your Master while you live, but meerly for the good of Your Soul and to partake of the Graces and Blessings promised to the Members of the Church of Jesus Christ.* One of the most Scandalous and common Crimes of our Slaves is their perpetual Changing of Wives and husbands, which occasions great disorders: I also tell them whom I baptise, *The Christian Religion dos not allow plurality of Wives, nor any changing of them: You promise truly to keep to the Wife you now have till Death dos part you.* I[t] has been Customary among them to have their ffeasts, dances, and merry Meetings upon the Lord's day, that practice is pretty well over in this Parish, but not absolutely: I tell them that present themselves to be admitted to Baptism, they must promise they'l spend no more the Lord's day in idleness, and if they do I'l cut them off from the Comunion.

These I most humbly Submit to the judgment of my Superiors whose Commands and instructions I will follow while I live: I see with an incredible joy the fervor of several of those poor Slaves. . . .

[February 19, 1710]— . . . We have but one single publick house in this vast parish, and hear of no Scandalous doings or at least of any habitual excesses. I have proposed to the Society in some of my former Letters, some difficulties about our joyning unbaptised persons in marriage; about the declaration I caused the baptised Negroes to make that they don't pretend to any freedome from their Masters Service, and will keep to their Wives and about promoting reading among all Slaves; in my last I troubled you with a trifling Narration of the Confusion our best Negroe Scholar was like to Create here among his fellow Slaves for having put his own Construction upon some Words of the Holy Prophet's which he had read; the thing indeed is inconsiderable in itself, but I fear the Consequences. I humbly submit to the Judgment of my Superiors in all Cases. . . .

[June 13, 1710]— . . . Permit me to assure My Lord President his Grace, My Lord of London and the Members of the Religious Society of my Obedience, respect & perfect gratitude. The Number of Our families the same 87. Since the 20th Octr. 1709. I baptised 19. among whom 3 Negroe Men; the Constant Number of Communicants 30. or 36, among whom 4 Negroe Men; all the Communicants together are still about 50. because some went to live in other places; Marriages 3; Buryals 2 Children; the Number of Our Negroe Slaves may be near 500. but above ⅓ part of 'em are Children.

Since it has pleased Almighty God to bless me with health I have upon Sundays, after our Divine Service invited the Negroes & Indian Slaves to stay for half an hour, the Invitation to my great Comfort has been joyfully reced by about 50 of 'em; We begin and end Our particular Assembly with the Collect *prevent us O Lord* &c. I teach 'em the Creed, the Lords Prayer, and the Commandments; I explain some portion of the Catechism, I give them an entire Liberty to ask questions, I endeavour to proportion my answers and all my Instructions to their want and Capacity: I must acknowledge that the hand of God dos visibly appear on this particular occasion. I had often attempted and proposed a time, a Method and means easy, as I thought, for the Instruction of those poor Souls, but all in vain, till this last was put in my mind by special mercy, the Most

Pious among their Masters stay also and hear; others not so zealous wou'd find fault, if possible, their Murmerings sometimes reach my Ears, but I am not discouraged: The Caution I have taken & which the Society is pleased to approve of, vizt. to do nothing without the Masters good testimony and consent, is a sufficient answer to them that oppose most the happyness of their Slaves; but the good example of some truely Religious Masters is a Check upon the others, the Alteration is so considerable of late that in general very few Masters excepted, the Slaves shall be fed and provided for by the Masters, and the whole time of the Slaves shall be their Masters; this is what I have continually urged; knowing how idly and criminally the Slaves spent the time given to them to Work for themselves. I bless God for having at last rendred the Masters sensible of their own Advantage in that respect. Four or 6 shall be soon baptised by the Consent of their Masters, and the others with the Children in time, except in danger of death, those Slaves behave themselves very well, and do better for their Masters profit than formerly, for they are taught to serve out of Christian Love & Duty; they tell me openly that they will ever bless God for their knowing good things which they knew not before. The Lord's day is no more profaned by their dancings at least about me: I asked once a pretty ancient and very fine Slave whether he cou'd read, his answer was he wou'd rather choose hereafter to practice the good he could remember. As I had the honour to represent in one of my last Letters the inconveniences which I perceive . . . I forbear urging too far the exercise of reading among them leaving to the discretion of their Masters to choose the fitest persons to learn till I receive further Instructions about that point. There are 3. or 4. Portuguese Slaves in this parish very desirous to receive the Communion amongst us; I framed a short Modell of Submission grounded upon some Popish Tenets which they told me of their own Accord, without troubling them with things they know not; I require of them their renouncing of those particular points, the Chief of which is praying to the Saints and that they must not return to the Popish Worship in case they shou'd be sent to Medera again. I gave them that fform of Submission in Writing and left it to their Consideration, they come constantly to Church and are very sensible. I have proposed to some Masters a thing that seems to me very easy to be done and will prevent horrid Crimes and Confusions amongst Negroes and Indian Slaves for the future, that none of those that are not yet marryed presume to do it without his Masters consent, and likewise those that are not Marryed do not part without the like Consent (I know some will transgress) but I hope 'twill do good to many, especially in time to come; This thought of mine I most humbly Submit to the Judgment of the Society to which I will ever yield with the utmost respect.

[July 14, 1710]— . . . The Spiritual State of my Parish till June the 13th. 1710. was thus; baptised 19 among whom 3 Negroe Men. Communicants about 50 in all; because some went out of the Parish, but no less than 30 constant Communicants every two Months among whom 4. Negroes: 3 Marriages and one Child buryed.

The great heat has thrown several persons and families into ffeavers; I was also sick and very weak which accident interrupted my duty of Cathechising the Poor Slaves: that Interruption has afforded to me the Comfort of seeing that those Slaves are sincerely desirous to do well, for they come constantly all of them near and about the Windows of Our Church, which cannot contain them when the Parishioners are met, and behave themselves very devoutly: I hope by the Blessing of God to begin again that beloved Work in a short time. Some Masters are come to me of their own Accord to signify their Consent and desire about the baptism of some of their Slaves. Some other Masters find difficulties which I endeavour to answer as I have opportunities: I most humbly intreat the Honorable Society that some Books and directions relating to the beginning and carrying on of the excellt. Work of Reformation of Manners may be sent to be distributed in my parish. . . .

[February 20, 1711/12]— . . . 2 Marriages. . 12 Children Baptised. 2 Adults. 4 Buryals 36 Communicants at Xtmas last among whome 5 new Communicants, and near 60 in the Parish, Children Catechised at a time 10 or 12 in all above 20 Negroes Catechised 40. or 50. The Mortality that begun to rage in Augt. is not yet over, especialy in Towne where the Commissary has attended with much zeal, and I thank God he has been preserved from dangerous sickness, the number of the

[31]

White People dead of late in the Province is near 200, and the slaves as many again, which is a Considble loss for a place, so thin Inhabited we have allso wanted Salt, and Provisions are very scarce chiefly in the Towne where no Body durst go from the Country. The Surgeons are of opinion that the Aire has been infected these 14 Yeares. I look upon a more immediat Cause that is the Irreligion and Lewdness of too many Persons, but chiefly the Barberous usage of the poor Slaves. I endeavour to urge the dutyes of mercy towards them as much as I am able, and I bless God things are upon a better ffoot in that respect about me—but still I am Contradicted by several Masters, but I trust in God these visitations will serve to make them mind better things than worldly advantages—

I have had of late an opportunity to oppose with all my might the putting of a very unhumane Law and in my Judgmt. very unjust it is in Execution, in Relation to run away Negroes, by a Law Enacted in this Province some years before I came; such an Negroe must be mutilated by amputation of Testicles if it be a man, and of Ears if a Woman. I have openly declared against such punishment grounded upon the Law of God, which setts a slave at liberty if he should loose an Eye or a tooth when he is Corrected. Exod. 21. and some good Planters are of my opinion. I must Informe you of a most Cruel Contrivance a man has Invented to punish small faults in slaves. he puts them in a Coffin where they are crushed almost to death, and he keeps them in that hellish Machine for 24 hours commonly with their ffeet Chained out, and a Lid pressing upon

their stomack, this is a matter of fact universally knowen, when I look upon the ordinary cause that makes those poor Souls run away, and almost dispaire I find it is imoderate labour and want of Victualls and rest.[1] God Alm: inspire the Honourable Society my most Illustrious Patrons to Consider those things so that they may be remedyed for the Encouragemt. of those poor Creatures, I will allso transmit to you what I observe Concerning our Indians, when I am Informed yt. you have received my Lres, and the papers I sent by Mrs Johnston, it is now 8 Months since I heard from any friend in Europe the last orders of the Society are of 18 Months date, the last Lre I had the Honour to receive from you was dated last Octobr. was twelve month. . . . I gave you an account in my last of the desolate Condition of Renoque. it was in Octobr. or the latter End of September that the Tuscararo's Indians liveing near Cape fair Cutt off 137 of our people, most of them Palatines and some Switzers. I am not able to declare whether they were sett on by some of the partys that have been long at variance in that place or whether they were provoked by some great Injustice & taking their Land by force, it is so reported among us. our forces are

1. Special courts were provided by law in 1690 for the trial of Negro slaves in South Carolina. Trial was without jury and punishment meted out consisted of whipping, branding, cutting off the ears, or the death penalty depending upon the severity and frequency of the offense. Despite minor changes, a slave code was enforced until the Civil War. See William R. Smith, *South Carolina as a Royal Province, 1719–1776* (New York, 1903), pp. 143–45. . . . (*Klingberg note*)

Actualy marched to Suppress those Murderers. Vizt. a Generall Called Barnewell and 16 White men, whome 6 or 700 Indians have Joined and they are to meet the Virginians many wise men in this Province doubt of the Success it is evident that our Traders have promoted Bloody Warrs this last Year to get slaves and one of them brought lately 100 of those poor Souls. It do's not belong to me to say any more upon those Melancholy Affaires I submit as to the Justice of those Proceedings to Your Wisdom. When I am asked how we are to deal with those unfortunate slaves, I content my selfe to Exhort that they be used with Xtian Charity and yt. we render their Condition as tollerable as we can. I don't know where the fault lyes but I see 30 Negroes at Church for an Indian slave, and as for our free Indians—they goe their own way and bring their Children like themselves with little Conversation among us but when they want something from us, I generaly Pceive something Cloudy in their looks, An argumt, I fear, of discontent. I am allso Informed yt. our Indian Allyes are grown haughty of late—. . .

[August 30, 1712]— . . . I hope through the mercy of God there will be in a Short time Some more Negroe Slaves Baptized: I take all the care I can that they Instruct one another when they have time; there are a few men in Sewall plantations to whom I have recommended to do that Good Service to the others, those men are Religious zealous, honest, they can read well, and by them I am inform'd when there is any disorder among their fellows slaves that it may be remedyed. I discountenance the changing of wives as much as it lyes in my power and I hope the Danceings upon Sundays are quite over in this Neighbourhood. There has been a very severe Act, to punish our Slaves, lately past in this province. Runaway Slaves are to be Mutilated; and at last put to death if they absent themselves for the fourth time for fourteen days. I have taken the Liberty to say Mutilation and Death too Great punishments in that respect But what I most complaine of is that upon Sundays they are Confin'd at home by the Letter of the Act I urg'd to the Magistrates in this parish these poor souls should have the liberty to come to Church. I was answered that it was so Implyed with their Masters leave, but I fear as the greatest part of the Masters is against their Slaves being Instructed they'll take an Advantage of the Tenour of the Act . . .

[December 11, 1712]— . . . I thought to have baptized some more Negro Slaves this Advent they are well Instructed and I hear no complaint concerning them. Their Masters Seem very much Averse to my Design, Some of them will not give them Leave to come to Church to learn how to Pray to God & to Serve him, I cannot find any reason for this New Opposition but the Old pretext that Baptism makes the Slaves proud and Undutifull: I endeavour to convince them of the Contrary From the Example of those I have baptized, and Chiefly those who are Admitted to our holy Comunion who behave themselves very well, I humbly ask that if the Society Orders any Thing to be Publisht to Induce the Masters to shew more Charity towards their Slaves I may have some Copies to distribute . . .

[February 23, 1713]— . . . I will not fail to Acquaint the Society with Some Particular Things wch I think it is my Duty to lay before them And I Submit to their wise Consideration & Judgemt. what Afflicts and Discourages me beyond Expression is to see the pious Designes of the Honrble Society very much Obstructed by the rash Conduct of Some of our Inhabitants. I humbly Apprehend That it is Expected the Missionaries should Endeavour to Promote the knowledge of Christ among the Ignorant Heathens begining with the Poor Negroe & Indian Slaves that live in our ffamilies, and Seeking all Opportunites to do good to the free Indians Scattered in the Province till God Gives us meanes to Instruct those Indian Nations that are our Neighbours, Which I firmly hope shall be Accomplished in his own time, But indeed few Masters appear Zealous or even pleased with what the Missionaries try to do for the Good of their Slaves, they are more Cruel Some of them of late Dayes than before, They hamstring maim & unlimb those poor Creatures for Small faults, A man within this Month had a very fine Negroe batized, Sensible Carefull & good in all Respects who being wearyed with Labour & fallen asleep had the Mischance to loose a parcell of Rice wch by the Oversetting of a Periogua fell into a River. The man tho Intreated by the Minister of the Parish, who is Brother Maule and some Persons of the best Consideration among us to forgive the Negroe, who had Offended only through Neglect without Malice,

thought fit to keep him for several Dayes in Chains, & I am told muffled up that he might not Eat, & Scourge him twice a Day, and at Night to put him into a hellish Machine contrived by him into the Shape of a Coffin where could not Stirr, The punishmt having continued Several Dayes & Nights and there being no Appearance when it should End, the poor Negroe through Despair Ask't one of his Children for a knife & manacled as he was Stabb'd himself with it; I am told this is the 5th Slave that Same man has destroyed by his Cruelty within 2 or 3 Yeares, but he is onely an hired Overseer the Owner of the Slaves lives out of this Province, I own I See everybody almost angry at So much Barbarity, Yet he pretends to go to Church, and they look upon the Man as Guilty of Murder, and So do great many of my Acquaintance who tho not So Barbarous take no Care at all of the Souls of their Slaves, and as little as the[y] can of their bodies I am at a loss when I see them in a praying posture knowing that at the same time they do not love their Neighbour, and what is most Amazeing I cannot make them Comprehend that their Neglect is an habitual state of Sin, I have Seen very Severe Judgemts. Since I came, Nothing Else almost but Judgemts. . . . .

[August 10, 1713]— . . . Communicants in all near 60. among whom 5 Negroe men and 2 Negro women.

With the Blessing of God I hope to Administer in a short time the holy Sacrament of Baptism to 2 Negroe men, and receive the abjuration of a Negroe woman that had been bred in Guadalupe, but now Expresses a great desire to serve God according to his Word. The Honble Society will I am persuaded, be very well pleased to hear that among many of our Inhabitants that are remiss in promoting the Instruction of their Slaves, and some who shew an absolute unwillingness that they should hear any thing of God and Jesus our Saviour, yet there is a good number of Honest Masters and Mistresses Sincerely Zealous in that Important point. I hear that upon all occasions they defend wth vigour the Cause of the Holy Gospel, and answer very well the objections of those uncharitable persons, who will not suffer their Slaves to come to Church to Learn their Prayers, because, say they, knowledge makes them worse, this is now their main Argument.

If the Society thinks fit to print anything by way of Admonition to the Masters that have Slaves I humbly ask a Sufficient Number to be distributed in our 11 Parishes. . . .

[January 22, 1714]— . . . Since the first of this month I baptized an old Sensible Negroe Man upon his death bed, and three Negroe children, and all of them with their masters consent some more come to me, Shewing an Earnest desire to receive that holy Sacrament. I Encourage them and instruct them the best I can by Divine Grace

It is a singular comfort to me to see that while so many professed Chriŝtians appear but Lukewarm, it pleases God to raise to himself faithfull and devout Servts from among the heathens, who are very zealous in the Practice of our Christian dutyes. I hear no Complaining of our Proselytes, their masters commend them for their faithfull-

ness, and from what I am going to relate, the Honble Society shall have a satisfactory Instance that their Pious designs are not fruitless, as Irreligious men would insinuate, when they pretend That the knowledge of the true God and Jesus his Son renders our Slaves worse.

About Christmas last past there was a rumour spread of an Intended Conspiracy of the Negro's against us all like that of New York. I was told that the Plot had been form'd in Goose Creek where there is a good number of fine Negro's. This News made me Inquire and observe being resolved to find out how true the thing might be. The matter has been examined very diligently by our Government this very week. 12 or 15 Negroes living on the North side of Cooper River, having been apprehended under suspicion it has appeared upon good evidence that a Negroe fellow brought hither some years ago from Martineco, and of a very stubborn temper, had Inticed some Slaves to joyn with him that they might get their liberty by force. the thing being proved against him he has been put to death for it, two more Slaves have been very severely chastis'd for hearkening to him, but there was not any sufficient proof to take their life and all denied the Crime, the other prisoners have been acquited but what I consider as a singular Providence there has not been so much as one of our Goose Creek Negroes accused of having knowledge of the Plot, far from having consented to so great a Crime. The most sensible of our Slaves whom I have admitted to the holy Sacrament have solemnly protested to me that if ever they hear of any Ill design of the Slaves I shall know it from them that it may be prevented, and I can't but depend upon the truth of their words, knowing them to be Exemplarily Pious and Honest.

I wish I could prevail upon the Inhabitants of this Place to make serious Reflexions upon the Judgments wch our Sins and in particular the want of Charity and the Love of this World bring down upon our heads from time to time. It is Miraculous how any of us came to escape from the great Hurricane we felt Sept 5th last past it continued for 12 hours, had the two rivers on both sides of Charles Town been joyned for some time that place would now be destroyed. . . .

---

7. The Reverend Jones Reports on Slavery in the Tobacco Country

---

As the eighteenth century wore on, life assumed a more settled aspect in the easterly regions that had been colonized earliest. With this new regularity came a clearer definition of the status of persons, and, slowly but surely, slave labor displaced the system of indentured servitude. Thus the link between chattel slavery and free status disappeared, and the colonies were left with a slave system that followed the color line. In the Southern colonies, devoted primarily to agriculture, slaves became the most desirable laborers, as their services were for life, and the slave trade responded all too well to the demands of colonial agriculture for labor.

On the eve of the two most vigorous decades of the slave trade, a young English clergyman arrived in Williamsburg to become mathematics professor at the College of William and Mary. It was the beginning of a long and active career for the Reverend Hugh Jones. Only twenty-five at the time he came to America, Jones left one of the most urbane and appreciative accounts of colonial life. Basically gregarious and outgoing, young Jones was soon involved in community affairs, serving as the chaplain of the House of Burgesses, as occasional "lecturer" at Bruton Parish Church, and as a companion of Gov. Alexander Spottswood when the Governor

Source: Hugh Jones, *The Present State of Virginia From Whence Is Inferred a Short View of Maryland and North Carolina*, ed. Richard L. Morton (Chapel Hill: University of North Carolina Press, 1956), pp. 74–77.

traveled the frontiers of the colony. After his move to Maryland in 1731 Jones put his mathematical abilities to further use by assisting Lord Baltimore to a settlement of the boundary dispute between Pennsylvania and Maryland. He was also recognized for his able arguments in favor of adoption of the Georgian calendar.

The following view of slavery in Virginia is taken from Jones's work of 1724, and through his sharp young eyes we see the new arrivals from Africa, the kinds of provisions made, and the conditions of labor. Jones even wrote in some detail about the tobacco culture, in which most slaves in the "Middle Plantation" region below Williamsburg were engaged. The wasteful agricultural methods associated with abundant land and slave labor were apparent from the beginning.

The whole country is a perfect forest, except where the woods are cleared for plantations, and old fields, and where have been formerly Indian towns, and poisoned fields and meadows, where the timber has been burnt down in fire-hunting or otherwise; and about the creeks and rivers are large rank morasses or marshes, and up the country are poor savannahs.

The gentlemen's seats are of late built for the most part of good brick, and many of timber very handsom, commodious, and capacious; and likewise the common planters live in pretty timber houses, neater than the farm houses are generally in England; with timber also are built houses for the overseers and out-houses; among which is the kitchen apart from the dwelling house, because of the smell of hot victuals, offensive in hot weather.

The Negroes live in small cottages called quarters, in about six in a gang, under the direction of an overseer or bailiff; who takes care that they tend such land as the owner allots and orders, upon which they raise hogs and

cattle, and plant Indian corn (or maize) and tobacco for the use of their master; out of which the overseer has a dividend (or share) in proportion to the number of hands including himself; this with several privileges in his salary, and is an ample recompence for his pains, and encouragement of his industrious care, as to the labour, health, and provision of the Negroes.

The Negroes are very numerous, some gentlemen having hundreds of them of all sorts, to whom they bring great profit; for the sake of which they are obliged to keep them well, and not overwork, starve, or famish them, besides other inducements to favour them; which is done in a great degree, to such especially that are laborious, careful, and honest; though indeed some masters, careless of their own interest or reputation, are too cruel and negligent.

The Negroes are not only encreased by fresh supplies from Africa and the West India Islands, but also are very prolifick among themselves; and they that are born there talk good English, and affect our language, habits, and customs; and though they be naturally of a barbarous and cruel temper, yet are they kept under by severe discipline upon occasion, and by good laws are prevented from running away, injuring the English, or neglecting their business.

Their work (or chimerical hard slavery) is not very laborious; their greatest hardship consisting in that they and their posterity are not at their own liberty or disposal, but are the property of their owners; and when they are free, they know not how to provide so well for themselves generally; neither did they live so plentifully nor (many of them) so easily in their own country, where they are made slaves to one another, or taken captive by their enemies.

The children belong to the master of the woman that bears them; and such as are born of a Negroe and an European are called Molattoes; but such as are born of an Indian and Negroe are called Mustees.

Their work is to take care of the stock, and plant corn, tobacco, fruits, etc. which is not harder than thrashing, hedging, or ditching; besides, though they are out in the violent heat, wherein they delight, yet in wet or cold weather there is little occasion for their working in the fields, in which few will let them be abroad, lest by this means they might get sick or die, which would prove a great loss to their owners, a good Negroe being sometimes worth three (nay four) score pounds sterling, if he be a tradesman; so that upon this (if upon no other account) they are obliged not to overwork them, but to cloath and feed them sufficiently, and take care of their health.

Several of them are taught to be sawyers, carpenters, smiths, coopers, etc. and though for the most part they be none of the aptest or nicest; yet they are by nature cut out for hard labour and fatigue, and will perform tolerably well; though they fall much short of an Indian, that has learned and seen the same things; and those Negroes make the best servants, that have been slaves in their own country; for they that have been kings and great men there are generally lazy, haughty, and obstinate; whereas the others are sharper, better humoured, and more laborious.

The languages of the new Negroes are various harsh jargons, and their religions and customs such as are best described by Mr. Bosman in his book intitled (I think) *A Description of the Coasts of Africa*.

The Virginia planters readily learn to become good mechanicks in building, wherein most are capable of directing their servants and slaves.

As for timber they abound with excellent good; having about eight sorts of oak, several kinds of walnut-tree and hickory and pignut, pine, cedar, and cypress for shingles; which covering is lighter than tiles, and being nailed down, are not easily blown off in any tempest or gust.

The oak, etc. is of quick growth, consequently will not last so long as ours; though it has a good grain, and is freer from knots, and will last long enough for shipping, and ordinary uses.

When a tract of land is seated, they clear it by felling the trees about a yard from the ground, lest they should· shoot again. What wood they have occasion for they carry off, and burn the rest, or let it lie and rot upon the ground.

The land between the logs and stumps they how up, planting tobacco there in the spring, inclosing it with a slight fence of cleft rails. This will last for tobacco some years, if the land be good; as it is where fine timber, or grape vines grow.

Land when tired is forced to bear tobacco by penning their cattle upon it; but cowpen tobacco tastes strong, and that planted in wet marshy land is called nonburning tobacco, which smoaks in the pipe like leather, unless it be of a good age.

When land is tired of tobacco, it will bear Indian corn, or English wheat, or any other European grain or seed, with wonderful increase.

Tobacco and Indian corn are planted in hills as hops, and secured by worm-fences, which are made of rails supporting one another very firmly in a particular manner.

Tobacco requires a great deal of skill and trouble in the right management of it.

They raise the plants in beds, as we do cabbage plants; which they transplant and replant upon occasion after a shower of rain, which they call a season.

When it is grown up they top it, or nip off the head, succour it, or cut off the ground leaves, weed it, hill it; and when ripe, they cut it down about six or eight leaves on a stalk, which they carry into airy tobacco houses; after it is withered a little in the sun, there it is hung to dry on sticks, as paper at the paper-mills; when it is in proper case, (as they call it) and the air neither too moist, nor too dry, they strike it, or take it down, then cover it up in bulk, or a great heap, where it lies till they have leisure or occasion to stem it (that is pull the leaves from the stalk) or strip it (that is take out the great fibres) and tie it up in hands, or streight lay it; and so by degrees prize or press it with proper engines into great hogsheads, containing from about six to eleven hundred pounds; four of which hogsheads made a tun, by dimension, not by weight; then it is ready for sale or shipping. . . .

8. William Fitzhugh Enlarges His Holdings

How many slaves were brought into Virginia before 1700 is a matter of scholarly dispute, with estimates ranging from six thousand to sixteen thousand. The lower figure is undoubtedly too low, but it is unlikely to be farther from the mark than two thousand. In the seventeenth century most of the slaves imported came from the West Indies, were already "seasoned," and the proportion of women to men was lower than it became during the next century. These slaves were at first scattered among many farmers and planters, and were not engrossed in large holdings. But during the last quarter of the century a changing pattern emerged. Importations increased under the stimulus of the Royal African Company, and certain planters began to accumulate large holdings of lands and slaves. For every importation a planter received a "headright" of land amounting to fifty acres.

William Fitzhugh (1651–1701) of Westmoreland County was such a planter, and an industrious merchant and lawyer as well. He owned twenty-nine Negroes in 1686, and left many slaves together with 54,000 acres of land when he died. He was a member of the House of Burgesses, and attorney for Major Robert Beverley in 1682 when Beverley as Clerk of the House was arrested for refusing to surrender the legislative journals to the Governor and the Council. Beverley's son was the Robert Beverley of document 5.

In a letter of June 19, 1681, Fitzhugh requested that Ralph Wormley buy slaves for him. "I understand there are some Negro ships expected into York [River] now every day[.] I am so remote that . . . they'll be all disposed of or at least none left but the refuse." The following letters concern that purchase, and show that already in the late seventeenth century the purchase of slaves had become a matter-of-fact business. In the excerpt from the second letter, Fitzhugh arranged for payment to the dealer in the complicated style of the day, using bills owed Fitzhugh for payment of his own obligations. The third excerpt is from a set of instructions to John Withers, who was serving as agent in Fitzhugh's affairs. The fourth letter shows Fitzhugh promising tobacco as security for another purchase.

Source: *Virginia Magazine of History and Biography*, 1 (1893–94):44–45, 51, 108.

William Fitzhugh to Ralph Wormley and others.

[1]

July 14th, 1681.

Hon'rd Sir:

. . . S^r your promise to assist me in the purchase of those Negroes I requested you to buy for me, only desire farther advice and more particular directions which I shall now do. I desired you in my former to buy me five or six, whereof three or four to be boys, a man and woman or men and women, the boys from eight to seventeen or eighteen, the rest as young as you can procure them, for price I cannot direct therein because boys according to there age and growth are valued in price, therefore S^r shall refer that wholly to yourself and doubt not your care therein and if you please to hire a messenger to come either way with them or to come immediately and give me notice thereof. I shall gladly pay the Messenger and readily come down myself to make payment for the same. . . .

Yr Wff.

To Ralph Wormley Esq.

[2]

Dec'r 3rd, 1681.

Mr. John Buckner

S'r: I was intended the last general court to have waited on you, in order to have taken care for your payment what I am indebted to you, but in my going was straitened in time and in my my coming home earnest to be here. I have now taken this opportunity by Mr. John Withers to send you bills of Maj^r Robert Beverlys for £20,5,00 which I suppose before this time he has taken care with you about his promised payment in your hands at the passing of the bills. Esqr Wormley likewise at the same time assured me that he would take care to pay you £20 more upon my account, which I doubt not but before this he has done; what remains I will hereafter take care honestly to pay but hope you will make me some abatement for your Dumb Negro that you sold me; had she been a new Negro, I must have blamed my fate not you; but one that you had two years, I must conclude you knew her qualities which is bad at work worse at talking and took the opportunity of the Softness of my Messenger to quit your hands of her. I will freely give you the £3,5,0, overplus of £20 that he gave for her to take her again and will get her convey'd to your hands or hope if my offer be not acceptable you will make me some abatement of so bad a bargain. I desire if you have not heard from Mr. Wormley and Maj. Beverly in order to the payment as above Mr. Withers will not scruple to stay a day while you send to them that thereby he may bring my Obligation with him and will pass himself for the Ballance which I'll see certainly paid. Sr. This Gentleman is come purposely to buy two or three Negro boys or girlls, men or women. Upon the Report the protested Bills has opened the Negro Market I advised him to you for your advice and instructions there, as well knowing that if such a thing be you can best advise him. I will also myself buy six or eight if the market be so low as is here reported, in both which your advice is desired by

Sr. Your Wff.

To Mr. Jno. Buckner,
p. Mr. Withers.

[3]

Instructions for Mr. Jn° Withers his proceedings in his York journey June 5th, 1682.

. . .

Eighthly. To purchase what likely Negroes you can either 1, 2, 3, 4, 5 or 6 what boys and men you possibly can, as few women as may be, but be sure not above two, to purchase neither man nor woman above thirty years old, not to exceed £20 for the price of a man unless he be extraordinary likely, to buy Mr. Walter's boy alone for £20 if you can or to give £54 for the three at most, what under you can, if you cannot purchase him alone. To proceed to £34 for Maj'r Peyton's two boys if you can't get them under or can't hear of a better purchase to do for me as for yourself in choosing and purchasing.

Ninthly, To pass Haverton's biils away in the purchase of Negroes if you Can.

Tenthly, To pass George Boyce his two bills in the Purchase of Negroes or any other swap to advantage nay though with loss. . . .

[4]

February 11th 1682–3.

Mr. Jackson,
As to your Proposal about the bring-

ing in Negroes next fall, I have this to offer and you may communicate the same to your owners and Employers, that I will deal with them for so many as shall amount to 50,000 lbs of Tob° and cask which will be about 20 hh^{ds} under the condition and at these ages and prices following, to say, to give 3,000 lbs Tob° for every Negro boy or girl, that shall be between the age of seven and eleven years old and to give 4,000 lbs Tob° for every youth or girl that shall be between the age of 11 to 15 and to give 5,000 lbs Tob° for every young man or woman that shall be above 15 years of age and not exceed 24, the said Negroes to be delivered at my landing some time in Septr next, and I to have notice whether they will so agree some time in August next. And I do assure you and so you may acquaint them, that upon your delivery and my receipt of the Negroes according to the ages above mentioned and that they be sound and healthfull at their Delivery, I will give such sufficient Caution for payment of the Tob° accordingly by the 20th Dec'r then next following as shall be approved of. The ages of the Negroes to be judged and determined by two or three such honest and reasonable men here as yourself shall nominate and appoint. The whole sum of the Tob° to be paid in the compass of twenty miles, perhaps not so remote, I am

Your Wff.

To Mr. Jackson of Piscataway
In New England These.

9. Robert Carter Assesses Slave Property

Robert Carter, "King" Carter of Corotoman, was one of the truly baronial landowners of eighteenth-century Virginia. In a letter to his London agent, Carter appraises an estate that he obviously hoped to purchase. In due course he describes the slaves, giving conservative estimates, one supposes. He also lines out the distinctions planters frequently made among the new Africans as to country of origin, and the "aptitude" for slavery of the blacks from those countries. When Carter refers to "small folks and middling people" he means, of course, neighboring farmers on the make, not grand planters like himself.

Carter served from time to time as an agent for the slave captains, selling slaves from the ships (which drew up to his plantation dock) and keeping record of the debts purchasing planters undertook. He had to be well-informed as to the credit of the buyers, and to make good himself for delinquent payments to the shipmaster.

Robert Carter to Micajah Perry.

July ye 13th, 1723.
Mr. Micaja[h] Perry:

Sir,—I have already sent you an inventory of ye _____ estate. That it may appear the clearer before you I now send it you distinguished under its several species by w'ch you and the gentl'n concerned be the better enabled to pass your judgments upon the value of it if they are in earnest to sell and can make a good title. However, I shall give you here the best acco't I can how the prices of Virginian estates run from man to man.

As for negroes I suppose you know the prices they are sold at well enough. Two years ago Colo. Page bought ——[1] Bombesa men slaves, the finest that I ever saw, between ab't 18 and 28 years of age, not one exceeding thirty I dare say, of Capt. Francis Willis, agent of the African Company, at seventeen pounds per head. Last year I bought men for twenty; women eighteen, and girls of 10 and 12 years of age for 10 pounds per head. This year I know of no large quantities having been sold together. The small folks and middling

1. The figures are illegible.

Source: *The Southern Planter* (Richmond, Va.), vol. 2, no. 2 (February 1842), pp. 40–41.

[43]

people have been the only buyers. I have known Leves all single choice men bought for 20£ apiece. The choicest have gone at 40£. This hath been the rule with the sellers as far as I have heard. I doubt not, would I have taken a quantity, I might have had them considerably cheaper. You must know, the slaves that come from Gambia, such as Colo. Page had, are of a much larger size and have more sense and are more used to work, than any other. I would freely give at any time 40 sh. a head more for them than for the Cites.

As for cattle, there is no such thing as selling a stock together, for money. The common price for any young, fat cow in killing time, is thirty-five shillings cash: and for a steer, seven years old, fifty shillings. This you may be informed of by your masters when they buy fresh meat.

The horses and mares, you must understand, are of very small value among us. They swarm upon us, and are degenerated into such runts, that you may buy them as they run almost for anything. Not many years ago I sold six out of my pasture, to Doctor Lomax, of three years old, for shipping off, at 20s. per head. Some of these, you will observe, are very old, and some very young.

For hogs, I do not know what to say of them. As they run in the woods we esteem them little better than vermin, and 'tis not common to put them into the inventory of our estates. Indeed, after we have spent a barrel of corn upon them per hog to make them fit for killing, they will fetch you from 20s. to 25s. per head, the barrows and speyed sows, current money.

For the household goods, 'tis very old and mean, as you may very well conceive, having been under the use of such various hands.

Nine of the negroes, as I have already observed, are so much past their labor that they are rather a charge than anything else. Their levy and clothes come to more than they make. There are three of them at one place put in for a share, and at no place under two for a share and a lusty girl or boy to help out with their work, to boot; and yet the overseers grumble very much to allow anything for them.

The lands and plantations you have often had a particular account of. When Carey has got that plantation away, as no doubt (if he can make his title good,) but he will, though I will defend it to the uttermost if you will send me such orders, there will be but nineteen hundred acres, or thereabout, every plantation cleared quite out, and no timber left for building.

This is a true representation of this estate. Old Capt. Willis knows as well the value of a Virginian estate as any man. Let him but consider the great difference there is between land in those parts of the country and Glos'ter, where he lived; the low ebb that Tob'o is at; and the little income we make at this day of our Virginian estates; and I could almost agree he should set the value upon it himself.

I must confess that in consideration of having had this estate so long under my government; that the best of the slaves went hence with my brother's daughter, Loyd's first wife, and are very much related to several of my families of slaves; and having lands in plenty to settle them upon; I am very desirous to be the purchaser, and will pay the money in as little time as they can reasonably desire it; and will give as much as any other person will offer *at* the estate entirely together: and I hope, if not for my sake, at least for my son, whom they seem to have very much in their esteem, and to whom

this estate may probably come, they will let me have the first refusal of it.

Thus you have this affair as fully before you as I can set it, until I hear further from you about it.

I am your most humble servant,

ROBERT CARTER.

10. Peter Kalm Observes Labor Conditions in Pennsylvania

The ways of making a livelihood were more various in the Middle Colonies than in the southerly ones. So were the ethnic strains composing their population more diverse. Germans and Swedes joined the English, Dutch, and Negroes in economic activities that ranged far beyond the planting of agricultural commodities for export. Although slavery continued in strength in the Middle Colonies through much of the eighteenth century, it existed as part of a more complex labor system that provided ready alternatives to slavery. Because of this diversity, the hopes of slaves in the colonies north of Maryland that the influence of Enlightenment ideas and the humanitarian impulses of the age might free them in time were better grounded in economic realities than were any expectations their brothers in bonds to the south may have had.

Dr. Peter Kalm, of the Swedish Academy of Sciences, and professor at the Academy of Äbo, wrote one of the most fascinating books about Colonial America, and the student of slavery will be glad that he included a brief but succinct description of the status of slaves in Pennsylvania in his account of his travels in this region. Kalm traveled in the Colonies between 1741 and 1751, looking specifically for a mulberry tree hardy enough to withstand the Swedish climate, and in general for all useful information on native American trees and shrubs. A student of Linnaeus, who later

Source: Adolf B. Benson, ed., *Peter Kalm's Travels in North America* (New York: Wilson-Erickson, 1937), 2 vols. 1:204–11.

named the mountain laurel *Kalmia Latifolia* in his honor, Kalm was a detached and scholarly observer. He gives evidence of his special interest in the study of poisonous roots and herbs in the account he gives here of the knowledge of poisons that the blacks were supposed to have had. It is also as a naturalist that he probes such questions as the effects of climate and racial intermixture on pigmentation.

Kalm's travels were first published in Stockholm between 1753 and 1761. The first English edition appeared in London in 1770, but that of Adolph Benson, from which our selection is drawn, the most complete edition in English, did not appear until 1937.

Servants. The servants which are employed in the English-American colonies are either free persons or slaves, and the former, again, are of two different classes.

1. Those who are entirely free serve by the year. They are not only allowed to leave their service at the expiration of their year, but may leave it at any time when they do not agree with their masters. However, in that case they are in danger of losing their wages, which are very considerable. A man servant who has some ability gets between sixteen and twenty pounds in Pennsylvania currency, but those in the country do not get so much. A maidservant gets eight or ten pounds a year. These servants have their food besides their wages, but they must buy their own clothes, and whatever they get of these as gifts they must thank their master's generosity for.

Indenture. 2. The second kind of free servants consists of such persons as annually come from Germany, England and other countries, in order to settle here. These newcomers are very numerous every year: there are old and young of both sexes. Some of them

have fled from oppression, under which they have labored. Others have been driven from their country by religious persecution, but most of them are poor and have not money enough to pay their passage, which is between six and eight pounds sterling for each person. Therefore, they agree with the captain that they will suffer themselves to be sold for a few years on their arrival. In that case the person who buys them pays the freight for them; but frequently very old people come over who cannot pay their passage, they therefore sell their children for several years, so that they serve both for themselves and for their parents. There are likewise some who pay part of their passage, and they are sold only for a short time. From these circumstances it appears that the price on the poor foreigners who come over to North America varies considerably, and that some of them have to serve longer than others. When their time has expired, they get a new suit of clothes from their master and some other things. He is likewise obliged to feed and clothe them during the years of their servitude. Many of the Germans who come hither bring money enough with them to pay their passage, but prefer to be sold, hoping that during their servi-tude they may get a knowledge of the language and character of the country and the life, that they may the better be able to consider what they shall do when they have gotten their liberty. Such servants are preferable to all others, because they are not so expensive. To buy a negro or black slave requires too much money at one time; and men or maids who get yearly wages are likewise too costly. But this kind of servant may be gotten for half the money, and even for less; for they commonly pay fourteen pounds, Pennsylvania currency, for a person who is to serve four years, and so on in proportion. Their wages therefore are not above three pounds Pennsylvania currency per annum. These servants are, after the English, called *servingar* by the Swedes. When a person has bought such a servant for a certain number of years, and has an intention to sell him again, he is at liberty to do so, but is obliged, at the expiration of the term of servitude, to provide the usual suit of clothes for the servant, unless he has made that part of the bargain with the purchaser. The English and Irish commonly sell themselves for four years, but the Germans frequently agree with the captain before they set out, to pay him a certain sum of money, for a certain number of persons. As soon as they arrive in America they go about and try to get a man who will pay the passage for them. In return they give according to their circumstances, one or several of their children to serve a certain number of years. At last they make their bargain with the highest bidder.

3. The *negroes* or blacks constitute the third kind. They are in a manner slaves; for when a negro is once bought, he is the purchaser's servant as long as he lives, unless he gives him to another, or sets him free. However, it is not in the power of the master to kill his negro for a fault, but he must leave it to the magistrates to proceed according to the laws. Formerly the negroes were brought over from Africa, and bought by almost everyone who could afford it, the Quakers alone being an exception. But these are no longer so particular and now they have as many negroes as other people. However, many people cannot conquer the idea of its being contrary to the laws of Christianity to keep slaves. There are likewise several free negroes in town, who have been lucky enough to get a very zealous Quaker for their master, and who gave them their liberty after they had faithfully served him for a time.

At present they seldom bring over any negroes to the English colonies, for those which were formerly brought thither have multiplied rapidly. In regard to their marriage they proceed as follows: in case you have not only male but likewise female negroes, they may intermarry, and then the children are all your slaves. But if you possess a male negro only and he has an inclination to marry a female belonging to a different master, you do not hinder your negro in so delicate a point, but it is of no advantage to you, for the children belong to the master of the female. It is therefore practically advantageous to have negro women. A man who kills his negro is, legally, punishable by death, but there is no instance here of a white man ever having been executed for this crime. A few years ago it happened that a master killed his slave. His friends and even the magistrates secretly advised him to make his escape, as otherwise they could not avoid taking him prisoner, and then he would be condemned to die according to the laws of the country, without any hopes of being saved. This leniency was granted toward him, that the negroes might not have the satisfaction of seeing a master executed for killing his slave. This would lead them to all sorts of dangerous designs against their masters, and to value themselves too much.

The negroes were formerly brought from Africa, as I mentioned before, but now this seldom happens, for they are bought in the West Indies, or American Islands, whither they were originally brought from their own country. It has been found that in transporting the negroes from Africa directly to these northern countries, they have not such good health as when they come gradually, by shorter stages, and are first carried from Africa to the West Indies, and from thence to North America. It has frequently been found, that the negroes cannot stand the cold here so well as the Europeans or whites; for while the latter are not in the least affected by the cold, the toes and fingers of the former are frequently frozen. There is likewise a material difference among them in this point; for those who come immediately from Africa, cannot bear the cold so well as those who are either born in this country, or have been here for a considerable time. The frost easily hurts the hands or feet of the negroes who come

from Africa, or occasions violent pains in their whole body, or in some parts of it, though it does not at all affect those who have been here for some time. There are frequent examples that the negroes on their passage from Africa, if it happens in winter, have some of their limbs frozen on board the ship, when the cold is but very moderate and the sailors are scarcely obliged to cover their hands. I was even assured that some negroes have been seen here who had excessive pain in their legs, which afterwards broke in the middle, and dropped entirely from the body, together with the flesh on them. Thus it is the same case with men here as with plants which are brought from the southern countries, before they accustom themselves to a colder climate.

The price of negroes differs according to their age, health and ability. A full grown negro costs from forty pounds to a hundred of Pennsylvania currency. There are even examples that a gentleman has paid a hundred pounds for a black slave at Philadelphia and refused to sell him again for the same money. A negro boy or girl of two or three years old, can hardly be gotten for less than eight or fourteen pounds in Pennsylvania money. Not only the Quakers but also several Christians of other denominations sometimes set their negroes at liberty. This is done in the following manner: when a gentleman has a faithful negro who has done him great services, he sometimes declares him independent at his own death. This is however very expensive; for they are obliged to make a provision for the negro thus set at liberty, to afford him subsistence when he is grown old, that he may not be driven by necessity to wicked actions, or that he may fall a charge to anybody, for these free negroes become very lazy and indolent afterwards. But the children which the free negro has begot during his servitude are all slaves, though their father be free. On the other hand, those negro children which are born after the parent was freed are free. The negroes in the North American colonies are treated more mildly and fed better than those in the West Indies. They have as good food as the rest of the servants, and they possess equal advantages in all things, except their being obliged to serve their whole lifetime and get no other wages than what their master's goodness allows them. They are likewise clad at their master's expense. On the contrary, in the West Indies, and especially in the Spanish Islands, they are treated very cruelly; therefore no threats make more impression upon a negro here than that of sending him over to the West Indies, in case he will not reform. It has likewise been frequently found by experience that when you show too much kindness to these negroes, they grow so obstinate that they will no longer do anything but of their own accord. Therefore a strict discipline is very necessary, if their master expects to be satisfied with their services.

In the year 1620 some negroes were brought to North America in a Dutch ship, and in Virginia they bought twenty of them. These are said to have been the first that came hither. When the Indians, who were then more numerous in the country than at present, saw these black people for the first time, they thought they were a real breed of devils, and therefore they called them *manito* for a long while. This word in their language signifies not only god but also devil. Some time before that, when they saw the first European ship on their coasts, they were quite convinced that God himself was in the ship. This account I got from some Indians, who preserved it among them as a tradition which they had received from their ancestors. Therefore the arrival of the negroes seemed to them to have confused everything; but since that time, they have entertained less disagreeable notions of the negroes, for at present many live among them, and they even sometimes intermarry, as I myself have seen.

The negroes have therefore been upwards of a hundred and thirty years in this country. As the winters here, especially in New England and New York, are as severe as our Swedish winter, I very carefully inquired whether the cold had not been observed to affect the color of the negroes, and to change it, so that the third or fourth generation from the first that came hither became less black than their ancestors. But I was generally answered that there was not the slightest difference of color to be perceived; and that a negro born here of parents who were likewise born in this country, and whose ancestors, both men and women had all been blacks born in this country, up to the third or fourth generation, was not at all different in color from those negroes who were brought directly from Africa. Hence many people concluded that a negro or his posterity did not change color, though they continued ever so long in a cold climate; but the union of a white man with a negro woman, or of a negro man with a white woman had an entirely different result. Therefore to prevent any disagreeable mixtures of the white people and negroes, and to hinder the latter from forming too great opinions of themselves, to the disadvantage of their masters, I am told there was a law passed prohibiting the whites of both sexes to marry negroes, under pain of almost capital punishment, with deprivation and other severer penalties for the clergyman who married them. But that the whites and blacks sometimes copulated, appears from children of a mixed complexion, which are sometimes born.

It is likewise greatly to be pitied that the masters of these negroes in most of the English colonies take little care of their spiritual welfare, and let them live on in their pagan darkness. There are even some who would be very ill pleased [with negro enlightenment], and would in every way hinder their negroes from being instructed in the doctrines of Christianity. To this they are led partly by the conceit of its being shameful to have a spiritual brother or sister among so despicable a people; partly by thinking that they would not be able to keep their negroes so subjected afterwards; and partly through fear of the negroes growing too proud on seeing themselves upon a level with their masters in religious matters.

Several writings are well known which mention that the negroes in South America have a kind of poison with which they kill each other,

though the effect is not sudden, and takes effect a long time after the person has taken it. The same dangerous art of poisoning is known by the negroes in North America, as has frequently been experienced. However, only a few of them know the secret, and they likewise know the remedy for it; therefore when a negro feels himself poisoned and can recollect the enemy who might possibly have given him the poison, he goes to him, and endeavors by money and entreaties to move him to deliver him from its effects. But if the negro is malicious, he not only denies that he ever poisoned him, but likewise that he knows an antidote for it. This poison does not kill immediately, as I have noted, for sometimes the sick person dies several years afterward. But from the moment he has the poison he falls into a sort of consumption state and enjoys but few days of good health. Such a poor wretch often knows that he is poisoned the moment he gets it. The negroes commonly employ it on such of their brethren as behave well [toward the whites], are beloved by their masters, and separate, as it were, from their countrymen, or do not like to converse with them. They have likewise often other reasons for their enmity; but there are few examples of their having poisoned their masters. Perhaps the mild treatment they receive, keeps them from doing it, or perhaps they fear that they may be discovered, and that in such a case, the severest punishments would be inflicted on them.

They never disclose the nature of the poison, and keep it inconceivably secret. It is probable that it is a very common article, which may be had anywhere in the world; for wherever the blacks are they can always easily procure it. Therefore it cannot be a plant, as several learned men have thought, for that is not to be found everywhere. I have heard many accounts here of negroes who have been killed by this poison. I shall only mention one incident which happened during my stay in this country. A man here had a negro who was exceedingly faithful to him, and behaved so well that he would not have exchanged him for twenty other negroes. His master likewise showed him a peculiar kindness, and the slave's conduct equalled that of the best servant. He likewise conversed as little as possible with the other negroes. On that account they hated him to excess, but as he was scarcely ever in company with them they had no opportunity of conveying the poison to him, which they had often tried. However, on coming to town during the fair (for he lived in the country) some other negroes invited him to drink with them. At first he would not, but they pressed him till he was obliged to comply. As soon as he came into the room, the others took a pot from the wall and pledged him, desiring him to drink likewise. He drank, but when he took the pot from his mouth, he said: "what beer is this? It is full of . . ." I purposely omit what he mentioned, for it seems undoubtedly to have been the name of the poison with which the malicious negroes do so much harm, and which is to be met with almost everywhere. It might be too much employed to wicked purposes, and it is therefore better that it remains unknown. The other negroes and negro-women began laughing at the complaints of their hated countryman, and danced and sang as if they had done an excellent thing, and had at last won the point so much wished for. The innocent negro went away immediately, and when he got home asserted that the other negroes had certainly poisoned him: he then fell into a decline, and no remedy could prevent his death.

11.   Philip Vickers Fithian Observes Slavery in Virginia

In October of 1773 the children of Robert Carter of Nomini Hall received a new tutor. Philip Vickers Fithian was a Princeton-trained divinity stu-

Source: *Philip Vickers Fithian, Journal and Letters 1767–1774,* ed. John Rogers Williams, 2 vols. (Princeton, N.J.: Princeton University Library, 1900), 1:68–69, 145, 190, 247–48, 255.

dent, and much that he saw among the great planters of Tidewater Virginia contrasted sharply with the values of his austere Presbyterianism. But Fithian accepted the games, the dancing, and the fox-hunting with commendable grace, and became much interested in life among the provincial aristocrats.

All that he saw is recorded with a fresh eye for detail, and a remarkable insight into personality. The institution of slavery exhausted his tolerance, however, and he states his opinions on the physical abuse of slaves in no ambiguous terms. Even here, nevertheless, he seems to have separated the evil of slavery as an institution from the particular evil of slaveholding—a nice distinction perhaps, but one that permitted Fithian to admire his employer, Robert Carter, and at the same time harbor the opinion that Carter did not furnish adequate provisions for his slaves. After the Revolution Carter emancipated many of his slaves, and provided them with economic security. Robert Carter of Nomini Hall was the grandson of Robert Carter of Corotoman (see document 8).

[December 23, 1773]— . . . —This Evening, after I had dismissed the Children, & was sitting in the School-Room cracking Nuts, none present but Mᵣ Carters Clerk, a civil, inoffensive, agreeable young Man, who acts both in the character of a Clerk and Steward, when the Woman who makes my Bed, asked me for the key of my Room, and on seeing the young Man sitting with me, she told him that her Mistress had this afternoon given orders that their Allowance of Meat should be given out to them to-morrow.—She left us; I then asked the young man what their allowance is? He told me that, excepting some favourites about the table their weekly allowance is a peck of Corn, & a pound of Meat a Head!—And Mᵣ Carter is allowed by all, & from what I have already seen of others, I make no Doubt at all but he is, by far the most humane to his Slaves of any in these parts!

Good God! are these Christians?—When I am on the Subject, I will relate further, what I heard Mᵣ Georges Lees Overseer, one Morgan, say the other day that he himself had often done to Negroes, and found it useful; He said that whipping of any kind does them no good, for they will laugh at your greatest Severity; But he told us he had invented two things, and by several experiments had proved their sucess.—For Sulleness, Obstinacy, or Idleness, says he, Take a Negro, strip him, tie him fast to a post; take then a sharp Curry-Comb, & curry him severely til he is well scraped; & call a Boy with some dry Hay, and make the Boy rub him down for several Minutes, then salt him, & unlose him. He will attend to his Business, (said the inhuman Infidel) afterwards!—But savage Cruelty does not exceed His next diabolical invention—To get a Secret from a Negro, says he, take the following

Method—Lay upon your Floor a large thick plank, having a peg about eighteen Inches long, of hard wood, & very Sharp, on the upper end, fixed fast in the plank—then strip the Negro, tie the Cord to a staple in the Ceiling, so as that his foot may just rest on the sharpened Peg, then turn him briskly round, and you would laugh (said our informer) at the Dexterity of the Negro, while he was relieving his Feet on the sharpened Peg!—I need say nothing of these seeing there is a righteous God, who will take vengeance on such Inventions! . . .

[April 4, 1774]— . . . After Supper I had a long conversation with Mrs Carter concerning Negroes in Virginia, & find that She esteems their value at no higher rate than I do. We both concluded, (I am pretty certain that the conclusion is just) that if in Mr Carters, or in any Gentlemans Estate, all the Negroes should be sold, & the Money put to Interest in safe hands, & let the Lands which these Negroes now work lie wholly uncultivated, the bare Interest of the price of the Negroes would be a much greater yearly income than what is now received from their working the Lands, making no allowance at all for the trouble & Risk of the Masters as to the Crops, & Negroes.—How much greater then must be the value of an Estate here if these poor enslaved Africans were all in their native desired Country, & in their Room industrious Tenants, who being born in freedom, by a laudable care, would not only enrich their Landlords, but would raise a hardy Offspring to be the Strength and the honour of the Colony.

[July 3, 1774] We were all to go to Church to day, but we were prevented by a storm of thunder & Rain; the Ground is now sufficiently wetted—I have not heard a Sermon on Sunday since the fifteenth of May; a longer Vacancy from publick worship than I have ever had since my first remembrance. About ten an old Negro Man came with a complaint to Mr Carter of the Overseer that he does not allow him his Peck of corn a Week—The humble posture in which the old Fellow placed himself before he began moved me. We were sitting in the passage, he sat himself down on the Floor clasp'd his Hands together, with his face directly to Mr Carter, & then began his Narration—He seem'd healthy, but very old, he was well dress'd but complained bitterly—I cannot like this thing of allowing them no meat, & only a Peck of Corn & a Pint of Salt a Week, & yet requiring of them hard & constant Service. We have several Rains this day so that the Ground is sufficiently wetted—I spent the greater part of the day writing at my Sermon.

[September 8, 1774]— . . . Something alarming happened a few nights ago in the Neighbourhood at Mr *Sorrels* a House in Sight—It is supposed that his Negres had appointed to murder him, several were found in his bed chamber in the middle of the night—his Wife waked—She heard a whispering, one perswading the other to go—On this She waked her Husband, who ran to his Gun; but they escaped in the dark—Presumption is so strong together with a small confession of the fellows, that three are now in Prison—

The ill Treatment which this unhappy part of mankind receives here, would almost justify them in any desperate attempt for gaining that *Civility*, & *Plenty* which tho' denied them, is here, commonly bestowed on Horses!—Now, Laura, I sleep in fear too, though my Doors & Windows are all secured! [1]

[September 17, 1774] . . . Ben returned about seven from Westmoreland Courthouse—He informed us that Mr. *Sorrels* Negroes had their trial there to Day, concerning their accusation of entering their Masters House in the night with an intention to murder Him—It

was there proved (so far as Negroes evidence will go) that a Brother of this Sorrel early last Spring bribed some Negroes to Poison his Brother; & when that diabolical Attempt could not succeed, he has since tried to perswade them to murder Him!—But all evidence against the Negroes was so weak & dark that the judges ordered them to be whiped & dismissed them—Though the Law considers all Testimony given by a Negro against a White-Man as weak & unsubstantial; yet what the Negro said to Day on Oath of the younger Mr. Sorrel, seems to gain much Belief with many who are candid & unbiased Judges; & with me beyond all Scruple, it fixes on him the cursed Character of *Fratricide!*—[2]

1. The "Laura" of Fithian's letters and diary was Miss Elizabeth Beatty, the young lady who became the tutor's wife soon after his return from Virginia on the eve of the American Revolution. (*Editor's note*)

2. After 1777, Negroes could not witness against white men in Virginia courts. (*Ed.*)

12. Benjamin West Sympathizes with Slaves in South Carolina

Throughout the eighteenth century conditions of living remained harsh, and the genuine suffering of slaves, who endured most, would be hard to exaggerate. Even within so miserable a general condition, however, there were varieties of treatment, and it appears that the exploitation of slave labor was much more thorough and debilitating for the slave where slaves were concentrated in large numbers, and engaged in agricultural labor in newly opened terrain where crops commanding high prices in the market

Source: Benjamin West, *Life in the South, 1778–1779: The Letters of Benjamin West*, ed. James S. Schoff (Ann Arbor, Mich.: William L. Clements Library, 1963), pp. 29–31.

were grown. Life was also more precarious for the slave in regions where disease and poor diet took an additional toll of life.

We are indebted to a New Englander, Dr. Benjamin West, for the following succinct account of slaves growing rice and indigo in South Carolina at the beginning of the American Revolution. Born in Massachusetts in 1746, young West was educated at Princeton and Harvard, and had tried his hand at teaching, the ministry, and the law before he decided to come to South Carolina. There he became the tutor of the children of Robert Gibbes. West liked much of what he saw in South Carolina, but slavery he detested, as is clear from the following account. Dr. West returned to the North after brief service in the Revolution, practiced law in New Hampshire, became a Federalist, and played an active part in the Hartford Convention. He died in 1817 in Charlestown, New Hampshire.

There is no difficulty in a man's employing a thousand Negros in planting rice and indigo, tho' there are but very few who own that number. But it is common for one man to own five, six or seven hundred. One hundred is tho't as many as it is profitable to work on one plantation. These are govern'd by an overseer, arm'd with a broad sword, and under him a black driver who always carries a whip, the inventor of which I presume never felt the least pain at the sufferings of his fellow creatures. They plant five acres for every Negro, so that a man who works a thousand plants five thousand acres. The Negroes are allow'd annually (i.e. if they have good masters) a short jacket and a pair of breeches of a coarse cloth call'd negro cloth, and a pair of shoes. They are fed either on corn, rice or peas, and the general rule is to allow them a bushel a month.

The planting of indigo is the most profitable. It is hard to determine the mean profits. The greatest I have known is of one Alstine, who sold his last year's crop of indigo for eighteen thousand pounds lawful money. He work'd two hundred and fifty Negros. Their clothing and shoes at the present price amount to £620, the overseer's wages to £80, the wear of their hoes perhaps twenty more. They raised their own provisions, and as the working of indigo employs them not more than eight months, they did much other service; so that deducting all expences there will remain (at least) seventeen thousand pounds clear profits. They make no use of ploughs but turn all their land with hoes.

The planting of rice is very destructive to their Negros, as it must be planted on low land where they can have the command of the water to flow it often; for which purpose they keep large bodies of water in reserve which being stagnant corrupt and become extremely unwholesome. But this is not so fatal as the excessive hard labor of beating the rice in mortars to separate it from a hard stiff hull which adheres to it. This (where there is a severe overseer) generally carries of[f] great numbers every winter. The servants that they keep about [the] house fare very differently from the field Negro[e]s. These are genteelly dressed and (in good families) well fed, but have their full share of flogging. . . .

I have many anecdotes of the behavior and treatment of Negros, but as they would rather give you pain then pleasure, I shall not relate them, but only observe that notwithstanding the despicable opinion which is generally entertain'd of that order of beings, there are many who give evident tokens of a courage, resolution and genious which in happier circumstances would transmit their names with honor to posterity. And yet a man will shoot a Negro with as little emotion as he shoots a hare, several instances of which have come within my own knowledge since I've been there. They have also a brief way of trying Negros for capital crimes. The court consists of one Justice and two freeholders, who order the Negro before them at any place, try him, and hang him up immediately. But there would perhaps be but few Negros prosecuted were it not from interested motives, for when a Negro is hanged by authority the government pay his master his full value, which if he shoots him he loses; this brings many to the gallows who would otherwise receive their pass to the other world from the musket of their masters.

13. Masters Describe Their Runaway Slaves

Among the most detailed descriptions of eighteenth-century slaves are those made by masters hoping to retrieve their absconding property, and by sheriffs, of slaves they had captured in flight. The "new Negroes," often described as "outlandish," were Africans not yet acculturated to plantation slavery and English ways. They often spoke little or no English, and they frequently bore their "country marks," or tribal cicatrizations. They were often less skillful in their attempts at escape than were the ac-

Source: Reprinted in Ulrich Bonnell Phillips, ed., Plantation and Frontier, vols. 1 and 2 of A Documentary History of American Industrial Society, ed. John R. Commons and others (Cleveland: A. H. Clark, 1909), 2:88–89, 93, 86–87.

culturated slaves, who had more knowledge of the country, disguised themselves more cleverly, and frequently had learned a trade or craft.

The following are typical eighteenth-century advertisements. When slaves were "outlawed" by their masters and the courts, they could be returned dead or alive. The casual barbarity of the advertisements of the period reveals much about general attitudes toward slave property and reflects a general insensitivity to pain as well.

[I]

Taken up on the 26th of July last, and now in Newbern goal [jail], North Carolina, Two New Negro Men, the one named Joe, about 45 years of age, about 5 feet 6 inches high, much wrinkled in the face, and speaks bad English. The other is a young fellow, about 5 feet 10 inches high speaks better English than Joe, who he says is his father, has a large scar on the fleshy part of his left arm, and says they belong to Joseph Morse, but can give no account where he lives. They have nothing with them but an old Negro cloth jacket, and an old blue sailors jacket without sleeves. Also on the 21st of September was committed to the said goal a Negro man named Jack, about 23 years of age, about 5 feet 4 inches high, of a thin visage, blear eyed, his teeth and mouth stand very much out, has six rings of his country marks round his neck, his ears full of holes, and cannot tell his master's name. And on the 27th of September two other Negro men, one named Sampson, about 5 feet 10 inches high, about 25 years of age, well made, very black, and is much marked on his body and arms with his country marks. The other named Will, about 5 feet 4 inches high, about 22 years of age, and marked on the chin with his country marks; they speak bad English, and cannot tell their masters names. Whoever own the said Negroes are desired to come and pay the fees and take them away.

RICHARD BLACKLEDGE, Sheriff.

Virginia Gazette (Williamsburg), Nov. 5, 1767.

[II]

Run away about the 15th of December last, a small yellow Negro wench named Hannah, about 35 years of age; had on when she went away a green plains petticoat, and sundry other clothes, but what sort I do not know, as she stole many from the other Negroes. She has remarkable long hair, or wool, is much scarified under the throat from one ear to the other, and has many scars on her back, occasioned by whipping. She pretends much to the religion the Negroes of late have practised, and may probably endeavour to pass for a free woman, as I understand she intended when she went away, by the Negroes in the neighbourhood. She is supposed to have made for Carolina. Whoever takes up the said slave, and secures her so that I get her again, shall be rewarded according to their trouble, by

STEPHEN DENCE.

Virginia Gazette (Williamsburg), March 26, 1767.

[III]

Run Away from the subscriber in Norfork, about the 20th of October last, two young Negro fellows, viz. Will, about 5 feet 8 inches high, middling black, well made, is an outlandish fellow, and when he is surprised the white of his eyes turns red; I bought him of Mr. Moss, about 8 miles below York, and imagine he is gone that way, or some where between York and Williamsburg. Peter, about 5 feet 9 inches high, a very black slim fellow, has a wife at Little Town, and a father at Mr. Philip Burt's quarter, near the half-way house between Williamsburg and York, he formerly belonged to Parson Fontaine, and I bought him of Doctor James Carter. They are both outlawed; and Ten Pounds a piece offered to any person that will kill the said Negroes, and bring me their heads, or Thirty Shillings for each if brought home alive.

JOHN BROWN.

Virginia Gazette (Williamsburg), April 23, 1767.

TWO
Slavery Survives the American Revolution

14. Saul, Revolution Veteran, Petitions for Freedom

During the American Revolution the institution of slavery was a formidable liability to the Southern colonies. Slavery was in conflict with the ideology of the natural rights of man, to be sure, but it also made the South vulnerable to insurrection and invasion from the British, if and when they chose to enlist the slaves on their side. The presence of a large concentration of slaves in the coastal regions virtually invited the British to throw the plantations into turmoil by holding out to the blacks the hope of emancipation. Lord Dunmore's invitation to the blacks to desert their masters, during the early months of the war, was successful enough in Virginia to establish emancipation of slaves as a significant British war measure. The British might, in fact, have proclaimed a general emancipation in the rebellious colonies but for the fear that a slave insurrection would have punished the loyalists as well as the rebellious colonials.

The colonials countered the British offer of freedom to fugitive slaves by offering freedom to those slaves who fought against the British. Many slaves served ably and enthusiastically, as did Saul, who stated his case in the document below. The claims of men like him were honored in most instances. Saul's petition, undated, was considered by the Virginia General Assembly on November 13, 1792, and Saul was granted his freedom. The state assumed the cost of his purchase from his master, George Kelly of Norfolk. More important for slaves than the emancipation of individuals was the philosophy of natural rights, basic to the American Revolution. Slaves could hope that this philosophy would shame their owners into striving for consistency by means of a general emancipation.

To the Honorable, the Speaker, and Members of the general Assembly.

The petition of Saul, a black slave, the property of Geo. Kelly, Esqr. Humbly sheweth.—In the beginning of the late War, that gave America Independence, Your Petitioner Shouldered his Musket and repaired to the American Standard. Regardless of the Invitation, trumpeted forth by British Proclamations, for slaves to Emancipate themselves, by becoming the Assassins of

Source: General Assembly, Petitions, Norfolk, August-October, 1792, Virginia State Library, Richmond, Va.

their owners, Your Petitioner avoided the rock, that too many of his colour were Shipwrecked on.—He was taught to know that War was levied upon America, not for the Emancipation of Blacks, but for the Subjugation of Whites, and he thought the number of Bond-men ought not to be augmented; Under those impressions, your Petitioner did actually Campaign it in both Armies,—in the American Army, as a Soldier,—In the British Army as a Spy, which will more fully appear, reference being had to certificates of Officers of respectability. In this double Profession, Your Petitioner flatters himself that he rendered essential service to his Country, and should have rendered much more had he not, in the Campaign of 1781, been betrayed by a Negro whom the British had employed upon the same business in Gen. Mulinburg's [1] Camp. Your Petitioner was at the time, in Portsmouth, a British Garrison, collecting Information for Colonel Josiah Parker, and his heels saved his neck.—He flew to the advance Post, commanded by Col Parker, and that very night led down the party, as a guide, who took off the British Picquett.—

Your Petitioner will trouble Your Honorable Body no further, with enumerating his different species of services, but begs a reference may be had to his ceritficates, and to the Honorable Thomas Matthews Esquire.—Hoping the Legislatures of a Republick will take his case in consideration and not suffer him any longer to remain a transferable property. And as in duty bound Your Petitioner will ever Pray.

Saul   X   (his mark)

1. Probably Maj. Gen. John Peter Muhlenberg.

15.   Virginia Authorizes Private Manumission

During the eighteenth century, slavery was in practice a more flexible institution that it became in the nineteenth, even though the specific physical conditions of life were harsher for most slaves, and the legal systems of the slave-holding colonies still permitted savage and barbarous punishments for recalcitrants.

In the eighteenth century the African slaves became better acculturated to English ways, and many became skilled artisans, enjoying considerable

Source: William Waller Hening, ed., The Statutes at Large: Being a Collection of All the Laws of Virginia, from the First Session of the Legislature in the Year 1619, 13 vols. (Richmond, 1809–23).

personal mobility in pursuit of their crafts. Alarm over this situation prompted the colonial legislators of Virginia to pass in 1723 a severe law making it impossible for individuals to emancipate slaves without the consent of the Governor and the Council. In 1782 the Revolutionary philosophy of the rights of man caused a reaction against that harsh policy, and the following law, facilitating private manumission, was enacted. During the two ensuing decades, the nucleus of a large free-black community was formed in the Upper South. For the significance of this development, consult Ira Berlin, *Slaves Without Masters* (New York, 1975).

An act to authorize the manumission of slaves.

I. WHEREAS application hath been made to this present general assembly, that those persons who are disposed to emancipate their slaves may be empowered so to do, and the same hath been judged expedient under certain restrictions: *Be it therefore enacted,* That it shall hereafter be lawful for any person, by his or her last will and testament, or by any other instrument in writing, under his or her hand and seal, attested and proved in the county court by two witnesses, or acknowledged by the party in the court of the county where he or she resides, to emancipate and set free, his or her slaves, or any of them, who shall thereupon be entirely and fully discharged from the performance of any contract entered into during servitude, and enjoy as full freedom as if they had been particularly named and freed by this act.

II. *Provided always, and be it further enacted,* That all slaves so set free, not being in the judgment of the court, of sound mind and body, or being above the age of forty-five years, or being males under the age of twenty-one, or females under the age of eighteen years, shall respectively be supported and maintained by the person so liberating them, or by his or her estate; and upon neglect or refusal so to do, the court of the county where such neglect or refusal may be, is hereby empowered and required, upon application to them made, to order the sheriff to distrain and sell so much of the person's estate as shall be sufficient for that purpose. *Provided also,* That every person by written instrument in his life time, or if by last will and testament, the executors of every person freeing any slave, shall cause to be delivered to him or her, a copy of the instrument of emancipation, attested by the clerk of the court of the county, who shall be paid therefor, by the person emancipating, five shillings, to be collected in the manner of other clerk's fees. Every person neglecting or refusing to deliver to any slave by him or her set free, such copy, shall forfeit and pay ten pounds, to be recovered with costs in any court of record, one half thereof to the person suing for the same, and the other to the person to whom such copy ought to have been delivered. It shall be lawful for any justice of the peace to commit to the gaol of his county, any emancipated slave travelling out of the county of his or her residence without a copy of the instrument of his or her emancipation, there to remain till such copy is produced and the gaoler's fees paid.

III. *And be it further enacted,* That in case any slave so liberated shall neglect in any year to pay all taxes and levies imposed or to be imposed by law, the court of the county shall order the sheriff to hire out him or her for so long time as will raise the said taxes and levies. *Provided* sufficient distress cannot be made upon his or her estate. *Saving nevertheless* to all and every person and persons, bodies politic or corporate, and their heirs and successors, other than the person or persons claiming under those so emancipating their slaves, all such right and title as they or any of them could or might claim if this act had never been made.

Statutes 11:39–40

16. Richard Randolph Explains His Act of Manumission

In 1782 there were only two thousand free Negroes in Virginia. Taking advantage of the opportunities available in Virginia after the 1782 law (see document 15), the owners of some ten thousand slaves freed their human property before the year 1790. By 1810 the number of free blacks had reached thirty thousand. Richard Randolph, elder brother of John Randolph of Roanoke, explained his inspiration and motives for emancipating his slaves in the preamble to his Last Will and Testament. Richard died in 1796, when his brother John was on the eve of his brilliant if erratic career as Representative and Senator from Virginia. Like his famous brother, Richard excelled in invective, as the denunciation of slavery in his will amply attests.

Because Richard Randolph emancipated his slaves before the law was passed requiring free blacks to leave the state, he established a community for them called Israel Hill. Neighbors complained that the community was a mistake, that the freedmen were lazy and corrupt, and that they set a

Source: William Cabell Bruce, *John Randolph of Roanoke: 1773–1833* (New York: Putnam, 1922), 1:104–5. The original is in the *Will Book for 1797,* Clerk's Office, Prince Edward County, Virginia.

bad example for slaves. Israel Hill was freely cited by those who opposed the policy of emancipation.

To make retribution, as far as I am able, to an unfortunate race of bondmen, over whom my ancestors have usurped and exercised the most lawless and monstrous tyranny, and in whom my countrymen (by their iniquitous laws, in contradiction of their own declaration of rights, and in violation of every sacred law of nature; of the inherent, inalienable and imprescriptible rights of man, and of every principle of moral and political honesty) have vested me with absolute property; to express my abhorrence of the theory as well as infamous practice of usurping the rights of our fellow creatures, equally entitled with ourselves to the enjoyment of liberty and happiness; to exculpate myself to those, who may perchance think or hear of me after death, from the black crime which might otherwise be imputed to me of voluntarily holding the above mentioned miserable beings in the same state of abject slavery in which I found them on receiving my patrimony at lawful age; to impress my children with just horror at a crime so enormous and indelible; to conjure them, in the last words of a fond father, never to participate in it in any the remotest degree, however sanctioned by laws (framed by the tyrants themselves who oppress them), or supported by false reasoning; used always to veil the sordid views of avarice and the lust of power; to declare to them and to the world that nothing but uncontrollable necessity, forced on me by my father (who wrongfully bound over them to satisfy the rapacious creditors of a brother who, for this purpose, which he falsely believed to be generous, mortgaged all his slaves to British harpies for money to gratify pride and pamper sensuality; by which mortgage, the said slaves being bound, I could not exercise the right of ownership necessary to their emancipation, and, being obliged to keep them on my land, was driven reluctantly to violate them in a great degree) (though I trust far less than others have done) in order to maintain them . . . ; for the aforesaid purposes and, with an indignation, too great for utterance, at the tyrants of the earth, from the throned despot of a whole nation to the most despicable, but not less infamous, petty tormentors of single wretched slaves, whose torture constitutes his wealth and enjoyment, I do hereby declare that it is my will and desire, nay most anxious wish that my negroes, all of them, be liberated, and I do declare them by this writing free and emancipated to all intents and purposes whatsoever.

17. Citizens of Halifax County Petition Against Emancipation

All too soon the rapid increase of the free black population induced a reaction to the policy of 1782, which eased private emancipation. Petitions like the following one from Halifax County, Virginia, signed by 261 citizens, soon had effect upon legislation. Free Negroes were forbidden to enter the state by an Act of 1793, and the right of private manumission, which seemed to some to "imperil" the white community, came under serious debate. The comings and goings of free blacks made the detection and apprehension of slave runaways difficult. Sometimes free blacks "harboured" runaways. (See document 20). Gabriel Prosser's plot for an insurrection (see document 27), exposed in 1800, added to the general alarm that was already accelerating in the 1790s. In 1806 the Virginia Assembly, although refusing to overturn the Act of 1782 directly, made manumission much less attractive to slave and master alike, by prescribing that slaves emancipated after that Act was passed be sent out of the state. Neighboring states soon threw up their own barriers against the immigration of free blacks, and manumission by private action declined sharply.

The petitions of the 1780s commonly employed three arguments that were associated with the fully developed pro-slavery argument of the post-1830 period: Biblical sanction, the sanctity of private property, the prosperity and safety of the community. One reason that the Biblical defense emerged so prominently was that Quakers and Methodists were moving rapidly toward general emancipation as a logical extension of the policy of 1782. I am indebted to Fredrika Teute for her analysis of these petitions.

To the honourable the General Assembly of Virginia the Remonstrance and Petition of the Free Inhabitants of Halifax County.

Gentlemen,

When the British Parliament usurped a Right to dispose of our Property without our Consent, we dissolved the Union with our Parent Country, & established a Constitution and Form of Government of our own,

Source: General Assembly, Petitions, Halifax County [November 10, 1785], Virginia State Library, Richmond, Va.

that our Property might be secure in Future. In order to effect this, we risked our Lives & Fortunes, and waded through Seas of Blood. Divine Providence smiled on our Enterprise, and crowned it with Success. And our Rights of Liberty and Property are now as well secured to us, as they can by any human Constitution & Form of Government.

But notwithstanding this, we understand, a very subtle and daring Attempt is on Foot to deprive us of a very important Part of our Property. An Attempt carried on by the Enemies of our Country, Tools of the British Administration, and supported by a Number of deluded Men among us, to wrest from us our Slaves by an Act of the Legislature for a general Emancipation of them. They have the Address, indeed to cover their Design, with the Veil of Piety, and Liberality of Sentiment. But it is unsupported by the Word of God, and will be ruinous to Individuals and to the Public.

It is unsupported by the Word of God. Under the Old Testament Dispensation, Slavery was permitted by the Deity himself. Thus it is recorded, Levit. Chap. 25. Ver. 44, 45, 46. "Both they Bond-men, and Bond-Maids, which thou shalt have, shall be of the Heathen that are round about you; of them shall ye buy Bond-men and Bond-maids. Moreover, of the Children of the Strangers, that do sojourn among you of them shall ye buy, and of their Families that are with you, which they beget in your Land, and they shall be your Possession, and ye shall take them, as an Inheritance for your Children after you, to inherit them for a Possession; they shall be

your Bond-men forever." This Permission to possess and inherit Bond Servants, we have Reason to conclude, was continued through all the Revolutions of the Jewish Government, down to the Advent of our Lord. And we do not find, that either he or his Apostles abridged it. On the Contrary, the Freedom which the Followers of Jesus were taught to expect, was a Freedom from the Bondage of Sin and Satan, and from the Dominion of their Lusts and Passions; but as to their outward Condition, whatever that was, whether Bond or Free, when they embraced Christianity, it was to remain the same afterwards. This Saint Paul hath expressly told us 1 Cor. Chap. 7. Ver. 20th. where he is speaking directly to this very Point; "Let every Man abide in the same Calling, wherein he is called"; and at Ver. 24. "Let every Man wherein he is called therein abide with God." Thus it is evident the above Attempt is unsupported by the Divine Word.

It is also ruinous to Individuals & to the Public. For it involves in it, and is productive of Want, Poverty, Distress, and Ruin to the Free Citizen; Neglect, Famine, and Death to the helpless black Infant & superannuated Parent; the Horrors of all the Rapes, Murders, and Outrages, which a vast Multitude of unprincipled, unpropertied, vindictive, and remorseless Benditti are capable of perpetrating; inevitable Bankruptcy to the Revenue, and consequently Breach of public Faith, and Loss of Credit with foreign Nations; and lastly Ruin to this now free and flourishing Country.

We therefore your Remonstrants, and Petitioners do solemnly adjure and humbly pray you, that you will discountenance and utterly reject every Motion and Proposal for emancipating our Slaves; that as the Act lately made, empowering the Owners of Slaves to liberate them, has been and is still productive, in some Measure, of sundry of the above pernicious Effects, you will immediately and totally repeal it; and that as many of the Slaves, liberated by the said Act, have been guilty of Thefts and Outrages, Insolences and Violences destructive to the Peace, Safety, and Happiness of Society, you will make effectual Provision for the due Government of them.

And your Remonstrants & Petitioners shall ever pray, &c.

18. Thomas Jefferson Condemns Slavery But Asserts Racial Differences

No philosopher of the Revolution was more devoted to the philosophy of the rights of man than Thomas Jefferson. In his famous *Notes on the State of Virginia*, written in 1782, and first published in 1787, Jefferson blasted the institution of slavery for its effects on slave owners. Yet the same book contains a close examination of racial characteristics that shows the author's troubled state of mind on the subject. His conclusions suggest strongly that he believed the differences he observed between white and black people to be innate, and uncomplimentary to blacks. Because the theory of racial inferiority became in time an important item in the proslavery argument, Jefferson's observations were prophetic. Believing that whites and blacks would be unable to live together on a basis of equality, Jefferson advocated colonization of free blacks as a solution to a problem that he feared could wreck the young republic.

Jefferson was himself one of the three men he mentions as having revised the laws. The others were George Wythe (Jefferson's former teacher) and Edmund Pendleton.

Source: Thomas Jefferson, *Notes on the State of Virginia.* 2d American ed. (Philadelphia: Mathew Carey, 1794), pp. 187, 198–210, 236–38.

Query XIV.
*The Administration of Justice and the
Description of the Laws?*
. . .

Many of the laws which were in force
during the monarchy being relative
merely to that form of government, or
inculcating principles inconsistent
with republicanism, the first assembly
which met after the establishment of
the commonwealth appointed a committee to revise the whole code, to reduce it into proper form and volume,
and report it to the assembly. This
work has been executed by three gentlemen, and reported; but probably
will not be taken up till a restoration of
peace shall leave to the legislature leisure to go through such a work.

The plan of the revisal was this. The
common law of England, by which is
meant, that part of the English law
which was anterior to the date of the
oldest statutes extant, is made the
basis of the work. It was thought dangerous to attempt to reduce it to a text:
it was therefore left to be collected
from the usual monuments of it. Necessary alterations in that, and so much
of the whole body of the British statutes, and of acts of assembly, as were
thought proper to be retained, were
digested into 126 new acts, in which
simplicity of style was aimed at, as far
as was safe. The following are the most
remarkable alterations proposed:

To change the rules of descent, so as
that the lands of any person dying in-
testate shall be divisible equally among
all his children, or other representatives, in equal degree.

To make slaves distributable among
the next of kin, as other moveables.

To have all public expences, whether

of the general treasury, or of a parish
or county, (as for the maintenance of
the poor, building bridges, courthouses, &c.) supplied by assessments
on the citizens, in proportion to their
property.

To hire undertakers for keeping the
public roads in repair, and indemnify
individuals through whose lands new
roads shall be opened.

To define with precision the rules
whereby aliens should become citizens, and citizens make themselves
aliens.

To establish religious freedom on the
broadest bottom.

To emancipate all slaves born after
passing the act. The bill reported by
the revisors does not itself contain this
proposition; but an amendment containing it was prepared, to be offered
to the legislature whenever the bill
should be taken up, and further directing, that they should continue with
their parents to a certain age, then be
brought up, at the public expence, to
tillage, arts or sciences, according to
their geniusses, till the females should
be eighteen, and the males twenty-one
years of age, when they should be colonized to such place as the circumstances of the time should render most
proper, sending them out with arms,
implements of household and of the
handicraft arts, feeds, pairs of the useful domestic animals, &c. to declare
them a free and independent people,
and extend to them our alliance and
protection, till they have acquired
strength; and to send vessels at the
same time to other parts of the world
for an equal number of white inhabitants; to induce whom to migrate
hither, proper encouragements were to

be proposed. It will probably be asked, Why not retain and incorporate the blacks into the state, and thus save the expence of supplying by importation of white settlers, the vacancies they will leave? Deep rooted prejudices entertained by the whites; ten thousand recollections, by the blacks, of the injuries they have sustained; new provocations; the real distinctions which nature has made; and many other circumstances, will divide us into parties, and produce convulsions, which will probably never end but in the extermination of the one or the other race. —To these objections, which are political, may be added others, which are physical and moral. The first difference which strikes us is that of colour. Whether the black of the negro resides in the reticular membrane between the skin and scarf-skin, or in the scarf-skin itself; whether it proceeds from the colour of the blood, the colour of the bile, or from that of some other secretion, the difference is fixed in nature, and is as real as if its seat and cause were better known to us. And is this difference of no importance? Is it not the foundation of a greater or less share of beauty in the two races? Are not the fine mixtures of red and white, the expressions of every passion by greater or less suffusions of colour in the one, preferable to that eternal monotony, which reigns in the countenances, that immoveable veil of black which covers all the emotions of the other race? Add to these, flowing hair, a more elegant symmetry of form, their own judgment in favour of the whites, declared by their preference of them, as uniformly as is the preference of the Oranootan for the black women over

those of his own species. The circumstance of superior beauty, is thought worthy attention in the propagation of our horses, dogs, and other domestic animals; why not in that of man? Besides those of colour, figure, and hair, there are other physical distinctions proving a difference of race. They have less hair on the face and body. They secrete less by the kidnies, and more by the glands of the skin, which gives them a very strong and disagreeable odour. This greater degree of transpiration renders them more tolerant of heat, and less so of cold than the whites. Perhaps too a difference of structure in the pulmonary apparatus, which a late ingenious [1] experimentalist has discovered to be the principal regulator of animal heat, may have disabled them from extricating, in the act of inspiration, so much of that fluid from the outer air, or obliged them in expiration, to part with more of it. They seem to require less sleep. A black after hard labour through the day, will be induced by the slightest amusements to sit up till midnight, or later though knowing he must be out with the first dawn of the morning. They are at least as brave, and more adventuresome. But this may perhaps proceed from a want of forethought, which prevents their seeing a danger till it be present. When present, they do not go through it with more coolness or steadiness than the whites. They are more ardent after their female: but love seems with them to be more an eager desire, than a tender delicate mixture of sentiment and sen-

1. Crawford. (Adair Crawford, *Experiments and Observations on Animal Heat.* London, 1779 [Editor's note].)

sation. Their griefs are transient. Those numberless afflictions, which render it doubtful whether heaven has given life to us in mercy or in wrath, are less felt, and sooner forgotten with them. In general, their existence appears to participate more of sensation than reflection. To this must be ascribed their disposition to sleep when abstracted from their diversions, and unemployed in labour. An animal whose body is at rest, and who does not reflect, must be disposed to sleep of course. Comparing them by their faculties of memory, reason, and imagination, it appears to me that in memory they are equal to the whites; in reason much inferior, as I think one could scarcely be found capable of tracing and comprehending the investigations of Euclid; and that in imagination they are dull, tasteless, and anomalous. It would be unfair to follow them to Africa for this investigation. We will consider them here, on the same stage with the whites, and where the facts are not apocryphal on which a judgement is to be formed. It will be right to make great allowances for the difference of condition, of education, of conversation, of the sphere in which they move. Many millions of them have been brought to, and born in America. Most of them indeed have been confined to tillage, to their own homes, and their own society: yet many have been so situated, that they might have availed themselves of the conversation of their masters; many have been brought up to the handicraft arts, and from that circumstance have always been associated with the whites. Some have been liberally educated, and all have lived in countries where the arts and sciences are cultivated to a considerable degree, and have had before their eyes samples of the best works from abroad. The Indians, with no advantages of this kind, will often carve figures on their pipes not destitute of design and merit. They will crayon out an animal, a plant, or a country, so as to prove the existence of a germ in their minds which only wants cultivation. They astonish you with strokes of the most sublime oratory; such as prove their reason and sentiment strong, their imagination glowing and elevated. But never yet could I find that a black had uttered a thought above the level of plain narration; never see even an elementary trait of painting or sculpture. In music they are more generally gifted than the whites with accurate ears for tune and time, and they have been found capable of imagining a small catch.[2] Whether they will be equal to the composition of a more extensive run of melody, or of complicated harmony, is yet to be proved. Misery is often the parent of the most affecting touches in poetry.—Among the blacks is misery enough, God knows, but no poetry. Love is the peculiar cestrum of the poet. Their love is ardent, but it kindles the senses only, not the imagination. Religion indeed has produced a Phyllis Whately; but it could not produce a poet. The compositions published under her name are below the dignity of criticism. The heroes of the Dunciad are to her, as Hercules to the author of that poem. Ignatius Sancho

2. The instrument proper to them is the Banjar, which they brought hither from Africa, and which is the original of the guitar, its chords being precisely the four lower chords of the guitar.

has approached nearer to merit in composition; yet his letters do more honour to the heart than the head. They breathe the purest effusions of friendship and general philanthropy, and shew how great a degree of the latter may be compounded with strong religious zeal. He is often happy in the turn of his compliments, and his stile is easy and familiar, except when he affects a Shandean fabrication of words. But his imagination is wild and extravagant, escapes incessantly from every restraint of reason and taste, and, in the course of its vagaries, leaves a tract of thought as incoherent and eccentric, as is the course of a meteor through the sky. His subjects should often have led him to a process of sober reasoning: yet we find him always substituting sentiment for demonstration. Upon the whole, though we admit him to the first place among those of his own colour who have presented themselves to the public judgment, yet when we compare him with the writers of the race among whom he lived and particularly with the epistolary class, in which he has taken his own stand, we are compelled to enroll him at the bottom of the column. This criticism supposes the letters published under his name to be genuine, and to have received amendment from no other hand; points which would not be of easy investigation. The improvement of the blacks in body and mind, in the first instance of their mixture with the whites, has been observed by every one, and proves that their inferiority is not the effect merely of their condition of life. We know that among the Romans, about the Augustan age especially, the condition of their slaves

was much more deplorable than that of the blacks on the continent of America. The two sexes were confined in separate apartments, because to raise a child cost the master more than to buy one. Cato, for a very restricted indulgence to his slaves in this particular,[3] took from them a certain price. But in this country the slaves multiply as fast as the free inhabitants. Their situation and manners place the commerce between the two sexes almost without restraint.—The same Cato, on a principle of œconomy, always sold his sick and superannuated slaves. He gives it as a standing precept to a master visiting his farm, to sell his old oxen, old waggons, old tools, old and diseased servants, and every thing else become useless. "Vendat boves vetulos, plaustrum vetus, ferramenta vetera, servum senem, servum morbosum, & si quid aliud supersit vendat." Cato de re rustica, c. 2. The American slaves cannot enumerate this among the injuries and insults they receive. It was the common practice to expose in the island Aesculapius, in the Tyber, diseased slaves, whose cure was like to become tedious.[4] The emperor Claudius, by an edict, gave freedom to such of them as should recover, and first declared that if any person chose to kill rather than expose them, it should be deemed homicide. The exposing them is a crime of which no instance has existed with us; and were it to be followed by death, it would be

3. *Tous doulous etaxen ōrismenou nomesmatos homilein tais therapainisin.* Plutarch, Cato. (He permitted male slaves to have intercourse with the female for a fee [Ed.].)
4. Suet. Claud, 25. (Gaius Suetonius Tranquillus, *Lives of The Caesars* [Ed.].)

punished capitally. We are told of a certain Vedius Pollio, who, in the presence of Augustus, would have given a slave as food to his fish, for having broken a glass. With the Romans, the regular method of taking the evidence of their slaves was under torture. Here it has been thought better never to resort to their evidence. When a master was murdered, all his slaves, in the same house, or within hearing, were condemned to death. Here punishment falls on the guilty only, and as precise proof is required against him as against a freeman. Yet notwithstanding these and other discouraging circumstances among the Romans, their slaves were often their rarest artists. They excelled too in science, insomuch as to be usually employed as tutors to their master's children. Epictetus, Terence, and Phaedrus, were slaves. But they were of the race of whites. It is not their condition then, but nature, which has produced the distinction. —Whether further observation will or will not verify the conjecture, that nature has been less bountiful to them in the endowments of the head, I believe that in those of the heart she will be found to have done them justice. That disposition to theft with which they have been branded, must be ascribed to their situation, and not to any depravity of the moral sense. The man, in whose favour no laws of property exist, probably feels himself less bound to respect those made in favour of others. When arguing for ourselves, we lay it down as a fundamental, that laws, to be just, must give a reciprocation of right: that, without this, they are mere arbitrary rules of conduct, founded in force, and not in con-

science: and it is a problem which I give to the master to solve, whether the religious precepts against the violation of property were not framed for him as well as his slave? And whether the slave may not as justifiably take a little from one, who has taken all from him, as he may slay one would slay him? That a change in the relations in which a man is placed should change his ideas of moral right and wrong, is neither new, nor peculiar to the colour of the blacks. Homer tells us it was so 2600 years ago.

'Emisu, ger t' aretes apoainutai europa Zeus
Haneros, eut' an min kata doulion ema elesin.

Od. 17.323.

Jove fix'd it certain, that whatever day Makes man a slave takes half his worth away.

But the slaves of which Homer speaks were whites. Notwithstanding these considerations which must weaken their respect for the laws of property, we find among them numerous instances of the most rigid integrity, and as many as among their better instructed masters, of benevolence, gratitude, and unshaken fidelity.—The opinion, that they are inferior in the faculties of reason and imagination, must be hazarded with great diffidence. To justify a general conclusion, requires many observations, even where the subject may be submitted to the anatomical knife, to optical glasses, to analysis by fire, or by solvents. How much more then where it is a faculty, not a substance, we are examining; where it eludes the research of all the senses; where the conditions of its existence are various and variously combined; where the effects of those which are present or absent bid defiance to calculation; let me add too, as a circumstance of great tenderness, where our conclusion would degrade a whole race of men from the rank in the scale of beings which their Creator may perhaps have given them. To our reproach it must be said, that though for a century and a half we have had under our eyes the races of black and of red men, they have never yet been viewed by us as subjects of natural history. I advance it therefore as a suspicion only, that the blacks, whether originally a distinct race, or made distinct by time and circumstances, are inferior to the whites in the endowments both of body and mind. It is not against experience to suppose, that different species of the same genus, or varieties of the same species, may possess different qualifications. Will not a lover of natural history then, one who views the gradations in all the races of animals with the eye of philosophy, excuse an effort to keep those in the department of man as distinct as nature has formed them? This unfortunate difference of colour, and perhaps of faculty, is a powerful obstacle to the emancipation of these people. Many of their advocates, while they wish to vindicate the liberty of human nature are anxious also to preserve its dignity and beauty. Some of these, embarassed by the question "What further is to be done with them?" join themselves in opposition with those who are actuated by sordid avarice only. Among the Romans emancipation required but one effort.

The slave, when made free, might mix with, without staining the blood of his master. But with us a second is necessary, unknown to history. When freed, he is to be removed beyond the reach of mixture. . . .

Query XVIII.
The particular *customs and manners that may happen to be received in that state?*

It is difficult to determine on the standard by which the manners of a nation may be tried, whether *catholic*, or *particular*. It is more difficult for a native to bring to that standard the manners of his own nation, familiarized to him by habit. There must doubtless be an unhappy influence on the manners of our people produced by the existence of slavery among us. The whole commerce between master and slave is a perpetual exercise of the most boisterous passions, the most unremitting despotism on the one part, and degrading submissions on the other. Our children see this, and learn to imitate it; for man is an imitative animal. This quality is the germ of all education in him. From his cradle to his grave he is learning to do what he sees others do. If a parent could find no motive either in his philanthropy or his self-love, for restraining the intemperance of passion towards his slave, it would always be a sufficient one that his child is present. But generally it is not sufficient. The parent storms, the child looks on, catches the lineaments of wrath, puts on the same airs in the circle of smaller slaves, gives a loose to the his worst of passions, and thus nursed, educated, and daily exercised in tyranny, cannot but be stamped by it with odious peculiarities. The man must be a prodigy who can retain his manners and morals undepraved by such circumstances. And with what execration should the statesman be loaded, who permitting one half the citizens thus to trample on the rights of the other, transforms those into despots, and these into enemies, destroys the morals of the one part, and the amor patriae of the other. For if a slave can have a country in this world, it must be any other in preference to that in which he is born to live and labour for another: in which he must lock up the faculties of his nature, contribute as far as depends on his individual endeavours to the evanishment of the human race, or entail his own miserable condition on the endless generations proceeding from him. With the morals of the people, their industry also is destroyed. For in a warm climate, no man will labour for himself who can make another labour for him. This is so true, that of the proprietors of slaves a very small proportion indeed are ever seen to labour. And can the liberties of a nation be thought secure when we have removed their only

firm basis, a conviction in the minds of the people that these liberties are of the gift of God? That they are not to be violated but with his wrath? Indeed I tremble for my country when I reflect that God is just: that his justice cannot sleep for ever: that considering numbers, nature and natural means only, a revolution of the wheel of fortune, an exchange of situation is among possible events: that it may become probable by supernatural interference! The almighty has no attribute which can take side with us in such a contest. —But it is impossible to be temperate and to pursue this subject through the various considerations of policy, or morals, of history natural and civil. We must be contented to hope they will force their way into every one's mind. I think a change already perceptible, since the origin of the present revolution. The spirit of the master is abating, that of the slave rising from the dust, his condition mollifying, the way I hope preparing, under the auspices of heaven, for a total emancipation, and that this is disposed, in the order of events, to be with the consent of the masters, rather than by their extirpation.

19. George Tucker Criticizes Jefferson's Views of Racial Differences

For a generation following the Revolution many Virginians still held to the Enlightenment philosophy and resisted the increasingly voluble arguments against emancipation. Nearly thirty years after Jefferson's *Notes* an anonymously published volume entitled *Letters from Virginia, Translated from the French* charged Jefferson with superficial reasoning in his discussion of racial characteristics. Although the authorship of this volume has been attributed to several persons, it is generally believed to have been written by George Tucker, a Virginia lawyer and the author of a number of works on political economy.

Born in Bermuda in 1775, at the age of twelve Tucker came to Virginia to live with relatives. He received his education as a lawyer at William and Mary College, and built his professional career in the state. He practiced law in Richmond, Chatham, and Lynchburg, served in the Virginia House of Delegates, and in the U.S. Congress from 1819 through 1825. He was appointed professor of moral philosophy at the newly created University of Virginia in 1825, and retained this position until his retirement in 1846. Tucker's opposition to slavery was unmistakable, but never militant, and not always consistent. In 1820, for instance, he argued that Congress could not constitutionally impose limits upon the expansion of slavery into the territories. But he never joined the broadening ranks of apologists for slavery. If Tucker is indeed the author of the *Letters* from which the following selection is taken, he evinced, for his time, an unusual ability to perceive the blighting effects of hereditary bondage on personality.

To Mr. Louis D—.

My dear Sir,
I hasten to answer your question, whether the blacks here are really inferior to the whites by nature as well as by law. I have examined the passage in Jefferson's Notes, to which you direct me, and can assure you, that as far as I have seen, there is no just excuse for his remarks. I am afraid, indeed, that his opinion is but too popular here, as

Source: [George Tucker], *Letters from Virginia, Translated from the French* (Baltimore: Fielding Lucas, 1816), pp. 73–103.

[76]

I have heard several masters ready to justify their severity to these poor wretches, by alleging, that they are an inferior race, created only to be slaves. What a horrible doctrine, my dear D——, and what a pity that any gentleman of Mr. J's reputation for talents, should lend it the countenance of his name. It is the more surprising from him too, because he has been so ready to refute a similar charge which Buffon has brought against the Indians, and Raynal against the Americans themselves. He confesses indeed, you see, towards the close of his remarks, that the subject is both difficult and delicate, and that his opinion of the inferiority of the blacks is rather a suspicion than a full belief. But even this indirect apology, is hardly sufficient to excuse him in the eye of reason and of heaven, for this libel upon so large a portion of his fellow-creatures. Do me the favour now to turn your eyes again upon the passage in his book, and suffer me to make a few notes upon his remarks.

He divides his strictures, you will observe, into "physical, and moral;" and maintains distinctly, that "the blacks are inferior to the whites in the endowment both of body and mind."

Now, as to his "physical" remarks upon their inferiority "in the endowment of body," it would hardly be necessary to notice them if there wasn't reason to apprehend, that he means to infer from the establishment of this point, their equal inferiority "in the endowment of mind." Indeed, he asserts in another place, that "the sympathy between body and mind, during their rise, progress, and decline, is too strict and obvious to endanger our

being misled while we reason from the one to the other." And accordingly we find him dexterously inferring from the allged equality of the Indians with Europeans in point of body, a similar equality in point of mind. A word or two then upon the supposed physical inferiority of the blacks.

As to our author's remarks, indeed, upon the comparative beauty of the two races, I must certainly agree with him in taste, (tho' I own I was a little surprised at his decision after the stories I have heard of him.) [1] I will never give up the lilies, and roses, and blushes of the whites, for the dull mask of the blacks. Nor shall I very readily consent to exchange our flowing hair for their woolly heads. I am not quite so satisfied, however, as he seems to be, about making my own judgment the standard of taste for all the world. Their preference of the whites, (in their amours I suppose he means, by his allusion to the obscene fable of the Oranootan,) can hardly be regarded as a concession of the point in our favour, as it may be very naturally ascribed to pride, and ambition to associate with superiors; for La Fontaine tells us, there is always a little grain of ambition in love. Nor is this supposed preference of theirs by any means universal, (whatever Mr. J's own experience may have been.) In Africa too, where artificial associations do not influence their natural notions in the same way, the blacks appear to discover no such partiality for the beauty of the whites. On the contrary,

---

1. The author refers to rumors that Jefferson fathered the children of his female slave Sally Hemings. (*Editor's note*)

we are told that, in their rude pictures, they are always sure to paint their angels black, and the devil white; which, to be sure, is rather a droll compliment to our superior beauty. And even in England, we are assured by intelligent travellers, that women of a lower order seem to feel no great qualms of taste in associating with woolly-headed husbands. But enough upon this point of beauty. For myself, tho' I shall certainly continue to prefer my own taste, I do not think it quite fair to insist upon their giving up the apple, without referring the matter to less partial judges than ourselves. After all, whether the blacks are uglier or handsomer than the whites, can prove nothing as to their inferiority in the endowments of the mind, unless we are to take it for granted that beauty and genius always go together, a proposition for which Mr. J. ought not to contend.

The observations upon other physical differences between the two races, are equally frivolous. If it is true that "they have less hair on the face and body," "secrete less by the kidneys," and have even "perhaps a difference of structure in the pulmonary apparatus"; all this will do nothing towards proving them inferior in mind, until we can first establish what precise quantity of hair, what kind of secretion, and what structure of the "pulmonary apparatus," are best adapted to make men poets and philosophers. And even then, I am afraid, those who consider the soul as incorporeal, and immaterial, wouldn't think the point entirely settled. But do these points of difference even establish the alleged inferiority of the blacks in the endowments of the body? Not at all. They only prove that the blacks are different, not that they are inferior; that they are better fitted for a warm climate, and we for a cold; that they would have the advantage over us in a hot day, and we over them in a freezing one. Besides, are there not very great differences, (if not as great,) between the constitutions and temperaments of different white races in different countries, between Laplanders and Italians, for example? Are they therefore of different species? And how often do we find that the constitution of the same individual, becomes altered upon his removal to another country. But does he change his species as often as he changes his climate? If so, who can tell us thro' what varieties of being a man might pass, in a journey from the Equator to the Poles, by this new and subtle doctrine of transmigration.

But enough of these remarks upon the inferiority of the blacks in the endowments of the body. I should really think, that after the essay of Dr. Smith,[1] no man can seriously doubt that even their striking difference in colour and structure of body, is purely the result of moral and physical causes, and not at all of any original distinction of nature. Indeed, the obvious change of the blacks since their importation into this commonwealth, and their gradual approach towards the colour and symmetry of the whites, would seem sufficient to establish the fact beyond debate.

1. Samuel Stanhope Smith's *Essay on the Causes of the Variety of Complexion and Figure in the Human Species* (1787 and 1810) assigned differences in color to varying climatic and social conditions. (*Editor's note*)

But Mr. J. suggests some other considerations to prove the natural inferiority of these people, (tho' perhaps it is not easy to tell to which branch of his proposition he would refer them.) Let us notice the most material.

"They seem to require less sleep." This must be allowed to be an original discovery. But, even if the fact were true, it might certainly be ascribed to very obvious moral causes. At least I am quite sure, it was never imagined that black *children* required less sleep than their little white masters, whatever may be the case with *adults*. It is true, indeed, that "a black, after hard labour thro' the day, will be induced by the slightest amusements, to sit up till midnight or later; though knowing he must be out with the first dawning of the morning." But this is only true of those slaves who have hard masters over them, and who are scarcely allowed a moment's respite from toil during the day. Like ourselves, they have a quick and lively relish for the pleasures of social intercourse. Is it wonderful then, that they seize the only moments in their power, to indulge this propensity of nature? The day was their masters; but the night is their own. And is it not even much to the credit of their minds, that they prefer spending the evening, and part of the night, in the "slightest amusement," rather than in the dull pleasure of sleep? And what are, not unfrequently, their amusements on these occasions. Such as would not suffer from a comparison with those of their more enlightened masters. Legendary ballads, narratives of alternate dialogue and singing, and things of that sort, rude indeed and coarse enough in all

conscience; but surely sufficient to show their taste for intellectual pleasures, and to prove "the existence of a germ in their minds which only wants cultivation." And, that the fact doesn't proceed from their naturally requiring less sleep, look at these same fellows the day after one of these nocturnal wakes, and see how ready they are to fall asleep over their work, whenever the whip of the overseer will suffer them. And consider too, that the slaves of more indulgent masters, are as regular in their sleeping hours as the whites. All indeed, when no labour forbids, and no amusement invites, are disposed to sleep with as much readiness, and certainly with as much tranquillity as their masters. Indeed, Mr. J. himself, you see, but a very few sentences afterwards, forgetting, or at least seeming to forget what he had just said, accuses them of having a great "disposition to sleep when abstracted from their diversions, and unemployed in labour." He even goes on to give us the philosophy of the fact, by saying, that "an animal whose body is at rest, and who doesn't reflect, must be disposed to sleep of course." But, how this strange class of beings, (or animals, if he will have it so,) can naturally require so little sleep, and yet perversely forgetting their own nature, feel obstinately disposed to require so much, and as a matter of course too, Mr. J. must help us to explain.

But, behold a compliment to the poor blacks in the midst of all the charges against them! "They are at least as brave, and more adventuresome." But stop, this compliment must have a little bitter to temper its sweetness. "This may perhaps proceed from a want of forethought, which prevents their seeing a danger till it be present." Thus their faults, it seems, are the faults of their nature; while their very virtues are but the consequences, or modifications of their faults. Humiliating hypothesis indeed! But, the praise is certainly due to these poor creatures, in its fullest extent. They are indeed, not unfrequently, the very first to brave toils and dangers, in heroic contempt of all those motives, which might naturally be supposed to wither their enterprise and exertion. I have myself often witnessed with astonishment, their resolute intrepidity on occasions of fire, in rescuing the property of the whites from the flames, without any prospect but of some paltry reward, (if they even thought of that,) while the timid owners of that very property, looked on and trembled at their daring. Indeed, there cannot be a doubt, that generous gratitude might rescue from oblivion, a thousand instances of sublime enterprise, in which these despised beings, *the forlorn hope* of human nature, have stormed dangers and difficulties, while their cowardly masters have fallen back, or fainted before the breach. But who is to record their exploits? Who "so poor to do them reverence," or even justice?

—Sed omnes illachrymabiles
Urgentur, ignotique, longa
Nocte, carent quia vate sacro.
Hor. Lib. 4. *Ca.* 9.

In endless night they sleep, unwept, unknown,
No bard had they to make all time their own.   *Francis.*

But let us pursue Mr. J. in his remarks. "They are more ardent after their females." If they appear to be so, (tho' I am by no means satisfied of the fact,) I think it may be fairly ascribed to the greater facilities of indulging a criminal intercourse which their situation allows, and the fewer restraints which their manners, morals, and mode of living impose upon the violence of their passions, rather than to any constitutional difference of nature. "But" it is added, "love seems with them to be more an eager desire, then a tender, delicate mixture of sentiment and sensation." And isn't this equally the case with the lower class of whites? Take a workman from the bench, or a labourer from his plough, and see what he will say to this "tender, delicate mixture of sentiment and sensation." Or what figure does Mr. J. think one of his own rustic neighbours would cut, as a commentator upon the sentimental graces of Anacreon, or Tibullus!—"Their griefs are transient. Those numberless afflictions which render it doubtful whether heaven has given life to us in mercy or in wrath, are less felt, and sooner forgotten with them." It is indeed, very true, that these poor blacks exhibit great patience, and even cheerfulness, under the hardships of their condition; but certainly not greater than the race of whites display in many despotic countries, not as great perhaps as the French, a volatile and sensible people, are manifesting at this moment under the execrable tyranny of Bonaparte. The truth is, hope is the food of liberty, as well as of love; and the food withdrawn, the passion expires. But what hope have these poor wretches of bettering their condition? Happy is it for them if with the hope, they have lost the wish of seeing fairer days. And it is certainly a most merciful provision of heaven, if they can always escape the pang of suffering, in the slumber of insensibility. But, after all, is their apathy quite as great as is supposed? If it is, why this feverish solicitude of the laws to guard against the spirit of insurrection and revenge? And why are so many innocent bosoms still agitated with fearful anticipations, and the slumbers of wives and mothers disturbed by visions of murder and conflagration?

Our author, however, is not yet satisfied, but still pursues his hostilities, and now advances to his main charge against these people. "Comparing them," says he, "by their faculties of memory, reason, and imagination, it appears to me, that in memory they are equal to the whites; in reason much inferior, as I think one could scarcely be found, capable of tracing, and comprehending, the investigations of Euclid; and, that in imagination they are dull, tasteless, and anomalous." He seems, indeed, to be aware of the very unequal ground on which they must stand, to be measured with the whites, and readily concedes, that it will be right to make great allowances for the difference of condition, of education, of conversation, of the sphere in which they move." But why, in the name of sense and justice, is not this difference quite sufficient, to account for any seeming inferiority in their intellectual faculties? Why, "many of them have been so situated, that they might have availed themselves of the conversation of their masters." And, is it then the fact, that the conversation of their masters is so strongly saturated with intelligence, that all who happen to breathe the same atmosphere must imbibe it of course, and almost of necessity? Has it lately been discovered, that knowledge may be communicated without the trouble of teaching, and that people may learn every thing without labour, and even in spite of themselves? Or, is it true, that these masters are careful to impart their redundant intelligence to their slaves, if not by any regular course of instruction, yet, at least, by the endearing familiarity, and winning ease of friendly conversation? "The whole commerce between master and slave," says our author himself, in another place, "is a perpetual exercise of the most boisterous passions: the most unremitting despotism on the one part, and degrading submissions on the other." Surely, intercourse of this kind cannot be very improving to these people, nor ought their minds to be condemned, if they happen to make but little progress under such discipline. Still, however, it may be thought, perhaps, that they ought to imbibe some portion of intelligence from the society of more humane and indulgent masters, and their guests. Certainly this is reasonable. And in general I think nothing is more apparent, than that the mental improvement of the blacks, keeps an even pace with that of the whites with whom they are brought in contact, allowing, only, for the great difference of situation always left between them. But, "many," it is further said, "have been brought up to the handicraft arts, and, from that circumstance, have always been associated with the whites." Yes, and in these cases, they have proved themselves quite equal to the whites in the same employments. They have not, indeed, started up philosophers and poets from the work-bench; but, neither have their masters. Still, "the Indians, with no advantages of this kind, will often carve figures on their pipes, not destitute of design and merit." "They astonish you with strokes of the most sublime oratory, &c." But, are not the Indians free—and is the want of freedom nothing to the negroes? Yet, is not the comparison so entirely in favour of the former, as our author's partiality for them may suppose. On the contrary, I think, if a fair estimate could be made, it would not be difficult to establish the superiority of the latter in almost every point of mental excellence, except perhaps in eloquence alone. "In music," he allows himself, "they are more generally gifted than the whites;" (still more than his darling Indians.) And doesn't this concession, by the by, sufficiently answer his own charge, of deficiency in taste and imagination. Surely, music and fancy are connected together, by pretty close ties of friendship and affinity. Thus, there is not one of the Muses, (and the Greeks had some judgment in their fictions,) but has a harp, or a lyre, or some other musical instrument at her command. Nor is there one of the poets, who most delight in the play of the imagination, but pipes on the reed or quavers on the string. The passion of the blacks then for music, is of itself sufficient to redeem them from the reproach, too hastily cast upon them, of being "in imagination, dull, tasteless, and anomalous." Still, it is said, there is no poetry among them. Nor is there much, I believe, among their masters. Neither

misery nor love, has yet inspired either race with any very extraordinary gifts in this fascinating art. But, perhaps, these will come in good time to both. Mr. J. continues: "The improvement of the blacks, both in body and mind, in the first instance of their mixture with the whites, has been observed by every one, and proves that their inferiority is not the effect merely of their condition of life." But how so? Surely, if this improvement of the breed follows from the cross, it can, at the utmost, only prove the *actual* superiority of the whites, without at all establishing the *cause* of that superiority as founded in original nature. A fruit-tree, which has degenerated in a bad soil, may be improved by a scion from its own native stock. But, there are moral causes enough, to explain the apparent superiority of the mulattoes over the blacks. It is notorious that, for reasons which may be easily imagined, they are almost invariably treated with more favours, and indulged with more liberty than their sable companions. Hence, naturally results a greater confidence in their own mental powers, most favourable to their developement; besides the sympathetic strength which they gain from the opinion of others. *Possunt quia posse videntur.*

Our author now proceeds to observe: "We know that among the Romans, about the Augustan age especially, the condition of their slaves was much more deplorable than that of the blacks on the continent of America." And "yet," it is afterwards added, "their slaves were often their rarest artists. They excelled too in science, insomuch, as to be usually employed as tutors to their master's children."

Now, in answer to all this, I observe in the first place, I am not quite satisfied that the condition of Roman slaves in general, was really so much worse than that of those in this state. That "the commerce between the two sexes is almost without restraint" among the latter, while it was considerably confined among the former, may be conceded at once without danger to our argument. *Abstinuit Venere* is a part of the character given to the man of great intellectual attainments, even by an Epicurean poet. Perhaps, indeed, no single circumstance has a more fatal efficacy in producing the debasement of their mental powers, than this very lawless commerce, which is strangely urged as an argument to prove their inferiority by nature. "Cato sold his sick and superannuated slaves," But are there no Catos in Virginia, Catos, I mean, in the worst sense of the name, in want of feeling and common charity to their slaves? Is there no farmer here who would give, or at least take the Roman's advice, "vendat servum senem, servum morbosum?" Diseased slaves indeed, thanks to the genius of Christianity, are never exposed to death on an island in the James, as they often were, partly, no doubt, from an absurd superstition, on the island of Æsculapius, in the Tyber. But, even this execrable practice, I am afraid, is not entirely without parallels of cruelty in this quarter. At least, when Mr. J. is so confident that such an exposure, if followed by death, would be punished capitally, it is fair to ask him how long it has been since it was found necessary to repeal a certain law of this Commonwealth which declared, in substance, that if a slave perished under the chastisement of his master, however wanton, the homicide should be considered only as manslaughter at the utmost. As to the case of Vidius Pollio, I am sorry to suspect, that it might not be altogether impossible to find a rival for him in the history of this state. But, individual examples prove nothing. The truth is, it is the natural consequence of tolerating slavery to harden the heart in cruelty, and that, whether at Rome, or in Virginia.

I am aware, however, and am perfectly ready to concede, that, judging by the laws alone, the Roman slaves were treated with most severity. Yet, I must still think, that their situation was far more favourable to the expansion of the intellectual faculties, than that of the blacks in this state. It is no new observation, that the state of a nation is not always to be estimated by its laws, which often remain dead letters upon the statute book, and are silently repealed by the manners of the people.—That this was actually the case with the Roman slaves, we have little reason to doubt, from the evidence of facts. At all events, we cannot fail to remark, that there were some striking advantages, in favour of their condition, over that of those in Virginia—advantages too secured, or at least indulged by law. Thus, the kind of *domestic* slaves, (called *Verna,*) were but few, in comparison with the great class of those who lived abroad, (called *Servi.*)—The former, from being brought up in the family of their masters, were treated with a degree of liberty not often allowed to the blacks in this quarter. This may be fairly inferred, from the characters of them scattered through our classics, as well as from the testimony of more grave historians.—The latter had, evidently, still greater advantages. They were generally born free, being foreigners, (barbarians, as the Romans chose to call them,) whom the chance of war, or the various casualties of human misfortune, had reduced to servitude, when the faculties of their minds were already blown, and could no longer be nipped in the bud by the blast of domestic tyranny. Even in slavery, they were generally removed from their master's eyes, and favoured with the privilege of living, in some measure, after their own will and fancy. Each one had his own *peculium*, or separate property, which he employed as he pleased—in farming, in trade, in commerce, or in some mechanic art, rendering a stipulated sum to his owner, instead of baser services, animated in his pursuit by the hope of gain, and liberty along with it. Will any one pretend, that their situation was not decidedly preferable to that of the negroes here, who are, generally, compelled to work under the eye of their masters, or low-bred overseers, with little or no motive to labour, but the dread of the impending lash over their heads? The Roman slave, too, might have the privilege, as it was doubtless considered in a warlike age and nation, of bearing arms in company with freemen, and his ransom, if taken prisoner, was half that of his master's. In this state, the law would punish even a free person of colour, for presuming to keep a gun, sword, or other instrument for self defence, without a special license from the court. Add to this, that the Roman slave might often hope for liberty, (as acts of emancipation were frequent among the Romans), and with it, the happiness of mingling with his former superiors, on some footing of equality. Here, the poor slave can hardly dream of liberty, or if he does, must feel the pleasure of the thought embittered by the horrible association of exile, and the harrowing reflection, that the disgrace of the scar will remain, when the galling of the fetter is removed.—The Romans encouraged their slaves to exert their talents, and rewarded their proficiency with the gift of freedom. The Virginians discountenance all efforts to enlighten theirs, and punish their ignorance with perpetual bondage.

Besides all this, is it not fair to suppose, that the Roman slaves would catch some improvement, from sympathy with a refined state of society around them? Mr. J. at least, certainly supposes so; when he makes it an argument, against the blacks, that "they have lived in countries where the arts and sciences are cultivated to a considerable degree, and have had before their eyes samples of the best works from abroad." But, will he seriously contend, that the literary character of Virginia can stand a comparison with that of Rome, and Rome, too, in the Augustan age? How long, pray, has it been, since he found it necessary to answer the reproach of Raynal:—On doit être étonné que l'Amérique n'ait pas encore produit un bon poète, un habil mathematicien, un homme de genie dans un seul art, ou une seule science,"—("one must be astonished, that America has not yet produced a good poet, an able mathematician, a man of genius in a single art, or a single science." And how many of his examples, to refute the calumny, did he find within the four corners of Virginia?

Our author continues: "Epictetus, Terence, and Phædrus were slaves. But they were of the race of whites." And, is it then perfectly fair to infer the superiority of a whole people from the eminence of a few individuals who must be admitted to be extraordinary? It is not, perhaps, possible for the greatest human understanding to explain the causes why such a man of genius has appeared in such an age or country. Indeed, as genius is obviously no mechanical thing, it is clear that we cannot determine its phenomena by any settled principles of calculation. The most rational account of the subject is, that God gives us a capacity at our birth, or conception if you please, and causes this seminal germ to be developed by a combination of natural and moral causes, too fine and secret for human eyes. Nothing then, I think, can be fairly concluded against the blacks, altho' they cannot boast an equal triumvirate.

And again, if the blacks are to be condemned as an inferior race, because they have not yet produced a Terence or a Phædrus, is not Mr. J. aware that his argument may be turned against his own fellow-citizens who have not yet produced, by his own confession, a single poet, whether of comedies or fables? But, perhaps, he would answer, as he has already done: "When we shall have existed as a people as long as the Greeks did before they produced a Homer, the Romans a Virgil, the French a Racine and Voltaire, the English a Shakspeare and Milton, should the reproach be still true, we will en-

quire from what unfriendly causes it has proceeded, that the other countries of Europe and quarters of the earth, shall not have inscribed any name in the roll of poets." Then would it not be at least equally just and reasonable to make the same concession of further time to the blacks, before we condemn them as absolutely mere lumps of prose? Or has the period already arrived when we may fairly plead the statute of limitations against their claims to intellect?

Once more, I would remark, that the individuals selected by Mr. J. as specimens of Roman slaves, were obviously placed in better circumstances of situation than most of the blacks in this region, so as to account, in part at least, for that superiority of theirs which is made an argument and reproach against the latter. Thus, Terence, in particular, was a native of Africa, born free, brought over from Carthage as a captive, and soon liberated on account of his talents and attainments, which therefore couldn't have been acquired during his slavery.—Here too, from the beauty of his person and the graces of his mind, he soon became the darling companion of Scipio Africanus and Lelius, spending his time with them in the elegant amusements of literature at their country seats. I pass over the common reports prevalent in his time, that his plays were actually composed by his illustrious friends, tho' he defends himself rather faintly against the charge in one of his prologues, and you remember our "downright Montaigne," (as Pope calls him,) positively insists upon it, that he never could have written them himself. Indeed, Boileau seems to adopt the same opinion in his verses to Moliere. But, throw the criticks away, and give the poet credit for his plays, was not his situation a little more favourable to literary exertions than that of any slave in Virginia, even within the philosophical atmosphere of Monticello, which shall be considered (for the sake of argument) as the seat of genius, the garden of taste, and, if you choose, the mountain of the muses into the bargain? Surely, this example at least, is a little unhappily chosen for our author's purpose. Perhaps too, (I will just add in passing,) a delicate critick might remark upon the examples which are cited, that all these authors are remarkable for the feminine delicacy of their style, rather than for the manly boldness of their judgment, or vigour of their invention. Would not this seem to excuse a suspicion at least, that their condition with all its comparative advantages, was not without some unfriendly influence upon their mental powers, and literary efforts? But enough of these discussions which are rather amusing than necessary to the argument. The state of Roman slaves, and the brilliant examples of Epictetus, Terence, and Phædrus will hardly justify our author's conclusion against the blacks: "it is not their condition then, but nature which has produced the distinction."

But to prove decisively that the inferiority of the negroes is the result of their situation alone, consider them in their childhood before they have learnt the painful lesson that they are slaves, and compare them with the whites of their own age. They are now the playfellows of their future masters, and share the sport with those who will one day refuse to share the toil with them. In this situation, though their infant minds are not very carefully cultivated, their thoughts shoot up wildly of themselves, for there is no one to prune them away. And though, even at this early period, the little imitative tyrants of the nursery cannot always repress the pride of domination, it would be hard to prove that their sable subjects exhibit less spirit, invention, or genius than themselves, in the games and amusements of their age. On the contrary, it is not at all uncommon to see these last taking the lead in their pursuits, and vindicating the full equality of their intellect in every mode of its exertion. Indeed, I am well persuaded, that if their masters would take but half the pains with them which they take with their horses or their pointers, they would have fewer imaginary causes of reproach against them, as well as fewer real ones against themselves. But pursue the progress of the child, and see the effect of slavery upon his mind. For my own part, I think there is not in nature a more melancholy picture than that of a little black when he first discovers that he is a slave. When the poor boy is taken from the street [2] to be disciplined for the house, he is welcomed with smiles by all the family, especially the children. A waiter is put in his hands which he receives with a bow of gratitude. A new livery is put upon him, which he views again and again with delight, because he is yet to learn that it is the badge of sorrow and disgrace. The whole scene is new to him, and charm-

2. By "street" the author means "slave quarter," the double row of cabins separated by a "street." (*Editor's note*)

ing from its novelty. To be sure he has something to learn, and something to do. But the pleasure of learning rewards the trouble, and a smile from his mistress overpays his work. He perceives too that he is the object of interest and amusement to the company, and feels a sympathy in their good humour. Perhaps even, if he behaves himself well, he may get the crust from the table which the good lady has promised, and this is a great encouragement to his little ambition. No wonder his motions are brisk, his spirits gay, and his sleep sweet; for indeed, except now and then an unlucky cuff from an envious fellow-waiter, or a rod from the cross cook, his life is pleasant enough. By and by however, the novelty of the scene wears off, and the pleasure with it. The smiles of encouragement grow less frequent, the customary crust is denied, and the voice of command begins to sound, he hardly knows how, a little harshly to his ear. Here the waiter that was once his pride, becomes a weight upon his arm, his thoughts will steal away to the kitchen or the street, the tears are in his eyes, and he longs to join his little play-fellows again. This is the time of transition from happy ignorance to painful knowledge. His carelessness and neglect of duty must be punished with the whip. With the first stroke the whole illusion of liberty vanishes never to return. The marks on his body indeed are soon effaced; but what time can obliterate the lashes from his mind? He is now a slave, and he feels that he is one. His mind soon sinks to the level of his condition, from which nothing, not even liberty at a subsequent period, shall ever raise it

again. After this, let no man tell me that "it is nature, and not their condition," which has made the blacks inferior to the whites.

Indeed, Mr. J. himself has been constrained to admit, that nature has done them full justice in the endowments of the heart. He even warmly declares, that notwithstanding the discouragements of their situation, "we find among them numerous instances of the most rigid integrity, and as many as among their better instructed masters, of benevolence, gratitude, and unshaken fidelity." He says too, "that disposition to theft with which they have been branded, must be ascribed to their situation, and not to any depravity of the moral sense." But, how long has it been discovered, that slavery operates with more injurious efficacy upon the moral, than upon the mental powers? Homer doesn't countenance such an idea, (whatever our author may have supposed when he made the quotation from him,) as you will see at a glance. He knew better. The truth is, the influence of slavery is the same upon the mind and heart, alike pernicious, and almost fatal to both.

But why pursue our author any further, when he seems to tremble himself at his own conclusion? "I advance it therefore," says he, after all his previous assertions, "as suspicion only, that the blacks, whether *originally a distinct race, or made distinct by time and circumstances,* are inferior to the whites in the endowments both of body and mind." So, then, all our dispute is *de lana caprina;* for I never doubted the *actual* inferiority of the blacks, and if it is now conceded that this may be ascribed to *"time and circumstances,"* it is all I contend for. Indeed, it is all that is worth contention. For surely if they have been made distinct only by *"time and circumstances,"* there is some reason to hope that *"time and circumstances"* may operate to abolish the distinction, and restore them to that rank in the creation from which they have been degraded.

After all, that they are not *"originally,"* that is by nature or creation, *"a distinct race,"* any christian I suppose may easily believe. In truth, if we look into our bible, as we ought to do upon this and every other question, the controversy is at an end. There we find it distinctly taught, that the whole race of mankind have sprung from one pair, the common parents of us all. Indeed, the doctrine of original sin, and that of

salvation through faith in the Redeemer, the sum and substance of our religion, all depend upon the admission of this fundamental truth, as all involve the relationship which the members of the great human family must bear to their federal head.

Let others, then, think as they please, or as they dare; for us, my dear D——, I am sure we shall not lightly change our faith for any thing that we have yet heard or read. And tho' I trust your belief requires no new confirmation, you may, perhaps, be pleased to find, that there is nothing in the race of blacks, or in Mr. J's remarks upon them, to disturb for a moment the tranquillity of our devotion.

Adieu, my good friend, and pardon the long letter which you have so innocently provoked.

20. Thomas Basye and Martha Turberville Protest Activities of Free Blacks

For several decades following 1782 the legal relations between whites and blacks in Virginia were not well defined, and the future course of the law, whether toward greater openness or greater restriction, was unpredictable. Free blacks were possessed of legal privileges that sometimes were enforced, and sometimes not. The position they occupied between slaves and white people was precarious at best, and what happened to them was a strong indicator of the sort of prospects slaves had for eventual liberty.

Whites came increasingly to resent the legal rights of free Negroes. The following letters of 1806 offer an intimate view of that resentment, a typi-

Source: Executive Department, Executive Papers, Box 142, Virginia State Library, Richmond.

cal instance of how free blacks incurred the wrath of whites, and how blacks could be caught between the animosities of feuding whites. Thomas Pope Basye and his mother-in-law implore Gov. William H. Cabell to urge the Legislature to curb the liberty of free blacks like Robert Williams, who has "harboured" eight of Martha Turberville's slaves.

[1]
Thomas Basye to William H. Cabell.

Peckatone (Westmoreland county) 14th December 1806
Wm. H. Cabell, Esquire,
Sir,
Although I have not the pleasure of a personal acquaintance with you, 'tis hoped the subject which superinduces this address will sufficiently apologize for the liberty used in making a communication thereon;—Your well-known patriotism will, no doubt, lead to a proper investigation of the points in question. It is deemed unnecessary however to give you a complete detail—having advised my friend General John Minor, by letter, under date hereof—the contents of which fully explains what should be represented in the [illegible]; and I have requested this Gentleman to exhibit the same to you—and have also written to my friend Ellison Currie Esq. (of the Senate) to the purpose. It may however be necessary to give the outlines, in order to [make?] a more immediate explanation. The subject relates in the first instance to the malconduct of some Magistrates of this county, to wit a John Murphy (Scotch fugitive) and a Mr. Stephen Baily, (an American:)—The partiality shown by these *pseudo majestrates* to a runaway negroe *harbourer* residing near this place—a mulatto man supposed to be *free,* but who actually is not, the Debts of his former master (Lewis [illegible]) having not been discharged, previous to the date of the Record of the emancipation of the said mulatto should be seriously noticed:—he the said mulatto, named Robert Williams harboured eight runaway negroes the property of Mrs. Martha Turberville, nearly six months in the year 1804 & 1805—and publicly *boasted of the act*—added to this consideration he had been previously apprehended as a leader of the *negroe* Conspiracy in 1802: [1]— & *arms & ammunition were found in his possession.* —Various other nefarious acts this mulatto has been guilty of, which it may not for the present be necessary to mention—Acting as a friend to my mother-in-law Mrs. Martha Turberville, I instructed the overseer at Peckatone, to chastise this mulatto, for *supporting the negroes* above mentioned, during the term of their elopement, which the said overseer, named Isaac Hutcheson did, by giving the said mulatto, the punishment which the laws of our State justly inflict on negroe slaves— An Indictment upon this account, was preferred against me at the county court of Westmoreland in July 1805:—an *Ignoramus* was found:—but John Campbell, the Commonwealth Atty, notorious for his deeprooted ma-

1. Basye probably meant the Gabriel plot of 1800; see document 27, below. (*Editor's note*)

lignity against the Turberville family, carried this Indictment to the North-umberland District Court where by the false testimony of a Hog-thief (by the name of William Williams, whom a man by the name of Parker is well ac-quainted with) the grand jury were so far imposed upon; that a true Bill was found—after which a decision was made by a *packed* Jury at the last *[illegible]* Court for said District, and a Fine assessed against myself, to the amount of $250 as also against the overseer (Isaac Hutcheson) of $50.

The Executive I well know, have not the power of remitting fines—but 'tis hoped, your solicitude for the *public good,* will suggest the propriety of ad-monishing the legislature of our state, now in session, of the expedience of framing some legal correctives, as bar-riers against the daily increasing en-croachments of negroes & mulattoes, upon the *Rights of White Persons.*

I have the honor to be
    with the highest respect,
        Your most obedient

                Thomas Pope Basye

[2]

ENCLOSURE FROM MARTHA
TURBERVILLE.

William H. Cabell, Esq.

Sir, I beg leave to annex a postscript to this letter & trust it will not be deemed a breach of decorum to state an opinion relative to the deportment of one of the members constituting the Court alluded to—The conduct of Judge Parker in my estimation was sin-gular, if unprecedented I believe in the annals of the jurisprudence of our country:—he admitted the testimony of this mulatto villain Robert Williams, alias Robin the Taylor to give evidence against my son in law Thomas Pope Basye, in open court—his corpororal *[sic]* oath was insisted on by Judge Parker, and opposed by Judge Holmes—but notwithstanding the re-sult had the intended effect—this mu-latto fellow was allowed to address the Court & Jury, giving testimony the fal-sity of which 'twas hoped the most de-praved character in the Com-monwealth would blush at—Judge Parker had the impertinence to enquire of one of the witnesses (who is a Gen-tleman) whether my daughter was married to Mr. Basye or not—I appeal to the world to say with what propriety Judge Parker could have made this in-terrogation—the question, in my mind was highly unbecoming the dignity of a Gentleman, and was calculated to add insult to injury—

I have, Sir, the honour to be
    with our respects
        Your most obedient

                Martha Turberville

21. A Richmond Editor Calls for a Military Corps

In the generation following the Revolution one seldom finds whites assuming that slaves were docile. As the following article clearly reveals, many eighteenth-century whites considered slaves a dangerous element in the population, and for that reason urged that slave owners be taxed for the support of a public guard. In time the defenders of slavery exploited the presumed docility of slaves as an indication that blacks were particularly suited to slave status.

When the piece below appeared in 1808, Virginians were still unable to forget the bloody uprising of the slaves of Santo Domingo in 1793, and their own near escape from Gabriel Prosser's attempted insurrection of the year 1800. The mobility of slave artisans—boatmen in particular—was an important means of spreading the news of the Gabriel plot among the slaves of the interior of the state. Clearly the editor of *The Virginian* believed that slaves should be confined to agricultural labor and isolated on the plantations. With every passing year more white people agreed with him. While inveighing against the freedom with which blacks circulated in 1808, the editor incidentally provides a picture of urban blacks and their diverse activities.

The benefits to be derived from the establishment of a military corps cannot be denied: nor can it be pretended, that under the actual state of society, some provision of that sort is not absolutely necessary.

And why absolutely necessary? it is because the state of slavery which exists, added to recent events, impresses it on the mind of every man of reflection, that some effectual and permanent means ought to be employed to guard against actual danger, as well as to ensure public tranquility.

If this be so; if the necessity of incurring a heavy public expence, proceeds altogether from the situation of society as relates to the slaves—then nothing can be more reasonable, than that the whole expense ought to be borne by the holders of that particular species of property.

It is foreseen that this will be immediately opposed upon the allegation of

Source: *The Virginian* (Richmond, Va.), January 1, 1808.

[91]

partiality and inequality—It will be alledged [sic] that all the expenses of government ought to be mutually borne by all descriptions of people, and that every tax calculated to serve one portion of society, from the burthens which are imposed on others, is not only in itself unjust and oppressive, but will trench upon the established principles of a free government. All that can be now said in relation to this objection, is to deny it. The design of the writer is merely to bring into notice those opinions which prevail in his own mind. He believes that a public guard is absolutely necessary; that the system which he has recommended is far superior to that which exists; and that a tax on slaves is not only just and reasonable in itself, but by no means inconsistent with the equal principles of our constitution, and he would willingly afford aids to widows, orphans, and other cases of extreme hardship.

With respect to the slaves, it is likely that a general change of policy would be productive of greater benefits, than could have been expected from the public guard—In order to invite the attention of the public to the subject, the following remarks are submitted to notice.

Two opposing opinions now distract the state. One set of men, with honest, generous, but imprudent zeal, aim at a general and unconditional emancipation—Others influenced by motives equally pure, not only thwart and oppose these humane innovators, but seem to take delight in oppressing and embittering the fate of the unfortunates. In both of these cases perhaps true policy is neglected. The general

weight and influence of public harmony is lost; the energies of the state are paralyzed; and men of equal respectability, of equal claims to public favour are arrayed against each other. Another course ought then to be adopted, promising not only to guard against general emancipation, but an amelioration of the condition of slaves.

Every slave ought to have some means of protection against the cruelty, injustice, and systematical oppressions of inhuman and flinty hearted masters; this may be done by competent tribunals, and upon terms dictated by justice and benevolence.

Indiscriminate and general emancipation at this time ought not to be countenanced, so far from it, the privilege ought to be extended, with care and caution, only to such as deserve so great a boon, by eminent service, or by a general course of a meritorious deportment.

Slaves ought to be solely employed in agricultural or other occupations of plain labour. It is also worthy of enquiry whether mechanics, house servants, waiters, waggoners, draymen, and water-men ought not to pay a higher tax, than those who are employed in agriculture, and whether in future, and by degrees the blacks should not be excluded from mechanical employments, and from being public carriers.

Innovations of this sort, would be at first attended with some inconvenience, but as soon as the regulations were known to be firmly settled and established, the labourers and industrious poor would very readily embrace those occupations, which are now, for the most part discharged by slaves—By this change alone, society would receive a much greater security than can result from the establishment of guards, even though their numbers and organization, should be equal to those ideas which have been partially unfolded. The dangers to be apprehended from slaves depend upon several causes; one is, they are the common carriers of the lower country —they have under their immediate care all the horses and accoutrements for horses—they are almost without exception good riders, and drivers, and among them may be found almost every kind of artist; Smiths and Carpenters without number. From these causes they have the means, without much exertion[,] of doing a great deal of mischief.

Now as the object of writing these sentences, is not to render the condition of the good and virtuous slave worse than heretofore, but to prevent the wicked from forming plots and conspiracies, the benevolent reader must not condemn what has been, or what may be said, before he looks through the vista of futurity, and impartially considers the different prospects which may be afforded. Peace, quiet industry on one hand—robbery, scourging, hanging, alarms and insurrections on the other.

If these or similar innovations are adopted, all the various duties now performed by slaves as carriers, artists, &c. will be performed by whites. The military strength of the city of Richmond alone, will be immediately doubled, and instead of danger from the black population, requiring a constant guard and patrol, there would be no other danger than that which is to be apprehended from the general depravity of mankind. The number of cultivators would be accordingly increased, and the general improvement of the country of course would be promoted.

Many other benefits would be obtained by this city. At present, there are at least one thousand black men, who are solely employed, some in bringing the produce to the city, by the means of the canal, and others in conveying it to tide water by the means of the drays. It is believed that at least every other boat which comes into the Basin, brings in it some articles which have been stolen—these are either sold or exchanged with draymen, or others in league with them; and although the boats may be pursued, the articles stolen will seldom be found. So likewise the plunder of Richmond is disposed of and conveyed away so as to escape detection. Besides these evils, there are in the city many retail shops, whose entire trade is with the dray-men and boat-men—Many of whom are always ready to receive stolen articles in exchange for ardent spirits, or perhaps a small pecuniary compensation. It is true that these dealers are frequently detected—but the means of proof is equally defective; because the testimony of a black man or mulatto cannot be received against a white man.

The complaint is as general as the wickedness is notorious—the inhabitants look to the magistrates, and the magistrates in vain try to check the evil; a few punishments to be sure are inflicted; but they bear no proportion to the extent of the mischief, and rather tend to irritate and harden the offenders, than to reclaim or deter them.

The notorious existence of such growing evils, ought of themselves, to excite the attention of the Legislature; but when they are coupled with the other, when the existence of so many black men in the city, in the employments which ought to be confided alone to whites, increase the common danger, these double inducements ought to exist for banishing them, not only from the city, but to employ them in future in agricultural or other occupations where the chances to commit depredations, and engage in conspiracies will be less frequent.

A great deal of this mischief might be remedied, if the Directors of the James River Canal and others to whose care the people confide the public interest would extend it to tide water, and thus deprive the drays of employment. The confederacy between boatmen and draymen would then cease to exist, and robbery would be less frequently committed because the articles of plunder could not be so easily concealed, and appropriated to useful purposes.

If these ideas should make the impression for which they were intended, it will be proper then to ascertain the amount of the tax and the description of slaves to which it ought to be confined. A general tax upon all slaves, the young and helpless, as well as the old and useless would be opposed—and in these relations unreasonable because the necessity for establishing any additional burthen, proceeds from the dangers to be apprehended from the males, who are in the active ages of life and therefore ought to be solely confined to those of that description. According to this idea, a tax ought to be imposed on all males, between the ages of 16 and 56—by these means the treasury would receive annually a sum of money, fully equal to the public exigency, and solely from that discription of property, the peculiar situation of which imposes it as a duty incident to self-preservation, to incur a heavy annual expense.

If this subject should obtain public notice, it will then be proper to unfold & illustrate some other ideas, such as will properly relate to the modifications of the plan.

All these considerations might be made not only subservient to each other, but without affording reasonable cause of complaint to any one, would promote public tranquility and prosperity, and at the same time ensure general happiness to society.

It will not be pretended that these propositions contain the most approved ideas of which the case is susceptible—but it will be strenuously insisted that they afford views which may be greatly improved, or enlarged according to the general impressions which a more mature examination may afford. All that is now intended, is to submit to notice the writer's impressions upon subjects of considerable magnitude, illustrated to such an extent only, as will induce those by whom they may be read, and have sufficient influence to devolve to them a reasonable portion of their time and reflection.

PHILOS.

22. White Artisans Claim Unfair Competition from Free Blacks

The reaction against free blacks was in part motivated by fear of competition from the better-educated and higher-skilled workers among them. In most states laws were enacted to restrict blacks from occupying certain positions, but these laws were apparently honored as much in the breach as in the observance. Yet the pressure to remove free blacks from the state was very strong following the Revolution. Although those who petitioned for this measure, like the citizens of St. Helena Parish (county) in the letter below, never got their wish, they did succeed in closing off the opportunities for slaves to become free unless they were willing to leave the state.

Petition of William J. Grayson, James R. Verdier, and 62 other citizens of St. Helena Parish to the Senate of South Carolina.

To the Honorbl the President and other members of the Senate, The undersigned inhabitances of St. Hellena Parish convinced of the perniceous consequences resulting to the State of So Car from the number of free persons of colour within her limits beg leave respectfully to bring the subject before you. The State not only derives no strength from the class of wich we complain, but is essentially injured, the example of indolence and vice exhibited by the coloured free persons is perpetually before the Slaves. They encourage insubordination by pricept as well as example. They are rapidly drawing from the country the valuable class of industrious mechanics, on whose intelegence and hardihood the safety of S° C^{ar} must mainly depend. What will be the condition of the State when your carpenters and painters and Blacksmiths, and the occupants of all the departments of mechanical industry are free men of colour. Yet such must be the consequences of the competition which the white mechanic encounters from the coloured labourer, the latter is able to work at a less price from obvious causes. He has very often no family to support, his wife and children are Slaves. He lives on the premises of their owner. He has no house rent to pay no clothing or food but his own to purchase. His expences are almost nothing, and he can therefore la-

Source: [*Post-Revolutionary File, ca.* 1831] South Carolina Department of Archives and History, Columbia, S.C.

[95]

bour for almost nothing. Your petitioners cannot believe that you will permit a class so useless, perniceous, and degrading, to the character of the State, to Supplant the intellegent industrious and vigorous freemen, who in the various mechanical departments would so essentially increase her physical and moral strength. Your petitioners therefore pray that you will take the whole subject into consideration, and make such provisions for the removal of the free coloured persons as to your wisdom may seem meet—and as in duty bound they will ever pray.—

THREE
Revolts, Plots, and Rumors of Plots

23. A Slave Conspiracy in New York, 1712

There were frequent sporadic slave insurrections in the colonial period, but the efforts do not appear to have been well organized, and they met with little success. They were invariably put down savagely, and punished in the barbaric modes of the day. On June 23, 1712, the Royal Governor of New York reported the details of a plot recently uncovered in the colony. Gov. Robert Hunter was among the most efficient of the colonial administrators, as his prompt vigor in handling the planned revolt attests. That he was also a man of more judgment than most is suggested by his hints that in this case justice perhaps had gone rather beyond the necessities of public security. The barbarity of the punishment is characteristic of the suppression of seventeenth-century and early eighteenth-century slave resistance.

Gov. Robert Hunter to the Lords of Trade, June 23, 1712.

I must now give your Lordships an account of a bloody conspiracy of some of the slaves of this place, to destroy as many of the Inhabitants as they could[.] It was put in execution in this manner, when they had resolved to revenge themselves, for some hard usage, they apprehended to have received from their masters (for I can find no other cause) they agreed to meet in the orchard of Mr Crook the middle of the Town, some provided with fire arms, some with swords and others with knives and hatchets, this was the sixth day of April, the time of meeting was about twelve or one o'clock in the night, when about three and twenty of them were got togeather, one coffee and negroe slave to one Vantilbrugh set fire to an out house of his Masters, and then repairing to the place where the rest were they all sallyed out togeather wth their arm's and marched to the fire, by this time the noise of fire spreeding through the town, the people began to flock to it upon the approach of severall the slaves fired and killed them, the noise of the guns gave the allarm, and some escaping their shot soon published the cause of the fire, which was the reason, that not above nine Christians were killed, and about five or six wounded, upon the first notice which was very soon after the mischeif was begun, I order'd a detachment from the fort under a proper officer to

Source: Edmund Bailey O'Callaghan, ed., *Documents Relative to the Colonial History of the State of New York*, 15 vols. (Albany: Weed, Parsons & Co., 1855), 5:341–42.

march against them, but the slaves made their retreat into the woods, by the favour of the night, having ordered centries the next day in the most proper places on the Island to prev^t their escape, I caused the day following the Militia of this town and of the county of west Chester to drive the Island, and by this means and strict searches in the town, we found all that put the design in execution, six of these having first laid violent hands upon themselves, the rest were forthwith brought to their tryal before ye Justices of this place who are authorized by Act of Assembly, to hold a Court in such cases, In that Court were twenty seven condemned whereof twenty one were executed, one being a woman with child, her execution by that meanes suspended, some were burnt others hanged, one broke on the wheele, and one hung a live in chains in the town, so that there has been the most exemplary punishment inflicted that could be possibly thought of, and which only this act of assembly could Justify, among these guilty persons severall others were apprehended, and again acquitted by the Court, for want of sufficient evidence, among those was one Mars a negroe man slave to one Mr Regnier, who was to his tryall and acquitted by the Jury, the Sheriffe the next day moving the Court for the discharge of such as were or should be soe acquitted, by reason hee apprehended they would attempt to make their escape but Mr Bickley who y^n executed the office of the Atter: Generall, for Mr Rayner opposed his motion, telling the Court that at that time, none but Mars being acquitted, the motion could be only intended in his favour,

against whom he should have some thing further to object, and therefore prayed he might not be discharg'd. so the sheriff did not obtain his motion, Mars was then indicted a second time and again acquitted, but not discharg'd, and being a third time presented was transferr'd (the Court of Justices not designing to sit again) to the supream Court, and there tryed and convicted on ye same evidence, on his two former tryals, this prosecution was carried on to gratify some private pique of Mr Bickleys against Mr Regnier, a gentleman of his own profession, which appearing so partial, and the evidence being represented to me as very defective, and being wholly acquitted of ever having known any thing of the Conspiracy by the Negroe witnesses, who were made use of in the tryals of all the criminals before the Justices, and without whose testimonies very few could have been punished, I thought fit to reprieve him till Her Majesties pleasure be known therein. if this supream court were likewise tryed, one Husea belonging to Mrs Wenham, and one John belonging Mr Vantilbourgh and convicted, these two are prisoners taken in a Spanish prize this war and brought into this Port by a Privateer, about six or seven years agoe and by reason of their colour which is swarthy, they were said to be slaves and as such were sold, among many others of the same colour and country, these two I have likewise reprieved till Her Majesties pleasure be signified. soon after my arrival in this government I received petitions from several of these Spanish Indians as they are called here, representing to me that they were free men subjects to the King of Spain, but sold here as slaves, I secretly pittyed their condition but haveing no other evidence of w^t they asserted then their own words, I had it not in my power to releive them, I am informed that in the West Indies where their laws against their slaves are most severe, that in case of a conspiracy in which many are engaged a few only are executed for an example, In this case 21 are executed, and six having done that Justice on themselves more have suffered than we can find were active in this bloody affair which are reasons for my repreiving these, and if your Lordships think them of sufficient weight, I beg you will procure Her Majesty's pleasure to be signifyed to me for their pardon, for they lye now in prison at their masters charge, I have likewise repreived one Tom a Negroe belonging to Mr Van Dam and Coffee a Negroe belonging to Mr Walton these two I have repreived at the instance of the Justices of the Court, who where of oppinion that the evidence against them, was not sufficient to convict them. . . . .

24. The Stono Insurrection in South Carolina, 1739

In coastal Georgia and South Carolina the black population was believed to be under the influence of the Spanish settled at St. Augustine, Florida, who offered asylum to runaways from the English colonies. The slaves often found help from the Indians of the region as well. The inducements to revolt under these circumstances were quite practical, and met with a certain amount of success. The following account of the Stono insurrection of September 1739 was an anonymous enclosure in a letter dated October 9, 1739, from Gen. James Oglethorpe, founder of the colony of Georgia, to Mr. Harman Verelst, treasurer to the Trustees of Georgia. Oglethorpe requested that the account be published in the English newspapers.

Sometime since there was a Proclamation published at Augustine, in which the King of Spain (then at Peace with Great Britain) promised Protection and

Source: Allen D. Candler [ed.], *The Colonial Records of the State of Georgia,* 26 vols. (Atlanta: Charles P. Byrd, 1913), vol. 22, pt. 2, pp. 232–36.

Freedom to all Negroes Slaves that would resort thither. Certain Negroes belonging to Captain Davis escaped to Augustine, and were received there. They were demanded by General Oglethorpe who sent Lieutenant Demere to Augustine, and the Governour assured the General of his sincere Friendship, but at the same time showed his Orders from the Court of Spain, by which he was to receive all Run away Negroes. Of this other Negroes having notice, as it is believed, from the Spanish Emissaries, four or five who were Cattel-Hunters, and knew the Woods, some of whom belonged to Captain Macpherson, ran away with His Horses, wounded his Son and killed another Man. These marched f [sic] for Georgia, and were pursued, but the Rangers being then newly reduced [sic] the Countrey people could not overtake them, though they were discovered by the Saltzburghers, as they passed by Ebenezer.[1] They reached Augustine, one only being killed and another wounded by the Indians in their flight. They were received there with great honours, one of them had a Commission given to him, and a Coat faced with Velvet. Amongst the Negroe Slaves there are a people brought from the Kingdom of Angola in Africa, many of these speak Portugueze [which Language is as near Spanish as Scotch is to English,] by reason that the Portugueze have considerable Settlement, and the Jesuits have a Mission and School in that Kingdom and many Thousands of the Negroes there

1. Ebenezer was the name of a religious community near Savannah, founded by German dissenters resettled in Salzburg. (Editor's note)

profess the Roman Catholic Religion. Several Spaniards upon diverse Pretences have for some time past been strolling about Carolina, two of them, who will give no account of themselves have been taken up and committed to Jayl in Georgia. The good reception of the Negroes at Augustine was spread about, Several attempted to escape to the Spaniards, & were taken, one of them was hanged at Charles Town. In the latter end of July last Don Pedro, Colonel of the Spanish Horse, went in a Launch to Charles Town under pretence of a message to General Oglethorpe and the Lieutenant Governour.

On the 9th day of September last being Sunday which is the day the Planters allow them to work for themselves, Some Angola Negroes assembled, to the number of Twenty; and one who was called Jemmy was their Captain, they suprized a Warehouse belonging to M[r]. Hutchenson at a place called Stonehow [sic—]; they there killed M[r]. Robert Bathurst, and M[r]. Gibbs, plundered the House and took a pretty many small Arms and Powder, which were there for Sale. Next they plundered and burnt M[r]. Godfrey's house, and killed him, his Daughter and Son. They then turned back and marched Southward along Pons Pons, which is the Road through Georgia to Augustine, they passed M[r]. Wallace's Tavern towards day break, and said they would not hurt him, for he was a good Man and kind to his Slaves, but they broke open and plundered M[r]. Lemy's House, and killed him, his wife and Child. They marched on towards M[r]. Rose's resolving to kill him; but he was saved by a

Negroe, who having hid him went out and pacified the others. Several Negroes joyned them, they calling out Liberty, marched on with Colours displayed, and two Drums beating, pursuing all the white people they met with, and killing Man Woman and Child when they could come up to them. Collonel Bull Lieutenant Governour of South Carolina, who was then riding along the Road, discovered them, was pursued, and with much difficulty escaped & raised the Countrey. They burnt Colonel Hext's house and killed his Overseer and his Wife. They then burnt M^r. Sprye's house, then M^r. Sacheverell's, and then M^r. Nash's house, all lying upon the Pons Pons Road, and killed all the white People they found in them. M^r. Bullock got off, but they burnt his House, by this time many of them were drunk with the Rum they had taken in the Houses. They increased every minute by new Negroes coming to them, so that they were above Sixty, some say a hundred, on which they halted in a field, and set to dancing, Singing and beating Drums, to draw more Negroes to them, thinking they were now victorious over the whole Province, having marched ten miles & burnt all before them without Opposition, but the Militia being raised, the Planters with great briskness pursued them and when they came up, dismounting; charged them on foot. The Negroes were soon routed, though they behaved boldly several being killed on the Spot, many ran back to their Plantations thinking they had not been missed, but they were there taken and [sic] Shot, Such as were taken in the field also, were after being examined, shot on the Spot, And this is to be said to the honour of the Carolina Planters, that notwithstanding the Provocation they had received from so many Murders, they did not torture one Negroe, but only put them to an easy death. All that proved to be forced & were not concerned in the Murders & Burnings were pardoned, And this sudden Courage in the field, & the Humanity afterwards hath had so good an Effect that there hath been no farther Attempt, and the very Spirit of Revolt seems over. About 30 escaped from the fight, of which ten marched about 30 miles Southward, and being overtaken by the Planters on horseback, fought stoutly for some time and were all killed on the Spot. The rest are yet untaken. In the whole action about 40 Negroes and 20 whites were killed. The Lieutenant Governour sent an account of this to General Oglethorpe, who met the advices on his return from the Indian Nation He immediately ordered a Troop of Rangers to be ranged, to patrole through Georgia, placed some Men in the Garrison at Palichocolas, which was before abandoned, and near which the Negroes formerly passed, being the only place where Horses can come to swim over the River Savannah for near 100 miles, ordered out the Indians in pursuit, and a Detachment of the Garrison at Port Royal to assist the Planters on any Occasion, and published a Proclamation ordering all the Constables &c. of Georgia to pursue and seize all Negroes, with a Reward for any that should be taken. It is hoped these measures will prevent any Negroes from getting down to the Spaniards.—

25. Samba's Conspiracy in Louisiana, 1763

Native Africans who had been leaders in their own country emerged from time to time as instigators of rebellion in the New World. In the pages of LePage du Pratz, a recorder of the early history of Louisiana, appears this account of a conspiracy led by Samba, an already seasoned revolutionary from Africa.

At the time the succours were expected from France, in order to destroy the Natchez, the Negroes formed a design to rid themselves of all the French at once, and to settle in their room, by making themselves masters of the Capital, and of all the property of the French. It was discovered in the following manner.

A female Negro receiving a violent blow from a French soldier, for refusing to obey him, said in her passion, that the French should not long insult Negroes. Some Frenchman, overhearing these threats, brought her before the Governor, who sent her to prison. The Judge Criminal not being able to draw anything out of her, I told the Governor, who seemed to pay no great regard to her threats, that I was of opinion, that a man in liquor, and a woman in passion, generally speak truth. It is therefore highly probable, said I, that there is some truth in what she said: And if so, there must be some conspiracy, ready to break out, which cannot be formed without many Negroes of the King's plantation being accomplices therein: And if there are any, I take upon me, said I, to find them out, and arrest them, if necessary, without any disorder or tumult.

The Governor and the whole Court approved of my reasons: I went that very evening to the camp of the Negroes, and from hut to hut, till I saw a light. In this hut I heard them talking together of their scheme. One of them was my first commander and my confidant, which surprized me greatly; his name was Samba.

I speedily retired for fear of being discovered; and in two days after, eight Negroes, who were at the head of the conspiracy, were separately arrested, unknown to each other, and clapt in irons without the least tumult.

The day after they were put to the torture of burning matches; which, tho' several times repeated, could not bring them to make any confession. In the mean time I learnt, that Samba

Source: LePage du Pratz, History of Louisiana (London, 1763), 1:131–33, reprinted in Ulrich B. Phillips, ed., Plantation and Frontier (Cleveland: A. H. Clark, 1909), 2:248–49.

had, in his own country, been at the head of the revolt, by which the French lost Fort Arguin; and when it was recovered again by M. Perier de Salvert, one of the principal articles of the peace was, that this Negro should be condemned to slavery in America: That Samba, on his passage, had laid a scheme to murder the crew, in order to become master of the ship; but that being discovered, he was put in irons, in which he continued, till he landed in Louisiana.

I drew up a memorial of all this; which was read before Samba by the Judge Criminal; who, threatening him again with the torture, told him, he had ever been a seditious fellow: Upon which Samba directly owned all the circumstances of the conspiracy; and the rest, being confronted with him, confessed also: After which, the eight Negroes were condemned to be broke alive on the wheel, and the woman to be hanged before their eyes; which was accordingly done, and prevented the conspiracy from taking effect.

26. A Small Plot in Louisiana, July 1776

Most plots uncovered during the colonial period appear to have been the work of small groups who probably did not seek wide support. Such plots had no larger apparent designs than the liberation of the slaves directly involved. In the wilder, less settled parts of Louisiana, making off into the forest was not impossible, and camps of runaways could be formed in the swamps.

The incident described below occurred on the plantation of William Dunbar, a Scotsman who came to Louisiana in 1773, settling near Baton Rouge. He had bought slaves in Jamaica to work on his plantation, and in his stave-making enterprise. In his diary he mentions frequent illness among the "new" Negroes, those not accustomed to the swampy terrain. Dunbar had problems with runaways, as this entry of a few days after the date of the selection below demonstrates: "This morning Kitty & Bessy runaway, because they had received a little correction the former evening for disobedience; the Negroes employed as usual—Bessy taken up at Mr. Francis' this evening; sent for her & put her in Irons."

Dunbar was a naturalist, a correspondent of Thomas Jefferson, and a

Source: Mrs. Dunbar Rowland, *Life, Letters and Papers of William Dunbar* (Jackson, Miss.: Mississippi Historical Society, 1930), pp. 26–28.

member of the American Philosophical Society. Here, in the month of the Declaration of Independence, is the record of an unsuccessful slave plot, and with it a small picture of the life of slaves on the Western frontier.

July, 1776.

Friday 12th.—A very disagreeable & unexpected accident hath interfered & prevented the keeping of my Journal with regularity as heretofore—On Sunday 23d of June I dined at Mr. Marshall's with Messrs. Poupet & Francis, & being all of us stave makers, we agreed the ensuing week to have a trial of skill & the Sunday following to compare notes—I intended regulating the work among my People in such a manner that I had not the smallest doubt / from former experiments / of making at least four thousand staves—The Monday following in the morning, I was visited by my Neighbors Messrs. Ross, Francis, [Gor]don; They informed me that a conspiracy among . . . Negroes had been discovered, & that it had taken [place] at my House; The Names of three were mentioned, who with a Negro of Watt's & Flowers, were said to be the principals—Judge my surprise! Of what avail is kindness & good usage when rewarded by such ingratitude; 'tis true indeed they were kept under due subordination & obliged to do their duty in respect to plantation work, but two of the three had always behaved so well that they had never once received a stroke of the whip—I immediately sent to the field where they were a making staves to call in one of the Principalls, whom I carried up with me to Mr. Poupets in company with Francis & Gordon. Upon our arrival there a Negro of Mr.

Poupets was taken up on suspicion & my Fellow was bound with Cords, still ignorant of the Discovery we had made. When questioned he seemed to know nothing of the matter, & when confronted by Mr. Ross' Negroes [the Informers] who had the story from himself, he still persisted in his Inocence & Ignorance & mentioned as an argument why it must be impossible; that he had now b[een] Considerable time with his Master, that he had fed & clothed him well & had never once struck him & of course it was absurd to suppose him guilty. In the afternoon we set out on our return down with Mr. Poupet to seize the rest of the criminals—My Negro was sitting in the bottom of the Boat with his arms pinioned; He was 'tis supposed stung with the heghnousness of his guilt, ashamed perhaps to look a Master in the face against whom he could urge no plea to paliate his intended Diabolical plan; for he took an oppy. in the middle of the River to throw himself overboard & was immediately drowned—This was sufficient evidence of his guilt. In the evening our other two negroes were seized, another with one of Rapalje's & one of Watt's & Flower's. The Monday following was appointed for the trial of the Criminals & notice was sent to the neighbouring settlements to be present on so solemn an occasion. Several other Negroes were taken up on suspicion in the interim; and the trial came on, When our two Negroes and one of Watt's &

Flower were condemned to be hanged & were accordingly executed the following Day—Lesser punishments were inflicted on the less guilty—By a law of this Province, Masters of Negroes executed by order of a proper Court are entitled to receive their value of the Receiver General agreeable to an appraisment made by the Court that condemned them—At present there is no Assembly & consequently no monies can be raised—The Gentlemen settlers, have therefor thought it equitable, that they should all bear a share of the burthen as these executions were for the general good of the Country: a Subscription hath been opened; the Gentlemen of Richmond have subscribed liberally: but after leaving this settlement, you move into a different Clime & it is feared the subscription will fall short of the sum required—There are however exceptions to this rule, as Mr. Clark & a few others—These accidents hath occasioned such fatigues both of body & mind, that Stave making hath been discontinued till the present time—5 C W. Oak [1] staves were made on the monday that the Discovery was made—The Negroes have been employed during this time in weeding the fields & cuting Canes—Nicholas the Carpenter was absent from Monday 21st June to Monday 1st July which with one Day before makes 13 working days to be made good.

1. Dunbar must mean 5 cords of water oak staves. (*Editor's note*)

27. Gabriel's Attempted Uprising in Richmond, 1800

In the year 1800 a slave of Thomas Prosser, named Gabriel, laid a plan for a general uprising of the slaves in the vicinity of Richmond, Virginia. A plot of formidable proportions developed, involving thousands of slaves, and it was the most sophisticated in political intention of all the slave plots uncovered. Gabriel's plan was frustrated by what the whites of Henrico County came to regard as the intervention of God. A vital footbridge by which the insurgents were to have approached Richmond was washed out by a torrential downpour of rain. The plot was revealed to the

Source: H. W. Flournoy, ed., *Calendar of Virginia State Papers and Other Manuscripts from January 1, 1799, to December 31, 1807; Preserved in the Capitol at Richmond,* 11 vols. (Richmond, 1890), 9: 140–44, 147, 150–52.

Richmond authorities by slave informers before Gabriel's plan could be revised.

How many slaves were involved is difficult to ascertain, with estimates ranging from one thousand to five thousand persons. It is likely that more than five thousand *knew* of the plot, but it is unlikely that even a thousand were armed and ready to fight with Gabriel. Even before Gabriel himself was captured, the trials of the conspirators began in Richmond. Some twenty slaves were executed, many others were exiled, and others acquitted. Gabriel was hanged on October 7, 1800, without having made a statement to the authorities.

The testimony of the conspirators in depositions taken by the court reveals many salient details of the plot and its social basis. Many of the leaders were skilled artisans who enjoyed much physical mobility, going about to barbecues, church meetings, and funerals, seizing these opportunities for organization.

At a court of Oyer and Terminer, called and held for the county of Henrico at the Courthouse, on Thursday the Eleventh day of September, 1800, for the trial of Michael alias Mike, a negro man slave the property of Judith Owen of the said county, charged with conspiracy and insurrection.

Present: Daniel L. Hylton, Miles Selden, Bowler Cocke, Hezekial Henley, Benjamin Goode, Pleasant Younghusband and George Williamson, Gent. Justices.

The said negro man Michael alias Mike, was set to the Bar in custody, and being arraigned of the premises said he was in nowise guilty of the crime with which he stands accused, whereupon sundry witnesses being charged, sworn and examined, and the prisoner heard in his defence by James Rind, Gent., counsel assigned him by the court, on consideration whereof, it is the opinion of the court that the said Michael alias Mike, is guilty of the crime with which he stands charged, and for the same that he be hanged by the neck until he be dead, and that execution of this sentence be done and performed on him the said Michael alias Mike, on tomorrow, being the twelfth instant, at the usual place of execution. The court valued the said slave at one hundred pounds.

The minutes of the foregoing trial and proceedings were signed by the above named justices.

A Copy—Teste:
ADAM CRAIG, C.H.C.

Henrico County Court, on September 11th, sentences John, a negro man slave, the property of Mary Jones, of Hanover, to death on charge of conspiracy and insurrection, and orders that he be hung at the usual place of execution on the 12th inst.

Henrico County Court, on Sept. 11th, sentences Solomon, a negro man slave, the property of Thomas H. Prosser, of Henrico, to death on charge of conspiracy and insurrection, and orders that he be hung on the 12th instant at the usual place of execution.

Henrico County Court, on September 11th, sentences Nat, a negro man slave, the property of Anne Parsons, of Henrico, to death on charge of conspiracy and insurrection, and orders that he be hung on the 12th instant at the usual place of execution.

Henrico County Court, on September 11th, sentences Isaac, a negro man slave, the property of Wm. Burton, of Henrico, to death on charge of conspiracy and insurrection, and orders that he be hung on the 12th instant at the usual place of execution.

Henrico County Court, on September 11th, sentences Will, a negro man slave, the property of John Mosby, Senior, of Henrico, to death on charge of conspiracy and insurrection, and orders that he be hung on the 12th instant at the usual place of execution.

EVIDENCE AGAINST THE NEGROES
TRIED SEPTEMBER 11TH.

Solomon's Case.—Ben, the property of Thos. H. Prosser, deposed: That the prisoner at the bar made a number of swords for the purpose of carrying into execution the plan of an insurrection which was planned by Gabriel, a negro man, the property of said Prosser, and that the said Solomon was to be Treasurer. In the first place, Mr. Prosser and Mr. Johnson were to be killed and their arms seized upon; then they were to resort to and kill all the White

Neighbours. This plan to be executed on the Saturday night on which there was such a great fall of rain. The place of meeting was near Prosser's Blacksmith's shop in the woods. After Murdering the Inhabitants of the Neighbourhood, the assembly were to repair to Richmond and Seize upon the Arms and Ammunition—to-wit, the Magazine. Gabriel was to command at commencement of the business. The swords made by the prisoner were to be distributed by s'd Gabriel; swords have been making ever since last Harvest. 1,000 men was to be raised from Richmond, 600 from Ground Squirrel Bridge, and 400 from Goochland. Meetings were frequently held at William Young's under pretext of attending preachment, and at other times— viz., at Fish feast and at Barbacues, to concert the plan of Insurrection. The Rain which fell on Saturday night, the 30th August, prevented the carrying the said plan into Execution. Swords made by the prisoner were to be used by Horsemen, two hundred of whom were appointed, but it was expected there would be 400. Gabriel and Solomon, the prisoner, kept lists of the names of the conspirators; that he heard Lewis Barrel spoken of as one of Town's Negroes concerned. That he in conversation with Jack Bowler, otherwise called Jack Ditcher, it appeared that two white Frenchmen was the first instigators of the Insurrection, but whose names he did not hear.

Pharoah, the property of Philip Sheppard, deposed: That the prisoner at the bar on Saturday, the 30th August, enquired of this deponent whether the light horse of Richmond were out, he being then from Richmond, who informed him that he had seen some at Col. Goodall's tavern. The prisoner remarked that the business of the insurrection had so far advanced that they were compelled, even if discovered, to go forward with it; that he had four swords then to finish, which he must complete by the time of his company meeting that evening, which would consist of 1,000 men, to wit: negroes.

Will's Case.—Ben, the property of T. H. Prosser, deposed: That the prisoner brought two scythe blades to Gabriel for the purpose of having them made into swords, and that four swords were made out of them by Solomon at request of Gabriel; that the said Will acknowledged in the presence of the deponent, in conversation with Gabriel, that he was concerned in the conspiracy and insurrection, and that he wanted the appointment of captain of the foot, but this being refused him, he was to act as a horseman; that the whites were to be murdered and killed indiscriminately, except [?] none of whom were to be touched.

Toby, the property of John Holman, deposed: That the prisoner proposed to join and fight the whites; that he had joined, and had to carry two scythe blades to Soloman to be made into swords; he was determined to kill his master; that he had his master's sorrel horse set apart for him to act upon as a horseman; that there was to be a grand meeting of the negroes near Prosser's, from whence they were to proceed and take the town; that 5,000 blacks were to meet the prisoner at the bar, and that all the blacks who did not join would be put to death; that he in-

tended to kill his master on Saturday night, the 30th August last; that the prisoner had an appointment as captain, but was turned out, being under size.

John's Case.—Daniel, property of John Williamson, deposed: That the deponent being at plough at home, the prisoner, who at that time worked at the penitentiary and was passing by, invited him to come to a great barbecue which was to be made by the negroes at Half Sink; and upon being informed that the purport of the barbecue was to concert measures for raising an insurrection and murdering and killing the whites and taking the country, of which he had no doubt, as Gabriel, and Solomon, and himself, being a captain, being at the head of the business; that the said John said he had a number of men at the Penitentiary, and was going up to Caroline, where he expected to raise several hundred; that they were to seize upon the arms at the penitentiary, and that all negroes who did not join in the insurrection would and should be put to death. That the whites were to be put to death indiscriminately.

Charles, property of Wm. Winston, deposed: That about three weeks ago the prisoner gave this deponent an invite to a barbecue to be at Mr. Moore's school-house, which was made on a particular occasion, but was not made known to him, the deponent, which invitation this deponent refused to accept.

Isaac's Case.—Ben, the property of T. H. Prosser, deposed, that the prisoner informed him the deponent, that he had joined Prosser's Gabriel, in order to take Richmond and that he the prisoner, was one of the foot soldiers; that he was if possible to supply himself with a sword which if he could not do, Gabriel was to furnish him, and he the prisoner, was determined either to kill or be killed.

Dan'l, the property of Wm. Burton, deposed, that the prisoner informed the deponent, on Friday the 29th August last, that he the prisoner, had been informed by Nanny, wife to Gabriel, that 1000 men were to meet said Gabriel near Prosser's Tavern the ensuing night, and that he also was to be one of them, for the purpose of murdering the White Citizens; that the Governor had in some measure, got an alarm of this business, and had caused the arms which had been kept in the Capitol to be removed to the Penitentiary—that they should not mind the guards which were placed over the arms as they were determined to rush through them and take both them and the magazine—that he communicated this information to the overseer that an army of negroes were raising aginst the whites, with an injunction to the said overseer to keep the communication secret, the blacks were determined to kill every black who should not aid in, and join them in the insurrection. The prisoner was much intoxicated at the time of the conversation and information above.

Michael's Case.—Ben, the property of T. H. Prosser, deposed: That about a fortnight before time appointed for the insurrection, the prisoner being on his way to Richmond, employed Gabriel to make him a sword, which was to be used by him in fighting the whites under the command of Gabriel, as a foot soldier; that he called on the Sat-

urday evening appointed for carrying the plot into execution, the prisoner applied at the house of Gabriel and obtained his sword, and promised to meet the Sunday night at the Tobacco house of Mr. Prosser, that being too rainy an evening for carrying their . . . .

Pharoah, the property of Philip Sheppard, deposed: That in the week preceding the Saturday appointed for an insurrection, the prisoner informed him that Gabriel was to furnish him a sword, which he would call and get on Saturday evening ensuing; that he had joined the party.

Ned, the property of Judith Owen, deposed: That the prisoner informed him he had been requested by Gabriel to join him in an insurrection, which he had rejected, promising said Gabriel should he see the business progress well he would afterward join him.

William Gentry deposed: That he and Mr. Glenn being in pursuit of Gabriel and just on the return from said Gabriel's habitation, fell in with the prisoner, who they were about to take up when he fled into the woods; that being pursued by Mr. Glenn, was taken some time before the deponent arrived, and that Mr. Glenn informed him that a scythe blade made into the form of a sword was produced by the prisoner, with which he made battle against said Glenn, who had overcome the prisoner and had then the said sword in his possession.

Nat's Case.—Ben, the property of T. H. Prosser, deposed: That the prisoner had joined Gabriel to fight the White people, and for that purpose purchased a sword from one William, belonging to Ben Mosby; that upon falling in with Gabriel and this deponent, he informed Gabriel that he had his sword, and left it at the warehouse; that he had a stick in his hand, and, flourishing it in his hand, observed that thus he would wield his sword. This was about three weeks previous to the time appointed for the commencement of the insurrection. That the said Gabriel and the prisoner agreed that the prisoner should bear the rank of a captain, the said prisoner remarking that all the Warehouse boys had joined, and he would go on to get as many as he could until the appointed time.

Washington, belonging to Benj. Mosby, deposed: That he sold a sword to the prisoner, who informed him he wanted to stand Guard with it at the Warehouse, where he then lived and had the care of.

[Sept. 12, Henrico]—Henrico County Court sentences Frank, a negro man slave, the property of Thos. H. Prosser, to death on charge of conspiracy and insurrection, and orders him to be hung on the 15th instant at the usual place of execution.

Henrico County Court sentences Martin, a negro man slave, the property of Thos. H. Prosser, to death on charge of conspiracy and insurrection, and orders him to be hung on the 15th instant at the usual place of execution.

Henrico County Court sentences Billy, a negro man slave, the property of Roger Gregory, of Henrico, to death on charge of conspiracy and insurrection, and orders that he be hung on the 15th instant at the usual place of execution.

Henrico County Court sentences Charles, a negro man slave, the property of Roger Gregory, of Henrico, to death on charge of conspiracy and insurrection, and orders him to be hung on the 15th instant at the usual place of execution.

. . .

CONFESSION OF SOLOMON.

Communications made to the subscribers by Solomon, the property of Thomas H. Prosser, of Henrico, now under sentence of death for plotting an insurrection.

My brother Gabriel was the person who influenced me to join him and others in order that (as he said) we might conquer the white people and possess ourselves of their property. I enquired how we were to effect it. He said by falling upon them (the whites) in the dead of night, at which time they would be unguarded and unsuspicious. I then enquired who was at the head of the plan. He said Jack, alias Jack Bowler. I asked him if Jack Bowler knew anything about carrying on war. He replied he did not. I then enquired who he was going to employ. He said a man from Caroline who was at the siege of Yorktown, and who was to meet him (Gabriel) at the Brook and to proceed on to Richmond, take, and then fortify it. This man from Caroline was to be commander and manager the first day, and then, after exercising the soldiers, the command was to be resigned to Gabriel. If Richmond was taken without the loss of many men they were to continue there some time, but if they sustained any considerable loss they were to bend their course for Hanover Town or York, they were not decided to which, and continue at that place as long as they found they were able to defend it, but in the event of a defeat or loss at those places they were to endeavor to form a junction with some negroes which, they had understood from Mr. Gregory's overseer, were in rebellion in some quarter of the country. This information which they had gotten from the overseer, made Gabriel anxious, upon which he applied to me to make scythe-swords, which I did to the number of twelve. Every Sunday he came to Richmond to provide ammunition and to find where the military stores were deposited. Gabriel informed me, in case of success, that they intended to subdue the whole of the country where slavery was permitted, but no further.

The first places Gabriel intended to attack in Richmond were, the Capitol, the Magazine, the Penitentiary, the Governor's house and his person. The inhabitants were to be massacred, save those who begged for quarter and agreed to serve as soldiers with them. The reason why the insurrection was to be made at this particular time was, the discharge of the number of soldiers, one or two months ago, which induced Gabriel to believe the plan would be more easily executed.

Given under our hands this 15th day of September, 1800.

Gervas Storrs,
Joseph Selden.

. . .

CONFESSIONS OF BEN ALIAS BEN WOOLFOLK.

[Sept. 17]—The first time I ever heard of this conspiricy was from Mrs. Ann Smith's George; the second person that gave me information was Samuel alias Samuel Bird, the property of Mrs. Jane Clarke. They asked me last spring to come over to their houses on a Friday night. It was late before I could get there; the company had met and dispersed. I inquired where they were gone, and was informed to see their wives. I went after them and found George; he carried me and William (the property of William Young) to Sam Bird's, and after we got there he (Sam) enquired of George if he had any pen and ink; he said no—he had left it at home. He brought out his list of men, and he had Elisha Price's Jim, James Price's Moses, Sally Price's Bob, Denny Wood's Emanuel. After this George invited me to come and see him the next night, but I did not go. The following Monday night William went over and returned with a ticket for me; likewise one for Gilbert. The Thursday night following, both George and Sam Bird came to see me. Bowler's Jack was with us. We conversed untill late in the night upon the subject of the meditated war. George said he would try to be ready by the 24th of August, and the following Sunday he went to Hungry meeting-house to enlist men. When I saw him again he informed me he had enlisted 37 men there. The Sunday after he went to Manchester, where he said he had recruited 50-odd men. I never saw him again untill the sermon at my house, which was about three weeks before the rising was to take place. On the day of the sermon, George called on Sam Bird to inform how many men he had; he said he had not his list with him, but he supposed about 500.

George wished the business to be deferred some time longer. Mr. Prosser's Gabriel wished to bring on the business as soon as possible. Gilbert said the summer was almost over, and he wished them to enter upon the business before the weather got too cold. Gabriel proposed that the subject should be referred to his brother Martin to decide upon. Martin said there was this expression in the Bible, delays breed danger; at this time, he said, the country was at peace, the soldiers were discharged, and the arms all put away; there was no patroling in the country, and that before he would any longer bear what he had borne, he would turn out and fight with his stick. Gilbert said he was ready with his pistol, but it was in need of repair; he gave it to Gabriel, who was put it in order for him. I then spoke to the company and informed them I wished to have something to say. I told them that I had heard in the days of old, when the Israelites were in service to King Pharoah, they were taken from him by the power of God, and were carried away by Moses. God had blessed him with an angel to go with him, but that I could see nothing of that kind in these days. Martin said in reply: I read in my Bible where God says if we will worship Him we should have peace in all our land; five of you shall conquer an hundred, and a hundred a thousand of our enemies. After this they went on consultation upon the time they should execute the plan. Martin spoke and appointed for them to meet in three weeks, which was to be of a Saturday night. Gabriel said he had 500 bullets made. Smith's George said he was done the corn and would then go on to make as many cross-bows as he could. Bowler's Jack said he had got 50 spiers or bayonets fixed at the end of sticks. The plan was to be as follows: We were all to meet at the briery spot on the Brook; 100 men were to stand at the Brook bridge; Gabriel was to take 100 more and go to Gregory's tavern and take the arms which were there; 50 more were to be sent to Rocketts to set that on fire, in order to alarm the upper part of the town and induce the people to go down there; while they were employed in extinguishing the fire Gabriel and the other officers and soldiers were to take the Capitol and all the arms they could find and be ready to slaughter the people on their return from Rocketts. Sam Bird was to have a pass as a free man and was to go to the nation of Indians called Catawbas to persuade them to join the negroes to fight the white people. As far as I understood all the whites were to be massacred, except the Quakers, the Methodists, and the Frenchmen, and they were to be spared on account as they conceived of their being friendly to liberty, and also they had understood that the French were at war with this country for the money that was due them, and that an army was landed at South Key, which they hoped would assist them. They intended also to spare all the poor white women who had no slaves.

The above communications are put down precisely as delivered to us by Ben, alias Ben Woolfolk. Given under our hands this 17th day of September, 1800.

GERVAS STORRS,
JOSEPH SELDEN.

28.   Denmark Vesey's Conspiracy in Charleston, 1822

Twenty-two years after Gabriel Prosser's futile attempt in Richmond, a second formidable conspiracy developed in Charleston, South Carolina. Nearly forty thousand slaves were imported into the state in the early nineteenth century, most of them just ahead of the federal ban on the slave trade, which became effective in 1808; and some were imported illegally after that date. Large numbers of these slaves came directly from Africa, and others arrived from the West Indies with their masters, who were in flight from the insurrections of San Domingo occurring at the turn of the century. The situation was conducive to the spread of revolutionary ideas among the blacks, especially in Charleston, where free blacks like Denmark Vesey had great freedom of movement in the black sections of the city.

Vesey was a brilliant mulatto who had purchased his freedom with the proceeds of a lottery jackpot, a man who then turned his trade as a carpenter into a comfortable living. But Vesey was dissatisfied with mere personal freedom, and humiliated that his people were enslaved. He read widely and spoke freely, rebuking fellow blacks who demonstrated servility by getting out of the street to accommodate white passers-by. In the back alleys of the city he told anyone who would listen about the white man's hypocrisy in reserving the Declaration of Independence for whites only. In the black church he reminded his fellows of how the Israelites dealt with the captured city of Jericho, after the walls came tumbling down: "And they utterly destroyed all that was in the city, both man and woman, young and old, and ox, and ass, with the edge of the sword," and they burned the city.

Vesey's most effective lieutenant in the task of arousing the black population was Gullah Jack, who had come directly from Angola, and claimed supernatural powers. Of grotesque physique and frightening countenance, Gullah Jack used the symbols of conjure, and invoked tribal gods. The combination of the adopted religion and the African heritage proved

Source: Letter of Gov. Thomas Bennett, August 10, 1822, printed with editor's comments in *Niles' Weekly Register,* September 7, 1822.

its potency, and by early summer of 1822 Charleston was sitting, all unaware, on the rim of destruction. On May 30, a loyal house servant informed authorities of the plot but was disbelieved. Two weeks later a second house servant confessed, fear gripped the city, and the Governor and mayor sprang into action, only two days before June 16, the zero hour. Troops in the city imperiled Vesey's carefully laid plan, and he called off the insurrection.

The trials began anyhow, and during the months that followed, one terrifying revelation after another shattered white nerves. The shocking discovery that highly placed and trusted personal servants were among those most deeply involved imparted fears that were never entirely allayed in South Carolina. The notable silence of the chief leaders under questioning meant that most of the participants remained at large in the city. It has also given several historians to believe that there was in fact no basis for the public alarm, that there had been no plot of any real importance in the first place. No doubt the hysteria was overdeveloped because of the trials, which lasted two months, but the evidence for a large plan is too convincing to be ignored. Before the case was closed, thirty-five blacks were hanged, and thirty-seven others sent out of the state.

To allay the continuing panic Gov. Thomas Bennett wrote the following public letter, and one supposes that he placed the most conservative estimate possible on the proportions of the conspiracy. Even so, his efforts met with modest success only, for South Carolina did not soon forget this close escape from what was perhaps the best-planned of all the slave conspiracies. The immediate results for the slave population was a harsh reaction in public policy, with the specific aim of limiting slaves' exposure to incendiary messages of any kind, written or spoken. Assembly in churches was curtailed and reading outlawed, black sailors were confined to ships in Charleston harbor, and incoming mails checked carefully.

Editor Hezekiah Niles, who published Governor Bennett's letter, followed it with a comment and excerpts from the report of the City Council of Charleston.

EXECUTIVE DEPARTMENT,
Charleston, August 10, 1822

SIR: After a prolonged and almost uninterrupted session of six weeks, the first court organized for the trial of slaves charged with an attempt to raise an insurrection in this city, was dissolved on the 20th ult. Another court was subsequently convened, and, after a session of three days, closed the unpleasant investigation with which it was charged, and adjourned on the 8th instant, *sine die.*

During the interesting period occupied by the court first organized, the public mind was agitated by a variety of rumors, calculated to produce great excitement and alarm. These had their origin in the nature of the transaction, and the secrecy and seclusion observed in the incipient stages of the inquiry; as but few of the circumstances were known to the community, and the number apprehended and sentenced to the severest punishment, beyond any former example. Certainty gave place to exaggeration, and the general impression sustained the rumor of a very extensive conspiracy.

The effects resulting from these reports, if uncontrolled by an exhibition of facts, are too obvious to require comment. The reputation of the state must suffer abroad, and a rapid deterioration of property occur within; while suspicion and anxiety will continue long to mar the public tranquility. It becomes, therefore, a duty imperiously obligatory on me, to represent the occurrences as they have transpired, and thus evidence to you that the attempt has not only been greatly magnified, but as soon as discovered it ceased to be dangerous.

A servant, prompted by attachment to his master, communicated to him that he had been requested to give his assent and subscribe his name to a list of persons already engaged in the conspiracy. The intendant immediately received the information, and caused the arrest of three slaves of Mr. Paul—one of whom was subsequently identified by the servant making the communication. The city council was convened, and after a very close and attentive examination, a general impression was produced that but little credence could attach to the statement. A prudent caution was nevertheless exercised, and the fellow charged committed to solitary imprisonment. A few days after his confinement, he made many disclosures to a member of council, but so amplified the circumstances that the utmost credulity was requisite to the belief of his tale.

Some consternation was obviously produced amongst a few of the conspirators by the arrest of these slaves, and I cannot doubt led to a detail more plausible and deserving of attention. Another servant, whose name is also concealed, from prudential motives, stated, generally, that such a combination actually existed, and mentioned the names of several who were most conspicuous in their exertions, adding, with great confidence, that the explosion of their schemes would occur on the ensuing Sunday night. This confession was given on Thursday, the 13th June, and contained the recital of several occurrences which would precede the attempt and evidence the intention. This suggested the propriety, while it sanctioned the effort, to conceal from the community the intelligence thus received, for the intervening time—during which extensive and efficient preparations were made for the safety and protection of the city. Saturday night and Sunday morning passed without the predicted demonstrations; doubts were again excited, and counter orders issued for diminishing the guard. The facts communicated were generally known to our fellow citizens on Sunday; producing a night of sleepless anxiety. But no one of the predicted (or any other) occurrences presented itself to disturb the general tranquility.

On the 18th June ten slaves were arrested, and on the 19th the court was organized for their trial. Investigation was retarded by the difficulty of procuring authentic evidence, and it was not until the 28th that the sentence of death was pronounced against six of the persons charged with the offence. Denmark Vesey, a free negro, was arrested on the 21st, and on the 22d put on his trial. Although he was unquestionably the instigator and chief of this plot, no positive proof of his guilt appeared until the 25th. This grew out of the confession of one of the convicts, and on the 27th his guilt was further established by a servant of Mr. Ferguson.

The progress made, and the expectations of immunity from punishment by confession, gradually developed the plot, and produced the arrest of several others, fortunately two who were principals, Monday Gell and Gullah Jack. These, with three others, John Horry, Charles Drayton and Harry Haig, were convicted, and sentenced to die on Friday, the 12th July last; but, at the suggestion of the court that important communications were expected from them, Monday Gell, Charles Drayton and Harry Haig were respited.

The arrest of Perault, a servant of Mr. Strohecker, which took place the day previous to the respite, and the general and very important discoveries made by him, enabled the committee of vigilance, not only to elicit the confirmation of his statement from the three convicts, but to apprehend a great number of persons engaged in the plot. Among others, William Gar-

ner, reputed to be one of the principals, the only one not then apprehended.

The number of persons at this period under arrest, evinced the necessity of such arrangements of the testimony as would enable the court to progress with more rapidity. This duty devolved on the committee of vigilance: and principally from the general information of Perault, and of the convicts Monday Gell and Charles Drayton, facility was given to the further proceedings of the court. In the short space of seven days thirty-two negroes were convicted; twenty-two of whom were executed on Friday, the 20th July: and within four days after, eleven others were convicted, four of whom have also been executed.

Having established the existence of a plot, and the places of rendezvous, all that was deemed requisite for conviction was to prove an association with the ringleaders, and an expression of their assent to the measure. On such, generally, the sentence of death has been executed. Others who, without actually combining, were proved to have known of the conspiracy, and to have given their sanction by any act, have been sentenced to die, and their punishment commuted to banishment from the United States, or sentenced, in the first instance to banishment from this state or from the United States. In this manner, the whole number, seventy-two, have been disposed of; thirty-five executed, and thirty-seven sentenced to banishment. With these we may reasonably conclude that we have reached the extremities of this conspiracy, and this opinion, if not conclusive, is entitled to great weight, when we advert to the extraordinary measures pursued to effect the object and the motives which influenced the accused.

No means which experience or ingenuity could devise were left unessayed, to eviscerate the plot. In the labors of investigation, the court was preceded by a committee formed by the city council, whose intelligence, activity, and zeal, were well adapted to the arduous duties of their appointment. Their assiduity, aided by the various sentiments which influenced the prisoners, produced a rapid development of the plot. Several of the conspirators had entered into solemn pledges to partake of a common destiny, and one, at least, was found, who, after his arrest, felt no repugnance to enforce the obligation, by surrendering the names of his associates. A spirit of retaliation and revenge produced a similar effect with others, who suspected that they were the victims of treachery; and this principle operated with full effect, as the hope or expectation of pardon predominated. To the last hour of the existence of several, who appeared to be conspicuous actors in this drama, they were pressingly importuned to make further confessions.

Among the conspirators, the most daring and active was Monday, the slave of Mr. Gell. He could read and write with facility, and thus attained an extraordinary and dangerous influence over his fellows. Permitted by his owner to occupy a house in a central part of the city, hourly opportunities were afforded for the exercise of his skill on those, who were attracted to his ship by business or favor. It was there that his artful and insidious delusions were kept in perpetual exercise. Materials were abundantly furnished in the seditious pamphlets brought into this state, by equally culpable incendiaries; while the speeches of the oppositionists in congress to the admission of Missouri, gave a serious and imposing effect to his machinations. This man wrote to Boyer (by his own confession) requesting his aid, and addressed the envelope of his letter to a relative of the person who became the bearer of it, a negro from one of the northern states.[1] He was the only person proved to have kept a list of those engaged; and the court considered his confession full and ample.—From such means and such sources of information, it cannot be doubted that all who were actually concerned, have been brought to justice. There is no exception within my knowledge; it has, however, been stated, that a plantation in St. John's was infected, but I do not know on what authority.

This plain detail of the principal incidents in this transaction, will satisfy you that the scheme has not been general nor alarmingly extensive. And it furnishes a cause for much satisfaction, that, although religion, superstition, fear, and almost every passion that sways the human mind, have been artfully used by the wicked instigators of this design, so few have been seduced from a course of propriety and obedience. Those who associated were unprovided with the means of attack or resistance. No weapons (if we except

1. Jean Pierre Boyer (1776–1850) was President of the black republic of Haiti 1818–42. (Editor's note)

thirteen hoop-poles) have been discovered; nor any testimony received but of six pikes, that such preparations were actually made. The witnesses generally agree in one fact, that the attempt was to have taken place on Sunday night, the 16th June, differing a little as to the precise time; 12 o'clock appears to have been the hour.

From the various conflicting statements made during the trials, it is difficult to form a plausible conjecture of their ultimate plans of operation; no two agreeing on general definite principles. That the first essay would be made with clubs against the state arsinal is inferrible, from their being unprovided with arms, and the concurrence of several witnesses. But whether the attack would be made simultaneously by various detachments, or whether the whole, embodied at a particular spot, would proceed to the accomplishment of their object, is very uncertain. Upon the whole, it is manifest that if any plan had been organized, it was never communicated by the principal conspirator to the leaders or the men, as they were wholly ignorant even of the places of rendezvous; although within two days of the time appointed, and but one man arrested prior to the day fixed on for the attempt.

When we contrast the numbers engaged with the magnitude of the enterprize, the imputation of egregious folly or madness is irresistible: and supposing the attempt to have been predicated on the probability, that partial success would augment their numbers, the utmost presumption would scarcely have hazarded the result. Servility long continued, debases the

mind and abstracts it from that energy of character, which is fitted to great exploits. It cannot be supposed, therefore, without a violation of the immutable laws of nature, that a transition from slavery and degradation to authority and power, could instantly occur. Great and general excitement may produce extensive and alarming effects; but the various passions which operate with powerful effect on this class of persons, impart a confident assurance of detection and defeat to every similar design. While the event is remote, they may listen with credulity to the artful tale of the instigator, and concur in its plausibility; but the approach of danger will invariably produce treachery, the concomitant of dastardly dispositions. In the fidelity and attachment of a numerous class of these persons, we have other sources of security and early information; from both of which, it is reasonable to conclude, that, in proportion to the number engaged, will be the certainty of detection; and that an extensive conspiracy cannot be matured in this state.

I have entered with much reluctance on this detail, nor would it have been considered requisite, but to counteract the number of gross and idle reports, actively and extensively circulated, and producing a general anxiety and alarm. And, although their authors may have no evil design, and may really be under the delusion, it is easy to perceive what pernicious consequences may ensue from not applying the proper corrective. Every individual in the state is interested, whether in relation to his own property, or the reputation of the state, in giving no more importance to the transaction than it justly merits. The legislature has wisely provided the means of efficient protection. If the citizens will faithfully perform the duty enjoined on them by the patrol laws, I fear not that we shall continue in the enjoyment of as much tranquility and safety as any state in the union.

I have the honor to be, very respectfully, sir, your obedient servant,

THO. BENNETT.

EDITOR NILES'S ADDENDUM.

A pamphlet has also been published, under the authority of the city council of Charleston, giving a long account of the intended insurrection in that city, and detailing the facts that appeared against individuals found guilty of being engaged in it. But, perhaps, enough has been said to show the nature and extent of the conspiracy. It appears that 131 blacks were arrested, of whom 35 were executed, 12 respited until the 25th of October, 21 sentenced to be transported out of the United States, 1 to be sent out of the state, 9 were acquitted, the propriety of transportation being suggested and agreed to, and 52 were acquitted and discharged.

"The following is the sentence that was pronounced on *Gullah Jack*, who affected great supernatural power by *charming* men and things, and declaring that he was invulnerable by white men, &c.

"The court, after deliberately considering all the circumstances of your case, are perfectly satisfied of your guilt. In the prosecution of your wicked designs, you were not satisfied with resorting to natural and ordinary means, but endeavored to enlist on your behalf, all the powers of darkness, and employed for that purpose the most disgusting mummery and superstition. You represented yourself as invulnerable; that you could neither be taken nor destroyed; that all who fought under your banners would be invincible. While such wretched expedients are calculated to *inspire* the confidence, or to alarm the fears of the ignorant and credulous, they excite no other emotion in the mind of the intelligent and enlightened, but contempt and disgust. Your boasted charms have not protected yourself, and of course could not protect others. 'Your altars and your Gods have sunk together in the dust.' The airy spectres, conjured by you, have been chased away by the special light of truth, and you stand exposed, the miserable and deluded victim of offended justice. Your days are literally numbered. You will shortly be consigned to the cold and silent grave, and all the powers of darkness cannot rescue you from your approaching fate! Let me then, conjure you to devote the remnant of your miserable existence, fleeing from the *wrath to come*. This can only be done by a full disclosure of the truth. The court is willing to afford you all the aid in their power, and to permit any minister of the gospel, whom you may select, to have free access to you. To him you may unburthen your guilty conscience. Neglect not the opportunity, for there is 'no device nor art beyond the tomb,' to which you must shortly be consigned."

29. Nat Turner's Revolt in Virginia, 1831

Eleven years after Vesey's plot was disclosed, a slave named Nat Turner launched a revolt in Southampton County, Virginia. Unlike Gabriel Prosser's and Vesey's attempts, this first major plot to cost white lives was primarily a rural affair. Like Vesey, however, Nat Turner called on religion to bring slaves to his side. Turner was a slave preacher and a mystic. He had, as he said, a kind master, but he felt himself called of God to liberate his people, and early in life developed the sense that his was a special destiny. He waited for signals, and when a solar eclipse occurred during February of 1831, Turner scheduled his revolution for the Fourth of July. He later postponed the date because of illness, but another signal came soon after, and on August 21 he began the insurrection. Turner's followers killed first his own master and his family, and then swept through the community, destroying entire families, leaving small possibility of survivors who could spread the alarm. Within twenty-four hours nearly sixty whites of all ages and both sexes had been killed. State and federal troops then overpowered Turner's band.

The state executed fifty-five persons, banished many more, and acquitted others. But the hysterical immediate reaction caused the death by mob action of upward of two hundred blacks, many of whom had been in no way connected with Nat Turner's war on slavery. The question of what Virginia would do in the face of this unprecedented threat to slavery hung briefly in the balance. The State Legislature in its next session discussed the problem thoroughly, and the voices raised against slavery were numerous and strong. The vote was close, but in the end Virginia took the same course South Carolina had taken earlier, and supported a repressive policy, one that continued until the outbreak of the Civil War. The following document is the statement Nat Turner made after his capture on October 30 to Dr. Thomas Gray, a physician who visited him in prison. It will readily occur to the reader that the prisoner may have told Dr. Gray rather more than the truth by way of explanation of his deed, and that Dr. Gray himself may have invested the insurrection with some of his own biases.

Source: The Confessions of Nat Turner, the Leader of the Late Insurrection in Southampton, Va., As Fully and Voluntarily Made to Thomas R. Gray (Richmond: Thomas R. Gray, 1832), pp. 7–22.

But the confession has an unmistakable consistency, has very little contrary evidence to confront, and remains the best and most credible complete account of Nat Turner's uprising. Turner was hanged on November 11, 1831.

The Confession.

Agreeable to his own appointment, on the evening he was committed to prison, with permission of the Jailor, I visited NAT on Tuesday, the 1st November, when, without being questioned at all, he commenced his narrative in the following words:

SIR—You have asked me to give a history of the motives which induced me to undertake the late insurrection, as you call it. To do so I must go back to the days of my infancy, and even before I was born. I was thirty-one years of age the 2d of October last, and born the property of Benj. Turner, of this county. In my childhood a circumstance occurred which made an indelible impression on my mind, and laid the groundwork of that enthusiasm, which has terminated so fatally to many, both white and black, and for which I am about to atone at the gallows. It is here necessary to relate this circumstance—trifling as it may seem, it was the commencement of that belief which has grown with time, and even now, sir, in this dungeon, helpless and forsaken as I am, I cannot divest myself of. Being at play with other children, when three or four years old, I was telling them something, which, my mother overhearing, said it had happened before I was born. I stuck to my story, however, and related some things which went, in her opinion, to confirm it. Others being called on were greatly astonished, knowing that these things had happened, and caused them to say in my hearing, I surely would be a prophet, as the Lord had shown me things that had happened before my birth. And my father and mother strengthened me in this, my first impression, saying in my presence, I was intended for some great purpose, which they had always thought from certain marks on my head and breast—[a parcel of excres-[c]ences, which I believe are not at all uncommon, particularly among negroes, as I have seen several with the same. In this case he has either cut them off or they have nearly disappeared.] My grandmother, who was very religious, and to whom I was much attached; my master, who belonged to the church, and other religious persons who visited the house, and whom I often saw at prayers, noticing the singularity of my manners, I suppose, and my uncommon intelligence for a child, remarked I had too much sense to be raised, and if I was, I would never be of any service to any one as a slave. To a mind like mine, restless, inquisitive, and observant of everything that was passing, it is easy to suppose that religion was the subject to which it would be directed, and although this subject principally occupied my thoughts, there was nothing that I saw or heard of to which my attention was not directed. The manner in which I learned to read and write, not only had great influence on my own mind, (as I acquired it with the most perfect ease, so much so, that I have no recollection whatever of learning the alphabet,) but to the astonishment of the family, one day when a book was shown me to keep me from crying, I began spelling the names of the different objects. This was a source of wonder to all in the neighborhood, particularly the blacks, and this learning was constantly improved at all opportunities. When I got large enough to go to work, while employed, I was reflecting on many things that would present themselves to my imagination, and whenever an opportunity occurred of looking at a book, when the school children were getting their lessons, I would find many things that the fertility of my own imagination had depicted to me before. All my time, not devoted to my master's service, was spent either in prayer, or in making experiments in casting different things in moulds made of earth; in attempting to make paper, gunpowder, and many other experiments, that although I could not perfect, yet convinced me of its practicability if I had the means. I was not addicted to stealing in my youth, nor have ever been, yet such was the confidence of the negroes in the neighborhood even at this early period of my life, in my superior judgment, that they would often carry me with them when they were going on any roguery, to plan for them. Growing up among them, with this confidence in my superior judgment, and when this, in their opinions, were perfected by Divine in-

spiration, from the circumstances already alluded to in my infancy, and which belief was ever afterwards zealously inculcated by the austerity of my life and manners, which became the subject of remark by white and black, having soon discovered to be great, I must appear so, and therefore studiously avoided mixing in society, and wrapped myself in mystery, devoting my time to fasting and prayer. By this time, having arrived to man's estate and hearing the scriptures commented on at meetings, I was struck with that particular passage which says: "Seek ye the kingdom of heaven and all things shall be added unto you." I reflected much on this passage, and prayed daily for light on this subject. As I was praying one day at my plough, the Spirit spoke to me, saying: "Seek ye the kingdom of heaven and all things shall be added unto you."

Question.—What do you mean by the Spirit.

Answer.—The Spirit that spoke to the Prophets in former days.

And I was greatly astonished, and for two years prayed continually, whenever my duty would permit; and then, again, I had the same revelation, which fully confirmed me in the impression that I was ordained for some great purpose in the hands of the Almighty. Several years rolled round, in which many events occurred to strengthen me in this, my belief. At this time I reverted in my mind to the remarks made of me in my childhood, and the things that had been shown me, and as it had been said of me in my childhood by those by whom I had been taught to pray, both white and black, and in whom I had the greatest confidence, that I had too much sense to be raised, and if I was, I would never be of any use as a slave. Now, finding I had arrived to man's estate, and was a slave, and these revelations being made known to me, I began to direct my attention to this great object, to fulfill the purpose for which, by this time, I felt assured I was intended. Knowing the influence I had obtained over the minds of my fellow-servants, (not by the means of conjuring and such like tricks, for to them I always spoke of such things with contempt,) but by the communion of the Spirit, whose revelations I often communicated to them, and they believed and said my wisdom came from God. I now began to prepare them for my purpose by telling them something was about to happen that would terminate in fulfilling the great promise that had been made to me. About this time I was placed under an overseer, from whom I ran away, and after remaining in the woods thirty days I returned, to the astonishment of the negroes on the plantation, who thought I had made my escape to some other part of the country, as my father had done before. But the reason of my return was, that the Spirit appeared to me and said I had my wishes directed to the things of this world, and not to the kingdom of heaven, and that I should return to the service of my earthly master—"For he who knoweth his Master's will, and doeth it not, shall be beaten with many stripes, and thus have I chastened you." And the negroes found fault and murmured against me, saying that if they had my sense they would not serve any master in the world. And about this time I had a vision—

and I saw white spirits and black spirits engaged in battle, and the sun was darkened—the thunder rolled in the heavens, and blood flowed in streams—and I heard a voice saying, "Such is your luck, such you are called to see, and let it come rough or smooth, you must surely bear it." I now withdrew myself as much as my situation would permit, from the intercourse of my fellow-servants, for the avowed purpose of serving the Spirit more fully; and it appeared to me and reminded me of the things it had already shown me, and that it would then reveal to me the knowledge of the elements, the revolution of the planets, the operation of tides, and changes of the seasons. After this revelation in the year 1825, and the knowledge of the elements being made known to me, I sought more than ever to obtain true holiness before the great day of judgment should appear; and then I began to receive the true knowledge of faith. And from the first steps of righteousness until the last, was I made perfect; and the Holy Ghost was with me and said, "Behold me as I stand in the heavens;" and I looked and saw the forms of men in different attitudes, and there were lights in the sky to which the children of darkness gave other names than what they really were, for they were the lights of the Saviour's hands, stretched forth from east to west, even as they were extended on the cross on Calvary for the redemption of sinners. And I wondered greatly at these miracles, and prayed to be informed of a certainty of the meaning thereof, and shortly afterwards, while laboring in the field, I discovered drops of blood on the corn, as though it were dew from heaven, and I communicated it to many, both white and black, in the neighborhood; and I then found on the leaves in the woods hieroglyphic characters and numbers, with the forms of men in different attitudes, portrayed in blood, and representing the figures I had seen before in the heavens. And now the Holy Ghost had revealed itself to me, and made plain the miracles it had shown me, for as the blood of Christ had been shed on this earth, and had ascended to heaven for the salvation of sinners, and was now returning to earth again in the form of dew; and as the leaves on the trees bore the impression of the figures I had seen in the heavens, it was plain to me that the Saviour was about to lay down the yoke he had borne for the sins of men, and the great day of judgment was at hand. About this time I told these things to a white man (Etheldred T. Brantley) on whom it had a wonderful effect, and he ceased from his wickedness and was attacked immediately with a cutaneous eruption, and blood oozed from the pores of his skin, and after praying and fasting nine days, he was healed; and the Spirit appeared to me again and said, "As the Saviour had been baptized so should we be also;"—and when the white people would not let us be baptized by the church, we went down into the water together, in the sight of many who reviled us, and were baptized by the Spirit. After this I rejoiced greatly, and gave thanks to God. And on the 12th of May, 1828, I heard a loud noise in the heavens, and the Spirit instantly appeared to me and said the Serpent was loosened, and Christ had laid down the yoke he had borne for the sins of men, and that I should take it on and fight against the Serpent, for the time was fast approaching when the first should be last and the last should be first.

Question.—Do you not find yourself mistaken now?

Answer.—Was not Christ crucified?

And by signs in the heavens that it would make known to me when I should commence the great work, and until the first sign appeared I should conceal it from the knowledge of men; and on the appearance of the sign (the eclipse of the sun last February,) I should arise and prepare myself and slay my enemies with their own weapons. And immediately on the sign appearing in the heavens the seal was removed from my lips, and I communicated the great work laid out for me to do, to four, in whom I had the greatest confidence, (Henry, Hark, Nelson, and Sam.) It was intended by us to have begun the work of death on the 4th of July last. Many were the plans formed and rejected by us, and it affected my mind to such a degree that I fell sick, and the time passed without our coming to any determination how to commence. Still forming new schemes and rejecting them, when the sign appeared again, which determined me not to wait longer.

Since the commencement of 1830, I had been living with Mr. Joseph Travis, who was to me a kind master and placed the greatest confidence in me; in fact, I had no cause to complain of his treatment to me. On Saturday evening, the 20th of August, it was agreed between Henry, Hark, and myself, to prepare a dinner the next day for the men we expected and then to concert a plan, as we had not yet determined on any. Hark, on the following morning, brought a pig, and Henry, brandy, and being joined by Sam, Nelson, Will, and Jack, they prepared in the woods a dinner, where, about three o'clock, I joined them.

Question.—Why were you so backward in joining them?

Answer.—The same reason that had caused me not to mix with them for years before.

I saluted them on coming up, and asked Will how came he there. He answered, his life was worth no more than others, and his liberty as dear to him. I asked him if he thought to obtain it. He said he would, or lose his life. This was enough to put him in full confidence. Jack, I knew, was only a tool in the hands of Hark. It was quickly agreed we should commence at home (Mr. J. Travis') on that night, and until we had armed and equipped ourselves, and gathered sufficient force, neither age nor sex was to be spared, (which was invariably adhered to.) We remained at the feast until about two hours in the night, when we went to the house and found Austin; they all went to the cider press and drank except myself. On returning to the house, Hark went to the door with an axe for the purpose of breaking it open, as we knew we were strong enough to murder the family if they were awaked by the noise; but reflecting that it might create an alarm in the neighborhood, we determined to enter the house secretly and murder them whilst sleeping. Hark got a ladder and set it against the chimney, on which I ascended, and hoisting a window, en-

tered and came down stairs, unbarred the door, and removed the guns from their places. It was then observed that I must spill the first blood, on which, armed with a hatchet, and accompanied by Will, I entered my master's chamber. It being dark I could not give a death blow; the hatchet glanced from his head; he sprang from the bed and called his wife; it was his last word; Will laid him dead with a blow of his axe, and Mrs. Travis shared the same fate, as she lay in bed. The murder of this family, five in number, was the work of a moment, not one of them awoke. There was a little infant sleeping in a cradle that was forgotten until we had left the house and gone some distance, when Henry and Will returned and killed it. We got here four guns that would shoot and several old muskets, with a pound or two of powder. We remained some time at the barn, where we paraded. I formed them in line as soldiers, and after carrying them through all the manœuvers I was master of, marched them off to Mr. Salathul Francis', about six hundred yards distant. Sam and Will went to the door and knocked. Mr. Francis asked who was there. Sam replied it was him, and he had a letter for him; on which he got up and came to the door. They immediately seized him, and dragging him out a little from the door, he was dispatched by repeated blows on the head. There was no other white person in the family. We started from there for Mrs. Reese's, maintaining the most perfect silence on our march, where, finding the door unlocked, we entered, and murdered Mrs. Reese in her bed while sleeping. Her son awoke, but it was only to

[127]

sleep the sleep of death; he had only time to say who is that, and he was no more. From Mrs. Reese's we went to Mrs. Turner's, a mile distant, which we reached about sunrise, on Monday morning. Henry, Austin, and Sam, went to the still, where, finding Mr. Peebles, Austin shot him, and the rest of us went to the house. As we approached the family discovered us and shut the door. Vain hope! Will, with one stroke of his axe, opened it, and we entered and found Mrs. Turner and Mrs. Newsome in the middle of the room, almost frightened to death. Will immediately killed Mrs. Turner with one blow of his axe. I took Mrs. Newsome by the hand, and with the sword I had when I was apprehended, I struck her several blows over the head, but not being able to kill her, as the sword was dull, Will turning around and discovering it, despatched her also. A general destruction of property and search for money and ammunition, always succeeded the murders. By this time my company amounted to fifteen, and nine men mounted, who started for Mrs. Whitehead's, (the other six were to go through a by-way to Mr. Bryant's, and rejoin us at Mrs. Whitehead's) As we approached the house we discovered Mr. Richard Whitehead standing in the cotton patch, near the lane fence. We called him over into the lane, and Will, the executioner, was near at hand, with his fatal axe, to send him to an untimely grave. As we pushed on to the house I discovered some one run around the garden, and thinking it was some of the white family, I pursued them, but finding it was a servant girl belonging to the house, I returned to

commence the work of death, but they whom I left had not been idle. All the family were already murdered but Mrs. Whitehead and her daughter Margaret. As I came round to the door I saw Will pulling Mrs. Whitehead out of the house, and at the step he nearly severed her head from her body with his broad axe. Miss Margaret, when I discovered her, had concealed herself in the corner, formed by the projection of the cellar cap from the house. On my approach she fled, but was soon overtaken, and after repeated blows with the sword, I killed her by a blow on the head with a fence rail. By this time the six who had gone by Mr. Bryant's rejoined us, and informed me they had done the work of death assigned them. We again divided, part going to Mr. Richard Porter's, and from thence to Nathaniel Francis'; the others to Mr. Howell Harris' and Mr. T. Doyle's. On my reaching Mr. Porter's he had escaped with his family. I understood there that the alarm had already spread, and I immediately returned to bring up those sent to Mr. Doyle's and Mr. Howell Harris'—the party I left going on to Mr. Francis' having told them I would join them in that neighborhood. I met those sent to Mr. Doyle's and Mr. Harris' returning, having met Mr. Doyle on the road and killed him; and learning from some who joined them that Mr. Harris was from home, I immediately pursued the course taken by the party gone on before, but knowing they would complete the work of death and pillage at Mr. Francis' before I could get there, I went to Mr. Peter Edwards' expecting to find them there, but they had been here also. I then went to Mr. John T.

Barrow's; they had been here and murdered him. I pursued on their track to Capt. Newit Harris', where I found the greater part mounted and ready to start. The men now amounting to about forty, shouted and hurrahed as I rode up. Some were in the yard loading their guns, others drinking. They said Captain Harris and his family had escaped; the property in the house they destroyed, robbing him of money and other valuables. I ordered them to mount and march instantly. This was about nine or ten o'clock Monday morning. I proceeded to Mr. Levi Waller's, two or three miles distant. I took my station in the rear, and as it was my object to carry terror and devastation wherever we went, I placed fifteen or twenty of the best armed and most to be relied on in front, who generally approached the houses as fast as their horses could run. This was for two purposes—to prevent their escape and strike terror to the inhabitants. On this account I never got to the houses after leaving Mrs. Whitehead's until the murders were committed, except in one case. I some times got in sight in time to see the work of death completed, viewed the mangled bodies as they lay, in silent satisfaction, and immediately started in quest of other victims. Having murdered Mrs. Waller and ten children, we started for Mr. William Williams', having killed him and two little boys that were there. While engaged in this, Mrs. Williams fled and got some distance from the house, but she was pursued, overtaken, and compelled to get up behind one of the company, who brought her back, and after showing her the mangled body of her lifeless husband, she

was told to get down and lay by his side, where she was shot dead. I then started for Mr. Jacob Williams', where the family were murdered. Here we found a young man named Drury, who had come on business with Mr. Williams; he was pursued, overtaken and shot. Mrs. Vaughan's was the next place we visited, and, after murdering the family here, I determined on starting for Jerusalem. Our number amounted now to fifty or sixty, all mounted and armed with guns, axes, swords and clubs. On reaching Mr. James W. Parker's gate, immediately on the road leading to Jerusalem, and about three miles distant, it was proposed to me to call there, but I objected, as I knew he was gone to Jerusalem, and my object was to reach there as soon as possible; but some of the men having relations at Mr. Parker's, it was agreed that they might call and get his people. I remained at the gate on the road with seven or eight, the others going across the field to the house, about half a mile off. After waiting some time for them, I became impatient, and started to the house for them, and on our return we were met by a party of white men, who had pursued our blood-stained track, and who had fired on those at the gate and dispersed them, which I knew nothing of, not having been at that time rejoined by any of them. Immediately on discovering the whites I ordered my men to halt and form, as they appeared to be alarmed. The white men, eighteen in number, approached us in about one hundred yards, when one of them fired, (this was against the positive orders of Captain Alexander P. Peete, who commanded, and who had directed the men to reserve their fire until within thirty paces,) and I discovered about half of them retreating. I then ordered my men to fire and rush on them. The few remaining stood their ground until we approached within fifty yards, when they fired and retreated. We pursued and overtook some of them, who, we thought, we left dead, (they were not killed;) after pursuing them about two hundred yards, and rising a little hill, I discovered they were met by another party and had halted, and were reloading their guns, (this was a small party from Jerusalem who knew the negroes were in the field and had just tied their horses to await their return to the road, knowing that Mr. Parker and family were in Jerusalem, but knew nothing of the party that had gone in with Captain Peete; on hearing the firing they immediately rushed to the spot and arrived just in time to arrest the progress of these barbarous villians, and save the lives of their friends and fellow-citizens;) thinking that those who retreated first, and the party who fired on us at fifty or sixty yards distant, had all only fallen back to meet others with ammunition. As I saw them reloading their guns and more coming up than I saw at first, and several of my bravest men being wounded, the others became panic-struck and squandered over the field; the white men pursued and fired on us several times. Hark had his horse shot under him and I caught another for him as it was running by me; five or six of my men were wounded, but none left on the field. Finding myself defeated here, I instantly determined to go through a private way, and cross the Nottoway

River at the Cypress Bridge, three miles below Jerusalem, and attack that place in the rear, as I expected they would look for me on the other road, and I had a great desire to get there to procure arms and ammunition. After going a short distance in this private way, accompanied by about twenty men, I overtook two or three who told me the others were dispersed in every direction. After trying in vain to collect a sufficient force to proceed to Jerusalem, I determined to return, as I was sure they would make back to their old neighborhood, where they would rejoin me, make new recruits, and come down again. On my way back I called at Mrs. Thomas', Mrs. Spencer's, and several other places; the white families having fled we found no more victims to gratify our thirst for blood. We stopped at Maj. Ridley's quarter for the night, and being joined by four of his men, with the recruits made since my defeat, we mustered now about forty strong. After placing out sentinels, I laid down to sleep, but was quickly roused by a great racket. Starting up I found some mounted, and others in great confusion. One of the sentinels having given the alarm that we were about to be attacked, I ordered some to ride round and reconnoitre, and on their return, the others being more alarmed, not knowing who they were, fled in different ways, so that I was reduced to about twenty again. With this I determined to attempt to recruit, and proceed to rally in the neighborhood I had left. Dr. Blunt's was the nearest house, which we reached just before day. On riding up the yard Hark fired a gun. We expected Dr. Blunt and his family were at Maj. Riley's, as I knew there was a company of men there; the gun was fired to ascertain if any of the family were at home. We were immediately fired upon and retreated, leaving several of my men. I do not know what became of them, as I never saw them afterwards. Pursuing our course back, and coming in sight of Captain Harris', where we had been the day before, we discovered a party of white men at the house, on which all deserted me but two, (Jacob and Nat.) We concealed ourselves in the woods until near night, when I sent them in search of Henry, Sam, Nelson, and Hark, and directed them to rally all they could at the place we had had our dinner the Sunday before, where they would find me, and I, accordingly, returned there as soon as it was dark and remained until Wednesday evening, when discovering white men riding around the place as though they were looking for some one, and none of my men joining me, I concluded Jacob and Nat had been taken and compelled to betray me. On this I gave up all hope for the present, and on Thursday night, after having supplied myself with provisions from Mr. Travis', I scratched a hole under a pile of fence rails in a field, where I concealed myself for six weeks, never leaving my hiding place but for a few minutes in the dead of night to get water, which was very near. Thinking by this time I could venture out, I began to go about in the night and eavesdrop the houses in the neighborhood; pursuing this course for about a fortnight and gathering little or no intelligence, afraid of speaking to any human being, and returning every morning to my cave before the

dawn of day. I know not how long I might have led this life if accident had not betrayed me. A dog in the neighborhood passing by my hiding-place one night while I was out, was attracted by some meat I had in my cave, and crawled in and stole it, and was coming out just as I returned. A few nights after, two negroes having started to go hunting with the same dog, and passed that way, the dog came again to the place, and having just gone out to walk about, discovered me and barked, on which, thinking myself discovered, I spoke to them to beg concealment. On making myself known they fled from me. Knowing then they would betray me, I immediately left my hiding place, and was pursued almost incessantly until I was taken a fortnight afterwards by Mr. Benjamin Phipps, in a little hole I had dug out with my sword, for the purpose of concealment, under the top of a fallen tree. On Mr. Phipps' discovering the place of my concealment, he cocked his gun and aimed at me. I requested him not to shoot, and I would give up, upon which he demanded my sword. I delivered it to him and he brought me to prison. During the time I was pursued I had many hair-breadth escapes, which your time will not permit me to relate. I am here, loaded with chains, and willing to suffer the fate that awaits me.

I here proceeded to make some inquiries of him, after assuring him of the certain death that awaited him, and that concealment would only bring destruction on the innocent, as well as the guilty of his own color, if he knew of any extensive or concerted plan. His answer was, I do not. When I questioned him as to the insurrection in North Carolina, happening about the same time, he denied any knowledge of it; and when I looked him in the face as though I would search his inmost thoughts, he replied, "I see, sir, you doubt my word; but can you not think the same ideas, and strange appearances about this time in the heavens might prompt others, as well as myself, to this undertaking." I now had much conversation with, and asked him many questions, having forborn to do so previously, except in the cases noted in parenthesis; but during his statement, I had, unnoticed by him, taken notes as to some particular circumstances, and having the advantage of his statement before me in writing, on the evening of the third day that I had been with him, I began a cross-examination, and found his statement corroborated by every circumstance coming within my own knowledge, or the confessions of others whom had been either killed or executed, and whom he had not seen nor had any knowledge since 22d of August last, he expressed himself fully satisfied as to the impracticability of his attempt. It has been said he was ignorant and cowardly, and that his object was to murder and rob for the purpose of obtaining money to make his escape. It is notorious, that he was never known to have a dollar in his life, to swear an oath, or drink a drop of spirits. As to his ignorance, he certainly never had the advantages of education, but he can read and write, (it was taught him by his parents,) and for natural intelligence and quickness of apprehension, is surpassed by few men I have ever seen. As to his being a

coward, his reason as given for not resisting Mr. Phipps, shows the decision of his character. When he saw Mr. Phipps present his gun, he said he knew it was impossible for him to escape, as the woods were full of men; he therefore thought it was better to surrender and trust to fortune for his escape. He is a complete fanatic, or plays his part most admirably. On other subjects he possesses an uncommon share of intelligence, with a mind capable of attaining anything, but warped and perverted by the influence of early impressions. He is below the ordinary stature, though strong and active, having the true negro face, every feature of which is strongly marked. I shall not attempt to describe the effect of his narrative, as told and commented on by himself in the condemned hole of the prison. The calm, deliberate composure with which he spoke of his late deeds and intentions, the expression of his fiend-like face when excited by enthusiasm; still bearing the stains of the blood of helpless innocence about him; clothed with rags and covered with chains, yet daring to raise his manacled hands to heaven; with a spirit soaring above the attributes of man, I looked on him and my blood curdled in my veins.

I will not shock the feelings of humanity, nor wound afresh the bosoms of the disconsolate sufferers in this unparalleled and inhuman massacre, by detailing the deeds of their fiend-like barbarity. There were two or three who were in the power of these wretches, had they known it, and who escaped in the most providential manner. There were two whom they thought they left dead on the field at

Mr. Parker's, but who were only stunned by the blows of their guns, as they did not take time to reload when they charged on them. The escape of a little girl who went to school at Mr. Waller's, and where the children were collecting for that purpose, excited general sympathy. As their teacher had not arrived, they were at play in the yard, and seeing the negroes approach, she ran up a dirt chimney, (such as are common to log houses,) and remained there unnoticed during the massacre of the eleven that were killed at this place. She remained in her hiding-place till just before the arrival of a party who were in pursuit of the murderers, when she came down and fled to a swamp, where, a mere child as she was, with the horrors of the late scene before her, she lay concealed until the next day, when, seeing a party go up to the house, she came up, and on being asked how she escaped, replied with the utmost simplicity, "The Lord helped her." She was taken up behind a gentleman of the party and returned to the arms of her weeping mother. Miss Whitehead concealed herself between the bed and the mat that supported it, while they murdered her sister in the same room without discovering her. She was afterwards carried off and concealed for protection by a slave of the family, who gave evidence against several of them on their trial. Mrs. Nathaniel Francis, while concealed in a closet heard their blows, and the shrieks of the victims of these ruthless savages. They then entered the closet where she was concealed, and went out without discovering her. While in this hiding-place she heard two of her women in a quarrel about the division of her clothes. Mr. John T. Barrow discovering them approaching his house, told his wife to make her escape, and scorning to fly, fell fighting on his own threshold. After firing his rifle, he discharged his gun at them, and then broke it over the villain who first approached him, but he was overpowered and slain. His bravery, however, saved from the hands of these monsters, his lovely and amiable wife, who will long lament a husband so deserving of her love. As directed by him, she attempted to escape through the garden, when she was caught and held by one of her servant girls, but another coming to her rescue, she fled to the woods and concealed herself. Few, indeed, were those who escaped their work of death. But, fortunate for society, the hand of retributive justice has overtaken them, and not one that was known to be concerned has escaped.

The Commonwealth vs. Nat Turner.

Charged with making insurrection and plotting to take away the lives of divers free white persons,&c., on the 22d of August, 1831.

The court composed of _____, having met for the trial of Nat Turner, the prisoner was brought in and arraigned, and upon his arraignment pleaded *not guilty;* saying to his counsel that he did not feel so.

On the part of the Commonwealth, Levi Waller was introduced, who, being sworn, deposed as follows: (*agreeably to Nat's own Confession.*) Col. Trezvant [1] was then introduced, who,

1. The Committing Magistrate. (*Gray note*)

being sworn, numerated Nat's Confession to him, as follows: (*his Confession as given to Mr. Gray.*) The prisoner introduced no evidence, and the case was submitted without argument to the court, who, having found him guilty, Jeremiah Cobb, Esq., Chairman, pronounced the sentence of the Court in the following words: "Nat Turner, stand up! Have you anything to say why sentence of death should not be pronounced against you?"

Answer.—I have not; I have made a full confession to Mr. Gray and I have nothing more to say.

Attend then to the sentence of the Court! You have been arraigned and tried before this Court, and convicted of one of the highest crimes in our Criminal Code. You have been convicted of plotting, in cold blood, the indiscriminate destruction of men, of helpless women, and of infant children. The evidence before us leaves not a shadow of doubt but that your hands were often imbued in the blood of the innocent; and your own confession tells us that they were stained with the blood of a master, in your own language, "too indulgent." Could I stop here your crime would be sufficiently aggravated. But the original contriver of a plan, deep and deadly, one that can never be effected, you managed so far to put it into execution as to deprive us of many of our most valuable citizens; and this was done when they were asleep and defenceless, under circumstances shocking to humanity. And while upon this part of the subject, I cannot but call your attention to the poor, misguided wretches who have gone before you. They are not few in number—they were your bosom associates—and the blood of all cries aloud and calls upon you as the author of their misfortune. Yes! You forced them unprepared, from time to eternity. Borne down by this load of guilt, your only justification is that you were led away by fanaticism. If this be true, from my soul I pity you; and while you have my sympathies, I am, nevertheless, called upon to pass the sentence of the Court. The time between this and your execution will necessarily be very short, and your only hope must be in another world. The judgment of the Court is, that you be taken hence to the jail from whence you came, thence to the place of execution, and on Friday next, between the hours of 10 A.M. and 2 P.M., be hung by the neck until you are dead! dead! dead! and may the Lord have mercy upon your soul.

FOUR
Slaves on the Block . . .
Slaves on the Road

30. Ethan Allen Andrews Visits a Slave Emporium in Alexandria

In the early nineteenth century most slaves were concentrated in the upper South, but as the new territories were opened to settlement in the Southwest, white men began the move to the interior, developing cotton plantations on the rich lands that stretched westward from central Georgia through Mississippi. After 1807 the slave laborers for these plantations could no longer be secured from Africa, because of the closing of the international trade. They came instead from the upper South, sometimes with their masters, but more often as a part of a "lot" or "parcel" assembled at a slave emporium such as that of Franklin & Armfield, described in the following selection. Alexandria, Virginia, was one of the central points for collection of slaves being sold in the East. From Alexandria the slaves were sent overland to Natchez, or by sea to New Orleans, for sale in the West. Franklin & Armfield had another establishment in Natchez, this for the sale of slaves to western purchasers.

Naturally enough, anti-slavery men and women recognized that the domestic slave trade was one of the most vulnerable aspects of slavery, because of the separations it caused within slave families. They also knew that its suppression and control would be a serious blow to the "peculiar institution" by reducing the mobility of this kind of property. It is plain from Ethan Allen Andrews's description of Franklin & Armfield's establishment that he opposes slavery, but also that he aspires to be objective in his investigation of the internal slave traffic. Andrews was a Latin teacher, and the author of textbooks and dictionaries for the use of students. He was born in 1787, graduated from Yale University in 1810, and died in New Britain, Connecticut, in 1858. Andrews taught in private academies in New Haven and Boston.

Letter XX.

Alexandria, July 24, 1835.
After spending four days at Washington, I took passage in the steamboat this morning for this place.

My principal object in coming to this city was, to visit the establishment of

Source: Ethan Allan Andrews, Slavery and the Domestic Slave Trade in the United States (Boston: Light & Stearns, 1836), pp. 135–43.

Franklin and Armfield, who have for some years been actively engaged in purchasing slaves for the southern market. From the gentlemen to whom I brought letters from friends in Washington, I have received every attention, and such directions as enabled me to accomplish the purpose of my visit.

The establishment to which I have alluded is situated in a retired quarter in the southern part of the city. It is easily distinguished as you approach it, by the high, white-washed wall surrounding the yards, and giving to it the appearance of a penitentiary. The dwelling-house is of brick, three stories high, and opening directly upon the street. Over the front door is the name of the firm, FRANKLIN & ARMFIELD. It was mid-day when I arrived. The day was excessively warm, and the door and windows were thrown wide open to admit the air. On inquiring at the door for Mr. Armfield, he came forward in a few minutes from the yard in the rear of the building, and invited me into his parlor.

Mr. Armfield is a man of fine personal appearance, and of engaging and graceful manners. He is still in the prime of life, though he has been for many years engaged in the traffic in human flesh, by which he is supposed to have acquired great wealth. I explained to him frankly my object in visiting him, accompanying my statement with a request that I might be allowed to see his establishment. It was an important object in my journey to gain access to such an establishment, to see the slaves collected for transportation, and to ascertain the details of the traffic. I was not wholly without fears, that, after all my labor, I

should meet with a refusal; but these apprehensions were soon dispelled, for he immediately, and apparently with great readiness, complied with my request.

Calling an assistant or clerk, he directed him to accompany me to every part of the establishment. We passed out at the back door of the dwelling-house, and entered a spacious yard nearly surrounded with neatly white-washed two story buildings, devoted to the use of the slaves. Turning to the left, we came to a strong grated door of iron, opening into a spacious yard, surrounded by a high, white-washed wall. One side of this yard was roofed, but the principal part was open to the air. Along the covered side extended a table, at which the slaves had recently taken their dinner, which, judging from what remained, had been wholesome and abundant. In this yard, only the men and boys were confined. The gate was secured by strong padlocks and bolts; but before entering we had a full view of the yard, and everything in it, through the grated door. The slaves, fifty or sixty in number, were standing or moving about in groups, some amusing themselves with rude sports, and others engaged in conversation, which was often interrupted by loud laughter, in all the varied tones peculiar to the negroes.

While opening the gate, my conductor directed the slaves to form themselves into a line, and they accordingly arranged themselves, in single file, upon three sides of the yard. They were in general young men, apparently from eighteen to thirty years old, but among them were a few boys whose age did not exceed ten or fifteen years.

They were all—except one or two, who had just been admitted, and whose purchase was not yet completed—neatly and comfortably dressed, and, in general, they looked cheerful and contented. As my conductor, however, was expatiating on their happy condition, when compared with that in which they had lived before they came to this place—a discourse apparently intended for the joint benefit of the slaves and their northern visiter—I observed a young man, of an interesting and intelligent countenance, who looked earnestly at me, and as often as the keeper turned away his face, he shook his head, and seemed desirous of having me understand, that he did not feel any such happiness as was described, and that he dissented from the representation made of his condition. I would have given much to hear his tale, but in my situation that was impossible. Still, in imagination, I see his countenance, anxiously and fearfully turning from the keeper to me, with an expression which seemed to say, like the ghost in Hamlet, "I could a tale unfold."

After a short time, spent in walking around this yard, and examining the appearance of the slaves, we "passed out by the iron gate," and crossing over to the right, we came to a similar one, which admitted us into a yard like that which we had just left. Here we found the female slaves, amounting to thirty or forty. These, too, were well dressed, and everything about them had a neat and comfortable appearance, *for a prison.* The inmates of this apartment were of about the same ages as those who occupied the yard which I had just left. There was but one mother with an infant; and my guide informed me, that they did not like to purchase women with young children, as they were less saleable than others, in the market to which they sent their slaves. In answer to my inquiries respecting the separation of families, he assured me that they were at great pains to prevent such separation in all cases, in which it was practicable, and to obtain, if possible, whole families. Married slaves, he said, were generally preferred by purchasers to those who were single, because their owners felt more sure that they would be contented, and stay at home. In one instance, he remarked, they had purchased, from one estate, more than fifty, in order to prevent the separation of family connections; and in selling them, they had been equally scrupulous to have them continue together. In this case, however, they had sacrificed not less than one or two thousand dollars, which they might have obtained by separating them, as they would have sold much better in smaller lots. The women, in general, looked contented and happy, but I observed a few who seemed to have been weeping.

Near the yard in which the women were confined, was the kitchen, where the food of the slaves was prepared. Here everything appeared neat and clean, and the arrangements for cooking resembled those which we usually see in penitentiaries. From the kitchen we went to the tailor's shop, where were stored great quantities of new clothing, ready for the negroes when they set off upon their long journey to the south. These clothes appeared to be well made, and of good materials; and in the female wardrobe considerable taste was displayed. Each negro, at his departure, is furnished with two entire suits from the shop. These he does not wear upon the road, but puts them on when he arrives at the market. In the rear of the yard, is a long building, two stories high, in which the slaves pass the night. Their blankets were then lying in the sun at the doors and windows, which were grated like those of ordinary prisons. In a corner of the yard, a building was pointed out to me as the hospital; but such was the health of the slaves at this time, that the building was unoccupied.

Passing out at a back gate, we entered another spacious yard, in which four or five tents were spread, and the large wagons, which were to accompany the next expedition, were stationed.

Having examined everything, so far as the excessive heat would permit, we returned to the parlor. Everywhere, as I passed along, I observed the most studied attention paid to cleanliness, continually reminding me of the penitentiary, which I visited yesterday at Washington. The fences and walls of the houses, both internally and externally, were neatly white-washed, and there was also the same apparatus of high walls, and bolts, and bars, to secure the prisoners. In most respects, however, the situation of the convicts at the penitentiary was far less deplorable than that of these slaves, confined for the crime of being descended from ancestors who were forcibly reduced to bondage. Most of the former are confined for a few years only, and then go forth as free as the judge by whose sentence they had been imprisoned. While in confinement, at morning and at evening, and upon each returning Sabbath, they assemble like a well ordered christian household, receive religious instruction, and unite in the songs of thanksgiving and praise which ascend to the common Parent of all. Far different is the condition of the slave. He is a prisoner for life; and in his long and hopeless bondage he may seldom hear the voice of the religious teacher.

In the parlor, I again met Mr. Armfield, who, during my absence, had been negotiating for the purchase of a slave, and had just concluded a bargain. Here I was again treated with great politeness, and refreshments of various kinds were offered me.

The number of slaves, now in the establishment, is about one hundred. They are commonly sent by water from this city to New Orleans. Brigs of the first class, built expressly for this trade, are employed to transport them. The average number, sent at each shipment, does not much exceed one hundred and fifty, and they ship a cargo once in two months. Besides these, they send a considerable number over land, and those which I saw were to set off in this way in a few days. A train of wagons, with the provisions, tents, and other necessaries, accompanies the expedition, and at night they all encamp. Their place of destination is Natchez, where Mr. Franklin resides, for the purpose of disposing of them on their arrival. Those which are sent by water, after landing at New Orleans, are sent up the rivers by steamboats to the general depot at Natchez, where they are exposed for sale.

As it is an object of the first importance, that the slaves should arrive at their place of destination "in good order and well-conditioned," every indulgence is shown to them, which is consistent with their security, and their good appearance in the market. It is true that they are often chained at night, while at the depot at Alexandria, lest they should overpower their masters, as not more than three or four white men frequently have charge of a hundred and fifty slaves. Upon their march, also, they are usually chained together in pairs, to prevent their escape; and sometimes, when greater precaution is judged necessary, they are all attached to a long chain passing between them. Their guards and conductors are, of course, well armed.

After resting myself a few minutes, I took leave of Mr. Armfield and of his establishment, and returned to my lodgings in the city, ruminating, as I went, upon the countless evils, which "man's inhumanity to man," has occasioned in this world of sin and misery.

---

31. William Chambers Attends a Slave Auction in Richmond

While all Southern cities had physical arrangements for the sale and purchase of slaves, the busiest markets were found at the eastern and western extremities of this trade, since these markets transferred black labor from less productive lands of the East to the fertile borders of the Mississippi River. Richmond, Virginia, was one of the eastern terminals, and the slave market there catered not only to the interstate traffic but to local demand as well.

William Chambers, a Scotsman who visited this country in 1853, wrote the following account of a slave auction in Richmond. It is more complete in its details than most such accounts, and the author apparently made a studied effort to keep his emotions in the background. Had he been able to pierce the black masks of the slaves on the block this might not have been possible. Chambers was born in Peebles, Scotland, in 1800, became a printer and publisher, and in time a philanthropist. He was the founder of

Source: William Chambers, *Things As They Are in America* (Philadelphia: Lippincott, Grambo, & Co., 1854), pp. 269–86.

Chambers's Journal and _Chambers's Encyclopædia_, author of several works of popular instruction, and Lord Provost of Edinburgh. He died in 1883.

Much of the country through which we passed was uncleared of woods, which had a wild appearance, and the land, where opened to agricultural operations, seemed to be of a poor description. Among the trees growing naturally in the patches of tangled forest, was the _arbor vitæ_, which here attains a considerable size. Rhododendrons hung their faded blossoms by the roadsides, where they grew like common weeds; and in other kinds of vegetation, there was still the lingering aspect of autumn. On crossing the Rappahannock, at Fredericksburg, the agricultural character of the country was much improved; but even at the best, and all the way to Richmond, a distance of sixty miles from the Potomac, it fell short of what I had seen in Western Canada and Ohio. Yet possessing, as it does, the elements of fertility, what might not be expected from the land, if put under an enlightened system of tillage! The ploughing, performed by slaves under the inspection of overseers riding about the fields on horseback, was very defective; for it seemed scarcely to tear up the soil, and left large pieces altogether untouched. As the train passed, the negro ploughmen invariably stopped in their labour to look at, and speculate on, the phenomenon, as if their heart was not in their work, and they took every opportunity of shirking it. From the way they seemed to be proceeding, I feel pretty safe in averring, that two ordinary Scotch ploughmen would get

through as much labour in a day as any six of them, and do the work, too, in a greatly superior manner.

. . .

The train arrived at Richmond about two o'clock in the afternoon; and by an omnibus in attendance, I was transferred to a hotel, which proved to be no way inferior to the establishments in the states further north. The whole of the waiters were negroes, in white jackets; but among the female domestics I recognised one or two Irish girls—the sight of them helping to make good what I had everywhere heard stated about the Irish dispossessing the coloured races. At Willard's Hotel, in Washington, all the waiters, as well as the female servants, were Irish; and here, also, they will probably be so in a short time.

Situated on a high and sloping bank on the left side of the James River, Richmond is much less regular in outline than the greater number of American cities. Its streets, straggling in different directions on no uniform plan, are of an old-established appearance, with stores, churches, and numerous public buildings. Besides the principal thoroughfares, there are many narrow streets or lanes of a dismal, half-deserted appearance, generally dirty, and seemingly ill drained and ventilated. Everywhere, the number of black faces is considerable; for in a population of 27,000, as many as 9000 are said to be slaves. The dwellings occupied by the lower classes of coloured people are of a miserable kind, resembling the worst brick-houses in the back-lanes of English manufacturing towns. In the upper part of the city, there are some rows of handsome villas, and in this quarter is a public square, with the Capitol, or seat of legislature, in a central and conspicuous situation. In walking through this public edifice towards dusk, I observed that it was guarded by an armed sentinel, the sight of whom had almost the startling effect of an apparition; for it was the first time I had seen a bayonet in the United States, and suggested the unpleasant reflection, that the large infusion of slaves in the composition of society was not unattended with danger.

.   .   .

Although, in many respects, inferior in point of appearance as compared with the smart New-England cities, Richmond shewed various symptoms of prosperity and progress. A species of dock for shipping was in process of excavation adjoining the bridges, and several large cotton-factories were in the course of erection. In the streets in this lower quarter, there was an active trade in the packing and sale of tobacco, quantities of which, like faded weeds, were being carted to the factories by negroes. The cotton manufacture is carried on in several large establishments, and will soon be extended, but principally, I was told, by means of northern capital, and the employment of hired white labourers, who, for factory purposes, are said to be preferable to persons of colour.

Richmond is known as the principal market for the supply of slaves for the south—a circumstance understood to originate in the fact that Virginia, as a matter of husbandry, breeds negro labourers for the express purpose of sale. Having heard that such was the case, I was interested in knowing by what means and at what prices slaves are offered to purchasers. Without introductions of any kind, I was thrown on my own resources in acquiring this information. Fortunately, however, there was no impediment to encounter in the research. The exposure of ordinary goods in a store is not more open to the public than are the sales of slaves in Richmond. By consulting the local newspapers, I learned that the sales take place by auction every morning in the offices of certain brokers, who, as I understood by the terms of their advertisements, purchased or received slaves for sale on commission.

Where the street was in which the brokers conducted their business, I did not know; but the discovery was easily made. Rambling down the main street in the city, I found that the subject of my search was a narrow and short thoroughfare, turning off to the left, and terminating in a similar cross thoroughfare. Both streets, lined with brick-houses, were dull and silent. There was not a person to whom I could put a question. Looking about, I observed the office of a commission-agent, and into it I stepped. Conceive the idea of a large shop with two windows, and a door between; no shelving or counters inside; the interior a spacious, dismal apartment, not well swept; the only furniture a desk at one of the windows, and a bench at one side of the shop, three feet high, with two steps to it from the floor. I say, conceive the idea of this dismal-looking place, with nobody in it but three negro children, who, as I entered, were playing at auctioning each other. An intensely black little negro, of four or five years of age, was standing on the bench, or block, as it is called, with an equally black girl, about a year younger, by his side, whom he was pretending to sell by bids to another black child, who was rolling about the floor.

My appearance did not interrupt the merriment. The little auctioneer continued his mimic play, and appeared to enjoy the joke of selling the girl, who stood demurely by his side.

"Fifty dolla for de gal—fifty dolla—fifty dolla—I sell dis here fine gal for fifty dolla," was uttered with extraordinary volubility by the woolly-headed urchin, accompanied with appropriate gestures, in imitation, doubtless, of the scenes he had seen enacted daily on the spot. I spoke a few words to the little creatures, but was scarcely understood; and the fun went on as if I had not been present: so I left them, happy in rehearsing what was likely soon to be their own fate.

At another office of a similar character, on the opposite side of the street, I was more successful. Here, on inquiry, I was respectfully informed by a person in attendance, that the sale would take place the following morning at half-past nine o'clock.

Next day, I set out accordingly, after breakfast, for the scene of operations, in which there was now a little more life. Two or three persons were lounging about, smoking cigars; and, looking along the street, I observed that three red flags were projected from the doors of those offices in which sales were to occur. On each flag was pinned a piece of paper, notifying the articles to be sold. The number of lots was not great. On the first, was the following announcement:—"Will be sold this morning, at half-past nine o'clock, a Man and a Boy."

It was already the appointed hour; but as no company had assembled, I entered and took a seat by the fire. The office, provided with a few deal-forms and chairs, a desk at one of the windows, and a block accessible by a few steps, was tenantless, save by a gentleman who was arranging papers at the desk, and to whom I had addressed myself on the previous evening. Minute after minute passed, and still nobody entered. There was clearly no hurry in going to business. I felt almost like an intruder, and had formed the resolution of departing, in order to look into the other offices, when the person referred to left his desk, and came and seated himself opposite to me at the fire.

"You are an Englishman," said he, looking me steadily in the face; "do you want to purchase?"

"Yes," I replied, "I am an Englishman; but I do not intend to purchase. I am travelling about for information, and I shall feel obliged by your letting me know the prices at which negro servants are sold."

"I will do so with much pleasure," was the answer. "Do you mean fieldhands or house-servants?"

"All kinds," I replied; "I wish to get all the information I can."

With much politeness, the gentleman stepped to his desk, and began to draw up a note of prices. This, however, seemed to require careful consideration; and while the note was preparing, a lanky person, in a wide-awake hat,[1] and chewing tobacco, entered, and took the chair just vacated. He had scarcely seated himself, when, on looking towards the door, I observed the subjects of sale—the man and boy indicated by the paper on the red flag—enter together, and quietly walk to a form at the back of the shop, whence, as the day was chilly, they edged themselves towards the fire, in the corner where I was seated. I was now between the two parties—the white man on the right, and the old and young negro on the left—and I waited to see what would take place.

The sight of the negroes at once attracted the attention of Wide-awake. Chewing with vigour, he kept keenly eyeing the pair, as if to see what they were good for. Under this searching gaze, the man and boy were a little abashed, but said nothing. Their appearance had little of the repulsiveness we are apt to associate with the idea of slaves. They were dressed in a gray woollen coat, pants, and waistcoat, coloured cotton neckcloths, clean shirts,

coarse woollen stockings, and stout shoes. The man wore a black hat; the boy was bareheaded. Moved by a sudden impulse, Wide-awake left his seat, and rounding the back of my chair, began to grasp at the man's arms, as if to feel their muscular capacity. He then examined his hands and fingers; and, last of all, told him to open his mouth and shew his teeth, which he did in a submissive manner. Having finished these examinations, Wide-awake resumed his seat, and chewed on in silence as before.

I thought it was but fair that I should now have my turn of investigation, and accordingly asked the elder negro what was his age. He said he did not know. I next inquired how old the boy was. He said he was seven years of age. On asking the man if the boy was his son, he said he was not—he was his cousin. I was going into other particulars, when the office-keeper approached, and handed me the note he had been preparing; at the same time making the observation that the market was dull at present, and that there never could be a more favourable opportunity of buying. I thanked him for the trouble which he had taken; and now submit a copy of his price-current:—

1. Chambers refers to a style of military cap popular during the decade. Its later use by Republican marching societies as a part of their uniform caused the clubs to be called "Wide-Awakes." (*Editor's note*)

Best Men, 18 to 25 years old, ...	1200 to 1300 dollars.
Fair do. do. do.	950 to 1050 "
Boys, 5 feet, ...	850 to 950 "
Do., 4 feet 8 inches, ...	700 to 800 "
Do., 4 feet 5 inches, ...	500 to 600 "
Do., 4 feet, ...	375 to 450 "
Young Women, ...	800 to 1000 "
Girls, 5 feet, ...	750 to 850 "
Do., 4 feet 9 inches, ...	700 to 750 "
Do., 4 feet, ...	350 to 452 "

(Signed) ———————

Richmond, Virginia

Leaving this document for future consideration, I pass on to a history of the day's proceedings. It was now ten minutes to ten o'clock, and Wide-awake and I being alike tired of waiting, we went off in quest of sales further up the street. Passing the second office, in which also nobody was to be seen, we were more fortunate at the third. Here, according to the announcement on the paper stuck to the flag, there were to be sold "A woman and three children; a young woman, three men, a middle-aged woman, and a little boy." Already a crowd had met, composed, I should think, of persons mostly from the cotton-plantations of the south. A few were seated near a fire on the right-hand side, and others stood round an iron stove in the middle of the apartment. The whole place had a dilapidated appearance. From a back-window, there was a view into a ruinous courtyard; beyond which, in a hollow, accessible by a side-lane, stood a shabby brick-house, on which the word *Jail* was inscribed in large black letters, on a white ground. I imagined it to be a depôt for the reception of negroes.

On my arrival, and while making these preliminary observations, the lots for sale had not made their appearance. In about five minutes afterwards they were ushered in, one after the other, under the charge of a mulatto, who seemed to act as principal assistant. I saw no whips, chains, or any other engine of force. Nor did such appear to be required. All the lots took their seats on two long forms near the stove; none shewed any sign of resistance; nor did any one utter a word. Their manner was that of perfect humility and resignation.

As soon as all were seated, there was a general examination of their respective merits, by feeling their arms, looking into their mouths, and investigating the quality of their hands and fingers—this last being evidently an important particular. Yet there was no abrupt rudeness in making these examinations—no coarse or domineering language was employed. The three negro men were dressed in the usual manner—in gray woollen clothing. The woman, with three children, excited my peculiar attention. She was neatly attired, with a coloured handkerchief bound round her head, and wore a white apron over her gown. Her children were all girls, one of them a baby at the breast, three months old, and the others two and three years of age respectively, rigged out with clean white pinafores. There was not a tear or an emotion visible in the whole party. Everything seemed to be considered as a matter of course; and the change of owners was possibly looked forward to with as much indifference as ordinary hired servants anticipate a removal from one employer to another.

While intending purchasers were proceeding with personal examinations of the several lots, I took the liberty of putting a few questions to the mother of the children. The following was our conversation:—

"Are you a married woman?"

"Yes, sir."

"How many children have you had?"

"Seven."

"Where is your husband?"

"In Madison county."

"When did you part from him?"

"On Wednesday—two days ago."

"Were you sorry to part from him?"

"Yes, sir," she replied with a deep sigh; "my heart was a'most broke."

"Why is your master selling you?"

"I don't know—he wants money to buy some land—suppose he sells me for that."

There might not be a word of truth in these answers, for I had no means of testing their correctness; but the woman seemed to speak unreservedly, and I am inclined to think that she said nothing but what, if necessary, could be substantiated. I spoke, also, to the young woman who was seated near her. She, like the others, was perfectly black, and appeared stout and healthy, of which some of the persons present assured themselves by feeling her arms and ankles, looking into her mouth, and causing her to stand up. She told me she had several brothers and sisters, but did not know where they were. She said she was a house-servant, and would be glad to be bought by a good master—looking at me, as if I should not be unacceptable.

I have said that there was an entire absence of emotion in the party of men, women, and children, thus seated preparatory to being sold. This does not correspond with the ordinary accounts of slave-sales, which are represented as tearful and harrowing. My belief is, that none of the parties felt deeply on the subject, or at least that any distress they experienced was but momentary—soon passed away, and was forgotten. One of my reasons for this opinion rests on a trifling incident which occurred. While waiting for the commencement of the sale, one of the gentlemen present amused himself with a pointer-dog, which, at command, stood on its hind-legs, and took pieces of bread from his pocket. These tricks greatly entertained the row of negroes, old and young; and the poor woman, whose heart three minutes before was almost broken, now laughed as heartily as any one.

"Sale is going to commence—this way, gentlemen," cried a man at the door to a number of loungers outside; and all having assembled, the mulatto assistant led the woman and her children to the block, which he helped her to mount. There she stood with her infant at the breast, and one of her girls at each side. The auctioneer, a handsome, gentlemanly personage, took his place, with one foot on an old deal-chair with a broken back, and the other raised on the somewhat more elevated block. It was a striking scene.

"Well, gentlemen," began the salesman, "here is a capital woman and her three children, all in good health—what do you say for them? Give me an offer. (Nobody speaks.) I put up the whole lot at 850 dollars—850 dollars—850 dollars (speaking very fast)—850 dollars. Will no one advance upon that? A very extraordinary bargain, gentlemen. A fine healthy baby. Hold it up. (Mulatto goes up the first step of the block; takes the baby from the woman's breast, and holds it aloft with one hand, so as to shew that it was a veritable sucking-baby.) That will do. A woman, still young, and three children, all for 850 dollars. An advance, if you please, gentlemen. (A voice bids 860.) Thank you, sir—860; any one bids more? (A second voice says, 870; and so on the bidding goes as far as 890 dollars, when it stops.) That won't do, gentlemen. I cannot take such a low price. (After a pause, addressing the mulatto): She may go down." Down from the block the woman and her children were therefore conducted by the assistant, and, as if nothing had occurred, they calmly resumed their seats by the stove.

The next lot brought forward was one of the men. The mulatto beckoning to him with his hand, requested him to come behind a canvas screen, of two leaves, which was standing near the back-window. The man placidly rose, and having been placed behind the screen, was ordered to take off his clothes, which he did without a word or look of remonstrance. About a dozen gentlemen crowded to the spot while the poor fellow was. stripping himself, and as soon as he stood on the floor, bare from top to toe, a most rigorous scrutiny of his person was instituted. The clear black skin, back and front, was viewed all over for sores from disease; and there was no part of his body left unexamined. The man was told to open and shut his hands, asked if he could pick cotton, and every tooth in his head was scrupulously looked at. The investigation being at an end, he was ordered to dress himself; and having done so, was requested to walk to the block.

The ceremony of offering him for competition was gone through as before, but no one would bid. The other two men, after undergoing similar examinations behind the screen, were also put up, but with the same result. Nobody would bid for them, and they were all sent back to their seats. It seemed as if the company had conspired not to buy anything that day. Probably some imperfections had been detected in the personal qualities of the negroes. Be this as it may, the auctioneer, perhaps a little out of temper

from his want of success, walked off to his desk, and the affair was so far at an end.

"This way, gentlemen—this way!" was heard from a voice outside, and the company immediately hived off to the second establishment. At this office there was a young woman, and also a man, for sale. The woman was put up first at 500 dollars; and possessing some recommendable qualities, the bidding for her was run as high as 710 dollars, at which she was knocked down to a purchaser. The man, after the customary examination behind a screen, was put up at 700 dollars; but a small imperfection having been observed in his person, no one would bid for him; and he was ordered down.

"This way, gentlemen—this way, down the street, if you please!" was now shouted by a person in the employment of the first firm, to whose office all very willingly adjourned—one migratory company, it will be perceived, serving all the slave-auctions in the place. Mingling in the crowd, I went to see what should be the fate of the man and boy, with whom I had already had some communication.

There the pair, the two cousins, sat by the fire, just where I had left them an hour ago. The boy was put up first.

"Come along, my man—jump up; there's a good boy!" said one of the partners, a bulky and respectable-looking person, with a gold chain and bunch of seals; at the same time getting on the block. With alacrity the little fellow came forward, and, mounting the steps, stood by his side. The forms in front were filled by the company; and as I seated myself, I found that my old companion, Wide-awake, was close at hand, still chewing and spitting at a great rate.

"Now, gentlemen," said the auctioneer, putting his hand on the shoulder of the boy, "here is a very fine boy, seven years of age, warranted sound—what do you say for him? I put him up at 500 dollars—500 dollars (speaking quick, his right hand raised up, and coming down on the open palm of his left)—500 dollars. Any one say more than 500 dollars. (560 is bid.) 560 dollars. Nonsense! Just look at him. See how high he is. (He draws the lot in front of him, and shews that the little fellow's head comes up to his breast.) You see he is a fine, tall, healthy boy. Look at his hands."

Several step forward, and cause the boy to open and shut his hands—the flexibility of the small fingers, black on the one side, and whitish on the other, being well looked to. The hands, and also the mouth, having given satisfaction, an advance is made to 570, then to 580 dollars.

"Gentlemen, that is a very poor price for a boy of this size. (Addressing the lot): Go down, my boy, and shew them how you can run."

The boy, seemingly happy to do as he was bid, went down from the block, and ran smartly across the floor several times; the eyes of every one in the room following him.

"Now, that will do. Get up again. (Boy mounts the block, the steps being rather deep for his short legs; but the auctioneer kindly lends him a hand.) Come, gentlemen, you see this is a first-rate lot. (590—600—610—620—630 dollars are bid.) I will sell him for 630 dollars. (Right hand coming down on left.) Last call. 630 dollars once—630 dollars twice. (A pause; hand sinks.) Gone!"

The boy having descended, the man was desired to come forward; and after the usual scrutiny behind a screen, he took his place on the block.

'Well, now, gentlemen,' said the auctioneer, 'here is a right prime lot. Look at this man; strong, healthy, able-bodied; could not be a better hand for field-work. He can drive a wagon, or anything. What do you say for him? I offer the man at the low price of 800 dollars—he is well worth 1200 dollars. Come, make an advance, if you please. 800 dollars said for the man (a bid), thank you; 810 dollars—810 dollars—810 dollars (several bids)—820—830—850—860—going at 860—going. Gentlemen, this is far below his value. A strong-boned man, fit for any kind of heavy work. Just take a look at him. (Addressing the lot): Walk down. (Lot dismounts, and walks from one side of the shop to the other. When about to reascend the block, a gentleman, who is smoking a cigar, examines his mouth and his fingers. Lot resumes his place.) Pray, gentlemen, be quick (continues the auctioneer); I must sell him, and 860 dollars are only bid for the man—860 dollars. (A fresh run of bids to 945 dollars.) 945 dollars once, 945 dollars twice (looking slowly round, to see if all were done), 945 dollars, going—going (hand drops)—gone!'

During this remarkable scene, I sat at the middle of the front form, with my note-book in my hand, in order to obtain a full view of the transaction. So strange was the spectacle, that I could hardly dispel the notion that it was all a kind of dream; and now I look back upon the affair as by far the most curious I ever witnessed. The more intelligent Virginians will sympathise in my feelings on the occasion. I had never until now seen human beings sold; the thing was quite new. Two men are standing on an elevated bench, one white and the other black. The white man is auctioning the black man. What a contrast in look and relative position! The white is a most respectable-looking person; so far as dress is concerned, he might pass for a clergyman or church-warden. There he stands—can I believe my eyes?—in the might of an Anglo-Saxon, sawing the air with his hand, as if addressing a missionary or any other philanthropic meeting from a platform. Surely that gentlemanly personage cannot imagine that he is engaged in any mortal sin! Beside him is a man with a black skin, and clothed in rough garments. His looks are downcast and submissive. He is being sold, just like a horse at Tattersall's, or a picture at Christie and Manson's—I must be under some illusion. That dark object, whom I have been always taught to consider a man, is not a man. True, he may be called a man in advertisements, and by the mouth of auctioneers. But it is only a figure of speech—a term of convenience. He is a man in one sense, and not in another. He is a kind of man—

stands upright on two legs, has hands to work, wears clothes, can cook his food (a point not reached by monkeys), has the command of speech, and, in a way, can think and act like a rational creature—can even be taught to read. But nature has thought fit to give him a black skin, and that tells very badly against him. Perhaps, also, there is something wrong with his craniological development. Being, at all events, so much of a man—genus *homo*—is it quite fair to master him, and sell him, exactly as suits your convenience—you being, from a variety of fortunate circumstances, his superior? All this passed through my mind as I sat on the front form in the saleroom of Messrs _____, while one of the members of that well-known firm was engaged in pursuing, by the laws of Virginia, his legitimate calling.

Such were a forenoon's experiences in the slave-market of Richmond. Everything is described precisely as it occurred, without passion or prejudice. It would not have been difficult to be sentimental on a subject which appeals so strongly to the feelings; but I have preferred telling the simple truth. In a subsequent chapter, I shall endeavour to offer some general views of slavery in its social and political relations.

32. Maria Perkins Writes of the Sale of Her Child

Beyond the economic forces that encouraged the domestic slave traffic lay the human sorrow of slaves whose families could be—and were—parted for so many causes: the failure of the planter, the spite of a jealous wife, misbehavior of a stubborn slave, or simple profit. Although the open condemnation of shocked white persons is often registered, it is seldom that the historian finds recorded the personal emotion of the *victims* of the internal slave trade. The following letter from a slave mother to her husband is an exception. Mrs. Perkins was naturally more alarmed at the prospect of being bought by a trader who might sell her far from home and family, than if he were a local person. Scottsville, mentioned in the letter, is a small town very near Charlottesville. Staunton is over the mountains and some forty miles farther away.

Maria Perkins to Richard Perkins

Charlottesville, Oct. 8th, 1852.
Dear Husband I write you a letter to let you know my distress   my master has sold albert to a trader on Monday court day and myself and other child is for sale also and I want you to let [me] hear from you very soon before next cort if you can I don't know when   I don't want you to wait till Chrismas I want you to tell dr Hamelton and your master if either will buy me they can attend to it know and then I can go afterwards. I don't want a trader to get me   they asked me if I had got any person to buy me and I told them no   they took me to the court houste too   they never put me up   a man buy the name of brady bought albert and is gone I don't know where   they say he lives in Scottesville   my things is in several places some is in staunton and if I should be sold I don't know what will become of them   I don't expect to meet with the luck to get that way till I am quite heartsick   nothing more   I am and ever will be your kind wife   Maria Perkins.

To Richard Perkins.

Source: Ulrich B. Phillips, ed., *Life and Labor in the Old South* (Boston: Little, Brown, 1929), p. 212.

33. Tyrone Power Sees Slavery Moving West

The scenes Ethan Allen Andrews saw in Alexandria (see document 30) were largely inspired by the demand for labor on the Southern frontier. After the expulsion of the Cherokees from their Georgia lands, the rich soil of the famous "Black Belt" in central Georgia and Alabama was opened to white settlement. The plantation system, replete in all its details—planter, slaves, cotton—moved rapidly into the vast region. In the early 1830s the roads into the new districts were dotted with arriving settlers, older planting families seeking new lands to replenish fortunes rapidly going downhill on the exhausted farms of the East, and aspiring planters-to-be setting out with a few slaves and a little property, hoping to build an estate on the frontier.

Nineteenth-century visitors to the United States came from every walk of life, but some of the most interesting were performing artists, such as Tyrone Power, an Irish actor who toured this country in the period of the great rush to open the Southwest. Power was born in Waterford, in 1797, of an affluent family, became stage-struck at the age of fourteen—much to his mother's chagrin—and joined a theater troupe. In time Power became famous for his Irish comic roles, and played to large audiences at Covent Garden. A writer of some ability, Power left several romances and many Irish farces.

On his visits to the United States, Power left the beaten path and traveled well into the interior. On one of his three journeys in the 1830s he saw slavery moving west. The selection below illustrates Power's descriptive ability, and no little capacity for economic analysis. His depiction of the planters is favorable, because he admires what they are doing, but he seems nonetheless to be trying to set things down as he sees them. In 1841, while returning from his fourth visit to the United States, Power was lost at sea.

Source: Tyrone Power, *Impressions of America During the Years 1833, 1834, and 1835*, 2 vols. (Philadelphia: Carey, Lea & Blanchard, 1836), 2:80–83, 136–38.

[December] 19th [1834].—At six P.M. quitted Augusta [Georgia], with nine other victims, in a stage otherwise laden with mail-bags and luggage. About an hour before we started rain set in, and the weather-wise prognosticate that the fine season is now at an end for this year, I certainly have no right to complain, but could desire the rain might yet be postponed for a few days. The roads were from the start as bad as could be, and the heavy fall was not likely to improve that part of our route which was to come.

We passed in the course of this night several camps of emigrants, on the move from the Carolinas and Georgia: they managed to keep their fires blazing in the forest, in spite of the falling shower; occasionally might be seen a hugh pine crackling and burning throughout as it lay on the ground, whilst, ranged to windward, stood the wagons and huts of the campers.

The rich alluvial lands of Alabama, recently belonging to the Indian reserves, and now on sale by government or through land-speculators, are attracting thousands of families from the washed-out and impoverished soil of the older Southern States; and during this and the preceding season, the numbers moving along this and the other great lines towards the Southwest are incredible, when viewed in reference to the amount of population given to the countries whence the emigrants are chiefly derived.

At a season like the present, the sufferings of these families must be considerable. The caravan usually consists of from two to four tilt wagons, long and low-roofed; each laden, first with the needful provisions and such household gear as may be considered indispensable; next, over this portion of the freight is stowed the family of the emigrant planter, his wife, and commonly a round squad of white-haired children, with their attendants: on the march these vehicles are preceded and surrounded by the field slaves, varying in numbers from half a dozen to fifty or sixty, according to the wealth of the proprietor; a couple of mounted travellers commonly complete the cavalcade, which moves over these roads at the rate of twelve or fifteen miles a day. At night, or when the team gives out, or the wagons are fairly stalled, or set fast, the party prepares to camp: the men cut down a tree for fire, and with its branches make such rude huts as their time and ingenuity may best contrive; the females prepare the evening meal, and perform such domestic duties as may be needful. On these occasions I have frequently passed amongst or halted by them, and have been surprised at the air of content and good-humour commonly prevailing in their rude camps, despite of the apparent discomfort and privation to which they were exposed.

Many of the negroes, however, I am informed, are exceedingly averse to a removal from the sites on which they have been bred, and where their connexions are formed: in these cases, planters who are uncertain of the personal attachment of their slaves, generally dispose of them amongst their neighbours: when they are really attached to their owners, however, there is little difficulty experienced in their removal.

In most of the parties I encountered,

I should say, judging fairly by their deportment and loud merriment, despite the great fatigue and constant exposure, the affair was taken in a sort of holiday spirit, no way warranted by their half-naked miserable appearance.

Thus they crawl onward from day to day, for weeks or months, until they have reached that portion of the forest, or cane-brake, fixed upon for the plantation: and here the enterprising settler has to encounter new toil, and a long series of privations, cheered however by the hope, seldom a delusive one, of ultimate wealth accumulating to the survivors of the party; for, unhappily, health is the sacrifice, I believe, generally paid for the possession of the fat soil lying along these sluggish rivers.

Along the whole line of our route from Augusta in Georgia to the banks of the Alabama, we found the road covered by parties of this description; and, according to the opinions of well-informed residents, with whom I conversed on this subject, not fewer than ten thousand families have quitted the two Carolinas and Georgia during the course of this season.

Amongst these families journeying to the land of promise, inspired by hopes for the future and cheered by the presence of those on whom they relied for their fulfilment, we now and then met little parties of broken-men retracing their sad steps toward the homes they had consigned to strangers: of these, one family, which we encountered camping near the banks of a swollen river whose bridge we were compelled to repair before we could cross it, excited deep commiseration. The establishment consisted of a single covered wagon, a small open cart, and half-a-dozen slaves, principally women: its conductress was a widow, not exceeding thirty years of age, having by her side five children, one an infant.

Within a year after the location of his family on the banks of the Black-warrior, her husband, we learned, had died; and the widow was thus far on her way back to Virginia, accompanied by such of her household as remained to her; this was the 22d of December, and there yet remained five hundred miles of her journey unperformed. I know my heart was sore as I contemplated her forlorn condition, and thought upon the toilsome way yet dividing her from the changed home she sought.

· · ·

[ca. February 24, 1835]—The grounds on which the vast and seemingly extravagant increase of the cotton crop of this State of Alabama may be justified, are to be found, not only in the great fertility of the virgin soil yearly brought under cultivation, but in the unprecedented increase of population. This very year, it is calculated, not less than twenty-five thousand slaves have been brought into this country from the older States on the Atlantic; this amount will, in all probability, be exceeded by the increase of next season, as there are many millions of acres of the most fertile land in the Union yet in the hands of Government for sale, lately conceded in exchange by the Indians of the Creek and Cherokee tribes.

The great cause of emigration from the Atlantic States is to be looked for in the temptation offered the planter by a soil of vastly superior fertility. In South

Carolina and in most parts of Georgia, it will appear that a good average crop will give one bale or bag of cotton, weighing 310 lbs. for each working-hand employed on the plantation; now, in Alabama, four or five bales, each weighing 430 lbs. is a fair average for an able-bodied slave engaged in the cultivation; and I have conversed with many planters, holding places upon the bottom-lands of the river, who assured me their crop was yearly ten bales of cotton for each full-grown hand.

When it is considered that this season the value of cotton has been ranging from sixpence-halfpenny to ninepence per pound, the enormous receipts of some of these persons, who make from four hundred to three thousand bales of 430 lbs. weight each, may be imagined.

These are the men who have been my companions on all my late steamboat trips, for this is the season that affords them *relâche* and brings them together; and in. . .*[Mobile]* especially, as at Natchez, it is by this singular class I am surrounded: they are not difficult to comprehend, and a slight sketch of their condition and habits may not be uninteresting, as they form the great mass now inhabiting this mighty region, and it is from them a probable future population of one hundred million of souls must receive language, habits, and laws.

We generally associate with the Southern planter ideas of indolence, inertness of disposition, and a love of luxury and idle expense: nothing, however can be less characteristic of these frontier tamers of the swamp and of the forest: they are hardy, indefati-

gable, and enterprising to a degree; despising and contemning luxury and refinement, courting labour, and even making a pride of the privations which they, without any necessity, continue to endure with their families. They are prudent without being at all mean or penurious, and are fond of money without having a tittle of avarice. This may at first sight appear stated from a love of paradox, yet nothing can be more stictly and simply true; this is, in fact, a singular race, and they seem especially endowed by Providence to forward the great work in which they are engaged—to clear the wilderness and lay bare the wealth of this rich country with herculean force and restless perseverance, spurred by a spirit of acquisition no extent of possession can satiate.

Most men labour that they may, at some contemplated period, repose on the fruits of their industry; adventurers in unhealthy regions, generally, seek to amass wealth that they may escape from their *pénible* abodes, and recompense themselves by after enjoyment for the perils and privations they have endured. Not so the planters of this south-western region; were their natures moulded after this ordinary fashion, these States, it is true, might long continue mines of wealth, to be wrought by a succession of adventurers; but never would they become what Providence has evidently designed they shall be,—great countries, powerful governments, and the home of millions of freemen yet unborn.

These men seek wealth from the soil to return it back to the soil, with the addition of the sweat of their brows tracking every newly-broken furrow.

Their pride does not consist in fine houses, fine raiment, costly services of plate, or refined cookery: they live in humble dwellings of wood, wear the coarsest habits, and live on the plainest fare. It is their pride to have planted an additional acre of canebrake, to have won a few feet from the river, or cleared a thousand trees from the forest; to have added a couple of slaves to their family, or a horse of high blood to their stable.

It is for these things that they labour from year to year. Unconscious agents in the hands of the Almighty, it is to advance the great cause of civilization, whose pioneers they are, that they endure toil for their lives, without the prospect of reaping any one personal advantage which might not have been attained in the first ten years of their labour.

It is not through ignorance either that they continue in these simple and rude habits of life. Most of these planters visit the Northern States periodically, as well as New Orleans; their wealth, and the necessity the merchant feels to conciliate their good-will, makes them the ready guests at tables where every luxury and refinement abounds; but they view these without evincing the least desire to imitate them, prefer generally the most ordinary liquids to the finest-flavoured wines, and, as guests, are much easier to please than to catch; for not only do they appear indifferent to these luxuries, but they seek to avoid them, contemn their use, and return to their loghouses and the canebrake to seek in labour for enjoyment.

There must, however, be a great charm in the unrestrained freedom of this sort of life; since I have frequently met women, who were bred in the North, well educated, and accustomed for years to all the *agrémens* of good society, who yet assure me that they were happiest when living in the solitude of their plantation, and only felt dull whilst wandering about the country or recruiting at some public watering-place.

34. George Featherstonhaugh Encounters a Slave Coffle

One of the most vivid descriptions of slave coffles on the move toward the frontier was written by George W. Featherstonhaugh, an English author

Source: George W. Featherstonhaugh, *Excursion through the Slave States, from Washington on the Potomac to the Frontier of Mexico: with Sketches of Popular Manners and Geological Notices* (New York: Harper & Bros., 1844), pp. 36–38, 46–47, 141–42.

and geographer who was employed by the U.S. War Department to make geological surveys of the lands west of the Great Lakes. His title is United States Geographer in the works of his published by Congress. Featherstonhaugh disliked slavery intensely, and was quick to note the awkwardness of American pretensions to democracy under the circumstances. And yet he also distrusted the plans of the abolitionists who advocated immediate and general emancipation. His unequivocal disgust with the internal slave traffic is plain from the following observations recorded during his travels from Virginia through Alabama to the Southwest in September of the year 1834. The reader may be interested in comparing his description of John Armfield with that of Ethan Allen Andrews (document 30). Justified or not, Featherstonhaugh's self-righteousness had its disagreeable side.

Many Americans resented this assumption of moral superiority so typical of British visitors of the period, and sometimes they pointed to the British record of involvement in the foundation of slavery in the New World. But after 1833, when the British passed an Emancipation Act for their islands in the West Indies, and in the light of British efforts to suppress the international slave trade, it was much harder for Americans to rebuke the British with hypocrisy.

Featherstonhaugh was born in London in 1780 and came to the United States in 1807. In 1835 he was made a Fellow of the Royal Society. From 1844 to 1866, the year of his death, he was British consul at Le Havre.

From Chapter X.

Just as we reached New River, in the early grey of the morning, we came up with a singular spectacle, the most striking one of the kind I have ever witnessed. It was a camp of negro slave-drivers, just packing up to start; they had about three hundred slaves with them, who had bivouacked the preceding night *in chains* in the woods; these they were conducting to Natchez, upon the Mississippi River, to work upon the sugar plantations in Louisiana. It resembled one of those coffles of slaves spoken of by Mungo Park, except that they had a caravan of nine waggons and single-horse carriages, for the purpose of conducting the white people, and any of the blacks that should fall lame, to which they were now putting the horses to pursue their march. The female slaves were, some of them, sitting on logs of wood, whilst others were standing, and a great many little black children were warming themselves at the fires of the bivouac. In front of them all, and prepared for the march, stood, in double files, about two hundred male slaves, *manacled and chained to each other.* I had never seen so revolting a sight before! Black men in fetters, torn from the lands where they were born, from the ties they had formed, and from the comparatively easy condition which agricultural labour affords, and driven by white men, with liberty and equality in their mouths, to a distant and unhealthy country, to perish in the sugar-mills of Louisiana, where the duration of life for a sugar-mill slave does not exceed seven years! To make this spectacle still more disgusting and hideous, some of the principal white slave-drivers, who were tolerably well dressed, and had broad-brimmed white hats on, *with black crape round them,* were standing near, laughing and smoking cigars.

Whether these sentimental speculators were, or were not—in accordance with the language of the American Declaration of Independence—in mourning "from a decent respect for the opinions of mankind," or for their own callous inhuman lives, I could not but be struck with the monstrous absurdity of such fellows putting on any symbol of sorrow whilst engaged in the exercise of such a horrid trade; so wishing them in my heart all manner of evil to endure, as long as there was a bit of crape to be obtained, we drove on, and having forded the river in a flat-bottomed boat, drew up on the road, where I persuaded the driver to wait until we had witnessed the crossing of the river by the "gang," as it was called.

It was an interesting, but a melancholy spectacle, to see them effect the passage of the river: first, a man on horseback selected a shallow place in the ford for the males slaves; then followed a waggon and four horses, attended by another man on horseback. The other waggons contained the children and some that were lame, whilst the scows, or flat-boats, crossed the women and some of the people belonging to the caravan. There was much method and vigilance observed, for this was one of the situations where the gangs—always watchful to obtain their liberty—often show a disposition to mutiny, knowing that if one or two of them could wrench their manacles off, they could soon free the rest, and either disperse themselves or overpower and slay their sordid keepers, and fly to the Free States. The slave-drivers, aware of this disposition in the unfortanate negroes, endeavour to mitigate their discontent by feeding them well on the march, and by encouraging them to sing "Old Virginia never tire," to the banjo.

The poor negro slave is naturally a cheerful, laughing animal, and even when driven through the wilderness in chains, if he is well fed and kindly treated, is seldom melancholy; for his thoughts have not been taught to stray to the future, and his condition is so degraded, that if the food and warmth his desires are limited to are secured to him, he is singularly docile. It is only when he is ill-treated and roused to desperation, that his vindictive and savage nature breaks out.[1] But these

1. This practice of driving gangs of slaves through the country to the southern markets has been to a great extent discontinued on account of the dangers and inconveniences it is unavoidably subject to: for the *drivers* are not all equally prudent and vigilant; often outraging the slaves by brutal treatment, and then trusting too implicitly to their apparent humility. Watching their opportunity, the slaves have sometimes overpowered them, put them to death, and dispersed themselves. The attention of

gangs are accompanied by other negroes trained by the slave-dealers to drive the rest, whom they amuse by lively stories, boasting of the fine warm climate they are going to, and of the oranges and sugar which are there to be had for nothing: in proportion as they recede from the Free States, the danger of revolt diminishes, for in the Southern Slave-States all men have an interest in protecting this infernal trade of slave-driving, which, to the negro, is a greater curse than slavery itself, since it too often dissevers for ever those affecting natural ties which even a slave can form, by tearing,

---

these speculators in men has thus become turned to the expediency of embarking them at some port in one of the slave-holding states, and sending them to New Orleans by sea.

This scheme, however, as far as regards the speculators, seems to be obnoxious to the same objection that applies to marching them by land, and amounts, in fact, to the introduction of the domestic slave-trade of the United States upon the great highway of nations. In the case of the Creole, slave-transport, which occasioned so much excitement in the United States, and led to a protracted negotiation between the Federal Government and the Government of Great Britain, the cargo of slaves overpowered their keepers whilst on the voyage, and took refuge in a British dependency. They were reclaimed as *property;* but as our laws admit of no property in human beings, the legality of the claim was denied, and the denial was acquiesced in. There seems to be no distinction, in the eyes of humanity, between chaining and transporting slaves by land or by sea, and any European government that would recognise claims for aid or compensation, founded upon the inability of slave-drivers to protect their interests upon the high seas, although when bound from one American port to another, would substantially give countenance to the slave-trade. (*Author's note*)

without an instant's notice, the husband from the wife, and the children from their parents; sending the one to the sugar plantations of Louisiana, another to the cotton-lands of Arkansas, and the rest to Texas.[2]

. . .

2. One day, in Washington, whilst taking a hasty dinner preparatory to a journey, I received a letter from a benevolent lady— *which letter I have preserved*—entreating me in the most pressing terms to endeavour to procure the enlargement of a slave called Manuel, who had been her servant. She stated that he had been decoyed to a public slave-depôt in the skirts of the city, had been seized and detained there, and was going to be sold into the Southern States, and that the delay of an hour perhaps would be too late for interference. This poor fellow was the *property* of the principal hotel-keeper in the place, a person called G——; who, when the Congress was not in session, and he had little or no occupation for his slaves, was in the habit of hiring them out to families by the month, as domestic servants. This Manuel, who was about twenty-six years old, had belonged to his present master a great many years, was very useful in the hotel, and had married a female slave born in G——'s house, by whom he had four or five little children. I had observed him when visiting at this lady's, and was struck with his pleasing manners. She informed me at the time that he was in everything exemplary in his conduct, and that on Sundays he always went to church with his wife and children, whom he was training up in the most admirable manner.

Inconvenient in many respects as it was for me to interfere at that time in a matter of this kind, I felt that I should not be satisfied with myself if I disregarded her entreaties, and, therefore, determined instantly to go to this slave-depôt. In a few minutes a carriage took me to a large brick edifice in the suburbs, and being directed to a room where the superintendent was, I went there, and found that it was neither more nor less than a jail that I was in; manacles, fetters, and all sorts of offensive things were

Revolting as all these atrocious practices are, still this "Institution"—a term with which some of the American statesmen dignify slavery and the circumstances inherent to it—as it exists in the United States, does not appear to me to have been fairly placed before the judgment of mankind by any of those who have written concerning it. All Christian men must unite in the wish that slavery was extinguished in every part of the world, and from my personal knowledge of the sentiments of many of the leading gentlemen in the Southern States, I am persuaded that they look to the ultimate abolition of slavery with satisfaction. Mr. Mad-

ison, the Ex-President, with whom I have often conversed freely on this subject, has told me more than once that he could not die in peace if he believed that so great a disgrace to his country was not to be blotted out some day or other. He once informed me that he had assembled all his slaves— and they were numerous—and offered to manumit them immediately; but they instantly declined it, alleging that they had been born on his estate, had always been provided for by him with raiment and food, in sickness and in health, and if they were made free they would have no home to go to, and no friend to protect or care for them. They preferred, therefore, to live and die as

---

lying about, and on casting a look at the hard features of the superintendent, I saw at once that he was the jailkeeper. Informing him that I wished to see a coloured man of the name of Manuel, he took up a ponderous key and conducted me to a door with chains drawn across it, and, unbarring and unlocking it, he called the poor fellow, whom I immediately recognised. This door opened into a very spacious prison, where several coloured people were walking about, but without manacles; and stepping into it, I asked Manuel what had happened. He then told me the following story:

His master had sent him to the depôt with a message to the superintendent, who, on his arrival, locked him in the prison. Towards evening his master told his wife that he was surprised Manuel had not returned, and she had better take the children a walk there to see what was the matter. Thus were these poor unsuspecting people all entrapped. Manuel on the arrival of his wife and family saw into the plot he had been the victim of, and coupling it with some other circumstances that had not struck him at the time, now perceived that his master, wanting to raise a sum of money, had sold them all. The poor fellow brought his wife and neat little children to me: she was a modest, well-dressed woman, appeared very wretched at the idea of being sold

away from her husband and her children, and implored me most earnestly not to leave them there. On seeing me, they had conceived the hope that I had come to buy them all, to prevent their being separated, and they both protested in the most vehement and affecting way that they would be faithful to me until death. I told them that was impossible, that I never did own a slave, and never intended to own one; that Mrs. ——, had written to inform me of their misfortune, and that I would do all I could to persuade some of my friends to do what they wished me to do.

Leaving a little money with them, I drove to the house of a gentleman who knew what it was most advisable to do in such a case, but he gave me a very little consolation. He said that he knew of several transactions of G—— of a similar character; that he had more than once purchased slaves to prevent their being sent to the South, and that he would interest himself in the affair, but that it would take some time to put anything in train for their relief. I left Washington that evening, and on my return some months afterwards, had the satisfaction of learning that the publicity I had given to the affair had prevented the separation of these unfortunate but respectable persons. (*Author's note*) his slaves, who had ever been a kind master to them. This, no doubt, is the situation of many humane, right-thinking proprietors in the Southern States; they have inherited valuable plantations with the negroes born upon them, and these look up to their master as the only friend they have on earth. The most zealous, therefore, of the Abolitionists of the Free States, when they denounce slavery, and call for its *immediate* abolition, overlook the conditions upon which alone it could be effected. They neither propose to provide a home for the slaves when they are manumitted, nor a compensation to their proprietors. Without slaves the plantations would be worthless: there are no white men to cultivate them; the newly-freed and improvident negroes could not be made available, and there would be no purchasers to buy the land, and no tenants to rent it. The Abolitionists, therefore, call upon the planters to bring ruin upon their families without helping the negro. In the mean time the Abolitionists, not uniting in some great practical measure to effect the emancipation of all salves at the national expense, suffer the evil to go on increasing; the negro population amounts now to about two millions, and the question—as to the Southern States—will, with the tide of time, be a most appalling one, viz, whether the white or the black race is to predominate.

The uncompromising obloquy which has been cast at the Southern planters, by their not too scrupulous adversaries, is therefore not deserved by them; and it is but fair to consider them as only indirectly responsible for such

scenes as arise out of the revolting traffic which is carried on by these sordid, illiterate, and vulgar slave-drivers—men who can have nothing whatever in common with the gentlemen of the Southern states. This land traffic, in fact, has grown out of the wide-spreading population of the United States, the annexation of Louisiana, and the increased cultivation of cotton and sugar. The fertile lowlands of that territory can only be worked by blacks, and are almost of illimitable extent. Hence negroes have risen greatly in price, from 500 to 1000 dollars, according to their capacity. Slaves being thus in demand, a detestable branch of business—where sometimes a great deal of money is made—has very naturally arisen in a country filled with speculators. The soil of Virginia has gradually become exhausted with repeated crops of tobacco and Indian corn; and when to this is added the constant subdivision of property which has overtaken every family since the abolition of entails, it follows of course that many of the small proprietors, in their efforts to keep up appearances, have become embarrassed in their circumstances, and, when they are pinched, are compelled to sell a negro or two. The wealthier proprietors also have frequently fractious and bad slaves, which, when they cannot be reclaimed, are either put into jail, or into those depots which exist in all the large towns for the reception of slaves who are sold, until they can be removed. All this is very well known to the slave-driver, one of whose associates goes annually to the Southwestern States, to make his contracts with those planters there who are in want of slaves for the next season. These fellows then scour the country to make purchases. Those who are bought out of jail are always put in fetters, as well as any of those whom they may suspect of an intention to escape. The women and grown-up girls are usually sold into the cotton-growing States, the men and the boys to the rice and sugar plantations. Persons with large capital are actively concerned in this trade, some of whom have amassed considerable fortunes. But occasionally these dealers in men are made to pay fearfully the penalty of their nefarious occupation. I was told that only two or three months before I passed this way a "gang" had surprised their conductors when off their guard, and had killed some of them with axes.

. . .

Chapter XI.

On resuming our places in the stage-coach, our companion in black pronounced a most decided eulogium upon *Gineral* Jackson, but in such language as was quite inimitable. With a strange solemnity of tone and manner, he said, "The old Gineral is the most greatest and most completest idear of a man what had ever lived. I don't mean to say nothing agin Washington—he was a man too; but Jackson *is* a man, I tell *you:* and when I see'd him in his old white hat, with the mourning crape on it, it made me feel a kind of particular curious." This mysterious sympathy betwixt the two white hats in mourning opened a vein of sentiment in our companion that presently took a very sublimated form, and he commenced thinking aloud as it were,

keeping his right hand pressed on the thigh of the Tuscaloosan. He now attempted to cover a farrago of bad grammar with an affected pronunciation of his words; and at last got into such a strain of talking fine, that my son and myself had great difficulty in suppressing our laughter. He spoke of a niece that he had, and said, in quite a staccato style, "She—is—a—most—complete—" and there he rather equivocally left the matter, adding, however, that he had given her "a most beautiful barouche," and that he expected to overtake her that night. By and by, he said he expected to overtake another barouche which belonged to him; and then told us what the two barouches had cost him. In short, he so thoroughly mystified us, that we could not make out what stratum in society he belonged to. If it had not been for these barouches, we might have conjectured, but they threw us out. We knew we had no barouches on the road, and were disposed to respect any one who had for a barouche is a barouche always; and what must a man be who has two on the road, and "a complete" in one of them?

A vague idea had once or twice crossed my mind that I had seen this man before, but where I could not imagine. On coming, however, to a long hill, where I got out to walk, I took occasion to ask the driver if he knew who the passenger was who had two barouches on before. "Why," said the man, "don't you know it's Armfield, the negur-driver?" "Negur-driver!" thought I, and immediately the mystery was cleared up. I remembered the white hat, the crape, the black, short-cut, round hair, and the barouches. It was one of the identical slave-dealers I had seen on the 6th of September, crossing his gang of chained slaves over New River. On re-entering the vehicle I looked steadily at the fellow, and recollecting him, found no longer any difficulty in accounting for such a compound of everything vulgar and revolting, and totally without education. I had now a key both to his manners and the expression of his countenance, both of them formed in those dens of oppression and despair, the negro prisons, and both of them indicating his abominable vocation.

As he had endeavoured to impose himself upon us for a respectable man, I was determined to let him know before we parted that I had found him out; but being desirous first of discovering what was the source of that sympathy which united his hat with that of General Jackson, I asked him plump who he was in mourning for. Upon this, drawing his physiognomy down to the length of a moderate horse's face, "Marcus Layfeeyate" (Marquis Lafayette) was his answer. "Do you mean General Lafayette?" [3] I inquired. "I reckon that's what I mean," said he. "Why General La-fayette," I replied, "gloried in making all men free, without respect of colour; and what are you, who I understand are a negro-driver, in mourning for him for? Such men as you ought to go into mourning only when the price of black men falls. I remember seeing you cross your gang in chains at New River; and I shouldn't be at all sur-

3. He died in the early part of the summer, and many of his friends in the United States were in mourning on the occasion. (Author's note)

prised if Lafayette's ghost was to set every one of your negroes free one of these nights."

The fellow did not expect this, and was silent, but my son burst into a violent fit of laughter; and, to add to our amusement, the negur-driver's black man—who had been vastly tickled with the idea of the ghost coming to help the negurs—boiled over into a most stentorious horse-laugh of the African kind. His enraged master now broke out, "What onder arth is the matter with you, I reckon? If you think I'll stand my waiter's sniggering at me arter that fashion, I reckon you'll come to a nonplush to-night." These awful words, which Pompey knew imported very serious consequences, brought him immediately into a graver mood, and he very contritely said, "Master, I warn't a larfing at you, by no manner of means; I was just a larfing at what dat ar gemmelman said about de ghose." Soon after this the fellow pretended he was taken ill, and determined to stop at a tavern on the road, a few miles from Bean's Station. He accordingly told Pompey to go on with the stage-coach until he overtook the gang, and then to return for him with one of the barouches.

Here we left him to digest our contempt as well as he could. Pompey now told us a great many things that served to confirm my abhorrence of this brutal land-traffic in slaves. As to his master, he said he really thought he was ill: "Master's mighty fond of ingeons," said he, "and de doctors in Alexandria tells him not to eat sich lots of ingeons; but when he sees 'em he can't stand it, and den he eats 'em, and dey makes him sick, and den he carries on jist like a house a fire; and den he drinks brandy upon 'em, and dat makes him better; and den he eats ingeons agin, and so he keeps a carrying on." From which it would appear that the sum total of enjoyment of a negro-driver, purchased at such a profligate expense of humanity, is an unlimited indulgence in onions and brandy.

Before we stopped for the night, but long after sunset, we came to a place where numerous fires were gleaming through the forest: it was the bivouac of the gang. Having prevailed upon the driver to wait half an hour, I went with Pompey—who was to take leave of us here—into the woods, where they were all encamped. There were a great many blazing fires around, at which the female slaves were warming themselves; the children were asleep in some tents; and the males, in chains, were lying on the ground, in groups of about a dozen each. The white men, who were the partners of Pompey's master, were standing about with whips in their hands; and "the complete" was, I suppose, in her tent; for I judged, from the attendants being busy in packing the utensils away, that they had taken their evening's repast. It was a fearful and irritating spectacle, and I could not bear long to look at it.

---

35. Joseph Holt Ingraham Describes a Slave Sale at Natchez

Natchez, Mississippi, was the western terminus for slaves sent overland by Franklin & Armfield and other eastern agencies. After seven or eight weeks of traveling through the wilderness, along a route that carried them through lands still held by Indians, the coffles reached the Mississippi, and on its banks the slaves were sold to the planters of the Southwest. One mile outside Natchez there was a settlement called "Forks of the Road," devoted exclusively to the display and sale of slaves.

Joseph Holt Ingraham, who describes the dealings at Forks of the Road in the selection following, was not an unbiased observer, as the reader will see for himself. Ingraham was a novelist, among other things: a New England man who came to Mississippi and liked his adopted home well

Source: Joseph Holt Ingraham, The South-West, by a Yankee, 2 vols. (New York: Harper & Bros., 1835), 2:192–97.

enough to romanticize even her worst feature. While Ingraham's idea of the slave's probable state of mind is subject to revision by the reader, his eye for detail is nevertheless keen, and for the overt facts of his description there is much corroborating evidence. It is interesting to compare what Ethan Allen Andrews thought he understood about the emotions of slaves who had just been sold, with what Ingraham felt about the probable emotions of slaves about to be sold again.

Ingraham was born in Portland, Maine, in 1809, was at one time a sailor, later a teacher at Jefferson College, Mississippi, and later still a Protestant Episcopal clergyman who served congregations in Alabama and Tennessee as well as in Mississippi. He was a prolific writer, widely known for his romantic novels and works of fiction based on biblical themes, the most popular of these last being *The Prince of the House of David* (1855). *The South-West, by a Yankee*, from which the following piece is taken, appeared in two volumes in 1835. *The Sunny South*, Ingraham's final book on the subject, appeared in 1860, the year of his death.

Having terminated my last letter with one of my usual digressions, before entering upon the subject with which I had intended to fill its pages, I will now pursue my original design, and introduce you into one of the great slave-marts of the south-west.

A mile from Natchez we came to a cluster of rough wooden buildings, in the angle of two roads, in front of which several saddle-horses, either tied or held by servants, indicated a place of popular resort.

"This is the slave market," said my companion, pointing to a building in the rear; and alighting, we left our horses in charge of a neatly dressed yellow boy belonging to the establishment. Entering through a wide gate into a narrow court-yard, partially enclosed by low buildings, a scene of a novel character was at once presented. A line of negroes, commencing at the entrance with the tallest, who was not more than five feet eight or nine inches

in height—for negroes are a low rather than a tall race of men—down to a little fellow about ten years of age, extended in a semicircle around the right side of the yard. There were in all about forty. Each was dressed in the usual uniform of slaves, when in market, consisting of a fashionably shaped, black fur hat, roundabout and trowsers of coarse corduroy velvet, precisely such as are worn by Irish labourers, when they first "come over the water;" good vests, strong shoes, and white cotton shirts, completed their equipment. This dress they lay aside after they are sold, or wear out as soon as may be; for the negro dislikes to retain the indication of his having recently been in the market. With their hats in their hands, which hung down by their sides, they stood perfectly still, and in close order, while some gentlemen were passing from one to another examining for the purpose of buying. With the exception of displaying their teeth when addressed, and rolling their great white eyes about the court—they were so many statues of the most glossy ebony. As we entered the mart, one of the slave merchants—for a "lot" of slaves is usually accompanied, if not owned, by two or three individuals—approached us, saying "Good morning, gentlemen! Would you like to examine my lot of boys? I have as fine a lot as ever came into market."— We approached them, one of us as a curious spectator, the other as a purchaser; and as my friend passed along the line, with a scrutinizing eye—giving that singular look, peculiar to the buyer of slaves as he glances from head to foot over each individual—the passive subjects of his observations betrayed no other signs of curiosity than that evinced by an occasional glance. The entrance of a stranger into a mart is by no means an unimportant event to the slave, for every stranger may soon become his master and command his future destinies. But negroes are seldom strongly affected by any circumstances; and their reflections never give them much uneasiness. To the generality of them, life is mere animal existence, passed in physical exertion or enjoyment. This is the case with the field hands in particular, and more so with the females than the males, who through a long life seldom see any other white person than their master or overseer, or any other gentleman's dwelling than the "great hus," the "white house" of these little domestic empires in which they are the subjects. To this class a change of masters is a matter of indifference;—they are handed from one to another with the passiveness of a purchased horse.

These constitute the lowest rank of slaves, and lowest grade in the scale of the human species. Domestic and city slaves form classes of a superior order, though each constitutes a distinct class by itself. I shall speak of these more fully hereafter.

"For what service in particular did you want to buy?" inquired the trader of my friend. "A coachman." "There is one I think may suit you, sir," said he; "George, step out here." Forthwith a light-coloured negro, with a fine figure and good face, bating an enormous pair of lips, advanced a step from the line, and looked with some degree of intelligence, though with an air of indifference, upon his intended purchaser.

"How old are you, George?" he inquired. "I don't recollect, sir, 'zactly— b'lieve I'm somewere 'bout twenty-dree.' " "Where were you raised?" "On master R____'s farm in Wirginny." "Then you are a Virginia negro." "Yes, master, me full blood Wirginny." "Did you drive your master's carriage?" "Yes, master, I drove ole missus' carage, more dan four year." "Have you a wife?" "Yes, master, I lef' young wife in Richmond, but I got new wife here in de lot. I wishy you buy her, master, if you gwine to buy me."

Then came a series of the usual questions from the intended purchaser. "Let me see your teeth—your tongue—open your hands—roll up your sleeves—have you a good appetite? are you good tempered? "Me get mad sometime," replied George to the last query, "but neber wid my horses." "What do you ask for this boy, sir?" inquired the planter, after putting a few more questions to the unusually loquacious slave. "I have held him at one thousand dollars, but I will take nine hundred and seventy-five cash. The bargain was in a few minutes concluded, and my companion took the negro at nine hundred and fifty, giving negotiable paper—the customary way of paying for slaves—at four months. It is, however, generally understood, that if servants prove unqualified for the particular service for which they are bought, the sale is dissolved. So there is in general perfect safety in purchasing servants untried, and merely on the warrant of the seller. George, in the meanwhile, stood by, with his hat in his hand, apparently unconcerned in the negotiations going on, and when the trader said to him, "George, the gentleman has bought you; get ready to go with him," he appeared gratified at the tidings, and smiled upon his companions apparently quite pleased, and then bounded off to the buildings for his little bundle. In a few minutes he returned and took leave of several of his companions, who, having been drawn up into line only to be shown to purchasers, were now once more at liberty, and moving about the court, all the visiters having left except my friend and myself. "You mighty lucky, George" said one, congratulating him, "to get sol so quick." Oh, you neber min', Charly," replied the delighted George; "your turn come soon too."

"You know who you' master be—whar he live?" said another. "No, not zactly; he lib on plantation some whar here 'bout." After taking leave of his companions, George came, hat in hand, very respectfully, to his purchaser, and said, "Young master, you never be sorry for buy George; I make you a good servant. But—beg pardon, master—but—if master would be so good as buy Jane—" "Who is Jane?"—"My wife, since I come from Wirginny. She good wife and a good girl—she good seamstress an' good nurse—make de nice shirts and ebery ting."

"Where is she, George?" "Here she be, master," said he, pointing to a bright mulatto girl, about eighteen, with a genteel figure and a lively countenance, who was waiting with anxiety the reply of the planter. Opposite to the line of males was also a line of females, extended along the left side of the court. They were about twenty in number, dressed in neat calico frocks, white aprons and capes, and fancy kerchiefs, tied in a mode peculiar to the negress, upon their heads. Their whole appearance was extremely neat and "tidy." They could not be disciplined to the grave silence observed by the males, but were constantly laughing and chattering with each other in suppressed voices, and appeared to take, generally, a livelier interest in the transactions in which all were equally concerned. The planter approached this line of female slaves, and inquired of the girl her capabilities as seamstress, nurse, and ironer. Her price was seven hundred and fifty dollars. He said he would take her to his family; and if the ladies were pleased with her, he would purchase her. The poor girl was as much delighted as though already purchased; and, at the command of the trader, went to prepare herself to leave the mart.

[167]

36.   Fredrika Bremer Sees the New Orleans Slave Market

Slaves sent by sea to the Southwest were usually sold in New Orleans. In the following selection Fredrika Bremer describes the New Orleans market as she saw it in December 1850, the year of the last effective compromise between the free and the slave states.

Miss Bremer was among the most interesting and interested of all foreign observers of the American scene during the last decade before the Civil War. Her interests ranged from the Senate debates on the Fugitive Slave Law, which constituted a part of the Compromise of 1850, to the contents of field slaves' dinner pails. Her curiosity took her into places and situations few travelers explored. Although there were a few things Miss Bremer criticized in America, including the taste of bananas ("somewhat insipid . . . like biting into soap"), she was impressed, even ecstatic, about much that she saw.

Slavery was another matter, and, as she complained, in the South "I hardly ever meet a man, or woman either, who can openly and honestly look the thing in the face." Actually, in Miss Bremer's rendering there is a certain amount of ambivalence, for she met slave-owning families who impressed her as being good and kind. She nevertheless regarded slavery as the worst aspect of American life, the thing that kept the South far behind the North in "moral and intellectual culture."

Fredrika Bremer was born in Finland in 1801, but her family moved to Sweden three years later. Brought up in Stockholm by affluent parents, young Fredrika developed a spirited and ambitious character, and chaffed at the limitations society placed on bright young women in her time. She read widely and turned her hand to writing, and in this activity she met early and continuous success. The domestic scenes sketched so carefully in her books constituted the introduction of the domestic novel into the literature of Sweden. Popular at home and abroad, financially successful, the novelist found time to interest herself in various social reforms, women's rights among the most important. Miss Bremer's visit to the United States

Source: Fredrika Bremer, *The Homes of the New World: Impressions of America*, trans. Mary Howitt, 2 vols. (New York: Harper & Bros., 1853), 2:202–9.

was inspired by her curiosity to witness at first hand the position of women in the New World. Her last years were brightened by the knowledge that slavery was abolished in the United States. She died in 1865.

And now, while the weather is bad, and the great world is paying visits and compliments, and polite gentlemen are sunning themselves in the beautiful smiles of elegant ladies, in gas-lighted drawing-rooms, I will, at my ease, converse with you about the occurrences of the last few days, about the slave-market and a slave-auction at which I have been present.

I saw nothing especially repulsive in these places excepting the whole thing; and I can not help feeling a sort of astonishment that such a thing and such scenes are possible in a community calling itself Christian. It seems to me sometimes as if it could not be reality—as if it were a dream.

The great slave-market is held in several houses situated in a particular part of the city. One is soon aware of their neighborhood from the groups of colored men and women, of all shades between black and light yellow, which stand or sit unemployed at the doors. Accompanied by my kind doctor, I visited some of these houses. We saw at one of them the slave-keeper or owner—a kind, good-tempered man, who boasted of the good appearance of his people. The slaves were summoned into a large hall, and arranged in two rows. They were well fed and clothed, but I have heard it said by the people here that they have a very different appearance when they are brought hither, chained together two and two, in long rows, after many days' fatiguing marches.

I observed among the men some really athletic figures, with good countenances and remarkably good foreheads, broad and high. The slightest kind word or joke called forth a sunny smile, full of good humor, on their countenances, and revealed a shining row of beautiful pearl-like teeth. There was one negro in particular—his price was two thousand dollars—to whom I took a great fancy, and I said aloud that "I liked that boy, and I was sure we should be good friends."

"Oh yes, Missis!" with a good, cordial laugh.

Among the women, who were few in number in comparison with the men (there might be from seventy to eighty of them), there were some very pretty light mulattoes. A gentleman took one of the prettiest of them by the chin, and opened her mouth to see the state of her gums and teeth, with no more ceremony than if she had been a horse. Had I been in her place, I believe that I should have bitten his thumb, so much did I feel myself irritated by his behavior, in which he evidently, no more than she, found any thing offensive. Such is the custom of the place.

My inquiries from these poor human chattels confined themselves to the question of whence they came. Most of them came from Missouri and Kentucky. As I was constantly attended by the slave-keeper, I could not ask for any biographical information, nor could I, in any case, have been certain

that what I here received was to be relied upon.

In another of these slave-houses I
saw a gentleman whose exterior and
expression I shall never forget. He
seemed to be the owner of the slaves
there, and my companion requested
permission for himself and me to see
them. He consented, but with an air,
and a glance at me, as if he would an-
nihilate me. He was a man of unusual
size, and singularly handsome. His
figure was Herculean, and the head
had the features of a Jupiter; but majesty and gentleness were there converted into a hardness which was really horrible. One might just as well
have talked about justice and humanity to a block of stone as to that man.
One could see by the cold expression
of that dark blue eye, by those firmly-
closed lips, that he had set his foot
upon his own conscience, made an end
of all hesitation and doubt, and bade
defiance both to heaven and hell. He
would have *money*. If he could. by
crushing the whole human race in his
hand, have converted them into
money, he would have done it with
pleasure. The whole world was to him
nothing excepting as a means of making money. The whole world might go
to rack and ruin so that he could but
rise above it—a rich man, as the only
rich and powerful man in the world. If
I wanted to portray the image of perfected, hardened selfishness, I would
paint that beautiful head. That perfectly dark expression of countenance,
the absence of light, life, joy, was only
the more striking because the complexion was fair; and the cheeks, although
somewhat sunken, had a beautiful
bloom. He seemed to be about fifty.

After having visited three slave-
houses or camps, and seen some of the
rooms in which the slaves were lodged
for the night, and which were great
garrets without beds, chairs, or tables,
I proceeded to the hospital of New Orleans. . . .

On the 31st of December I went with
my kind and estimable physician to
witness a slave-auction, which took
place not far from my abode. It was
held at one of the small auction-rooms
which are found in various parts of
New Orleans. The principal scene of
slave-auctions is a splendid rotunda,
the magnificent dome of which is
worthy to resound with songs of freedom. I once went there with Mr.
Lerner H., to be present at a great
slave-auction; but we arrived too late.

Dr. D. and I entered a large and
somewhat cold and dirty hall, on the
basement story of a house, and where
a great number of people were assembled. About twenty gentlemenlike
men stood in a half circle around a
dirty wooden platform, which for the
moment was unoccupied. On each
side, by the wall, stood a number of
black men and women, silent and
serious. The whole assembly was silent, and it seemed to me as if a heavy
gray cloud rested upon it. One heard
through the open door the rain falling
heavily in the street. The gentlemen
looked askance at me with a gloomy
expression, and probably wished that
they could send me to the North Pole.

Two gentlemen hastily entered; one
of them, a tall, stout man, with a gay
and good-tempered aspect, evidently a
bon vivant, ascended the auction platform. I was told that he was an Eng-

lishman, and I can believe it from his blooming complexion, which was not American. He came apparently from a good breakfast, and he seemed to be actively employed in swallowing his last mouthful. He took the auctioneer's hammer in his hand, and addressed the assembly much as follows:

"The slaves which I have now to sell, for what price I can get, are a few home-slaves, all the property of one master. This gentleman having given his bond for a friend who afterward became bankrupt, has been obliged to meet his responsibilities by parting with his faithful servants. These slaves are thus sold, not in consequence of any faults which they possess, or for any deficiencies. They are all faithful and excellent servants, and nothing but hard necessity would have compelled their master to part with them. They are worth the highest price, and he who purchases them may be sure that he increases the prosperity of his family."

After this be beckoned to a woman among the blacks to come forward, and he gave her his hand to mount upon the platform, where she remained standing beside him. She was a tall, well-grown mulatto, with a handsome but sorrowful countenance, and a remarkably modest, noble demeanor. She bore on her arm a young sleeping child, upon which, during the whole auction ceremonial, she kept her eyes immovably riveted, with her head cast down. She wore a gray dress made to the throat, and a pale yellow handkerchief, checked with brown, was tied round her head.

The auctioneer now began to laud this woman's good qualities, her skill, and her abilities, to the assembly. He praised her character, her good disposition, order, fidelity; her uncommon qualifications for taking care of a house; her piety, her talents, and remarked that the child which she bore at her breast, and which was to be sold with her, also increased her value. After this he shouted with a loud voice, "Now, gentlemen, how much for this very superior woman, this remarkable, &c., &c., and her child?"

He pointed with his outstretched arm and fore-finger from one to another of the gentlemen who stood around, and first one and then another replied to his appeal with a short silent nod, and all the while he continued in this style:

"Do you offer me five hundred dollars? Gentlemen, I am offered five hundred dollars for this superior woman and her child. It is a sum not to be thought of! She, with her child, is worth double that money. Five hundred and fifty, six hundred, six hundred and fifty, six hundred and sixty, six hundred and seventy. My good gentlemen, why do you not at once say seven hundred dollars for this uncommonly superior woman and her child? Seven hundred dollars—it is downright robbery! She would never have been sold at that price if her master had not been so unfortunate," &c., &c.,

The hammer fell heavily; the woman and her child were sold for seven hundred dollars to one of those dark, silent figures before her. Who he was; whether he was good or bad; whether he would lead her into tolerable or intolerable slavery—of all this, the bought and sold woman and mother knew as little as I did, neither to what part of the world he would take her. And the father of her child—where was he?

With eyes still riveted upon that sleeping child, with dejected but yet submissive mien, the handsome mulatto stepped down from the auction-platform to take her stand beside the wall, but on the opposite side of the room.

Next, a very dark young negro girl stepped upon the platform. She wore a bright yellow handkerchief tied very daintily round her head, so that the two ends stood out like little wings, one on each side. Her figure was remarkably trim and neat, and her eyes glanced round the assembly both boldly and inquiringly.

The auctioneer exalted her merits likewise, and then exclaimed,

"How much for this very likely young girl?"

She was soon sold, and, if I recollect rightly, for three hundred and fifty dollars.

After her a young man took his place on the platform. "He was a mulatto, and had a remarkably good countenance, expressive of gentleness and refinement. He had been servant in his former master's family, had been brought up by him, was greatly beloved by him, and deserved to be so—a most excellent young man!"

He sold for six hundred dollars.

After this came an elderly woman, who had also one of those good-natured, excellent countenances so common among the black population, and whose demeanor and general appearance showed that she too had been in the service of a good master, and, having been accustomed to gentle treatment, had become gentle and happy. All these slaves, as well as the young girl, who looked pert rather than good, bore the impression of having been accustomed to an affectionate family life.

And now, what was to be their future fate? How bitterly, if they fell into the hands of the wicked, would they feel the difference between then and now—how horrible would be their lot! The mother in particular, whose whole soul was centered in her child, and who, perhaps, would have soon to see that child sold away, far away from her—what would then be her state of mind!

No sermon, no anti-slavery oration could speak so powerfully against the institution of slavery as this slave-auction itself!

The master had been good, the servants good also, attached, and faithful, and yet they were sold to whoever would buy them—sold like brute beasts!

FIVE
The Slave and the Law

37. The Louisiana Slave Code of 1824

Each Southern state regulated the conditions of slavery through codes of law that defined the precarious position of a human being who was also property. Although each state had unique provisions, all shared a common feature in placing the slave completely under his master's control, and in assigning the master the responsibility for his care. The slave could not own property in his own name, or make any civil contract. His position before the courts was seriously limited in every respect: thus, he could not witness against his master, nor could he institute a suit in his own behalf. The law assumed that the master's interests were synonymous with the physical well-being of his slave, and the master's property rights in the slave were assumed to be the slave's appropriate defense from injury from all others.

The fallacy of these assumptions is readily demonstrable, but slavery would not have been slavery without them. There was in fact a ruthless legal consistency in the concept, given that fundamental assumption. There were, for example, two reasons why masters were reimbursed by the state if their slaves were executed for crime: the slave represented property confiscated and destroyed by the state, of course, but it was also thought necessary to detach the master's pecuniary interest from the slave on trial for offenses against the state. Otherwise masters might obstruct the course of justice. Some, in fact, did encourage slaves to run away in the face of criminal charges that might result in execution. Given the legal circumstances, and the inability of the slave to sue in his own behalf, it followed that most cases involving the abuse of slaves were instituted by the master against some other person, usually the employer or overseer of his slave, for property damages.

The following provisions are from the Louisiana Code of 1824, which came through the French *Code Noir*, and more remotely from the Roman Civil Law. The Louisiana code was less severe than most of the state codes, and is certainly less complete than the Alabama Code of 1852 (document 38). In practice, however, there were more similarities than divergences in the control of slaves throughout the Southern states.

Source: *Civil Code of the State of Louisiana Preceded by the Treaty of Cession with France, the Constitution of the United States of America and of the State* (Published by a citizen of Louisiana, 1825), pp. 90–94.

The Slave and the Law

ART. 172.—The rules prescribing the police and conduct to be observed with respect to slaves in this State, and the punishment of their crimes and offences, are fixed by special laws of the Legislature.

ART. 173.—The slave is entirely subject to the will of his master, who may correct and chastise him, though not with unusual rigor, nor so as to maim or mutilate him, or to expose him to the danger of loss of life, or to cause his death.

ART. 174.—The slave is incapable of making any kind of contract, except those which relate to his own emancipation.

ART. 175.—All that a slave possesses, belongs to his master; he possesses nothing of his own, except his *peculium,* that is to say, the sum of money, or moveable estate, which his master chooses he should possess.

ART. 176.—They can transmit nothing by succession or otherwise; but the succession of free persons related to them which they would have inherited had they been free, may pass through them to such of their descendants as may have acquired their liberty before the succession is opened.

ART. 177.—The slave is incapable of exercising any public office, or private trust; he cannot be tutor, curator, executor nor attorney; he cannot be a witness in either civil or criminal matters, except in cases provided for by particular laws. He cannot be a party in any civil action, either as plaintiff or defendant, except when he has to claim or prove his freedom.

ART. 178.—When slaves are prose-

cuted in the name of the State, for offences they have committed, notice must be given to their masters.

ART. 179.—Masters are bound by the acts of their slaves done by their command, as also by their transactions and dealings with respect to the business in which they have entrusted or employed them; but in case they should not have authorised or entrusted them, they shall be answerable only for so much as they have benefitted by the transaction.

ART. 180.—The master shall be answerable for all the damages occasioned by an offence or quasi-offence committed by his slave, independent of the punishment inflicted on the slave.

ART. 181.—The master however may discharge himself from such responsibility by abandoning his slave to the person injured; in which case such person shall sell such slave at public auction in the usual form, to obtain payment of the damages and costs; and the balance, if any, shall be returned to the master of the slave, who shall be completely discharged, although the price of the slave should not be sufficient to pay the whole amount of the damages and costs; provided that the master shall make the abandonment within three days after the judgment awarding such damages, shall have been rendered; provided also that it shall not be proved that the crime or offence was committed by his order; for in case of such proof the master shall be answerable for all damages resulting therefrom, whatever be the amount, without being admitted to the benefit of the abandonment.

ART. 182.—Slaves cannot marry

without the consent of their masters, and their marriages do not produce any of the civil effects which result from such contract.

ART. 183.—Children born of a mother then in a state of slavery, whether married or not, follow the condition of their mother; they are consequently slaves and belong to the master of their mother.

ART. 184.—A master may manumit his slave in this State, either by an act *inter vivos* [1] or by a disposition made in prospect of death, provided such manumission be made with the forms and under the conditions prescribed by law; but an enfranchisement, when made by a last will, must be express and formal, and shall not be implied by any other circumstances of the testament, such as a legacy, an institution of heir, testamentary executorship or other dispositions of this nature, which, in such case, shall be considered as if they had not been made.

ART. 185.—No one can emancipate his slave, unless the slave has attained the age of thirty years, and has behaved well at least for four years preceding his emancipation.

ART. 186.—The slave who has saved the life of his master, his master's wife, or one of his children, may be emancipated at any age.

ART. 187.—The master who wishes to emancipate his slave, is bound to make a declaration of his intentions to the judge of the parish where he resides; the judge must order notice of it to be published during forty days by advertisement posted at the door of the

1. Between living persons. (*Editor's trans.*)

court house; and if, at the expiration of this delay, no opposition be made, he shall authorise the master to pass the act of emancipation.

ART. 188.—The act of emancipation imports an obligation on the part of the person granting it, to provide for the subsistence of the slave emancipated, if he should be unable to support himself.

ART. 189.—An emancipation once perfected, is irrevocable, on the part of the master or his heirs.

ART. 190.—Any enfranchisement made in fraud of creditors, or of the portion reserved by law to forced heirs is null and void; and such fraud shall be considered as proved, when it shall appear that at the moment of executing the enfranchisement, the person granting it had not sufficient property to pay his debts or to leave to his heirs the portion to them reserved by law; the same rule will apply if the slave thus manumitted, was specially mortgaged; but in this case the enfranchisement shall take effect, provided the slave or any one in his behalf shall pay the debt for which the mortgage was given.

ART. 191.—No master of slaves shall be compelled, either directly or indirectly, to enfranchise any of them, except only in cases where the enfranchisement shall be made for services rendered to the State, by virtue of an act of the Legislature of the same, and on the State satisfying to the master the appraised value of the manumitted slave.

ART. 192.—In like manner no master shall be compelled to sell his slave, but in one of two cases, to wit: the first, when being only co-proprietor of the slave, his co-proprietor demands the sale in order to make partition of the property; the second, when the master shall be convicted of cruel treatment of his slave, and the judge shall deem proper to pronounce, besides the penalty established for such cases, that the slave shall be sold at public auction, in order to place him out of the reach of the power which his master has abused.

ART. 193.—The slave who has acquired the right of being free at a future time, is from that time, capable of receiving by testament or donation. Property given or devised to.him must be preserved for him, in order to be delivered to him in kind, when his emancipation shall take place. In the mean time it must be administered by a curator.

ART. 194.—The slave for years [2] cannot be transported out of the State. He can appear in court to claim the protection of the laws in cases where there are good reasons for believing that it is intended to carry him out of the State.

ART. 195.—If the slave for years dies before the time fixed for his enfranchisement, the gifts or legacies made him revert to the donor or to the heirs of the donor.

ART. 196.—The child born of a woman after she has acquired the right of being free at a future time, follows the condition of its mother, and becomes free at the time fixed for her enfranchisement, even if the mother should die before that time.

2. A slave "for years" was one whose servitude was to end at a specified age, or after a specified number of years. (*Editor's note*)

38.   The Alabama Slave Code of 1852

By the time the new states of the Southwest organized their governments, the white South was generally committed to slavery as a necessary institution, and had determined that it was not in conflict with justice or religion. Therefore, many of the early contradictions and ambiguities were resolved and the laws of slavery became more systematic. One of the most complete codes was that of Alabama in effect during the last decade before the Civil War. The Alabama Code of 1852, along with regulations governing free blacks, is given below.

Although the basic humanity of the slave was acknowledged, and strict

Source: *The Code of Alabama*, prepared by John J. Ormand, Arthur P. Bagby, and George Goldthwaite (Montgomery: Brittan and DeWolf, 1852), pp. 234–45, 390–93, 589–97.

laws were included obliging masters to decent care of their human property, the restrictions on slave testimony made enforcement difficult. Relations between slaves and free blacks are outlined with great exactness, and free black sailors, who were frequently suspected of disseminating incendiary ideas, were confined to their vessels. The duties of white patrols are outlined carefully, and penalties set for failure to perform duty when called. In peaceful times strict codes like that of Alabama appear to have been honored as much in the breach as the observance, but whenever the white community was alarmed the regulations were stringently enforced.

The sections, chapters, and articles that do not have to do with slavery have been omitted here.

[PART ONE]

Chapter III. Patrols.

§ 983. All white male owners of slaves, below the age of sixty years, and all other free white persons, between the ages of eighteen and forty-five years, who are not disabled by sickness or bodily infirmity, except commissioned officers in the militia, and persons exempt by law from the performance of militia duty, are subject to perform patrol duty.

§ 984. During the second week of the month of March, in each year, the justices of each precinct in the state, must make out a complete list of all the persons within their precinct, subject to patrol duty; and make division of the whole number, into detachments of not less than four, nor more than six, one of which number must be designated leader of the patrol.

§ 985. After such enumeration and division is made, a record must be made thereof, which must be retained by the senior justice, who must cause lists to be made of the names of the persons composing each detachment, with the leader thereof, numbering the

list from number one, consecutively, and designating, on each list, when the term of service of the detachment will commence; each detachment being required to serve as patrol, not less than two nor more than three weeks.

§ 986. The list, so made out, must be delivered to the constable, during the second week in March, and must be by him served on the leader of each detachment, within ten days thereafter, either personally, or by leaving the list at his place of residence.

§ 987. If the leader of the patrol is sick or absent, the constable must notify the next person on the list, informing him that he is the leader of the patrol detachment.

§ 988. When the term of service of all the detachments is exhausted, the justice must again cause notice to be given by the constable, to the leader of each detachment, stating when the term of service of each detachment will commence; which must be served in the same manner as the previous notice.

§ 989. Upon receiving such notice, with a list of the persons comprising the detachment, the leader must, within five days thereafter, notify each member thereof, personally, or by leaving written notice at his place of residence; and designate the time and place of the meeting of the patrol.

§ 990. Each detachment must patrol such parts of the precinct as in their judgment is necessary, at least once a week at night, during their term of service, and oftener, when required so to do by a justice of the peace; or when informed, by a credible person, of evidences of insubordination, or threatened outbreak, or insurrection of the slaves; or of any contemplated unlawful assembly of slaves or free negroes.

§ 991. Any member of a patrol detachment may send a substitute, who, if accepted by the leader, may patrol in his stead.

§ 992. The patrol has power to enter, in a peaceable manner, upon any plantation; to enter by force, if necessary, all negro cabins or quarters, kitchens and out houses, and to apprehend all slaves who may there be found, not belonging to the plantation or household, without a pass from their owner or overseer; or strolling from place to place, without authority.

§ 993. The patrol has power to punish slaves found under the circumstances recited in the preceding section, by stripes, not exceeding thirty-nine.

§ 994. It is the duty of the patrol, on receiving information that any person is harboring a runaway slave, to make search for such slave, and if found, to apprehend and take him before a justice of the peace, who, if the owner is unknown, must commit him to jail.

§ 995. If the patrol find any slave from home without a pass, and under circumstances creating the belief that he is a runaway, they must detain him in custody, and give information thereof to the owner, if known; and if unknown, or without their precinct, deliver him up to a justice, who must commit him to jail for safe keeping.

§ 996. If there is but one justice in the precinct, he must perform all the duties required by this chapter; and if there be no justices in office in the precinct on the second Monday in March, the duties here enjoined must be performed the week succeeding his election.

§ 997. The leader, or any member of the detachment, failing to appear according to the notice, and perform patrol duty, must be fined ten dollars by the justice of the precinct.

§ 998. The leader of each patrol must, at the expiration of each term of service, make report in writing, and upon oath, to the justice, of the number of times his detachment has patrolled, and of the absence, without sufficient excuse, of any member of the detachment at the times designated for patrolling, and failure to perform patrol duty; and thereupon it is the duty of the justice to cite such delinquents to appear at a time and place designated by him, and show cause why a fine should not be imposed against him; and upon their failure to appear, or to render a sufficient excuse, they must each be fined ten dollars for each omission, for which execution may issue.

§ 999. If the leader of the patrol fails to make such report, within one month after the expiration of his term of service, he is guilty of a misdemeanor, and, on conviction, must be fined in a sum not less than twenty dollars, at the discretion of the jury.

§ 1000. The justice must make report in writing, to the solicitor of his circuit, of all omissions on the part of patrol leaders, to make the reports referred to in the two preceding sections.

§ 1001. Every person appointed a leader of the patrol, who refuses, without sufficient excuse, to act as such, must be fined twenty dollars by the justice appointing him; being first cited to appear and show cause against it.

§ 1002. Every justice and constable failing or refusing to perform any of the duties required of them by this chapter, are guilty of a misdemeanor, and, on conviction, must be fined, the justice not less than fifty, and the constable not less than twenty dollars, at the discretion of the jury.

§ 1003. All fines collected for a violation of the provisions of this chapter, must be paid by the justice or constable collecting it, into the county treasury; and failing to do so, may be proceeded against by motion in the name of the county treasurer, as for other money collected in their official capacity.

§ 1004. The patrol, if sued for any act done in the performance of patrol duty, may give this law in evidence under the general issue; but are liable in damages, to any person aggrieved, for any unnecessary violence committed under color of performing patrol duty, either by unnecessarily breaking or entering houses, or for excessive punishment inflicted on any slave.

Chapter IV. Slaves and Free Negroes.

ARTICLE I.
Slaves.

§ 1005. No master, overseer, or other person having the charge of a slave, must permit such slave to hire himself to another person, or to hire his own time, or to go at large, unless in a corporate town, by consent of the authorities thereof, evidenced by an ordinance of the corporation; and every such offence is a misdemeanor, punishable by fine not less than twenty nor more than one hundred dollars.

§ 1006. No master, overseer, or head of a family must permit any slave to be or remain at his house, out house, or kitchen, without leave of the owner or overseer, above four hours at any one time; and for every such offence he forfeits ten dollars, to be recovered before any justice of the peace, by any person who may sue for the same.

§ 1007. Any owner or overseer of a plantation, or householder, who knowingly permits more than five negroes, other than his own, to be and remain at his house, plantation, or quarter, at any one time, forfeits ten dollars for each and every one over that number, to the use of any one who may sue for the same, before any justice of the peace; unless such assemblage is for the worship of almighty God, or for burial service, and with the consent of the owner or overseer of such slaves.

§ 1008. No slave must go beyond the limits of the plantation on which he resides, without a pass, or some letter or token from his master or overseer, giving him authority to go and return from a certain place; and if found violating this law, may be apprehended and punished, not exceeding twenty stripes, at the discretion of any justice before whom he may be taken.

§ 1009. If any slave go upon the plantation, or enter the house or out house of any person, without permission in writing from his master or overseer, or in the prosecution of his lawful business, the owner or overseer of such plantation or householder may give, or order such slave to be given ten lashes on his bare back.

§ 1010. Any railroad company in whose car or vehicle, and the master or owner of any steamboat, or vessel, in which a slave is transported or carried, without the written authority of the owner or person in charge of such slave, forfeits to the owner the sum of fifty dollars; and if such slave is lost, is liable for his value, and all reasonable expenses attending the prosecution of the suit.

§ 1011. In any action under the preceding section, it devolves on the defendant to prove that the owner has regained possession of the slave.

§ 1012. No slave can keep or carry a gun, powder, shot, club, or other weapon, except the tools given him to work with, unless ordered by his master or overseer to carry such weapon from one place to another. Any slave found offending against the provisions of this section, may be seized, with such weapon, by any one, and carried before any justice, who, upon proof of the offence, must condemn the weapon to the use of such person, and direct that the slave receive thirty-nine lashes on his bare back.

§ 1013. Any justice of the peace may,

within his own county, grant permission in writing to any slave, on the application of his master or overseer, to carry and use a gun and ammunition within his master's plantation.

§ 1014. No slave can, under any pretence, keep a dog; and for every such offence must be punished by any justice of the peace with twenty stripes on his bare back. If such dog is kept with the consent of the owner or overseer, he must pay five dollars for every dog so kept, to the use of any person who will sue for the same before any justice: and is also liable to any person for any injury committed by said dogs.

§ 1015. Riots, routs, unlawful assemblies, trespasses, and seditious speeches by a slave, are punished, by the direction of any justice before whom he may be carried, with stripes not exceeding one hundred.

§ 1016. Any person having knowledge of the commission of any offence by a slave against the law, may apprehend him, and take him before a justice of the peace for trial.

§ 1017. Any slave fire hunting [1] in the night time, must be punished with thirty-nine lashes, by order of any justice before whom he may be carried. If such fire hunting by the slave is by the command of the master or overseer, the slave must not be punished, but the master or overseer forfeits the sum of fifty dollars, one half to the county, and the other half to any person who may sue for the same before any justice of the peace.

§ 1018. No slave can own property, and any property purchased or held by

1. To fire-hunt was to set fires in woods or brush to flush out game. (*Editor's note*)

a slave, not claimed by the master or owner, must be sold by order of any justice of the peace; one half the proceeds of the sale, after the payment of costs and necessary expenses, to be paid to the informer, and the residue to the county treasury.

§ 1019. Any slave who writes for, or furnishes any other slave with any pass or free paper, on conviction before any justice of the peace, must receive one hundred lashes on his bare back.

§ 1020. Not more than five male slaves shall assemble together at any place off the plantation, or place to which they belong, with or without passes or permits to be there, unless attended by the master or overseer of such slaves, or unless such slaves are attending the public worship of God, held by white persons.

§ 1021. It is the duty of all patrols, and all officers, civil and military, to disperse all such unlawful assemblies; and each of the slaves constituting such unlawful assembly, must be punished by stripes, not exceeding ten; and for the second offence, may be punished with thirty-nine stripes, at the discretion of any justice of the peace before whom he may be brought.

§ 1022. Any slave who preaches, exhorts, or harangues any assembly of slaves, or of slaves and free persons of color, without a license to preach or exhort from some religious society of the neighborhood, and in the presence of five slave-holders, must, for the first offence, be punished with thirty-nine lashes, and for the second, with fifty lashes; which punishment may be inflicted by any officer of a patrol company, or by the order of any justice of the peace.

§ 1023. Runaway slaves may be apprehended by any person, and carried before any justice of the peace, who must either commit them to the county jail, or send them to the owner, if known; who must, for every slave so apprehended, pay the person apprehending him six dollars, and all reasonable charges.

§ 1024. Any justice of the peace receiving information that three or more runaway slaves are lurking and hid in swamps, or other obscure places, may, by warrant, reciting the names of the slaves, and their owners, if known, direct a leader of the patrol of the district, and if there be none, then any other suitable person, to summon, and take with him such power as may be necessary to apprehend such runaway; and if taken, to deliver them to the owner or commit them to the jail of his proper county.

§ 1025. For such apprehension and delivery to the owner, or committal to jail, the parties so apprehending shall be entitled to twenty dollars for each slave, to be paid by the owner.

§ 1026. The justice committing a runaway, must endeavor to ascertain from the slave, and from all other sources within his reach, the true name of the slave, and his owner's name, and residence; and must include all such information in the commitment, which must be preserved and filed by the justice.

§ 1027. On the reception of a runaway slave, the sheriff must, without delay, cause advertisement to be made in a newspaper, published in the county, if there be one, if not, in the one published nearest to the court house of such county, giving an accurate description of the person of the slave, his supposed age, the information contained in the warrant in relation to the slave, and his owner, and such other facts important to the identification of the slave, as the sheriff may be able to obtain from the slave, or from any other source, which must be continued for six months, once a week, if the slave is not sooner reclaimed by the owner.

§ 1028. If the slave is not reclaimed within six months, the sheriff must advertise and sell him for cash, in the manner slaves are sold under execution. The proceeds of the sale, after all expenses are paid, must be paid to the county treasurer for the use of the county.

§ 1029. The owner may regain the possession of the slave before sale, or the proceeds after sale, by appearing before the judge of probate of the county, and proving, by an impartial witness, his title to the slave; which proof must be reduced to writing, sworn to, subscribed, and filed in the office of the probate judge.

§ 1030. Thereupon, and upon the payment by the owner of the costs of advertising, and all other expenses attending the imprisonment, the judge of probate must, by order in writing, direct the jailor, if the slave has not been sold, to deliver him to the applicant. If he has been sold, then the order must be directed to the county treasurer, to pay him over the proceeds of such sale received in the treasury.

§ 1031. The title of the purchaser of such slave is not affected by the claim of the owner, or by an irregularity in the advertisement or sale.

§ 1032. The fee of probate judge is two dollars, and the sheriff is allowed the same commissions as on sales under execution.

ARTICLE II.
Free negroes.

§ 1033. Every free colored person who has come to this state since the first day of February, one thousand eight hundred and thirty-two, and has been admonished by any sheriff, justice of the peace, or other judicial officer, that he cannot, by law, remain in this state; and does not, within thirty days, depart therefrom, must, on conviction, be punished by imprisonment in the penitentiary for two years; and shall have thirty days after his discharge from the penitentiary to leave the state; and on failing to do so, must be imprisoned in the penitentiary for five years.

§ 1034. All sheriffs, justices of the peace, and other judicial officers, knowing of any free person of color being within the state, contrary to the provisions of the preceding section, are hereby required to give the warning therein prescribed.

§ 1035. If any free person of color is at any time found at an unlawful assembly of slaves, he forfeits twenty dollars, to any person who will sue for the same, before any justice of the peace; and for the second offence, must, in addition thereto, be punished with ten stripes. All justices of the peace, sheriffs, and constables, are charged with the execution of this law.

§ 1036. No free person of color must retail, or assist in retailing, or vending, spirituous or vinous liquors; and for every such offence, forfeits twenty dollars, to be recovered before any justice of the peace, by any one who will sue for the same; and for the second offence, having been once convicted and fined, must be punished by stripes, not exceeding twenty-five, at the discretion of the justice.

§ 1037. The preceding sections of this article do not apply to, or affect any free person of color, who, by the treaty between the United States and Spain, became a citizen of the United States, or the descendants of such.

§ 1038. Any free person of color who writes for, or furnishes a slave with a pass, is guilty of a misdemeanor, and, on conviction, must be fined not less than fifty dollars, and be imprisoned not less than six months.

§ 1039. Any free person of color who writes for, or furnishes any slave a pass, with the intent to enable such slave to escape from his master, is guilty of a felony, and, on conviction, must be imprisoned in the penitentiary not less than three, nor more than seven years.

§ 1040. Any free person of color imprisoned in the penitentiary, must leave the state in one month after his discharge, unless pardoned; and failing to do so, or having left returns again, on conviction, must be imprisoned in the penitentiary five years.

§ 1041. Any free person of color, who buys of, or sells to, any slave, any article, or commodity whatever, without a written permission from the master, or overseer of such slave, designating the article so to be bought, or sold, is guilty of a misdemeanor, and must, upon conviction, before any justice of the peace of the county where such offence is committed, be punished with thirty-nine stripes.

§ 1042. Any free person of color, found in company with any slave, in any kitchen, out house, or negro quarter, without a written permission from the owner, or overseer of such slave, must, for every such offence, receive fifteen lashes; and for every subsequent offence, thirty-nine lashes; which may be inflicted by the owner or overseer of the slave, .or by any officer or member of any patrol company.

§1043. If any free person of color permits a slave to be, or remain in his house, or out house, or about his premises, without permission, in writing, from the owner, or overseer of the slave, he shall be punished as provided in the preceding section.

§ 1044. Any free person of color, who preaches, exhorts, or harangues any assembly of slaves, or of slaves and free persons of color, unless in the presence of five slaveholders, and licensed to preach or exhort by some religious society of the neighborhood, must, for the first offence, receive thirty-nine lashes, and for the second offence, fifty lashes, by the order of any justice of the county, before whom the offender may be carried.

ARTICLE III.
Free colored mariners.

§ 1045. The master or consignee of any vessel, coming into any port in this state, having on board any free person of color, as cook, steward, or mariner, must, within three days thereafter, furnish the mayor, or intendant of the place, a list of the free persons of color on board such vessel, and enter into bond, payable to the state of Alabama, in such sum, not less than two thousand dollars, and with such surety as the mayor or intendant may prescribe, which must be filed in his office; and upon a breach thereof, judgment may be rendered by motion of the solicitor of the circuit, in the circuit court of the county, or in the city court of Mobile, ten days' notice thereof being given, for the penalty of such bond.

§ 1046. The condition of the bond is, that such free colored persons shall remain on board the vessel, and not leave the same during the stay of the vessel in the waters of this state; and upon its departure, that such free colored persons will depart with the vessel. That such vessel, with such persons on board, shall not come within three miles of the town or city attached to the port, nor within one mile of the shore, except in passing out of the bay of Mobile; and that during the stay of such vessel, no communication will be permitted between the free colored persons on board the vessel and slaves, or free persons of color within the state.

§ 1047. If any such free persons of color are dangerously ill, they may be conveyed to any hospital of the United States; or if there be none, to a private hospital; and as soon as discharged therefrom, must return to the vessel.

§ 1048. If within three days after the arrival of a vessel within the waters of this state, the list of such free colored persons, and the bond required by this article is not made, and delivered as herein provided for, the sheriff of the county must apprehend all such free persons of color, and lodge them in jail, where they must be kept until the vessel is ready to proceed to sea; and it is the duty of the harbor master to give information to the sheriff of the arrival of any vessel containing such free persons of color.

§ 1049. It is the duty of the master of such vessel, when ready for sea, to take such free persons of color with him, and carry them beyond the limits of this state, paying the expenses of their arrest and detention; and upon failure to do so, he is guilty of a misdemeanor, and must be fined in a sum not exceeding one thousand dollars, and may, in the discretion of the jury, be imprisoned, not exceeding six months.

§ 1050. If such free persons of color are not carried away by the master of the vessel bringing them into this state, they must, after the departure of the vessel, be discharged from jail, and warned to leave the state; the expenses of their arrest and detention to be paid by the county.

§ 1051. If they do not depart within ten days after being discharged, or if, having left, they return to the state, they must, on conviction, be punished by confinement in the penitentiary not less than two, nor more then five years.

§ 1052. Fees to the sheriff, three dollars for each free colored person apprehended.

§ 1053. To the mayor one dollar, for taking and filing of bond, and list of sailors.

§ 1054. To the jailor same fees as allowed by law for sustenance of prisoners.

Chapter V. Retailers.

§ 1055. No free negro must be licensed to keep a tavern, or to sell vinous or spirituous liquor.

§ 1056. No license must be granted to sell vinous, or spirituous liquor, unless the applicant produce to the judge of probate of his county, the recommendation of six respectable freeholders or householders thereof, residing within five miles of such applicant, stating that they are acquainted with him, that he is possessed of a good moral character, and in all respects a proper person to be licensed.

§ 1057. The applicant must also, before obtaining his license, take and subscribe the following affidavit: "I do solemnly swear, that I will not sell any vinous or spirituous liquor to, or sell to, or purchase from, any slave, any article, or commodity, without the permission of the owner, master, or overseer, of such slave; and that I will not knowingly suffer the same to be done by my partner, clerk, agent, or any other person, upon, or about my premises, if in my power to prevent the same; and further, that I will not allow any gaming of any kind to be carried on, on or about my premises, if in my power to prevent the same;" which affidavit must be filed in the office of the judge of probate.

§ 1058. Any person selling vinous, or spirituous liquor, in quantities less than one quart, or by the quart to any person of known intemperate habits, or in any quantity, if the same is drank on, or about the premises, are retailers within the meaning of this code.

§ 1059. In all indictments for retailing without a license, it is sufficient to charge, that the defendant sold vinous, or spirituous liquor, without a license, and contrary to law; and on the trial, any act of retailing, in violation of the law, may be proved.

§ 1060. No person must obtain a judgment in any court of this state, upon any account, any item of which is for vinous or spirituous liquor in less quantities than one quart, without producing to the court a license, showing his authority to retail, at the date of such item.

§ 1061. All justices, whenever they have good reasons to believe, or whenever informed on oath, that any person has violated any of the provisions of this chapter, must forthwith issue a warrant against such person, and bind him over to answer therefor, to the next term of the circuit court.

·   ·   ·

[PART TWO]

Chapter IV. Master and Slave.

§ 2042. The state or condition of negro or African slavery is established by law in this state; conferring on the master property in and the right to the time, labor and services of the slave, and to enforce obedience on the part of the slave, to all his lawful commands. This authority he may delegate to another.

§ 2043. The master must treat his slave with humanity, and must not inflict upon him any cruel punishment; he must provide him with a sufficiency of healthy food and necessary clothing; cause him to be properly attended during sickness, and provide for his necessary wants in old age.

§ 2044. The master may emancipate

his slave by application to the judge of probate of his county, in writing, with the name, age and sex of the slave, a description of his person, and the reasons for desiring his emancipation.

§ 2045. Thereupon the judge of probate must cause an advertisement to be made in a newspaper, published in the county, if there be one, if not, in the nearest adjacent county, which shall be continued for sixty days, giving notice of the application, and of the time fixed for its determination.

§ 2046. Upon the hearing of the application, if it be shown that the slave has served his master with fidelity, or other good cause be shown for his emancipation, and no sufficient objection be made, the probate judge may make an order that the slave be emancipated, which, with the application, must be recorded on the minutes of the court, and is evidence of the right of the slave to freedom.

§ 2047. The slave so emancipated, must leave the state within six months thereafter, and failing so to do, or returning thereafter, must be seized and sold as a slave for life. The proceeds of the sale, after the payment of the necessary expenses, must be paid into the county treasury of the county in which he may be seized; and the county treasurer, sheriff, and all the justices of the peace, and constables, are charged with the execution of this law.

§ 2048. No such emancipation affects the rights of creditors, or can be made, unless it be shown that the master is unembarrassed in his pecuniary affairs, and has paid the costs of advertising.

The fee to the probate judge is five dollars for each slave emancipated.

§ 2049. A slave claiming his freedom, must proceed by petition, in the circuit court of the county in which the reputed owner resides, or that in which he retains the petitioner as a slave; setting forth succinctly the facts upon which the right to freedom is asserted, and the name of the person claiming him as a slave.

§ 2050. Upon the filing of the petition, the clerk must issue a summons commanding the reputed owner to appear at the next term of the court to answer to the petition: and if the summons is returned "not found," or if it be shown that such owner is a nonresident, the court must direct publication to be made, which is equivalent to a service of the summons.

§ 2051. If the defendant appear, he must be required to plead to the petition. If he make default, the trial proceeds as if appearance had been entered, and the truth of the allegations of the petition denied.

§ 2052. If the slave is in the possession of the reputed owner, he must be required to enter into bond, in such sum, and with such surety as may be required by the court, payable to the state of Alabama, with condition to abide by the judgment rendered in the premises; and thereupon the master is entitled to the possession of the alleged slave, until the determination of the cause: or the court may require a bond according to the provisions of the following section, in which case the possession of such slave must be given to his sureties, until the cause is determined.

§ 2053. If the slave is not in the possession of the reputed owner, he must in like manner execute bond with surety, under the direction of the court, with condition to pay the owner all costs and damages incurred by the institution of the suit, if he fail therein; and that the petitioner will be forthcoming to abide the judgment of the court. These bonds may be taken by the court in vacation, or in term time.

§ 2054. If the slave fail in his suit, judgment must be rendered in favor of the master; and if the slave has given bond and surety, as provided in the two preceding sections, judgment shall also be rendered on motion against the sureties, for the costs of the suit, and the damages the master has sustained by the institution thereof.

§ 2055. If judgment be rendered in favor of the slave, he is thenceforth entitled to his freedom.

§ 2056. No execution can be levied on a child, or children, under the age of ten years, without including the mother; or upon the mother, without including the child, or children, as aforesaid, if living, and belonging to the defendant in execution; and the mother and child, or children, must be sold together, unless the parties in interest, or one of them, make affidavit and delivers the same to the officer, that he believes his interest will be materially prejudiced, by selling the slaves together, when they may be sold separately; but no levy or sale shall be made, by which a child under five years of age shall be separated from its mother.

§ 2057. In all sales of slaves under any decree, or order of the chancery or probate court, or under any deed of trust, or power of sale in a mortgage, the slaves must be offered, and, if practicable, sold in families; unless affidavit be made, as required in the preceding section, and delivered to the officer, or other person, having the charge or management of such sale.

§ 2058. If any slaves, or persons of color, have been or are hereafter brought into this state in violation of the laws of the United States prohibiting the slave trade, the governor of the state must appoint an agent to take possession of such slaves, who has authority to sue in the name of the state of Alabama for the possession thereof.

§ 2059. The agent is required to execute bond payable to the state of Alabama, to be approved by the governor, in such sum as he may direct, with conditions to treat the slaves humanely and have them forthcoming to abide any decree which may be rendered in reference to such slaves, which must be filed in the office of the secretary of state.

§ 2060. Pending any controversy about the slaves, the agent must hire them out, and after deducting the sum necessary for their maintenance, must account with the comptroller for his trouble, and pay the residue into the state treasury.

§ 2061. It is the duty of the agent, after obtaining possession of the slaves, to file a libel in any circuit court of the state, in the nature of proceedings in admiralty praying a sale thereof; and upon his failure or neglect for thirty days to file such libel, any other person has the power.

§ 2062. If it be made to appear that the said slaves have been imported or brought into the United States contrary to the laws thereof, the court must decree that they be sold for cash, to the highest bidder, as slaves for life; and after deducting the costs and expenses, one-fourth part of the proceeds must be paid to the agent or informer, the residue into the state treasury.

§ 2063. Any person claiming title to such slave, may interpose as claimant, and, on motion to the court, must be made defendant, according to the practice in courts of admiralty, and be liable for costs.

[PART FOUR]
Chapter II. Indictable Offenses
ARTICLE VI
Miscellaneous Offenses

. . .

§ 3278. Any person who sells and delivers any poisonous substance, without having the word "poison" written or printed on the label attached to the vial, box or parcel in which the same is sold; or sells and delivers any tartar emetic, laudanum or morphine, without having the common name thereof, written or printed upon a label attached to the vial, box or parcel, containing the same, must, on conviction, be fined not more than one hundred dollars.

§ 3279. Any person who sells to any slave, or free child under ten years of age, any drug, poisonous in its nature, without an order in writing from the owner or master of such slave, or the parent, guardian, or person standing in that relation to such child, designating the drug, either by name or by its effects, must, on conviction, be fined not more than two hundred dollars, and may be imprisoned not more than three months.

§ 3280. Any licensed retailer or other person, keeping fermented, vinous or spirituous liquors for sale, who sells, gives or delivers to any student of any college, or pupil of any school or academy, or to any other person for the use of such student or pupil, any of such liquors, knowing the use for which it was intended, without the consent of the parent or guardian, or the person having the charge of such student or pupil, such retailer, or the person so selling, giving or delivering, must, on conviction, be fined not less than fifty or more than five hundred dollars.

§ 3281. Any licensed retailer or other person who sells, gives, or delivers to any minor any of the liquors specified in the preceding section, after notice from the parent, guardian, or person in charge of such minor, forbidding such sale, gift, or delivery, must, on conviction, be fined not less than fifty or more than five hundred dollars.

§ 3282. Any licensed retailer, who, after taking the affidavit prescribed in section 1057, knowingly sells any vinous or spirituous liquors to any slave; or knowingly sells to or purchases from any slave any article or commodity, without the permission of the master or overseer of such slave; or knowingly permits the same to be done by his partner, clerk, or any other person about his premises; or knowingly permits any gaming to be carried on on his premises, must, on conviction, be imprisoned in the penitentiary not less than two or more than five years.

§ 3283. Any person who sells, gives, or delivers to any slave any vinous or spirituous liquor, except on an order in writing, signed by the overseer or master of such slave, specifying the quantity to be sold, given, or delivered, must, on conviction, be fined not less than fifty dollars.

§ 3284. The provisions of the above section apply to licensed retailers as well as other persons.

§ 3285. Any person who sells to or buys or receives from any slave, any other article or commodity of any kind or description, without the consent of the master, owner, or overseer of such slave, verbally or in writing, expressing the articles permitted to be sold to, or bought or received from such slave, first obtained, must, on conviction, be fined in not less than ten or more than two hundred dollars, and may be imprisoned not more than six months.

§ 3286. Upon the trial of indictments under the preceding and section 3283, evidence that the slave was seen in the night time, or on Sunday, going into a place where spirituous or vinous liquors or merchandize are sold, with an article of traffic, and coming out without the same; or that such slave was seen at such time, or on such day, immediately after coming out of such place, in possession of spirituous or vinous liquor, or merchandize of any kind, is presumptive evidence of the guilt of the defendant.

§ 3287. Any person keeping spirituous liquor for sale, who employs any slave or free person of color in drawing off or selling such liquor, must, on conviction, be fined not less than twenty-five or more than fifty dollars.

§ 3288. Any justice or magistrate, whenever he has good reason to believe, or upon information on oath that any of the laws of this state against retailing or trading with slaves have been violated by any person, must forthwith issue a warrant of arrest against such person, and if the evidence proves the offence, must bind him over to answer therefor at the next circuit court, and on his failing to give bond must commit him.

§ 3289. Any person who employs or knowingly permits any slave or free person of color to sample any cotton, must, on conviction, be fined not less than fifty or more than one thousand dollars.

§ 3290. In indictments under the preceding section, the defendant may show in defence he was the owner of the cotton.

§ 3291. Any person who prosecutes a suit in any of the courts in this state, in the name of another person, without his consent, must, on conviction, be fined not less than five hundred dollars.

§ 3292. The provisions of the preceding section do not apply to a person having the beneficial interest using the name of the person having the legal right, in cases where he cannot bring the action in his own name.

§ 3293. Any person summoned by any sheriff, or other officer having authority, for the purpose of enabling such officer to make an arrest, or to execute any duty devolving upon him under any law in relation to public offences, who refuses obedience to such summons, must, on conviction, be fined not less than fifty or more than three hundred dollars.

§ 3294. It is the duty of the officer summoning such person to present the offender to the next grand jury, and failing so to do, he must, on conviction, be fined not less than twenty dollars.

The Slave and the Law

ARTICLE VII.
Offences against slaves.

§ 3295. Any person who with malice aforethought causes the death of a slave, by cruel whipping or beating, or by any inhuman treatment, or by the use of any weapon in its nature calculated to produce death, is guilty of murder in the first degree.

§ 3296. Any owner, overseer, or other person having the right to correct any slave, who causes the death of such slave by cruel whipping or beating, or by any other cruel or inhuman treatment, or by the use of any instrument in its nature calculated to produce death, though without any intention to kill, is guilty of murder in the second degree, and may be guilty of murder in the first degree.

§ 3297. Any master, or other person standing towards the slave in that relation, who inflicts, or allows another to inflict on him any cruel punishment, or fails to provide him with a sufficiency of healthy food, or necessary clothing, or to provide for him properly in sickness or old age, or treats him in any other way with inhumanity, on conviction thereof must be fined not less than twenty-five or more than one thousand dollars.

§ 3298. In indictments under the preceding section, it is sufficient to charge that the defendant did inflict on a slave any cruel punishment, or that he failed to provide him with a sufficiency of healthy food, or necessary clothing, or to provide for him properly in sickness or old age; or if for any other species of inhuman treatment, it may be charged that he treated such slave with inhumanity, without speci-

fying in what such inhumanity consists, and the jurors are the judges of what constitutes cruel punishment, a sufficiency of healthy food, necessary clothing, and proper provision in sickness and old age.

§ 3299. On the trial of indictments under section 3297, the defendant is entitled to a jury, two-thirds of whom are slaveholders.

§ 3300. Any person other than the master, or person occupying that relation, who commits an assault and battery on a slave, without just cause or excuse, to be determined by the jury, is guilty of a misdemeanor.

ARTICLE VIII.
Of misdemeanors at common law, not provided for by the provisions of this code.

§ 3301. All misdemeanors at common law, the punishment of which is not expressly provided for in this code, are indictable offences, and must, on conviction, be punished by a fine and imprisonment, the fine not to exceed two thousand dollars, in any case in which the party whose person or property has been injured, has a civil remedy; in all other cases, such an amount as the jury may assess, and the imprisonment not to exceed six months.

ARTICLE IX.
Petty offences cognizable before a justice of the peace.

§ 3302. Any person who on Sunday compels his apprentice, servant, or slave, to perform any labor, except the customary household duties of daily necessity, comfort, or charity, must for each offence be fined, by any justice of the county, ten dollars.

§ 3303. Any person who engages in shooting, hunting, gaming, racing, or in any other sport, diversion, or pastime, on Sunday, or any merchant, or shop-keeper, except druggists, who keeps open store, or disposes of any goods on Sunday, for each offence must be fined, by any justice before whom complaint is made, twenty dollars.

§ 3304. The provisions of the two preceding sections do not apply to steam boats, or other vessels navigating the waters of this state, or to any manufacturing establishment which requires to be kept in constant operation.

Article X.
Offences committed by slaves, and in certain cases by free persons of color, and proceedings in relation thereto.

§ 3305. The previous provisions of this title in relation to the punishment of and disqualification for the commission of offences, do not apply to slaves; the other provisions of this title apply to slaves, except so far as they are inconsistent with the other provisions of this code in relation to that class of persons, and with the character of the institution; free persons of color are subject to its provisions, except so far as they are excepted therefrom, either expressly, or by the application of a different law respecting them.

§ 3306. Every slave who consults or conspires to rebel, or is in anywise concerned in an insurrection or rebellion of the slaves against the white inhabitants of this state, or the laws and government thereof, must, on conviction, suffer death.

§ 3307. Every slave or free negro who commits, or attempts to commit, a rape on any white female, must, on conviction, suffer death.

§ 3308. Every slave who breaks into and enters a dwelling house in the night time, with the intention to steal or commit a felony, must, on conviction, suffer death.

§ 3309. No building must be deemed a dwelling house, or any part thereof, unless some white person is in such house at the time the act is done or offence committed; and no building which is not joined to and parcel of such dwelling house, must be considered as included in the preceding section.

§ 3310. Any slave who breaks into and enters a dwelling house in the day time, or any other building in the day or night time, must, on conviction, be punished by stripes, not exceeding one hundred, and by branding in the hand, one or both.

§ 3311. Every slave who robs, or commits an assault and battery with intent to rob, any white person, or willfully maims, puts out an eye, or cuts or bites off the lip, ear, or nose, of any white person, or attempts to poison, or to deprive any white person of life, by any means not amounting to an assault, must, on conviction, suffer death.

§ 3312. Every slave who is guilty of murder, or of assault with intent to kill any white person, or who is guilty of the voluntary manslaughter of a white person, or the involuntary manslaughter of a white person, in the commission of any unlawful act, must, on conviction, suffer death.

§ 3313. Every slave who willfully and maliciously sets fire to or burns any dwelling house, or out house appurtenant thereto, store house, office, banking house, ware house, or other edifice, public or private, corn crib, gin house, cotton house, stable, barn, cotton in the heap to the value of one hundred dollars, or in bale to any value, or any ship or steam boat, must, on conviction, suffer death.

§ 3314. Every slave who is guilty of the manslaughter of a slave or free negro, must, on conviction, be punished by any number of stripes, not exceeding one hundred, or be branded in the hand, one or both, at the discretion of the jury.

§ 3315. Every slave who is guilty of the crime of perjury must, on conviction, be punished with stripes not exceeding one hundred, at the discretion of the jury, and be branded in the hand with the letter P.

§ 3316. All offences committed by a slave, of a higher grade than petit larceny, and not capitally punished, and which, if committed by a white person, are punished by imprisonment in the penitentiary, may be tried by the judge of the probate court and two justices of the peace, according to the provisions of sections 3322, 3323, 3324, 3325, 3326, and 3327, and the jury shall, by their verdict, direct the punishment to be inflicted, not to exceed one hundred lashes, and branding in the hand, one or both.

§ 3317. For the offence of petit larceny, or any other offence of the same or less grade, any slave may be tried by a justice of the peace on warrant, and

may be sentenced to receive any number of stripes, not exceeding one hundred; but no justice is authorized to inflict more than thirty-nine stripes, unless he associates with him two respectable freeholders, who concur in the propriety of the sentence.

§ 3318. Whenever a slave is a witness in any cause, the presiding judge must explain to him the nature of the oath about to be administered, and also state to him the punishment for swearing falsely; it must direct him to be taken into custody, if the court before whom any slave is sworn has reason to believe he or she has sworn falsely, and as soon as practicable to cause a jury to be empanelled to try the fact; and if the slave is found guilty, the court must, without delay, cause the proper punishment to be inflicted.

§ 3319. The trial of all slaves for capital offences must, except in the cases provided for by this chapter, be by the circuit court of the county having jurisdiction, and in the mode provided by law for the trial of white persons, except that the slave is allowed but twelve peremptory challenges, and the state but four, and at least two-thirds of the jury must be slaveholders.

§ 3320. In indictments against slaves for capital offences, it is not necessary to allege the name of the owner, or that the slave belongs to any person.

§ 3321. In cases of an actual or threatened rebellion or insurrection of slaves, any justice of the peace before whom a slave or free negro is brought, charged with a capital offence, if there is probable ground for believing him guilty of the offence charged, must commit him to jail, and may appoint a day for the trial of the offence, not more than fifteen days from the commitment.

§ 3322. Such justice must give notice of the day appointed, to the judge of probate, and some other justice, and to attend the trial, which notice may be served by the sheriff, or any constable; and if there is no judge of probate, or he is absent, some other justice must supply his place; and if neither attend, two other justices may be summoned, and a majority of the officers thus summoned constitute a court for the trial of the offender.

§ 3323. The justice making the commitment must also require the sheriff in writing to summon a jury, to appear at the time appointed for the trial of the accused, possessing the qualifications of grand and petit jurors, under the provisions of Chapter six of Title two of this Part, to consist of twenty-four persons, at least two-thirds of whom must be slaveholders; and if the persons attending, so summoned, are exhausted by challenges or otherwise, the deficiency may be made up from the by-standers; but no person having an interest in such slave is a competent juror.

§ 3324. In all trials had under the three preceding sections, it is sufficient for the prosecuting officer to write out a brief statement of the offence, and sign his name thereto, to which the accused is required to plead, and failing to plead, the plea of not guilty must be entered.

§ 3325. The trial must be had at the court house of the county, and it is the duty of the sheriff and clerk of the circuit court to attend and enter the proceedings of record.

§ 3326. The clerk of the circuit court or committing magistrate, must issue subpœnas or other legal process, as well for the prisoner as the state; which must be executed by the sheriff, or any constable.

§ 3327. Whenever on the trial of any slave for a capital offence, the jury returns a verdict of guilty, the presiding judge must cause the same, or another jury to be empannelled, and sworn to assess the value of such slave; the verdict must be entered on the minutes of the court, and the owner of such slave, or his personal representative, on producing to the comptroller a transcript from the records of the court, duly certified by the clerk, and the certificate of the sheriff, that such slave has been executed according to his sentence, is entitled to receive a warrant on the state treasurer for one-half the amount assessed by the jury, to be paid out of the fund assessed for that purpose.

§ 3328. Whenever the prosecuting officer has good cause to believe that the owner is to blame for the offence committed by the slave, it is his duty to introduce evidence to establish the fact; and if the jury so find, the master shall receive no compensation; and when a slave is executed on a charge of insurrection or rebellion, the owner is not entitled to receive from the state any compensation.

§ 3329. In all trials of slaves for capital offences, if the owner refuses or neglects to employ counsel for his defence, the court must assign counsel for that purpose, who must be paid twenty dollars therefor, to be taxed as costs, for which execution may issue; and if any free negro, in a capital case, is unable to employ counsel, the court must assign counsel, who is entitled to a fee of twenty dollars, to be paid out of the state treasury.

§ 3330. If any slave or free person of color is found guilty of a capital offence, the court must pronounce sentence, which must be executed in the manner prescribed by this code for white persons; and not more than twenty or less than ten days must elapse between the passing of sentence and the execution, unless the trial is had in the circuit court, and points of law are reserved for the decision of the supreme court, in which case the same time is allowed as in case of white persons; or unless a writ of error is allowed under the provisions of Chapter twelve, of Title two of this Part, in which case the execution must be stayed as in case of white persons; but in case of a conviction for conspiracy, insurrection or rebellion, the court, if satisfied of the guilt of the defendant, and it is necessary for the public interest, may sentence him to be executed forthwith; and in such case the sentence must be executed accordingly.

§ 3331. In all convictions of slaves for any offence not capital, the slave is liable to be sold in ten days after conviction, for the costs of prosecution, by the sheriff or any constable, unless the costs are paid by his owner.

§ 3332. Slaves are bailable before conviction, except for capital offences, when the proof is evident or the presumption great.

§ 3333. Any person entitled to the control or possession of such slave, may be allowed to bail him, in cases deemed bailable, upon giving such bond and surety as the judge or justice having jurisdiction may require.

§ 3334. Justices of the peace, before commitment, have jurisdiction to commit to jail, bail or discharge, any slave charged with any offence, as the law or circumstances of the case may require.

§ 3335. Judges of probate and of the circuit courts have jurisdiction on application, to commit to jail, bail or discharge, any slave, as the justice of the case may require, notwithstanding any previous order made by a justice of the peace.

39. Thomas R. R. Cobb on the Legal Foundations of Slavery

Thomas Reade Roots Cobb was one of the most learned legal scholars of his time, and he left a very complete study of Southern laws concerning

Source: Thomas Reade Roots Cobb, *An Inquiry into the Law of Negro Slavery in the United States of America* (Philadelphia: T. & J. W. Johnson & Co., 1858), 1:82–115.

slavery and the slave's standing before the courts. The three chapters from his *Inquiry into the Law of Negro Slavery* given below deal with state laws concerning the slave and homicide, abuses against slaves by the master and other whites, and the interpretation of these laws in the Southern state courts. Because he believed slavery to be a good and viable institution, Cobb had special difficulties in explaining what he called "one of the most vulnerable points" in slavery: the slave's legal impotence before a cruel master. In paragraphs 104–7 in the following document Cobb evinces his uneasiness by suggesting reform in state laws.

While Cobb's basic sympathy with slavery as an institution is plainly revealed in his defensive explanation of the historical background of slavery, in which he expands on Southern slavery as an advance in humanity over the "absolute" slavery of Africa and the ancient world, and in the voluminous precedents he cites to justify Southern claims that fugitive slaves must be returned to their masters from wherever they were discovered, his work nonetheless constitutes for the careful modern reader a blazing revelation of the slave's weakness before the law whenever his own safety came in conflict with the master's will.

Thomas Cobb (1832–62) was born in Jefferson County, Georgia, of a prominent family, and was a graduate of the University of Georgia. He was admitted to the Georgia bar in 1842. Like his older brother Howell Cobb, the famous United States Senator, Thomas Cobb was a defender of slavery and a prominent advocate of secession. He quickly made his reputation as a lawyer, and was court reporter for the Supreme Court of the state for eight years. He became chairman of a committee for the revision of the state constitution, and wrote many books on legal topics. His digest of the laws of Georgia was so accurate and thorough that it amounted to a codification. Cobb's writings on law are distinguished for their clarity and precision.

Chapter IV.
Of the slave as a person—
personal security.

§ 83. Having ascertained the origin and sources of negro slavery, and having traced that origin to the pure or absolute slavery existing among the tribes of Africa, and having seen that negro slavery is in no wise opposed to the law of nature, except so far as the power to kill or to maim may be claimed therefrom, it follows, that no actual enactment of the legislative power is necessary for its introduction into any country where no municipal law is thereby infringed. Hence, we find it true, that, with the exception of Georgia (where it was at first prohibited), no law is found on our statute books authorizing its introduction.

§ 84. The condition of these slaves in

their native country having been one of absolute slavery, including the power over life, such would be their condition in the country to which they were removed, except so far as the same may be modified by the existing laws of their new domicile, and such subsequent legislative enactments as may have been made for their benefit. The law of nature, denying the power over life and limb, being a part of the law of every civilized state, such power never existed in any of the United States, although it required municipal law to prescribe the punishment for such offences. Many subsequent legislative enactments have been made, regulating the power of the master, and protecting and giving rights to the slave. Having none prior to these enactments, to the municipal law we look for all his rights.

§ 84 a. In the Roman law, a slave was a mere chattel (*res*). He was not recognized as a person. But the negro slave in America, protected as above stated by municipal law, occupies a double character of person and property. Having now ascertained who are and may be slaves in America, a natural division of our subject suggests itself in considering the slave,—first, AS A PERSON, and then, AS PROPERTY.

§ 85. In treating of slaves as persons, we shall inquire of their rights and disabilities, of the authority and rights of the master, and of the relation of slaves to persons other than their masters. To a great extent, these necessarily will be considered together, yet, as far as possible, we shall endeavor to treat them in the order in which they are named.

§ 86. Of the three great absolute rights guaranteed to every citizen by the common law, viz., the right of personal security, the right of personal liberty, and the right of private property, the slave, in a state of pure or absolute slavery, is totally deprived, being, as to life, liberty, and property, under the absolute and uncontrolled dominion of his master, so that infringements upon these rights, even by third persons, could be remedied and punished only at the suit of the master for the injury done him in the loss of service or the diminution in value of his slave. As before remarked, however, no such state of slavery exists in these States. And so modified is the slavery here, partly by natural law, partly by express enactment, and more effectually by the influence of civilization and Christian enlightenment, that it is difficult frequently to trace to any purely legal sources many of those protecting barriers, the denial of whose existence would shock an enlightened public sense.

§ 87. Statute law has done much to relieve the slave from this absolute dominion, and the master from this perilous power, more especially so far as regards the first great right of personal security. In all of the slaveholding States, the homicide of a slave is held to be murder, and in most of them, has been so expressly declared by law. In Georgia, Alabama, Texas, and Arkansas, the provisions for the protection of the person of the slave are inserted in their respective Constitutions, thus making it a part of the fundamental law, and beyond the reach of ordinary legislation. Nor has the legislation of the States stopped at the protection of their lives, but the security of limbs and the general comfort of the body are, in most of the States, amply provided for, various penalties being inflicted on masters for their cruel treatment; which will be more particularly considered in a subsequent chapter.

§ 88. The question has been much mooted, whether in the absence of statute laws, the homicide of a slave could be punished under the general law prescribing the penalty for murder. By some courts it has been held, that so soon as the progress of civilization and Christian enlightenment elevated the slave from the position of a mere chattel, and recognized him for any purpose as a person, just at that moment, the homicide of him, a human being, in the peace of the State, with malice aforethought, was murder. So long as he remained purely and unqualifiedly property, an injury upon him was a trespass upon the master's rights. When the law, by providing for his proper nourishment and clothing, by enacting penalties against the cruel treatment of his master, by providing for his punishment for crimes, and other similar provisions, recognizes his existence as a person, he is as a child just born, brought for the first time within the pale of the law's protecting power; his existence as a person being recognized by the law, that existence is protected by the law.

§ 89. It has been objected to this conclusion, that if the general provision of the law against murder should be held to include slaves, why would not all other penal enactments, by the same course of reasoning, be held to include similar offences when committed on slaves, without their being specifically named? The reply made is twofold. 1st. The law, by recognizing the existence

of the slave as a person, thereby confers no rights or privileges except such as are necessary to protect that existence. All other rights must be granted specially. Hence, the penalties for rape would not and should not, by such implication, be made to extend to carnal forcible knowledge of a slave, the offence not affecting the existence of the slave, and that existence being the extent of the right which the implication of the law grants. 2d. Implications of law will always be rebutted by the general policy of the law, and it is clearly against the policy of the law to extend over this class of the community, that character of protection which many of the penal statutes are intended to provide for the citizen.

§ 90. In addition to these reasons, some of the courts have striven to assimilate the condition of the slave to that of the villain in Britain, and thence to apply to slavery here such rules as were applicable to villanage there. That no such identity exists as would justify this conclusion, has been as strenuously demonstrated. Other courts have applied to the master and slave, the principles of law applicable to masters and apprentices. This proposition, however, has not been adhered to with any tenacity. Another able judge assumes the position, that "the true state of the slave must be ascertained by reference to the disabilities of an alien enemy, in which light the heathen were anciently regarded."

§ 91. To all of this reasoning and these conclusions other courts have withheld their assent, and while they acknowledge that the feelings of humanity, and the dictates of conscience enlightened by Christianity, would lead them to these conclusions, yet they have been unable in the law itself to feel themselves justified in so declaring it. In their view, the slave remains in a state of pure slavery, until relieved by legislative anactment, and the provisions of those enactments are the extent of their rights and protection; that by the rules for the construction of statutes, which are adopted to regulate the conduct of citizens, slaves are not included within their provisions unless specifically named; that though murder is defined to be the killing of a human being, &c., yet rape is defined to be the carnal forcible knowledge of a female, and if the killing of a slave be murder, the carnal forcible knowledge of a female slave is rape; and further, that the fact that every slaveholding State has, by penal enactment, provided punishment for such offences when committed on the persons of slaves, is a legislative declaration that such offences were before that time unprovided for. That the Colonies having adopted the common law, and negro slavery having no existence in Great Britain, there could be necessarily no provision of that law in reference to it, and consequently the power of the master until limited by legislation was absolute. This view of the question seems to have prevailed in the courts of the British West Indies, as appears from the act passed in Jamaica, in 1792, providing punishments for the murder and maiming of slaves.

§ 92. The view we have taken of the law of nature leads us to a different conclusion from either of these, viz., that by that law, and without statutory enactment, the homicide or maiming of a negro slave is prohibited and un-

lawful, but that it requires statutory enactment to provide punishment for such offences. Such statutes having been passed long since in all the slave-holding States, the question arises now only collaterally; and generally upon the point whether the master is bound to prosecute criminally, before entering his civil complaint for damages.

§ 93. The same course of reasoning that would make the killing of a slave murder, without statutory enactment, would extend to the offences of man-slaughter, mayhem, wounding, and assault with intent to murder, all of these affecting the life of the slave. It would not extend to an ordinary battery, and it would seem clear upon principle, that the battery of a slave, without special enactment, could not be prosecuted criminally. The master's civil remedy would be the only mode of redress against a stranger. Where the battery was committed by the master himself, there would be no redress whatever, for the reason given in Exodus 21: 21, "for he is his money." The powerful protection of the master's private interest would of itself go far to remedy this evil. Legislators, however, have taken care, as before remarked, in all the States, to protect by stringent enactments, the slave from the cruel treatment of his master.

§ 94. The protection of the person of the slave depending so completely upon statute law, it becomes a question of importance, what words in a statute would extend to this class of individuals? Generally, it would seem that an Act of the Legislature would operate upon every person within the limits of the State, both natural and artificial, yet, where the provisions of the statute evidently refer to *natural* persons, the courts will not extend them to *artificial*. Nor will statutes ever be so construed as to lead to absurd and ridiculous conclusions. Experience has proved what theory would have demonstrated, that masters and slaves cannot be governed by the same laws. So different in position, in rights, in duties, they cannot be the subjects of a common system of laws. Hence, the conclusion, that statutory enactments never extend to or include the slave, neither to protect nor to render him responsible, unless specifically named, or included by necessary implication.

§ 95. Statutes having declared and affixed penalties to the offences affecting the personal security of slaves, it behooves us to inquire, how far the peculiar relation of the slave may affect the defences of those charged with a violation of these statutes. It would seem that from the very nature of slavery, and the necessarily degraded social position of the slave, many acts would extenuate the homicide of a slave, and reduce the offence to a lower grade, which would not constitute a legal provocation if done by a white person. Thus, in The State v. Tackett, it was held competent for one charged with the murder of a slave to give in evidence that the deceased was turbulent, and insolent, and impudent to white persons. And an assault or striking by a slave would, in many cases, amount to a justification of a homicide, which, in a white person, would only mitigate the offence. If the slave is in a state of insurrection, the homicide is justifiable, in most of the States, by statute. And if a slave is killed, who, being found at an unlawful assembly, combining to rebel, refuses to surrender and resists by force, the homicide is justifiable.

§ 96. But while the law, from the necessity of the case, will thus subject the slave to the partial control of all the freemen of the country, yet it will not sanction any wanton violation of the person of the slave. Thus, it has been held, that a white citizen is not justified in shooting a negro who he orders to stop, and who refuses to do so, even though the negro be a fugitive or runaway. And in the case of Witsell v. Earnest and another, it was held, that even though the negro be suspected of a felony, and be a fugitive, a person not clothed with the authority of law to apprehend him, cannot lawfully kill such slave while flying from him, nor would an overseer be justified in shooting a negro who fled from punishment.

And so, also, the mere fact that the party committing the homicide was a patrolman, and in the exercise of his duties as such, will not justify the killing of a slave flying from him.

§ 97. No settled rule can be laid down as to the extent of the justification which the circumstances of each case may unfold. This we may say, the law looks favorably upon such conduct as tends to the proper subordination of the slave; but at the same time looks with a jealous eye upon all such conduct as tends to unnecessary and cruel treatment.

§ 98. The personal security of the slave being thus protected by express law, becomes *quasi* a right belonging to the slave as a person. How far may the slave go to protect that right? Subordination on the part of the slave is absolutely necessary, not only to the existence of the institution, but to the peace of the community. The policy of the law, therefore, requires that the slave should look to his master and the courts to avenge his wrongs. The rule, therefore, that justifies the freeman in repelling force by force, applies not to the slave.

If, however, the life or limb of the slave is endangered, he may use sufficient force to protect and defend himself, even if in so doing he kills the aggressor. Such seems to have been the civil law.

§ 99. The law in its mercy goes still farther, and while it will not justify the slave in resisting force by force, except in the case stated, yet, in regard for the frailty of human nature, if the passions of the slave be excited into unlawful violence by the inhumanity of his master or others, it will extenuate the offence, and if a homicide be committed, will hold these circumstances as a rebuttal of the presumption of malice. This extenuation has been by some courts confined to cases of homicide by a slave of one of his own condition, the reason given being "a stern and unbending necessity." I cannot yield my assent fully to this proposition as being well-founded in law. The duty of the slave to obey, and his habit of subordination, would require a greater provocation to justify an "infirmity of temper or passion;" but still there are circumstances, where such provocation might be given, especially by others than the master, as to reduce the offence by the slave from murder to manslaughter.

§ 100. In some of the States the statutes provide only for the punishment

of the murder of a slave, without specifying or referring to the minor offences of manslaughter, or an assault with intent to murder, being most probably an oversight on the part of the draughtsman. In such a case, a verdict of guilty of manslaughter, it would seem, would leave the Court to pass judgment as if no statute had been enacted.

§ 101. The law is different, however, as to the offence of an assault with intent to murder, for the statute, by making the killing of a slave murder, constituted the offence, at the same time, a felony. And, according to the common law, an attempt to commit a felony, even though the felony be created by statute, is indictable: such attempt being a misdemeanor.

§ 102. Before leaving the subject of the homicide of slaves, it is, perhaps, well to remark, that where a slave is killed, the presumption of law is the same as in other cases of homicide, that it was done maliciously. On account of the frequent and necessarily private relation of master and slave, remote most generally from the presence and view of any white person competent to be a witness, this presumption may and must often operate to the prejudice of the slayer, there being no means of proving the provocation given. Under this view, the Act of South Carolina provides, that where the homicide is committed, and no competent witness is present at the time to testify to the whole transaction, the affidavit of the accused is admitted before the jury, explanatory and exculpatory of his conduct on the occasion. In the other States, upon principle, it would seem, that while the presumption is admitted, the jury should consider the peculiar relations of master and slave, as to some extent rebutting its force and effect.

Chapter V.
Of personal security—Continued.

§ 103. With reference to the minor offences created by statute, protecting the person of the slave from torture, wounding, maiming, and cruel and inhuman treatment, the great diversity of the statutory provisions and penalties prescribed in the different States, renders it impossible, within the limits of this treatise, to analyze carefully each statute, and consider its practical operation. A few general remarks, upon the general current of legislation, will suffice our purpose.

§ 104. On account of the perfectly unprotected and helpless position of the slave, when his master is placed in opposition to him: not being allowed to accumulate property, with which to provide means for the prosecution of his rights; his mouth being closed as a witness in a court of justice; his hands being tied, even for his own defence, except in the extreme cases before alluded to; his time not being at his service, even for the purpose of procuring testimony; and his person and conduct being entirely under the control of him against whom he stands arrayed, the courts should, and do, feel themselves to be his guardian and protector, and will provide for the defence of his rights, as for a ward of the Court. Hence, in some of the States, by statute, the court is required to assign him counsel learned in the law, and, in oth-

ers, the very penalty affixed to a conviction for cruel treatment by the master, is the emancipation of the slave. In others, the penalty is, in part, the sale of the slave.

§ 105. This is one of the most vulnerable points in the system of negro slavery, and should be farther guarded by legislation. Large compensation should be provided for informers, upon the conviction of the master of cruel treatment; and perhaps the best penalty that could be provided upon conviction, would be not only the sale of the particular slave cruelly treated, but of all the slaves owned by the offender, and a disqualification forever of owning or possessing slaves.

§ 106. As to what amounts to cruel treatment, is a question which necessarily, to some extent, must be submitted to the jury. The general principle would be, that the master's right to enforce obedience and subordination on the part of the slave should, as far as possible, remain intact. Whatever goes beyond this, and from mere wantonness or revenge inflicts pain and suffering, especially unusual and inhuman punishments, is cruelty, and should be punished as such. And though the statute creating the offence specifies particular acts of cruelty, yet it has been held, that other acts of cruelty, though of a minor grade than those specified, were indictable under the general description of cruel punishment.

§ 107. Another consequence of slavery is, that the violation of the person of a female slave, carries with it no other punishment than the damages which the master may recover for the trespass upon his property. Among the

Romans there was also given the master, an action for the corruption of his slave, in which double damages were given. This, however, was founded also upon the idea of the injury to the property. Among the Lombards, if a master debauched his slave's wife, the slave and his wife were restored to their freedom. The laws of King Alfred provided a pecuniary compensation to the master for the ravishment of his slave. These laws are suggestive of defects in our own legislation.

It is a matter worthy the consideration of legislators, whether the offence of rape, committed upon a female slave, should not be indictable; and whether, when committed by the master, there should not be superadded the sale of the slave to some other master. The occurrence of such an offence is almost unheard of; and the known lasciviousness of the negro, renders the possibility of its occurrence very remote. Yet, for the honor of the statute-book, if it does occur, there should be an adequate punishment.

§ 108. Having thus inquired into the condition of the slave in reference to personal security under the laws of the United States, it might be profitable to compare this condition with that of slaves in other countries and at other ages. Among the Jews the killing of a slave went unpunished, unless the death was immediate. If the master maimed the slave by putting out an eye or knocking out a tooth, the slave was thereby emancipated. A similar law was enacted by Alfred the Great, as to the murder of a slave by his master, though no civil punishment was prescribed. Among the Anglo-Saxons the murder of a slave by his own master was entirely unpunished by the civil courts. If the homicide was committed by a stranger, the punishment was the payment to the master of *a pound*. So also, the laws of Henry I, of England. "Qui servum suum occiderit suum peccatum est et dampnum; si ipso die, quo vulneratus est, vel alio modo afflictus, tanquam in manibus domini sui moriatur crudelius est et gravius, sicut in lege Moysis scriptum est." [1] When Saxon slavery became modified, and feudal villanage took its place, the murder or maiming of a villain was indictable, but no other cruel treatment was within the interdict of the law. The Roman law gave the master absolute power over the life and limbs of the slave. He might maim or destroy them at pleasure. It is related of a citizen that he caused the head of a slave to be cut off, for the gratification of a guest who had never witnessed such an exhibition.

Subsequently, however, by a constitution of Claudius, the killing of a slave was declared murder; and certain cruel treatment worked an emancipation of the slave. And by a previous constitution of Antoninus, if the master was convicted of cruel treatment to his slave, he was compelled to sell him, and the slave was empowered to make his complaint to the proper authority.

§ 109. In ancient Athens, the life and person of a slave were protected

1. The killing of one's own serf is a sin and condemnation; if on the day in which the serf is wounded or harmed in any other way, so that he dies in the hands of his own master, this is more cruel and serious, just as it is written in the law of Moses. (*Editor's trans.*)

by law. And in case of cruel treatment by his master, the slave could take shelter in the temple of Theseus, and there claim the privilege of being sold by him.

By the provisions of the Code Noir, a negro slave in the French West Indian Islands, by cruel treatment, was forfeited to the crown, and owners convicted of such offences were obliged to sell all the slaves they had, and incapacitated from afterwards holding such property.

In the Spanish and Portuguese colonies the laws seem still more favorable for the slave. Ill-usage entitled the slave to enfranchisement, or else a sale to another master, or the purchase of his own freedom upon a fair valuation.

Among the German states, the *jurisdictio patrimonialis* [2] gave to the lord or patron the right to chastise in moderation (*modice castigandi*) their serfs or prædial slaves. But among the ancient Germans and Franks, the master exercised the "jus vitæ necisque," though we are told, "non atrociter, sed tum demum si servi hostilem induissent animum." [3]

After the introduction of Christianity, though the homicide of a slave was unpunished by law, the Church inflicted penalties therefor. Subsequently, about the twelfth century, it was modified by law, as stated by Heineccius, into the *jurisdictio patrimonialis*.

§ 110. The law of slavery in the British East Indies (being the Hindoo and Mohammedan Law, adopted and enforced by the British courts), treated the slave as the absolute property of the master, made no provision for the protection of the slave from the cruelty of his master, not limiting the master's power, even over the life and limb of the slave.

In ancient Spain, Gaul, Poland, Russia, Bohemia, Denmark, Sweden, Belgium, and Helvetia, the power of the master or lord over his slave or serf was absolute, he being the sole judge in all cases, and being allowed to coerce "verberibus flagellis, aliisque pœnis." [4] This differed from the condition of the slave at Rome in later days in this, that the master's power over the latter, though recognized by law, was subject to the supervision of the civil courts, while among the German nations and those of German extraction, the master or lord had jurisdiction independent of other courts, of all questions touching the vassal or slave.

Chapter VI.
Of personal liberty.

§ 111. The right of personal liberty in the slave is utterly inconsistent with the idea of slavery, and whenever the slave acquires this right, his condition is *ipso facto* changed. Hence, the enjoyment of it for a number of years has been held to be strong presumptive evidence of former emancipation.

§ 112. Blackstone defines this personal liberty to "consist in the power of locomotion, of changing situation or moving one's person to whatsoever

2. Jurisdiction of the father. (*Editor's trans.*)
3. "The right of life and death," though we are told, "not cruelly, unless the slave demonstrates a hostile demeanor." (*Editor's trans.*)

4. Beating, whipping, or any other punishment. (*Editor's trans.*)

place one's own inclination may direct, without imprisonment or restraint, unless by due course of law." The slave, while possessing the power of locomotion, moves not as his own inclination may direct, but at the bidding of his master, who may, of his own will, imprison or restrain him, unless he thereby infringes some provision of statute law. So utterly opposite is the position of the slave from that of the freeman in respect to this right, that we could not better define his condition, than to say it is the reverse of that of the freeman.

§ 122 *a*. But while the slave's power of locomotion is thus within the absolute control of the master, no third person has any right to restrain or imprison him, except by order of the master, or in cases provided by law. Hence, disobedience of a slave to the order of a person who has no right to control him, in the absence of statute law, would be no justification to such person for a battery or other injury committed on the slave.

§ 113. Reasons of policy and necessity, however, require that so long as two races of men live together, the one as masters and the other as dependents and slaves, to a certain extent, *all* of the superior race shall exercise a controlling power over the inferior. If the slave feels that he is solely under the power and control of his immediate master, he will soon become insolent and ungovernable to all others. If the white man had, then, no right by law to control, the result would be, the excitement of angry passions, broils, and bloodshed. Hence have arisen, in the States, the various police and patrol regulations, giving to white persons other than the master, under certain circumstances, the right of controlling, and, in some cases, correcting slaves. But if the white person exceeds the authority given, and chastises a slave who has given no provocation, he is liable for the trespass.

§ 114. Necessarily, much of the time of the slave is not employed in his master's service. The long hours of the night, the Sabbath day, and the various holidays, are times when, by the permission of masters, slaves enjoy a *quasi* personal liberty. At such times, it cannot be expected that the watchful eye of the master can follow them. Frequent and large collections of them would necessarily occur, and, having no business to occupy their thoughts and conversation, mischief and evil would be the consequence of their assemblage. It has been found expedient and necessary, therefore, in all the slaveholding States, to organize, in every district, a body of men, who, for a limited time, exercise certain police powers, conferred by statute, for the better government of the slave, and the protection of the master. Upon these policemen or patrol, for the time, greater powers and privileges are necessarily conferred, for the execution of their office, in controlling the liberty and movements of the slave.

§ 115. The power and authority of the patrol, however, are limited by the statutes prescribing them, and they are not at liberty to overleap these bounds. Hence, in South Carolina, it was held, that under the authority to disperse unlawful assemblies of negroes, the patrol had no right to interfere with an open assemblage, for the purpose of religious worship, where white persons were also assembled. Nor with an orderly meeting of slaves, with the consent of their masters, upon the premises of a slaveholder, with his permission and occasional presence. Nor can the patrol correct a slave giving no provocation, who is without his master's inclosure, with a permit or ticket authorizing it.

If the patrol inflict excessive punishment upon a slave, they will be liable to the master for the trespass. Some degree of discretion, however, is necessarily allowed them.

§ 116. The necessity for patrol regulations being to control slaves when not under the control of their masters, it would seem that the patrol, upon principle, could never interfere with the master's control of his own slave, and upon his own premises. It would require very express enactment to justify such interference.

§ 117. Yet the master's privilege extends only to his own slaves, and he cannot so act towards them as to interfere or injure his neighbors. Hence, the enactments in many States, against persons permitting assemblages of the slaves of others upon their premises, without the consent of their owners. Hence, also, a master, in many States, is prohibited from furnishing spirituous liquors to his own slaves in such quantities as to enable them to furnish others. Hence, also, in almost all the States, the penalties against the master for permitting his slaves to hire their own time, or to go at liberty, to the injury of others.

§ 118. To restrain the slave altogether from leaving his master's premises, during the time that he is not employed in his master's business,

would be unnecessarily harsh towards that dependent class. Hence, by the permission of the master, the slave may be allowed to travel the highway, or to visit and remain at other places; in which event, he is not subject to be controlled or corrected by the patrol, unless found violating some provision of law. The evidence of such permission is called a *permit* or *pass*. The particularity with which it should be written, and what it should contain, must necessarily depend upon the requisition of the statutes regulating patrols. A substantial compliance with the statute is sufficient. On the other hand, the master is not permitted to violate the whole policy of the legislation of a State by giving his slave a "permit" or "pass" for an indefinite or unreasonable period of time, especially if it professes to allow the slave privileges forbidden to the slave, and penal in the master.

§ 119. From this *quasi* liberty of the slave, during the Sabbath and other holidays, flow many interesting questions as to the liability of the master or hirer for the acts of the slave at such times, which will be considered hereafter.

§ 120. The slave being deprived of the right of personal liberty, cannot, by any act of his, obtain it without the consent of his master. Hence, though he escapes from the actual personal control of the master, and while a fugitive enjoys actual liberty, he is at all times subject to be retaken, and placed again under the power of the master. In fact, by placing himself beyond the pale of the master's protecting power, and being, for the time and *pro tanto*, in a state of rebellion to his lawful authority, he deprives himself of the exemption from the interference of strangers, which at home he enjoys, and becomes, to a limited extent, an outlaw in the community. As such, he may be arrested and imprisoned by any one, even on the Sabbath day, just as a criminal caught *flagrante delicto*.

§ 121. Any person harboring or concealing him, or aiding or abetting him in making his escape, is not only liable to the master civilly, but, in all the States, is made responsible criminally.

Any person hiring or employing a runaway slave, is responsible to the master for his services; and this is true with or without notice to the employer, of the fact of his being a fugitive, the rule in such cases being analogous to that adopted in reference to masters and apprentices. And although the master is bound to furnish necessary food and clothing to his slave, yet the wrongdoer, in such a case, could not set-off against the master's claim, advances made to the slave, however necessary they were.

§ 122. The master may recapture his slave at any time or place, whether in a slaveholding or non-slaveholding State; and in order to do so, he may enter upon the premises of another without being guilty of a trespass, provided he does so peaceably, and without committing any breach of the peace. Such was the rule in reference to a master and his apprentice at common law; and an advertisement, by the master, in a public newspaper, of his runaway apprentice, has been held sufficient authority to justify a third person in entering upon the premises of another to arrest the apprentice. Such was the rule, also, in reference to

the lord and his villain, provided the recapture was within a year and a day; and this privilege extended to any portion of the realm to which the villain may have escaped. Thus Fleta: "Servus fugitivus non solum infra annum et diem capi poterit in feodo domini, sed ubicunque inventus fuerit in regno, dum tamen recenter post fugam sequatur, comprehendi poterit, etiam impune retineri." [5] Fugitive villains, upon recaption, were branded in the forehead.

§ 123. According to the Roman law, the master's rights over his slaves were in no wise affected by his running away. A class of persons called *Fugitivarii* made it their business to recover runaway slaves. The master's right of recaption extended everywhere in the realm, and it was the duty of all authorities to give him aid in recovering the slave. The fugitive slave when captured was branded in the forehead. Such cruel punishment was sometimes added, that Ulpian relates an instance of one who killed himself for fear of returning to his master. No length of time nor acquisition of honors debarred the master's right of recovery. It was otherwise, however, if another possessed him as a slave. An action was given to the master against any one who persuaded the slave to fly to a statue for refuge.

§ 124. Fugitive slaves were the subject of recapture in the French Empire during the middle ages. And the Em-

5. The fugitive serf may be captured within a year and a day not only in the fief of his lord, but wherever he is found in the realm. So long as he is followed promptly after flight, he may be captured and even confined without retaliation. (*Editor's trans.*)

peror Charlemagne is applauded for providing, that if a lord claimed his villain or slave (*colonus sive servus*), who had escaped beyond his territory, he was not to be given up until strict inquiry was made as to the truth of the claim.

§ 125. In all the German states fugitive slaves were the subjects of recapture. And no length of prescription could bar the master's claim. Thirty years' possession by another master was subsequently declared a bar. Among the Lombards, thirty years' enjoyment of freedom prescribed the master's claim. The law of the Visigoths enacted severe penalties against those who concealed a slave, refused to deliver him to a judge, released him from his chains, aided him in his flight, or gave him a refuge. It also prescribed the condition of his wife, who married him supposing him to be free, and also of the children born of such a marriage. In some cases, *stripes* were provided as the punishment. Most of the German states made provision by law for the delivery of the fugitives from other states. If the delivery of the fugitive slave was refused, a war frequently ensued. To avoid these controversies, the emperors at different times prescribed a certain length of time to peaceable residence, after which the master's rights were barred. Some of the emperors refused to receive fugitives within their states to the prejudice of their masters.

§ 126. The right of recapture existed in ancient Greece, and branding was a common punishment for a runaway slave.

In the West Indies, the punishment of a fugitive was very severe. By the "Code Noir" he was branded and his ears cut off, for the first and second offences, and for the third, he lost his life. In the Spanish colonies he was hung, if absent longer than six months. Up to the year 1819, a fugitive slave who had been absent for thirty days, was hung in the English colony of Barbadoes.

§ 127. The Church, since the apostolic day, has ever followed the example of Paul in restoring to his master the fugitive Onesimus, and in which Paul only pursued the teaching of the Spirit of the Lord, that instructed Hagar in the wilderness to return and submit herself to the hand of her mistress. Saint Basil gave full instructions on the subject of fugitive slaves, requiring all the inferior clergy, where refuge was sought in the convents or other sacred places, after having enlightened and made them better, to restore them to their masters. So, by the decrees of several councils, any person advising a slave to abandon the service of his master, or advising him not to serve with good faith and the most profound respect, was subject to the anathema of the Church.

40. Thomas B. Chaplin Sits on a Jury of Inquest

During the nineteenth century the penalties for the homicide of a slave were raised, and in cases of premeditated murder of a slave the death penalty was assigned. In South Carolina, where such legal reforms came later than in the other states, this law was not enacted until 1821. Under its operation white persons, even masters, were occasionally executed for murder of slaves, but in most instances whites indicted for this crime escaped lightly.

The difficulties of enforcement of the law, and securing a conviction of offenders, were enormous, because of two factors: the law assigned the masters an almost unlimited power to *chastise* slaves; and slaves were legally incapable, except under very restricted circumstances, to witness against white persons. A conviction against the master for murder of his slave was hardest of all to secure, since the law assumed that the master's property interest would deter him from harming his own slave unnecessarily. It is significant that in such instances as convictions were won, the murder had been accompanied by torture or extreme cruelty, inescapably identifiable as "cruel and unusual" punishment.

Although judgments rendered in the highest courts of the Southern states are studded with judicial regrets that slaves stood so poorly protected against their masters, all efforts to correct this legal injustice involved some reduction of the master's authority over his slave property, and hence produced no result. Nevertheless, in numerous instances juries were called on, just as were judges, to decide whether a given "chastisement" or "correction" was unreasonable, or whether it could have been expected to cause death.

The following document presents such an instance, which occurred in 1849 in South Carolina. South Carolina provided that when a master had caused the death of his slave, the case should be promptly investigated by a jury of inquest, the members of which were to present the charges in court if after investigating the facts they determined that a crime had been

Source: Thomas B. Chaplin, Manuscript Diary, South Carolina Historical Society, Charleston, S.C.

committed. Thomas B. Chaplin (see also documents 50 and 75) was called upon for such jury service in the death of a slave named Roger as a result of "correction." It must be remembered that the jury was composed of neighboring planters. The slaves themselves were questioned by the jury-men, and they answered boldly, perhaps at some risk to themselves. Al-though it is obvious from planter Chaplin's account that he did not like the verdict, his use of the subjunctive voice leaves some doubt about how he himself voted, and it seems clear enough that Roger's death was deter-mined to have been accidental and that no charges were made.

Feb 19th [1849] Monday. Clear and very cold, freezing. 3 women choping fennell in root patch, Isaac tracking out same. Carts carrying the cotton over to the River Side to go to Beaufort.—I received a summons while at Breakfast to go over to J. H. Sandiford's at 10 O'clock A.M. this day, and sit on a jury of inquest, on the body of Roger, a negro man belonging to Sandiford. Accordingly I went. About 12 M[eridian] there were 12 of us together—(the number required to form a jury)—viz. Dr. Scott, foreman, J. J. Pope,—J. E. L. Fripp—W. O. P. Fripp—Dr. M. M. Sams, Henry Fripp, Dr. Jenkins, Jno. McTurio[u]s, Henry McTurious, P. W. Perry—W. Perry, & myself. We were sworn by J. D. Pope, Magistrate, and proceeded to examine the body. We found it in an out house used as a corn house, and meat house, (for there were both in the house,) Such a shocking sight never before met my eyes, there was the poor negro, who all his life had been a compleat cripple, being hardly able to walk, & used his knees more than his feet, in the most shock-ing situation—but *stiff dead.* He was placed in this situation by his *master,* to punish him, as he sais *for imperti-nence,*—and what [was] this punish-

ment [for?] This *poor cripple* was sent by his master (as Sandifords evidence goes) on Saturday the 17th inst *before day light* (cold & bitter weather, as every one knows, tho Sandiford sais, "it was *not very* cold") in a Paddling boat down the river to get Oisters, and ordering him to return before high water, & cut a bundle of marsh. The poor fellow did not return before ebb tide, but he brought 7 baskets of oi-sters—& a small bundle of marsh (more than the primest of my fellows would have done, Anthony never brought me more than 5 baskets of Oi-sters & took the whole day). His mas-ter asked him why he did not return sooner & cut more marsh—he said that the wind was too high—his master said he would whip him for it, & set to work with a cowhide to do the same, the fellow hollowed & when told to stop—said, He would not as long as he was being whiped for which imperti-nence he rec d 30 cuts. He went to the kitchen, and was talking to another negro—when Sandiford sliped up & overheard their confab, heard Roger, as he sais, say, that if he had sound limbs, he would not take a flogging from any white man, but would shoot them down, and turn his back on

[211]

them. (another witness, the negro that Roger was talking to, sais that Roger did not say this—but—"that he would turn his back on them if they shot him down," which I think is much the most probable of the two speaches.) Sandiford then had him confined, in the manner I will describe. Even if the fellow had made the speach that Sandiford said he did, and even worse—it by no means warranted the punishment he received, the fellow was a cripple, & could not escape from a slight confinement—besides—I dont think he was ever known to use a gun, or even knew how to use one. So there was little apprehension of his putting his threat, (if it can be called one) into execution. for These *Crimes*—this man—, this demon in human shape, this pretended Christian member of the Baptist Church—had this poor cripple negro—placed in an open out house—the wind blowing through a hundred cracks—his clothes wet to his waist—without a single blanket—& in freezing weather, with his back against a partition—shackles on his wrists, & chained to a bolt in the floor, and a chain around *his neck*—the chain passing through a partition behind him, & fastened on the other side—in this position this poor wretch

was left for the night, a position that none but the most *blood thirsty* Tyrant could have placed a human being. My heart chills at the idea—and my blood boils at the base tyranny—The wretch returned to his victim about day light the next morning—& found him, as any one might expect, dead—*chocked—strangled—*frozen to death, <u>murdered</u>.—The verdict of the jury was, that Roger came to his death by chocking by a chain put around his neck by his master—*having sliped from the position in wich he was placed.*—The verdict should have been—, that Roger came to his death by inhuman treatment to him by his master—by placing him—in very cold weather—in a cold house—with a chain about his neck—& fastened to the wall—& otherways chained so that he could in no way assist himself—should he slip from the position in which he was placed, & must consequently choke to death without immediate assistance. Even should he escape from being frozen to death —which we believe would have been the case—from the fact of his clothes being wet & the severity of the weather.

My *individual* verdict would be *Deliberately,* but *unpremeditately*—Murdered by his master James H. Sandiford.

41. The Killing of Nath: A Matter of Property

Among the most interesting primary sources for the study of slavery are the reports of cases heard before the state supreme courts—cases brought on appeal from lower decisions. Frequently these cases arose in contests between white men over slave property.

In the Arkansas case given below, a slave owner named R. A. Brunson withheld the salary of his overseer, James Martin, on the ground that Martin had killed Brunson's slave, a valuable man named Nath, who was worth, according to his master, fifteen hundred dollars. In the Hempstead County Court Martin had sued Brunson in *assumpsit* (meaning merely that the law assumes that salary is owed where services have been performed), for his salary. Planter Brunson pled *non-assumpsit,* charged Martin with having broken contract in killing Nath without good cause, and notified Martin of his intention to seek a judgment against him for the balance of Nath's assessed value, beyond the overseer's salary for 1853. The circuit court of Hempstead had given a verdict in favor of Martin, the plaintiff, and Planter Brunson appealed.

After a brief discussion of legal means of recovery for lost property in such cases as Brunson's, involving "recoupment," "set-off," and "abatement," Judge Shelton Watson for the Supreme Court of Arkansas refused to take the case, declaring that he found no fault with the instructions to the jury made in the Hempstead court. It was on these grounds that Brunson had made his appeal. Brunson would be obliged to take other means for his "recoupment" against Martin for the loss of Nath. Judge Watson was convinced that the Hempstead jury had correctly understood that they were deciding whether Nath had been killed without reasonable cause, and they had decided in overseer Martin's favor. Quite apart from the legal fine points, the reader of this case gets a view of slave resistance among what the overseer labeled "a rough and saucy set of hands."

Source: L. E. Barber, [ed.], *Reports of Cases at Law and in Equity Argued and Determined in the Supreme Court of Arkansas at the January Term, 1856* (Little Rock: James Battle, 1857), 17:270–78.

Brunson vs. Martin.

Where a defendant elects to use his claim against the plaintiff for damages, by way of recoupment, he cannot have a balance found in his favor, as in case of set-off.

To an action by an overseer and manager of a plantation and negroes for his wages such, the employer may recoup any damages he may have sustained by an imperfect performance of the contract on the part of the overseer—as where he has violated the contract in its terms and spirit.

In such action the claim for damages being on account of the killing of one of the slaves of the employer by the overseer, to authorize recoupment for such damages it must appear, from the evidence, that the killing arose from the overseer's mismanagement—that he killed the slave negligently and without necessity.

At common law, a party could not maintain an action for damages arising out of a felony, until after a trial upon a criminal prosecution; but our Legislature has changed this rule. (*Dig.*, p. 428.)

Appeal from Hempstead Circuit Court.

HON. SHELTON WATSON, Circuit Judge.

CURRAN & GALLAGHER, for appellant.

S. H. HEMPSTEAD, for appellee.

Mr. Justice SCOTT delivered the opinion of the Court.

Martin sued Brunson, in the Hempstead Circuit Court, to recover, in assumpsit, the value of services rendered as overseer, in the year 1853. The latter pleaded *non-assumpsit*, and with his plea, filed a notice to the plaintiff, as follows, *to wit:*

"Take notice, that at, and upon the trial of this cause, I shall introduce testimony, and prove that you did not keep and perform the contract between us, in said suit specified, but on the contrary, did break and violate the same, in this; that you, without necessity, and contrary and against your duty, as my overseer, and manager upon my farm, did wrongfully kill and destroy my property, then under your care and control, as my overseer and manager, by virtue of the contract in said suit specified, *to wit:* a negro slave named *Nathan,* of great value, *to wit:* of the value of fifteen hundred dollars, and that I shall cut-off, and keep back, the entire sum claimed by you in the suit aforesaid, for the damages by me sustained in this behalf, *and take judgment against you for the balance to which I am entitled on account of the same,* when and where you can controvert my claim to damages in this behalf, if you think proper.

ROBERT A. BRUNSON."

Although there is no question upon the record as to this notice, it may be remarked, in response to observations about it by the counsel on both sides, that it seems proper that it should be filed at the same time that the plea of *non-assumpsit,* which it accompanies, is filed; as it appears was done in this case. If the plaintiff should, in fact, be surprised by the notice, it would, of course, be a ground upon which he might apply to the court for a continuance, to enable him to prepare to repel the defence.

With regard to so much of the notice as we have marked in italics, it may be further remarked, that it has been held in New York, (*Batterman vs. Price,* 3 *Hill's Rep.* 171) that, where a defendant elects to use his claim by way of *recoupment,* he cannot have a balance certified in his favor, as in case of set-off; but he must be content to have it go in abatement, in whole or in part of the plaintiff's demand: And in Alabama, (*McLane vs. Miller*, 12 *Ala. Rep.* 643,) and New Hampshire, (*Britton vs. Turner*, 6 *N. H. Rep.* 481,) that after making such election, he cannot afterwards bring his cross-action for damages.

The cause was tried by a jury, who, after having heard the evidence, and receiving the instructions of the court, rendered a verdict for the plaintiff, Martin, and judgment was given accordingly.

Brunson moved for a new trial upon the ground, that the instructions given on the motion of the plaintiff, were improper, and that the finding of the jury was contrary to law, and to the instructions, and to the evidence, and was without evidence to support it. The court overruled his motion, and taking a bill of exceptions, in which all the instructions given to the jury, and all the evidence produced before them, are contained, appealed to this court.

The matter of the instructions may be as well considered, under the circumstances of this case, before the evidence is stated, as afterwards. There were but three given to the jury; two of them upon the motion of the plaintiff, and the other upon the motion of the defendant. The former were both excepted to, and it is upon them that the only question of law, as to the instructions, arises in the cause. They were as follows, *to wit:*

1st. "That to enable the defendant to recoup, it must appear to the jury that the death of the negro was the result of the plaintiff's mismanagement, as overseer for the defendant.

2d. In order to enable the defendant to recoup, it must appear from the testimony, that plaintiff, negligently and without necessity, killed the defendant's slave."

The instruction given on the defendant's motion was, "if the jury believe, from the evidence, that Martin did not perform his contract to oversee and manage for Brunson the slaves and farm of Brunson, but did break and violate the same in its terms and spirit, they should recoup the damage sustained by Brunson in that behalf, from the amount of the plaintiff's claim against Brunson, for overseeing."

These instructions distinctly informed the jury, when they are all taken together: 1st. That, if from the evidence, they should believe, that the plaintiff violated his contract with the defendant, in its terms and spirit, the former was liable to the latter, and that the latter was entitled to recoup the damages arising from such breach of the plaintiff's undertaking: 2d. That in reference to the alleged violation of the contract, as connected with the killing of the slave, in order to authorize them to find the contract so violated, it must appear from the evidence that that arose from the plaintiff's mismanagement as overseer. And 3d. That unless it did appear from the evidence that the plaintiff, negligently and without necessity, killed the slave, the defendant was not entitled to recoup.

Thus, the jury were not only instructed that a negligent killing of the slave authorized recoupment, but they were instructed strongly inferentially, that a killing without necessity would constitute such negligent killing.

We think it clear enough, that there is nothing in these instructions of which the appellant can complain; because, so far as they may be considered erroneous at all, that error is in his favor. And we can but find it very difficult to say that they are erroneous at all, in view of the just protection of the slave, which the common law of slavery, as it has grown up in the slave States of this Union, humanely affords to him. And yet, while we cannot see that we can safely displace that word *"necessity,"* as it appears in the charge of the court, with any other word, the stern mandates of that same common law of slavery, does, in truth, mitigate it in that connection, of some of its absoluteness of signification, in the absolute right it recognizes, not only of the master or his representative, but also of a stranger, as against the slave, to overcome by proper means, graduated upon principles of humanity and law, the slave's rebellion against the awful authority of his master. See *Austin vs. The State,* 14 *Ark. Rep.* 567, as to the last point considered in that case. And in that sense, doubtless, the court and jury understood the word, or the verdict and the judgment could not have been rendered, nor the action for a new trial have been overruled.

To determine from the evidence, whether the means used for overcoming the rebellion in this case, were graduated upon the principles of humanity, was the appropriate province of the jury, as matter of fact and law, of which latter, *necessity* in the slayer, as thus understood, was given them by the court as a standard.

And although we cannot but say that we would be loath to subscribe to the verdict, is is still more difficult to say, that it is totally unsupported by the ev-

idence, when we regard the legitimate province of the jury to judge exclusively of its weight.

In support of the verdict and judgment, the facts, which the evidence in the record conduces to prove, may be thus stated: 1st. Those preceding the killing of the slave. The slaves of the defendant "were a hard set to manage," and often found idle, in the absence of the overseer. The overseer of the previous year had found it necessary to flog some of them for idleness and other faults common to negroes, and he also had found them "harder to manage than some negroes he had managed."

In the morning of the day of the killing (which occurred in the afternoon of that day) the plaintiff said, at a store in the neighborhood of the plantation, in a conversation about the management of negroes on a farm, that he "had a rough and saucy set of hands to manage, and that, after that, if he ever overseed again, he would make the negroes obey him, or he would kill them." This was about 11 o'clock, and he appeared perfectly calm and in no way excited. Another witness stated that he remained at the store until two or three o'clock, and "was drinking," but "seemed to be in a good humor, and laughed and talked a good deal," and among other things, said, he was going to prove a mule for his employer, which had been taken up as an estray. Another witness, however, proved that, at three o'clock, the plaintiff showed no signs of being intoxicated.

The killing seems to have occurred about, or soon after this hour, and the facts attendant are, 2d. about, in substance, these: The plaintiff, having his whip in his hand, went into the field where the hands were picking cotton, and when approaching near to them, said to *Nath*, the slain, that he had "come for his shirt;" to which, *Nath* replied, that he "had pulled off his shirt to the last overseer." The plaintiff, drawing a revolver, repeated to him that he "had come for his shirt, and intended to have it or hurt him." To which *Nath* replied, *"shoot and be damned,"* the plaintiff simultaneously exploding a cap in his first effort to shoot, and at the same moment Nath commenced advancing upon the plaintiff, with some cotton in one hand, and nothing in the other, the plaintiff firing his pistol upon him, three or four times; until, at the last fire, *Nath* was near enough to knock the pistol up— *Nath* at the same moment himself falling down. The physician, who was called in, states, that there were upon the person of *Nath*, the wounds of three balls. "One, passing near his privates, lodged in his right thigh, on its way slightly wounding the penis. Another hit him near the left hip joint, but a little above and behind it; and the third struck him on the left side of the abdomen, and ranged rather down. This latter ball produced his death." And the same witness further states as his opinion, formed from the examination of the person of *Nath*, that "all the shots were made by some one, on the left side of the negro. The wounds could not have been made upon one who advanced directly to the shooter; if at all, while advancing, it must have been done while advancing with his left side to the shooter."

It was also proven, that Nath was a stout negro, weighing about 200 pounds, "with bodily strength enough to crush the plaintiff down," while the latter, it seems, was at the time "a cripple," and that it was the general custom of overseers to carry weapons.

In other respects the testimony makes out, fully, the case for the plaintiff, and that for the defendant —showing the plaintiff to have rendered services as an overseer for the defendant, from the spring of the year, from about the first of March, until he was discharged by the defendant, upon the killing of *Nath*, which was about the 15th of October: That they were worth from two hundred and fifty, to four hundred and fifty dollars; and that the value of Nath, at the time when he was killed, was from twelve to fifteen hundred dollars.

Brunson also read in evidence, without objection, a paper which was admitted by the plaintiff to have been signed by himself, which was in words and figures, as follows, *to wit:* "This is to certify, that I only claim of R. A. Brunson, two hundred and fifty dollars, as my wages for overseeing for him in the year 1853. This 15th day of May, 1854.

JAMES MARTIN."

There was also evidence to the effect, that Brunson's crop was, in the year 1853, a tolerably good one, although it did not turn out as well as the crops upon the adjoining farms. There was no testimony, otherwise, conducing to show that Martin had been negligent, or had otherwise imperfectly discharged his duties as overseer.

Under such a state of proof, we do not feel authorized to disturb the verdict, upon the ground that it is not supported by the evidence, in view of the province of the jury to judge exclusively of the weight of that adduced before them without exceptions to its competency; no question as to which latter was made on the motion for new trial.

As to the validity of the defence attempted to be sustained on the part of the defendant, it could not have been maintained upon the principles of the common law, until after the slayer had been first tried upon an indictment for the *homicide;* the excellent policy of that law preventing the person injured by the trespass, from seeking his own redress, until it should be first ascertained and determined by the proper tribunal what the justice of the State requires of the accused for the deed. If the law were otherwise, the common law supposed that persons injured would often obtain compensation for such trespasses, upon an agreement not to complain of the public wrong; and reparation would be made for the civil injury, to escape the justice of the country. *Morgan vs. Rhodes,* 1 *Stew. Ala. Rep.* 70; *Middleton vs. Holmes,* 3 *Porter's Rep.* 424. But our Legislature has changed this rule, and the civil injury is no longer merged in the felony. Our statute provides, that "in no case shall the right of action of any party, injured by the commission of a felony, be deemed or adjudged to be merged in such felony; but damages sustained thereby may be recovered in an action brought for that purpose. *Dig., chap.* 53, *sec.* 269, *page* 428.

The only remaining doubt would be, whether, although the owner could maintain his action for the value of his slave, he could insist upon it by way of recoupment. And as to this, there can be no doubt, we think, but that the principle upon which recoupment proceeds, is amply broad enough to sustain the defence. The latter was unquestionably based upon a supposed breach of one of the stipulations of the contract, upon which the plaintiff sought to recover. *Van Buren vs. Diggs,* 11 *How. U.S. Rep.* 475. And it has been frequently held in other courts, that where an overseer sues for his wages, the employer may recoup any damages he may have sustained by an imperfect performance of the contract on the part of the overseer. *Hunter vs. Waldron.* 7 *Ala.* 753; *McLane vs. Miller,* 12 *Ala. Rep.* 643; *Jones vs. Deyer,* 16 *Ib.* 221. And in Pennsylvania it was held, in the case of *Hicks vs. Shener,* 4 *Serg. & Raw.* 249, that, in an action to recover compensation for services as housekeeper, evidence that the plaintiff had been guilty of the malfeasance of embezzling the goods of the defendant, might be given to defeat the action: Chief Justice TILGHMAN remarking, in that case: "whatever be the nature of the services for which the plaintiff demands compensation, I may show that those services were ill performed; for by such evidence, I do no more than meet the plaintiff in his own allegation. I prove that he did badly, what he ought to have done well.

"The plaintiff claimed compensation for services as a house keeper. It is the duty of the house keeper to take care of the house-hold goods. The defendant offered to prove that the plaintiff did not take care of his goods, and to show the particular manner in which she violated her trust, *viz:* that she sent sundry articles to her daughter's house, and suffered her to make use of them. How is neglect of duty to be shown, but by showing the particular acts of negligence or malfeasance?" And Mr. Justice GIBSON, said: "I grant that a mere tort, unconnected with the plaintiff's conduct as house-keeper, could not have any effect on her claim in that character. But the evidence rejected went to show, that, during the time she was in the defendant's service, she gave away various articles belonging to him, without his knowledge, &c. This was a breach, on her part, of the contract implied by the law, that she would behave herself in the execution of her office or trust with integrity and fidelity. 3 *Com.* 163. It, therefore, appears unjust that he should be compelled to treat her in the first instance as a person having faith-

fully executed her trust, and be turned round to an action against her, for a breach of her part of the agreement. This unnecessary circuity ought to be avoided. The merits of the defence can be tried in this form with as much convenience to the parties, as in a separate suit, and the judgment, if pleaded with proper averments, would be a bar to another action for the same cause." See, also, *Crowninshield vs. Robinson et al.,* 1 *Mason* 93; *Austin vs. Foster,* 9 *Pick.* 342; *The Allair Works vs. Guion,* 10 *Barb. Sup. Ct. Rep.* 55.

Upon the whole record, then, we find no error of law, for which the judgment ought to be reversed; and sustaining the verdict of the jury as we have done, there was no error in the court below, in refusing the motion for a new trial. Affirmed.

42.   Assault and Battery on Lydia

In the following case, which arose on appeal from Chowan County to the Supreme Court of North Carolina, one of the harshest statements of the power of masters over slaves is provided by Judge Thomas Ruffin, who professed reluctance to reach a decision at variance with his own sense of natural justice and previous decisions made in North Carolina. Ruffin, who was born in Virginia in 1787, moved to North Carolina in 1807, and was admitted to the bar the next year. Over a long judicial career in North

Source: Thomas P. Devereaux [ed.], *Cases Argued and Determined in the Supreme Court of North Carolina from December Term, 1828, to December Term, 1830* (Raleigh: J. Gales & Sims, 1831), 2:263–68.

Carolina, stretching from 1816 through 1858, Ruffin was noted for his strict interpretation of law, his failure to consult precedents in preference to his own reasoning, and for the plain and forceful language in which his decisions were couched. When the case of the *State v. John Mann* was decided in 1829, Ruffin was Associate Justice of the Superior Court.

In this famous case the defendant is John Mann, who had hired a slave woman named Lydia from Elizabeth Jones. Elizabeth Jones prosecuted Mann for having committed assault and battery on Lydia during her term of service. Generally speaking, the lower courts were more inclined than the higher courts to leniency to whites who had injured slaves, but in this instance the lower court had convicted Mann, and Mann then appealed to the Superior Court, where Judge Ruffin wrote the opinion reversing the decision. Ruffin declared his belief that slavery was becoming a milder institution in practice as a result of statutes ameliorating slavery and because of the "frowns and deep imprecations" of society upon barbarous owners of slaves.

Actually Judge Ruffin's opinion was sterner than the high court of North Carolina usually rendered. Only six years later in the case of the *State Vs. Will* [I Devereaux and Battle, 12] the Superior Court overturned a circuit court's conviction of a slave for murder of his overseer. In this much discussed decision Judge Gaston appealed to common law and determined that Will had slain the overseer while in fear for his own life, and without malice. "It is confidently contended," wrote Judge Gaston, "that a master [and by extension the overseer] has not, by the law of the land, the right to kill a slave for a simple act of disobedience, however provoking may be the circumstances under which it is committed."

The State

v.

John Mann.

From Chowan [County].

The Master is not liable to an indictment for a battery committed upon his slave.

One who has a right to the labor of a slave, has also a right to all the means of controlling his conduct which the owner has.

Hence one who has hired a slave is not liable to an indictment for a battery on him, committed during the hiring.

But this rule does not interfere with the owner's right to damages for an injury affecting the value of the slave, which is regulated by the law of bailment.

The Defendant was indicted for an assault and battery upon *Lydia*, the slave of one *Elizabeth Jones*.

On the trial it appeared that the Defendant had hired the slave for a year—that during the term, the slave had committed some small offence, for which the Defendant undertook to chastise her—that while in the act of so doing, the slave ran off, whereupon the Defendant called upon her to stop, which being refused, he shot at and wounded her.

His honor Judge DANIEL charged the Jury, that if they believed the punishment inflicted by the Defendant was cruel and unwarrantable, and disproportionate to the offence committed by the slave, that in law the Defendant was guilty, as he had only a special property in the slave.

A verdict was returned for the State, and the Defendant appealed.

No Counsel appeared for the Defendant.

The Attorney-General contended, that no difference existed between this case and that of the *State v. Hall*, (2 *Hawks*, 582.) In this case the weapon used was one calculated to produce death. He assimilated the relation between a master and a slave, to those existing between parents and children, masters and apprentices, and tutors and scholars, and upon the limitations to the right of the superiors in these relations, he cited *Russell on Crimes*, 866.

RUFFIN, Judge.—A Judge cannot but lament, when such cases as the present are brought into judgment. It is impossible that the reasons on which they go can be appreciated, but where institutions similar to our own, exist and are thoroughly understood. The struggle, too, in the Judge's own breast between the feelings of the man, and the duty of the magistrate is a severe one, presenting strong temptation to put aside such questions, if it be possible. It is useless however, to complain of things inherent in our political state. And it is criminal in a Court to avoid any responsibility which the laws impose. With whatever reluctance therefore it is done, the Court is compelled to express an opinion upon the extent of the dominion of the master over the slave in North-Carolina.

The indictment charges a battery on *Lydia*, a slave of *Elizabeth Jones*. Upon the face of the indictment, the case is the same as the *State* v. *Hall*. (2 *Hawks* 582.)—No fault is found with the rule then adopted; nor would be, if it were now open. But it is not open; for the question, as it relates to a battery on a slave by a stranger, is considered as settled by that case. But the evidence makes this a different case. Here the slave had been *hired* by the Defendant, and was in his possession; and the battery was committed during the period of hiring. With the liabilities of the hirer to the general owner, for an injury permanently impairing the value of the slave, no rule now laid down is intended to interfere. That is left upon the general doctrine of bailment.[1] The enquiry here is, whether a cruel and unreasonable battery on a slave, by the hirer, is indictable. The Judge below instructed the Jury, that it is. He seems to have put it on the ground, that the Defendant had but a special property. Our laws uniformly treat the master or other person having the possession and command of the slave, as entitled to the same extent of authority. The object is the same—the services of the slave; and the same powers must be confided. In a criminal proceeding, and indeed in reference to all other persons but the general owner, the hirer and possessor of a slave, in relation to both rights and duties, is, for the time being, the owner.

1. The laws of bailment are concerned with complications that may arise when one person has delivered property or goods to a second person in expectation that some service or trust will be performed. (*Editor's note*)

This opinion would, perhaps dispose of this particular case; because the indictment, which charges a battery upon the slave of *Elizabeth Jones*, is not supported by proof of a battery upon Defendant's own slave; since different justifications may be applicable to the two cases. But upon the general question, whether the owner is answerable *criminaliter*,[2] for a battery upon his own slave, or other exercise of authority or force, not forbidden by statute, the Court entertains but little doubt.— That he is so liable, has never yet been decided; nor, as far as is known, been hitherto contended. There have been no prosecutions of the sort. The established habits and uniform practice of the country in this respect, is the best evidence of the portion of power, deemed by the whole community, requisite to the preservation of the master's dominion. If we thought differently, we could not set our notions in array against the judgment of every body else, and say that this, or that authority, may be safely lopped off. This has indeed been assimilated at the bar to the other domestic relations; and arguments drawn from the well established principles, which confer and restrain the authority of the parent over the child, the tutor over the pupil, the master over the apprentice, have been pressed on us. The Court does not recognise their application. There is no likeness between the cases. They are in opposition to each other, and there is an impassable gulf between them.—The difference is that which exists between freedom and slavery—

2. To be answerable "criminaliter" for an offense is to be subject to a criminal prosecution as opposed to a civil prosecution. (*Editor's note*)

and a greater cannot be imagined. In the one, the end in view is the happiness of the youth, born to equal rights with that governor, on whom the duty devolves of training the young to usefulness, in a station which he is afterwards to assume among freemen. To such an end, and with such a subject, moral and intellectual instruction seem the natural means; and for the most part, they are found to suffice. Moderate force is superadded, only to make the others effectual. If that fail, it is better to leave the party to his own headstrong passions, and the ultimate correction of the law, than to allow it to be immoderately inflicted by a private person. With slavery it is far otherwise. The end is the profit of the master, his security and the public safety; the subject, one doomed in his own person, and his posterity, to live without knowledge, and without the capacity to make any thing his own, and to toil that another may reap the fruits. What moral considerations shall be addressed to such a being, to convince him what, it is impossible but that the most stupid must feel and know can never be true—that he is thus to labour upon a principle of natural duty, or for the sake of his own personal happiness, such services can only be expected from one who has no will of his own; who surrenders his will in implicit obedience to that of another. Such obedience is the consequence only of uncontrolled authority over the body. There is nothing else which can operate to produce the effect. The power of the master must be absolute, to render the submission of the slave perfect. I most freely confess my sense of the harshness of this proposition, I feel it as deeply as any man can. And as a principle of moral right, every person in his retirement must repudiate it. But in the actual condition of things, it must be so. There is no remedy. This discipline belongs to the state of slavery. They cannot be disunited, without abrogating at once the rights of the master, and absolving the slave from his subjection. It constitutes the curse of slavery to both the bond and free portions of our population. But it is inherent in the relation of master and slave.

That there may be particular instances of cruelty and deliberate barbarity, where, in conscience the law might properly interfere, is most probable. The difficulty is to determine, where a *Court* may properly begin. Merely in the abstract it may well be asked, which power of the master accords with right. The answer will probably sweep away all of them. But we cannot look at the matter in that light. The truth is, that we are forbidden to enter upon a train of general reasoning on the subject. We cannot allow the right of the master to be brought into discussion in the Courts of Justice. The slave, to remain a slave, must be made sensible, that there is no appeal from his master; that his power is in no instance, usurped; but is conferred by the laws of man at least, if not by the law of God. The danger would be great indeed, if the tribunals of justice should be called on to graduate the punishment appropriate to every temper, and every dereliction of menial duty. No man can anticipate the many and aggravated provocations of the master, which the slave would be constantly stimulated by his own passions, or the instigation of others to give; or the consequent wrath of the master, prompting him to bloody vengeance, upon the turbulent traitor—a vengeance generally practised with impunity, by reason of its privacy. The Court therefore disclaims the power of changing the relation, in which these parts of our people stand to each other.

We are happy to see, that there is daily less and less occasion for the interposition of the Courts. The protection already afforded by several statutes, that all-powerful motive, the private interest of the owner, the benevolences towards each other, seated in the hearts of those who have been born and bred together, the frowns and deep execrations of the community upon the barbarian, who is guilty of excessive and brutal cruelty to his unprotected slave, all combined, have produced a mildness of treatment, and attention to the comforts of the unfortunate class of slaves, greatly mitigating the rigors of servitude, and ameliorating the condition of the slaves. The same causes are operating, and will continue to operate with increased action, until the disparity in numbers between the whites and blacks, shall have rendered the latter in no degree dangerous to the former, when the police now existing may be further relaxed. This result, greatly to be desired, may be much more rationally expected from the events above alluded to, and now in progress, than from any rash expositions of abstract truths, by a Judiciary tainted with a false and fanatical philanthropy, seeking to redress an acknowledged evil, by means still more wicked and appalling than even that evil.

I repeat, that I would gladly have avoided this ungrateful question. But being brought to it, the Court is compelled to declare, that while slavery exists amongst us in its present state, or until it shall seem fit to the Legislature to interpose express enactments to the contrary, it will be the imperative duty of the Judges to recognise the full dominion of the owner over the slave, except where the exercise of it is forbidden by statute. And this we do upon the ground, that this dominion is essential to the value of slaves as property, to the security of the master, and the public tranquillity, greatly dependent upon their subordination; and in fine, as most effectually securing the general protection and comfort of the slaves themselves.

Per Curiam.—Let the judgment below be reversed, and judgment entered for the Defendant.

43. Blacks and Whites May Celebrate Together—Sometimes

Color prejudice was deeply rooted in the slave system, and thus caused otherwise harmless social occasions to be suspect in the eyes of neighbors when blacks and whites congregated. In the following North Carolina case Jacob Boyce appealed a conviction in a lower court on the charge of keeping a disorderly house "for his own lucre and gain." The evidence rested largely on the fact that the dancing and general hilarity of a Christmas celebration was racially mixed. The patrollers who broke up the gathering were witnesses for the state.

In this instance Judge Ruffin, who rendered such a severe definition of relations between slaves and masters (and by extension hirers of slaves) in the case of *The State v. John Mann* (see document 42), evinced a kinder aspect. "As far as appears," he wrote for the Court, the dancing "was but a harmless merriment." With notable condescension, Judge Ruffin reversed the judgment of the lower court.

Source: James Iredell [ed.], Reports of Cases at Law Argued and Determined in the Supreme Court of North Carolina from August Term, 1849, to December Term, 1849. 13 vols. (Raleigh: Seaton & Gales, 1850), 10:536–42.

The State vs. *Jacob Boyce*

Permitting a man's slaves to meet and dance on his premises on Christmas Eve or other holidays, even though other slaves, with the permission of their masters, participate in the enjoyment, and though some of the younger members of the owner's family occasionally join in the dance, does not constitute the offence of keeping a disorderly house nor any other offence.

The case of the *State* v. *Matthews,* 2 Dev. & Bat. 424. cited and approved.

Appeal from the Superior Court of Law of Perquimons County, at the Spring Term 1848, his Honor Judge SETTLE presiding.

The indictment charges, that the defendant, on the 1st day of September 1847, and on divers other days before the taking of the inquisition, did keep and maintain a certain common, ill governed, and disorderly house, and in said house, for his own lucre and gain, certain persons, both men and women, and white and black, of evil name and fame and of dishonest and lewd conversation, to frequent and come together at unlawful times, as well in the night as the day, and on Sundays, and there to be and remain, drinking, tippling, and otherwise misbehaving themselves and other evil practices to carry on, did unlawfully and wilfully permit, to the common nuisance, &c and evil example, &c.

On not guilty pleaded, the evidence was as follows. A witness stated, that at Christmas 1845 he went to a negro quarter on the defendant's plantation and about 200 yards from his dwelling house, and there found a quilting going on and dancing by negroes; and that a daughter of the defendant was there at the time and some of the ne-groes did not belong there—that he heard the noise of dancing some distance before he reached the house; but that he did not see the defendant, nor know that he was at home. Another witness stated, that he was once at the defendant's negro quarters and found more negroes there than belonged to him, and that there was more noise than he had ever heard at any place.

Another witness for the State named Roberts deposed, that on Christmas night 1846, he and other patrollers went to the defendant's plantation between 8 and 9 o'clock: that for three quarters of a mile before he reached the house he heard much noise in that direction: that they went to the negro quarter first and found several negroes dancing there: that they then went to the house in which Boyce lived, and found therein twelve or fifteen ne-groes, of whom one was fiddling, and the others dancing and talking loud; and that some of them acted as if they were drunk, and he smelt spirits: that Boyce was in the house, and with him were a neighboring white man named Hollowell, a brother of the defendant, named Baker, and a married daughter of the defendant and her husband, (all of whom were visitors) and several children of the defendant, who lived with him and were enjoying themselves in the dance with the negroes: that several of the negroes did not belong to Boyce, but they all had papers to go to Boyce's, and yet were whipped by the patrol, except the fid-dler, who had been sent there by one of the patrol: that when the patrol seized the negroes to whip them, Goodwin, the defendant's son-in-law, had high words, and got into a fight with the patrol, but the defendant did not interfere.

Another witness for the State, named Simpson, stated, that he was one of the patrol, who went with Roberts at Christmas 1846 to the defendant's: that he heard no noise until they got to the defendant's gate, about 200 yards from the houses, and that the defendant resided in a very private situation, not being within a mile of any public road. And another of the patrol stated, that they bursted open the door and were in the house before the defendant knew they were on the land: that they immediately began to tie the negroes, when Goodwin remarked to Roberts, that a person who would act as he was doing, was no better than a negro: and that brought on a fight between them.

On the part of the defendant, Hollowell stated, that the defendant and his children, his brother, son-in-law and daughter, and the witness, were sitting quietly in conversation, when the patrol broke into the house: that all the negroes belonged to the defendant except four, and that those four had belonged to him and came there by the permission of their owners to pay a Christmas visit to their old master, and their parents and relations, who belonged to the defendant: that some of the negroes were dancing, but they were not drunk, and, indeed, they had no spirits, and made but little noise: that the defendant permitted the negroes to come into the house to dance one reel, for the amusement of his children and visitors, and there was no disorder: and that he had lived within a mile of the defendant for many years, and was familiarly acquainted with the habits of his family, and never knew

any disorder there. Baker Boyce gave the same account in substance.

The defendant then called five witnesses, all of whom had for many years, and still, lived near the defendant—some within a quarter, and the furthest within three quarters of a mile—who stated, that they were at home on Christmas night 1846, and were not disturbed by, nor did they hear, any noises or tumult at the defendant's: that they had not at any time heard any great noises there or more than is usual in families in the country, and those were upon such occasions as log rollings or holidays, and that the defendant's household was orderly, peaceable, and quiet.

The Court instructed the jury, that, in order to convict the defendant, they must be satisfied, that he had done, or permitted others to do, acts in his house, which violated the public morals, or that he made, or permitted others to make there, such a noise and confusion as annoyed and disturbed the public: that, if they found upon the evidence, that the defendant had upon two or three occasions suffered white persons and negroes, of both sexes, to meet together at his house and fiddle and dance together, and get drunk and make a noise, so as to disturb the public, they should find the defendant guilty; and further, that, if they believed the witnesses for the State, they ought to convict him. The jury accordingly found the defendant guilty, and after sentence be appealed.

Attorney General, for the State.
No counsel for the defendant.

RUFFIN, C. J. The conviction seems to be a hard one; and we own, we do not see enough in the evidence to support it. Up to Christmas 1846, nothing appears to have been done at the defendant's house, tending to the corruption of the public morality. At Christmas 1845 there was a quilting, as it is called, and dancing by negroes in a negro quarter, accompanied by such noise as arises from a negro dance; and it happened, that a daughter of the defendant was seen there and that some of the negroes did not belong to the defendant; but why the daughter went there, or how long she staid, or what she did, or how many strange negroes there were, or that they were unlawfully there, or that there was any drunkenness or drinking, or any thing else improper, did not appear. At another time, it is stated, that negroes, not belonging to the defendant, were in his negro quarters, and that a very great noise was made. But it is not stated, when that was, nor that those-negroes were improperly there, nor that it was at an unseasonable hour, nor what was the nature or occasion of the noise. The case is, then, brought down to the affair of Christmas night 1846; and the question is, whether that constitutes the defendant the keeper of a disorderly house. According to the case of *Mathews,* 2 Dev. and Bat. 424. it does not, as far as the collecting of people and their drinking go; for it was there held, that a private person, living half a mile from any other house and at a distance from a highway, was not guilty of keeping a disorderly house, though on two occasions he took in company for pay, who set up all night, played cards, and got drunk and committed affrays. The criminality here, then, must consist, if in any thing, in the assemblage of negroes and their dancing and thereby making a noise— for no other kind of noise or disorder is suggested—and in the mingling of the two colors together in the same house and dance, as stated by the witness, Roberts. It would really be a source of regret, if contrary to common custom it were to be denied to slaves, in the intervals between their toils, to indulge in mirthful pastimes, or if it were unlawful for a master to permit them among his slaves, or to admit to the social enjoyment the slaves of others, by their consent. But it is, clearly, not so. The statute law recognises the usage, and only forbids under a penalty any person from permitting slaves to meet on his plantation to dance or drink, unless they have the written permission of the owner. When the law tolerates such merry makings among these people, it must be expected in the nature of things, that they will not enter into them with the quiet and composure, which distinguish the gaieties of a refined society, but with somewhat of that hearty and boisterous gladsomeness and loud laughs, which are usually displayed in rustic life, even where the peasantry are much in advance of our negroes in the power and habit of restraining the exhibition of a keen sense of such pleasures. One cannot well regard with severity the rude pranks of a laboring race, relaxing itself in frolic, though they may seem to some to be at times somewhat excessive. If slaves would do nothing, tending more to the corruption of their morals or to the annoyance of the whites, than seeking the exhiliration [sic] of their simple music and romping dances, they might be set down as an innocent and happy class. We may let them make the most of their idle hours, and may well make allowances for the noisy out-pourings of glad hearts, which providence bestows as a blessing on corporeal vigor united to a vacant mind. In the assemblage at the defendant's there seems to have been nothing more; no brawls, no profane swearing, nor other vicious disorder. It was but the dancing in a retired situation of the negroes of the plantation, to which the greater hilarity was probably imparted by the participation of a few others, who had been of the same family and by the leave of their owners came, at the season of Christmas, to receive the affections belonging to the ties of kindred and former association. There was nothing contrary to morals or law in all that—adding, as it did, to human enjoyment, without hurt to any one, unless it be that one feel aggrieved, that these poor people should for a short space be happy at finding the authority of the master give place to his benignity, and at being freed from care and filled with gladness. Then, as to the ingredient, that the negroes were allowed to dance in their master's dwelling house, and that some of the white people also joined in their dance. Taking the testimony for the State altogether, there is much question as to the truth of this last circumstance. But, supposing it to be so, we yet must say, though it be not according to the custom of this part of our country, that there is nothing in it forbidden by law—nothing that, of itself, can constitute a disorderly house. The presence of the family might be a safe guard against riotous conduct in the negroes, rather than authorise the inference, that it contributed to create disorder; and it is very possible, that the children of the family might in Christmas times, without the least impropriety, countenance the festivities of the old servants of the family by witnessing, and even mingling in them. As far as appears, it was but harmless merriment; which, indeed, is the character given to it by the concurring testimony of all those, who lived nearest to the defendant, and knew best the nature and periods of these merry-makings.

PER CURIAM. Judgment reversed and a *venire de novo*.

44. Manslaughter or Murder?

In April of 1850 the case of the slave Nelson, convicted in a lower court of murdering a white man, was heard by the Supreme Court of Tennessee.

Source: West H. Humphreys [ed.], *Reports of Cases Argued and Determined in the Supreme Court of Tennessee*, 11 vols. (St. Louis: G. I. Jones and Co., 1879), 10:518–35.

Nelson was able to appeal his conviction on the ground that five of the jurymen in the lower court trial claimed that they had been induced to render the guilty verdict only because they believed the judge intended to order a punishment short of hanging. They claimed that they had been thus misinformed by the judge, and had also been led to believe that the charge of manslaughter could not be brought against a slave. The Supreme Court accepted the case, and Judge Nathan Green gave the opinion of the court that the jury had indeed been misled by the circuit judge. He reversed the judgment and ordered a new trial.

While refraining from comment on the testimony, Judge Green stated at the same time that the State of Tennessee did admit manslaughter as a possible charge against a slave, that manslaughter was not punishable by death, and that in cases of extreme provocation manslaughter, not murder, was the proper charge. In all the Southern states, however, the provocation for slaves would have to be the fear of death, and there were distinctions in favor of whites as to what constituted sufficient provocation.

Judge Green, who served on the Supreme Court between 1831 and 1852, was one of the great justices of the Tennessee bench, commanding the respect of fellow judges and lawyers alike, even though his decisions were unusually liberal for his time. He astonished many by holding that the Congress had the right to abolish slavery in the District of Columbia. He was a Unionist, and came to support the Confederacy only after the breach appeared inevitable.

Nelson v. *the State.*
Jackson, April, 1850.

HOMICIDE BY A SLAVE—MANSLAUGHTER. If a slave, who by insolence and misconduct has provoked chastisement, is assaulted and beaten by a stranger having no authority over him, and he kill the person so beating him, such killing will be extenuated to manslaughter if the blows of the stranger were inflicted with a weapon, and in a manner cruel and excessive, in view of the prisoner's insolence. [Cited on this, or other points thrown out in the opinion touching the criminal liability of slaves, in Ann *v.* State, 11 Humph. 166; Walker *v.* Brown, 11 Humph. 181; James *v.* Carper, 4 Sneed, 401; Brothers *v.* State, 2 Coldw. 205.]

AFFIDAVIT OF JURORS. The affidavit of five of the jury was that they were induced to find a verdict of guilty of murder in the second degree, and submit him (the prisoner) to the mercy of the court, under the belief that the court could adjudge a punishment short of death, and, if they had not so believed they would never have consented to a verdict of guilty; and the Supreme Court say: "We do not think a verdict ought to stand, when the life of a human being is involved, which has been rendered under the influence of such manifest misconceptions of the legal effect of it, especially where these misconceptions have been produced and fortified by the action of the court. [Cited in Galvin *v.* State, 6 Coldw. 287.]

This case was tried by Hardin, special judge, in the county of Perry. Defendant was found guilty, by a jury, of murder in the second degree, and judgment of death was entered against him. He appealed.

L. M. Jones, for plaintiff in error; Attorney-General, for the State.

GREEN, J., delivered the opinion of the court.

The plaintiff in error was indicted in the circuit court of Hardin county, for the murder of David Sellars, a free white man, on the 11th of November, 1845.

The case was transferred to Perry county by change of venue, and at the September term, 1849, of said court, the prisoner was brought to the bar and put upon his trial. The prisoner challenged the panel for cause, and upon the examination of the jurors it appeared that several of them were only householders, and not freeholders. The court ruled that the said jurors were competent; whereupon, they were put to the prisoner, and a jury was elected by him, he having challenged peremptorily only thirty-two jurors. Two of the jurors elected were householders only.

It was then proved, that on the night of the 11th of November, 1845, the prisoner and a number of other negroes were at a corn-husking, at the house of John Nesbit, having been invited to assist in husking and putting up the corn and husks. After the husking was over, and while the hands were employed in putting away the husks, a quarrel arose between some of the negroes, of whom Nelson was one. The deceased (who was the son-in-law of Nesbit, and had been requested by

Nesbit to superintend the putting away of the husks), procured a stick and struck one of the negroes. Nelson thereupon spoke in an abrupt manner to Sellars, who then struck Nelson two or three blows with the stick or club. It was a hickory stick as large as a chair-post. Some of the negroes, and Nelson among them, then went off, twenty or thirty yards, in the direction of their home. They were called back to get their supper, by Ellis Nesbit, the son of the owner of the corn. When they went back to the place where the corn had been husked, Sellars, the deceased, spoke to Nelson, who was in front, saying, "You have come back again, have you?" To which Nelson replied, "Yes, and if you will give me a white man's chance, I will whip you like damnation." The deceased then struck Nelson several times with the stick, knocking him down or to his knees; and as Nelson recovered, the deceased struck him with the stick again, and Nelson, pressing up towards the deceased, stabbed him with a long knife which had been made by grinding a file to an edge or point. The deceased cried out, "I am stabbed;" and Nelson was pulled away and then ran off. The deceased lived but a short time after the stab was given. He was an athletic man, weighing 160 or 170 pounds, and had been overseer for Mr. Elliot, (but was not his overseer at the time of the stabbing.) When Nelson and others started towards home, they were not gone more than a minute or two before they were back again.

Joe, a slave, a witness for the defendant, proved that Nelson is a basket-maker, and had the knife with which the stabbing was done, to work in white oak, and that he usually carried it about him. Nelson had one or two bad cuts on his head, made by the blows inflicted by the deceased, and the blood was running down his face. This is all the material testimony.

The court charged the jury, "That the distinction made by the statute between murder in the first, and murder in the second degree, did not apply to the defendant; that if the proof satisfied the jury that the defendant was guilty of murder as defined by the common law, it would require them to find him guilty as charged in the bill of indictment; that malice was the distinguishing characteristic between murder and manslaughter, so far as the defendant was concerned; that murder in a slave, according to the common law definition, was a capital offence; and that the court knew of no punishment authorized by law that the court could inflict for the offence of manslaughter in a slave.

The court further charged the jury, "That a white man was authorized by law to correct the slave of another, in a reasonable manner, for insolence, with a view of stopping the insolence; but when the insolence ceased, the correction should cease. That a slave may resist a stranger who attacks him in a manner to endanger his life or limb, or to do him some great bodily harm; that to make a slave excusable for killing a white man who has no right of control over him, but who attacks him in a manner dangerous to life or limb, or calculated to do him some great bodily harm, he must retreat as far as he can, unless the attack is so fierce that it would be more dangerous to retreat than to resist."

The court charged the jury, "That the great distinction between homicide committed with malice, and that committed in a transport of passion suddenly excited by a grievous provocation, is as steadily to be kept in view in the trial of a slave charged with the murder of a white man, as in that of a white man charged with the murder of his equal, or of a slave. But the same matters which would be deemed in law a sufficient provocation to free a white man who has committed homicide in a moment of passion, from the guilt of murder, will not have the same effect when the party slain is a white man and the offender a slave. For though among equals the general rule is, that words are not, but blows are a sufficient provocation; yet there may be words of reproach so aggravating when uttered by a slave, as to excite in a white man the temporary fury which negatives the charge of malice." The court also charged the jury, "That so far as the offence of murder was concerned, the defendant was entitled in all respects to be treated as if he were a white man."

Upon this evidence, and charge of the court, the jury returned the following verdict: "We find Nelson, a slave, guilty of murder in the second degree, and submit him to the mercy of the court."

The defendant moved for a new trial, and offered the affidavit of William Horner, A. J. Taylor, Thomas Fortner, Caswell Cotham, and Richard Tucker, five of the jurors before whom the prisoner was tried, who state, "that they agreed to render the verdict of murder in the second degree, with a recommendation to the mercy of the court, upon the ground only that they believed, from the argument of their fellow-jurors and the charge of the court, that the court had the power to commute the punishment from hanging to any less punishment." They state that when they agreed first to offer the verdict above spoken of, in conjunction with their fellow-jurors, and the court refused to receive the same, they supposed that the court had refused to accept the verdict and exercise any power to commute the punishment. But when they were sent for the last time, they then supposed that the court had come to the determination to receive the verdict and commute the punishment according to the former views; and it was in this view of the case, and this only, that they would ever have been induced to join in the verdict rendered in this case. They further state, that all the jurors generally seemed to be of opinion that the court, by sending for them, had agreed to accept their verdict with the understanding stated above."

While the argument for a new trial was pending, the prisoner offered the affidavit of A. J. Taylor, one of the jurors, who states, "that at the rendition of the verdict, he did not believe that the defendant was guilty of murder, or any higher offence than manslaughter, and only agreed to said verdict for the causes stated in the former affidavit."

The court overruled the motion for a new trial, and pronounced sentence of death upon the prisoner; from which judgment the prisoner appealed to this court.

Several questions of considerable importance are raised by this record.

And first, has a stranger a right to chastise the slave of another person?

In South Carolina, it is held that the criminal offense of assault and battery cannot be committed upon a slave. State v. Minor, 2 Hill, 453; State v. Chentwood, 2 Hill, 459; Hilton v. Carton, 2 Baily, 98; White v. Chambers, 2 Bay, 70. The slave is not regarded as being within the peace of the State; and, therefore, the peace of the State is not broken by an assault and battery on him. He can look alone to his master for protection, who may maintain trespass for a battery on his slave.

But, in North Carolina, a different doctrine prevails, and one much more consonant to our feelings of humanity, and much more calculated to preserve the peace and good order of society. It is there held, that the principles of the common law, where there is no legislation on the subject, moulded and suited to our social condition, must be held to apply to offences committed upon a slave.

In the case of the State v. Hale, 2 Hawks. 582, Chief Justice Taylor says: "It would be a subject of regret to every thinking person, if courts of justice were restrained, by any austere rule of judicature, from keeping pace with the march of benignant policy and provident humanity, which for many years has characterised every legislative act relative to the protection of slaves, and which christianity, by the mild diffusion of its light and influence, has contributed to promote." And, again, he says, "When the authority of the master is usurped by a stranger, nature is disposed to assert her rights, and prompt the slave to resistance. The public peace is thus as much broken as if a free man had been beaten. A wanton injury committed by a slave is a great provocation to the owner, awakens his resentment, and has a direct tendency to a breach of the peace, by inciting him to seek immediate vengeance; and, if resented in the heat of blood, it would probably extenuate a homicide to manslaughter. These offences are usually committed by men of dissolute habits, hanging loose upon society, who, being repelled from association with well-disposed citizens, take refuge in the company of colored persons and slaves, whom the deprave by their example, embolden by their familiarity, and then beat, under the expectation that a slave dare not resent a blow from a white man." In view of these considerations, the court rule, that an assault and batter upon a slave by a stranger is indictable. But in view of the actual condition of society, and the difference that exists between the two races, many circumstances that would not constitute a legal provocation for a battery by one white man on another, would justify it if committed on a slave, provided the battery were not excessive.

We fully concur with this view of the subject taken by the supreme court of North Carolina. We think it alike necessary to secure the rights of the master, to protect the slave from wanton abuse, and to save white men from injury and insult.

2. The next question is, may homicide committed by a slave on a free white man, not excusable in self-defence, be reduced below the grade of murder?

Upon this subject, the charge of his honor, the circuit judge, is vague and indistinct. It is true that in one part of the instruction, it is said, "that the great distinction between homicide committed with malice, and that committed in a transport of passion, excited by a grievous provocation, is as steadily to be kept in view in the trial of a slave charged with the murder of a white man, as in that of a white man charged with the murder of his equal." And again, in conclusion, he says, "that, so far as murder is concerned, the defendant is to be treated as if he were a white man."

These passages of instruction to the jury, taken alone, indicate pretty clearly that the judge was of opinion that manslaughter might be committed by a slave. But in another part of the instruction he says, "the court knows of no punishment authorized by law, that the court could inflict for the offence of manslaughter in a slave." Again he says, "a white man is authorized by law to correct the slave of another, in a reasonable manner, for insolence; that a slave may resist a stranger who attacks him in a manner to endanger his life or limb, or to do him some great bodily harm; that to make a slave excusable in killing a white man, who has no right or control over him, but who attacks him in a manner dangerous to life or limb, or calculated to do him some great bodily harm, he must retreat as far as he can, unless the attack is so fierce that it would be more dangerous to retreat than to resist."

The sense of these latter passages seem applicable alone to a case of excusable self-defence. The judge says, in substance, that a white man may correct the slave of another for insolence, but if the attack on the slave endanger his life or limb, or put him in danger of great bodily harm, and he cannot retreat, he is excusable, if he slay his assailant; but that the court knows of no punishment for manslaughter committed by a slave.

The case put by his honor would be clearly a case of self-defence, and, as stated by him, the slave would be excusable, and he excludes the consideration of a case of manslaughter altogether, not only by failing to put a possible case in which it may be committed, but by expressly stating that there was no punishment provided by law for that offence; thus leaving it to be inferred by the jury that the offence did not exist.

The question then is, did his honor err in this view of the subject? And it may be observed here, that the question is not, whether the owner of a slave may be guilty of an assault and battery, by the immoderately beating his slave, or whether, if a slave slay his master while he is enduring a cruel and inhuman chastisement, such killing could be mitigated to manslaughter.

We are aware that the supreme court of North Carolina, in the case of the State *v.* Mann, 2 Dev. 263, held that the master is not liable to an indictment for a battery committed on his slave, no matter how cruel and excessive such battery may be. And Judge Turley, in the case of The State *v.* Jacob, 3 Humph. 920, says, "The right to obedience and submission in all lawful things, on the part of the slave, is perfect in the master, and the power to inflict any punishment, not affecting

life or limb, which he may consider necessary for the purpose of keeping him in such submission, and enforcing such obedience to his commands, is secured to him by law, and if, in the exercise of it, with or without cause the slave resist and slay him, it is murder and not manslaughter, because the law cannot recognize the violence of the master as a legitimate cause of provocation." But Green, judge, in the same case, says, "I think proper to announce distinctly as my opinion, that there may exist cases in which the killing a master by a slave would be manslaughter. What circumstances of torture, short of endangering life or limb, would so reduce a homicide, it is not easy to indicate. Every such case must rest upon its peculiar facts. The rights and duties of the parties must form the *criteria* by which an enlightened court and jury should act."

Judge Reese expressed no opinion upon this point, nor was there anything in the case to call for the *dicta* above referred to. The whole court concurred in the opinion that there was no mitigating circumstance in the case, and that it was most clearly a case of murder.

But the case now before the court is of a different character altogether. The man who was killed, was neither the master, nor overseer of the slave. He received the wound while he was inflicting severe blows, with a heavy cudgel, upon the prisoner's head. It becomes necessary, therefore, that we determine whether, in such a case, manslaughter may be committed. In Jacob's case, before referred to, it is asserted, that the principles of the common law are applicable to the relations that exist between the slave and his master, and with much more reason may we assert, that those principles are applicable when the slave inflicts an injury on a white man, who is a stranger. The statute (1819, ch. 35, sec. 1) declares, that murder, when committed by a slave, shall be punished with death. Now, what murder is, we learn from the definition of the common law. It is, "where a person of sound memory and discretion, unlawfully killeth any reasonable creature in being, with malice aforethought." 3d Inst. 47. A slave, then, who commits a homicide, is punishable with death, if it be done "with malice aforethought." And, unless it be so done, he is not guilty of murder. But, the killing being established, the law presumes that it was done maliciously, and circumstances of alleviation, or excuse, must be shown by the accused.

In general, if a party that is struck, strikes again, and death ensues, it is only manslaughter. The law regards the blow as a sufficient provocation to excite the passions, so that the party acts under the influence of the sudden heat, and not from malice. But a slight assault will not always extenuate a killing to manslaughter; much depends upon the character of the weapon used, in reference to the provocation. There must be a reasonable proportion between the mode of resentment, and the provocation to reduce the offence of killing to manslaughter. Archb. Crim. L. 392. So if there be proof of malice, at the time of the killing, the existence of provocation will not reduce it to manslaughter. For, although the provocation usually repels the presumption of malice, yet,

if its actual existence be established, notwithstanding the provocation, it is murder, and not manslaughter. 1 Russ. on Cr. 440; Roscoe's Cr. Ev. 627.

How then shall these principles be applied to the case of a slave who kills a white man?

The common law is the breast of the judges, and must be expounded under the influence of enlightened reason. Thus guided, it is manifest, that the same indignity which would excite the passions of a white man, would not have a like effect upon a slave. That which would be a grievous provocation to the one, would provoke the other but slightly. This difference arises from the different habits of feeling, and modes of thought, of the two races. In view of reason, then, the common law cannot hold that an act, constituting a provocation, which would mitigate a homicide committed by a white man to manslaughter, shall have a like effect when the homicide is committed on a white man, by a slave. So to hold, would be a perversion of the principles of the common law by sticking to its letter. It would be to disregard entirely the character and condition of this portion of our population, and would be as repugnant to reason, as it would be mischievous in practice.

It does not, however, follow that a provocation may not be so grievous as that, if the slave slay the white man, it will be but manslaughter, although the life or limb of the party killing, is not endangered. On the contrary, we think there is no doubt but the cases may exist, where the slave committing the homicide, although not excusable, as having acted in self-defence, yet he cannot be deemed to have done the act with malice aforethought.

In the case of the The State *v.* Will (1 Dev. & B. 121), Judge Gaston, delivering the opinion of the court, held the killing to be manslaughter only. In that case, too, the person killed was the overseer, and had authority to punish the prisoner. The deceased had attempted to punish the prisoner, who ran off, refusing to submit. The deceased got a gun, loaded with shot, and firing on the prisoner inflicted wounds in his back. He then pursued and overtook the prisoner, and a scuffle ensued, and the prisoner inflicted a fatal stab on the arm of the deceased with a knife, the overseer then being unarmed. Here the prisoner was not acting in self-defence, but in the heat of blood, occasioned by the smarting wounds, the act was done, and the court held that it was not done with malice.

The court cannot point out with precise accuracy, what particular extent of provocation will reduce such homicide to manslaughter. Each case must depend very much on its own circumstances, and must be left to the enlightened judgment of the jury.

If the slave has misbehaved, and by his insolence has provoked merited chastisement, and punishment be reasonably inflicted upon him, it is his duty to submit; and if he resist, and slay the person chastising him, it will be murder. But if the punishment be unreasonable and excessive, the killing will only be manslaughter.

If a slave, not having misbehaved or given cause for offence, is assaulted and beaten by a stranger, who has no authority over him, and he kill the person so beating him, such killing will be extenuated to manslaughter, in cases where such extenuation would not exist, if by insolence and misconduct, the slave had provoked chastisement.

Having thus stated our opinion, that by our law, manslaughter may be perpetrated by a slave, it follows that if the charge of the court to the jury, excluded the investigation of the question of manslaughter, in this case, his honor erred. And that it was so excluded, we think has been made apparent, by the review of the charge we have presented in the former part of this opinion.

The court also misled the jury, when he told them, in effect, that there was no law in this State by which manslaughter could be punished.

It is true, the indictment of a slave for murder, does not include a charge of manslaughter, because by the act of 1819, ch. 35, sec. 1, murder, committed by a slave, is declared to be capital, and by the act of 1835, ch. 19, sec. 9, exclusive original jurisdiction is given to the circuit courts, of all offences committed by slaves which are punishable with death, and as manslaughter is not so punishable, the circuit court has no jurisdiction thereof, and, therefore, it cannot be included in the indictment filed in that court.

But if it exists as an offence, it is punishable. By the act of 1741, ch. 24, sec. 48 (1 Scott Rev. 74,75), any crime committed by a slave, was to be tried before three justices, and four freeholders and slaveholders, and punished at their discretion. By the act of 1783, ch. 14, sec. 2 (1 Scott Rev. 279), trivial offences were to be tried before one justice alone, and punished not exceeding forty lashes. But if the justice was of opinion that the offender deserved a greater punishment, he was to commit him to jail to be tried as theretofore. By the act of 1815, ch. 138, sec. 1 (2 Scott Rev. 246, 247), the 48th section of the act of 1741 is repealed, and it is provided, ["] that offences committed by slaves shall be tried before three justices and nine freeholders and slaveholders, and if found guilty they shall pass such judgment, according to their discretion, as the nature of the crime or offence shall require." By the act of 1819, ch. 35, sec. 1, murder, arson, burglary, rape, and robbery, are declared capital, to be punished with death, and all other offences are to be punished as heretofore; provided that the punishment in no case shall extend to life or limb, except in the cases above enumerated. It will be seen from this review of the statutes, that all offences committed by slaves, the punishment of which is not specifically provided for by statute, may be punished at the discretion of the court and jury; provided such punishment extend not to life or limb. The act of 1815, ch. 138, is not in the compilation of Nicholson and Caruthers, and the act of 1783, ch. 14, is entirely misconceived by them, and we suppose his honor was misled by that work.

The jury were led to the inevitable conclusion, by the charge of the court, that unless the prisoner was convicted of murder, he would be excused altogether from any punishment, and thus, doubtless, were influenced by this misdirection to render the verdict returned by them.

3. The verdict of the jury is wholly inapplicable to the case before them. They say, the "find Nelson, a slave, guilty of murder in the second degree, and submit him to the mercy of the court."

There is no second degree of murder, as to slaves, and perhaps, if the case depended alone upon the form of the verdict, the court might pronounce judgment upon it, regarding as surplusage, the words "second degree." But when we remember, that the law of murder as to white men, is divided into the first and second degree—the first, punishable with death, and the second, not so punishable—and that this law is expounded and acted on every day in our courts, and is familiar to the minds of men generally, we cannot fail to perceive that the jury were laboring under erroneous impressions as to the law of the case then before them. They unquestionably supposed, that under their finding, a punishment short of death, would be inflicted. And this reference from the form of the verdict alone, is rendered still more certain, by the affidavit of five of the jurors. They say, that from the arguments of their fellow jurors, they were induced to believe, that if they found such a verdict, the court could adjudge a punishment short of death, and that if they had not so believed, they never would have consented to a verdict of guilty. They say, when they came into court with their verdict, the court refused to receive it, and sent them back, but soon after, sent for them again, and did receive the verdict; thereby confirming their first impression, that the court would not pronounce sentence of death on the prisoner.

We think this is a stronger case than

that of Crawford, in 2 Yerg. The affidavit of the jurors, when taken alone, constitutes it very analogous to Crawford's case. But when we connect with their affidavit, the form of the verdict, by which the facts they state are rendered certainly true, all the danger which would otherwise exist, in receiving affidavits of jurors to impeach their verdict, is obviated. We do not think, that a verdict ought to stand, when the life of a human being is involved, which has been rendered under the influence of such manifest misconceptions of the legal effect of it; especially where these misconceptions have been produced, and fortified by the action of the court.

In the first place, the charge of the court left the jury under the impression, that unless the prisoner were punished for murder, he could not be punished at all, and they, acting under that mistaken opinion, resorted to this form of a verdict, to effect what they were led to suppose was the judgment of the law, and, at the same time, to save the life of the prisoner. Besides it is seriously doubted by some members of the court, whether the verdict is an answer to the indictment.

The indictment is a charge for murder, simply. It includes no different grades of crime. The verdict could only be "guilty" or "not guilty." But this verdict has manifest reference to an entirely different character of indictment; one which includes three grades of felonious homicide. The jury had in their minds, therefore, an indictment wholly different from that actually before them, and intended their verdict as an answer to that, and not to the case now before us.

4. Upon the facts of the case, we forbear any commentary. If Nelson, after leaving, and starting towards home, conceived the design to inflict injury on the deceased, in revenge for the blows he had received, and returned armed, and intending, by insolence, to provoke blows again, and then to stab, it would be an aggravated case of murder. But if, without any such purpose, he returned, because he had been invited to come back to supper, and his insolent reply was prompted on a sudden, by the address of the deceased, and the previous infliction of blows, then it will be for the jury to determine whether the blows inflicted on him, exceeded a proper chastisement for his insolence. If they did not, it would be still a case of murder. But if the blows were inflicted with a weapon, and in a manner cruel and excessive, in view of the prisoner's insolence, the killing would be only manslaughter, and of this the jury must judge.

5. As to the qualification of the jurors, there is no error. By the act of 1835, ch. 19, sec. 11, it is provided that all persons who would be competent jurors on the trial of a free person, shall be competent on the trial of a slave. On the trial of a free person, householders are competent jurors, and therefore, householders were competent to try this case.

Upon the whole, we think there is error in the record, and that the judgment should be reversed, and the prisoner remanded for another trial.

45. Hanging and Quartering in 1733

By English law dismemberment was a regular feature of punishment for petty treason, and the murder of whites by slaves was defined as petty treason. This punishment could not be assigned by county courts, but by special courts of oyer and terminer. P. G. Miller, who secured the copies of the following proceedings and sent them to the *Virginia Magazine of History and Biography* in 1893, did so to prove that such harsh penalties were actually set in the eighteenth century in Virginia. In 1749 two slaves were also executed for treason in Cambridge, Massachusetts, by being hung in chains and burned, respectively; and further cases in Virginia were reported in the *Virginia Magazine of History and Biography* in 1899 (vol. 7, P. 304). See also document no. 23. In short, while in the eighteenth century such barbarous punishments were undoubtedly common throughout the Colonies, it is plain that more offenses were punishable in this way for slaves than for free persons.

At a Court called for Goochland County the twenty-fifth day of June MDCCXXXIII, for the tryall of Champion a Negro man slave, Lucy, a Negro woman slave, both belonging to Hutchins Burton, Sampson, Harry, & George, three Negro men slaves belonging to William Randolph, Esq'r, & Valentine, a negro man slave belonging to Bowler Cocke gent.

A commission from the Hon'ble William Gooch Esq'r His Majesty's Lieut Governor & Commander in chief of this Dominion to John Fleming, William Mayo, Daniel Stoner, Tarlton Fleming, Allen Howard, Edward Scott, George Payne, William Cabbell, James Holman, Isham Randolph, James Skelton, George Raine, & Anthony Hoggatt, gent. to be Justices of Oyer and Terminer for the tryall of Champion a Negro man slave, Lucy a Negro woman slave both belonging to Hutchins Burton, Sampson, Harry, & George, three Negro men slaves belonging to William Randolph Esq'e & Valentine a Negro man slave belonging to Bowler Cocke gent. being read as also the Dedimus for administering the Oaths & Test therein mentioned George Payne & Anthony Hoggatt gent. administter the oaths appointed by Act of Parliament to be taken instead of the Oaths of Allegiance and Supremacy the Oath appointed to be taken by an Act of Parliament made in the first year of the reign of his late

Source: *Virginia Magazine of History and Biography*, 3 (January 1894):328–30.

Ordered that the heads & quarters of Champion & Valentine be set up in severall parts of this County.

A Copy—Teste:

P. G. MILLER,
Deputy Clerk Goochland County Court.

November 23d, 1893.

At a Court held for Goochland County the ninth day of October Anno Domi MDCCXXXIII for laying the County leevy.

Present:

John ffleming, Daniel Stoner, Tarlton ffleming, George Payne, William Cabbell, James Skelton, Gent. Justices.

Goochland County	Dr.	Tobacco.

To Thomas Walker & Joseph Dabbs sub-sherifs for a mistake in the levey in 1732. — 10

To Do. For going to Williamsburg for a Comission of Oyer & Terminer to try Champion, Lucy, Valentine, Sampson, Harry & George, Negros 90 miles going at 2lb and 90 miles returning at 2lb p. mile — 360

To Do. for sumoning the Justices and attending the Court for the tryal of the said Negros — 200

To Do. for Executing Champion & Valentine, 250lb each — 500

To Do. for providing Tarr, burying the trunk, cutting out the quarters a Pott, Carts & horses, carrying and setting up the heads & quarters of the two Negros at the places mentioned by order of Court — 2000

To Do. for gallows & ropes to hang the two said Negros — 60

To Do. for 24 days imprisonment of Champion @ 5lb p. day — 120

To Do. for 22 days imprisonment of Lucy @ 5lb — 110

To Do. for Comitment & releasment of Lucy, Sampson, George & Harry — 80

To Do. for 12 days imprisonment of Valentine @ 5lb — 60

To Do. for 4 days imprisonment of Sampson @ 5lb — 20

To Do. for 4 days imprisonment of Harry @ 5lb — 20

To Do. for 4 days imprisonment of George @ 5lb — 20

An Extract—Teste

P. G. MILLER,
Dep. Clerk Goochland Co. Ct.

Nov. 23d, 1893.

Majesty King George the ffirst Entitled An Act for the further security of his Majesty's person and Government and the Succession of the Crown in the Heirs of the late Princess Sophia being Protestants and for extinguishing the hopes of the pretended Prince of Wales and his open & secret abettors, unto John ffleming & Daniel Stoner, gent. who Subscribe the Test take the Oath for duly executing the Office of a Commissioner of Oyer and Terminer, and then administer the said Oaths & Test unto Tarlton ffleming, George Payne, James Skelton & Anthony Hoggatt, gent.

Champion being brought to the Barr an Indictment against him for feloniously murdering Robert Allen of this County is read the prisoner confesses himself guilty of the said murder and it is thereupon considered by the court that he return to the place from whence he came and from thence to the place of Execution there to be hanged by the neck on Wednesday next between the hours of eleven and two till he be dead. The Court value the said Negro at thirty pounds Curr't money.

George, Sampson & Harry, being brought to the Barr several Indictments against them for feloniously murdering Robert Allen of this County are read the prisoners plead not guilty whereupon the Witnesses & the prisoners defence being heard it is the opinion of the Court that they are not guilty and they are thereupon acquitted.

Valentine being brought to the Barr an Indictment against him for feloniously murdering Robert Allen of this County is read the prisoner pleads not guilty whereupon the Witnesses & the prisoners defence being heard it is the opinion of the Court that he is guilty and it is considered that he return to the place from whence he came and from thence to the place of Execution there to be hanged by the neck on Wednesday next between the hours of eleven & two till he be dead. The Court value the said Negro at forty pounds Curr't money.

Lucy being brought to the Barr an Indictment against her for feloniously murdering Robert Allen of this County is read the prisoner pleads not guilty and whereupon the Witnesses and the prisoners defence being heard it is the opinion of the Court that she is not guilty of the murder but upon Consideration that she is supposed to have known of the murder after it was committed & did not discover [1] the same it is Ordered that she receive on her bare back twenty one lashes well laid on at the Comon whipping post & that she be then discharged.

---

1. "Discover" in this usage means "disclose."

===

46. Punishing Black Thieves in 1802

===

Stealing was the most frequent violation of the law charged against slaves. In rural areas depredation of livestock was a constant annoyance for planters. In the cities clothing and small articles disappeared. Sometimes thieves were very bold, as in the case reported below. The barbarous punishments of the eighteenth century had not disappeared in 1802, as the reader of this notice in the *Virginia Recorder* will see.

Source: *Virginia Recorder* (Richmond, Va.), January 30, 1802.

Negro Theft.

In last Saturday's "RECORDER," we took some notice of one GEORGE, a negro fellow, who attempted to rob the cellar of Robert Gordon, of this city. He walked into it in broad day, stripped off his own great coat, put on a new one which he found in the cellar, and then his own above it. He was marching out of the cellar with an armfull of plunder, and with all the cool appearance of a person that belonged to it. Unfortunately for this veteran thief, he was met in the teeth by a person belonging to Gordon, who stopt him. He was immediately stript and examined; and it was found, that the coat, which he called *his own*, had been stolen by Mr. George from the very same cellar about a year ago. Nobody doubts that he is a consummate hardened villain. He will certainly receive a good whipping; besides being burnt upon the hand. It would be much better to hang him at once; for society can never lose any thing by the death of a rascal. His master says, that he has been a perpetual plague to his family, as the fellow could never be kept from stealing every thing that came within his reach.

This amiable unit of the human race has, within this fortnight past, been twice, besides this time, in the hands of justice. One of the charges was supported by testimony truly diverting. A man had got his store robbed; and had lost out of it a few tobacco pipes, and some gingerbread. A negro girl, of five years of age, told him that she had seen George coming out of the store, and that he had given her some of the gingerbread. The fellow was apprenhended. The magistrates were convened. The *witness* was examined; and the suit dismissed.

The other charge was of a more serious nature. A robbery was committed some weeks ago, at the Eagle Tavern; and George was intercepted with the whole, or a great part of the plunder in his possession. He was taken to a store, where the property was deposited, while the thief was sent to prison. The gentlemen to whom the articles belonged, went to the store, and took them away. At the trial, the only evidence produced was that of the person who apprehended George, and one of the gentlemen who had been robbed. The former looked into the breast of a shirt which the latter had on, and swore that he believed this shirt to be one of those which had been found in the possession of George. The gentleman attested that the shirt was his. But no other part of the stolen property was produced. Mr. Munford, of the house of assembly, who was one of the principal sufferers, declined to appear. The store-keeper, with whom the goods had been deposited, was likewise absent. The whole evidence, therefore, turned upon the belief, of the person who apprehended the robber, that the shirt which he saw upon the gentleman's back was positively one of the shirts stolen. Now, it is very common for a person to have a dozen shirts, of which neither the maker, nor the owner can distinguish any one from the rest. This, therefore, was the loosest evidence imaginable.

By laws of this state, when a negro is tried before five judges, it is necessary for his condemnation, that they should be unanimous against him. In the present case, the infamy of the prisoner's character, and the strong circumstantial evidence, convinced every one in the court that George was guilty; but there was not a sufficiency of direct evidence to convict him. Four of the magistrates were for sending the fellow to the whipping-post. His back was saved, for that time, by the justice, or humanity of capt. Richardson. One of the gentlemen, who was in the majority, has since altered his opinion, and thought that capt. R. was in the right.

In London, this ingenious adventurer would not always have escaped with so readiness. His person perhaps, would have been described and advertised, and all people, who wished to see him, would have been invited to come and look at him. In the present case, it signifies very little to let such a culprit escape with a bare whipping. In six weeks after his discharge, both his hand and his shoulders will be again *fit for business;* and after six, eight, or ten fresh robberies, he will, possibly, be whipped a second time.[1]

1. *Since this article was written, George has been tried, branded, and completely whipt.*

---

47.   On the Treadmill in Charleston Jail

Imprisonment was never the standard means of punishment for slaves, because loss of time was the master's loss and not that of the slaves. Whipping was more logical. But in Southern cities owners often sent slaves to prison for the administration of lashing or other punishments. In some cities they were required to make punishments through the penal institution, rather than privately.

Prisoners of the state were of course incarcerated. Karl Bernhard, Duke of Saxe-Weimar, visited the United States in 1825–26, and because of his interest in prison reform, he took special note of arrangements in Charleston for the punishment of offenders. From his account it is clear that the treadmill was a recent innovation, that two prisoners from the Denmark Vesey plot (see document 28) were still in jail, and that the Duke regarded idleness as a bad thing in prisons. Most slaves who found themselves in jail were there because their masters sent them there for some offense against household discipline.

Source: Karl Bernhard, Duke of Saxe-Weimar Eisenach, *Travels through North America during the Years 1825 and 1826,* 2 vols. (Philadelphia: Carey, Lea & Carey, 1828), 2:8–10.

The state prison is a small building. The prisoners are too much crowded together, and have no employment. The atrocious criminals live in the upper story, and are immured two together in a cell, without ever being permitted to come into the open air. This is allowed only to those dwelling in the first story, consisting of debtors, and persons who are imprisoned for breaches of the peace. The walls within, as well as the flooring, are of strong oak wood. In each apartment is an iron ring in the floor, for the purpose of securing dangerous prisoners. In the upper story there is a negro confined, who, implicated in one of the late conspiracies, had not committed himself so far as to allow of his being hung; nevertheless, his presence appeared so dangerous to the public tranquillity, that he is detained in prison till his master can find some opportunity to ship him to the West Indies, and there sell him. In another room was a white prisoner, and it is not known whether he be an American or Scotchman, who involved himself by his writings deeply in the last negro conspiracy. The prisoners received their food while we were present: it consisted of very good soup, and three-quarters of a pound of beef. Upon the ground floor is the dwelling of the keeper, who was an Amsterdam Jew, and the state-rooms in which gentlemen, who are lodged here, receive accommodation for money and fair words. The cleanliness of the house was not very great; upon the whole it left an unfavourable impression upon me.

I found the other prison, destined for the punishment of minor offences of the negro slaves, in a better condition. In it there were about forty individuals of both sexes. These slaves are either such as have been arrested during the night by the police, or such as have been sent here by their masters for punishment. The house displays throughout a remarkable neatness; black overseers go about every where armed with cow-hides. In the basement story there is an apparatus upon which the negroes, by order of the police, or at the request of their masters, are flogged. The latter can have nineteen lashes inflicted on them according to the existing law. The machine consists of a sort of crane, on which a cord with two nooses runs over pullies; the nooses are made fast to the hands of the slave and drawn up, while the feet are bound tight to a plank. The body is stretched out as much as possible, and thus the miserable creature receives the exact number of lashes as counted off! Within a year, flogging occurs less frequently: that is to say, a tread-mill has been erected in a back building of the prison, in which there are two tread-wheels in operation. Each employs twelve prisoners, who work a mill for grinding corn, and thereby contribute to the support of the prison. Six tread at once upon each wheel, while six rest upon a bench placed behind the wheel. Every half minute the left hand man steps off the tread-wheel, while the five others move to the left to fill up the vacant place; at the same time the right hand man sitting on the bench, steps on the wheel, and begins his movement, while the rest, sitting on the bench, uniformly recede. Thus, even three minutes sitting, allows the unhappy being no repose.

The signal for changing is given by a small bell attached to the wheel. The prisoners are compelled to labour eight hours a day in this manner. Order is preserved by a person, who, armed with a cow-hide, stands by the wheel. Both sexes tread promiscuously upon the wheel. Since, however, only twenty-four prisoners find employment at once on both wheels, the idle are obliged in the interval to sit upon the floor in the upper chambers, and observe a strict silence. One who had eloped several times from a plantation, was fastened by a heavy iron ring, that passed over his leg to the floor. To provide against this state of idleness, there should be another pair of tread-wheels erected. The negroes entertain a strong fear of the tread-mills, and regard flogging as the lighter evil! Of about three hundred and sixty, who, since the erection of these treadmills, have been employed upon them, only six have been sent back a second time.

SIX
The Slave's Protest: Resistance Short of Rebellion

48. Bewitching Master and Mistress in South Carolina

Telling a pointed story is the mildest form of resistance available to the oppressed, especially if it is told in the third person, with a passable remoteness from specific persons. Storytelling could be very effective, however, as an outlet for bruised feelings, as the following "pointed" tales suggest. In each instance the master or the mistress, and in two instances both of them, become the victims of cunning and witchcraft.

The first three of these stories from slave days were told by Maria Middleton, who was born on Edisto Island in South Carolina several years before the Civil War. The fourth tale was written down by Louise Green, of St. Helena Island, who was much younger than Maria Middleton. They were taken down by Elsie Clews Parsons, as she heard them, for the American Folk-Lore Society. On the basis of much study of Caribbean folk tales, Parsons judged the "hag" stories to have been of African origin. There is no reason to doubt the spirit or authenticity of these stories as having originated as a mild protest of slavery.

[I]

Wen' to a witch-man. When his master 'mence to whip him, eve'y cut he give de man, his [master's] wife way off at home feel de cut. Sen' wor' please stop cut lick de man. When he [master] got home, his wife was wash down wid blood.

[II]

His master beat him so sevare, so de man went to a witch. De witch said, "Never min'! you go home. To-morrow you will see me." When de man got up in de mornin', de white man was jus' as happy as happy as happy can be; but de more de sun goes down, he commence ter sleep. At de same time he call to his Negro, "To-morrow you go an' do such an' such a tas'." Givin' out his orders kyan hardly hol' up his head. As soon as de sun was down, he down too, he down yet. De witch done dat. He [witch] come, but he stay in his home an' done dat.

[III]

A white man had a wife. Eve'y night his wife go, but he don' know where

Source: Elsie Clews Parsons, *Folk-Lore of the Sea Islands, South Carolina* (Cambridge, Mass., and New York: American Folk-Lore Society, 1923), p. 61–63.

his wife go to. He had a servant to wait on dem. So de servant whispered to his master, "Master, don' you know mistress kill all my chil'run?" Say, "Mistress is a hag."—"You think you can prove it? You think you can ketch her?"—"Yes, suh! you let me sleep here one night. I kyan ketch her." So de servant an' his master make de agreement how to ketch 'em. He said to his servan', "Don' you go home tonight. You sleep hyere. I'm goin' away soon in de mornin'." Dey bof (de man an' de wife) dey went to baid, de servan' on de watch. Late in de night de mistress woke up. De servan' watch her. Somet'in' she put on her flesh an' take off her skins. After take off her skins, she roll it up an' put it in her dirty clo'es in de back o' de baid. An' she gone out. After she gone out, de servan' call to her master, said, "Master, mistress is gone. To proof to you dat mistress is a hag, I come now an' show you what she done." She went back ob de baid an' get de clo'es what de skin in, an' bring it to her master, an' say, "Here is mistress skin." An' he said to his servan', "What shall we do wid de skin to ketch her?" She said, "Put black pepper an' salt in de skin on de inside." So de master did dat. So later on de mistress came an' get her skin. An' she 'mence to put it on; an' eve'y time de skin bu'n her so much, she said to de skin, "Skin, skin, you don' know me? 'Tis me." Still she couldn' get it on. So she went to her

baid an' wrapped up. Master was out now. She lay down till late. Her husband 'mence to p'ovoke her to get up. Still she won't get up. Jus' keep po'-vokin'. All at oncet he snatched off de cover off her, an' dere she was raw like a beef. So he called witnesses to prove. So dey make a kil' of lime an' put her in it, an' bu'n her down. But as much as de fire a-bu'nin', she never holler 'til dey t'row de skin in. De skin 'mence to scream. So dat was de en' of his wife.

[IV]

Once upon a time there was a old man in slavery. He told his master that he was cripple and couldn't work. So the man let him stay home to take care of his children. One day the master went away. When he came home, he find the man play on his banjo,—

"I was fooling my master seventy-two years,
And I am fooling him now."

He was singing this song away on his bango. His master caught him, and start to kill him by whipping him. So the old man went to the doctor Negro. The next day he was to be kill'. When his master started to whip him, every time the man start to whip him, none of the licks touch. And he had freedom.

49. Stealing from Old Master, Vicariously, in Louisiana

Stealing from the master was a predictable result of the slave system, and required small rationalization on the part of the slaves, especially where food was concerned. They reasoned that, in any case, master's property was merely being transferred. Cleverness in the transfer was much admired, however, and was often elevated to an art form in the tales told by slaves about the fireside, tales in which not the faintest sign of guilt or punishment appears for the astute thief. Bunglers are nevertheless punished, as the first of the following folk stories from Louisiana makes clear.

It was taken down by Professor Alcée Fortier of Tulane University sometime before 1888, and it concerns Brer Rabbit, always known in Louisiana as "Compair Lapin," and his inept friend Compair Bouki, who is the foolish victim of many of Compair Lapin's startling schemes. Although the storyteller ascribes feathers and a bill to Bouki, he is apparently taking literary license. In almost every story Bouki seems actually to be the foolish and cowardly victim—the American version of the hyena or jackal of African folk stories, who behaves the same way. Bouki is definitely too stupid to double for Brer Fox, who is "Compair Renard" in Louisiana anyhow; nor is he so bold or persistent as Brother Wolf, who sometimes gets the better of Brer Rabbit in Georgia and South Carolina.

To understand the second story it is only necessary to recognize in the phrase "Choal Djé" the phrase "cheval de Dieu," or "the Horse of God." He is, of course, a stand-in for Old Master, just as is the carter in the first story.

[I]
Compair Bouki and Compair Lapin.

One day, Compair Bouki, who was dying of hunger, went to see his old friend, Compair Lapin. He found him thinking of nothing, and occupied in cleaning some fish. Bouki asked where he had taken that. His old friend related his story to him. He told him: "You see, daddy, I went to watch for the fish cart on the road. I saw it com-

Source: Alcée Fortier, *Louisiana Folk-Tales in French Dialect and English Translation* (Boston and New York: Houghton Mifflin, 1895), pp. 110–11, 115–16.

ing; I lay down in the road, as if I was dead. The master of the cart came down right off to pick me off. He shook me up a little; and after that, he threw me in his cart, on a pile of fish. I did not move my feet, like Mr. Fox. I watched well the old master, until I saw he had forgotten me. I began quietly to throw all the fish in the road until we had nearly gone a mile further; then, when I thought I had enough, I jumped down and picked up all the fish which I had thrown in the road. There were one hundred or a thousand—I did not count; I was in such a hurry. I put them all by myself on my back, faster than I could; and I came straight here to eat them." Compair Bouki reflected a long while; he was a little afraid that if he tried to do the same thing, he would put himself again in trouble. Compair Lapin, who was looking at him with his good eyes, saw that his friend was reflecting too long. He told him: "Old friend, you are dying of hunger; do like me; go and watch for the cart on the road, steal as much as you can, and we shall have a grand festival."

Old Bouki, who was greedy, could not resist; he started, he lay down on the road as if he was dead for true, he lifted his feet in the air to deceive people better. When the master of the cart came very near, he saw old Bouki, who was playing his tricks to catch him. He came down with a big plantation whip, and gave him a whipping which had red pepper, black pepper, and salt, it burned so much. Compair Bouki remained one month in his bed after that. He did not have a single feather left, and had colics to his very beak. They gave him a great deal of tafia to give him strength; they put him in a large bath made with gumbo, and they made him drink some laurel tea all the time after that. When Compair Bouki was cured, he swore, but too late, that Compair Lapin would never deceive him again.

All the goats which are not rascals
Ought to fear the old rabbits.

[II]
Choal Djé

Choal Djé had a pond, and he allowed all the comrades to drink from it, except Compair Lapin and his comrades. One day he caught Compair Lapin near his pond. "If I catch you drinking from my pond, I shall make you pay a fine." Compair Lapin replied: "Well-ordained charity begins with one's self, and as you are the master I am not going to drink from your pond." But one day they killed a deer, and after having skinned it, they threw away the skin. Compair Lapin picked up the skin and passed his head in it; he then went to drink in Choal Djé's pond. When Choal Djé saw that, he advanced nearer and asked Compair Chévreil who it was that had marked him in that way. Compair Chévreil answered: "It is Compair Lapin who made the sign of the cross on me, and who put me in this condition, and if you don't let him drink in your pond, he will do the same thing with you."—"Well, you may tell Compair Lapin that he can come to drink in my pond with all his comrades. I don't want him to do the same thing with me."—Compair Lapin ran to his house, took off the skin, and came back with his comrades to drink in Choal Djé's pond. When Choal Djé saw him coming, he said to him:

"Drink as much as you want, Compair Lapin, with your comrades."—Compair Lapin was always more cunning than everybody else.

---

50. "Sheep-stealing" and "Lying Out" on St. Helena Island

Slave-owners who lived in the proximity of swamps where runaways were often "lurking" were not surprised when they lost livestock, as the following entries in a South Carolina planter's diary reveal. The casual nature of the references indicates that running away for a short time was not unusual in this coastal region of the state, and tends to confirm the often expressed opinion of the Southern gentry that most of the running away of slaves was within the neighborhood, and not to the North Star. The entries also show that slaves frequently received help, including supplies of food, from slaves who were not "lying out."

Thomas B. Chaplin, author of the diary from which these entries come, was an obscure ante-bellum planter who owned property on St. Helena Island, a man of modest education, but an instinctive diarist, who left a revealing record of value for the 1840s and 1850s. With a farmer's anxious eye to the weather, he faithfully recorded the vagaries of his hurricane-ridden coast, the condition of crops, and the management of slave labor. Of malingering and runaway slaves he once observed resignedly that they would "have their time out." Documents 40 and 75 are also from Chaplin's diary, which has not been published. Slave-owner Sandiford of the following entry is the same planter whose slave died under correction in document 40 above.

May 15th [1845]—

Went very early in the morning to take a cat hunt with the Major, but in-stead of starting a wild cat we started 2 runaways belonging to James San-diford—Charles & Peter. We got a

Source: Thomas B. Chaplin, Manuscript Diary, South Carolina Historical Society, Charleston, S.C.

number of fellows working in a[d]jacent fields & gave chase, but they were too cunning for us—& gave us the slip, by taking to the marsh—after dropping their bag of provisions—cooking utensils &c &c. . . .

May 16th [1845]—

As soon as I was up, heard that a sheep had been killed in the pen last night, went to investigate the matter, found the meat in old Sancho's house. Rode in the field after breakfast, had Sancho tied. As soon as he found that he was found out he said that Mr. Sandiford's Charles, (the fellow that we started yester-day), came and gave him the meat, but after several doubtful tales I came to the conclusion that Sancho was leagued with the runaways, as he sais that Charles was to return the same night, & eat some of the meat with him, & that he had retired to Toomer's woods for the day. Rode over to

the Majors, got the Capt & himself to ride with me in search of the fellow. We traversed the woods & hedges in vain—Saw nothing of the runaway— So returned home. . . .

May 17th [1845]—

Anthony did not catch Charles last night—but saw the other fellow that is out with Charles named Dick—did not catch him. But I am convinced that my man Sancho harbours the pair of them, as they have both been to see him. ———What shall be done with this old rascall. . . .

June 8th [1845] Sunday . . .

Heard that man Bidcome, driver on the estate of W. S. Chaplin, had caught runaway Dick, belonging to Mr. Sandiford, he & Charles his companion, were in the sheep pen, had two sheep tied. Charles escaped by nocking down one of the men. . . .

51. Helping the Overseer Lose the Crop

The phrase for work badly done in cases where an individual laborer's responsibility could not be readily discerned was "eye service," indicating that a particular slave performed well only so long as he or she was closely watched. The instance reported below seems to have been a case of collective "eye service" with the object of causing the overseer, a Mr. Carter, to lose the cotton crop. The slaves must have disliked him, and hoped that

Source: John Hartwell Cocke Papers, Alderman Library, University of Virginia, Charlottesville, Va.

he might, if discredited, be replaced by an overseer more to their liking.

Richard D. Powell, the writer of the letter reporting the slaves' scheme, was a manager of Gen. John Hartwell Cocke's estates in Mississippi and Alabama, and he had been associated with the General for many years as supervisor of the overseers, purchaser of supplies, and seller of Cocke's cotton crop. By 1857 General Cocke was well advanced in years, and living at his Virginia home, Bremo Bluff. For more details about Cocke's life, see the introduction to document 91.

Richard D. Powell to John Hartwell Cocke, August 14, 1857.

Columbus[,] Miss. 14th Aug. 1857
Dear Genl:
. . . I have written to Carter twice lately & from what he writes to me, all hands are getting on very well, & think you will make a plenty of Corn & as much, or more Cotton than you made last year, at hopewell. The negroes attempted in a very friendly way in May to make Carter loose the crop. After finding himself in the grass he took the place of his head man, or Driver, & put him to work the first row & all the other hands to follow him, & all hands slighted their work be covering up the grass lightly, & not Cutting it up when small, & he became so restless that he did not take time to see how the work was done, & had his plows run[n]ing about, & plowing a spot here, & a spot there, & where they did plow, they would let the plows run over the grass, & not plow it up. All hands found I understood all about it, & from the first of June Overseer & negroes have done well—Carter never did have such a plain talking from any man before, I reckon as I gave him & it has made [him] see plainly all his foolish ways & C —The negroes understood me fully too, & all was done in friendship, & love, with a promise of punishment when the Crop was Laid by, or a good barbacue, & one or two days rest. They had the barbacue last Saturday. I will go down in a few days if Mrs. Powells' health continues to improve, & will write you again from Hopewell— . . .
Yr. friend & Bro. in Christ
R. D. Powell Sr.
Genl. J. H. Cocke

52. Carpenter Ned: "Doing Literally Nothing"

In the following letter to his sister, Mrs. Howell Cobb, wife of Sen. Howell Cobb of Georgia, John B. Lamar of Macon (see also document 83) explains his troubles with an "idling" servant. He concludes that it is better not to send Ned where "there is no one he fears."

John B. Lamar to Mrs. Howell Cobb, April 17, 1846.

Yours of the 22nd came duly to hand. With reference to the building of your negro house, I expect it would be best under all the circumstances to have it done as John proposed, let some one find all the materials & do the work at a specific price. But $250 is a high price for a negro house & unless it is to be a mighty fine negro house.

Whoever does the work ought to furnish certain specifications, such as the dimensions of the house, the number of lights &c so that you can have some means of judging if you are not paying double price.

My man Ned the carpenter is idle or nearly so at the plantation. He is fixing gates & like the idle groom in Pickwick trying to fool himself into the belief that he is doing something. But on considering his general character for intemperance & disobedience, & quarrelsomeness I have concluded it would be best to pay a little too much for the house, rather than inflict him on you at this time. While I was gone I had him in town & on returning found that he had been drunk & fighting, and misbehaving in every way, so that I have banished him to rural life. He is an eye servant. If I was with him I could have the work done soon & cheap, but I am afraid to trust him off where there is no one he fears. He is doing literally nothing at home, and sparing him would not be a cents expense as to that, but I conclude that you do not feel like being annoyed, just now, as I fear & almost know he would annoy you, by getting drunk & raising a row on the lot. I shall sell the rascal the first chance I get.

Source: Ulrich B. Phillips, ed., Plantation and Frontier (Cleveland: A. H. Clark, 1909), 2:38.

53.   Colonel Carter's *Mr.* Toney, and Others: Malingering, Bad Work, Lying, and Drunkenness

In March of 1770 Col. Landon Carter of Sabine Hall engaged in a sustained trial of wills with a slave whom he referred to sarcastically as "Mr. Toney." Colonel Carter was an industrious, slightly dyspeptic, and ever-watchful planter who expected a lot—and was often disappointed. He succeeded enough of the time to run a highly effective plantation, but often commented in his voluminous diary on his difficulties with slaves. Problems of health (his own, his family's, his slaves') occupied much of his time, and he kept a keen eye open to discern whether a slave was malingering or really ill. Colonel Carter's complaints were continuous. "Mr. Toney's" failings only began the list of ways in which, to use the Colonel's language, a slave could be inhumane to his master!

Landon Carter, born in 1710, was the son of Robert "King" Carter of document 9, and the uncle of Robert Carter of Nomini Hall, Philip Fithian's employer (see document 11). Colonel Carter died in 1778.

The numeral at the beginning of the dateline of each entry selected refers to the day of the month.

5. *Monday* [September 1757]

Before day wind came to Northeast and rain and at day a great probability of Gust and so it continues. A good deal of tobacco on scaffolds cut down the 2d and 3d of the month. More Sicke people come in and so it has been every monday morning for near 3 weeks, but this peculiar to negroes who refuse to complain on Sundays because they look on that as holy day and don't care to be confined by phys-ick let their Sickness. Rain all day and gusty.

25. *Friday* [April 1766]

. . .

My man Bart came in this day, he has been gone ever since New year's day. His reason is only that I had ordered him a whipping for saying he then brought in two load of wood when he was coming with his first load only. This he still insists on was truth

Source: Jack P. Greene, ed., *The Diary of Colonel Landon Carter of Sabine Hall, 1752–1778,* 2 vols. (Charlottesville, 1965), 1:174; 290–92, 369–70, 373, 378, 429–30, 496.

Although the whole plantation asserts the contrary, and the boy with him. He is the most incorrigeable villain I beleive alive, and has deserved hanging; which I will get done if his mate in roguery can be tempted to turn evidence against him.

Bart broke open the house in which he was tyed and locked up; he got out before 2 o'clock but not discovered till night. Talbot is a rogue. He was put in charge of him. I do imagine the gardiner's boy Sam, a rogue I have suspected to have maintained Bart and Simon all the while they have been out And I sent this boy with a letter to the Island ferry at breakfast, but he never returned although he was seen coming back about 12 and was seen at night by Hart George at night pretending to be looking for his Cattle. I kept this fellow up two nights about these fellows before And have given Rit the Miller a light whipping as having fed them by the hands of Gardiner Sam.

5 Cattle died yesterday and 3 or 4 more in a decaying Situation. I have had them up to my Lucern field. Perhaps that may save them. My overseer Davis was advised to give me notice of the Poverty of the creatures before they faltered; but he is a sorry fellow and I beleive does not care though he pretends he does. He pretended the Creatures were out in the woods but they never went there; the wench never carried them out there at all in this day but he says it was his orders. I shall direct otherwise and get a man to see my orders obeyed.

27. *Sunday* [April 1766].

Yesterday my son brought a story from Lansdown old Tom, that Johnny

my gardiner had harboured Bart and Simon all the while they were out, Sometimes in his inner room and sometimes in my Kitchen Vault. Tom had this from Adam his wife's grandson That they were placed in the Vault in particular the day my Militia were hunting for them.

This Simon owned, and the boy Adam repeated it to me; but Tom of Landsdown said that George belonging to Capn. Beale[1] saw them in my quarter when he came from setting my Weir. It seemed to me so plausible that I sent Johnny [to] Goal [jail] and locked his son in Law Postilion Tom up. Note: every body denyed they had ever seen them and in Particular Mrs. Carter's wench Betty, wife to Sawney, brother of Simon, denyed that she had ever seen them; as she did to me with great impudence some days agoe. However Capn. Beale's George this day came to me and before Mrs. Carter told the story and in Simon's hearing That coming from the Weir he went into Frank's room and then into Sawney's room, when Simon came in to them. So that favourites and all are liars and villains.

These rogues could not have been so entertained without some advantage to those who harboured them; from whence I may conclude the making away of my wool, wheat etc., and the death of my horses. I never rightly saw into the assertion that negroes are honest only from a religious Principle. Johny is the most constant churchgoer I have; but he is a drunkard, a thief

1. Capt. William Beale (d. 1778), Richmond Co. planter and father of Winifred Travers Beale, wife of Robert Wormeley Carter. (*Greene note*)

and a rogue. They are only through Sobriety, and but few of them. . . .

15. *Thursday* [March 1770]

· · ·

Mr. Toney shall as certainly receive ample correction for his behaviour to me as that he and I live. The day before yesterday he began to pale in the garden and only fitted the rails to seven posts. When he began to put them up I was riding out and ordered him to leave the gateway into the garden as wide as the two piers next the gate on each side. Nay, I measured the ground off to him and showed him where the two concluding posts where to stand and the rest at 8 feet asunder from post to post to answer to the tenons of his rails and I asked him if he under stood me. He said he did and would do it so. I had been 2 hours out and when I came home nothing was done and he was gone about another jobb. I asked him why he served me so. He told me because it would not answer his design. The villain had so constantly interrupted my orders that I had given him about every jobb this year that I struck him upon the shoulders with my stick which having had ten year made out of hiccory so very dry and light had been long split and tied with packthread therefore shivered all to pieces and this morning, for that stroke which did not raise the least swelling nor prevent the idle dog from putting up the posts as I directed in which I convinced him that every thing answered, I say this morning he has laid himself up with a pain in that shoulder and will not even come out to take off a lock that he carried but 2 days agoe to Buckland's

smith on purpose to get the spring mended which broke again this morning. I might as well give up every Negroe if I submit to this impudence.

16. *Friday* [March 1770].

Yesterday was a bad day all day indeed. Abundance of rain and a good deal of snow which melted as it fell.

I do believe my old Carpenters intend to be my greatest rascals. Guy does not go about any jobb be it ever so trifling that he does not make three weeks or a month of it at least. The silling my Mudhouse, a jobb of not more than 3 days, he has already been above a fortnight about, and this morning when my people went to help to put the sills in, though he said he was ready for them, he had the rotten sills to cut out and because I told him he should certainly be called to account for it as I came back truly he was gone and no body knew where and had been gone for sometime but not about my house.

Mr. Tony, another rascal, pretends he is full of pain though he looks much better than any Negroe I have.

17. *Saturday* [March 1770].

Tony came abroad and was well entertained for his impudence. Perhaps now he may think of working a little . . .

23. *Friday* [March 1770]

· · ·

I came home but without Nassau or Nat, a drunken father and Son. The latter first mired my horse up to his saddle in crossing a marsh that none but a blind drunkard could ever venture upon and Mr. Nat so engaged with boon companions as never to get my chariot by which means I was to plung home 5 or 6 miles upon this mired horse without one person to assist me. I got home near sunset and about 8 o'clock came the Chariot with the drunken father and Son. This morning I ordered the son his deserts in part. The father I shall leave till another opportunity for though my old Servant I am too old a Master to be thus inhumanely treated.

31. *Saturday* [March 1770]

    · · ·

I think my man Tony is determined to struggle whether he shall not do as he pleases. He has with McGinis been 2 days only pailing in the dairy and henhouse yard with the posts ready hewed and morticed for him. I told him when I rode out this morning he would certainly get another whipping. He was ranging the pales at least one pannel above another full a foot pretending the ground was uneven. I asked him if he could not pare the ground away. He stoopt down like falling but I imagined it was the Negroe's foolish way of hearing better. I rode out. When I came home the pales were all laid slanting. I asked him why he did that. He still laid the fault on the ground and as his left shoulder was to me I gave him one small rap upon it. He went to breakfast afterwards and no complaint. This evening I walked there and then he pretended he could not drive a nail, his arm was so sore. I made Nassau strip his Cloaths off and examined the whole arm. Not the least swelling upon it and every now and then he would tremble. I asked him if I hit him upon the legs he said his

stroke was in his bone which made all his body ach. At last, looking full upon him, I discovered the Gentleman compleatly drunk. This I have suspected a great while. I then locked him up for monday morning's Chastisement for I cannot bear such a rascal. I thought this a truly religious fellow but have had occasion to think otherwise and that he is a hypocrite of the vilest kind. His first religion that broke out upon him was new light and I believe it is from some inculcated doctrine of those rascals that the slaves in this Colony are grown so much worse. It behoves every man therefore to take care of his own. At least I am determined to do what I can. Mine shall be brought to their [p]iety though with as little severity as [possible].

28. *Thursday* [June 1770]

    · · ·

I think I have the clearest evidence in the world that kindness to a Negroe by way of reward for having done well is the surest way to spoil him although according to the general observation of the world most men are spurred on to diligence by rewards. However this species of gratitude is seldom experienced in a slave.

My man George at the fork whose care and diligence had carried on the plantation to a very fine prospect in Corn, the only thing they tend there, has been rewarded by me very frequently with meat from my Smoak house to encourage his continuance in doing well. And now his weeds are come upon him he takes double the time to do any one thing. Yesterday I was pretty early there. They had but 17 rows in the morning to weed out to get to the other Corn field which was little better than 2 rows a hand and George himself had but 1 row to do, these rows shorter than all the rest by the depth of the Cotton patch. And in the others they used to do 4 rows apiece per day and this morning when I went there the women had better than a row apiece to finish that field and Mr. George was but in his second row in the other field. I looked particularly and carefully to see the work yesterday that was to be done. It was perfectly light and far from being as foul as what had been done when he did 5 rows the day and the rest 4. Therefore, I ordered them all a sound whipping and George should have been well paid only he had an excuse of removing the Cowpenn. The wench Judy sent to my house for broad hoes full an hour by sun did not get here till I was going to bed. I gave her a sound basting and Mr. George, instead of being rewarded with meat for doing well as before shall receive a sound correction, if by tomorrow I find he has not mended his pace.

Mary Ann worming my Tobacco had but a few rows this morning to finish the ground she was in and has not at 12 o'clock got into the other piece. Indeed she laid a foundation for this lazyness for after I came away she sent me word there were abundance of worms and she wanted Sukey, I suppose to keep her company in her lazyness. But she shall have but one reproof more and the next shall be a sound whipping. . . .

21. *Friday* [September 1770]

. . .

I discovered this day what I never knew before, nay what I had positively forbid years ago, but negroes have the impudence of the devil. Last year the suckling wenches told the overseers that I allowed them to go in five times about that business; for which I had some of them whipt and reduced it to half an hour before they went to work, half an hour before their breakfast; and half an hour before they go in at night. And Now they have made the simpletons believe I allow them to eat their morning's bit. So that a wench goes out to bake for that, then they must have time to eat it, then another bakes for their breakfast. But these things I have forbid upon their Peril.

54. John J. Audubon Encounters a Runaway in Louisiana Swamps

Much running away was expected by masters who held slaves in the vicinity of swamps and deep woods. They knew where slaves would be "lurking," as the expression went. Sometimes regular encampments of runaways were maintained for years by groups of slaves. There are also astonishing sagas of runaway individuals and families who secreted themselves for long periods of time.

It was such a situation that John James Audubon stumbled upon in the fastnesses of a Louisiana swamp late in the 1820s when he was engaged in one of the hunting expeditions that preceded his paintings of the birds of America. On this occasion he had been shooting wood ibis. The story reflects, no doubt, a certain amount of romanticism, as well as the painter's love of a good story. But the essential facts seem plausible enough. Notable, and to Audubon's credit, is the complete absence of those stereotypical attributions of docility that marked portraits of blacks in a later period. Audubon's final sentence shows that he did not understand how limited Louisiana law was in the defense of slave families.

Never shall I forget the impression made on my mind by the *rencontre* which forms the subject of this article, and I even doubt if the relation of it will not excite in the mind of my reader emotions of varied character.

Late in the afternoon of one of those sultry days which render the atmosphere of the Louisiana swamps pregnant with baneful effluvia, I directed my course towards my distant home, laden with a pack consisting of five or six Wood Ibises, and a heavy gun, the weight of which even in those days when my natural powers were unimpaired, prevented me from moving with much speed. Reaching the banks of a miry bayou, only a few yards in breadth, but of which I could not ascertain the depth, on account of the muddiness of its waters, I thought it might be dangerous to wade through it with my burden; for which reason, throwing to the opposite side each of

Source: John James Audubon, *Ornithological Biography, or an Account of the Habits of the Birds of the United States of America; Accompanied by Descriptions of the Objects Represented in the Work Entitled The Birds of America, and Interspersed with Delineations of American Scenery and Manners.* 5 vols. (Edinburgh: Adam Black, 1831–39), 2 (1834):27–32.

my heavy birds in succession, together with my gun, powder-flask, and shot-bag, and drawing my hunting-knife from its scabbard, to defend myself, if need should be, against alligators, I entered the water, followed by my faithful dog. As I advanced carefully and slowly, "Plato" swam around me, enjoying the refreshing influence of the liquid element that cooled his fatigued and heated frame. The water deepened, as did the mire of its bed; but with a stroke or two I gained the shore.

Scarcely had I stood erect on the opposite bank, when my dog ran to me, exhibiting marks of terror, his eyes seeming ready to burst from their sockets, and his mouth grinning with the expression of hatred, while his feelings found vent in a stifled growl. Thinking that all this was produced by the scent of a wolf or bear, I stooped to take up my gun, when a stentorial voice commanded me to "stand still, or die!" Such a *"qui vive"* in these woods was as unexpected as it was rare. I instantly raised and cocked my gun; and although I did not yet perceive the individual who had thus issued so peremptory a mandate, I felt determined to combat with him for the free passage of the grounds. Presently a tall firmly-built Negro emerged from the bushy underwood, where, until that moment, he must have been crouched, and in a louder voice repeated his injunction. Had I pressed a trigger, his life would have instantly terminated; but observing that the gun, which he aimed at my breast, was a wretched rusty piece, from which fire could not readily be produced, I felt little fear, and therefore did not judge it neces-

sary to proceed at once to extremities. I laid my gun at my side, tapped my dog quietly, and asked the man what he wanted.

My forbearance, and the stranger's long habit of submission, produced the most powerful effect on his mind. "Master," said he, "I am a runaway. I might perhaps shoot you down; but God forbids it, for I feel just now, as if I saw him ready to pass his judgment against me for such a foul deed, and I ask mercy at your hands. For God's sake, do not kill me, master!" And why, answered I, have you left your quarters, where certainly you must have fared better than in these unwholesome swamps? "Master, my story is a short, but a sorrowful one. My camp is close by, and as I know you cannot reach home this night, if you will follow me there, depend upon *my honour* you shall be safe until the morning, when I will carry your birds, if you choose, to the great road."

The large intelligent eyes of the Negro, the complacency of his manner, and the tones of his voice, I thought, invited me to venture; and as I felt that I was at least his equal, while, moreover, I had my dog to second me, I answered that I would *follow him*. He observed the emphasis laid on the words, the meaning of which he seemed to understand so thoroughly, that, turning to me, he said, "There, master, take my butcher's knife, while I throw away the flint and priming from my gun!" Reader, I felt confounded: this was too much for me; I refused the knife, and told him to keep his piece ready, in case we might accidentally meet a cougar or a bear.

Generosity exists everywhere. The

greatest monarch acknowledges its impulse, and all around him, from his lowliest menial to the proud nobles that encircle his throne, at times experience that overpowering sentiment. I offered to shake hands with the runaway. "Master," said he, "I beg you thanks," and with this he gave me a squeeze, that alike impressed me with the goodness of his heart, and his great physical strength. From that moment we proceeded through the woods together. My dog smelt at him several times, but as he heard me speak in my usual tone of voice, he soon left us, and rambled around as long as my whistle was unused. As we proceeded, I observed that he was guiding me towards the setting of the sun, and quite contrary to my homeward course. I remarked this to him, when he with the greatest simplicity replied, "merely for our security."

After trudging along for some distance, and crossing several bayous, at all of which he threw his gun and knife to the opposite bank, and stood still until I had got over, we came to the borders of an immense cane brake, from which I had, on former occasions, driven and killed several deer. We entered, as I had frequently done before, now erect, then on "all fours." He regularly led the way, divided here and there the tangled stalks, and, whenever we reached a fallen tree, assisted me in getting over it with all possible care. I saw that he was a perfect Indian in the knowledge of the woods, for he kept a direct course as precisely as any "Red-skin" I ever travelled with. All of a sudden he emitted a loud shriek, not unlike that of an owl, which so surprised me, that I

once more instantly levelled my gun. "No harm, master, I only give notice to my wife and children that I am coming." A tremulous answer of the same nature gently echoed through the tree-tops. The runaway's lips separated with an expression of gentleness and delight, when his beautiful set of ivory teeth seemed to smile through the dusk of evening that was thickening around us. "Master," said he, "my wife, though black, is as beautiful to me as the President's wife is to him; she is my queen, and I look on our young ones as so many princes:—but you shall see them all, for here they are, thank God!"

There, in the heart of the cane-brake, I found a regular camp. A small fire was lighted, and on its embers lay gridling some large slices of venison. A lad nine or ten years old was blowing the ashes from some fine sweet potatoes. Various articles of household furniture were carefully disposed around, and a large pallet of bear and deer skins seemed to be the resting-place of the whole family. The wife raised not her eyes towards mine, and the little ones, three in number, retired into a corner, like so many discomfited racoons; but the Runaway, bold and apparently happy, spoke to them in such cheering words, that at once one and all seemed to regard me as one sent by Providence to relieve them from all their troubles. My clothes were hung up by them to dry, and the Negro asked if he might clean and grease my gun, which I permitted him to do, while the wife threw a large piece of deer's flesh to my dog, which the children were already caressing.

Only think of my situation, reader!

Here I was, ten miles at least from home, and four or five from the nearest plantation, in the camp of runaway slaves, and quite at their mercy. My eyes involuntarily followed their motions, but as I thought I perceived in them a strong desire to make me their confidant and friend, I gradually relinquished all suspicion. The venison and potatoes looked quite tempting, and by this time I was in a condition to relish much less savoury fare; so, on being humbly asked to divide the viands before us, I partook of as hearty a meal as I had ever done in my life.

Supper over, the fire was completely extinguished, and a small lighted pine-knot placed in a hollowed calabash. Seeing that both the husband and wife were desirous of communicating something to me, I at once and fearlessly desired them to unburden their minds; when the Runaway told me a tale of which the following is the substance.

About eighteen months before, a planter residing not very far off, having met with some losses, was obliged to expose his slaves at a public sale. The value of his negroes was well known, and on the appointed day, the auctioneer laid them out in small lots, or offered them singly, in the manner which he judged most advantageous to their owner. The Runaway, who was well known as being the most valuable next to his wife, was put up by himself for sale, and brought an immoderate price. For his wife, who came next, and alone, eight hundred dollars were bidden and paid down. Then the children were exposed, and, on account of their breed, brought high prices. The rest of the slaves went off at rates corresponding to their qualifications.

The Runaway chanced to be purchased by the overseer of the plantation; the wife was bought by an individual residing about a hundred miles off, and the children went to different places along the river. The heart of the husband and father failed him under this dire calamity. For awhile he pined in deep sorrow under his new master; but having marked down in his memory the names of the different persons who had purchased each dear portion of his family, he feigned illness, if indeed he whose affections had been so grievously blasted could be said to feign it, refrained from food for several days, and was little regarded by the overseer, who felt himself disappointed in what he had considered a bargain.

On a stormy night, when the elements raged with all the fury of a hurricane, the poor negro made his escape, and, being well acquainted with all the neighboring swamps, at once made directly for the cane brake, in the centre of which I found his camp. A few nights afterwards he gained the abode of his wife, and the very next after their meeting he led her away. The children one after another he succeeded in stealing, until at last the whole objects of his love were under his care.

To provide for five individuals was no easy task in those wilds, which, after the first notice was given of the wonderful disappearance of this extraordinary family, were daily ransacked by armed planters. Necessity, it is said, will bring the wolf from the forest. The Runaway seems to have well understood the maxim, for under night he approached his first master's plantation, where he had ever been treated with the greatest kindness. The house servants knew him too well not to aid him to the best of their power, and at the approach of each morning he returned to his camp with an ample supply of provisions. One day, while in search of wild fruits, he found a bear dead before the muzzle of a gun that had been set for the purpose. Both articles he carried to his home. His friends at the plantation managed to supply him with some ammunition, and in damp and cloudy days he first ventured to hunt around his camp. Possessed of .courage and activity, he gradually became more careless, and rambled farther in search of game. It was on one of his excursions that I met him, and he assured me that the noise which I made in passing the *bayou* had caused him to lose the chance of killing a fine deer, although, said he, "my old musket misses fire sadly too often."

The runaways, after disclosing their secret to me, both rose from their seat, with eyes full of tears. "Good master, for God's sake, do something for us and our children," they sobbed forth with one accord. Their little ones lay sound asleep in the fearlessness of their innocence. Who could have heard such a tale without emotion? I promised them my most cordial assistance.

They both sat up that night to watch my repose, and I slept close to their urchins, as if on a bed of the softest down.

Day broke so fair, so pure, and so gladdening, that I told them such heavenly appearances were ominous of good, and that I scarcely doubted of obtaining their full pardon. I desired them to take their children with them, and promised to accompany them to the plantation of their first master. They gladly obeyed. My Ibises were hung around their camp, and, as a memento of my having been there, I notched several trees, after which I bade adieu, perhaps for the last time, to that cane brake. We soon reached the plantation, the owner of which, with whom I was well acquainted, received me with all the generous kindness of a Louisiana planter. Ere an hour had elapsed, the Runaway and his family were looked upon as his own. He afterwards re-purchased them from their owners, and treated them with his former kindness; so that they were rendered as happy as slaves generally are in that country, and continued to cherish that attachment to each other which had led to their adventures. Since this event happened, it has, I have been informed, become illegal to separate slave families without their consent.

55. Arson by a Virginia House Servant

House servants were in many instances looked up to by other slaves on the plantation, sometimes because of their closer connection with the privileged world of the master and his family, but more often, one would guess, because the house servants frequently possessed superior gifts of one sort or another. In any case it is not true that all slaves envied and preferred the big house to the field. For one thing there was much closer surveillance; and undoubtedly social relations among fellow slaves became more constrained as white contacts multiplied.

In 1844 the central part of Mt. Airy, the ancestral home of the Tayloe family in the Virginia Tidewater, was set afire, presumably by a slave named Lizzie Flood. The Tayloe family believed that the slave was prompted to this extreme act because of her displeasure at being brought into the house and assigned to domestic duties.

At the time of the fire William H. Tayloe, the master of the house, was far away in Alabama on business, and the following letters were written to him to describe the circumstances, and the investigation undertaken to uncover the real facts concerning Lizzie Flood's involvement. The evidence is circumstantial, and dependent largely on slave testimony. It probably would not, as the lawyers suggested at the time, have held up in court. But the instance does show the informal ways in which information was taken from slaves, and that even for the purposes of safety, the white community had to regard slaves as being more than property.

[I]
Benjamin D. Rust to William H. Tayloe.

Mt. Airy Warsaw, Va December 22nd [18]44
My Dear Sir
It is with grief & pain I write to you to communicate bad news, the burning of the center building of Mt. Airy house. all else safe, all the furniture saved the bedsteads & curtains, the wardrobe & the desk on each side of the fireplace in your room, in the [illegible] many articles taken out, the gold watch, the rings safe & all the other houses & [illegible]

all your family safe & well
your papers safe, all in the cellar

Source: Tayloe Family Papers, Virginia Historical Society, Richmond, Va.

safe, The iron chest has been recovered. from the ruins 30 [illegible] of money found in it only, no jewelry found in it, it was siting on its bottom in the cellar, In hacking it out it opened, the [illegible] being unlached, every effort will be made to recover from the ruins, any thing that may have been droped from the chest, or otherwise.

There is not the least doubt but that the house was set on fire, by an incendiary. Lizzy is suspected.

This morning about half past 11 oclock we all started to church, the ladies in the carriage, & I on horse back, Rolf driving & Armstead behind, we got there during service, in about 15 minutes Albert arrivd from Mt. A . . . . , saying that the roof of the house was in a blaze, we all started in the greatest haste, as hard as our horses could run, Armstead first, McKinny and many others directly after, all at the house, all the negroes on the farms soon there, Col Carter very soon. As I came in sight, I saw the blaze very large from the roof of the house. On reaching the stairs I found the fire just over them, and over my room door, the fire burning over the head of the stairs prevented our saving the things just above. I was about 20 minutes going to church, about 15 there, & less than five minutes returning, absent less than 40 minutes. the carriage came with the ladies rapidly, but being much alarmed went back to Mr. Wards immediately.

Jenny informs me that as soon as we left, she went to all the rooms & saw that the fire in the ladies rooms was safe then went to her house, first locking the doors leading to the building from the covered ways, lached the garden saloon door, & pushed the bolt of the oposite one but thinks it did not catch. In a short time she sent Kitty to the house to see after the fires, went to Miss Goodwins room, & found her bed on fire, gave the alarm, which brought Jenny & Ruffin to the room Jenny says that they threw the burning bed out of the window, & thus rid the room of fire, that, in the hearth [was] entirely down, but a chunk of fire [was] under the bed. McKinny saw that all the fire was out in the room, & no possible communication from this room to any part of the house, by the fire found in it. other gentlemen say the same that went in the roon—Jenny says, hearing a noise in the garret, she looked for the keys where they are usually hid, but could not find them, ran to the garret door in the passage, found it closed, but not locked, the key not in it, the garret & roof then on fire, so that fire must have been communicated to it & Miss G's room at the same time, as there was no connection between them. The ladies left their rooms & waited in the parlor 15 minutes waiting for the carriage hop[p]ing all of us in & out of the house several times, looking for the carriage. The incendiary may have got in the house before J locked the doors, & the fire must have been put as soon as we left. . . .

Six of us are sitting up all night keeping watch. All the furniture shall be sorted out tomorrow & put away in the best order I will make every [illegible] & sacrifice of comfort & convenience for the benefit of your family & safety of your property

[The following interstitial comment, like the paragraph above, was written in the fold of the letter. (Editor)]

Liz & her father did not come to the house till all was over, says she thought she could do no good, & had no curiosity to see, contradicts herself by her tales tomorrow we shall investigate the matter & do what is best. The walls have not fallen in, only slightly cracked at the top A very thick fog lasted till the rain & a calm which with our cuting away a part of the covered way, saved the wings.

[II]

Edward J. Tayloe to William H. Tayloe.

To W^m. H. Tayloe, Esq.
Walnut Grove, Alab.

Powhatan Hill, 30th Dec. 1844

My Dear Brother,

. . . There remains not a doubt on the minds of all of us who have investigated the matter, that Lizzy Flood set fire to the Mt. Airy House on the 22^d inst. It has, also, leaked out during the investigation, that she was suspected by the servants of having set fire to the curtain in October last. After ascertaining from Mr. Stuman, that he would ask of the Court, & no doubt, obtain a continuance of her case until you returned home, or we could hear from you, I had her committed to jail. It is very probable, that further evidence will be obtained during her confinement. I will give you a brief statement of the testimony, most of which was collected by Col. Carter, Col. Brockenbrough & Mr. Ward on the day succeeding the fire—some of it, next day, by Mr Ward & myself. All these gentlemen are convinced of Lizzy's guilt—but they think that the proof thus far

elicited, is insufficient for her conviction.

Kitty was first examined. "First person saw the fire in Miss Goodwin's room, under the bed, which was on fire—a chunk of about 6 or 8 inches long under the foot of the bed—first told Jenny—discovered the fire about 10 minutes after the family left for the church. They were hardly at church when I saw the fire. Found the garret door unlocked, & could not find the key which staid generally under the head of Henry's bed. They were always hid in the same place—thinks no one but herself & Jenny knew where they were hid. Not usual for Lizzie Flood to be at the House—was there in the morning directly after breakfast, & went upstairs—1st saw her as she came up the steps, and went down with her. She went out the covered way, back door where she was standing, & I went back with Miss Goodwin to the room next Miss G's—I saw her no more that day till evening, after she was sent for. Miss G's room was not on fire, but I saw the fire in the corner of Col. Rust's room. (she meant to say in the cornice). This is the 1st time Lizzie has bro't the clothes since master left home—they were generally bro't on Saturday evening. Cook W^m., Albert, Sam Flood, Enoch, Martha, Ruffin and grandmother, Jenny & myself were all that were at the house when I saw the fire. Lizzy said she was not going anywhere." (Miss G. confirms Kitty's statements as to Lizzy, having met her in the covered way at about 10 o'clock. Left them conversing as she went up the cov^d. way stairs.)

Jenny said, "When the family went to church I went upstairs, & saw a little fire [in the fireplace] in the young ladies room, which I covered up. Kitty told me about the fire when I got in Miss G's room, the bed was on fire—a chunk was under the bed—no part of the room was burnt. Garret door locked on Monday eveg. by me—the key put under the head of Henry's bed. I did not know that anyone but Kitty knew where the keys were hid. Lizzie Flood knew that the keys were hid upstairs somewhere. Celia also knew that the keys were hid upstairs in some of the rooms. The fire was in the garret in a parcel of old lumber—& I don't think. it had been there more than 15 minutes. It was all smothered— & I saw the smoke bursting thro' the cornice of Col. Rust's room."

It thus appears, that the house was fired in two opposite points. It was first discovered in Miss G's room & wholly extinguished, the bed being thrown out of the window. It was now found that the garret was on fire, & all efforts were in vain to subdue it, for it soon burst thro' into Col. Rust's room.

Lizzie's statement to Col. Carter & Mr. Ward. "She bro't clothes to the House about breakfast time. Miss G. met her—& Kitty took the clothes from her—did not go upstairs (contradicted most strongly by Kitty) but returned by the back way thro' the park home where she remained & got her breakfast & then left for Nominy meeting. When she got as far as the branch near the mill it began to rain, & she stopped awhile & then returned home—met no one going or returning—(it began to rain between 12 1/2 & 1 P.M. after the house had been burning an hour or more—too late to go to Nominy Meeting—Shoemaker James was at [the] mill

when he heard of the fire—ran to the house by the road Lizzie s^d. she was going—& met no person—"Anyone going, said he, to Nominy could, by starting at the usual time, have got there before the rain.") but [Lizzy resumes] saw some people going from the house through the field—heard some one cry murder, as she thought, & supposed it was the children, come home, & saw the house burning, & was told the house was on fire—didn't go to the house because it was raining— & she could do no good. She has a suspicion that the house was set on fire & suspects somebody, but afraid to say who,—is on good terms with all the servants (this is contradicted by almost all & it is proved that she was very angry & sent various angry messages to Jenny on Saturday by young Jane)—if anybody is on bad terms with her, does not know it. Her father went to the cuthouse."

I copy the material parts of Lizzy's examination by me next day. "Came over to the house early—about breakf^t. time—Miss G. opened backdoor in cov^d. way—met Kitty on cov^d. way stairs (Kitty says, hearing someone go upstairs, she went to see who it was & she met Lizzy at top of the stairs in main building)—did not go into main house. Kitty asked where I was going—sd. to Nominy if it didn't rain (Kitty says she s^d. she was going nowhere & did not say a word of Nominy)—returned home & took breakf^t. at the same time with her Father (Tom Flood denies this & says he saw nothing of Lizzy until Sunday night when he returned home, having breakfasted with his wife—& left home for Col. Brockenbrough's from 1/4 to 1/2 an hour before the carriage started for church)—then dressed to go to Nominy meeting House—got to run this side of tannery—& it began to rain—waited awhile—& heard a noise behind me—got a little wet & changed my clothes. Brother spoke of fire. I went towards house by way of the spring, & met Albert, who told me that Mt. Airy house was burnt down & then I returned home—got home to breakfast a smart while before Tom returned from the house—we all eat together & I started first for meeting. Never had difference with any of the servants—spoke last with Jenny on Monday Morng. before the fire—& told her then "good morng." Never sent any messages to Jenny (contradicted by Nancy & Jane).

It is seen, that Lizzy can give no account of herself from soon after 10, when she & Kitty parted, until after the rain, when she returned home wet (the house had then fallen in) which is not contradicted by her Father & other persons & by circumstances inconsistent with her statements. Other matters will probably be elicited during her confinement. If testimony to convict her cannot be procured, Mr. Stuman will ask the court to enter a nolle prosequi, & she will again be at your disposal. Whatever may be your wishes, we will endeavor to execute them. In my opinion you sh^d get rid of all that family of Floods." . . .

Yours ever affly,
Ed. J. Tayloe

56.   Henry Brown Escapes in a Box

The decision to attempt escape to the North was a more conclusive demonstration of slave resistance than short-term "lurking" in the woods or swamps, or seeking a local hideaway. A slave who took this step was leaving behind him the only world he knew, and the only people who mattered in his personal life, for an unknown future. The penalties for failure could be severe, and except for the bright lure of freedom, the rewards could only be guessed. For this reason the motives prompting fugitives are especially interesting. They often fit into the category of the proverbial last straw.

For the slave, the final outrage was most often based on his conviction

Source: Henry Box Brown, *Narrative of the Life of Henry Box Brown, Written by Himself,* 1st Eng. ed. (Manchester: Lee and Glynn, 1851), pp. 49–57.

that the master had broken some unspoken rule of fair dealing, that he had broken his word to the slave, that even within the warped justice of the slave system, the master had betrayed the slave's expectation of him. Such was the case of Henry "Box" Brown, whose master had been unwilling to purchase Brown's wife, the slave of another owner who was on the point of selling her to a dealer. Brown's indignation burned slowly and deeply into his heart, threatening to sour his religious faith. Especially galling in Brown's mind was his knowledge of the sums of money his master had received for his own labor when he was hired out as a tobacconist in Richmond.

Brown's escape was among the most dramatic of all the fugitive experiences, and better authenticated than most. James Miller McKim, a distinguished Unitarian minister and abolitionist, declared that he might have been doubtful of this story had he not been present when "Box" Brown arrived in Philadelphia, an eyewitness to the "uncrating."

I now began to get weary of my bonds; and earnestly panted after liberty. I felt convinced that I should be acting in accordance with the will of God, if I could snap in sunder those bonds by which I was held body and soul as the property of a fellow man. I looked forward to the good time which every day I more and more firmly believed would yet come, when I should walk the face of the earth in full possession of all that freedom which the finger of God had so clearly written on the constitutions of man, and which was common to the human race; but of which, by the cruel hand of tyranny, I, and millions of my fellow-men, had been robbed.

I was well acquainted with a storekeeper in the city of Richmond, from whom I used to purchase my provisions; and having formed a favourable opinion of his integrity, one day in the course of a little conversation with him, I said to him if I were free I would be able to do business such as

he was doing; he then told me that my occupation (a tobacconist) was a money-making one, and if I were free I had no need to change for another. I then told him my circumstances in regard to my master, having to pay him 25 dollars per month, and yet that he refused to assist me in saving my wife from being sold and taken away to the South, where I should never see her again; and even refused to allow me to go and see her until my hours of labour were over. I told him this took place about five months ago, and I had been meditating my escape from slavery since, and asked him, as no person was near us, if he could give me any information about how I should proceed. I told him I had a little money and if he would assist me I would pay him for so doing. The man asked me if I was not afraid to speak that way to him; I said no, for I imagined he believed that every man had a right to liberty. He said I was quite right, and presenting it again to Mr. Allen I obtained the permission required, with the advice that I should go home and get a poultice of flax-meal to it, and keep it well poulticed until it got better. I took him instantly at his word and went off directly to the store-keeper who had by this time received an answer from his friend in Philadelphia, and had obtained permission to address the box to him, this friend in that city, arranging to call for it as soon as it should arrive. There being no time to be lost, the store-keeper, Dr. Smith, and myself, agreed to meet next morning at four o'clock, in order to get the box ready for the express train. The box which I had procured was three feet one inch wide, two feet six inches high, and two feet wide: and on the morning of the 29th. day of March, 1849, I went into the box—having previously bored three gimlet holes opposite my face, for air, and provided myself with a bladder of water, both for the purpose of quenching my thirst and for wetting my face, should I feel getting faint. I took the gimlet also with me, in order that I might bore more holes if I found I had not sufficient air. Being thus equipped for the battle of liberty, my friends nailed down the lid and had me conveyed to the Express Office, which was about a mile distant from the place where I was packed. I had no sooner arrived at the office than I was turned heels up, while some person nailed something on the end of the box. I was then put upon a waggon and driven off to the depôt with my head down, and I had no sooner arrived at the depôt, than the man who drove the waggon tumbled me roughly into the baggage car, where, however, I happened to fall on my right side.

The next place we arrived at was Potomac Creek, where the baggage had to be removed from the cars, to be put on board the steamer; where I was again placed with my head down, and in this dreadful position had to remain nearly an hour and a half, which, from the sufferings I had thus to endure, seemed like an age to me, but I was forgetting the battle of liberty, and I was resolved to conquer or die. I felt my eyes swelling as if they would burst from their sockets; and the veins on my temples were dreadfully distended with pressure of blood upon my head. In this position I attempted to lift my hand to my face but I had no power to move it; I felt a cold sweat coming over me which seemed to be a warning that death was about to terminate my earthly miseries, but as I feared even that, less than slavery, I resolved to submit to the will of God, and, under the influence of that impression, I lifted up my soul in prayer to God, who alone, was able to deliver me. My cry was soon heard, for I could hear a man saying to another, that he had travelled a long way and had been standing there two hours, and he would like to get somewhat to sit down; so perceiving my box, standing on end, he threw it down and then two sat upon it. I was thus relieved from a state of agony which may be more easily imagined than described. I could now listen to the men talking, and heard one of them asking the other what he supposed *the box contained;* his companion replied he guessed it asked me how much money I would give him if he would assist me to get away. I told him that I had 166 dollars and that I would give him the half; so we ultimately agreed that I should have his service in the attempt for 86. Now I only wanted to fix upon a plan. He told me of several plans by which others had managed to effect their escape, but none of them exactly suited my taste. I then left him to think over what would be best to be done, and, in the mean time, went to consult my friend Dr. Smith, on the subject. I mentioned the plans which the storekeeper had suggested, and as he did not approve either of them very much, I still looked for some plan which would be more certain and more safe, but I was determined that come what may, I should have my freedom or die in the attempt.

One day, while I was at work, and my thoughts were eagerly feasting upon the idea of freedom, I felt my soul called out to heaven to breathe a prayer to Almighty God. I prayed fervently that he who seeth in secret and knew the inmost desires of my heart, would lend me his aid in bursting my fetters asunder, and in restoring me to the possession of those rights, of which men had robbed me; when the idea suddenly flashed across my mind of shutting myself *up in a box*, and getting myself conveyed as dry goods to a free state.

Being now satisfied that this was the plan for me, I went to my friend Dr. Smith and, having aquainted him with it, we agreed to have it put at once into execution not however without calculating the chances of danger with which it was attended; but buoyed up by the prospect of freedom and [in]creased hatred to slavery I was wil[ling] to dare even death itself rather t[han] endure any longer the clanking [of] those galling chains. It being still [nec]essary to have the assistance of [the] storekeeper, to see that the box [was] kept in its right position on its p[as]sage, I then went to let him know [my] intention, but he said although he w[as] willing to serve me in any way [he] could, he did not think I could live i[n the] box for so long a time as would be ne[c]essary to convey me to Philadelph[ia,] but as I had already made up n[y] mind, he consented to acompany n[e] and keep the box right all the way.

My next object was to procure a bo[x] and with the assistance of a carpent[er] that was very soon accomplished, an[d] taken to the place where the packin[g] was to be performed. In the mean time the storekeeper had written to a friend in Philidelphia, but as no answer had arrived, we resolved to carry out our purpose as best we could. It was deemed necessary that I should get permission to be absent from my work for a few days, in order to keep down suspicion until I had once fairly started on the road to liberty; and as I had then a gathered finger I thought that would form a very good excuse for obtaining leave of absence; but when I showed it to one everseer, Mr. Allen, he told me it was not so bad as to prevent me from working, so with a view of making it bad enough, I got Dr. Smith to procure for me some oil of vitriol in order to drop a little of thi[s] on it, but in my hurry I dropped rathe[r] much and made it worse than the[re] was any occasion for, in fact it w[as] very soon eaten in to the bone, and [?]

was "THE MAIL." I too thought it was a mail but not such a mail as he supposed it to be.

The next place at which we arrived was the city of Washington, where I was taken from the steam-boat, and again placed upon a waggon and carried to the depôt right side up with care; but when the driver arrived at the depôt I heard him call for some person to help to take the box off the waggon, and some one answered him to the effect that he might throw it off; but, says the driver, it is marked "this side up with care;" so if I throw it off I might break something, the other answered him that it did not matter if he broke all that was in it, the railway company were able enough to pay for it. No sooner were these words spoken than I began to tumble from the waggon, and falling on the end where my head was, I could hear my neck give a crack, as if it had been snapped asunder and I was knocked completely insensible. The first thing I heard, after that, was some person saying, "there is no room for the box, it will have to remain and be sent through to-morrow with the luggage train; but the Lord had not quite forsaken me, for in answer to my earnest prayer He so ordered affairs that I should not be left behind; and I now heard a man say that the box had come with the express, and it must be sent on. I was then tumbled into the car with my head downwards again, but the car had not proceeded far before, more luggage having to be taken in, my box got shifted about and so happened to turn upon its right side; and in this position I remained till I got to Phila-

delphia, of our arrival in which place I was informed by hearing some person say, "We are in port and at Philadelphia." My heart then leaped for joy, and I wondered if any person knew that such a box was there.

Here it may be proper to observe that the man who had promised to accompany my box failed to do what he promised; but, to prevent it remaining long at the station after its arrival, he sent a telegraphic message to his friend, and I was only twenty seven hours in the box, though travelling a distance of three hundred and fifty miles.

I was now placed in the depôt amongst the other luggage, where I lay till seven o'clock, P.M., at which time a waggon drove up, and I heard a person inquire for such a box as that in which I was. I was then placed on a waggon and conveyed to the house where my friend in Richmond had arranged I should be received. A number of persons soon collected round the box after it was taken in to the house, but as I did not know what was going on I kept myself quiet. I heard a man say "let us rap upon the box and see if he is alive;" and immediately a rap ensued and a voice said, tremblingly, "Is all right within?" to which I replied—"all right." The joy of the friends was very great; when they heard that I was alive they soon managed to break open the box, and then came my resurrection from the grave of slavery. I rose a freeman, but I was too weak, by reason of long confinement in that box, to be able to stand, so I immediately swooned away. After my recovery from the swoon the first thing, which arrested my attention, was the presence of a number of friends, every one seeming more anxious than another, to have an opportunity of rendering me their assistance, and of bidding me a hearty welcome to the possession of my natural rights. I had risen as it were from the dead; I felt much more than I could readily express; but as the kindness of Almighty God had been so conspicuously shown in my deliverance, I burst forth into the following him of thanksgiving,

I waited patiently, I waited patiently for the Lord, for the Lord;

And he inclined unto me, and heard my calling:
I waited patiently, I waited patiently for the Lord,
And he inclined unto me, and heard my calling:
And he hath put a new song in my mouth,
Even a thanksgiving, even a thanksgiving, even a thanksgiving unto our God.
Blessed, Blessed, Blessed, Blessed is the man, Blessed is the man,
Blessed is the man that hath set his hope, his hope in the Lord;
O Lord my God, Great, Great, Great.

---

57. Colonel Alexander's Slaves Resist the Patrol

Slave patrols, a regular feature of plantation communities, were designed to maintain order among slaves, and charged particularly with seeing to it that slaves did not go abroad at night without written passes from their masters, nor congregate for unauthorized meetings. These patrols were authorized by statute (see, for example, the chapter on patrols in the Alabama Slave Code reproduced in document 38), but were much more active in time of public disturbance than at other times. All white males were subject to patrol duty, but as a matter of fact slave-owners, being men of power and influence, were often able to evade patrol duty, a situation which frequently aroused the resentment of the poorer whites who had to serve, and who often took it out on the slaves who were caught. Sometimes there was drinking among the patrollers, and often there was cruelty

Source: Austin Steward, *Twenty-Two Years a Slave, and Forty Years A Freeman; Embracing a Correspondence of Several Years, While President of Wilberforce Colony, London, Canada West.* 2d ed. (Rochester, N.Y.: Allings & Cory, 1859), pp. 27–39.

enough to warrant the anger of the slave-owners. Some owners' slaves were watched more carefully than others, and this appears to have been the case in the story Austin Steward told of a patrol resisted by a certain Colonel Alexander's slaves in Virginia in the first decade of the nineteenth century.

Austin Steward was a well-known leader of free blacks in Rochester, Cincinnati, and in the Wilberforce community in Canada, of which he was president for many years. Born in Prince William County, Virginia, Steward was carried into western New York State early in the nineteenth century. He managed to make good his own escape from slavery ahead of the general emancipation in New York, which occurred in 1827, and by 1817 had established himself at Rochester in the butcher's trade. Steward was himself a good exemplar of the doctrine he always preached to other free blacks as the best policy for success: the Calvinist doctrine of frugality, hard work, and sobriety.

Slaves are never allowed to leave the plantation to which they belong, without a written pass. Should any one venture to disobey this law, he will most likely be caught by the *patrol* and given thirty-nine lashes. This patrol is always on duty every Sunday, going to each plantation under their supervision, entering every slave cabin, and examining closely the conduct of the slaves; and if they find one slave from another plantation without a pass, he is immediately punished with a severe flogging.

I recollect going one Sunday with my mother, to visit my grand-mother; and while there, two or three of the patrol came and looked into the cabin, and seeing my mother, demanded her pass. She told them that she had one, but had left it in another cabin, from whence she soon brought it, which saved her a whipping but we were terribly frightened.

The reader will obtain a better knowledge of the character of a Virginia patrol, by the relation of an affair, which came off on the neighboring plantation of Col. Alexander, in which some forty of Capt. Helm's [1] slaves were engaged, and which proved rather destructive of human life in the end.

But I must first say that it is not true, that slave owners are respected for kindness to their slaves. The more tyrannical a master is, the more will he be favorably regarded by his neighboring planters; and from the day that he acquires the reputation of a kind and indulgent master, he is looked upon with suspicion, and sometimes hatred, and his slaves are watched more closely than before.

Col. Alexander was a very wealthy planter and owned a great number of slaves, but he was very justly suspected of being a kind, humane, and

1. Captain Helm was Austin Steward's owner. (*Editor's note*)

indulgent master. His slaves were always better fed, better clad, and had greater privileges than any I knew in the Old Dominion; and of course, the patrol had long had an eye on them, anxious to flog some of "those pampered niggers, who were spoiled by the indulgence of a weak, inefficient, but well-meaning owner."

Col. A. gave his slaves the liberty to get up a grand dance. Invitations were sent and accepted, to a large number of slaves on other plantations, and so, for miles around, all or many of the slaves were in high anticipation of joining in the great dance, which was to come off on Easter night. In the mean time, the patrol was closely watching their movements, and evinced rather a joyful expectancy of the many they should find there without a pass, and the flogging they would give them for that, if not guilty of any other offence, and perhaps they might catch some of the Colonel's slaves doing something for which they could be taught "to know their place," by the application of the cowhide.

The slaves on Col. A.'s plantation had to provide and prepare the supper for the expected vast "turn out," which was no light matter; and as slaves like on such occasions to pattern as much as possible after their master's family, the result was, to meet the emergency of the case, they *took*, without saying, "by your leave, Sir," some property belonging to their master, reasoning among themselves, as slaves often do, that it can not be *stealing*, because "it belongs to massa, and so do *we*, and we only use one part of his property to benefit another. Sure, 'tis all massa's." And if they do not get detected in this

removal of "massa's property" from one location to another, they think no more of it.

Col. Alexander's slaves were hurrying on with their great preparations for the dance and feast; and as the time drew near, the old and knowing ones might be seen in groups, discussing the matter, with many a wink and nod; but it was in the valleys and by-places where the younger portion were to be found, rather secretly preparing food for the great time coming. This consisted of hogs, sheep, calves; and as to master's *poultry*, that suffered daily. Sometimes it was missed, but the disappearance was always easily accounted for, by informing "massa" that a great number of hawks had been around of late; and their preparation went on, night after night, undetected. They who repaired to a swamp or other by-place to cook by night, carefully destroyed everything likely to detect them, before they returned to their cabins in the morning.

The night for the dance *came* at last, and long before the time, the road leading to Col. Alexander's plantation presented a gay spectacle. The females were seen flocking to the place of resort, with heads adorned with gaudy bandanna turbans and new calico dresses, of the gayest colors,—their whole attire decked over with bits of gauze ribbon and other fantastic finery. The shades of night soon closed over the plantation, and then could be heard the rude music and loud laugh of the unpolished slave. It was about ten o'clock when the *aristocratic slaves* began to assemble, dressed in the cast-off finery of their master and mistress, swelling out and putting on airs in imitation of those they were forced to obey from day to day.

When they were all assembled, the dance commenced; the old fiddler struck up some favorite tune, and over the floor they went; the flying feet of the dancers were heard, pat, pat, over the apartment till the clock warned them it was twelve at midnight, or what some call "low twelve," to distinguish it from twelve o'clock at noon; then the violin ceased its discordant sounds, and the merry dancers paused to take breath.

Supper was then announced, and all began to prepare for the sumptuous feast. It being the pride of slaves to imitate the manners of their master and mistress, especially in the ceremonies of the table, all was conducted with great propriety and good order. The food was well cooked, and in a very plentiful supply. They had also managed in some way, to get a good quantity of excellent wine, which was sipped in the most approved and modern style. Every dusky face was lighted up, and every eye sparkled with joy. However ill fed they might have been, here, for once, there was plenty. Suffering and toil was forgotten, and they all seemed with one accord to give themselves up to the intoxication of pleasurable amusement.

House servants were, of course, "the stars" of the party; all eyes were turned to them to see how they conducted, for they, among slaves, are what a military man would call "fugle-men." The field hands, and such of them as have generally been excluded from the dwelling of their owners, look to the house servant as a pattern of politeness and gentility. And indeed, it is often the only method of obtaining any knowledge of the manners of what is called "genteel society;" hence, they are ever regarded as a privileged class; and are sometimes greatly envied, while others are bitterly hated. And too often justly, for many of them are the most despicable tale-bearers and mischiefmakers, who will, for the sake of the favor of his master or mistress, frequently betray his fellow-slave, and by tattling, get him severely whipped; and for these acts of perfidy, and sometimes downright falsehood, he is often rewarded by his master, who knows it is for his interest to keep such ones about him; though he is sometimes obliged, in addition to a reward, to send him away, for fear of the vengeance of the betrayed slaves. In the family of his master, the example of bribery and treachery is ever set before him, hence it is, that insurrections and stampedes are so generally detected. Such slaves are always treated with more affability than others, for the slaveholder is well aware that he stands over a volcano, that may at any moment rock his foundation to the center, and with one mighty burst of its long suppressed fire, sweep him and his family to destruction. When he lies down at night, he knows not but that ere another morning shall dawn, he may be left mangled and bleeding, and at the mercy of those maddened slaves whom he has so long ruled with a rod of iron.

But the supper, like other events, came to an end at last. The expensive table service, with other things, which had been secretly brought from the "great house," was hurriedly cleansed by the slaves, and carefully returned. The floor was again cleared, the violin sounded, and soon they were performing another "break down," with all the wild abandon of the African character, —in the very midst of which, the music suddenly ceased, and the old musician assumed a listening attitude. Every foot was motionless; every face terrified, and every ear listening for the cause of the alarm.

Soon the slave who was kept on the "look-out," shouted to the listeners the single word "patrol!" and then the tumult that followed that announcement, is beyond the power of language to describe! Many a poor slave who had stolen from his cabin, to join in the dance, now remembered that they had no pass! Many screamed in affright, as if they already felt the lash and heard the crack of the overseer's whip; others clenched their hands, and assumed an attitude of bold defiance, while a savage frown contracted the brow of all. Their unrestrained merriment and delicious fare, seemed to arouse in them the natural feelings of self-defence and defiance of their oppressors. But what could be done? The patrol was nearing the building, when an athletic, powerful slave, who had been but a short time from his "fatherland," whose spirit the cowardly overseer had labored in vain to quell, said in a calm, clear voice, that we had better stand our ground, and advised the females to lose no time in useless wailing, but get their things and repair immediately to a cabin at a short distance, and there remain quiet, without a light, which they did with all possible haste. The men were terrified at this bold act of their leader; and many with dismay at the thought of resistance, began to skulk behind fences and old buildings, when he opened the door and

requested every slave to leave who felt unwilling to fight. None were urged to remain, and those who stood by him did so voluntarily.

Their number was now reduced to twenty-five men, but the leader, a gigantic African, with a massive, compact frame, and an arm of great strength, looked competent to put ten common men to flight. He clenched his powerful fist, and declared that he would resist unto death, before he would be arrested by those savage men, even if they promised not to flog him. They closed the door, and agreed not to open it; and then the leader cried, "Extinguish the lights and let them come! we will meet them hand to hand!" Five of the number he stationed near the door, with orders to rush out, if the patrol entered, and seize their horses, cut the bridles, or otherwise unfit them for use. This would prevent them from giving an alarm and getting a reinforcement from surrounding plantations. In silence they awaited the approach of the enemy, and soon the tramping of horses' feet announced their approach, but when within a few yards of the house they halted, and were overheard by one of the skulking slaves, maturing their plans and mode of attack. There was great hesitancy expressed by a part of the company to engage in the affair at all.

"Coming events cast their shadow before."

The majority, however, seemed to think it safe enough, and uttered expressions of triumph that they had got the rascals at last.

"Are you not afraid that they will resist?" said the weaker party.

"Resist?" was the astonished answer. "This old fellow, the Colonel, has pampered and indulged his slaves, it is true, and they have slipped through our fingers whenever we have attempted to chastise them; but they are not such fools as to dare resistance! Those niggers know as well as we, that it is *death*, by the law of the State, for a slave to strike a white man."

"Very true," said the other, "but it is dark and long past midnight, and beside they have been indulging their appetites, and we cannot tell what they may attempt to do."

"Pshaw!" he answered, contemptuously, "they are unarmed, and I should not fear in the least, to go in among them *alone*, armed only with my cowhide!"

"As you please, then," he said, rather dubiously, "but look well to your weapons; are they in order?"

"In prime order, Sir." And putting spurs to their horses, were soon at the house, where they dismounted and requested one of the party to remain with the horses.

"What," said he, "are you so chicken-hearted as to suppose those d____d cowardly niggers are going to get up an insurrection?"

"Oh no," he replied, carelessly, but would not consent to have the horses left alone. "Besides," said he, "they may forget themselves at this late hour; but if they do, a few lashes of the cowhide will quicken their memory, I reckon."

The slaves were aware of their movements, and prepared to receive them.

They stepped up to the door boldly, and demanded admittance, but all was silent; they tried to open it, but it was fastened. Those inside, ranged on each side of the door, and stood perfectly still.

The patrol finding the slaves not disposed to obey, burst off the slight fastening that secured the door, and the chief of the patrol bounded into their midst, followed by several of his companions, all in total darkness!

Vain is the attempt to describe the tumultuous scene which followed. Hand to hand they fought and struggled with each other, amid the terrific explosion of fire-arms,—oaths and curses, mingled with the prayers of the wounded, and the groans of the dying! Two of the patrol were killed on the spot, and lay drenched in the warm blood that so lately flowed through their veins. Another with his arm broken and otherwise wounded, lay groaning and helpless, beside the fallen slaves, who had sold their lives so dearly. Another of his fellows was found at a short distance, mortally wounded and about to bid adieu to life. In the yard lay the keeper of the horses, a stiffened corpse. Six of the slaves were killed and two wounded.

It would be impossible to convey to the minds of northern people, the alarm and perfect consternation that the above circumstance occasioned in that community. The knowledge of its occurrence was carried from one plantation to another, as on the wings of the wind; exaggerated accounts were given, and prophecies of the probable result made, until the excitement became truly fearful. Every cheek was blanched and every frame trembled when listening to the tale, that "insurrection among the slaves had commenced on the plantation of Col. Alexander; that three or four of the patrol had been killed, &c." The day after, people flocked from every quarter, armed to the teeth, swearing vengeance on the defenceless slaves. Nothing can teach plainer than this, the constant and tormenting fear in which the slaveholder lives, and yet he repents not of his deeds.

The kind old Colonel was placed in the most difficult and unenviable position. His warm heart was filled with sorrow for the loss of his slaves, but not alone, as is generally the case in such instances, because he had lost so much property. He truly regretted the death of his faithful servants, and boldly rebuked the occasion of their sudden decease. When beset and harrassed by his neighbors to give up his slaves to be tried for insurrection and murder, he boldly resisted, contending for the natural right of the slaves, to act in their own defence, and especially when on his own plantation and in their own quarters. They contended, however, that as his slaves had got up a dance, and had invited those of the adjoining plantations, the patrol was only discharging their duty in looking after them; but the gallant old Colonel defended his slaves, and told them plainly that he should continue to do so to the extent of his ability and means.

The poor slaves were sad enough, on the morning after their merry meeting, and they might be seen standing in groups, conversing with a very different air from the one they had worn the day before.

Their business was now to prepare the bodies of their late associates for the grave. Robert, the brave African, who had so boldly led them on the night before, and who had so judi-ciously provided for their escape, was calmly sleeping in death's cold embrace. He left a wife and five slave children. Two of the other slaves left families, whose pitiful cries it was painful to hear.

The Colonel's family, deeply afflicted by what was passing around them, attended the funeral. One of the slaves, who sometimes officiated as a minister, read a portion of Scripture, and gave out two hymns;—one of which commences with

"Hark! from the tomb a doleful sound."

Both were sung with great solemnity by the congregation, and then the good old man offered a prayer; after which he addressed the slaves on the shortness of human life and the certainty of death, and more than once hinted at the hardness of their lot, assuring, however, his fellow-slaves, that if they were good and faithful, all would be right hereafter. His master, Col. Alexander, was deeply affected by this simple faith and sincere regard for the best interests of all, both master and slave.

When the last look at their fellow-servants had been taken, the procession was formed in the following manner: First, the old slave minister, then the remains of the dead, followed by their weeping relatives; then came the master and his family; next the slaves belonging to the plantation; and last, friends and strangers, black and white; all moved on solemnly to the final resting-place of those brave men, whose descendants may yet be heard from, in defence of right and freedom.

58. Bereaved Father Avenges Himself by Self-Mutilation

How often the accidents slaves encountered were purposeful, designed to avoid field work, or to punish a cruel master or overseer for punishment perceived as unjust, is very hard to determine. But the record gives ample evidence that some slaves found this a not unacceptable means of getting even with their oppressors. The degree of embitterment that would precede such an act is an appalling testimony of the basic humanity of the slave, and of his capacity for abandoned self-sacrifice that might be compared, not unfairly, with the *hauteur* of certain young "blooded" aristocrats who flung themselves into duels with far less cause.

Fredrika Bremer, who met one such proud young slave in a Richmond jail, may well have been right in telling him that no Christian could commit such an act. Yet who can deny that the combination of grief, frustration, and raw anger will often produce such a result? For Miss Bremer, see the introduction to document 36.

July 3rd [1851]

. . . I have to-day, in company with an estimable German gentleman, resident at Richmond, visited some of the negro jails, that is, those places of imprisonment in which negroes are in part punished, and in part confined for sale. I saw in one of these jails a tall, strong-limbed negro, sitting silent and gloomy, with his right hand wrapped in a cloth. I asked if he were ill.

"No," replied his loquacious keeper, "but he is a very bad rascal. His master, who lives higher up the river, has parted him from his wife and children, to sell him down South, as he wanted to punish him, and now the scoundrel, to be revenged upon his master, and to make himself fetch a less sum of money, has cut off the fingers of his right hand! The rascal asked me to lend him an ax to knock the nails into his shoes with, and I lent it him without suspecting any bad intention, and now has the fellow gone and maimed himself for life!"

I went up to the negro, who certainly had not a good countenance, and asked him whether he were a Christian. He replied curtly "No!" Whether he ever had heard of Christ? He again replied "No!" I said to him, that if he

Source: Fredrika Bremer *The Homes of the New World: Impressions of America,* 2 vols. (New York: Harper & Bros., 1853), 2:533–34.

had known him, he would not have done this act; but that even now he ought not to believe himself abandoned, because He who has said "Come unto me, all ye that are weary and heavy laden," had spoken also to him, and would console and recreate even him.

He listened to me at the commencement with a gloomy countenance, but by degrees he brightened up, and at the close looked quite melted. This imbittered soul was evidently still open and accessible to good. The sun shone into the prison-yard where he sat with his maimed hand, and the heavy irons on his feet, but no Christian had come hither to preach to him the Gospel of Mercy.

59. London Commits Suicide

The suicide of slaves recently brought from Africa was more common than among those who were born slaves in the New World, and suicide was less common among acclimated slaves in the United States than it was in Brazil and the sugar islands. It was nonetheless a form of ultimate protest that some slaves chose, and it was something that masters and overseers wished to make as unattractive as possible. This explains the refusal of William Capers, overseer at Charles Manigault's plantation in Chatham County, Georgia, to give poor London's body a decent burial. This was probably an effective deterrent, because the blacks attached very great importance to proper funerals.

William Capers to Charles Manigault, June 13, 1860.

[On my return to the plantation] All things found going on quite well excepting the death of London who was drowned on Monday morning about 9 ocl. The cause of this sad calamity is this, viz., George brought London & Nat to Ralph,[1] saying they deserved punishment, they were taken to the Barn, when Ralph went for the key to put them in George allowed London to leave him, an when spoken to by Ralph about not making an exertion to stop London his answer was he would not dust his feet to stop him. London went on to Racoon sq[r] then took the

Source: Ulrich B. Phillips, ed., *Plantation and Frontier* (Cleveland: A. H. Clark, 1909), 2:94.

River at the mouth of the canal, in the presents of some of Mr. Barclay's negroes and Ralph who told him to return, George should not whip him until my return, his ans[wer] was he would drown himself before he would and he sank soon after, the remains of

him is now quite near no 15 Trunk, Gowrie. My orders have been no one is to touch the corpse and will there remain if not taken off by the next tide, this I have done to let the negroes see when a negro takes his own life they will be treated in this manner. My advice to you about George is to ship him, he is of no use to you as a driver and is a bad negro, he would command a good price in Savannah where he can be sold in a quiet manner.

1. Ralph was apparently the negro foreman, George, a subforeman, and London and Nat were members of George's gang. (*Phillips note*)

SEVEN
The Slave's Work

60. Labor and Discipline on a Mississippi Cotton Plantation

In the years immediately preceding the Civil War, thoughtful Northern readers looking for solid information about social and economic conditions in the slave South would probably have turned to the works of Frederick Law Olmsted. Olmsted, more than other travelers, will remind twentieth-century readers of skilled modern journalists who strive for objectivity. Educated as an engineer, the Connecticut-born writer had a keen respect for industrial innovations, and his own considerable experience with modern farming techniques on his Staten Island property gave him a certain confidence in assessing the plantation system.

In 1852 Olmsted was commissioned to report to the *New York Times* on conditions of life and labor in the Southern states. His books on the South came out in a steady succession, beginning in 1856 with the publication of *A Journey through the Seaboard Slave States*. *A Journey through Texas* followed in 1857, and in 1860 *A Journey in the Back Country* appeared. In 1862 these works were reduced to two volumes entitled *The Cotton South*. Judicious and fair on a subject seldom treated objectively, Olmsted won a wide readership, and his works have become classics. His steadily mounting conviction that slavery was inefficient as a labor system was registered more strongly in each successive book. Some readers have believed that his moral revulsion from slavery as an iniquitous system caused him to undervalue the efficiency of the slaves themselves as agricultural workers. In any case Olmsted believed with most modern thinkers of his own time that enlightened self-interest was the key to productivity.

In the following selection from Olmsted's third book the author shows singular qualities of observation on labor and management on a very large and highly regimented cotton plantation on the Mississippi River. Olmsted's investigation of the health care and diet of slaves and the role of overseers makes his work a valuable supplement to Solomon Northup's account of a smaller plantation in the same general region (document 62).

Source: Frederick Law Olmsted, *A Journey in the Back Country* (New York: Mason Bros., 1860), pp. 70–93.

SLAVERY AS AN EDUCATIVE SYSTEM.

The benefit to the African which is supposed to be incidental to American slavery, is confessedly proportionate to the degree in which he is forced into intercourse with a superior race and made subject to its example. Before I visited the South, I had believed that the advantages accruing from slavery, in this way, far outweighed the occasional cruelties, and other evils incidental to the system. I found, however, the mental and moral condition of the negroes, even in Virginia, and in those towns and districts containing the largest proportion of whites, much lower than I had anticipated, and as soon as I had an opportunity to examine one of the extensive plantations of the interior, although one inherited by its owner, and the home of a large and virtuous white family, I was satisfied that the advantages arising to the blacks from association with their white masters were very trifling, scarcely appreciable indeed, for the great majority of the field-hands. Even the overseer had barely acquaintance enough with the slaves individually, to call them by name; the owner could not determine with confidence if he were addressing one of his own chattels, by its features. Much less did the slaves have an opportunity to cultivate their minds by intercourse with other white people. Whatever of civilization, and of the forms, customs and shibboleths of Christianity they were acquiring by example, and through police restraints might, it occurred to me, after all, but poorly compensate the effect of the systematic withdrawal from them of all the usual influences which tend to nourish the moral nature and develop the intellectual faculties, in savages as well as in civilized free men.

This doubt, as my northern friends well know, for I had habitually assumed the opposite, in all previous discussions of the slavery question, was unexpected and painful to me. I resisted it long, and it was not till I had been more than twelve months in the South with my attention constantly fixed upon the point that I ceased to suspect that the circumstances which brought me to it were exceptional and deceptive. It grew constantly stronger with every opportunity I had of observing the condition, habits and character of slaves whom I could believe to present fair examples of the working of the system with the majority of those subject to it upon the large plantations.

The laborers we see in towns, at work on railroads and steamboats, about stations and landings; the menials of our houses and hotels, are less respectable, moral and intelligent than the great majority of the whole laboring class of the North. The traveler at the South has to learn that there the reverse is the case to a degree which can hardly be sufficiently estimated. I have been obliged to think that many amiable travelers who have received impressions with regard to the condition of the slaves very different from mine, have failed to make a sufficient allowance for this. The rank-and-file plantation negroes are not to be readily made acquaintance with by chance or through letters of introduction.

SLAVE MANAGEMENT ON THE
LARGEST SCALE.

The estate I am now about to describe, was situated upon a tributary of the Mississippi, and accessible only by occasional steamboats; even this mode of communication being frequently interrupted at low stages of the rivers. The slaves upon it formed about one twentieth of the whole population of the county, in which the blacks considerably out-number the whites. At the time of my visit, the owner was sojourning upon it, with his family and several invited guests, but his usual residence was upon a small plantation, of little productive value, situated in a neighborhood somewhat noted for the luxury and hospitality of its citizens, and having a daily mail, and direct railroad and telegraphic communication with New York. This was, if I am not mistaken, his second visit in five years.

The property consisted of four adjoining plantations, each with its own negro-cabins, stables and overseer, and each worked to a great extent independently of the others, but all contributing their crop to one gin-house and warehouse, and all under the general superintendence of a bailiff or manager, who constantly resided upon the estate, and in the absence of the owner, had vice-regal power over the overseers, controlling, so far as he thought fit, the economy of all the plantations.

The manager was himself a gentleman of good education, generous and poetic in temperament, and possessing a capacity for the enjoyment of nature and a happiness in the bucolic life, unfortunately rare with Americans. I found him a delightful companion, and I have known no man with whose natural tastes and feelings I have felt, on so short acquaintance, a more hearty sympathy. The gang of toiling negroes to him, however, was as essential an element of the poetry of nature as flocks of peaceful sheep and herds of lowing kine, and he would no more appreciate the aspect in which an Abolitionist would see them than would VIRGIL have honored the feelings of a vegetarian, who could only sigh at the sight of flocks and herds destined to feed the depraved appetite of the carnivorous savage of modern civilization. The overseers were superior to most of their class, and, with one exception, frank, honest, temperate and industrious, but their feelings toward negroes were such as naturally result from their occupation. They were all married, and lived with their families, each in a cabin or cottage, in the hamlet of the slaves of which he had especial charge. Their wages varied from $500 to $1,000 a year each.

These five men, each living more than a mile distant from either of the others, were the only white men on the estate, and the only others within several miles of them were a few skulking vagabonds. Of course, to secure their own personal safety and to efficiently direct the labor of such a large number of ignorant, indolent, and vicious negroes, rules, or rather habits and customs, of discipline, were necessary, which would in particular cases be liable to operate unjustly and cruelly. It is apparent, also, that, as the testimony of negroes against them would not be received as evidence in court, that there was very little probability that any excessive severity would be restrained by fear of the law. A provision of the law intended to secure a certain privilege to slaves, was indeed disregarded under my own observation, and such infraction of the law was confessedly customary with one of the overseers, and was permitted by the manager, for the reason that it seemed to him to be, in a certain degree, justifiable and expedient under the circumstances, and because he did not like to interfere unnecessarily in such matters.

In the main, the negroes appeared to be well taken care of and abundantly supplied with the necessaries of vigorous physical existence. A large part of them lived in commodious and well-built cottages, with broad galleries in front, so that each family of five had two rooms on the lower floor, and a loft. The remainder lived in log-huts, small and mean in appearance, but those of their overseers were little better, and preparations were being made to replace all of these by neat boarded cottages. Each family had a fowl-house and hog-sty (constructed by the negroes themselves), and kept fowls and swine, feeding the latter during the summer on weeds and fattening them in the autumn on corn *stolen* (this was mentioned to me by the overseers as if it were a matter of course) from their master's corn-fields. I several times saw gangs of them eating the dinner which they had bought, each for himself, to the field, and observed that they generally had plenty, often more than they could eat, of bacon, corn-bread, and molasses. The allowance of food is weighed and measured under the eye of the manager by the drivers, and distributed to the head of each family weekly: consisting of—for each person, 3 pounds of pork, 1 peck of meal; and from January to July, 1 quart of molasses. Monthly, in addition, 1 pound tobacco, and 4 pints salt. No

drink is ever served but water, except after unusual exposure, or to ditchers working in water, who get a glass of whisky at night. All hands cook for themselves after work at night, or whenever they please between nightfall and daybreak, each family in its own cabin. Each family had a garden, the products of which, together with eggs, fowls and bacon, they frequently sold, or used in addition to their regular allowance of food. Most of the families bought a barrel of flour every year. The manager endeavored to encourage this practice, and that they might spend their money for flour instead of liquor, he furnished it to them at rather less than what it cost him at wholesale. There were many poor whites within a few miles who would always sell liquor to the negroes, and encourage them to steal, to obtain the means to buy it of them. These poor whites were always spoken of with anger by the overseers, and they each had a standing offer of much more than the intrinsic value of their land, from the manager, to induce them to move away.

The negroes also obtain a good deal of game. They set traps for raccoons, rabbits and turkeys, and I once heard the stock-tender complaining that he had detected one of the vagabond whites stealing a turkey which had been caught in his pen. I several times partook of game while on the plantation, that had been purchased of the negroes. The stock-tender, an old negro, whose business it was to ride about in the woods and keep an eye on the stock cattle that were pastured in them, and who was thus likely to know where the deer ran, had an ingenious way of supplying himself with venison. He lashed a scythe blade or butcher's knife to the end of a pole so that it formed a lance; this he set near a fence or fallen tree which obstructed a path in which the deer habitually ran, and the deer in leaping over the obstacle would leap directly on the knife. In this manner he had killed two deer the week before my visit.

The manager sent to him for some of this venison for his own use, and justified himself to me for not paying for it on the ground that the stock tender had undoubtedly taken time which really belonged to his owner to set his spear. Game taken by the field-hands was not looked upon in the same light, because it must have been got at night when they were excused from labor for their owner.

The first morning I was on the estate, while at breakfast with the manager, an old negro woman came into the room and said to him, "Dat gal's bin bleedin' agin dis mornin'."

"How much did she bleed?"

"About a pint, sir."

"Very well; I'll call and see her after breakfast."

"I come up for some sugar of lead, master; I gin her some powdered alum 'fore I come away."

"Very well; you can have some."

After breakfast the manager invited me to ride with him on his usual daily round of inspection through the plantations.

PLANTATION WORK-HOUSE.

On reaching the nearest "quarters," we stopped at a house, a little larger than the ordinary cabins, which was called the loom-house, in which a dozen negroes were at work making shoes, and manufacturing coarse cotton stuff for negro clothing. One of the hands so employed was insane, and most of the others were cripples, invalids with chronic complaints, or unfitted by age, or some infirmity, for field-work.

MEDICAL SURVEY.

From this we went to one of the cabins, where we found the sick woman who had been bleeding at the lungs, with the old nurse in attendance upon her. The manager examined and prescribed for her in a kind manner. When we came out he asked the nurse if any one else was sick.

"Oney dat woman Carline."

"What do you think is the matter with her?"

"Well, I don't tink dere's anyting de matter wid her, masser; I mus' answer you for true, I don't tink anyting de matter wid her, oney she's a little sore from dat whippin' she got."

We went to another cabin and entered a room where a woman lay on a bed, groaning. It was a very dingy, comfortless room, but a musquito bar, much patched and very dirty, covered the bed. The manager asked the woman several times what was the matter, but could get no distinct reply. She appeared to be suffering great pain. The manager felt her pulse and looked at her tongue, and after a few more inquiries, to which no intelligible reply was given, told her he did not believe she was ill at all. At this the woman's groans redoubled. "I have heard of your tricks," continued the manager; "you had a chill when I came to see you yesterday morning; you had a chill when the mistress came here, and you had a chill when the master came. I never knew a chill to last the whole day. So you'll just get up now and go to the field, and if you don't work smart, you'll get a dressing; do you hear?"

We then left. The manager said that he rarely—almost never—had occasion to employ a physician for the people. Never for accouchements; the women, from their labor in the field, were not subject to the difficulty, danger, and pain which attended women of the better classes in giving birth to their offspring.

Near the first quarters we visited there was a large blacksmith's and wheelwright's shop, in which a number of mechanics were at work. Most of them, as we rode up, were eating their breakfast, which they warmed at their fires. Within and around the shop there were some fifty plows which they were putting in order. The manager inspected the work, found some of it faulty, sharply reprimanded the workmen for not getting on faster, and threatened one of them with a whipping for not paying closer attention to the directions which had been given him. He told me that he once employed a white man from the North, who professed to be a first-class workman, but he soon found he could not do nearly as good work as the negro mechanics on the estate, and the latter despised him so much, and got such high opinions of themselves in consequence of his inferiority, that he had been obliged to discharge him in the midst of his engagement.

The overseer of this plantation rode up while we were at the shop, and reported to the manager how all his hands were employed. There were so many at this and so many at that, and they had done so much since yesterday. "There's that girl, Caroline," said the manager; "she's not sick, and I told her she must go to work; put her to the hoeing; there's nothing the matter with her, except she's sore with the whipping she got. You must go and get her out." A woman was passing at the time, and the manager told her to go and tell Caroline she must get up and go to work, or the overseer would come and start her. She returned in a few minutes, and reported that Caroline said she could not get up. The overseer and manager rode toward the cabin, but before they reached it, the girl, who had probably been watching us from the window, came out and went to the field with her hoe. They then returned to me and continued their conversation. Just before we left the overseer, he said, "I think that girl who ran away last week was in her cabin last night." The manager told me, as we rode on, that the people often ran away after they have been whipped, or something else had happened to make them angry. They hide in the swamp, and come in to the cabins at night to get food. They seldom remain away more than a fortnight, and when they come in they are whipped. The woman, Caroline, he said, had been delivered of a dead child about six weeks before, and had been complaining and getting rid of work ever since. She was the laziest woman on the estate. This shamming illness gave him the most disagreeable duty he had to perform. Negroes were famous for it. "If it was not for her bad character," he continued, "I should fear to make her go to work to-day; but her pulse is steady, and her tongue perfectly smooth. *We have to be sharp with them; if we were not, every negro on the estate would be abed.*"

CLOTHES AND CLEANLINESS.

We rode on to where the different gangs of laborers were at work, and inspected them one after another. I observed, as we were looking at one of the gangs, that they were very dirty. "Negroes are the filthiest people in the world," said the manager; "there are some of them who would not keep clean twenty-four hours at a time if you gave them thirty suits a year." I asked him if there were any rules to maintain cleanliness. There were not, but sometimes the negroes were told at night that any one who came into the field the next morning without being clean would be whipped. This gave no trouble to those who were habitually clean, while it was in itself a punishment to those who were not, as they were obliged to spend the night in washing.

They were furnished with two suits of summer, and one of winter clothing each year. Besides which, most of them got presents of some holiday finery (calico dresses, handkerchiefs, etc.), and purchased more for themselves, at Christmas. One of the drivers now in the field had on a splendid uniform coat of an officer of the flying artillery. After the Mexican war, a great deal of military clothing was sold at auction in New Orleans, and much of it was bought by planters at a low price, and given to their negroes, who were greatly pleased with it.

HOURS OF LABOR.

Each overseer regulated the hours of work on his own plantation. I saw the negroes at work before sunrise and after sunset. At about eight o'clock they were allowed to stop for breakfast, and again about noon, to dine. The length of these rests was at the discretion of the overseer or drivers, usually, I should say, from half an hour to an hour. There was no rule.

OVERSEERS.

The number of hands directed by each overseer was considerably over one hundred. The manager thought it would be better economy to have a white man over every fifty hands, but the difficulty of obtaining trustworthy overseers prevented it. Three of those he then had were the best he had ever known. He described the great majority as being passionate, careless, inefficient men, generally intemperate, and totally unfitted for the duties of the position. The best overseers, ordinarily, are young men, the sons of small planters, who take up the business temporarily, as a means of acquiring a little capital with which to purchase negroes for themselves.

PLOW-GIRLS.

The plowing, both with single and double mule teams, was generally performed by women, and very well performed, too. I watched with some interest for any indication that their sex unfitted them for the occupation. Twenty of them were plowing together, with double teams and heavy plows. They were superintended by a male negro driver, who carried a whip, which he frequently cracked at them, permitting no dawdling or delay at the turning; and they twitched their plows around on the head-land, jerking their reins, and yelling to their mules, with apparent ease, energy, and rapidity. Throughout the Southwest the negroes, as a rule, appear to be worked much harder than in the eastern and northern slave States. I do not think they accomplish as much daily, as agricultural laborers at the North usually do, but they certainly labor much harder, and more unremittingly. They are constantly and steadily driven up to their work, and the stupid, plodding, machine-like manner in which they labor, is painful to witness. This was especially the case with the hoe-gangs. One of them numbered nearly two hundred hands (for the force of two plantations was working together), moving across the field in parallel lines, with a considerable degree of precision. I repeatedly rode through the lines at a canter, with other horsemen, often coming upon them suddenly, without producing the smallest change or interruption in the dogged action of the laborers, or causing one of them to lift an eye from the ground. A very tall and powerful negro walked to and fro in the rear of the line, frequently cracking his whip, and calling out, in the surliest manner, to one and another, "Shove your hoe, there! shove your hoe!" But I never saw him strike any one with the whip.

DISCIPLINE.

The whip was evidently in constant use, however. There were no rules on the subject, that I learned; the overseers and drivers punished the negroes whenever they deemed it necessary, and in such manner, and with such severity, as they thought fit. "If you do n't work faster," or "If you do n't work better," or "If you do n't recollect what I tell you, I will have you flogged," are threats which I have often heard. I said to one of the overseers, "It must be very disagreeable to have to punish them as much as you do?" "Yes, it would be to those who are not used to it—but it's my business, and I think nothing of it. Why, sir, I would n't mind killing a nigger more than I would a dog." I asked if he had ever killed a negro? "Not quite," he said, but overseers were often obliged to. Some negroes are determined never to let a white man whip them, and will resist you, when you attempt it; of course you must kill them in that case. Once a negro, whom he was about to whip in the field, struck at his head with a hoe. He parried the blow with his whip, and drawing a pistol tried to shoot him, but the pistol missing fire he rushed in and knocked him down with the butt of it. At another time a negro whom he was punishing, insulted and threatened him. He went to the house for his gun, and as he was returning, the negro, thinking he would be afraid of spoiling so valuable a piece of property by firing, broke for the woods. He fired at once, and put six buck-shot into his hips. He always carried a bowie-knife, but not a pistol, unless he anticipated some unusual act of insubordination. He always kept a pair of pistols ready loaded over the mantel-piece, however, in case they should be needed. It was only when he first came upon a plantation that he ever had much trouble. A great many overseers were unfit for their business, and too easy and slack with the negroes. When he succeeded such a man, he had hard work for a time to break the negroes in, but it did not take long to teach them their place. His conversation on this subject was exactly like what I have heard said, again and again, by northern shipmasters and officers, with regard to seamen.

PUNISHMENT.

The severest corporeal punishment of a negro that I witnessed at the South, occurred while I was visiting this estate. I suppose however, that punishment equally severe is common—in fact, it must be necessary to the maintenance of adequate discipline on every large plantation. It is much more necessary than on shipboard, because the opportunities of hiding away and shirking labor, and of wasting and injuring the owner's property without danger to themselves, are far greater in the case of the slaves than in that of the sailors, but above all, because there is no real moral obligation on the part of the negro to do what is demanded of him. The sailor performs his duty in obedience to a voluntary contract; the slave is in an involuntary servitude. The manner of the overseer who inflicted the punishment, and his subsequent conversation with me about it,

indicated that it was by no means an unusual occurrence with him. I had accidentally encountered him, and he was showing me his plantation. In going from one side of it to the other, we had twice crossed a deep gully, at the bottom of which was a thick covert of brushwood. We were crossing it a third time, and had nearly passed through the brush, when the overseer suddenly stopped his horse exclaiming, "What's that? Hallo! who are you there?"

It was a girl lying at full length on the ground at the bottom of the gully, evidently intending to hide herself from us in the bushes.

"Who are you there?"

"Sam's Sall, sir."

"What are you skulking there for?"

The girl half rose, but gave no answer.

"Have you been here all day?"

"No sir."

"How did you get here?"

The girl made no reply.

"Where have you been all day?"

The answer was unintelligible.

After some further questioning, she said her father accidentally locked her in, when he went out in the morning.

"How did you manage to get out?"

"Pushed a plank off, sir, and crawled out."

The overseer was silent for a moment, looking at the girl, and then said, "That won't do—come out here." The girl arose at once, and walked towards him; she was about eighteen years of age. A bunch of keys hung at her waist, which the overseer espied, and he said, "Ah, your father locked you in; but you have got the keys." After a little hesitation, the girl replied that these were the keys of some other locks; her father had the door-key.

Whether her story were true or false, could have been ascertained in two minutes by riding on to the gang with which her father was at work, but the overseer had made up his mind as to the facts of the case.

"That won't do," said he, "get down on your knees." The girl knelt on the ground; he got off his horse, and holding him with his left hand, struck her thirty or forty blows across the shoulders with his tough, flexible, "raw-hide" whip. They were well laid on, as a boatswain would thrash a skulking sailor, or as some people flog a baulking horse, but with no appearance of angry excitement on the part of the overseer. At every stroke the girl winced, and exclaimed, "Yes, sir!" or "Ah, sir!" or "Please, sir!" not groaning or screaming. At length he stopped and said, "Now tell me the truth." The girl repeated the same story. "You have not got enough yet," said he, "pull up your clothes—lie down." The girl without any hesitation, without a word or look of remonstrance or entreaty, drew closely all her garments under her soulders, and lay down upon the ground with her face toward the overseer, who continued to flog her with the rawhide, across her naked loins and thigh, with as much strength as before. She now shrunk away from him, not rising, but writhing, groveling, and screaming, "Oh, do n't sir! oh, please stop, master! please, sir! please, sir! oh, that's enough, master! oh, Lord! oh, master, master! oh, God, master, do stop! oh, God, master, oh, God, master!"

A young gentleman of fifteen was with us; he had ridden in front, and now, turning on his horse looked back with an expression only of impatience at the delay. It was the first time I had ever seen a woman flogged. I had seen a man cudgeled and beaten, in the heat of passion, before, but never flogged with a hundredth part of the severity used in this case. I glanced again at the perfectly passionless but rather grim business-like face of the overseer, and again at the young gentleman, who had turned away; if not indifferent he had evidently not the faintest sympathy with my emotion. Only my horse chafed with excitement. I gave him rein and spur and we plunged into the bushes and scrambled fiercely up the steep acclivity. The screaming yells and the whip strokes had ceased when I reached the top of the bank. Choking, sobbing, spasmodic groans only were heard. I rode on to where the road coming diagonally up the ravine ran out upon the cotton-field. My young companion met me there, and immediately afterward the overseer. He laughed as he joined us, and said,

"She meant to cheat me out of a day's work—and she has done it, too."

"Did you succeed in getting another story from her?"

"No; she stuck to it."

"Was it not perhaps true?"

"Oh no, sir, she slipped out of the gang when they were going to work, and she's been dodging about all day, going from one place to another as she saw me coming. She saw us crossing there a little while ago, and though we had gone to the quarters, but we turned back so quick, we came into the gully before she knew it, and she could do nothing but lie down in the bushes."

"I suppose they often slip off so."

"No, sir; I never had one do so before—not like this; they often run away to the woods and are gone some time, but I never had a dodge-off like this before."

"Was it necessary to punish her so severely?"

"Oh yes, sir," (laughing again.) "If I had n't punished her so hard she would have done the same thing again to-morrow, and half the people on the plantation would have followed her example. Oh, you've no idea how lazy these niggers are; you northern people do n't know any thing about it. They'd never do any work at all if they were not afraid of being whipped."

We soon afterward met an old man, who, on being closely questioned, said that he had seen the girl leave the gang as they went to work after dinner. It appeared that she had been at work during the forenoon, but at dinner-time the gang was moved and as it passed through the gully she slipped out. The driver had not missed her. The overseer said that when he first took charge of this plantation, the negroes ran away a great deal—they disliked him so much. They used to say 'twas hell to be on his place; but after a few months they got used to his ways, and liked him better than any of the rest. He had not had any run away now in some time. When they ran away they would generally return within a fortnight. If many of them went off, or if they staid out long, he would make the rest of the force work Sundays, or deprive them of some of their usual privileges until they returned. The negroes on the plantation could always bring them in if they chose to. They depended on them for their food, and they had only to stop the supplies to oblige them to surrender.

NAMES.

Afterward, as I was sitting near a gang with an overseer and the manager, the former would occasionally call out to one and another by name, in directing or urging their labor. I asked if he knew them all by name. He did, but the manager did not know one fifth of them. The overseer said he generally could call most of the negroes on a plantation by their names in two weeks after he came to it, but it was rather difficult to learn them on account of there being so many of the same name, distinguished from each other by a prefix. "There's a Big Jim here, and a Little Jim, and Eliza's Jim, and there's Jim Bob, and Jim Clarisy."

"What's Jim Clarisy?—how does he get that name?"

"He's Clarisy's child, and Bob is Jim Bob's father. That fellow ahead there, with the blue rag on his head, his name is Swamp; he always goes by that name, but his real name is Abraham, I believe; is it not, Mr. [Manager]?"

"His name is Swamp on the plantation register—that's all I know of him."

"I believe his name is Abraham," said the overseer; "he told me so. He was bought of Judge ———, he says, and he told me his master called him Swamp because he ran away so much. He is the worst runaway on the place."

MORAL EDUCATION OF THE NEGROES.

I inquired about the increase of the negroes on the estate, and the manager having told me the number of deaths and births the previous year, which gave a net increase of four per cent— on Virginia estates it is often twenty per cent—I asked if the negroes began to have children at a very early age. "Sometimes at sixteen," said the manager. "Yes, and at fourteen," said the overseer; "that girl's had a child"— pointing to a girl that did not appear older than fourteen. "Is she married?" "No." "You see," said the manager, "negro girls are not remarkable for chastity; their habits indeed rather hinder them from having children. They'd have them younger than they do if they would marry or live with but one man, sooner than they do. They often do not have children till they are twenty-five years old." "Are those who are married true to each other?" I asked. The overseer laughed heartily at the idea, and described a disgustingly "Free Love" state of things. "Do you not try to discourage this?" "No, not unless they quarrel." "They get jealous and quarrel among themselves sometimes about it," the manager explained, "or come to the overseer and complain, and he has them punished." "Give all hands a damned good hiding," said the overseer. "You punish for adultery, then, but not for fornication?" "Yes," answered the manager, but "No," replied the overseer, "we punish them for quarreling; if they do n't quarrel I do n't mind any thing about it, but if it makes a muss, I give all four of 'em a warming."

BLACK, WHITE, AND YELLOW.

Riding through a large gang of hoers, with two of the overseers, I observed that a large proportion of them appeared to be thorough-bred Africans. Both of them thought that the "real black niggers" were about three fourths of the whole number, and that this would hold as an average on Mississippi and Louisiana plantations. One of them pointed out a girl—"That one is pure white; you see her hair?" (It was straight and sandy.) "She is the only one we have got." It was not uncommon, he said, to see slaves so white that they could not be easily distinguished from pure-blooded whites. He had never been on a plantation before, that had not more than one on it. "Now," said I, "if that girl should dress herself well, and run away, would she be suspected of being a slave?"

"Oh, yes; you might not know her if she got to the North, but any of us would know her."

"How?"

"By her language and manners."

"But if she had been brought up as house-servant?"

"Perhaps not in that case."

The other thought there would be no difficulty; a slave girl would always quail when you looked in her eyes.

I asked if they thought the mulattoes or white slaves were weaker or less valuable than the pure negroes.

"Oh, no; I'd rather have them a great deal," said one. "Well, I had not," said the other; "the blacker the better for me." "The white ones," added the first, "are more active, and know more, and I think do a good deal the most work." "Are they more subject to illness, or do they appear to be of weaker constitutions?" One said they were not, the other that they did not seem to bear the heat as well. The first thought that this might be so, but that, nevertheless, they would do more work. I afterwards asked the manager's opinion. He thought they did not stand excessive heat as well as the pure negroes, but that, from their greater activity and willingness, they would do more work. He believed they were equally strong, and no more liable to illness; had never had reason to think them of weaker constitution. They often had large families, and he had not noticed that their children were weaker or more subject to disease than others. He thought that perhaps they did not have so many children as the pure negroes, but he had supposed the reason to be that they did not begin bearing so young as the others, and this was because they were more attractive to the men, and perhaps more amorous themselves. He knew a great many mulattoes living together, and they generally had large and healthy families.

Afterwards, at one of the plantation nurseries, where there were some twenty or thirty infants and young children, a number of whom were evidently the offspring of white fathers, I asked the nurse to point out the healthiest children to me, and of those she indicated, more were of the pure, than of the mixed breed. I then asked her to show me which were the sickliest, and she did not point to any of the latter. I then asked if she noticed any difference in this respect between the black and the yellow children. "Well, dey do say, master, dat de yellow ones is de sickliest, but I can't tell for true dat I ever see as dey was."

RELIGION.

Being with the proprietor and the manager together, I asked about the religious condition of the slaves. There were "preachers" on the plantations, and they had some religious observances on a Sunday; but the preachers were the worst characters among them, and, they thought, only made their religion a cloak for habits of especial depravity. They were, at all events, the most deceitful and dishonest slaves on the plantation, and oftenest required punishment. The negroes of all denominations, and even those who ordinarily made no religious pretensions, would join together in exciting religious observances. These gentlemen considered the religious exercises of the negroes to be similar, in their intellectual and moral character, to the Indian feasts and war-dances, and did not encourage them. Neither did they like to have white men preach on the estate; and in future they did not intend to permit them to do so. It excited the negroes so much as to greatly interfere with the subordination and order which were necessary to obtain the profitable use of their labor. They would be singing and dancing every night in their cabins, till dawn of day, and utterly unfit themselves for work.

I remarked that I had been told that a religious negro was considered to be worth a third more, because of his greater honesty and steadiness.

"Quite the contrary," they both assured me, for a religious negro generally made trouble, and they were glad to get rid of him.

I have no doubt these opinions were sincere. Probably these gentlemen held different views of the intellectual and moral capabilities of the African race from those entertained by the Liberty planters.[1] I did not infer, however, that

1. The planters of Liberty County, Georgia, were known throughout the South for their religious piety and educational attainments.

they shared the most advanced views of southern philosophers on this subject. . . .

Olmsted assessed Liberty as "a district in which more is done for the elevation of the slaves than in any other of the South." (*Editor's note*)

61. On a South Carolina Rice Plantation

In the tidal areas of the Southeast, long-staple cotton and rice were the principal staple crops; both were limited to the coastal areas because of their cultivation requirements. Rice was especially challenging, by reason of the complexity of its culture, involving as it did great care in the timing of operations, and a system of dikes for the periodic flooding of the fields. It was also an unhealthful crop for slaves, who suffered much from pulmonary diseases associated with exposure.

Capt. Basil Hall of the British Navy visited a sea island rice plantation northeast of Charleston in the 1820s, and reported in some detail about the crop and about plantation social structure. Captain Hall's account has particular interest for another reason: in the nineteenth century only on board ship was the discipline of a severity roughly comparable to that of slavery. Hall, who was born in Edinburgh in 1788, and died in 1844, left several volumes recording his many travels in Asia and North America.

Although Hall opposed slavery in principle, and was much criticized when his books were published for his severe strictures on the institution, the modern reader may reach the conclusion that Hall was bending over backward in his effort to be fair to the planters. He was obviously exerting himself to remain objective about an institution that few could be objective about. He rated the intelligence of skilled slave laborers as being very

Source: Basil Hall, *Travels in North America in the Years 1827 and 1828.* 2 vols. (Philadelphia: Carey, Lea & Carey, 1829), 2:212–17.

high. His observation concerning the preferences of slaves for field labor is interesting, and contrary to the views of some travelers.

After dinner we strolled over the plantation, under our friend Solomon's direction, and a most intelligent and agreeable guide he proved—more so, indeed, than it had ever occurred to us any slave-driver could possibly be. The imagination pictures such a character flourishing his whip, and so far it is true, for this symbol of office is never laid down—but he made no use of it during our stay, and he appeared to be any thing but stern or tyrannical in his deportment, to the people under his orders. We found the principal body of the negroes making a dam to keep back the waters of an adjacent river, which had invaded some of the rice fields. The negroes were working in a long string, exactly like a row of ants, with baskets of earth on their heads, under the superintendence of two under drivers, likewise blacks. This labour appeared to be heavy, and as the day declined, some of the poor people, especially the women, looked tired enough.

This plantation, at the time of our visit, consisted of 270 acres of rice, 50 of cotton, 80 of Indian corn, and 12 of potatoes, besides some minor plots for vegetables; the whole being cultivated by eighty working hands. A shovel plough is used at certain seasons for weeding; but all the essential and laborious work of preparing the soil, as well as that of sowing and reaping the crops, is done exclusively by hand.

Next day we left our hospitable friend's plantation, and proceeded to the southward. We had no difficulty in again finding shelter, for the considerate people of Charleston had supplied us amply with introductions, enjoining us, at the same time, to consider every house we came to, as open to receive us, if we had any wish to occupy it. An experienced traveller on this road, had given us a hint where we should be best entertained, and we accordingly drove up to a very promising establishment, which fully answered the description given of it. The master of the place was walking about the grounds, but the servants had orders, they said, to receive us, and begged us to walk in.

The day being hot and calm, all the doors and windows were thrown open, and we walked through the house to a pleasant garden, overhanging the Combahee River, flowing majestically past, in a direction from the sea. Our host, who soon joined us, explained that the current we saw, was caused by the flood tide, though the sea was distant full 30 miles. This ebb and flow of the rivers intersecting the level parts of South Carolina, is of the greatest consequence to the rice growers, as it enables them to irrigate their fields at the proper season, and in the proper quantity; an advantage which leads to the production of those magnificent crops, with which all the world is familiar.

During our stay at this extensive and skilfully managed plantation, we had an opportunity of being initiated into the mysteries of the cultivation of rice, a staple of Carolina. This grain is sown in rows, in the bottom of trenches made by slave labour entirely. These ridges lie about seventeen inches apart, from centre to centre. The rice is put in with the hand, generally by women, and is never scattered, but cast so as to fall in a line. This is done about the 17th of March. By means of flood-gates, the water is then permitted to flow over the fields, and to remain on the ground five days, at the depth of several inches. The object of this drenching is to sprout the seeds, as it is technically called. The water is next drawn off, and the ground allowed to dry, until the rice has risen to what is termed four leaves high, or between three and four inches. This requires about a month. The fields are then again overflowed, and they remain submerged for upwards of a fortnight, to destroy the grass and weeds. These processes bring matters to the 17th of May, after which the ground is allowed to remain dry till the 15th of July, during which interval it is repeatedly hoed, to remove such weeds as have not been effectually drowned, and also to loosen the soil. The water is then, for the last time, introduced, in order that the rice may be brought to maturity—and it actually ripens while standing in the water. The harvest commences about the end of August, and extends into October. It is all cut by the male slaves, who use a sickle, while the women make it up into bundles. As it seems that no ingenuity has yet been able to overcome the difficulty of thrashing the grains out by machinery, without breaking them, the whole of this part of the process is done with hand flails in a court-yard.

The cultivation of rice was described to me as by far the most unhealthy work in which the slaves were employed; and, in spite of every care, that they sank under it in great numbers. The causes of this dreadful mortality, are the constant moisture and heat of the atmosphere, together with the alternate floodings and dryings of the fields, on which the negroes are perpetually at work, often ankle-deep in mud, with their bare heads exposed to the fierce rays of the sun. At such seasons every white man leaves the spot, as a matter of course, and proceeds inland to the high grounds; or, if he can afford it, he travels northward to the springs of Saratoga, or the Lakes of Canada.

Each plantation is furnished with a mill; and in most cases that fell in my way, the planters contrived to make this and every thing else, or very nearly every thing else which they require, on their own estates. All the blacksmiths' and carpenters' work, for example, was done by the slaves of each plantation; nor did it appear, from all I could learn, that there was any deficiency of intellect in the negro, so far as these mechanical operations went. The contrary is stoutly maintained in the non-slave-holding States; but this, I think, is in some degree to be accounted for by the admitted fact, of the free negro population—with which alone persons in the north are personally acquainted—being a degraded, dissolute class. But on a well-regulated plantation, such as the one I am describing, where the proprietor is a man of sense, temper, and discrimination, and where he has somewhat more than a thousand slaves to choose from, the experiment—as to the lower walks of intellect, at least—has more fair play given it. The negroes themselves feel this very strongly, I was told, and whenever they are under the management of such a person as our judicious host, they exert themselves greatly, from the hope of being distinguished. While he and I were in the act of discussing this topic, I happened to break the bolt joining the triple legs of the camp stool I used when drawing with the Camera Lucida. "Do you think, now," I said, "you have any man on your plantation who could repair this, for it is rather a nice matter?"

"O yes.—Caesar! come here," he called out to the blacksmith. "Don't you see this bolt is broken—can you put it to rights?"

"I can, sir," was his answer; and though he was rather hurried, he executed the job in a very neat and business-like style. The rest of the party having walked on, I staid to have some conversation with Caesar, whose correct acquaintance not only with his own mechanical operations, but with many other things, surprised me a good deal, and I left the smithy, with my opinion of the whole black race raised in the scale by this trivial incident. Of such flimsy materials is prejudice built!

I think it right to mention, that as far as my own experience has gone, I have invariably noticed that precisely in proportion as the negro has a fair chance given him, so he proves himself equal in capacity to the white man. Perhaps the only place in the world where a black has, to all intents and purposes, an equal chance with the rest of mankind, is on board a ship-of-war. He is there subjected to the same discipline, has the same favour shown if he behaves well, and suffers a like punishment for the like faults. I think it is generally allowed in the English navy, that under like circumstances, black seamen are as useful and as trust-worthy as the rest of the crew. I am led to infer, also, from a recent American work—the Red Rover—that the author, who is a naval officer, agrees with me in this view of the matter. At all events, he makes his admirable seaman, 'Fid,' not superior, if equal, to his sable companion 'Guinea,'—both characters, however, being so exquisitely drawn, that it would almost be worth a landsman's while to make a voyage or two merely to understand them.

Generally speaking, though by no means always, I found the most sensible planters of opinion, that there was not naturally and essentially any intellectual difference between the two races.

Our hospitable friend next showed us the slave village of his plantation, where every thing was neat and comfortable. In answer to our questions, he told us, that he interfered as little as possible with their domestic habits, except in matters of police. "We don't care what they do when their tasks are over—we lose sight of them till next day. Their morals and manners are in their own keeping. The men may have, for instance, as many wives as they please, so long as they do not quarrel about such matters."

I asked if they had any religion?

"I know little about that," he said; "there may perhaps be one or two methodists in a hundred. Preachers are never prevented, by me at least, from coming amongst the negroes, upon a distinct and express stipulation, however, that they do not interfere with the duties of the slaves, towards their master."

"Can any of them read and write?"

"Certainly none," he answered; "that is entirely contrary to usage here, and contrary to law in some places. Such things would only make them discontented with their lot, and in fact would be quite repugnant to the whole system of slave discipline in this country."

Domestic slaves, he told me, were better fed and clothed, and generally better treated, than those employed out of doors; but, what was odd enough, he added, that every where the slaves preferred the field-work, chiefly, as far as I could learn, from its being definite in amount, which left them a certain portion of the day entirely to themselves. This privilege has become, virtually a right in many places; and so far, is a spark of freedom in their dark night of bondage; whereas the house slave, from being liable to every call, early and late, sometimes fancies himself less free. A negro, however, who has been regularly bred in that line, generally becomes so much attached to the children and to the other members of the family, and falls so completely into the ways of the house, that he would feel it an intolerable hardship to be sent to the field-work.

The laws direct that the overseer of the plantation shall always be a white man. He is a very important personage, as may be supposed, since much of the success of an estate, as well as the happiness or misery of the negroes—which appears to be nearly the same thing—depend upon his character. The details of superintendence pass under his eye, and he has the power of directing punishments, which ought always to be inflicted in his presence on the spot, by the driver. It is very disagreeable to think of such things, but it is obvious to every one who has reflected at all on this painful subject, that there must be a certain amount of prompt and vigorous discipline exercised over people who are influenced by so few of the ordinary motives to exertion.

It is the popular fashion in America, and I think elsewhere, to abuse these overseers as a class. But none of my enquiries led me to think so ill of them by any means as I had heard them reported. Their interest, as well as that of the planters, in the long run, is, unquestionably, to use the slaves well. An overseer who acquires a character for undue severity, is much scouted, and sooner or later discovers that his services are not valued or sought after, merely because he produces less effective work than a more judicious person would do. Negroes, like many other people, may be driven to perform a certain portion of labour; but as no amount of tyranny can carry things permanently beyond that point, custom seems to have established in the slave-holding States of America, a particular method of treatment, which is found to produce the greatest result. I have much satisfaction accordingly, in stating, that after many careful enquiries, I have no reason to suppose unnecessary severity is by any means general in America.

62. Growing Cotton and Sugar Cane in Louisiana

The first cotton to be grown commercially in the United States was the long-staple sea island cotton raised near the Atlantic Coast. The seed was readily separable from the fibre, but this cotton could not be grown in the interior, and the short-staple cotton that could be grown in the uplands could not be grown commercially because of the difficulty of separating the short fibre from the seed. The invention in 1793 of the cotton gin opened the way for the widespread culture of short-staple cotton in the interior of the South. In the early decades of the nineteenth century, upland cotton rapidly gained ascendency over other crops, and by the 1830s was the great commercial crop of the South. Most slaves were employed in cotton fields. Therefore, conditions controlling the life and labor in the cotton crop were the conditions most familiar to Southern blacks.

In the following document Solomon Northup describes the culture of cotton on a large plantation on the Bayou Bœuf in Avoyelles Parish in Louisiana. Northup's narrative of his experience as a slave is unique for its clarity and detail, as well as for the circumstances that prompted his story. Born a free man in New York State, Northup earned money as a fiddler for entertainments before two white men drugged and kidnapped him, and then sold him as a slave. Northup was bought by a Louisiana slave-master named Ford, who hired him out—under his new name of "Platt"—to the "Master Epps" of the following account.

Northup's family never gave up the search for him, and after twelve years his freedom was restored by their efforts and the intercession of the Governor of New York. Many details of Northup's account have been verified by Sue Eakin and Joseph Logsden, who in 1968 edited for Louisiana State University Press a new edition of Northup's narrative.

During his long ordeal in slavery Northup was singularly observant of the manner in which work of all kinds was done, and occasionally made inventions that eased chores. Since he was hired out to work in sugar cane

Source: Solomon Northup, *Twelve Years a Slave. Narrative of Solomon Northup, a Citizen of New-York, Kidnapped in Washington City in 1841, and Rescued in 1853, From a Cotton Plantation Near the Red River, in Louisiana* (Auburn, N.Y.: Derby and Miller, 1853), pp. 163–75, 208–12.

as well as in cotton, he could describe the activities that went into producing the sugar and getting it ready for the market.

Chapter XII.
[on cotton]

· · ·

When "in his cups," Master Epps was a roystering, blustering, noisy fellow, whose chief delight was in dancing with his "niggers," or lashing them about the yard with his long whip, just for the pleasure of hearing them screech and scream, as the great welts were planted on their backs. When sober, he was silent, reserved and cunning, not beating us indiscriminately, as in his drunken moments, but sending the end of his rawhide to some tender spot of a lagging slave, with a sly dexterity peculiar to himself.

He had been a driver and overseer in his younger years, but at this time was in possession of a plantation on Bayou Huff Power, two and a half miles from Holmesville, eighteen from Marksville, and twelve from Cheneyville. It belonged to Joseph B. Roberts, his wife's uncle, and was leased by Epps. His principal business was raising cotton, and inasmuch as some may read this book who have never seen a cotton field, a description of the manner of its culture may not be out of place.

The ground is prepared by throwing up beds or ridges, with the plough—back-furrowing, it is called. Oxen and mules, the latter almost exclusively, are used in ploughing. The women as frequently as the men perform this labor, feeding, currying, and taking care of their teams, and in all respects doing the field and stable work, precisely as do the ploughboys of the North.

The beds, or ridges, are six feet wide, that is, from water furrow to water furrow. A plough drawn by one mule is then run along the top of the ridge or center of the bed, making the drill, into which a girl usually drops the seed, which she carries in a bag hung round her neck. Behind her comes a mule and harrow, covering up the seed, so that two mules, three slaves, a plough and harrow, are employed in planting a row of cotton. This is done in the months of March and April. Corn is planted in February. When there are no cold rains, the cotton usually makes its appearance in a week. In the course of eight or ten days afterwards the first hoeing is commenced. This is performed in part, also, by the aid of the plough and mule. The plough passes as near as possible to the cotton on both sides, throwing the furrow from it. Slaves follow with their hoes, cutting up the grass and cotton, leaving hills two feet and a half apart. This is called scraping cotton. In two weeks more commences the second hoeing. This time the furrow is thrown towards the cotton. Only one stalk, the largest, is now left standing in each hill. In another fortnight it is hoed the third time, throwing the furrow towards the cotton in the same manner as before, and killing all the grass between the rows. About the first of July, when it is a foot high or thereabouts, it is hoed the fourth and last time. Now the whole space between the rows is ploughed, leaving a deep water furrow in the center. During all these hoeings the overseer or driver follows the slaves on horseback with a whip, such as has been described. The fastest hoer takes the lead row. He is usually about a rod in advance of his companions. If one of them passes him, he is whipped. If one falls behind or is a moment idle, he is whipped. In fact, the lash is flying from morning until night, the whole day long. The hoeing season thus continues from April until July, a field having no sooner been finished once, than it is commenced again.

In the latter part of August begins the cotton picking season. At this time each slave is presented with a sack. A strap is fastened to it, which goes over the neck, holding the mouth of the sack breast high, while the bottom reaches nearly to the ground. Each one is also presented with a large basket that will hold about two barrels. This is to put the cotton in when the sack is filled. The baskets are carried to the field and placed at the beginning of the rows.

When a new hand, one unaccustomed to the business, is sent for the first time into the field, he is whipped up smartly, and made for that day to pick as fast as he can possibly. At night it is weighed, so that his capability in cotton picking is known. He must bring in the same weight each night following. If it falls short, it is considered evidence that he has been laggard, and a greater or less number of lashes is the penalty.

An ordinary day's work is two hundred pounds. A slave who is accustomed to picking, is punished, if he or she brings in a less quantity than that. There is a great difference among them as regards this kind of labor. Some of them seem to have a natural knack, or quickness, which enables them to pick with great celerity, and with both hands, while others, with whatever practice or industry, are utterly unable to come up to the ordinary standard. Such hands are taken from the cotton field and employed in other business. Patsey, of whom I shall have more to say, was known as the most remarkable cotton picker on Bayou Bœuf. She picked with both hands and with such surprising rapidity, that five hundred pounds a day was not unusual for her.

Each one is tasked, therefore, according to his picking abilities, none, however, to come short of two hundred weight. I, being unskillful always in that business, would have satisfied my master by bringing in the latter quantity, while on the other hand, Patsey would surely have been beaten if she failed to produce twice as much.

The cotton grows from five to seven feet high, each stalk having a great many branches, shooting out in all directions, and lapping each other above the water furrow.

There are few sights more pleasant to the eye, than a wide cotton field when it is in the bloom. It presents an appearance of purity, like an immaculate expanse of light, new-fallen snow.

Sometimes the slave picks down one side of a row, and back upon the other, but more usually, there is one on either side, gathering all that has blossomed, leaving the unopened bolls for a succeeding picking. When the sack is filled, it is emptied into the basket and trodden down. It is necessary to be extremely careful the first time going through the field, in order not to break the branches off the stalks. The cotton will not bloom upon a broken branch. Epps never failed to inflict the severest chastisement on the unlucky servant who, either carelessly or unavoidably, was guilty in the least degree in this respect.

The hands are required to be in the cotton field as soon as it is light in the morning, and, with the exception of ten or fifteen minutes, which is given them at noon to swallow their allowance of cold bacon, they are not permitted to be a moment idle until it is too dark to see, and when the moon is full, they often times labor till the middle of the night. They do not dare to stop even at dinner time, nor return to the quarters, however late it be, until the order to halt is given by the driver.

The day's work over in the field, the baskets are "toted," or in other words, carried to the gin-house, where the cotton is weighed. No matter how fatigued and weary he may be—no matter how much he longs for sleep and rest—a slave never approaches the gin-house with his basket of cotton but with fear. If it falls short in weight—if he has not performed the full task appointed him, he knows that he must suffer. And if he has exceeded it by ten or twenty pounds, in all probability his master will measure the next day's task accordingly. So, whether he has too little or too much, his approach to the gin-house is always with fear and trembling. Most frequently they have too little, and therefore it is they are not anxious to leave the field. After

weighing, follow the whippings; and then the baskets are carried to the cotton house, and their contents stored away like hay, all hands being sent in to tramp it down. If the cotton is not dry, instead of taking it to the gin-house at once, it is laid upon platforms, two feet high, and some three times as wide, covered with boards or plank, with narrow walks running between them.

This done, the labor of the day is not yet ended, by any means. Each one must then attend to his respective chores. One feeds the mules, another the swine—another cuts the wood, and so forth; besides, the packing is all done by candle light. Finally, at a late hour, they reach the quarters, sleepy and overcome with the long day's toil. Then a fire must be kindled in the cabin, the corn ground in the small hand-mill, and supper, and dinner for the next day in the field, prepared. All that is allowed them is corn and bacon, which is given out at the corncrib and smoke-house every Sunday morning. Each one receives, as his weekly allowance, three and a half pounds of bacon, and corn enough to make a peck of meal. That is all—no tea, coffee, sugar, and with the exception of a very scanty sprinkling now and then, no salt. I can say, from a ten years' residence with Master Epps, that no slave of his is ever likely to suffer from the gout, superinduced by excessive high living. Master Epps' hogs were fed on *shelled* corn—it was thrown out to his "niggers" in the ear. The former, he thought, would fatten faster by shelling, and soaking it in the water—the latter, perhaps, if treated in the same manner, might grow too fat to labor.

Master Epps was a shrewd calculator, and knew how to manage his own animals, drunk or sober.

The corn mill stands in the yard beneath a shelter. It is like a common coffee mill, the hopper holding about six quarts. There was one privilege which Master Epps granted freely to every slave he had. They might grind their corn nightly, in such small quantities as their daily wants required, or they might grind the whole week's allowance at one time, on Sundays, just as they preferred. A very generous man was Master Epps!

I kept my corn in a small wooden box, the meal in a gourd; and, by the way, the gourd is one of the most convenient and necessary utensils on a plantation. Besides supplying the place of all kinds of crockery in a slave cabin, it is used for carrying water to the fields. Another, also, contains the dinner. It dispenses with the necessity of pails, dippers, basins, and such tin and wooden superfluities altogether.

When the corn is ground, and fire is made, the bacon is taken down from the nail on which it hangs, a slice cut off and thrown upon the coals to broil. The majority of slaves have no knife, much less a fork. They cut their bacon with the axe at the wood-pile. The corn meal is mixed with a little water, placed in the fire, and baked. When it is "done brown," the ashes are scraped off, and being placed upon a chip, which answers for a table, the tenant of the slave hut is ready to sit down upon the ground to supper. By this time it is usually midnight. The same fear of punishment with which they approach the gin-house, possesses them again on lying down to get a snatch of rest. It is the fear of oversleeping in the morning. Such an offence would certainly be attended with not less than twenty lashes. With a prayer that he may be on his feet and wide awake at the first sound of the horn, he sinks to his slumbers nightly.

The softest couches in the world are not to be found in the log mansion of the slave. The one whereon I reclined year after year, was a plank twelve inches wide and ten feet long. My pillow was a stick of wood. The bedding was a coarse blanket, and not a rag or shred beside. Moss might be used, were it not that it directly breeds a swarm of fleas.

The cabin is constructed of logs, without floor or window. The latter is altogether unnecessary, the crevices between the logs admitting sufficient light. In stormy weather the rain drives through them, rendering it comfortless and extremely disagreeable. The rude door hangs on great wooden hinges. In one end is constructed an awkward fire-place.

An hour before day light the horn is blown. Then the slaves arouse, prepare their breakfast, fill a gourd with water, in another deposit their dinner of cold bacon and corn cake, and hurry to the field again. It is an offence invariably followed by a flogging, to be found at the quarters after daybreak. Then the fears and labors of another day begin; and until its close there is no such thing as rest. He fears he will be caught lagging through the day; he fears to approach the gin-house with his basket-load of cotton at night; he fears, when he lies down, that he will oversleep himself in the morning. Such is a true, faithful, unexaggerated picture and description of the slave's daily life, during the time of cotton-picking, on the shores of Bayou Bœuf.

In the month of January, generally, the fourth and last picking is completed. Then commences the harvesting of corn. This is considered a secondary crop, and receives far less attention than the cotton. It is planted, as already mentioned, in February. Corn is grown in that region for the purpose of fattening hogs and feeding slaves; very little, if any, being sent to market. It is the white variety, the ear of great size, and the stalk growing to the height of eight, and often times ten feet. In August the leaves are stripped off, dried in the sun, bound in small bundles, and stored away as provender for the mules and oxen. After this the slaves go through the field, turning down the ear, for the purpose of keeping the rains from penetrating to the grain. It is left in this condition until after cotton-picking is over, whether earlier or later. Then the ears are separated from the stalks, and deposited in the corncrib with the husks on; otherwise, stripped of the husks, the weevil would destroy it. The stalks are left standing in the field.

The Carolina, or sweet potato, is also grown in that region to some extent. They are not fed, however, to hogs or cattle, and are considered but of small importance. They are preserved by placing them upon the surface of the ground, with a slight covering of earth or cornstalks. There is not a cellar on Bayou Bœuf. The ground is so low it would fill with water. Potatoes are worth from two to three "bits," or shillings a barrel; corn, except when there is an unusual scarcity, can be purchased at the same rate.

As soon as the cotton and corn crops are secured, the stalks are pulled up, thrown into piles and burned. The ploughs are started at the same time, throwing up the beds again, preparatory to another planting. The soil, in the parishes of Rapides and Avoyelles, and throughout the whole country, so far as my observation extended, is of exceeding richness and fertility. It is a kind of marl, of a brown or reddish color. It does not require those invigorating composts necessary to more barren lands, and on the same field the same crop is grown for many successive years.

Ploughing, planting, picking cotton, gathering the corn, and pulling and burning stalks, occupies the whole of the four seasons of the year. Drawing and cutting wood, pressing cotton, fattening and killing hogs, are but incidental labors.

In the month of September or October, the hogs are run out of the swamps by dogs, and confined in pens. On a cold morning, generally about New Year's day, they are slaughtered. Each carcass is cut into six parts, and piled one above the other in salt, upon large tables in the smokehouse. In this condition it remains a fortnight, when it is hung up, and a fire built, and continued more than half the time during the remainder of the year. This thorough smoking is necessary to prevent the bacon from becoming infested with worms. In so warm a climate it is difficult to preserve it, and very many times myself and my companions have received our weekly allowance of three pounds and a half, when it was full of these disgusting vermin.

Although the swamps are overrun

with cattle, they are never made the source of profit, to any considerable extent. The planter cuts his mark upon the ear, or brands his initials upon the side, and turns them into the swamps, to roam unrestricted within their almost limitless confines. They are the Spanish breed, small and spike-horned. I have known of droves being taken from Bayou Bœuf, but it is of very rare occurrence. The value of the best cows is about five dollars each. Two quarts at one milking, would be considered an unusual large quantity. They furnish little tallow, and that of a soft, inferior quality. Notwithstanding the great number of cows that throng the swamps, the planters are indebted to the North for their cheese and butter, which is purchased in the New-Orleans market. Salted beef is not an article of food either in the great house, or in the cabin.

Master Epps was accustomed to attend shooting matches for the purpose of obtaining what fresh beef he required. These sports occurred weekly at the neighboring village of Holmesville. Fat beeves are driven thither and shot at, a stipulated price being demanded for the privilege. The lucky marksman divides the flesh among his fellows, and in this manner the attending planters are supplied.

The great number of tame and untamed cattle which swarm the woods and swamps of Bayou Bœuf, most probably suggested that appellation to the French, inasmuch as the term, translated, signifies the creek or river of the wild ox.

Garden products, such as cabbages, turnips and the like, are cultivated for the use of the master and his family. They have greens and vegetables at all times and seasons of the year. "The grass withereth and the flower fadeth" before the desolating winds of autumn in the chill northern latitudes, but perpetual verdure overspreads the hot lowlands, and flowers bloom in the heart of winter, in the region of Bayou Bœuf.

There are no meadows appropriated to the cultivation of the grasses. The leaves of the corn supply a sufficiency of food for the laboring cattle, while the rest provide for themselves all the year in the evergrowing pasture.

There are many other peculiarities of climate, habit, custom, and of the manner of living and laboring at the South, but the foregoing, it is supposed, will give the reader an insight and general idea of life on a cotton plantation in Louisiana. The mode of cultivating cane, and the process of sugar manufacturing, will be mentioned in another place.

Chapter XV.
[on sugar]

In consequence of my inability in cotton-picking, Epps was in the habit of hiring me out on sugar plantations during the season of cane-cutting and sugar-making. He received for my services a dollar a day, with the money supplying my place on his cotton plantation. Cutting cane was an employment that suited me, and for three successive years I held the lead row at Hawkins', leading a gang of from fifty to an hundred hands.

In a previous chapter the mode of cultivating cotton is described. This may be the proper place to speak of the manner of cultivating cane.

The ground is prepared in beds, the

same as it is prepared for the reception of the cotton seed, except it is ploughed deeper. Drills are made in the same manner. Planting commences in January, and continues until April. It is necessary to plant a sugar field only once in three years. Three crops are taken before the seed or plant is exhausted.

Three gangs are employed in the operation. One draws the cane from the rick, or stack, cutting the top and flags from the stalk, leaving only that part which is sound and healthy. Each joint of the cane has an eye, like the eye of a potato, which sends forth a sprout when buried in the soil. Another gang lays the cane in the drill, placing two stalks side by side in such manner that joints will occur once in four or six inches. The third gang follows with hoes, drawing earth upon the stalks, and covering them to the depth of three inches.

In four weeks, at the farthest, the sprouts appear above the ground, and from this time forward grow with great rapidity. A sugar field is hoed three times, the same as cotton, save that a greater quantity of earth is drawn to the roots. By the first of August hoeing is usually over. About the middle of September, whatever is required for seed is cut and stacked in ricks, as they are termed. In October it is ready for the mill or sugar-house, and then the general cutting begins. The blade of a cane-knife is fifteen inches long, three inches wide in the middle, and tapering towards the point and handle. The blade is thin, and in order to be at all serviceable must be kept very sharp. Every third hand takes the lead of two others, one of whom is on each side of

him. The lead hand, in the first place, with a blow of his knife shears the flags from the stalk. He next cuts off the top down as far as it is green. He must be careful to sever all the green from the ripe part, inasmuch as the juice of the former sours the molasses, and renders it unsalable. Then he severs the stalk at the root, and lays it directly behind him. His right and left hand companions lay their stalks when cut in the same manner, upon his. To every three hands there is a cart, which follows, and the stalks are thrown into it by the younger slaves, when it is drawn to the sugar-house and ground.

If the planter apprehends a frost, the cane is winrowed. Winrowing is the cutting the stalks at an early period and throwing them lengthwise in the water furrow in such a manner that the tops will cover the butts of the stalks. They will remain in this condition three weeks or a month without souring, and secure from frost. When the proper time arrives, they are taken up, trimmed and carted to the sugar-house.

In the month of January the slaves enter the field again to prepare for another crop. The ground is now strewn with the tops, and flags cut from the past year's cane. On a dry day fire is set to this combustible refuse, which sweeps over the field, leaving it bare and clean, and ready for the hoes. The earth is loosened about the roots of the old stubble, and in process of time another crop springs up from the last year's seed. It is the same the year following; but the third year the seed has exhausted its strength, and the field must be ploughed and planted again. The second year the cane is sweeter and yields more than the first, and the third year more than the second.

During the three seasons I labored on Hawkins' plantation, I was employed a considerable portion of the time in the sugar-house. He is celebrated as the producer of the finest variety of white sugar. The following is a general description of his sugar-house and the process of manufacture:

The mill is an immense brick building, standing on the shore of the bayou. Running out from the building is an open shed, at least an hundred feet in length and forty or fifty feet in width. The boiler in which the steam is generated is situated outside the main building; the machinery and engine rest on a brick pier, fifteen feet above the floor, within the body of the building. The machinery turns two great iron rollers, between two and three feet in diameter and six or eight feet in length. They are elevated above the brick pier, and roll in towards each other. An endless carrier, made of chain and wood, like leathern belts used in small mills, extends from the iron rollers out of the main building and through the entire length of the open shed. The carts in which the cane is brought from the field as fast as it is cut, are unloaded at the sides of the shed. All along the endless carrier are ranged slave children, whose business it is to place the cane upon it, when it is conveyed through the shed into the main building, where it falls between the rollers, is crushed, and drops upon another carrier that conveys it out of the main building in an opposite direction, depositing it in the top of a chimney upon a fire beneath, which

consumes it. It is necessary to burn it in this manner, because otherwise it would soon fill the building, and more especially because it would soon sour and engender disease. The juice of the cane falls into a conductor underneath the iron rollers, and is carried into a reservoir. Pipes convey it from thence into five filterers, holding several hogsheads each. These filterers are filled with bone-black, a substance resembling pulverized charcoal. It is made of bones calcinated in close vessels, and is used for the purpose of decolorizing, by filtration, the cane juice before boiling. Through these five filterers it passes in succession, and then runs into a large reservoir underneath the ground floor, from whence it is carried up, by means of a steam pump, into a clarifier made of sheet iron, where it is heated by steam until it boils. From the first clarifier it is carried in pipes to a second and a third, and thence into close iron pans, through which tubes pass, filled with steam. While in a boiling state it flows through three pans in succession, and is then carried in other pipes down to the coolers on the ground floor. Coolers are wooden boxes with sieve bottoms made of the finest wire. As soon as the syrup passes into the coolers, and is met by the air, it grains, and the molasses at once escapes through the sieves into a cistern below. It is then white or loaf sugar of the finest kind—clear, clean, and as white as snow. When cool it is taken out, packed in hogsheads, and is ready for market. The molasses is then carried from the cistern into the upper story again, and by another process converted into brown sugar.

63. Weighing In the Cotton and Measuring Out the Punishment

The following detailed description of raising a crop of cotton, from sowing to picking, was written by Dr. John Wesley Monette (1803–51), an authority on diseases of the Mississippi Delta. Here Dr. Monette is primarily concerned with the process of cotton production, not slavery, but all the tasks connected with the process were performed by slaves. The reader will perhaps be surprised to learn of the variety of tasks involved, as well as the degree of regimentation on individual operations that comprised the yearly round of labor. The description of the nightly "weighing-in" during the press of the cotton picking season speaks volumes about the slave system. Dr. Monette's digression, as he calls it, on the subject of whipping, is approximate, in detail and detachment, to his description of the cotton crop itself. One is therefore not entirely surprised to learn that he was one of the numerous apologists for slavery who regarded blacks as inferior beings. He did not, however, go so far as to suppose that blacks were the product of a separate creation, as did some of his contemporaries.

Dr. Monette was not only a physician but an historian as well, and a serious student of physical anthropology, whose ideas in several respects anticipated those of Charles Darwin. The selection appearing below was published originally as an Appendix to Joseph Holt Ingraham's *South-West, by a Yankee* (see document 35).

The Cotton Crop.

Having finished or relinquished the miscellaneous business of winter, such as clearing, building, ditching, and splitting rails, the hands are actively employed in making preparation for another crop. The first thing to be attended to, is the repairing of all the fences, with the light force, such as boys and women; while the strong hands are employed in chopping, and log-rolling in the new grounds. These operations are commenced generally about the middle of February, and continued two or three weeks, unless the

Source: John Wesley Monette, "The Cotton Crop," Appendix to Joseph Holt Ingraham, *The South-West, by a Yankee*, 2 vols. (New York: Harper & Bros., 1835), 2:281–91.

farm is mostly new; in which case the clearing of the new ground continues four or five weeks until it is time to plant corn, generally from the first to the twentieth of March. During all this time several ploughs, in a well opened place, are kept constantly running (unless prevented by rain), in "listing up" corn and cotton ground. The distance between the ridges for cotton varies according to the strength of the soil, and the consequent size to which the plant grows. In the rich bottoms the distance between the middle or tops of the ridges must be from five to seven feet; while in the thin upland soil, a space of three or four feet is amply sufficient. In the latter soil, the cotton plant attains the height of three or four feet, and branches laterally about half that distance. But in the rich alluvial lands, the stalk not unfrequently shoots up to six and eight feet, and branches so as to interlock with the other rows six or eight feet apart.

Early in April, and sometimes even in the last days of March, the cotton-planting commences. To open the ridges, a narrow plough is run by one horse along the middle of the ridge, so as to open a narrow shallow furrow, in the mellow ground first ploughed. Immediately behind the opening plough, follows the sower, with his sack of cotton-seed suspended from his neck, walking at the same pace with the plough-man before. At every step or two he throws the seed so as to strew it four or five feet ahead in the furrow, at each dash of the hand. The quantity sown is often unnecessarily large, being frequently twenty times more numerous than the stalks permitted to remain growing. This profusion of seed is sown for the purpose of obtaining a "good stand," after allowing for defective seeds as well as some which may not be covered, and others that may be covered too deep, and also for many plants that may sicken and die after they have vegetated and come above the ground. This latter circumstance frequently occurs: a stand may be amply sufficient when first up, but from drought, excessive rain, or chilling winds, one half in the rows, and sometimes whole acres together, die with the "rust," "sore skin," or "yellow fever."

After the sower another hand follows closely with a light horse harrow, drawn over the furrow, for the purpose of covering the seed. This throws in the loose earth over the seed, and covers them so lightly that often one-third of them are still visible, yet this covering is sufficient, for no seeds require less covering than cotton-seed. They will sprout and take root, when left on the surface of the ground, if a slight shower follows.

On a large plantation where there are, say, fifty effective hands, there will probably be three or four sets of hands engaged at the same time in planting; each set, however, not in any way interfering with the other; but all pushing on with a constant brisk motion. As a medium task, each set, of three hands, will very easily plant ten acres, but oftener fifteen in old well broken land. During the planting season, or between the first of April and the middle of May, there are always from one to three wet or rainy spells, continuing from one to four days each, so that the planting is necessarily interrupted. This, however, is an advantage which none complain of, as it facilitates and expedites the vegetation of the seed already planted; while it causes the several portions of the crop to vary eight or ten days in age, and thereby renders the working more convenient. Twenty planting days are sufficient to put in the whole cotton crop, or at least as much as can be properly tended and secured. On the rich bottom lands, when the growth of the cotton is very luxuriant, it is desirable to finish planting always before the first of May; but in the hills, especially where the soil is thin, and the cotton plant attains but a small comparative size, it is preferable to plant between the fifteenth of April and the twentieth of May. Cotton thus planted in thin soil, will mature and open as soon as that which has been planted three weeks sooner in bottom lands.

When the earth is moist and warm, cotton-seed will sprout, and be up in about five or six days; but if the soil be dry it takes much longer—or until there is rain sufficient to saturate the loose earth: for the seed, being covered with a thick coat of coarse wool, is not so readily, as some other seeds, acted upon by slight moisture. As the plant first comes out of the ground, it has somewhat the appearance of a young bean, or of the okra plant, being composed at first of two lobate leaflets, which continue, gradually enlarging, until about the end of the first week, when a leaf or two begins to put out between the lobules. The young cotton-plant is extremely tender, and sensible to the most moderate degrees of cold: the slightest frost cuts it off— while it withers and dies from the ef-

fects of a few hours of chilling winds.

From the profusion of seed planted, the cotton plant of course comes up very thick and crowded in the row; in which condition it is allowed to remain a week or ten days, and often of necessity much longer, when it is thinned out, or as it is called, "scraped." During scraping time there is one constant rush, and every hand that can use a hoe is brought into the field. The process of scraping commences by running a light furrow close on each side of the row of young cotton, with the share of the plough next it, so as to throw the dirt from the cotton and trim off the scattering plants: the space left unbroken between these two furrows is about eight or ten inches wide, ready for the hoes. If there are many hoe-hands there are several ploughs "barring off" as it is called. The hoe hands follow close upon the ploughs, each hand upon a separate row, and with hoes sharp, and set particularly for "scraping." Experienced cotton hands run over the rows with great rapidity, and evince great dexterity in striking out all to a single stalk, which is left at the distance, from its next neighbour, of at least the width of the hoe; and in bottom land, at double that distance. Thus, in thin land, the stalks are desired to be ten or twelve inches apart, and in the rich lands about eighteen or twenty inches, in the row. The cotton plant thus thinned out, continues to grow slowly until the hot weather of June sets in, when it begins to grow rapidly, putting out a blossom at each new joint formed on the branches. This successive florescence continues until frost puts a stop to the growth of the plant, which is generally in October. The pericarp or boll of cotton, from the first bloom, is generally matured in eight or ten weeks, when it begins to crack at the four seams in the bolls, until the four valves spread wide open, remaining attached only at the base or extremity next the *stem*. When the valves are thus open, the cotton with the seed, to which it adheres in a kind of cluster, hangs down from one to four inches. From June until October, the cotton exhibits a successive and continued florescence, while the plant is loading itself with green bolls, from the size of a young peach, having just dropped its blossom, to that of a small hen's egg. About the last of August the matured bolls begin to burst or open their valves and suspend their cotton; and from that time the plant exhibits at the same time, blossoms, and bolls of every size, and every stage of maturity. Toward fall, when the heat of the sun is constant and intense, the bolls will mature and open in six weeks from the blossom.

After the first "scraping out," the cultivation is carried on much in the same manner as in the cultivation of corn, until about the first of August, when it ceases, and the crop is laid by. The same kind of cultivation that would make good corn would make good cotton. In this however there is a difference of opinion: some will hill, or heap the earth up in high ridges with both corn and cotton, while others will keep the soil loose and level about both; the latter is decidedly the proper mode for either.

When the blossom is first unfolded, which generally occurs in the night, in form it resembles the white hollyhock, but is smaller, and is of a faint yellowish white colour, which it retains until about noon; the heat of the sun then being intense, the corolla partially closes, not unlike the four-o'clock-flower, and at the same time its hue is changed to a delicate rose, or lilac. On the following day the flowers become more deeply tinged; toward the close of the second evening they are of a deep crimson, or violet hue. During the succeeding night, and morning, that is, about forty-eight hours after they first open, they always drop off, while of a deep violet colour, leaving the young capsule or boll. The blossoms generally open, as well as fall off, during the night, and early in the morning. Thus a cotton field in July, August, September, and October, exhibits the singular appearance of a continued crop of opening, closing, and falling blossoms, with an almost equal mixture of white, lilac, and purple flowers; while each morning the ground is seen covered with the latter, and the branches replenished with the white.

As the ploughing generally ceases and the crop is "laid by" about the last of July, when the plant is large and brittle, there is but little done in the field during the first three weeks in August, except that a few light hands are kept employed in cutting, or pulling up the "tie-vines" which are sometimes very troublesome: the tie-vine is nothing more or less than the morning-glory, so carefully cultivated in gardens at the north, for the purpose of shading arbours and summer houses.

Toward the last of August, or as soon as there is sufficient open cotton for a hand to pick fifteen or twenty pounds during the day, the light force, consisting of women and children, is put to picking for a week or ten days; when there being sufficient cotton opened, to make a full day's work, all hands are engaged without exception. Then begins another push, which continues until the whole crop is gathered and housed. During "picking time" which continues where full crops are made until the first of December, and in river lands, until the first of January, the hands are regularly roused, by a large bell or horn, about the first dawn of day, or earlier so that they are ready to enter the field as soon as there is sufficient light to distinguish the bolls. As the dews are extremely heavy and cool, each hand is provided with a blanket coat or wrapper, which is kept close around him until the dew is partially evaporated by the sun. Without this protection they would be completely wet from head to feet, in a very short time; and as they would be in the field at least two hours before the sun's rays would be felt, they would be perfectly chilled, if no worse consequence attended. The hands remain in the field until it is too dark to distinguish the cotton, having brought their meals with them. For the purpose of collecting the cotton, each hand is furnished with a large basket, and two coarse cotton bags about the size of a pillow case, with a strong strap to suspend them from the neck or shoulders. The basket is left at the end of a row, and both bags taken along: when one bag is as full as it can well be crammed, it is laid down in the row, and the hand begins to fill the second in the same way. As soon as the second is full, he returns to the basket, taking the other bag as he passes it, and emptying both

into the basket, treading it down well, to make it contain his whole day's work. The same process is repeated until night; when the basket is taken upon his head and carried to the scaffold-yard, to be weighed. There the overseer meets all hands at the scales, with the lamp, slate, and whip. On the left hand margin of the slate is pasted a strip of paper, with the name of each written in fair large hand. As soon as their baskets are set upon the ground, the weighing commences. Each basket is carefully weighed, and the nett weight of cotton set down upon the slate, opposite the name of the picker. The negroes stand round, to remove and replace the baskets as they are weighed; and occasionally the countenance of an idler may be seen to fall. Then is the time for the overseer to watch close or he may be greatly imposed upon by the cunning and lazy, who are apt, in the crowd, to prevent their baskets from being weighed, by substituting a heavier one which has been passed, or they may fill up their baskets from one already weighed. Sometimes a negro, known to be lazy, will have heavy weight and will probably extort from the overseer expressions of praise and encouragement, unless he examines the basket, when perchance he may find one of his sacks full of moist earth snugly covered up at the bottom; such tricks as these will be continually practised upon an overseer, who is careless or "soft"; a quality or character, which none can more readily and properly appreciate than the negro. It is not an uncommon occurrence for an overseer, who is even vigilant, amid the crowd of negroes and baskets, with only one lamp, held close to the scales and slate, to weigh some of the heavier baskets several times, their exact weight being changed by taking out, or putting in a few pounds; while the lighter ones pass entirely unnoticed. No inconvenience arises to any one from such incidents, except that the crop is not gathered in as good time as it might otherwise have been, and a portion consequently is wasted.

After the weighing is over, and the baskets are emptied, or turned bottom upward, upon the scaffolds, the overseer takes the slate, and examines the weights attached to each name. Those who are found to have brought in less their usual quantity, unless for good reasons, are called in the order of their names: the individual advances, and if his reasons are insufficient, he is ordered to lie down upon his face, with his back exposed; when he receives ten, twenty, or fifty stripes with the whip, according to his deserts. In this way the overseer goes over the list, punishing only those who have idled away their time.

No one knows that he is to be punished until his name is called, when he has an opportunity of giving his reasons for his imperfect day's work. As to the quantity which a hand can pick in a day, there is a great difference; some will pick only from 75 to 100 lbs., others from 150 to 200 lbs., while some extraordinary pickers can pick as high as 4 or 500 lbs. in one day. But to pick these last weights requires such brisk and incessant motion, that it could not be done two days in succession without danger of life or health; and is only attempted for a wager, or such like reason. The average weight picked by all

the hands on a place, will seldom exceed 150 or 160 lbs., in good picking. Children from ten to fifteen years of age generally pick nearly as much as grown hands. The scaffolds for drying cotton are mostly temporary, being made anew every summer, of common boards or plank. Upon these the cotton is suffered to lie spread out to the sun, at least one day to dry; while some old or decrepid hand stays at the scaffold, to turn and spread it, as well as to pick out leaves and trash.

It may not be improper to make a remark or two relative to whipping. This is generally performed with as much care and humanity as the nature of the case will admit. A person standing at the distance of two hundred yards, being unacquainted with the mode, and hearing the loud sharp crack of the whip upon the naked skin, would almost tremble for the life of the poor sufferer. But what would be his surprise, after hearing fifty or one hundred stripes thus laid on, to go up and examine the poor fellow, and find the skin not broken, and not a drop of blood drawn from him! Yet this is the way in which the whip is generally used here upon slaves: very few planters would permit them to be whipped on the bare back with a rawhide, or cow-skin, as it is called. Though, as in every thing else, there is a great difference in the degree of severity exercised by different masters: yet we must take the general rule, as applicable to the great class of planters. The common overseer's whip consists of a stout flexible stalk, large at the handle, tapering rapidly to the distance of about eighteen inches, and thence continued with cord or leather;

the whole is covered with a leather plat, which continues tapering into, and forms the lash—the whole together being about three feet and a half long. To the end of the lash is attached a soft, dry, buckskin cracker, about three eights of an inch wide and ten or twelve inches long, which is the only part allowed to strike, in whipping on the bare skin. So soft is the cracker, that a person who has not the sleight of using the whip, could scarcely hurt a child with it. When it is used by an experienced hand it makes a very loud report, and stings, or "burns" the skin smartly, but does not bruise it. One hundred lashes well laid on with it, would not injure the skin as much as ten moderate stripes with a cow-skin.

But to return from this digression:— Every day, when the weather will admit, beholds a repetition of the ceremony of picking, weighing, and drying, as before detailed. Those who have gins, as all planters should have, generally keep the stand running during the picking season, so as to gin out the cotton as fast as it is picked. If there are forty or fifty good pickers, it requires one stand to be kept running constantly to keep up with them. In such cases, during wet weather, when the hands cannot pick cotton, the ablest of them are kept baling the cotton which has been ginned since the last rain, or within the last eight or ten days. When there are not more than twenty, or twenty-five, the gin will be able to keep up, by ginning the last three days in the week, in addition to all rainy weather; and the able-bodied hands will be able to do all the pressing and baling during the wet days.

Gin, in the common acceptation, sig-nifies the house and all the machinery required to separate the *lint* from the seed, and to press it into large bales, weighing generally from 400 to 500 pounds. The house is a large enclosed roof, resting upon blocks or posts, which support it at about eight or nine feet from the ground. The common area covered is about forty by sixty feet, the rafters resting upon plates, and the plates upon flooring beams, or joists, upon which the floor is laid. About the distance of one-third the length of the house, two gearing beams are laid across, for supporting the machinery. These rest upon the top of the blocks, or on posts framed into them. On the ground floor is the horse-path for drawing the main wheel and counter wheel; the last of which carries a broad band, which passes over and turns the cylinder and brush of the gin-stand alone. The large plantations are adopting steam engines, and erect for the purpose very large and expensive buildings, in which are placed two, three, or four stands. A gin-stand is a frame, in which runs a wooden cylinder with an iron shaft running through it; this cylinder is encircled at every inch by a very thin circular saw, with sharp hooked teeth, upon which the seed cotton is thrown, running through parallel grates. The teeth of the saws catch and carry through the lint from the seed. Just behind the cylinder is a fly-wheel brush—that is, a fan, with a brush on its extreme circumference; this brush, running considerably faster than the cylinder, takes off the cotton from the teeth, and blows it back. The space or room above is divided into two apartments; one for the stand and seed cotton, and the other for ginned cotton; the latter of which will contain cotton for twenty or thirty bales. A good gin-stand, with sixty or sixty-five saws, running constantly from daybreak in the morning until eight or nine o'clock at night, will gin out as much as will make three or four bales.

At the other end of the house, and immediately under the room containing ginned cotton, is the press. It consists of two large wooden screws, twelve or sixteen inches in diameter, with reversed threads cut on each end to within eighteen inches or two feet of the middle, through which there is a mortice for the lever. These screws stand perpendicularly, and about ten feet apart, and work into a large heavy beam above, and into another firmly secured below. The upper moves up or down (when the screws are turned), between four strong upright posts, framed together, two on each side, so as to come down strait and steady when pressing.

The lower sides of the press are composed of very strong batten doors; when the beam is brought sufficiently low, a spring is struck, and they fly open; when they are removed, leaving the naked bale standing on its edge under the press. A piece of bagging, cut to the proper size and shape, was put in the bottom of the press-box, before filling in the cotton, and another on top, immediately under the follower. These two pieces are brought together in such manner as to cover the cotton neatly, and there sewed with twine. The rope passed under and over it, through the grooves left in the bed-sill and in the follower, by means of a windlass, is drawn extremely tight and

tied with double loop knots. When all is finished, the screws are turned backward, the beam rises, and the bale is rolled out. Notwithstanding there are seven bands of strong rope around it, the bale will swell and stretch the rope, until its breadth is at least two or three inches more than when in the press. To press and bale expeditiously requires at least four or five hands and one horse. When the box has been sufficiently filled, generally eight or nine feet deep, the men bring down the beam by turning the screws with hand levers as long as they can turn them; then a large lever is placed in the screw, with a strong horse attached to one end, and a few turns of the screws by the horse bring the beam down to the proper point, within thirty or thirty-four inches of the sill.

The requisite number of hands will put up and bale with a common press about ten or twelve bales a day, by pushing. After the bales are properly put up, the next thing is to mark and number them on one end. For this purpose a plate of copper, with the initials, or such mark as is fancied, cut in it, is applied to the end of the bale and the letters and figures painted through it with black marking ink.

The next trouble is to haul them to market, or the nearest landing for boats; sometimes this is a very troublesome and difficult task, especially in wet weather, when the roads, from the immense quantity of heavy hauling, in getting the crops to market, are much cut up, and often almost impassable. The planter who is careful to take all proper advantages of season and weather, will have his cotton hauled early in the fall, as fast as it is ginned, when the roads are almost certainly good.

The quantity of cotton produced to the acre, varies with the quality of the soil and the season. The best kind of river and alluvial lands, when in a complete state of cultivation, and with a good season, will produce on an average from 1500 to 2000 lbs. of cotton in the seed per acre; while new land of the same quality will not yield more than 1200 or 1400 lbs. per acre. The highlands, where the soil is fertile, will yield under the most favourable circumstances about 1400 lbs., while those lands which have been many years in cultivation, where the soil is thin, will not yield more than from 800 to 1000 lbs. per acre; and some not more than 600 lbs. As a general rule 1300 or 1400 lbs. of seed cotton, will, when ginned out, make a bale of 400 lbs. or more. This is according to the correct weight of the daily picking in the cotton book; although after being weighed, it must lose some weight by drying.

The quantity of cotton raised and secured by good management most commonly averages about five or six bales to the hand: and the quantity, among the mass of planters, more frequently falls below, than rises above this estimate. Some, with a few choice hands, may sometimes average nine or ten bales to the hand by picking until January.

When the crop is all secured, which, as we observed before, varies from the first of December until some time in January, according to the season, hands, and extent of the crop, the hands are employed during the winter in clearing, chopping logs in the field, splitting rails, or ditching, if necessary. About the middle of February they resume preparations for "another crop."

---

64. Women's Work in Field and Kitchen

The larger Southern plantation was a community within itself, providing nearly all the necessities of life, and some of the accoutrements of elegant living for the family of the master. One of the best descriptions of the unity of this life, and the conditions of the men and women on whose labor it rested, was left by Emily Burke, a Northern schoolteacher who

Source: Emily P. Burke, *Reminiscences of Georgia* (n.p.: James M. Fitch, 1850), pp. 111–13, 115–17, 120–24.

served in Georgia for a number of years during the 1830s and 1840s. As the following account reveals, Miss Burke was especially sensitive to the plight of slave women. Her description of women at hard labor and the trials of the family cook show aspects of life that many travelers failed to observe. The plantation described here was not far from Savannah.

Letter XVI.

Agreeable to my promise in my last letter, I will now go on with my description of the buildings belonging to a Southern plantation.

In the first place there was a paling enclosing all the buildings belonging to the family and all the house servants. In the centre of this enclosure stood the principal house, the same I have already in a previous letter described. In this the father of the family and all the females lodged. The next house of importance was the one occupied by the steward of the plantation, and where all the white boys belonging to the family had their sleeping apartments. The next after this was a school house consisting of two rooms, one for a study, the other the master's dormitory. Then the cook, the washer-woman, and the milk-maid, had each their several houses, the children's nurses always sleeping upon the floor of their mistress' apartment. Then again there was the kitchen, the store-house, corn-house, stable, hen-coop, the hound's kennel, the shed for the corn mill, all these were separate little buildings within the same enclosure. Even the milk-safe stood out under one great tree, while under another the old washer woman had all her apparatus arranged; even her kettle was there suspended from a cross-pole. Then to increase the beauty of the scene, the whole establishment was completely shaded by ornamental trees, which grew at convenient distances among the buildings, and towering far above them all. The huts of the field servants formed another little cluster of dwellings at considerable distance from the master's residence, yet not beyond the sight of his watchful and jealous eye. These latter huts were arranged with a good deal of order and here each slave had his small patch of ground adjacent to his own dwelling, which he assiduously cultivated after completing his daily task. I have known the poor creatures, notwithstanding "tired nature" longed for repose, to spend the greater part of a moonlight night on these grounds. In this way they often raise considerable crops of corn, tobacco, and potatoes, besides various kinds of garden vegetables. Their object in doing this is to have something with which to purchase tea, coffee, sugar, flour, and all such articles of diet as are not provided by their masters, also such clothing as is necessary to make them appear decent in church, but which they can not have unless they procure it by extra efforts.

From this you see the slave is obliged to work the greater part of his time, for one coarse torn garment a year, and hardly food enough of the coarsest kind to support nature, without the least luxury that can be named. Neither can they after the fatigues of the day repose their toil worn bodies upon a comfortable bed unless they have earned it by laboring many a long, weary hour after even the beasts and the birds have retired to rest. It is a common rule to furnish every slave with one coarse blanket each, and these they always carry with them, so when night overtakes them, let it be where it may, they are not obliged to hasten home to go to rest. Poor creatures! all the home they have is where their blanket is, and this is all the slave pretends to call his own besides his dog. . . .

I found after I had been in the country a few months that the season when I first went there was the most gloomy part of the year. At this time there were but few slaves upon the plantation, many of them being let out to boatmen who at this season of the year are busily engaged in the transportation of goods and produce of all kinds up and down the rivers. The sweet singing birds, too, were all gone to their winter quarters still farther South, but when they had all returned, and the trees began to assume the freshness of summer, and the plants to put forth their blossoms, I found it was far from being a dull and gloomy place. During the greater part of the winter season the negro women are busy in picking, ginning, and packing the cotton for market.

In packing the cotton, the sack is suspended from strong spikes, and while one colored person stands in it to tread the cotton down, others throw it into the sack. I have often wondered how the cotton could be sold so cheap when it required so much labor to get it ready for the market, and certainly it could not be if all their help was hired at the rate of northern labor.

The last of January the servants began to return to the plantation to repair the fences and make ready for planting and sowing. The fences are built of poles arranged in a zigzag manner, so that the ends of one tier of poles rests upon the ends of another. In this work the women are engaged as well as the men. They all go into the woods and each woman as well as man cuts down her own pine sapling, and brings it upon her head. It certainly was a most revolting sight to see the female form scarcely covered with one old miserable garment, with no covering for the head, arms, or neck, nor shoes to protect her feet from briers and thorns, employed in conveying trees upon her head from one place to another to build fences. When I beheld such scenes I felt culpable in living in ease and enjoying the luxuries of life, while so many of my own sex were obliged to drag out such miserable existences merely to procure these luxuries enjoyed by their masters. When the fences were completed, they proceeded to prepare the ground for planting. This is done by throwing the earth up in ridges from one side of the field to the other. This work is usually executed by hand labor, the soil is so light, though sometimes to facilitate the process a light plough, drawn by a mule, is used. The ground there is reckoned by tasks instead of acres. If a person is asked the extent of a certain piece of land, he is told it contains so many tasks, accordingly so many tasks are assigned for a day's work. In hoeing corn, three tasks are considered a good day's work for a man, two for a woman and one and a half for a boy or girl fourteen or fifteen years old. . . .

I have, in a previous letter, spoken of the slaves grinding corn; this is done by hand-mills constructed of two round flat stones, the upper one being turned around upon the other by hand labor. One person can, though, with a good deal of difficulty, grind corn alone, but it is customary for two at a time to engage in this labor. This mill is probably the same in kind with those used in Oriental countries, respecting which our Savior said, "Two women shall be grinding at the mill, the one shall be taken the other left." The time for the grinding of corn was always in the evening after the daily tasks were done.

About seven o'clock, in the summer season, the colored people would generally begin to assemble in the yard belonging to the planter's residence. Here they would kindle little bonfires, not only to ward off the musquitoes, but because they are considered essential in the hot season to purify the air when it is filled with feverish vapors that arise from decayed vegetable matter. Then while two of their number are engaged at the mill, all the rest join in a dance around the burning fagots. In this manner were spent the greater part of the summer evenings, and it was usual for the white members of the family to assemble on the piazza to witness their pastimes, and sometimes at the request of a favorite slave, I have seen the white children engage in the waltz, or take their places in the quadrille. Slaves from adjoining plantations would often come to spend an evening with their acquaintances, and bring their corn with them to grind. The grinding generally commences at about six in the evening, and the hoarse sound of the mill seldom ceased much before midnight.

Though the slaves in general, notwithstanding all their hard toils and sorrows, had their happy hours, there was one old woman on the plantation who always looked cast down and sorrowful, and never appeared to take any interest in what caused the joy and mirth of those around her. She was one of Afric's own home born daughters, and she had never forgotten those who nursed her in infancy, nor the playmates of her childhood's happy hours. She told me she was stolen one day while gathering shells into a little basket on the sea shore, when she was about ten years old, and crowded into a vessel with a good many of her own race, who had also been stolen and sold for slaves, and from that hour when she left her mother's hut to go out to play she had never seen one of her own kindred, though she had always hoped that Providence might bring some of them in her way; "but now," she replied, "I begin to despair of ever seeing those faces which are still fresh in my memory, for now I am an old woman, and shall soon get through all my troubles and sorrows, and I only think now of meeting them in heaven." When requested she would favor us with a song in her own language, learned before she was stolen, but when she came to sing of her native hills and sparkling streams, the tears would trickle down her sunburnt and furrowed cheeks, and my heart could but ache for this poor creature, stolen away in the innocence of youth, from parents, kindred, home, and country, which were as dear to her as mine to me.

Of all the house-servants, I thought the task of the cook was the most laborious. Though she did no other housework she was obliged to do every thing belonging to the kitchen department, and that, too, with none of those conveniences without which a Northern woman would think it was impossible for her to prepare a meal of victuals. After having cooked the supper and washed the dishes she goes about making preparations for the next morning's meal. In the first place she goes into the woods to gather sticks and dried limbs of trees, which she ties in bundles and brings to the kitchen on her head, with which to kindle the morning fire; to get as much fuel as she will want to use in preparing the breakfast she is often obliged to go into the woods several times. When this is done she has all the corn to grind for the hommony and bread, then the evening's preparations are completed. In the morning she is obliged to rise very early, for she has every article of food that comes on to the table to cook, nothing ever being prepared till the hour it is needed. When she has gone through with all the duties connected with the morning's repast, then she goes about the dinner, bringing fuel from the woods, grinding corn, etc. In this manner the cook spends her days, for in whatever department the slaves are educated, they are generally obliged to wear out their lives.

65. A Manager Negotiates Hiring for an Iron Furnace

Although most slaves were engaged in agricultural labor, there were many who found their way into the Southern factories. Not only were slaves employed in towns, at textile mills, tobacco factories, and iron works; many others worked in small industrial concerns that were scattered about the countryside. One such enterprise, Cloverdale Furnace in Botetourt County, Virginia, where the following group of letters originated, hired

Source: Letters in possession of the Editor.

white men as well as slaves whose masters could not use their services at home.

The letters are from the owner to a slaveholder whose slave, Nathan, they have hired. Hiring out sometimes proved a means of joining husband and wife, as these letters reveal. Because of Nathan's leg injury, the company he would work for at Cloverdale had to make clear the not inconsiderable flexibility in the terms of hire available. To "find" oneself meant that the person hired in this way received more pay, but had to find his own room and board.

[I]

Cloverdale Furnace
Jany 11th /59

Green B. Martin Esq
  Dear Sir—
  We have hired the wife of your Boy Nathan, & he is anxious that we should hire him—We are willing to take him at the rates of $125– per year, the hire to begin when he gets able to go to work, & will charge you no board until that time, should it not exceed two or three weeks after he arrives— We understand he is getting better, but should it turn out that he would not likely be able to do much work during the year, or should his knee become stiff from the effects of the cut, we would not be willing to give the above amount for him, if indeed we would want him at all—We don't apprehend much danger of this but mention it to prevent any difficulty hereafter—If you conclude to let us have him inform us at once—Direct your letter to "Blue Ridge P.O. Botetourt County Vᵃ"
                  Yrs Very Resptly
  (signed)   Anderson & Patton

[II]

Cloverdale Furnace
May 12th 1859

Green B. Martin Esq
  Dear Sir—
  To gratify Nathan I acceeded to your proposition to board him 1 month for his work—He has been cutting wood for the last two or three weeks, & I delayed writing to you in order to see what he could do—He chop[p]ed last week 6 cords & I presume will be able to continue at that & possibly do more—He thinks his leg is better when he works than when he does nothing— I will make this proposition to you, that we will pay 37½ cts per cord for all the wood he cuts, & he or you pay him for his provision, clothing &c—in other words we will place him on the same footing with our white choppers—
  By this arrangement we pay for what he does, & you get pay for what he does—In his condition we are unwilling to hire him for the rest of the year at a specific price—For whilst he might be able to work all the time, his leg might give way & be of no service to us—
  Please inform us whether you accede

[329]

to our proposition, to commence when he began chopping wood—

Yrs Resptly
(signed) Wm T. Patton

Blue Ridge PO
Botetourt C^o
V^a

[III]

Cloverdale Furnace
June 3^d 1859

Green B. Martin Esq
  Dear Sir—
  I send Nathan on today, & hope he may arrive safely at home—He was improving in his chopping weekly—He seems anxious to return & I have told him he might say to you that we will allow him 40 cts per cord for cutting wood, he find himself—

  You can talk with him about it & if you conclude to let him come back send him on as soon as convenient—

Yrs Respectly
(signed) Wm T. Patton

66. Whites and Blacks in a Textile Factory

James Silk Buckingham (1786–1855) was an English reformer and temperance advocate who traveled widely in the United States during the 1830s, and turned out eight volumes of description of the country, with emphasis on social customs and morals. Much interested in slavery, Buckingham gave the following account of slaves working with whites in a cotton mill in Athens, Georgia. That Buckingham was far from friendly toward slavery lends some credibility to his assertion that little friction was observable between the races. This was not always the case in factories, however. The managers of the Tredegar iron works in Richmond, for example, encountered difficulty in launching such an experiment.

On the banks of the Oconee river—one fork of which runs close by the town of Athens, in a deep valley, the town itself being on a hill, and the other forks

Source: James Silk Buckingham, The Slave States of America, 2 vols. (London: Fisher, 1842), 2:111–14.

[330]

at a distance for a few miles only—are three cotton factories, all worked by water-power, and used for spinning yarn, and weaving cloth of coarse qualities for local consumption only. I visited one of these, and ascertained that the other two were very similar to it in size and operations. In each of them there are employed from 80 to 100 persons, and about an equal number of white and black. In one of them, the blacks are the property of the mill-owner, but in the other two they are the slaves of planters, hired out at monthly wages to work in the factory. There is no difficulty among them on account of colour, the white girls working in the same room and at the same loom with the black girls; and boys of each colour, as well as men and women, working together without apparent repugnance or objection. This is only one among the many proofs I had witnessed of the fact, that the prejudice of colour is not nearly so strong in the South as in the North. Here, it is not at all uncommon to see the black slaves of both sexes, shake hands with white people when they meet, and interchange friendly personal inquiries; but at the North I do not remember to have witnessed this once; and neither in Boston, New York, or Philadelphia would white persons generally like to be seen shaking hands and talking familiarly with blacks in the streets.

The negroes here are found to be quite as easily taught to perform all the required duties of spinners and weavers as the whites, and are just as tractable when taught; but their labour is dearer than that of the whites, for whilst the free boys and girls employed receive about 7.00 dollars per month, out of which they find themselves, the slaves are paid the same wages (which is handed over to their owners) and the mill-owner has to feed them all in addition; so that the free labour is much cheaper to him than the slave; and the hope expressed by the proprietor to me was, that the progressive increase of white population by immigration, would enable him to employ wholly their free labour, which, to him would be more advantageous. The white families engaged in these factories, live in loghuts clustered about the establishment on the river's bank, and the negroes repair to the huts allowed them by their owners when they are near, or stay at the mill, when their master's plantation is far off.

The whites looked miserably pale and unhealthy; and they are said to be very short-lived, the first symptoms of fevers and dysenteries in the autumn appearing chiefly among them at the factories, and sweeping numbers of them off by death. Under the most favourable circumstances, I think the Factory system detrimental to health, morals, and social happiness; but in its infant state, as it is here, with unavoidable confinement in a heated temperature, and with unwholesome associations, it is much worse, and I do not wonder that the most humane members of the community deplore the introduction of factories in the South, and wish that the labours of the people should be confined to agriculture, leaving manufactures to Europe or to the States of the North. The machinery of these establishments is made at Frankford in New Jersey, the cotton is grown here, and the wool, of which they use large quantities in the production of a coarse cloth of cotton and wool mixed, for negro clothing, is imported from Africa to New York, being coarser but much cheaper than wool from any part of Europe, and answering their purpose equally well.

67. Working at a Richmond Tobacco Factory

Masters often hired slaves out when they owned more men than they could employ profitably in agriculture. In Virginia, slaves were often hired to work at the tobacco factories in Richmond. They frequently "found" themselves, which means simply that they engaged their own lodgings and meals, paid for their own clothing, and acted more independently in all respects than plantation slaves. Sometimes slaves were hired out simply because they had become unmanageable at home.

For the following brief account of slaves at work in a tobacco factory, we are indebted to Charles Weld, who was Secretary to England's Royal Society, a lawyer, a scientist, and an authority on polar expeditions. Weld was a half-brother of Isaac Weld, who in 1799 had published a book on America that became very popular and influential. Charles Weld regarded his own book as being in some sense a sequel to the earlier work.

I was much struck by a forcible illustration of the loss attending the employment of slaves, by a visit to one of the largest tobacco factories in Richmond. . . .

Down the centre of a long room were twenty large presses, at each of which some dozen slaves, stripped to the waist (it was very hot), were tugging and heaving at long iron arms, which turned screws, accompanying each push and pull by deep-drawn groans. Within a few yards of the factory runs, or rather rushes, an illimitable supply of water, the merest fraction of which would furnish power to turn the screws of all the tobacco pressed in Richmond. On suggesting the desir-

Source: Charles Weld, *A Vacation Tour of the United States and Canada* (London: Longman, Brown, Green and Longman's, 1855), pp. 313–14.

ableness of using this great natural force, instead of the numerous Negroes now employed, thus saving their labor, the proprietor of the factory, who kindly acted as my guide, assured me the slaves did the work far better than it could be done by machinery, as the overseer could direct them to apply precisely as much pressure as the tobacco required.

EIGHT
Master and Man

68. Master Bruce Inventories His Slave Property

As David Brion Davis pointed out so cogently in his work *The Problem of Slavery in Western Culture* (Ithaca, 1966), the essential contradiction in slavery has always been that, even though slaves were property under its terms, because they were also human beings they could not always be managed (or even exploited efficiently) unless some aspects of their humanity were taken into account. Since the slave was the legal property of his master, it seems reasonable to begin the exploration of relations between master and man at its basic level. The clearest manifestation of the slave's status as property is the slave inventory.

Like other property, human chattels had to be counted and evaluated from time to time, assessed at their market value under ever-changing conditions of the economy. Good business required it. Accordingly, inventories were necessary when properties were divided among heirs to estates, or when planters had to borrow money. Few documents are more revealing to the social historian. Not only is the essential relation of master to slave registered in the market value of the slave, but also the comparative value of slaves by age, sex, and occupation is revealed. Even the humanity of slave "property" is acknowledged indirectly when the quality of personality is thrown into the account. Economic historians have made particular use of slave inventories in monitoring the changing value of prime field hands over the decades. Usually a correlation existed between the price of cotton and the value of slaves.

The following inventory comes from the business papers of James Coles Bruce (1806–65), one of the largest slave-owners in the South in the decades preceding the Civil War. Although Bruce's possessions were truly baronial, the inventory to follow includes only slaves of a sugar plantation in Louisiana, owned by Bruce jointly with two relatives. One of them, brother-in-law James A. Seddon, became a high-ranking Cabinet officer in the Confederate Government. A close reading of this inventory will show that Dr. Wilkins, the third owner, was in residence at the plantation, with six slaves he owned personally, at the time the inventory was made.

Source: "List and Inventory of the Negro[e]s on the Plantation of Messrs Bruce, Seddon, & Wilkins[.] St. James [Parish, La.] Nov. 22nd 1849," in Papers of the James Coles Bruce Family of Berry Hill, Alderman Library, University of Virginia.

Bruce was educated at the University of South Carolina, Harvard University, and the University of Virginia. As a member of the General Assembly of Virginia, Bruce supported slavery, but lived to regret doing so. He was a Whig and a Unionist in the secession crisis, but switched after Lincoln called for troops. Ultimately he contributed more than $50,000 to the Confederacy.

This inventory, made in 1849, is especially interesting for the brief characterizations of the slaves. "Full hands" were those capable of the work load of a mature slave in good health; "half-hands" were those too young, too old, or physically incapable of a full work load. It is apparent that skilled slaves were of a higher market value than others, and that men were valued more highly than women. "Africans" were those who were not fully acculturated to plantation life, either because they were recent imports (unlikely in 1849), or because they had not learned English well, or bore the tribal markings, or otherwise gave evidence of what was called "outlandishness."

List of Negro Men & Boys, also their ages & Value

Names	Ages	Full Hands	Half Hands	Value	Remarks
Perry— Driver	40 Years	1″		$900 00	Disposed to medle with women
Old Daniel	70 ″		½	100 00	old and decriped
John Miller	28 ″	Full Hand		600 00	a Runaway
Jim Bassy	25 ″	″		600 00	Sickly
Claiborn West	28 ″	″		800 00	good Negro
Jack Page	35 ″	″		700 00	has Runaway
Claiborn Anderson	35 ″	″ * 1		400 00	has runaway
Orange	28 ″	″		800 00	good Hand
Anderson. M	25 ″	″		800 00	good Negro
Bob. Scooner	28 ″	″		700 00	Well disposed but Sloe
Izor M	45 ″	″		500 00	African, good but Sloe
George. M.	25 ″	″		600 00	a cooper, Sickly but good
Jin. Wilbot	45 ″	″ *		400 00	a Runaway no account

1. Sometime after the inventory was made, someone lightly wrote the word "dead" alongside the four names asterisked here. (*Editor's note*)

Names	Ages	Full Hands	Half Hands	Value	Remarks
Carter Allen	23 [Years]	"		400 00	a Runaway, verry Sloe
Charles Mena	45 "	"		500 00	African, verry good
Randle	45 "	"		800 00	Sugar Maker, good hand
Edmond	40 "	"		600 00	A great drunkard
Sam Williams	25 "	"		600 00	A good hand
Gallant	45 "	"		500 00	rather trifling, but will do
Old Mat M.	35 "		½	300 00	Sickly consumption
Bill Kenty	45 "	"		700 00	good hand
Fleming	45 "	"		400 00	a runaway
Jefferson	28 "	"		800 00	Superior Hand
Simond (Carpenter)	45 "	"		800 00	the greatest rascal on Plantation
Friday	40	*	½	350 00	Sickly Subject to fits
Milton	20 "	"		700 00	good hand
Ezekiel	25 "	"		800 00	good hand
John Davis	45 "	"	½	400 00	Sickly, & a runaway
Jackson Tailor	28 "	"		800 00	good hand
Sam Briggs	23 "	"		700 00	good hand
David	44 "	"		700 00	well disposed but sloe
John Henderson	20 "	"		700 00	a fine hand
Richmond	23 "	"		800 00	a good hand
Simond Melacha	25 "	"		700 00	good hand but tricky
Ned Duck	35 "	"		500 00	not much account
Granison	26 "	"		600 00	good hand
Ransom	25 "	"		800 00	good hand
Tellemark	50 "		½	200 00	African King, no account
Charles Sims	28 "	"		700 00	good hand
Jack Coopper	30 "	"		1000 00	Jack Cooper, good hand
Bill Pleasant	28 "	"		700 00	good hand
Bill Sprague	30 "	"		600 00	good hand
Wyatt	30 "	"		700 00	good hand

List of Negro Men & Boys, also their ages & Value (*Continued*)

Names	Ages	Full Hands	Half Hands	Value	Remarks
Isaac Pascal	35 [Years]	"		700 00	verry Sloe and high tempe[red]
Bill Berry	35 "	"		700 00	Sugar Maker, a great Liar
Squire	50 "		½	200 00	not much account
Ceazor	50 "		½	200 00	well disposed but no account
Little Daniel	40 "	" *		600 00	disposed to fein sickness
Patrick	50 "		½	200 00	gardner no account
Ephraim	30 "	"		800 00	excelent hand
Old Champ	50 . "		¼	100 00	most Blind, but well disposed
Washington	20 "	"		600 00	a Runaway
Carter M.	35 "	"		600 00	verry deceptive
John Comedy	45 "	" *		600 00	a great Rascal & Runaway
Jack Allen	18 "		½	300 00	Sickly (Breast complaint)
Jo Blacksmith	30 "	"		1200 00	Blacksmith good hand
Old Luis	50 "		½	200 00	water hauler no account
Richard	15 "	"	½	500 00	good hand
One Leg Bob	50 "		0	000 00	no earthly use
John Robinson	16 "	"	½	500 00	assistant Black-smith good
Emmanuel	45 "		½	100 00	criple, (in the Doct yard)
Old Charles	60 "		0	5 00	wore out, no account
General	30 "	"		800 00	No 1 hand
Little Mat M.	17 "		½	300 00	reumatic (but well disposed)
Little Jo	15 "		½	500 00	excelent Boy
Israel	20 "	"		600 00	Brick layer fair hand
Willson	22 "	"		600 00	Brick layer fair hand

Names	Ages	Full Hands	Half Hands	Value	Remarks
Pleasant	26 [Years]	"		1000 00	Carpenter fine Negro
Moses	27 "	"		1000 00	Engineer good Negro
Phill	10 "		1/3	300 00	wants much watching
Sandy	9 "		1/3	300 00	verry fine Boy
Jo	8 "		1/3	250 00	verry trifling
Anderson M	25 "	"		900 00	good hand
Will Shoemaker	28 "	"		800 00	good hand
Jim Wilkins	27 "	"		700 00	good hand
Little Bob	12 "		1/2	300 00	a verry good Boy
Julius	12 "		1/2	300 00	good Boy
One hand Luis	30 "		1/2	400 00	Bad Negro Runaway
Old Jake	50 "		1/2	300 00	well disposed
John Wilkins	30 "	"		600 00	verry good
Ballard Doct	12 "		1/2	300 00	good Boy but Sloe
Little Jack Doct	10 "		1/2	300 00	verry Smart Boy
William	6 "	o	o	200 00	verry good Boy
Nelson	4 "	o	o	150 00	rather young to Judge
Lunon	3 "	o	o	150 00	" "
Maldry	4 "	o	o	150 00	" "
Mose	4 "	o	o	200 00	" "
Ceazor	4 "	o	o	200 00	" "
George	2 "	o	o	100 00	" "
Pier	5 "	o	o	250 00	" "
Henry Lewis (Louisa child 9 months)	o "	o	o	100 00	" "
Prince (Araminta child 8 months)	o "	o	o	100 00	" "
92 Men & Boys &					
44 Women & Children					
136 in all					

A List Women their ages & value

Names	Ages	Full Hands	Half Hands	Value	Remarks
Letha	20 [Years]	"		500 00	good hand
Elmira	25 "		½	400 00	Sickly
Eliza Ann	18 "	"		500 00	good hand
Nanny	16 "	"		500 00	good hand
Long Mariah	45 "		½	200 00	not much account
Tena	40 "	"		400 00	well disposed fair hand
Eliza	20 "	"		400 00	fair hand
Amy	35 "	"		400 00	fair hand
Jennette	35 "	"		400 00	verry good cook
Peggy	30 "	"		500 00	good hand
Fanny	18 "	"		500 00	good hand
Nancy	16 "	"		500 00	good hand
Harriet (Black)	25 "	"		500 00	good hand
Olive	20 "	"		500 00	good hand
Hager	50 "		½	200 00	excells in telling lies
Angelina	30 "	"		400 00	verry good hand
Mariah (Cook)	40	"		300 00	all mouth. plantation cook
Polly	40	"		300 00	verry Bad woman (great temper)
Lucy	20	"		500 00	good hand
Martha	35	"		500 00	good hand
Lydia	25	"		400 00	good hand
Yellow Harriet	18		¼	100 00	verry little account sickly
Cathrine	20	"		400 00	fair hand
Penelopy	60		½	200 00	Plantation Nurse
Mary Jose	55		½	100 00	wash woman, no account
Little Mary	14 "		½	400 00	good Girl
Dina	40 "	"		400 00	Hospital nurse. fair
Julia	20 "	"		400 00	fair hand
Vina	30 "		½	200 00	Sickly
Tamor	30 "	"		400 00	fair hand
Matilda	16 "	"		500 00	good hand

Names	Ages	Full Hands	Half Hands	Value	Remarks
Rose	10[Years]		o	300 00	a great Liar (but will do)
Mary Creole	20 "	"		500 00	good hand
Hannah	45 "		½	300 00	mischief maker (all talk)
Terese	11 "		½	300 00	will Lie & Steal
Farma	30 "	"		500 00	good hand
Louisa (Doctors)	22 "	"		500 00	good hand
Araminta "	22 "	"		500 00	good hand
Micky	5 "	o	o	150 00	well disposed
Eliza	7 "	o	o	250 00	great Liar (but will do)
Rebecca 6 mo	0 "	o	o	100 00	to young to Judge
Nancy (5 months)	0 "	o	o	100 00	" " " "
Rachael (3 months)	0 "	o	o	100 00	" " " "
Delphy 2 months	0 "	o	o	100 00	" " " "

List of Negros that does not work in the field

Sawmill Hands
Mose, Anderson, Carter[,] Izor[,] Friday (½)[,] old Mat (½), Little Mat (½), Charles [,] Louis[,] Little Jack (½)
4 of which are half Hands which make 10 in number
& onely 8 full Hands   10 in Number

Pleasant, Little Jo, (Anderson Wilkins) old Davy & Simond are the carpenters
                                                                       5 in Number

Jack, George, & Jim Bassy are the Coopers   3 in Number

Jo Blacksmith & John Robison are the Blacksmiths   2 in Number

John Comedy [,] Ned Duck, Sandy (½), Phill (½), & Joe (½) are the Stable Boys
                                                                       5 in Number

Dina, is Hospital Nurse   1 in Number

Penelopy is Plantation washwomen   1 in Number

Mary Jose is a Nurse for children	1 in Number
Mariah & Harriet are Plantation Cooks	2 in Number
Fanny is the Doct Cook	1 in Number
Polly is at Mr Knowltons House	1 in Number
Jennett is at the overseers House	1 in Number

old Bob, Old Dan, Old Champ, Old Charles, & Old Patrick, employed in various ways Such as gardening Shingle makeing Shaveing hoops &c all together will not do more than one good hand but are called ½ Hands

5 in Number

Making in Number 37 Negros who does not work in the field except in Rooling [sugar rolling] Season and in the Said 37 Negroes their are 27 full Hands

Their are	45	men full hands in the field &
their are	25	women in the field full Hands
makeing	70	in Number for the field
&	27	full hands employed in various ways as above stated
makeing	97	full hands on the Plantation

The men & Boys are worth in the agrigate as per inventory $47,005.00
The Women & Girls are worth 15,600.00

$62,605.00
Off for Dr Wilkins Negros 1 800.00

60 805.00

Average value of each $460.33 & a fraction
130 in all after deducting 6 for Dr Wilkins

69. Governor Hammond's Instructions to His Overseer

Plantation owners frequently committed to paper the general regulations they intended their overseers to follow in the management of slaves and their other farm property. This was true especially of large owners who occasionally had more than one overseer. These regulations were sometimes followed, and sometimes they were not, as the letters and diaries of planters make clear. If a master rewarded the overseer too well for producing extraordinary crops, and was not too careful to inquire into the condition of his slave property, the overseer would sometimes be tempted to overwork his labor force. This was more likely to happen if the owner was an absentee from his plantation for long periods.

The manuals are nonetheless valuable in indicating what was regarded by the community at large as being respectable conditions of labor; and one assumes that what is respectable is what one would customarily encounter, except during periods of urgency on the plantation, when loss of the crop seemed imminent, or when a crisis in interpersonal relations drove out balanced judgment. Employing a manual of rules, it may be added, gave the planter support before the law in case cruelty or bad judgment on the part of his overseer caused him to lose the life or service of a field hand.

The following manual of rules drawn up by Gov. James Henry Hammond of South Carolina, designed for use on a large estate in the 1840s and 1850s, is unusually particular in its details. Hammond was called a stern master by some of his contemporaries, but he considered himself to be a fair man. He was certainly a staunch supporter of slavery, and apparently the originator of the famous line, "Cotton is king."

CROP.

1 A good crop means one that is good taking into consideration every thing—negroes, land, mules, stock, fences, ditches, farming utensils, &c., &c., all of which must be kept up & improved in value. The effort therefore must not be merely to make *so many* cotton bales or such an amount of

Source: MS Manual of Rules [ca. 1840/50], James Henry Hammond Papers, Library of Congress.

other produce, but as much as can be made without interrupting the steady increase in value of the rest of the property.

Remarks.—There should be an increase in number, & improvement in condition & value of negroes; abundant provisions of all sorts for every thing, made on the place, carefully saved & properly housed; an improvement in the productive qualities of the land, & general condition of the plantation; mules, stock, fences & farming utensils in fine order at the close of the year; as much produce as could possibly be made under these circumstances, ready for market in good season, & of prime quality.

OVERSEER.—

2 The Overseer will never be expected to work in the fields, but he must always be with the hands when not otherwise engaged in the Employer's business, & will be required to attend on occasion to any pecuniary transaction connected with the plantation.

Remarks.—The Overseer should never give away, sell or exchange, nor buy, order or contract for any thing without the full knowledge of the Employer & positive orders to do so.

3 The Overseer must never be absent a single night nor an entire day, without permission previously obtained. Whenever absent at church, or elsewhere, he must be on the plantation by sundown without fail.

4 He must attend every night & morning at the stables, & see that the mules are watered, cleaned & fed, & the doors locked. He must keep the stable keys at night, & all the keys, in a safe place, & never allow any one to unlock a barn, smoke house, or other depository of plantation stores but himself. He must endeavor, also, to be with the plow hands always at noon.

5 The Overseer must see that all the negroes leave their houses promptly after hornblow in the morning. Once, or more, a week he must visit every house after horn blow at night to see that all are in.

Remarks.—He should not fall into a regular day or hour for night visit but should go so often and at such times that he may be expected at anytime.

6 The Overseer will be expected not to degrade himself by charging any negro with carrying news to the Employer. There must be no news to carry. The Employer will not encourage tale-bearing, but will question every negro indiscriminately whenever he thinks proper about all matters connected with the plantation, & require him to tell the truth. Whenever he learns anything derogatory to the Overseer he will immediately communicate it to him.

Remarks.—The Overseer must show no favoritism among negroes.

7 The Overseer must ride but one horse & must never allow any member of his family, or other person, on any

occasion, to use a horse without he obtains permission: And as the Employer's business will require his whole attention he is expected to see but little company.

8 He will be expected to obey strictly all instructions of the Employer. His opinion is requested on all questions relative to plantation matters as they arise, & will be treated with respect, but when not adopted, he must cheerfully & faithfully carry into effect the views of the Employer, & with a sincere desire to produce a successful result. He must carry on all experiments with fidelity, & note the results carefully, & must give, when instructed by the Employer, a fair trial to all new methods of culture, & new implements of agriculture.

9 The whole stock is under his charge. He must attend personally at feeding the hogs at laest [least] four times a week, & count them once a week: & count & salt the cattle twice a month.

Remarks.—He must fall into no routine in looking after the stock, but so arrange that the stockminder will always expect him.

10 The Overseer must keep the plantation Diary regularly & carefully, note the number of hands engaged each day in various operations under proper heading, the number of sick, weather, allowances & implements given out, articles received at or sent from the plantation, births, deaths & whatever other information or remarks which

may be valuable, together with an accurate summary of every thing on the plantation once a month. He must also inform the Employer, without being asked, of every thing going on that may concern or interest him.

11 The negroes must be made to obey & to work, which may be done by an Overseer, who attends regularly to his business, with very little whipping. Much whipping indicates a bad tempered, or inattentive manager, & will not be allowed. The Overseer must never on any occasion—unless in self defence—kick a negro, or strike with his hand, or a stick, or the butt-end of his whip. No unusual punishment must be resorted to without the Employer's consent.

Remarks.—He must never threaten a negro, but punish offences immediately on knowing them; otherwise he will soon have run-aways.

12 It is distinctly understood in the agreement with every Overseer that whenever dissatisfied he can quit the Employer's service on giving him one month's notice in writing, & that the Employer may discharge him at any time by paying him for his services up to that period at the same rates as he agreed to pay for the year. All use of spirituous liquors by the Overseer is objected to, & should he get drunk he must expect to be instantly discharged.

ALLOWANCES.—

1 Allowances are given out once a week. No distinction is made among

work-hands, whether they are full-hands or under, field hands or adjuncts about the yard, stables, &c.

Remarks.—Negroes are improvident with a longer interval between allowances many will consume, waste or barter their provisions before it closes & must commit thefts, or have insufficient & unwholesome food during a portion of the time; demoralyzing & rendering them physically incapable of doing full work, if not producing sickness. They should, also, be brought into that contact with the master, at laest [least] once a week, of receiving the means of subsistence from him.—

2 Each work-hand gets a peck of meal every Sunday morning—the measure filled & piled as long as it will stand on it, but not packed or shaken.

Remarks.—Every negro must come in person for meal allowance, & in clean clothes.— Sweet potato[e]s may be given in the winter after Christmas in part for meal, where preferred, at the rates of one bushel of potatos for a peck of meal. There must be a watch kept that they do not sell the potatos.

3 Each work hand gets 3 lbs. of bacon or pickled pork every Monday night. Fresh meat may be substituted at the rates of 3½ lbs. of fresh pork, (uncured, but salted) or 4 lbs. of beef or mutton, or 4½ of pork offal. When 1 pint of molasses is given the meat is reduced to 2½ lbs. of bacon or pickled pork, beef or mutton, or 3½ lbs. of pork offal. Mixed allowances of bacon & fresh meat are given in the same proportions. The entire amount of

meat is weighed out from the smoke-house & divided satisfactorily in the presence of the Overseer. Fresh beef may be given late in summer & on 'till spring—never in full allowances unless in cold weather. Fresh pork & pork offal only at hog-killing times. Each ditcher, who gives full satisfaction in his work for a week, receives an extra pound of meat on Wednesday night. The Drivers are allowed a small extra of meat whenever they may apply for it—which is rarely done. They receive also an extra pint of molasses every week.

Remarks.— If meat was given on Sunday many would consume it the same day in entertaining or eating in consequence of having nothing else to do. Frequent cases of sickness have resulted on Mondays from this cause.— Daily allowances would be better than weekly, but is troublesome. By giving it daily & cooking it there will be the advantages of regularity in the hours, quantity & quality of their meals, with the certainty of its being perfectly done. It is said to make full return to have an appointed cook for twenty hands.—All fresh meat should be well salted before given out & mutton at no time for over two days allowance. A little salt should be given out from time to time. Negroes are apt to hang fresh meat in their chimneys where the smoke preserves the outside from putrifying until the inner part is perfectly rotten. This should be guarded against.— In the long hot days of summer an extra pound of meat should be given occasionally.

4 Each ditcher receives every night, when ditching, a dram [jigger] consist-

ing ⅔ whiskey & ⅓ water, with as much asafoetida as it will absorb & several strings of red peppers added in the barrel. The dram is a large wine-glass-full. In cotton picking time, when sickness begins to be prevalent, every field hand gets a dram in the morning before leaving for the field.— After a soaking rain all exposed to it get a dram before changing their clothes: also those exposed to the dust from the sheller & fan in corn shelling on reaching the quarter at night, or any one required at any time to keep watch in the night. Drams are never given as rewards but only as medecinal.

5 From the second hoeing, or early in May, every work hand, who uses it, gets an occasional allowance of tobacco—about ⅙ of a pound, usually after some general operations as a hoeing, plowing, &c. This is continued until their crops are gathered, when they can provide for themselves.

CLOTHING.—

6 Each man gets in the fall 2 shirts of cotton drilling, a pair of woolen pants & a woolen jacket. In the Spring 2 shirts of cotton shirting & 2 pr of cotton pants.

Remarks.— Jackets or pants may be substituted for each other whenever the wish is expressed before making them. Often done.

7 Each woman gets in the fall 6 yds. of woolen cloth, 6 yds. of cotton drilling & a needle, skein of thread & ½ doz buttons. In the Spring 6 yds. of cotton shirting & 6 yds. of cotton cloth similar to that for men's pants, needle, thread & buttons.

8 Each worker gets a stout pr. of shoes every fall, & a heavy blanket every third year.

CHILDREN.—

9 There is a separate building [in] the charge of a trusty nurse, where the children are kept during the day. Weaned children are brought to it at the last horn-blow in the morning— about good day light. The unweaned are brought to it at sun rise, after suckling, & left in cradles in charge of the nurse.

10 Allowance is given out daily to the children, at the rates for each child, of ⅓ of meal & meat that [is] given to work-hands. An abundant supply of vegetables should be always at hand, in a garden cultivated for the especial purpose, to be cooked with their meat. Each child must have daily at laest [least] 1 pint of skimmed milk. Their food should be cooked by the nurse, & consist, for breakfast & supper, of hominy & milk and cold corn bread: their dinner of vegetable soup—usually pot-liquor or okra soup—& dumplings or bread. Cold bread or potatos should be kept on hand for occasional demands between meals. Their meat may be the same as that given to work hands, except that the only fresh meat allowed them is the beef bones for soup. They should have a little molasses once or twice a week, & a well roasted sweet potato every day. Each child is provided with a pan & spoon, placed in charge of a nurse.

11 Each child gets 2 shirts of drilling every fall, & 2 of shirting in the spring, made very long. The girls get 2 frocks, & the boys 2 pr of pants reaching the neck & with sleeves, in the fall, & 1 each in the spring—of lighter woolens in the fall than that given to the work hands.

12 Each child gets a blanket every 3rd year. Children born in the interval can have a blanket at the time, or the fall following, according to the necessities of the Mother. Mothers are required to put entirely clean clothes on their children twice a week, & it is the duty of the nurse to report any omission to do so.

SUCKLERS.—

13 Sucklers are not required to leave their houses until sun-rise, when they leave their children at the children's house before going to field. The period of suckling is 12 mos. Their work lies always within ½ mile of the quarter. They are required to be cool before commencing to suckle—to wait 15 minutes, at laest, in summer, after reaching the children's house before nursing. It is the duty of the nurse to see that none are heated when nursing, as well as of the Overseer & his wife occasionally to do so. They are allowed 45 minutes at each morning to be with their children. They return 3 times a day until their infants are 8 mos. old—in the middle of the forenoon, at noon, & in the middle of the afternoon: till the 12th mo. but twice a day, missing at noon: during the 12th mo. at noon only. On weaning, the child is removed entirely from its

Mother for 2 weeks, & placed in charge of some careful woman without a child, during which time the Mother is not to nurse it at all.

Remarks.— The amount of work done by a Suckler is about ³/₅ of that done by a full-hand, a little increased toward the last.

OLD & INFIRM.—

15 Those, who from age & infirmities are unable to keep up with the prime hands, are put in the suckler's gang.

PREGNANT.—

16 Pregnant women, at 5 mos. are put in the suckler's gang. No plowing or lifting must be required of them.

Sucklers, old, infirm & pregnant, receive the same allowances as full-work hands.

CONFINEMENT.—

17 The regular plantation midwife shall attend all women in confinement. Some other woman learning the art is usually with her during delivery. The confined woman lies up one month, & the midwife remains in constant attendance for 7 days. Each woman on confinement has a bundle given to her containing articles of clothing for the infant, pieces of cloth & rag, & some extra nourishment, as sugar, coffee, rice & flour for the Mother.

SICKNESS.—

18 No negro will be allowed to remain at his own house when sick, but

must be confined to the hospital. Every reasonable complaint must be promptly attended to, & with any marked or general symptom of sickness, however trivial, a negro may lie up a day or so at laest [least]. Homoeopathy is exclusively practiced. As no physician is allowed to practice on the plantation—there being no Homoeopathist convenient—each case has to be examined carefully by the master or overseer to ascertain the disease. The remedies next are to be chosen with the utmost discrimination. The vehicles, (tumblers & aprons) for preparing & administering with, are to be thoroughly cleansed. The directions for treatment, diet, &c. most implicitly followed; the effects & changes cautiously observed, & finally the medecines securely laid away from accidents & contaminating influences. In cases, where there is the slightest uncertainty, the books must be taken to the bed-side, & a careful & thorough examination of the case, & comparison of remedies, made before administering them. The Overseer must record in the prescription book every dose of medicine administered.

HOURS.—

19 The first morning horn is blown an hour before day-light. All work-hands are required to rise & prepare their cooking, &c. for the day. The second horn is blown just at good day-light, when it is the duty of the driver to visit every house & see that all have left for the field. The plow hands leave their houses for the stables, at the summons of the plow driver, 15 minutes earlier than the gang, the Overseer opening the stable doors to them. At 11 1/2 M. the plow hands repair to the nearest weather house. At 12 M. the gang stop to eat dinner. At 1 P.M. through the greater part of the year, all hands return to work. In summer the intermission increases with the heat to the extent of 3 1/2 hours. At 15 minutes before sun-set the plow-hands, & at sun-set the rest, knock off work for the day. No work must ever be required after dark. No negro will be allowed to go hunting at night. The negroes are allowed to visit among themselves until the night horn is blown, after which no negro must be seen out of his house, & it is the duty of the driver to go around & see that he is in it. The night horn is blown at 8 1/2 P.M. in winter, & at 9 P.M. in summer. The head driver has charge of & blows the horn.

DRIVER.—

20 The head driver is the most important negro on the plantation, & is not required to work like the other hands. He is to be treated with more respect than any other negro by both master & overseer. He is on no occasion to be treated with any indignity calculated to lose the respect of the other negroes, without breaking him. He is required to maintain proper discipline at all times. To see that no negro idles or does bad work in the field & to punish it with discretion on the spot. The driver must never be flogged, except by the master, but in emergencies that will not admit of delay. Of this, however, he is to be kept in entire ignorance. He is permitted to visit the master at any time without being required to get a card,

though, in general, he is expected to inform the Overseer when he leaves the place, & present himself on returning. He is expected to communicate freely whatever attracts his attention, or he thinks information of interest to the master. He is a confidential servant & may be a guard against any excuses or omissions of the Overseer.

MARRIAGE.—

21 Marriage is to be encouraged as it adds to the comfort, happiness & health of those who enter upon it, besides insuring a greater increase. Permission must always be obtained from the master before marriage, but no marriage will be allowed with negroes not belonging to the master. When sufficient cause can be shewn on either side, a marriage may be annulled, but the offending party must be severely punished. Where both are in wrong both must be punished, & if they insist on separating must have 100 lashes apiece. After such a separation neither can marry again for 3 years. For first marriage a bounty of $5.00 to be invested in household articles, shall be given. If either has been married before, the bounty shall be $3.50. A third marriage shall not be allowed but in extreme cases, & in such cases, or where both have been married before, no bounty will be given.

CHURCH.—

22 All are privileged & encouraged to go to Church on Sundays, but no religious meeting is allowed on the plantation beyond singing & praying, & at such times as will not conflict with the plantation hours, & always with the permission of the Master or Overseer. Church members are privileged to dance on all holyday occasions, & the class leader or deacon who may report them shall be reprimanded or punished at the discretion of the master.

VISITING.—

23 All visiting with strange negroes is positively forbidden. Negroes living at one plantation & having wives at the other can visit them only between Saturday night & Monday morning, & must get a pass card at each visit. The pass consists of a card with the full name of the place of destination on it & the first letter of the place of leaving below. The card must be delivered to the Overseer immediately on reaching the place named on it, & a return card asked for just before returning. The card is the recognized & required permit in all visiting & any negro leaving the plantation without it, or off the most direct route, shall be punished on detection by the Overseer, & is liable to punishment from any one meeting him. Not more than 6 ordinary at a time can leave the quarter, except for Church. Negroes are subject to the regulations of the place they are at any moment upon, & it is as much the duty of the Overseer & driver to observe them as those under their ordinary charge.

TOWN.—

24 Each work-hand is allowed to go to Town once a year (the women always selecting some of the men to go for them) on a Sunday between crop gathering & Christmas. Not more than

10 shall be allowed to go the same day. The head driver may have a cart some Saturday after Christmas that it is convenient for him to go to Town.

This rule is objectionable & must be altered.[1]

NEGRO PATCHES.—

Adjoining each negro house is a piece of ground convenient for a fowl-yard & garden. No fowl-yard or garden fence shall reach nearer than 60 feet to the negro houses. Negroes may have patches in various parts of the plantation (always getting permission from the master) to cultivate crops of their own. A field of suitable size shall be planted in pindars,[2] & cultivated in the same manner as the general crop, the produce of which is to be divided equally among the work-hands. Negroes are not allowed to grow crops of corn or cotton for themselves, nor to have any cattle or stock of any kind of their own.

HOLYDAYS.—

At Christmas a holyday of three or four days is given, commencing on Christmas day. On that day, if not a Sunday, a barbacue is given, beef or mutton & pork, coffee & bread being bountifully provided. Each plantation shall have its barbacue separate, unless there is a general desire on both places

1. Governor Hammond added this line at some later period than that of the original composition of his manual. (*Editor's note*)
2. Ground-nuts, or peanuts, very popular with blacks. The word "pindar" is of African origin and was in wide use in southeastern United States and the West Indies. (*Ed.*)

to have it united. There is also a barbacue & one day's holyday in August. No strange negroes are allowed to attend, nor shall any of the neighbors be invited by the Overseer without the Employer's consent.

CLEANING UP.—

A day shall be allowed in the Spring, after planting, for a thorough cleansing of the negro quarter. The Overseer must see that every house is completely emptied of everything, the articles removed exposed to the sun, & the floors & walls scoured in the morning so as to be dried by night. No lofts are allowed in any of the houses, & all accumulations under the roof are to be removed. The mattresses are to be emptied in the stable lot & fresh hay or shucks put in them. The yard & fowl yards to [be] cleaned, & all trash burnt or removed. One pint of lime is to [be] sprinkled under each house. Another cleaning up takes place after fodder pulling. Each house is white-washed inside & outside once every year. The sucklers must, also, clean the entire yard from time to time, & always remove all litter & trash. Negroes must appear once a week in clean clothes, & any negro habitually uncleanly in person must by [be] washed & scrubbed by order of the Overseer—the driver & two other negroes officiating.

REWARDS.—

The head driver receives on Christmas day $5.00 from the master; the plow driver $3.00; the midwife $2.00 & the nurse $1.00 for every actual increase of two on the place; the ditch driver $1.00 & the Stock Minder $1.00. Any of these rewards may be with-held where any negligence or misbehavior has occurred in the various departments, attributable to, or not promptly reported or corrected by the recipients. For every infant 13 months old & in sound health, that has been properly attended to the Mother shall receive a muslin or calico frock.

PUNISHMENTS.—

The following is the order in which offences must be estimated & punished: 1st Running away.—2nd Getting drunk or having spirits.—3rd Stealing hogs.— 4th Stealing.—5th Leaving plantation without permission.—6th Absence from house after horn blow at night.— 7th Unclean house or person.—8th Neglect of tools.—9th Neglect of work.— The highest punishment must not exceed 100 lashes in one day & to that extent only in extreme cases. The whip lash must be one inch in width or a strap of one thickness of leather 1 1/2 inches in width, & never severely administered. In general 15 to 20 lashes will be a sufficient flogging. The hands in every case must be secured by a cord. Punishment must always be given calmly & deliberately & never when angry or excited.

---

70. How To Manage Negroes, By "A Planter"

The management and control of slaves was an absorbing subject for all planters, and a subject of endless debate and not a little controversy. Were blacks healthier in brick or clapboard houses, or in log cabins? What kind of discipline was most effective? Was it preferable to have the cooking done by a plantation cook, or by the slave families? How could planters best secure the necessary care of infants? Was sexual morality important, and if so, how could it be secured? Were slaves better workers if taught religion? Or did they become rebellious?

The popular agricultural magazines frequently carried articles exploring these topics, and important essays or letters were frequently reprinted in more than one magazine. Obviously the size of the plantation had much

Source: *The Farmer's Register* (Petersburg, Va.), vol. 4, no. 8 (December 1, 1836), pp. 492–96, and no. 9 (January 1, 1837), pp. 574–75.

to do with how a slave-owner would resolve many of these questions, and, just as obviously, good advice was not always heeded. But the proffer of advice on certain questions indicates that a certain importance was attached to them. Was medical attention best secured by contracting with a physician for the entire plantation for a fixed sum? Was a given plantation large enough for a cookhouse and a hospital, and a nursery? Should a separate church or meeting house be built for slaves? How much freedom were the slaves to be allowed in the form of their worship? Most planters who wrote on these topics expressed a respect for cleanliness, firmness, and order.

The significance of personal example is stressed by the following writer, whose letter to *The Southern Agriculturist* was picked up by Edmund Ruffin, editor of *The Farmer's Register*, and reprinted. When this letter appeared, Ruffin was in the process of becoming a stout defender of slavery; yet on the whole, his famous agricultural journal, called by one authority "one of the very best agricultural publications ever issued in Europe or in this country," remained remarkably free of Ruffin's extreme view on slavery and Southern rights.

Notions on the Management of Negroes, &c.

1. *Cleanliness* is a matter which cannot be too closely attended to. Every owner should make it a rule to appoint a certain day in the week, for reviewing his negroes and their habitations, to see that both are clean and in good order. For myself, I select Sunday, as the best day for this purpose. My mode of making such reviews, is the following:

I appoint a certain hour for attending to this matter on each Sabbath, say nine o'clock in the morning. Every negro distinctly understands, that at this hour he will be reviewed. An hour or so previous to the review, I make it the business of the driver to sound the horn, for the negroes to prepare themselves and houses for inspection.

When the hour for review has arrived, it is also his business to attend upon me, and report the plantation ready for inspection. This being done, I repair to the negro houses. At the door of each house, the occupants thereof are seen standing with their children, if they have any. My business here is to call their respective names, and to see that every one has had his head well combed and cleaned, and their faces, hands, and feet well washed. The men are required, in addition to this, to have themselves shaved. That they may have no excuse for neglecting this requirement, those that need them are provided with combs and razors. I now see that their blankets, and all other body and bed clothing, have been hung out to air, if the weather be fine. Their pots are also examined. I particularly see that they have been well cleaned, and that nothing like "caked hominy," or potatoes is suffered to remain about them. I next enter their houses, and there see that every thing has been cleansed—that their pails, dressers, tables, &c. have all been washed down—that their chimneys have been swept and the ashes therefrom removed to one general heap in the yard, which serves me as an excellent manure for my lands. Being situated where my negroes procure many oysters, I make them save the shells, which they place in one pile, of which I burn lime enough each year, to white-wash my negro houses, both outside and inside. This not only gives a neat appearance to the houses, but preserves the boards of the same, and destroys all vermin which might infest them. From the inspection of the negro houses, I proceed to their *well,* and there see that the water is pure and healthy.

I should here state, that I repeat on Sunday what I do every time that I see any of my negroes viz. to examine that their clothes are not ragged or broken. Recollecting that a "stitch in time saves nine," I suffer none of them ever to appear with broken clothes. I give them the best clothes and I see that they do not suffer them to be ruined from carelessness. In all of my inspections I have a little book, in which I note down every thing that I see amiss. The negro who has been the cause, is called up on the morrow, and receives such reprimand or punishment as his case may require.

Having mentioned their own duties, it will, perhaps, not be amiss to state what I owe them also. Exacting as I do, the utmost *cleanliness* of them, I particularly observe *cleanliness* in my own person. For instance, I never appear before my negroes unshaved, or negligently dressed, and every thing that I have to do, I do with as much punctuality and exactness as I am capable of. Ignorant minds are ever apt to imitate their superiors, and upon this principle it will be found, that if the master is negligent in the observance of his duties, the slaves will also become so.

2. *Diet.*—This is a matter of more importance than most planters are aware of. It is only necessary to inquire of the physician, or to consult any medical work, to be convinced that an improper attention to diet, is one of the most prolific causes of disease among our negroes, as well as whites. It is the almost universal custom in this state, to give out to each negro a weekly allowance of corn or potatoes, and to suffer them to cook it as they please. For many reasons, this plan is the most agreeable to the negroes. I shall show, however, that it is far from being the most advantageous either to their health, or comfort. Every planter knows that there are many negroes, who rather than be at the trouble of cooking their own victuals, will trade away their allowance with their more industrious fellow-workers, for one-half; and even where this is not the case, they are always found ready to barter away their whole weekly allowance to some neighboring dram shop, for a gallon of whiskey, or a pound or two of tobacco, or bread. Where negroes are permitted to cook their own food, they neither have the time, nor capability to do it properly. It cannot be expected that the slave who is all day at hard work, can pay a proper at-

tention to preparing his food after the day's labor. He generally comes home tired, and before he has half cooked his meal, hunger induces him to devour it. It is true that some negroes cook their food in the field, while at work, but even this mode, must at once strike everyone as very improper. In nine cases out of ten, they cook with bad water, in dirty pots, and without salt. But I shall not enlarge upon the many ill effects arising from permitting negroes to have their allowance, and to cook it themselves. One of your correspondents, in a former number in an article on this subject, has pointed out many of the evils; I shall, therefore, detail a remedy which I have been applying for many years; and let me assure you, Mr. Editor, each year has caused me to be better pleased with its observance. First, then, when I give out corn as an allowance, I have it all ground into grist. And that this might be done with ease, I at first procured myself a corn mill worked by horse power, which, while it grinds and cracks all the corn on my plantation, only cost me a couple of hundred dollars. The corn being ground, I allow to each negro ten quarts of grist. Seven quarts of this I retain to be cooked for them, by a cook appointed for the purpose. The balance, three quarts, I give them to feed their poultry, or to do with, what they please. I have a person appointed to cook for all my negroes, who amount to about fifty in all. It is her business to prepare two meals per day; and for each meal she cooks a pint of grist to each grown hand, and in a smaller proportion for the younger negroes. That the food may be well done, she is required to cook in two or three

distinct pots. Both for breakfast and dinner, I allow a small portion of meat of some kind, to boil with their food. And here let me observe, that a bit of meat, which when divided among them all, would not afford a taste for anyone, will when cooked together, make soup enough to satisfy the whole plantation. In winter I require of the cook to have their breakfast ready at 8 o'clock, at which time the horn is sounded, and each negro comes with his piggin or bowl, and receives his portion, which is measured out to him by the driver. Dinner is required to be ready at 2 o'clock, and the same rules are observed as at breakfast. Since I have been cooking for the negroes of my plantation, I have never known one of them to complain of not having enough to eat. When I first adopted this rule, my negroes objected to it very much. But in a year or so they saw the utility of the practice, and now I am convinced, that they would not abandon it for a great deal, so much does it contribute to their comfort and health.

LITTLE NEGROES.

I have a nurse appointed to superintend all my little negroes, and a nursery built for them. If they are left to be protected by their parents, they will most assuredly be neglected. I have known parents take out an allowance for their children, and actually steal it from them, to purchase articles at some shop. Besides, when they would be honest to their offspring, from their other occupations, they have not the time to attend to them properly. The children get their food irregularly, and when they do get it, it is only half done. They are suffered, by not having one to attend to them, to expose themselves; and hence many of the deaths which occur on our plantations.

I have just stated that I have a nursery for my little negroes, with an old woman or nurse to superintend and cook for them, and to see that their clothes and bedding are well attended to. She makes the little ones, generally speaking, both girls and boys, mend and wash their own clothes, and do many other little matters, such as collecting litter for manure, &c. In this they take great pleasure, and it has the tendency to bring them up to industrious habits. The nurse also cooks for them three times a day; and she always has some little meat to dress for them, or the clabber or sour milk from the dairy to mix with their food. In *sickness* she sees that they are well attended to; and from having many of them together, one is taught to wait upon the other. My little negroes are consequently very healthy; and from pursuing the plan I have laid down, I am confident that I raise more of them, than where a different system is followed.

Having laid down some rules for preserving cleanliness among negroes, and attending to their diet, I proceed next, to the regulation of their morals and habits.

As soon as the negro is convinced that cleanliness adds to his comfort and ease, at home, he will unconciously practice the same, in discharging all his master's work. The slave, who has his head combed, and his face washed, and his clothes cleaned, will seldom be found neglecting his work

in the field, or scratching his head, as is too often the case, when he should be at his task. Niceness and exactness in discharging his duties, will imperceptibly creep into all his habits.

ORDER.

To observe order in all things, is a precept of Solomon; and the planter who will cause his negroes to adhere to this wise admonition, will live an easy and agreeable life throughout the year. I have seen a certain planter, who always has his negroes at work: they are never idle; and yet, he is always behind the seasons. Now, this arises from the non-observance of order. If he would only cause his negroes to do every thing as the time, the place, and the circumstance demanded, every thing would be done right, and he would get along well. Preserve order yourself, in all your actions, and your negroes will imitate you. For instance, if you ride by a fence that has been broken down, and you have a boy with you, make him stop and repair it; if you have no boy, get down, and do it yourself. Let every negro about you, and on your plantation, be made to observe this. I make it an offence, severely punishable, for any of my slaves to pass by any thing out of repair, without either stopping to put it to rights, or informing the proper person whose business it is to do so. One rail supplied, when the fence demands it, will save a supply of perhaps twenty or thirty, a week afterwards. I have seen negroes pass over bridges which had great holes in them, fifty times, and never take the trouble to mend them, when one log of wood could easily have done so. If negroes of mine did the like, be they male or female, if they were old enough to have discretion, I would punish them for the negligence. Let it not be said that such exactness is severe. Practice makes such things easy to the slaves, and they find it much better for their own comfort in the long run. The master should make it his business to show his slaves, that the advancement of his individual interest, is at the same time an advancement of theirs. Once they feel this, it will require but little compulsion to make them act as becomes them.

MORALS.

The planter should endeavor, as much as possible, to make his negroes adhere to moral rules. I know that to lay down any general code for them is idle. But then, a few particular rules may be strictly attended to. Among these, I particularly enjoin upon my slaves, the observance of their marriage contracts. In no instance do I suffer any of them to violate these ties—except where I would consider myself justified in doing so. Independently of the excellence of such an institution itself, it has the additional advantage of keeping your negroes at home.

If there be a church in the vicinity of the planter's residence, he should oblige all of his negroes to attend it, at least once a day. This has an excellent effect. Most negroes take Sunday as their day of visiting; and it not unfrequently happens, that they do more mischief on that day, by colleagueing themselves, than on any other. Now, the attendance upon church permits them to meet their relatives and friends there, and, at the same time, keeps them out of all mischief. It is rarely that any one can attend a house of religious worship without gaining some wholesome information. And the slave will generally learn, at such places, the reasons which sanction the master to exact of him his respective duties.

Upon their return from church, I generally employ them in regaling themselves in different healthful and innocent amusements—such as will tend to keep them in good spirits with each other. I know that some persons will object to this, as a desecration of the sabbath; but, for my own part, I cannot be persuaded that God's holy laws are violated in the innocent recreations of his creatures. But no more of this at present.

I have now, Mr. Editor, concluded my notions upon the management of negroes. I feel that I have said far less than the importance of the subject demands: but I hope that the little I have said, and the very imperfect manner in which it has been said, may induce others to give their notions likewise. We live by example, and, let me add, that much which is borrowed in this way, is immensely valuable. That every planter may recollect this, and that we may all do more than we have done, is the earnest wish of

A PLANTER.

71. A Small Farmer Describes His Slave Management

James Dunwoody Brownson DeBow, editor of the famous *DeBow's Review*, was an ardent and vocal supporter of the movement to industrialize the South, and his journal, published at New Orleans, became a forum for his ideas on the subject. DeBow was nonetheless interested in improved methods of plantation management as well, and when he drew up a three-volume work entitled *The Industrial Resources, Etc., of the Southern and Western States*, he included articles on the proper management of slave property. Among many other essays on the subject, the following piece by a "Small Farmer" may offer some contrasts with the instructions of Governor Hammond and the "Planter" of the two preceding documents.

NEGROES—MANAGEMENT OF.—The public may desire to know the age of the writer, the length of time he has been managing negroes, and how long he has tried the mode of management he recommends. It is sufficient to say, I have had control of negroes in and out of the field for thirty years, and have been carrying out my present system, and improving it gradually, for twenty years.

I do not deem it needful to follow "A Planter," nor shall I strike a blow at book-farming or theories, as I am an advocate for both, believing that even an error has its advantages, as it will frequently elicit inquiry and a good article in reply, whereas a statement of facts will sometimes pass unnoticed.

Housing for negroes should be good;

each family should have a house, 16 by 18 feet in the clear, plank floor, brick chimney, shingle roof; floor elevated two feet above the earth. There should be no loft, no place to stow away any thing, but pins to hang clothes upon. Each house should be provided with a bedstead, cotton mattress, and sufficient bed-clothes for comfort for the heads of the family, and also for the young ones.

Clothing should be sufficient, but of no set quantity, as all will use or waste what is given, and many be no better clad with four suits than others with two. I know families that never give more than two suits, and their servants are always neater than others with even four.

My rule is to give for winter a linsey

Source: James DeBow, ed., *The Industrial Resources, Etc., of the Southern and Western States,* 3 vols. (New Orleans, 1852), 2:336–37.

suit, one shirt of best towelling, one hat, one pair of shoes, a good blanket, costing $2 to $2 50, every other year, (or I prefer, after trying three years, a comfort.) In the summer, two shirts, two pair pants, and one straw hat. Several of my negroes will require two pair pants for winter, and occasionally even a third pair, depending mostly upon the material. Others require another shirt and a third pair of pants for summer. I seldom give two pair of shoes.

Food is cooked by a woman, who has the children under her charge. I do not regard it as good economy, to say nothing of any feeling, to require negroes to do any cooking after their day's labor is over.

The food is given out daily, a half pound to each hand that goes to the field, large and small, water carriers and all; bread and vegetables without stint, the latter prepared in my own garden, and dealt out to the best advantage, endeavoring to have something every day in the year. I think four pounds of clear meat is too much. I have negroes here that have had only a half pound each for twenty years, and they bid fair to outlive their master, who occasionally forgets his duty, and will be a gourmand. I practise on the plan, that all of us would be better to be restrained, and that health is best subserved by not over-eating.

My cook would make cotton enough to give the extra one pound. The labor in making vegetables would make another pound. I say this to show I do not dole out a half pound per day from parsimony.

My hours of labor, commencing with pitching my crop, is from daylight until 12 M.; all hands then come in and remain until 2 o'clock P.M., then back to the field until dark. Some time in May we prolong the rest three hours; and if a very hot day, even four hours. Breakfast is eaten in the field, half an hour to an hour being given; or they eat and go to work without being driven in and out—all stopping when my driver is ready.

I give all females half of every Saturday to wash and clean up, my cook washing for young men and boys through the week. The cabins are scoured once a week, swept out every day, and beds made up at noon in summer, by daylight in winter. In the winter, breakfast is eaten before going to work, and dinner is carried to the hands.

I do not punish often, but I seldom let an offense pass, making a lumping settlement, and then correct for the servant's remembrance. I find it better to whip very little. Young ones being rather treacherous in their memory, pulling an ear, or a sound box, will bring every thing right. I am almost afraid I will subject myself to the "chimney-corner theorist's" animadversion if I say more, but I will risk it. Put up a hewed log-house, with a good substantial door, lock and key, story 12 feet high, logs across above, so as to make a regular built jail. Have airholes near the ceiling, well protected by iron bars. The first negro that steals, or runs away, or fights, or who is hard to manage in order to get a day's work, must be locked up every night as soon as he comes in from work, and turned out next morning; kept up every Sunday. Negroes are gregarious; they dread solitariness, and to be deprived from the little weekly dances and chit-chat. They will work to death rather than be shut up. I know the advantage, though I have no jail, my house being a similar one, yet used for other purposes.

I have a fiddle in my quarters, and though some of my good old brethren in the church would think hard of me, yet I allow dancing; ay, I buy the fiddle and encourage it, by giving the boys occasionally a big supper.

I have no overseer, and do not manage so scientifically as those who are able to lay down rules; yet I endeavor to manage so that myself, family and negroes may take pleasure and delight in our relations.

It is not possible in my usual crude way to give my whole plans, but enough is probably said. I permit no night-work, except feeding stock and weighing cotton. No work of any kind at noon, unless to clean out cabins, and bathe the children when nursing, not even washing their clothes.

I require every servant to be present each Sabbath morning and Sabbath evening at family prayers. In the evening the master, or sometimes a visitor, if a professor,[1] expounds the chapter read. Thus my servants hear 100 to 200 chapters read each year anyhow. One of my servants, a professor, is sometimes called on to close our exercises with prayer.

Owning but few slaves, I am probably able to do a better part by them than if there were one or two hundred. But I think I could do better if I had enough to permit me to systematize better.

1. A "professing" Christian. (*Editor's note*)

I would keep a cook and a nurse. I would keep a stock feeder, whose whole duty should be to attend to stock in general, to clean out the stable, have troughs filled with food, so that the plough hands would have nothing to do but water, clean down, and tie up the teams. I would build a house large enough, and use it for a dance-house for the young, and those who wished to dance, as well as for prayer-meetings, and for church on Sunday—making it a rule to be present myself occasionally at both, and my overseer always. I know the rebuke in store about dancing, but I cannot help it. I believe negroes will be better disposed this way than any other. I would employ a preacher for every Sabbath. One of my negroes can read the Bible, and he has prayer-meeting every Sabbath at four o'clock P.M.; all the negroes attend regularly, no compulsion being used.

I have tried faithfully to break up immorality. I have not known an oath to be sworn for a long time. I know of no quarelling, no calling harsh names, and but little stealing. "Habits of amalgamation" I cannot stop; I can check it, but only in the name. I am willing to be taught, for I have tried every thing I know. Yours, truly,

A SMALL FARMER.

P.S.—I endeavor to have regularity on going to bed; forbid sitting or lying by the fire after bed-time. I require fire-makers to be up before day in winter, but forbid getting up before day, trotting off to the field, and waiting for daylight, as some persons are said to do. I forbid my driver from keeping hands in the field when there is an appearance of rain.

My negroes get baits of fresh meat occasionally, but always seasoned high with red pepper. At times I give molasses, sugar, coffee and flour, generally laying out about $10 per hand for such luxuries.

---

72. A Scottish Weaver Compares Slavery to English Labor

Most ante-bellum visitors to the South were from the classes who could best afford the expense of travel: either middle-class intellectuals or aristocrats. Their opinions varied considerably, but they were at a necessary disadvantage in judging the working world of the slave, and frequently their reports seem rather abstract. An interesting exception to this pattern appeared when William Thomson, a working-class Scottish weaver, came to the United States in the 1840s to examine the advantages to men like himself of coming to America to ply their craft.

Thomson was a keen observer of detail, and was more alert to the relations between slaves and their owners than many others visitors. He commended the paternalistic aspect of the masters' responsibilities, and contrasted the provisions owners made for their slaves in old age with the lonely and exposed position of English workmen. He also thought the lives of slave children were not so harsh and bitter as those of children of the English working class. Thomson was, however, unable to empathize with slaves—probably because of color. He mentions their seeming acquiescence in their lot, shows inadvertently that some were capable of violent reactions, avers his own preference for freedom in any case, and ends in a vaguely polemical plea that philanthropists in their emancipation efforts should do the planters justice. His account is valuable for what he observed, rather than for the conclusions he draws from his observations.

Source: William Thomson, A Tradesman's Travels, in the United States and Canada, in the Years 1840, 41, & 42. (Edinburgh: Oliver & Boyd, 1842), pp. 181–95.

After the services of the day were over, I was amused with their [the slaves'] appearance and manners, when they congregated in crowds and groups around the church, after the manner of the people in country parishes in Scotland, but with much more of light-hearted happiness in their black and glistening faces. Their politeness, too, was pleasing, though it amounted to the ridiculous—a shaking of hands, such bowing and scraping; the young wenches kissing each other for very joy. "How you do, Miss Diana?" "Pretty well, Massa Talleyrand; how you do?" Curtseying, chattering, and laughing, and showing rows of pearly teeth that a duchess might envy. What a contrast appears between these and their task-masters, as they lead their ladies to their carriages, through the crowd,—thin and delicate, with care and disease written upon their wrinkled but haughty brows. Surely, I said to myself, these men suffer more of the evils and the curses that always follow slavery than the slaves themselves.

The negroes are allowed to do as they please, with regard to marrying and becoming members of churches. Their masters prefer that they should marry, as it is favourable to increase; and I found, more frequently than might be expected, that they choose a wife from a different plantation. The reason of this is to give them an apology for getting away when their task is done; or, on Sundays, to see their neighbours, which they are very fond of.

The slave owners are not apt to separate families, although they are always liable to be sold; but, in reality, they are not so much scattered as the families of working men in Scotland, whose necessities compel them to separate at an age when the American slave is running about, gathering health and strength, and playing mischief. In the slave states there is something of the spirit of the ancient feudal times. The planters like to keep up the number of their slaves; and it is considered, if not disgraceful, at least an evidence of failing credit and respectability to be obliged to sell their negroes.

When a man and his wife, or a mother and her daughter, who love each other, are separted [sic], they complain of it to their owners, who make an arrangement either to "buy or sell." This is frequently done. Sometimes slaves are bought at private sale, but more frequently at auction. In several southern cities, I observed shops full of negroes for sale. In New Orleans they were most numerous; where there is a street with nothing in it but stores for the sale of negroes. They are tricked off to the best advantage, sitting on seats all round the store, and under the shade at the doors. I tried to screw up my courage to go in and ask the price of some of them, but could not do it. However, I frequently saw them selling at auction in the streets and market-places. Good house servants and mechanics frequently bring one thousand dollars; field hands and labourers, five hundred. The value of negroes on a plantation, including old and young, may average about 350 dollars each. The value of this kind of *property*, as they call it, is very fluctuating. It is considered real property, and is conveyed by regular articles and title-deeds. Money is borrowed on it by mortgage, and it is willed away the same as houses or land.

According to law, a slave cannot hold any property; but in practice, many of those who are hired out make more money than the stipulated wages their owners require. With this they are allowed to do as they please.

I took particular notice how masters treated the old slaves after they were unable to work in the fields. Their laws provide that they shall be fed and clothed; but I found that a better feeling than necessity prompted the planters to minister to the wants of their aged servants. They have their houses, blankets, shoes, clothing, and their allowance of corn, the same as prime hands. I knew some of them that had been toddling about for twenty years after they were unable to work. Many of these old hands keep themselves in tobacco, molasses, &c., by feeding a pig, or raising a few chickens. To feed them, they will cultivate a little patch of ground, but as frequently steal corn from "Massa" for this purpose; and, after all, if the planter's family want to buy any of their eggs or chickens, they will not sell them to them one cent cheaper than the regular market price. These old hands are a sort of privileged persons, and are never abused or neglected. I was acquainted with a planter on Beaufort Island, who had a little wrinkled slave called "Old Saw." He was so old that he remembered the "war of independence." He had been his father's coachman, and his own for many years. When a boy, this negro attended him when he went out; taught him to ride and hunt; and, although the planter's head was now silvered over

with the frost of years, "Old Saw" still looked upon him as a boy, and often spoke to him as such. One day "Old Saw" did something that displeased the planter very much. He gave the old man a scolding, and told him he deserved to be whipped for it. "Old Saw" bristled up like fire, exclaiming—"You whip me!—you whip me! You little rascal, I knew you 'fore you was born. I knew your daddy a *picayune*. You little rascal, you whip me!" The gentleman retreated into the house; but "Old Saw" followed him into the drawing-room amongst the ladies, who, by their laughter, encouraged the old fellow till the planter was fairly obliged to leave the room. "Old Saw" retired, not even deigning to reply to the ladies, who tried to pacify him, muttering to himself, "Little rascal, whip me!"

A negro, whether he is bound or free, cannot bear evidence against a white man in any of the slave states; but when he commits any grievous offence, he has the benefit of trial by jury, but not by his peers, any more than the labourers of this country can be tried by theirs. However, I believe they get a fair chance for their lives. To illustrate this, I shall mention the case of a planter who was murdered by one of his own slaves in Beaufort District, in the spring of the present year. It is a custom with those planters, who do not live upon their estates to go once a-week and serve out provisions to the people. This gentleman found that his corn-house had been entered in his absence. He suspected his driver or head slave, and taxed him with having stolen his corn. The negro denied that he had anything to do with it. The planter told him if, on his return, he found the practice continued, he would not serve him out his allowance. But, poor gentleman, he never returned; for this same slave waylaid him on the road, in the dusk of the evening, and coming suddenly behind him with a club or grubbing hoe, beat out his brains—mangling him in a shocking manner, after which, he threw the dead body into a neighbouring swamp. The cunning of the slave was remarkable. He joined in the search that was immediately made for the missing planter; and, I believe, actually had the nerve to be the first to discover the mangled corpse. It was a fortnight after this before suspicion rested on him. When apprehended, he confessed all. Counsel was assigned him; and, when brought to trial, he pleaded guilty. The court advised him to retract his plea of guilt, and take his trial; but he would not. He said he had murdered his Massa, and could not deny it. When asked his reason for committing so horrid a crime, he said it was the devil that put it into his mind, and he was now sorry for what he had done; for Massa was always good to him. He was executed on the spot where the murder was committed. All the slaves in the neighborhood were turned out to witness the execution; and when the sheriff asked if any of them would assist to run him up the limb of a tree, a number of them came forward very readily, and gave their assistance—evidently satisfied with the justice of the sentence.

On plantations, each family has a small house, generally built of wood, in rows, and mostly with some show of taste or regularity. I have inspected plantations where they work from ten to one hundred hands; and shall describe one house, which will serve for a specimen in general:—Built of wood, covered with shingles, ten feet wide, twelve or fourteen feet long; a chimney and fireplace at one end, sometimes made of lath and plaster, sometimes built of brick, without any stove or grate, which, indeed, there is no use for; a few boards in one corner, sometimes raised a little from the floor, to lie on; and this, with a blanket, constitutes their bed. They have frequently an old trunk or box for holding their clothes, although many of them have little occasion for such a convenience; a pot, an iron spoon or two; some firewood in the corner; a little black negro lying naked in the floor, scrambling about, as plump and shining as the hair bottom of a new chair; a seat at the door of the cabin, where they sit, sometimes nursing, sometimes sleeping. They have locks on their doors, which are necessary, for they steal like rats. They frequently have a few chickens, or a pig or two, in a little crib before their houses, which they sell, or trade away for tobacco, molasses, &c.

In their persons they are dirty. They have a nasty smell, commonly called *negro funk,* which is quite perceptible, and not very agreeable, "when they pass between the wind and your nobility." They are very careless of their clothes,—careless of the houses, or whether they be clean and comfortable; so much so, that I knew one who shifted his bed from one corner to another, when the rain came in, to save him the trouble of putting a shingle on the roof. But the fact is, when it rains they cannot mend the house, and when it does not rain, it is not necessary to have them water-tight. They have stated tasks to perform. Custom has established great uniformity in the amount of work they have to perform; and, as far as I could judge, from the physical condition of the slaves, and the length of time they are generally in the field, they are not overwrought. I have seen them finish their task [1] by mid-day, and some may not have finished their task when it is dark, in which case the deficiency is carried forward and added to their next day's work; but, in general, they have no difficulty in accomplishing their tasks. Those of them who are employed as house servants have not one-fourth so much work as a Scotch servant lass: but they do not sleep very soft at night—which, indeed, is no luxury in a warm climate, generally laying themselves down, with their blanket about them, in the hall or lobby of the house, or about the landings of the stairs. The "cow-skin" is not much used in the field. The driver is always a black man, who has the immediate oversight of the hands in the field. Sometimes he carries a bundle of small wands, perhaps five or six; some have a horse-whip, which they apply to the shoulders of the women, and the bare buttocks of the men, when they make bad work or misbehave in any way; but this sort of punishment is not very severe. It is when the "cow-skin," a piece of hide twisted into the appearance of a riding-switch, sometimes *painted red*, is applied to their bare back for some heinous offence, that

1. Thomson was visiting in coastal South Carolina, where work was assigned in customary units of labor called "tasks" rather than by the hour or the sun. (*Editor's note*)

they make the woods ring with their cries, which I have heard; but I never saw the punishment inflicted, and I hope never shall.

But truth is all the end I aim at in writing these pages. Truth, then, compels me to say that the planters in general treat their slaves with great humanity. Would to God the aristocracy or the government of this country would interest themselves half as much to improve the physical condition of the factory slave of England! After I got acquainted with the planters, I used to speak freely on the subject with some of them; and some of the more moderate and reasonable did not pretend to defend slavery, on principle or from nature. It is a curse entailed on them: and how are they to get clear of it? No practicable plan has been proposed to them. If the philanthropists throughout the world want to free the negro race, and assert the inalienable rights of human nature, they ought to follow the example of the Government of Great Britain, in freeing the West India negroes, at least as far as indemnity goes. It is too much to put the planters to great pecuniary loss for the pleasure of those who wish to rescue the negroes from domestic slavery. From what I have said, it will appear to those who knew my opinions on slavery before I visited that country, that, like most others, who can judge dispassionately, I have changed my opinions considerably. Although there are many cases of great cruelty, domestic slavery, in the southern and slave states of America, is not that horrid system of cruelty and oppression that is represented in this country. It is true slaves can neither read nor write, have no intellectual cultivation, and yet, I believe, they laugh and sing more than any class of men on earth. I have seen them laughing at the jokes of the auctioneer who was selling them at at [sic] public auction, like the beasts that perish. This, by some, will be called strong evidence of the great evils of the system. Well, be it so. I only wish, without being in their stead, I could laugh as hearty and as often as they do.

I must bring this chapter on slavery to a conclusion, although I have not expressed one half of the observations I made in my travels through the southern states. Yet, one remark more.—I have seen children in factories, both in England and Scotland, under ten years of age, working twelve hours a-day, till their little hands were bleeding. I have seen these children whipped, when their emaciated limbs could no longer support them to their work; and I believe there is not a planter in America whose blood would not rise, and whose arm would not be lifted up to defend even the negroes from such cruelty; especially the native planter, who is much better to his negroes than the planters that have been brought up in free states. This is an acknowledged fact, and therefore I need not illustrate it. If I were to look for the cause of the comparative kindly feeling of the native planter, it would partly be found in his having been nursed and tended in infancy by some careful negro, and having made playmates of the little black fellows of his father's house. I acknowledge that the miserably degraded state of the factory slave, or the equally unnatural condition of the miners, is no apology for the con-

tinuance of negro slavery; and I only make the comparison to show how difficult it is, under the present irrational state of society, to render pleasant the condition of the "hewers of wood and drawers of water." I consider myself in some degree qualified to make this comparison, for I have witnessed negro slavery in mostly all the slave-holding states in America; having lived for weeks on cotton plantations, observing closely the actual condition of the negroes; and can assert, without fear of contradiction from any man who has any knowledge of the subject, that I have never witnessed one-fifth of the real suffering that I have seen in manufacturing establishments in Great Britain. In regard to their moral condition, let those who have had the temerity, who have dared to lay their hands on fellow-men, to claim them as property, let them answer for themselves in this matter to the Almighty, who still permitteth this extraordinary condition of society to exist.

Let none suppose that my object is to defend slavery: but, dearly as I love personal liberty, I love justice and truth as well, which compel me to say that the condition of the negroes is not so anomalous as that of the labouring men of this country. They have no responsibility, no fear that their children may be left to want, no provision to make for age, no fear of being neglected in sickness, or of being compelled, in their old age to beg their bread from door to door. Whereas the labouring men of this boasted country have all the care and responsibility of freemen, and none of theri [their] valued privileges. They are used as animals of burden, and have not even the right of shifting the load from one shoulder to the other, without the consent of their task-masters. I do not make these comparisons between the negro and the worst-off class of manufacturing people for any invidious purpose, but only to enable me to convey a correct idea of their condition, by comparing them with a class that live amongst ourselves, and whose condition we know.

73. A Trial of Wills between a Slave and a Prospective Employer

In the first week of the New Year, slaves who were to be hired out by their owners often congregated in the towns or at the County Courthouses, sometimes in their masters' company, and sometimes alone, seeking the most favorable terms of employment for the coming year.

Although many talented slaves showed a preference for being hired out to work in the cities and towns, on account of the greater independence they were able to secure, these same slaves were not always pleased to go to work in iron furnaces and mills, often located deep in the countryside. There the slaves were removed from the plantation community, family perhaps, and lacked the more lively society of the free-black community of the towns as well. In such situations the particular conditions of work were a subject of concern for the slave being hired out.

Always the destiny of the "hired-out" slave was complicated by the introduction of a second, or surrogate, master. Good care was a prime condition for the owner, not only because the life and health of his slave was at stake, but also because the slave might run away if he were too much dissatisfied. The following letter originates with James C. Davis, who is recruiting slave labor in the upper Piedmont section of central Virginia for his father's iron furnace near Staunton, west of the Blue Ridge mountains.

Davis is writing to his father of his problems gathering the necessary labor force, and especially of his difficulty with a slave named "Elick," whose master "Dickenson" has reason to believe that "Elick" and his

Source: William W. Davis Manuscripts, Alderman Library, University of Virginia, Charlottesville, Va.

other hands do not want to return to the Davis furnace to work another year. While Davis's reluctance to defy his slaves on the point was pure common sense, it forced the prospective employer to think of an elaborate ruse to detach Elick from his obvious role as leader of the dissatisfied slaves. The incident serves as a reminder that masters in dealing with slaves were wise to consider their preferences, and foolish to defy them on slight provocation.

James C. Davis to William W. Davis.

Seclusion Jan 5th 1856

Dear Father:

Yours of the 2nd Inst . came to the P.O. day before yesterday. I answer by John because, he, starting tomorrow, will take it to you Monday which will be as quick as the mail will carry it. It came too late to mail anything with reference to that matter for Bryan started back the day before I received it. Hands are hiring a little higher this year than last; the cause of it is the high price of the produce of farms & the consequent demand for their labor in that direction. I have hired 11, the same as last year except Jim & Ben; the one besides is a wagoner belonging to old Mr. Nunn near the C[our]t House. I want to get one more. I could not get as many *such* hands as I wanted because there were very few for hire at the Ct House which was the only place I went to— there were plenty of half way hands, but them I did not want. The hiring came off the same days at the Ct House as at Waller's & Mt Pleasant & I, hiring most of last year's hands at the Ct House, went there. It seems that somebody has just put Massie up to the idea of charging extra prices for Bob & Mose on account of their being a wagoner & colier; he asked me $360 for the three & would not put them a cent lower. Dickenson's two Elick & Minor cost me $215; Nester's $190, same as last year; old Mr Nunn's boy $125: he is said to be a first rate wagoner, & has been driving at B[uena] Vista Furnace for the last 6 or 7 years. Blacksmith John $100; & Garland $75. The old Lady put him at that this year but would not knock off a single cent for last year. I was on my way to Orange Ct. House to hire Blacksmith John when John Jordan told me at L[ouisa?] Ct H[ouse] that he had hired him to go back to us & also asked whether we were going to hire them Nelson again. You can do as you please about it, but I think that if we do not hire more than 12 hands we will need him at home. If you do hire him you ought to get at least $100. Uncle Keefer gets that from B & W. N. Jordan for his boy, William, who is about the same age,—& that too on condition that he shall work in the shop and be taught the trade. I haven't heard anything from or about Coleman. I have'nt [sic] been in Spottsylvania at all as I had to be at the Ct House on the days that there was hiring in that county. From what I can hear I think I got my hands cheaper than the most of Iron masters; they gave about $120 for common hands, i.e. hands without any particular vocation, except it be wood chopping.

I hear that old Mr McCormack gave Norrell Trice $150 a piece for 7, and, that the Jordans gave Capt Jim Trice $130 a piece for 12. There is some difficulty about Dickenson's hands & I hardly know how to act. When they came from over the mountains they wished to go back: & under the impression that they still wished so I hired them of Dickenson at the Ct House Tuesday. Shortly after I hired them he came & told me that Elick did not wish to go, that a railroad man had offered him five dollars cash in his hands to go with him & that tickled his fancy, but says "I believe he will get over that & be willing to go with you & if he doesn't I will not ask him any odds but send them on" and the subject dropped. But yesterday I recieved [sic] a letter from him saying that his boys had come to him & avowed they would not go, & if they did go they would run off after they got there. Now I believe that this is nothing but an empty threat for the purpose of scaring their master & that it only requires decisive measures to bring them straight. But even if they were in earnest they would be apt to run before they got there & not after they crossed the blue [sic] Ridge, for they know that they dont understand the country well enough to start when so far from home. Should they do this they will come down in Dickenson's neighborhood & he will be perfectly willing to take them back & so no harm will result in that case. But should they on the other hand run off after they get there, which I dont believe they will

do, they, not being used to the country, nor skilled in the wiles of running away, will be taken before they get far. All this is on the hypothesis that Elick goes with them. If he is cooled down & kept in Jail until I choose to let him off & the others sent on I dont apprehend any difficulty whatever: because he is the ringleader and has persuaded the other's [sic] (I mean Hester's too for I have no doubt but he has infected them too) who are willing to go back up to last Monday when I saw them at the Ct House. Should I let these hands off it is now too late to get others in their places, for the hands through the country are hired: else I would not care so much to let them off. Moreover I got them cheaper than I could get hands again even if I could find any for hire. In consideration of all these things I wrote to Mr Dickinson by this morning's mail that I could not let them off, but for him to take them to the Ct House Monday morning, put Elick in Jail before the eyes of the others without saying a word as to the meaning of it, then take the others & send them on the cars for Staunton with a pass to Gibralter: and after they are gone to take Elick out of Jail & hire him out there at the Ct House by the day, letting on to him that he [Dickinson] will hire him where he wishes to go when he finds a place which he might do if I found I could make it suit to let him off; if not, I would take him over when I went. I think this plan will work. The boys, if he sends them Monday as I wrote to him to do, ought to get there Tuesday night & will get there (at the farthest) [in] time enough on wednesday for you to write me by that day's mail, which do & if they have not come give me your views: or, if they have, tell me what you think about keeping Elick if I cannot get another hand.

This negro's perversity is but another instance of the [assimilation?] of the negro to the dog. In order to make a dog like and follow you you must whip him occasionally & be sparing of favors, or he will turn at last & bite the hand that feeds him. So with this boy. Of all those five negroes he was the only one that escaped the lash: & frequently recieved [sic] favors that I would have denied the others. Now he not only turns from me, but tries to lead them away likewise. I have not been able to come across an old man

for hire yet. I think it would be best to employ Wright even if you have to pay him 37½ cts cash for every cord; but you can get him for less cash than that, for when I saw him at the Forge that day he only asked half money at 37½ cts & the rest trade at 40 cts. I believe that will [be?] equally as cheap if not cheaper than black labor. We are all well down here; but the weather is mighty bad. There has been a sleet on the ground for more than a week, & it is now snowing very fast & has been ever since day[light] this morning—the snow is now about a foot deep. My love to all. Your affectionate Son

Jas C Davis

74. Slaves Tell Masters What Masters Want To Hear

From time immemorial, slaves, like all dependent classes, have been charged with hypocrisy and deceit. This is perhaps the reason that "honesty" in a slave was so extravagantly praised. Because hypocrisy, deceit, and theft were the obvious ways for otherwise powerless individuals to manipulate the powerful, these charges have doubtless been based over time on a substantial stratum of fact.

Frederick Douglass once wrote that he had never heard a slave, while *still* a slave, say that he had a bad master. White visitors were sometimes baffled by this phenomenon, but Ethan Allen Andrews (see document 30) understood that a slave could not safely express himself on this matter,

Source: Ethan Allen Andrews, *Slavery and the Domestic Slave-Trade in the United States* (Boston: Light and Stearns, 1836), pp. 97–102.

and concluded that slave-owners—all protests of slave loyalty aside—actually slept "upon the verge of the volcano" of insurrection. The rigors of the patrol system, which good men could not otherwise have tolerated, were justified only because constant surveillance seemed essential to the safety of whites.

Letter XV.

Washington, July 21, 1835.

The real sentiments and feelings of the negroes, in respect to their situation, it is very difficult for any white person to ascertain, and for a stranger, it is nearly impossible. They regard the white man as of a different race from themselves, and as having views, feelings and interests which prevent his sympathizing fully with theirs. Distrust, even of their real friends, is no unnatural consequence of the relation which they and their ancestors have so long borne to the whites.

When therefore a white man approaches them with inquiries concerning their condition, they are at once put upon their guard, and either make indefinite and vague replies, or directly contradict their real sentiments. The following is the substance of many a conversation of the kind to which I allude.

"You have a kind master, I think, Jack." "O yes, massa, he very kind, he very good to de niggers." "You always have enough to eat and drink, I suppose." "Yes, massa, plenty to eat:— massa give all de niggers plenty to eat." "Do you have to work very hard, Jack?" "O no, massa, me no work hard—only sometimes." "Have you a wife?" "Yes, massa, she live at Major B.'s in W. county." "Why, that is a great way off: how often does your master let you go to see her?" "Me go to see her and de children once t' a month." "And how long does he allow you to be absent from the plantation, when you go to see your wife and children?" "I always goes a Friday, and stays till Monday." "And suppose you should not come back till Tuesday, what then?" "Why, massa no give me pass only to Monday; must come back den." "Or else anybody will flog you that finds you?" "Yes, massa." "Do n't you wish, Jack, that Major B. would buy you, so that you could live with your wife?" "Massa good massa, me no like to leave him—no leave massa." "Well, do n't you wish then that your master would buy your wife, and bring her here?" "O yes, massa, me like dat very much." "Well, Jack, suppose your master would give you your liberty; I suppose you would like that best of all, would you not?" "O no, massa, me no want to be free, have good massa, take care of me when I sick, never 'buse nigger; no, me no want to be free."

All this is said with an air of sincerity well fitted to produce the impression that the slave does not wish for freedom, and that he would not accept it, even if offered to him. The master himself, accustomed to hear such replies, though at heart aware that no dependence can be placed upon declarations made in such circumstances, half forgets that they are untrue, and repeats them to others, and especially to northern men, as evidence that no change is necessary in the situation of the slave, in order to render him as happy as his nature will permit. Nor is it others only who are deceived; the slave himself is probably not always aware of the insincerity of his replies. He has perhaps never viewed his own emancipation as possible, and does not know in what manner he would receive a proposition sincerely made of restoring him to freedom.

But even when he has fully awaked to a sense of the value of liberty, and when he sighs in secret to obtain the direction of his own conduct, and to pursue his own happiness without the control of others, he is fully conscious of the danger of expressing his new feelings and the visions inspired by hope. He knows that he shall be less valued if he is suspected of being discontented, and that the danger of exchanging his present lot for one still worse, will in such case be greatly increased. He looks, too, upon all white men, and especially strangers, as the friends of his master, and does not dare to trust his secret wishes to those who may immediately betray him.

Thus all continue to slumber upon the verge of the volcano; but it is only a feverish sleep, from which the slightest sound, which may be mistaken for the rumbling of the fires in the abyss beneath, is sufficient instantly to arouse them. Then they look around them, for a moment, with dismay; but the alarm soon subsides, and all sink again into repose. Not so however in case of actual insurrection. Then the apprehensions and consequent sufferings of all classes and all ages surpass

description. The strong and courageous master, whom no merely personal danger could appal, who would go calmly to meet a foreign enemy, trembles when he remembers that his wife and children are exposed to a foe who will show no mercy, and with whom war is only another name for massacre. Women and children, the aged and the helpless, tremble before a savage foe, from whom they expect not even the generosity which belongs to war in general, though indeed the tender mercies of ordinary wars are but cruelties. No more enviable is the situation of the slave himself. If indisposed to join in the revolt, he is apprehensive that he shall be suspected by both parties; and is terrified by fear of the insurgents, upon the one hand, and of the whites, upon the other. In such circumstances, the slightest suspicion is often a passport to instant death. To repel such dangers the strongest measures are felt to be necessary; and when those who are suspected cannot be kept in safety till the danger is past, death is called in to afford that security which nothing else can give.

In general, however, no danger is felt in the villages or large towns, except upon occasions of peculiar alarm. The timid mother may indeed "clasp her infant closer to her bosom, when she hears the sound of the midnight fire-bell," because her fears at such an hour excite the image of robbery and massacre, but commonly little apprehension of personal danger is felt, except in more lonely situations.

In every town and village an active and vigilant patrol is abroad at such hours of the night as they judge most expedient, and no negro dares, after the prescribed hour, to be found at a distance from his quarters. Great cruelty is often practised by the patrols, and such as is not only hard for the slaves, but even for the humane master to bear, when exercised towards his unoffending slaves. Often have I known a company of licentious and inebriated young men sally forth after an evening's carousal, and in the stillness of night commence their round of domiciliary visits to the quarters of the negroes, while their inmates were buried in sleep. The principal object of such visits is to terrify the slaves, and thus secure their good behavior, and especially to prevent their wandering about at night. If in such case a slave is found at any distance from his own home without a *pass*, he is often whipped upon the spot, without judge or jury, and with no other limit to the severity of the infliction, than such as the drunken caprice of the patrols may prescribe. I have known the husband thus chastised for being found in company with his wife, if he was not able to produce his pass or permit to visit her on that night. The state of a family thus violently disturbed during their slumbers, by the curses, and execrations, and violence of irresponsible men, may be in some measure conceived. The husband and father is dragged out and flogged before his terrified wife and children, while the females fear every indignity that such ruffians may please to perpetrate. Thus they proceed, until exhausted by fatigue and dizzy with the fumes of their debauch, when they return to their homes, leaving weeping, and dismay, and terror, where they found peace and repose.

75. Master Chaplin, In Debt, Must Sell Ten Slaves

The unpublished journal of Thomas B. Chaplin (see documents 40 and 50) is a rare and revealing document. A planter of long-staple cotton in the island country southwest of Charleston, Chaplin lived an entirely private life, seldom traveling farther from his estate than to Beaufort, the nearest coastal town, where local planters transacted their business affairs. Coming into his property in land and men very young, Chaplin soon enough

Source: Thomas B. Chaplin, Manuscript Diary, South Carolina Historical Association, Charleston, S.C.

discovered that his own talent for management was insufficient for the challenges of raising cotton in the older eastern districts during the panicky 1840s. Competition from the new lands farther west, where costs of production were low, created vast problems for eastern growers, problems that only the ablest and luckiest could surmount.

In the selection to follow we find Chaplin under the necessity of raising cash immediately to settle his debts. We may suppose that some among the ten slaves he was obliged to sell to meet these obligations found their way to Mississippi and Louisiana, where their labor upon the fresh lands of the West would bring a larger money return to their new owners. Pain for the fate of his Negroes was not unmixed with fear of public opinion, but Chaplin's guilty recognition of the role of his own unbridled, expensive, and often destructive tastes in the catastrophe, is fully confessed. It is to his credit that he did not claim youth or inexperience, as he might have done, for Chaplin was only twenty-three years old at this first debacle, already married six years, and father of a rapidly increasing family. Not the least significant aspect of his journal, however, is the steady attrition it reveals of the finer human instincts of Chaplin's youth, as he copes daily through the years with the special harassments of holding bondsmen.

Our diarist was a better educated man than his spelling and syntax would in themselves attest, but I have changed neither, and have placed my own comments and explanations in brackets.

May 3rd [1845] . . . [Chaplin complains of drought and crop damage likely to result] . . .

Trouble gathers thicker & thicker around me. I will be compelled to send about ten prime negroes to Town on next Monday, to be sold. I do this rather than have them seized and sold in Beaufort, by the Sheriff or rather sacrificed.—I never thought that I would be driven to this very unpleasant extremity,—nothing can be more Mortifying and grieving to a man, than to select out some of his negroes to be sold—you know not to whom, or how they will be treated by their new owners. And negroes that you find no fault with—to separate families [,] Mothers & daughters—Brothers & sisters—all to pay for your own extravagances. People will laugh at your distress—and say it serves you right—you lived beyond your means, though some of the same never refused to partake of that hospitality and generosity which caused me to live beyond my means. Those beings I shall find out, and will then know how to treat them.

May 4th Sunday—Did not go to Church; Tooth ache all day. The negroes pulled up the floor to some of out houses & killed 56 rats—fine Sunday's

work. A few clouds flying about—wind very fresh but no rain. Things look worse & worse. Rode over to J. L. Chaplins to get him to take the negroes up to Beaufort for me tomorrow——
May 4ᵗʰ [continued] Just as [I] had finished the foregoing sentence I perceived J. L. Chaplin [and] James Clark coming down the road.

After they had eaten dinner, they went to the negro houses & took 10 negroes—viz Prince—Sib—Moses—Louisa — Tom — Hannah — Paul — Titus—Marcus & Joe. Carried them over to the river side where Clarks boats was [,] got them on board, but it was so ruff that the boat was nearly swamped, so they had to come on shore & stop until the next day. I cannot express my feelings on seeing so many faithful negroes going away from me forever, not for any fault of their own but for my extravagance. . . . it is a dearly bought lesson, and I hope I will benefit by it. The negroes did not appear at all inclined to get off—but [were] apparently quite willing and in good spirits, particularly Prince & Paul.—I hope they will bring a good price in Charleston where I have sent them under the charge of Wᵐ B. Fickling, to be sold, and that I will not have to sell any more. Micklen the deputy levied on them as soon as they got in Beaufort but Fickling jockied him and got them onboard the steamboat quite safe.

May 5ᵗʰ Went to Beaufort. Could not go down to the boat to see the negroes off,—but am glad it is all over for it is the most unpleasant thing I have ever had to do, and truly hope it may never again occur.—The negroes at home are quite disconsolate—but this will soon blow over. They may see their children again in time.——
Returned home after dark. Da Costa rode from the ferry [from Beaufort to the island] with me.[1]

[Four years later, the following interesting entry appears in Chaplin's diary.]

"April 26ᵗʰ [1849] . . . When going in the field who should I meet but Paul, a fellow I sold some years ago—now belongs to B. M. Bride, he is a runaway. & has been out some months. He took good care to keep the fence between us when talking—he sais he came to see me knowing that I would not take him, & wants me to buy him. That is next to an impossibility."

1. In an undated comment to his diary, entered in the margins some years after the Civil War, Chaplin wrote: "It was a trying time then. But could I or any one [have] foreseen how things would be in 19 years after, when every negro was set free by force of war, I & every one else would have gladly put them all in their pockets. Besides I would not have felt bad about it, for in truth the negroes did not care as much about us as one did for them." (Editor's note)

76.   A Slave-Owner's Black Supervisors' Report

While slavery was for the common field hand all too often a brutalizing institution offering little opportunity for the development—or indeed the discovery—of any special ability, no account of the relations between master and man could omit the numerous exceptions to the pattern of wasted talents. Without the opportunities for development of leadership and management skills opened for numbers of able slaves, it would be difficult to explain the way slaves seized the greater opportunities that came with emancipation. The modern reader can easily afford a certain cynicism about claims of trust and mutual interdependence when they appear in the hand of the slave-owner, but it is difficult to dismiss evidence from the hand of the slave himself. The following rare pair of letters from slaves who were able stewards of their master's affairs reveals that the slaves Jacob and Isaac were trusted to borrow and loan in their master's name (which also attests something affirmative about their community standing), to make important decisions about crops, even to comment on the family's social affairs. Isaac Stephens also felt free to assess the merits of a particular white overseer.

William Elliott, whose "servants" wrote these letters, owned thousands of acres in the rich long-staple cotton and rice country of coastal South Carolina. These lands were plagued with malarial swamps, and during the summers Elliott usually traveled to a northern spa or to the up-country of North Carolina to escape the fevers. He appears to have had more confidence in his slave overseers than in white ones, for on at least one occasion he was fined for not retaining a white man on one of his large estates, as the law of South Carolina required. It would be difficult to miss, running beneath the surface of servile manners implicit in these letters, a certain bluff camaraderie, which could hardly have existed without a mutual confidence and respect between master and man.

Source: Elliott-Gonzales Papers, Southern Historical Collection, Chapel Hill, N.C.

[I]
Isaac Stephens to William Elliott.

Beaufort Oct 22ᵈ-[18]49
To Master

On the 16ᵗʰ of October I was at pon pon[plantation] and all the rice had been don harvisting 24 fine ricks—the overseer thinks it will run 2 thousand 8 hundred the stacker says 2 thousand 9 hundred—and I think 3 thousand—a fine crop of root potatoes for I think they will last until Christmass. I would not say the slip [potatoes] will turn out well for the want of the season. A fine crop of corn they have not taken it in as yet. I think things are going on well at the place all appear to be in good order[.] Mistress flour garden are in good order. I wish Master had such an overseer at Social Hall [plantation] for I think him fine[.] The cotton have been much injured with the drouth. I do not think they will make more than 2 or three bags—and last of all I think Mistress will raise but a few poultry— as regards Seder Grove [Cedar Grove?] on the 19th I got in 20 bags—the crop of cotton may run 30 bags though the crop has been much injured by the drouth—I am about taken in the peas [,] a fine crop—the root potatoes are don—I have begun to eat ¹ the slips they are small and bad—the corn has made 30 Barrels[.] as far as the cotton seed whent they wear fine—I may get 2 or three hundred oringes—Turkeys one hundred—as I have lost some of them—the vessel is still hear on account of the yellow fever being so bad

1. Stephens means that he was giving out the "slips" to the slaves to eat. (*Editor's note*)

in Charleston——Edward has been quite sick but better at this time.

Old Mistress and Miss Mary are quite well I was quite sorry some of my young mistress and masters wear not in Beaufort to enjoy themselves at some of the fine dinner and Tea partys old Mistress has been giving for her grandchildren in Beaufort—as every party remind me of Master William and the Doctor.

The Miss Smith's are quite well but know not how they will get thear servant back on the Main[land]—every thing on the Main are green having no frost thear—

Master will be so kind as to give my love to my wife—all her friends are will and say howdey to her and myself just like an old Buck hearty and prime. Not forgetting the old man to Mistress Snow

from Master
Servant Isaac Stephens

[II]
"Jacob" to William Elliott.

Chisolmville July 31 st 1862
My dear Master:

We are very much in want of rain, and as we have had little or none for nearly a month, the crops are suffering very much. There is a great deal of fever on the place and I would thank you to send me one pound of salts as we have none here. The salts I need for children, and as I had to borrow some for this purpose I will have to have some to return.

I will send Frank over to you tomorrow with the mule Betty. If you are going away you would oblige me by sending Betty back as she is one of the best workers.

I would like very much master if you would come over before you go away, for Mr. Grant says he cannot attend to the place and I need advise on several matters. I would be much oblige to you if I sould let me have a carpenter for a few days before you leave as there is several thinks which need fixing. We are now striping corn and working the rice field over again. We are going to make a short crop of potatoes as every thing is so dry. The rice is still fine but I have found some caterpilers among it and as I have no water with which to flow it I fear it will proove serious particularly on the side of the hill. Please give my love to brother John. By the way master tell John he has not sent that which he promised me, so I will expect it soon.

I sent to the Dixie Rangers 116 bags and delivered them to Lent Green, all that they have returned to me is 65.

Hoping that this will find you, mistress, and all the children well I remain

Your faithful Servant
Jacob.

If you will send me some powder and shot I can get you some summer ducks.

77. Frederick Douglass Breaks A Slave-Breaker

Resisting chastisement came so close to overt attack on a white man that few slaves were ready and willing to try it. When driven to desperation they did resist, however, as the following incident from the early life of Frederick Douglass attests. Douglass wrote three autobiographies in the course of a long and distinguished public career. In several respects the first of the three is the most remarkable, because it is the work of a young man of twenty-eight, written not long after his escape from slavery in Maryland. Douglass was born in 1817 in Talbot County, the slave of Aaron Anthony, an overseer for the great estate of Col. Edward Lloyd. As a child, in the midst of riches and plenty, Douglass experienced hunger and privation.

Fortunately, at the age of eight Douglass was sent to Baltimore, where

Source: Frederick Douglass, *Narrative of the Life of Frederick Douglass, An American Slave. Written by Himself* (Boston: Anti-Slavery Office, 1845), pp. 56–73.

he served as a houseboy; later he worked in a shipyard and learned something of city ways. The greatest thing that happened to him was learning to read and write. These relatively happy conditions were abruptly ended, however, when Captain Anthony died and Douglass had to report to his new owner, Thomas Auld, at St. Michael's, Maryland, a place some forty miles distant from Baltimore.

Not surprisingly, Douglass was never satisfied as a plantation slave again. In the eyes of his owner the city life had all but ruined Douglass, and so when Douglass provoked him once too often, he was hired to a small farmer named Edward Covey, who was famous for bringing obstreperous slaves into meek subordination. In the portion of his early biography quoted below, Douglass recounted how Covey's cruelty eventually goaded him to resistance, and he dates his own knowledge of himself as a potentially free man from that time.

Soon Douglass's master gave up trying to curb Douglass and sent him back to Baltimore to hire himself out on his own time as a caulker in the shipyards. Within two years Douglass made a successful escape, disguised as a seaman, and using the "free papers" of a friendly black sailor. Douglass became a leading abolitionist, and one of the great orators of his time, a friend of Presidents, and a powerful advocate of freedom and equality for blacks. The first of his three autobiographical works, *The Narrative* . . . , appeared in 1845, and its style and content, coming from Douglass's own pen, made it a bestseller and a signal contribution to the anti-slavery movement.

From Chapter IX.

My master and myself had quite a number of differences. He found me unsuitable to his purpose. My city life, he said, had had a very pernicious effect upon me. It had almost ruined me for every good purpose, and fitted me for every thing which was bad. One of my greatest faults was that of letting his horse run away, and go down to his father-in-law's farm, which was about five miles from St. Michael's. I would then have to go after it. My reason for this kind of carelessness, or carefulness, was, that I could always get something to eat when I went there. Master William Hamilton, my master's father-in-law, always gave his slaves enough to eat. I never left there hungry, no matter how great the need of my speedy return. Master Thomas at length said he would stand it no longer. I had lived with him nine months, during which time he had given me a number of severe whippings, all to no good purpose. He resolved to put me out, as he said, to be broken; and, for this purpose, he let me for one year to a man named Edward Covey. Mr. Covey was a poor man, a farm-renter. He rented the place upon which he lived, as also the hands with which he tilled it. Mr. Covey had acquired a very high reputation for breaking young slaves, and this reputation was of immense value to him. It enabled him to get his farm tilled with much less expense to himself than he could have had it done without such a reputation. Some slaveholders thought it not much loss to allow Mr. Covey to have their slaves one year, for the sake of the training to which they were subjected, without any other compensation. He could hire young help with great ease, in consequence of this reputation. Added to the natural good qualities of Mr. Covey, he was a professor of religion— a pious soul—a member and a class-leader in the Methodist church. All of this added weight to his reputation as a "nigger-breaker." I was aware of all the facts, having been made acquainted with them by a young man who had lived there. I nevertheless made the change gladly; for I was sure of getting enough to eat, which is not the smallest consideration to a hungry man.

Chapter X.

I left Master Thomas's house, and went to live with Mr. Covey, on the 1st of January, 1833. I was now, for the first time in my life, a field hand. In my new employment, I found myself even more awkward than a country boy appeared to be in a large city. I had been at my new home but one week before Mr. Covey gave me a very severe whipping, cutting my back, causing the blood to run, and raising ridges on my flesh as large as my little finger. The details of this affair are as follows: Mr. Covey sent me, very early in the morning of one of our coldest days in the month of January, to the woods, to get a load of wood. He gave me a team of unbroken oxen. He told me which was the in-hand ox, and which the off-hand one. He then tied the end of a large rope around the horns of the in-hand ox, and gave me the other end of it, and told me, if the oxen started to run, that I must hold on upon the rope. I had never driven oxen before, and of course I was very awkward. I, however, succeeded in getting to the edge of the woods with little difficulty; but I had got a very few rods into the woods, when the oxen took fright, and started full tilt, carrying the cart against trees, and over stumps, in the most frightful manner. I expected every moment that my brains would be dashed out against the trees. After running thus for a considerable distance, they finally upset the cart, dashing it with great force against a tree, and threw themselves into a dense thicket. How I escaped death, I do not know. There I was, entirely alone, in a thick wood, in a place new to me. My cart was upset and shattered, my oxen were entangled among the young trees, and there was none to help me. After a long spell of effort, I succeeded in getting my cart righted, my oxen disentangled, and again yoked to the cart. I now proceeded with my team to the place where I had, the day before, been chopping wood, and loaded my cart pretty heavily, thinking in this way to tame my oxen. I then proceeded on my way home. I had now consumed one half of the day. I got out of the woods safely, and now felt out of danger. I stopped my oxen to open the woods gate; and just as I did so, before I could get hold of my ox-rope, the oxen again started, rushed through the gate, catching it between the wheel and the body of the cart, tearing it to pieces, and coming within a few inches of crushing me against the gate-post. Thus twice, in one short day, I escaped death by the merest chance. On my return, I told Mr. Covey what had happened, and how it happened. He ordered me to return to the woods again immediately. I did so, and he followed on after me. Just as I got into the woods, he came up and told me to stop my cart, and that he would teach me how to trifle away my time, and break gates. He then went to a large gum-tree, and with his axe cut three large switches, and, after trimming them up neatly with his pocket-knife, he ordered me to take off my clothes. I made him no answer, but stood with my clothes on. He repeated his order. I still made him no answer, nor did I move to strip myself. Upon this he rushed at me with the fierceness of a tiger, tore off my clothes, and lashed me till he had worn out his switches, cutting me so savagely as to leave the marks visible for a long time after. This whipping was the first of a number just like it, and for similar offences.

I lived with Mr. Covey one year. During the first six months, of that year, scarce a week passed without his whipping me. I was seldom free from a sore back. My awkwardness was almost always his excuse for whipping me. We were worked fully up to the point of endurance. Long before day we were up, our horses fed, and by the first approach of day we were off to the field with our hoes and ploughing teams. Mr. Covey gave us enough to eat, but scarce time to eat it. We were often less than five minutes taking our meals. We were often in the field from the first approach of day till its last lingering ray had left us; and at saving-fodder time, midnight often caught us in the field binding blades.

Covey would be out with us. The way he used to stand it, was this. He would spend the most of his afternoons in bed. He would then come out fresh in the evening, ready to urge us on with his words, example, and frequently with the whip. Mr. Covey was one of the few slaveholders who could and did work with his hands. He was a hard-working man. He knew by himself just what a man or a boy could do. There was no deceiving him. His work went on in his absence almost as well as in his presence; and he had the faculty of making us feel that he was ever present with us. This he did by surprising us. He seldom approached the spot where we were at work openly, if he could do it secretly. He always aimed at taking us by surprise. Such was his cunning, that we used to call him, among ourselves, "the snake." When we were at work in the cornfield, he would sometimes crawl on his hands and knees to avoid detection, and all at once he would rise nearly in our midst, and scream out, "Ha, ha! Come, come! Dash on, dash on!" This being his mode of attack, it was never safe to stop a single minute. His comings were like a thief in the night. He appeared to us as being ever at hand. He was under every tree, behind every stump, in every bush, and at every window, on the plantation.

He would sometimes mount his horse, as if bound to St. Michael's, a distance of seven miles, and in half an hour afterwards you would see him coiled up in the corner of the wood-fence, watching every motion of the slaves. He would, for this purpose, leave his horse tied up in the woods. Again, he would sometimes walk up to us, and give us orders as though he was upon the point of starting on a long journey, turn his back upon us, and make as though he was going to the house to get ready; and, before he would get half way thither, he would turn short and crawl into a fence-corner, or behind some tree, and there watch us till the going down of the sun.

Mr. Covey's *forte* consisted in his power to deceive. His life was devoted to planning and perpetrating the grossest deceptions. Every thing he possessed in the shape of learning or religion, he made conform to his disposition to deceive. He seemed to think himself equal to deceiving the Almighty. He would make a short prayer in the morning, and a long prayer at night; and, strange as it may seem, few men would at times appear more devotional than he. The exercises of his family devotions were always commenced with singing; and, as he was a very poor singer himself, the duty of raising the hymn generally came upon me. He would read the hymn, and nod at me to commence. I would at times do so; at others, I would not. My non-compliance would almost always produce much confusion. To show himself independent of me, he would start and stagger through with his hymn in the most discordant manner. In this state of mind, he prayed with more than ordinary spirit. Poor man! such was his disposition, and success at deceiving, I do verily believe that he sometimes deceived himself into the solemn belief, that he was a sincere worshipper of the most high God; and this, too, at a time when he may be said to have been guilty of compelling his woman slave to commit the sin of adultery. The facts in the case are these: Mr. Covey was a poor man; he was just commencing in life; he was only able to buy one slave; and, shocking as is the fact, he bought her, as he said, for *a breeder*. This woman was named Caroline. Mr. Covey bought her from Mr. Thomas Lowe, about six miles from St. Michael's. She was a large, able-bodied woman, about twenty years old. She had already given birth to one child, which proved her to be just what he wanted. After buying her, he hired a married man of Mr. Samuel Harrison, to live with him one year; and him he used to fasten up with her every night! The result was, that, at the end of the year, the miserable woman gave birth to twins. At this result Mr. Covey seemed to be highly pleased, both with the man and the wretched woman. Such was his joy, and that of his wife, that nothing they could do for Caroline during her confinement was too good, or too hard, to be done. The children were regarded as being quite an addition to his wealth.

If at any one time of my life more than another, I was made to drink the bitterest dregs of slavery, that time was during the first six months of my stay with Mr. Covey. We were worked in all weathers. It was never too hot or too cold; it could never rain, blow, hail, or snow, too hard for us to work in the field. Work, work, work, was scarcely more the order of the day than of the night. The longest days were too short for him, and the shortest nights too long for him. I was somewhat unmanageable when I first went there, but a few months of this discipline tamed me. Mr. Covey succeeded in breaking me. I was broken in body, soul, and spirit. My natural elasticity was crushed, my intellect languished, the disposition to read departed, the cheerful spark that lingered about my eye died; the dark night of slavery closed in upon me; and behold a man transformed into a brute!

Sunday was my only leisure time. I spent this in a sort of beast-like stupor, between sleep and wake, under some large tree. At times I would rise up, a flash of energetic freedom would dart through my soul, accompanied with a faint beam of hope, that flickered for a moment, and then vanished. I sank down again, mourning over my wretched condition. I was sometimes prompted to take my life, and that of Covey, but was prevented by a combination of hope and fear. My sufferings on this plantation seem now like a dream rather than a stern reality.

Our house stood within a few rods of the Chesapeake Bay, whose broad bosom was ever white with sails from every quarter of the habitable globe. Those beautiful vessels, robed in purest white, so delightful to the eye of freemen, were to me so many shrouded ghosts, to terrify and torment me with thoughts of my wretched condition. I have often, in the deep stillness of a summer's Sabbath, stood all alone upon the lofty banks of that noble bay, and traced, with saddened heart and tearful eye, the countless number of sails moving off to the mighty ocean. The sight of these always affected me powerfully. My thoughts would compel utterance; and there, with no audience but the Almighty, I would pour out my soul's complaint, in my rude way, with an apostrophe to the moving multitude of ships:—

"You are loosed from your moorings, and are free; I am fast in my chains, and am a slave! You move merrily before the gentle gale, and I sadly before the bloody whip! You are freedom's swift-winged angels, that fly round the world; I am confined in bands of iron! O that I were free! O, that I were on one of your gallant decks, and under your protecting wing! Alas! betwixt me and you, the turbid waters roll. Go on, go on. O that I could also go! Could I but swim! If I could fly! O, why was I born a man, of whom to make a brute! The glad ship is gone; she hides in the dim distance. I am left in the hottest hell of unending slavery. O God, save me! God, deliver me! Let me be free! Is there any God? Why am I a slave? I will run away. I will not stand it. Get caught, or get clear, I'll try it. I had as well die with ague as the fever. I have only one life to lose. I had as well be killed running as die standing. Only think of it; one hundred miles straight north, and I am free! Try it? Yes! God helping me, I will. It cannot be that I shall live and die a slave. I will take to the water. This very bay shall yet bear me into freedom. The steamboats steered in a north-east course from North Point. I will do the same; and when I get to the head of the bay, I will turn my canoe adrift, and walk straight through Delaware into Pennsylvania. When I get there, I shall not be required to have a pass; I can travel without being disturbed. Let but the first opportunity offer, and, come what will, I am off. Meanwhile, I will try to bear up under the yoke. I am not the only slave in the world. Why should I fret? I can bear as much as any of them. Besides, I am but a boy, and all boys are bound to some one. It may be that my misery in slavery will only increase my happiness when I get free. There is a better day coming.''

Thus I used to think, and thus I used to speak to myself; goaded almost to madness at one moment, and at the next reconciling myself to my wretched lot.

I have already intimated that my condition was much worse, during the first six months of my stay at Mr. Covey's, than in the last six. The circumstances leading to the change in Mr. Covey's course toward me form an epoch in my humble history. You have seen how a man was made a slave; you shall see how a slave was made a man. On one of the hottest days of the month of August, 1833, Bill Smith, William Hughes, a slave named Eli, and myself, were engaged in fanning wheat. Hughes was clearing the fanned wheat from before the fan, Eli was turning, Smith was feeding, and I was carrying wheat to the fan. The work was simple, requiring strength rather than intellect; yet, to one entirely unused to such work, it came very hard. About three o'clock of that day, I broke down; my strength failed me; I was seized with a violent aching

of the head, attended with extreme dizziness; I trembled in every limb. Finding what was coming, I nerved myself up, feeling it would never do to stop work. I stood as long as I could stagger to the hopper with grain. When I could stand no longer, I fell, and felt as if held down by an immense weight. The fan of course stopped; every one had his own work to do; and no one could do the work of the other, and have his own go on at the same time.

Mr. Covey was at the house, about one hundred yards from the treading-yard where we were fanning. On hearing the fan stop, he left immediately, and came to the spot where we were. He hastily inquired what the matter was. Bill answered that I was sick, and there was no one to bring wheat to the fan. I had by this time crawled away under the side of the post and rail-fence by which the yard was enclosed, hoping to find relief by getting out of the sun. He then asked where I was. He was told by one of the hands. He came to the spot, and, after looking at me awhile, asked me what was the matter. I told him as well as I could, for I scarce had strength to speak. He then gave me a savage kick in the side, and told me to get up. I tried to do so, but fell back in the attempt. He gave me another kick, and again told me to rise. I again tried, and succeeded in gaining my feet; but, stooping to get the tub with which I was feeding the fan, I again staggered and fell. While down in this situation, Mr. Covey took up the hickory slat with which Hughes had been striking off the half-bushel measure, and with it gave me a heavy blow upon the head, making a large wound, and the blood ran freely; and with this again told me to get up. I made no effort to comply, having now made up my mind to let him do his worst. In a short time after receiving this blow, my head grew better. Mr. Covey had now left me to my fate. At this moment I resolved, for the first time, to go to my master, enter a complaint, and ask his protection. In order to do this, I must that afternoon walk seven miles; and this, under the circumstances, was truly a severe undertaking. I was exceedingly feeble; made so as much by the kicks and blows which I received, as by the severe fit of sickness to which I had been subjected. I, however, watched my chance, while Covey was looking in an opposite direction, and started for St. Michael's. I succeeded in getting a considerable distance on my way to the woods, when Covey discovered me, and called after me to come back, threatening what he would do if I did not come. I disregarded both his calls and his threats, and made my way to the woods as fast as my feeble state would allow; and thinking I might be overhauled by him if I kept the road, I walked through the woods, keeping far enough from the road to avoid detection, and near enough to prevent losing my way. I had not gone far before my little strength again failed me. I could go no farther. I fell down, and lay for a considerable time. The blood was yet oozing from the wound on my head. For a time I thought I should bleed to death; and think now that I should have done so, but that the blood so matted my hair as to stop the wound. After lying there about three quarters of an hour, I nerved myself up

again, and started on my way, through bogs and briers, barefooted and bareheaded, tearing my feet sometimes at nearly every step; and after a journey of about seven miles, occupying some five hours to perform it, I arrived at master's store. I then presented an appearance enough to affect any but a heart of iron. From the crown of my head to my feet, I was covered with blood. My hair was all clotted with dust and blood; my shirt was stiff with blood. My legs and feet were torn in sundry places with briers and thorns, and were also covered with blood. I suppose I looked like a man who had escaped a den of wild beasts, and barely escaped them. In this state I appeared before my master, humbly entreating him to interpose his authority for my protection. I told him all the circumstances as well as I could, and it seemed, as I spoke, at times to affect him. He would then walk the floor, and seek to justify Covey by saying he expected I deserved it. He asked me what I wanted. I told him, to let me get a new home; that as sure as I lived with Mr. Covey again, I should live with but to die with him; that Covey would surely kill me; he was in a fair way for it. Master Thomas ridiculed the idea that there was any danger of Mr. Covey's killing me, and said that he knew Mr. Covey; that he was a good man, and that he could not think of taking me from him; that, should he do so, he would lose the whole year's wages; that I belonged to Mr. Covey for one year, and that I must go back to him, come what might; and that I must not trouble him with any more stories, or that he would himself *get hold of me*. After threatening me thus, he gave me a very large dose of salts, telling me that I might remain in St. Michael's that night, (it being quite late,) but that I must be off back to Mr. Covey's early in the morning; and that if I did not, he would *get hold of me,* which meant that he would whip me. I remained all night, and, according to his orders, I started off to Covey's in the morning, (Saturday morning,) wearied in body and broken in spirit. I got no supper that night, or breakfast that morning. I reached Covey's about nine o'clock; and just as I was getting over the fence that divided Mrs. Kemp's fields from ours, out ran Covey with his cowskin, to give me another whipping. Before he could reach me, I succeeded in getting to the cornfield; and as the corn was very high, it afforded me the means of hiding. He seemed very angry, and searched for me a long time. My behavior was altogether unaccountable. He finally gave up the chase, thinking, I suppose, that I must come home for something to eat; he would give himself no further trouble in looking for me. I spent that day mostly in the woods, having the alternative before me,—to go home and be whipped to death, or stay in the woods and be starved to death. That night, I fell in with Sandy Jenkins, a slave with whom I was somewhat acquainted. Sandy had a free wife who lived about four miles from Mr. Covey's; and it being Saturday, he was on his way to see her. I told him my circumstances, and he very kindly invited me to go home with him. I went home with him, and talked this whole matter over, and got his advice as to what course it was best for me to pursue. I found Sandy an old adviser.

He told me, with great solemnity, I must go back to Covey; but that before I went, I must go with him into another part of the woods, where there was a certain *root,* which, if I would take some of it with me, carrying it *always on my right side,* would render it impossible for Mr. Covey, or any other white man, to whip me. He said he had carried it for years; and since he had done so, he had never received a blow, and never expected to while he carried it. I at first rejected the idea, that the simple carrying of a root in my pocket would have any such effect as he had said, and was not disposed to take it; but Sandy impressed the necessity with much earnestness, telling me it could do no harm, if it did no good. To please him, I at length took the root, and, according to his direction, carried it upon my right side. This was Sunday morning. I immediately started for home; and upon entering the yard gate, out came Mr. Covey on his way to meeting. He spoke to me very kindly, bade me drive the pigs from a lot near by, and passed on towards the church. Now, this singular conduct of Mr. Covey really made me begin to think that there was something in the *root* which Sandy had given me; and had it been on any other day than Sunday, I could have attributed the conduct to no other cause than the influence of that root; and as it was, I was half inclined to think the *root* to be something more than I at first had taken it to be. All went well till Monday morning. On this morning, the virtue of the *root* was fully tested. Long before daylight, I was called to go and rub, curry, and feed, the horses. I obeyed, and was glad to obey. But whilst thus engaged, whilst in the act of throwing down some blades from the loft, Mr. Covey entered the stable with a long rope; and just as I was half out of the loft, he caught hold of my legs, and was about tying me. As soon as I found what he was up to, I gave a sudden spring, and as I did so, he holding to my legs, I was brought sprawling on the stable floor. Mr. Covey seemed now to think he had me, and could do what he pleased; but at this moment—from whence came the spirit I don't know—I resolved to fight; and, suiting my action to the resolution, I seized Covey hard by the throat; and as I did so, I rose. He held on to me, and I to him. My resistance was so entirely unexpected, that Covey seemed taken all aback. He trembled like a leaf. This gave me assurance, and I held him uneasy, causing the blood to run where I touched him with the ends of my fingers. Mr. Covey soon called out to Hughes for help. Hughes came, and, while Covey held me, attempted to tie my right hand. While he was in the act of doing so, I watched my chance, and gave him a heavy kick close under the ribs. This kick fairly sickened Hughes, so that he left me in the hands of Mr. Covey. This kick had the effect of not only weakening Hughes, but Covey also. When he saw Hughes bending over with pain, his courage quailed. He asked me if I meant to persist in my resistance. I told him I did, come what might; that he had used me like a brute for six months, and that I was determined to be used so no longer. With that, he strove to drag me to a stick that was lying just out of the stable door. He meant to knock me down. But just as he was leaning over to get the stick, I seized him with both hands by his collar, and brought him by a sudden snatch to the ground. By this time, Bill came. Covey called upon him for assistance. Bill wanted to know what he could do. Covey said, "Take hold of him, take hold of him!" Bill said his master hired him out to work, and not to help whip me; so he left Covey and myself to fight our own battle out. We were at it for nearly two hours. Covey at length let me go, puffing and blowing at a great rate, saying that if I had not resisted, he would not have whipped me half so much. The truth was, that he had not whipped me at all. I considered him as getting entirely the worst end of the bargain; for he had drawn no blood from me, but I had from him. The whole six months afterwards, that I spent with Mr. Covey, he never laid the weight of his finger upon me in anger. He would occasionally say, he didn't want to get hold of me again. "No," thought I, "you need not; for you will come off worse than you did before."

This battle with Mr. Covey was the turning-point in my career as a slave. It rekindled the few expiring embers of freedom, and revived within me a sense of my own manhood. It recalled the departed self-confidence, and inspired me again with a determination to be free. The gratification afforded by the triumph was a full compensation for whatever else might follow, even death itself. He only can understand the deep satisfaction which I experienced, who has himself repelled by force the bloody arm of slavery. I felt as I never felt before. It was a glorious resurrection, from the tomb of slavery, to the heaven of freedom. My long-crushed spirit rose, cowardice departed, bold defiance took its place; and I now resolved that, however long I might remain a slave in form, the day had passed forever when I could be a slave in fact. I did not hesitate to let it be known of me, that the white man who expected to succeed in whipping, must also succeed in killing me.

From this time I was never again what might be called fairly whipped, though I remained a slave four years afterwards. I had several fights, but was never whipped.

It was for a long time a matter of surprise to me why Mr. Covey did not immediately have me taken by the constable to the whipping-post, and there regularly whipped for the crime of raising my hand against a white man in defence of myself. And the only explanation I can now think of does not entirely satisfy me; but such as it is, I will give it. Mr. Covey enjoyed the most unbounded reputation for being a first-rate overseer and negro-breaker. It was of considerable importance to him. That reputation was at stake; and had he sent me—a boy about sixteen years old—to the public whipping-post, his reputation would have been lost; so, to save his reputation, he suffered me to go unpunished.

78. Lucy Andrews Petitions To Enter Slavery

In 1794 St. George Tucker, a Virginia lawyer who opposed slavery, wrote a disquisition on the subject, outlining a plan for gradual emancipation. In the course of his argument he identified three forms of slavery: political slavery he illustrated by the case of the American Colonies vis-à-vis England; civil slavery he illustrated by the case of the "free" black population in the United States; but domestic slavery was the lot of the black chattels of the Southern states. Only by grasping entirely the difficulties of *civil* slavery can a person understand the voluntary choice of some free blacks to become slaves. Denied most legal defenses available to free whites, and segregated as thoroughly as the slave-owners could manage to do, from the majority of slaves who had the protection that their masters' interests provided, "free" blacks were almost pariahs in communities of dense

Source: South Carolina Department of Archives and History, Columbia, S.C.

slaveholding. Aside from the right to own property and to make contracts, free blacks had few civil rights. They experienced particular hardship after the reaction of the 1830s, when some states made emancipated blacks leave the state in order to avail themselves of their freedom.

All this said, one supposes that a dash of *white* philosophy is included in the following petition of Lucy Andrews to the legislature of South Carolina in 1859, which was probably framed by her approving "protectors." And yet it is necessary in fairness to the scruples of the Legislature to add that Lucy Andrews's petition was not acted upon affirmatively in 1859, the year of its first presentation, for it reappears regularly every year following that until 1862, when it appears for the last time. I am much in the debt of Mr. R. Nicholas Oldsberg, formerly of the South Carolina Department of Archives and History, for his help in dating this petition.

Petition of Lucy Andrews, 1859.

To the Honorable, the Senate, and House of Representatives, of the Legislature, of the State of South Carolina. The humble Petition of Lucy Andrews, a free Person of color, would respectful[l]y represent unto your Honorable Body that she is now sixteen years of age (and the Mother of an Infant Child) being a Descendant, of a White Woman, and her Father a Slave; That she is dissatisfied with her present condition being compelled to go about from place to place, to seek employment for her support, and not permitted to stay at any place, more than a week or two at a time, no one caring about employing her. That she expects to raise a family, and will not be able to support them. That she sees, and knows, to her own sorrow, and regret, that Slaves are far more happy, and enjoy themselves far better, than she does, in her present isolated condition of freedom; and are well treated, and cared for by their Masters, whilst she

is going about, from place, to place, hunting employment for her support. That she cannot enjoy herself, situated as She now is, and prefers Slavery, to freedom, in her present condition. Your Petitioner therefore prays, that your Honorable Body, would enact a law, authorizing, and permitting her, to go voluntarily, into Slavery, and select her own Master; and your Petitioner will, as in duty bound, ever pray &C—In the presence of—

her
Lucy   X   Andrews
mark

J. R. Trusdel
H. H. Duncan
Jas. Vinson

We the undersigned Citizens, of Lancaster District, are well acquainted with the Petitioner, Lucy Andrews, and believe the facts stated in the Petition to be true, and we are well satisfied in our own minds, that the Petitioner would be in a far better condition in a State of Slavery, than in

a State of freedom—and that her Petition ought to be granted—
[Fifty signatures follow.]

The Committee on Coloured Population to whom was referred the Petition of Lucy Andrews praying the passage of an Act making herself and her two children slaves beg leave to

Report

That they have considered the same and reccommend [sic] that the prayer of the Petition be granted and for this purpose they recommend the passage of the accompanying Bill

Respectfully Submitted
Randell Croft for The Committee [1]

1. This report must surely have been made not on the first, but on a subsequent, petition of Lucy Andrews, since it refers to her two children. (*Editor's note*)

NINE
Men, Women, and Children

79. Slaves Had "A Sense of the Moral Law"

Gaining an intimate view of family life in slavery has been a great challenge for historians. Slavery posed so many problems for domestic happiness that for a time some scholars held that the slave family was necessarily weak, if not altogether shattered. Because the marriage contract was not legally binding, masters had the right to separate couples, and the overpowering authority of the master in any case threatened the relation between parents—especially that of the father—and their children. The separation of families was an inevitable part of the interstate slave trade, and by general consent its most deplorable aspect.

The older view that slaves had no real family life is presently under vigorous revision, however, and historians have discovered that, pressures notwithstanding, the family was an important sustaining force for survival in slavery. How many of the thousands of slaves who moved from east to west during the 1820s, 1830s, and 1840s represented the separation of man and wife and children is not as yet an entirely settled subject, and the new scholarship tends to the conclusion that earlier estimates have been exaggerated. In any event, the slave family was stronger than the pressures upon it would lead one to suppose.

Undefended by law, or indeed by anything beyond the attitude of the master himself, the slave family apparently grew stronger rather than weaker during the last decades of the slave era. The narratives of fugitive slaves, the observations of travelers, plantation records, all tend to that conclusion. Especially suggestive of strong family feeling among slaves was the massive search for lost relatives during the first two years following emancipation. Plagued in every way, the slave family endured, and was undoubtedly the best comfort available to an abused people.

The role of father was undoubtedly weaker among slaves than among the slaveholding whites, for the primary task of protector was officially denied him. Nevertheless, there is ample evidence that he had an important position in the family. There were slaves whose wives were never beaten, because their slave husbands would surely be avenged; there were slave children who enjoyed better health because their fathers supplemented

Source: Jacob Stroyer, *My Life in the South,* New and Enlarged [3d] Edition (Salem, Mass.: Salem Observer Book and Job Print, 1885), pp. 9–27.

their diets by fishing and trapping and gardening. Yes, there were also slave fathers who secured order (or disorder) in their own cabins by the venerable dictum: "Spare the rod and spoil the child."

The story of Jacob Stroyer's early life as a slave on a South Carolina plantation illustrates many of the constraints on the slave family, psychological as well as physical. But it illustrates also consultation between parents, their concern, and the hope of freedom a patient and self-controlled father instilled in his son. Stroyer became an African Methodist Episcopal minister after the Civil War, serving in Salem, Massachusetts. He published his memoirs first in 1879, and the book went into several editions. It has an authentic ring, and is told in Stroyer's own language.

My father was born in Sierra Leone, Africa. Of his parents, and his brothers and sisters, I know nothing, I only remember that it was said that his father's name was Moncoso, and his mother's Mongomo, which names are known only among the native Africans. He was brought from Africa when but a boy and sold to old Colonel Dick Singleton, who owned a great many plantations in South Carolina, and when the old colonel divided his property among his children, father fell to his second son, Col. M. R. Singleton.

Mother never was sold, but her parents were; they were owned by one Mr. Crough, who sold them and the rest of the slaves, with the plantation, to Col. Dick Singleton, and mother was born on that place. I was born on this extensive plantation twenty-eight miles southeast of Columbia, South Carolina, in the year 1849. I belonged to Col. M. R. Singleton, and was held in slavery up to the time of the emancipation proclamation issued by President Lincoln.

THE CHILDREN.

My father had fifteen children: four boys and three girls by his first wife, and eight by his second. Their names were as follows: of the boys,—Toney, Aszerine, Duke and Dezine; of the girls,—Violet, Priscilla, and Lydia. Those of his second wife were as follows: Footy, Embrus, Caleb, Mitchell, Cuffey and Jacob; and of the girls, Catherine and Retta.

SAND-HILL DAYS.

Col. M. R. Singleton was like many other rich slave owners in the South, who had summer seats four, six or eight miles from the plantation, where they carried the little negro boys and girls while they were too small to work.

Our summer seat, or the sand hill, as the slaves used to call it, was four miles from the plantation. Among the four hundred and sixty-five slaves owned by the colonel, there were a great many children. If my readers had visited Col. Singleton's plantation the last of May or the first of June in the days of slavery, they would have seen three or four large plantation wagons loaded with little negroes of both sexes, of various complexions and conditions, who were being carried to this summer residence, and among them they would have found the author of this little work, in his sand-hill days.

My readers would naturally ask, how many seasons these children were taken to the summer seats? I answer, until, in the judgment of the overseer, they were large enough to work; then they were kept at the plantation. How were they fed? There were three or four women who were too old to work on the plantation, who were sent as nurses at the summer seats with the children; they did the cooking. The way in which these old women cooked for 80, and sometimes 150 children, in my sand-hill days, was this,—they had two or three large pots, which held about a bushel each, in which they used to cook corn flour, stirred with large wooden paddles. The food was dealt out with the paddles into each child's little wooden tray or tin pail, which was furnished by the parents according to their ability.

With this corn flour, which the slaves called mush, each child used to get a gill of sour milk, brought daily from the plantation in a large wooden pail on the head of a boy or a man. We children used to like the sour milk, or hard clabber as it was called by the slaves; but that seldom changed diet, namely the mush, was hated worse than medicine. Our hatred was increased against the mush from the fact that they used to give us molasses to eat with it instead of clabber. The hate-

ful mixture made us anxious for Sundays to come, when our mothers, fathers, sisters and brothers would bring something from the plantation, which, however poor, we considered very nice, compared with what we had during the week days. Among the many desirable things our parents brought us, the most delightful was cow pease, rice, and a piece of bacon, cooked together; the mixture was called by the slaves, "Hopping John."

THE STORY OF GILBERT.

A few large boys were sent yearly to the sand-hill among the smaller ones, as guides for them. At the time to which I am referring, there was one by the name of Gilbert, who used to go around with the smaller boys in the woods to gather bushes and sticks for the old women to cook our food with.

Gilbert was a cruel boy. He used to strip the little fellow negroes while in the woods, and whip them two or three times a week, so that their backs were all scarred, and threatened them with severer punishment if they told it; this state of things had been going on for quite a while. As I was a favorite of Gilbert, I always had managed to escape a whipping, with the promise of keeping the secret of the punishment of the rest, which I did, not so much that I was afraid of Gilbert, as because I always was inclined to mind my own business. But finally, one day Gilbert said to me, "Jake," as he used to call me, "you am a good boy, but I'm gwine to wip you some to-day, as I wip them toder boys." Of course I was required to strip off my only garment, which was an Osnaburg linen shirt, worn by both sexes of the negro children in the summer. As I stood trembling before my merciless superior, who had a switch in his hand, thousands of thoughts went through my little mind as to how to get rid of the whipping. I finally fell upon a plan which I hoped would save me from a punishment that was near at hand. There were some carpenters in the woods, some distance from us, hewing timber; they were far away, but it was a clear morning, so we could hear their voices and the sound of the axes. Having resolved in my mind what I would do, I commenced reluctantly to take off my shirt, and at the same time pleading with Gilbert, who paid no attention to my prayer, but said, "Jake, I is gwine to wip you to-day as I did dem toder boys." Having satisfied myself that no mercy was to be found with Gilbert, I drew my shirt off and threw it over his head, and bounded forward on a run in the direction of the sound of the carpenters. By the time he got from the entanglement of my garment, I had quite a little start of him; between my starting point and the place where the carpenters were at work, I jumped over some bushes five or six feet high. Gilbert soon gained upon me, and sometimes touched me with his hands, but as I had on nothing for him to hold to, he could not take hold of me. As I began to come in sight of the carpenters, Gilbert begged me not to go to them, for he knew that it would be badd [sic] for him, but as that was not a time for me to listen to his entreaties I moved on faster. As I got near to the carpenters, one of them ran and met me, into whose arms I

jumped. The man into whose arms I ran, was Uncle Benjamin, my mother's uncle. As he clasped me in his arms, he said, "bres de Lo, my son, wat is de matter?" But I was so exhausted that it was quite a while before I could tell him my trouble; when recovered from my breathless condition, I told him that Gilbert had been in the habit of stripping the boys and whipping them two or three times a week, when we went into the woods, and threatened them with greater punishment if they told it. I said he had never whipped me before, but I was cautioned to keep the secret, which I did up to this time; but he said he was going to whip me this morning, so I threw my shirt over his head and ran here for protection. Gilbert did not follow me after I got in sight of the carpenters, but sneaked away. Of course my body was all bruised and scratched up by the bushes. Acting as a guide for Uncle Benjamin, I took him to where I left my garment.

At this time the children were scattered around in the woods, waiting for what the trouble would bring; they all were gathered up and taken to the sand-hill house, examined, and it was found, as I have stated, that their backs were all scarred up. Gilbert was brought to trial, severely whipped, and they made him beg all the children to pardon him for his treatment to them. But he never was allowed to go into the woods with the rest of the children during that season. My sand-hill associates always thanked me for the course I took, which saved them and myself from further punishment by him.

MASTER AND MISTRESS VISITING.

When master and mistress were to visit their little negroes at the sand-hill, the news was either brought by the overseer, who resided at the above named place, and went back and forth to the plantation, or by one of master's house servants, a day ahead. The preparation required to receive our white guest[s] was that each little negro was to be washed, and clad in the best dress he or she had. But before this was done, however, the unsuccessful attempt was made to straighten out our unruly wools with some small cards, or Jim-crows as we called them.

On one occasion an old lady, by the name of Janney Cuteron, attempted to straighten out my wool with one of those Jim-crows; as she hitched the teeth of the instrument in my unyielding wool with her great masculine hand, of course I was jerked flat of my back. This was the common fate of most of my associates, whose wools were of the same nature, but with a little water, and the strong application of the Jim-crow, the old lady soon combed out my wool into some sort of shape.

As our preparations were generally completed three quarters of an hour before our guests came, we were placed in line, the boys together and the girls by themselves. We were then drilled in the art of addressing our expected visitors. The boys were required to bend the body forward with head down, and rest the body on the left foot, and scrape the right foot backward on the ground, while uttering the words, "how dy Massa and Missie." The girls were required to use the same words, accompanied with a courtesy [curtsey]. But when master and mistress left, the little African wools were neglected until the news of their next visit.

Our sand-hill days were very pleasant, outside of the seldom changed diet, namedly the mush, which we had to sometimes eat with molasses; the treatment of Gilbert, and the attempt to straighten out our unruly wools.

I said that my father was brought from Africa when but a boy, and was sold to old Col. Dick Singleton; and when his children were of age, he divided his plantations among them, and father fell to Col. M. R. Singleton, who was the second son.

On this large plantation there were 465 slaves; there were not so many when first given to Col. M. R., but increased to the above stated number, up to the time of emancipation.

My father was not a field hand; my first recollection of him was that he used to take care of horses and mules, as master had a great many for the use of his farm.

I have stated that father said that his father's name was Moncoso, and his mother's Mongomo, but I never learned what name he went by before he was brought to this country. I only know that he stated that Col. Dick Singleton gave him the name of William, by which he was known up to the day of his death. Father had a surname, Stroyer, which he could not use in public, as the surname Stroyer would be against the law; he was known only by the name of William Singleton, because it was his master's name. So the title Stroyer was forbidden him, and could be used only by his children after the emancipation of the slaves. There were two reasons given by the slave holders why they did not allow a slave to use his own name, but rather that of the master. The first was that if he ran away, he could not be so easily detected by using his own name, as if he used that of his master instead. The second was, that to allow him to use his own name would be sharing an honor which was due only to his master, and that would be too much for a negro, said they, who was nothing more than a servant. So it was held as a crime for a slave to be caught using his own name which would expose him to severe punishment. But thanks be to God that those days have passed, and we now live under the sun of liberty.

MOTHER.

My mother's name was Chloe. She belonged to Col. M. R. Singleton too; she was a field hand, and never was sold, but her parents were once.

As I have said, that one Mr. Crough owned this plantation on which mother lived, and he, Mr. C., sold the plantation to Col. Dick Singleton, with mother's parents on it, before she was born. The family from which mother came, the most of them had trades of some kind; some were carpenters, some blacksmiths, some house servants, and others were made drivers over the other negroes. Of course the negro drivers would be under a white man who was called the overseer. Sometimes the negro drivers were a great deal worse to their fellow negroes than the white men.

Mother had an uncle by the name of Esau, whom master thought more of than he did the overseer. Uncle Esau was more cruel than any white man master ever had on his plantation. Many of the slaves used to run away in the woods from him, instead of from the overseer. I have known some of the negroes to run away from the cruel treatment of Uncle Esau, and to stay off eight or ten months. They were so afraid of him that they used to say that they would rather see the devil than to see him; they were glad when he died. But while so much was said of Uncle Esau, which was also true of many other negro drivers, yet the overseers were not free from their portion of cruelty practised upon the defenceless slaves in gone by days.

I have said that the family from which mother came, most of them had trades of some kind; but she had to take her chance in the field with those who had to weather the storm. But my readers are not to think that those whom I have spoken of as having trades were free from punishment, for they were not; some of them had more troubles than the field hands. At times the overseer, who was a white man, would go to the shop of the blacksmith or carpenter, and would pick a quarrel with him, so as to get an opportunity to punish him. He would say to the negro, "Oh, ye think yourself as good as ye master, ye _____" Of course he knew what the overseer was after, so he was afraid to speak; the overseer, hearing no answer, would turn to him and cry out, "ye so big ye can't speak to me, ye _____," and then the conflict would begin, and he would give that man such a punishment as would disable him for two or three months. The merciless overseer would say to him, "Ye think because ye have a trade ye are as good as ye master, ye _____; but I will show ye that ye are nothing but a nigger."

I said that my father had two wives and fifteen children: four boys and three girls by the first, and six boys and two girls by the second wife. Of course he did not marry his wives as they do now, as it was not allowed among the slaves, but he took them as his wives by mutual agreement. He had my mother after the death of his first wife. I am the third son of his second wife.

My readers would very naturally like to know whether some of the slaves did not have more than one woman; I answer, they had; for as they had no law to bind them to one woman, they could have as many as they pleased by mutual agreement. But notwithstanding, they had a sense of the moral law, for many of them felt that it was right to have but one woman. They had different opinions about plurality of wives, as have the most educated and refined among the whites.

I met one of my fellow negroes one day, who lived next neighbor to us, and I said to him, "Well, Uncle William, how are you, to-day?" his answer was, "Thank God, my son, I have two wives now, and must try to make out with them until I can get some more." But while you would find many like him, others would rebuke the idea of having more than one woman for wife. But, thanks be to God, that day has come when no one need plead ig-

norance, for the master and slave are both bound by the same law, which knows no man by condition of color.

I did not go to the sand-hill, or summer seat, my allotted time, but stopped on the plantation with father, as I said that he used to take care of horses and mules. I was around with him in the barn yard when but a very small boy; of course that gave me an early relish for the occupation of hostler, and I soon made known my preference to Col. Singleton, who was a sportsman, and had fine horses. And, although I was too small to work, the Colonel granted my request; hence I was allowed to be numbered among those who took care of the fine horses, and learned to ride. But I soon found that my new occupation demanded a little more than I cared for.

It was not long after I had entered my new work before they put me upon the back of a horse which threw me to the ground almost as soon as I reached his back. It hurt me a little, but that was not the worse of it, for when I got up there was a man standing over me with a switch in hand, and he immediately began to beat me. Although I was a very bad boy, this was the first time I had been whipped by any one except father and mother, so I cried out in a tone of voice as if I would say, this is the first and last whipping you will give me when father gets hold of you.

When I got away from him I ran to father with all my might, but soon found my expectation blasted, as father very coolly said to me, "go back to your work and be a good boy, for I cannot do anything for you." But that did not satisfy me, so on I went to mother with my complaint and she came out to the man who whipped me; he was a groom, a white man whom master hired to train his horses, as he was a man of that trade. Mother and he began to talk, then he took a whip and started for her, and she ran from him, talking all the time. I ran back and forth between mother and him until he stopped beating her. After the fight between the groom and mother, he took me back to the stable yard and gave me a severe flogging. And although mother failed to help me at first, still I had faith that when he took me back to the stable yard, and commenced whipping me, that she would come and stop him, but I looked in vain, for she did not come.

Then the idea first came to me that I with my dear father and mother and the rest of my fellow negroes, was doomed to cruel treatment through life, and was defenceless. But when I found that father and mother could not save me from punishment, as they themselves had to submit to the same treatment, I concluded to appeal to the sympathy of the groom, who seemed to have had full control over me; but my pitiful cries never touched his sympathy, for things seemed to grow worse rather than better; so I made up my mind to stem the storm the best I could[.]

I have said that Col. Singleton had fine horses, which he kept for racing, and he owned two very noted ones, named Capt. Miner and Inspector. Perhaps some of my readers have already heard of Capt. Miner, for he was widely known, and won many races in Charleston and Columbia, S.C., also in Augusta, Ga., and New York. He was a dark bay, with short tail. Inspector was a chestnut sorrel, and had the reputation of being a very great horse. These two horses have won many thousand dollars for the colonel. I rode these two horses a great many times in their practice gallops, but never had the opportunity to ride them in a race before Col. Singleton died, for he did not live long after I had learned to ride for money. The custom was, when a boy learned the trade as a rider, he would have to ride what was known as a trial in the presence of a judge, who would approve or disapprove his qualifications to be admitted as a race rider, according to the jockey laws of South Carolina at that time.

This white man who trained horses for Col. Singleton was named Boney Young; he had a brother named Charles, who trained for the colonel's brother, John Singleton. Charles was a good man, but Boney, our trainer was as mean as Charles was good; he could smile in the face of one who was suffering the most painful death at his hands.

One day, about two weeks after Boney Young and mother had the conflict, he called me to him, as though he was in his pleasantest mood; he was singing. I ran to him as if to say by action, I will do anything you bid me, willingly. When I got to him he said, "go and bring me a switch sir." I answered, "yes, sir," and off I went and brought him one; then he said, "come in here, sir;" I answered, "yes, sir;" and I went into a horse's stall, but while I was going in a thousand thoughts passed through my mind as to what he wanted me to go in the stall for, but when I got in I soon learned, for he gave me a first class flogging.

A day or two after that he called me in the same way, and I went again, and he sent me for a switch. I brought him a short stubble that was worn out, which he took, beat me on the head, and then said to me, "go and bring me a switch, sir;" and off I went the second time, and brought him one very little better than the first; he broke that one over my head, also saying, "go and bring me a switch, sir;" I answered, "yes, sir," and off I went the third time, and brought one which I supposed suited him. Then he said to me, "Come in here, sir," I answered, "yes, sir." When I went into the stall, he told me to lie down; he kicked me around for awhile, then making me lie on my face, he whipped me to his satisfaction.

That evening when I went home to father and mother, I said to them, "Mr. Young is whipping me too much now; I shall not stand it, I shall fight him. Father said to me, "You must not do that, because if you do he will say that your mother and I advised you to do it, and it will make it hard for your mother and me, as well as for yourself. You must do as I told you, my son: do your work the best you can, and do not say anything." I said to father, "but I don't know what I have done that he should whip me; he does not tell me what wrong I have done, he simply calls me to him and whips me when he gets ready." Father said, "I can do nothing more than to pray to the Lord to hasten the time when these things shall be done away; that is all I can do." When mother stripped me and looked at the wounds that were upon me, she burst into tears, and said, "if he were not so small I would not mind

it so much; this will break his constitution; I am going to master about it, because I know he will not allow Mr. Young to treat this child so."

And I thought to myself that had mother gone to master about it, it would have helped me some, for he and she grew up together and he thought a great deal of her. But father said to mother, "you better not go to master, for while he might stop the child from being treated badly, Mr. Young may revenge himself through the overseer, for you know that they are very friendly to each other." So said father to mother, "you would gain nothing in the end; the best thing for us to do is to pray much over it, for I believe that the time will come when this boy with the rest of the children will be free, though we may not live to see it."

When father spoke of liberty his words were of great comfort to me, and my heart swelled with the hope of a future, which made every moment seem an hour to me.

Father had a rule, which was strictly carried out as far as possible under the slave law, which was to put his children to bed early; but that night the whole family sat up late, while father and mother talked over the matter. It was a custom among the slaves not to allow their children under certain ages to enter into conversation with them; hence we could take no part with father and mother. As I was the object of their sympathy, I was allowed the privilege of answering the questions about the whipping the groom gave me.

When the time came for us to go to bed we all knelt down in family prayer, as was our custom; father's prayer seemed more real to me that night than ever before, especially in the words, "Lord, hasten the time when these children shall be their own free men and women."

My faith in father's prayer made me think that the Lord would answer him at the farthest in two or three weeks, but it was fully six years before it came, and father had been dead two years before the war.

After prayer we all went to bed; next morning father went to his work in the barn yard, mother to hers in the field, and I to mine among the horses; before I started, however, father charged me carefully to keep his advice, as he said that would be the easiest way for me to get along.

But in spite of father's advice, I had made up my mind not to submit to the treatment of Mr. Young as before, seeing that it did not help me any. Things went smoothly for a while, until he called me to him, and ordered me to bring him a switch. I told him that I would bring him no more switches for him to whip me with, but that he must get them himself. After repeating the command very impatiently, and I refusing, he called to another boy named Hardy, who brought the switch, and then taking me into the stall he whipped me unmercifully.

After that he made me run back and forth every morning from a half to three quarters of an hour, about two hundred and fifty yards, and every now and then he would run after me, and whip me to make me run faster. Besides that, when I was put upon a horse, if it threw me he would whip me if it were five times a day. So I did

not gain anything by refusing to bring switches for him to whip me with.

One very cold morning in the month of March, I came from home without washing my face, and Mr. Young made two of the slave boys take me down to a pond where the horses and mules used to drink; they threw me into the water and rubbed my face with sand until it bled, then I was made to run all the way to the stable, which was about a quarter of a mile. This cruel treatment soon hardened me so that I did not care for him at all.

A short time after I was sent with the other boys about four or five miles from home, up the public road, to practise the horse, and they gave me a very wild animal to ride, which threw me very often. Mr. Young did not go with us, but sent a colored groom every morning, who was very faithful to every task allotted him; he was instructed to whip me every time the horse threw me while away from home. I got many little floggings by the colored groom as the horse threw me a great many times, but the floggings I got from him were very feeble compared with those of the white man; hence I was better content to go away with the colored groom than to be at home where I would have worse punishment.

But the time was coming when they ceased to whip me for being thrown by the horses. One day, as I was riding along the road, the horse that I was upon darted at the sight of a bird, which flew across the way, throwing me upon a pile of brush. The horse stepped on my cheek, and the head of a nail of his shoe went through my left cheek and broke a tooth, but it was done so quickly that I hardly felt it. It happened that he did not step on me with his whole weight, if he had my jaw would have been broken. When I got up the colored groom was standing by me, but he could not whip me when he saw the blood flowing from my mouth, so he took me down to the creek, which was but a short distance from the place, and washed me, then taking me home, sent for a doctor who dressed the wound.

When Mr. Young saw my condition, he asked how it was done, and upon being told he said it ought to have killed me. After the doctor had dressed my face, of course I went home, thinking they would allow me to stay until I got well, but I had no sooner arrived than the groom sent for me; I did not answer, as my jaw pained me very much. When he found that I did not come, he came after me himself, and said if I did not come to the stable right away, he would whip me, so I went with him. He did not whip me while I was in that condition, but he would not let me lie down, so I suffered very much from exposure.

When mother came that night from the farm and saw my condition, she was overcome with grief; she said to father, "this wound is enough to kill the child, and that merciless man will not let him lie down until he gets well; this is too hard." Father said to her, "I know it is very hard, but what can we do? for if we try to keep this boy in the house it will cause us trouble." Mother said, "I wish they would take him out of the world, then he would be out of pain, and we should not have to fret about him for he would be in heaven." Then she took hold of me and said,

"does it hurt you, son?" meaning my face, and I said, "yes, mamma," and she shed tears; but she had no little toys to give me to comfort me; she could only promise me such as she had, which were eggs and chickens.

Father did not show his grief for me as mother did, but he tried to comfort mother all he could, and at times would say to me, "never mind, my son, you will be a man bye and bye." But he did not know what was passing through my mind at that time. Though I was very small I thought that, if while a boy my treatment was so severe, it would be much worse when I became a man, and having had a chance to see how men were being punished, it was very poor consolation to me.

Finally the time came for us to go to bed, and we all knelt in family prayer. Father thanked God for having saved me from a worse injury, and then he prayed for mother's comfort, and also for the time which he predicted would come, that is the time of freedom, when I and the rest of the children should be our own masters and mistresses; then he commended us to God, and we all went to bed. The next morning I went to my work with a great deal of pain. They did not send me up the road with the horses in that condition, but I had to ride the old horses to water them, and work around the stable until I was well enough to go with the other boys. But, I am happy to say, that from the time I got hurt by that horse I was never thrown except through carelessness, neither was I afraid of a horse after that.

80. The White Boys Outgrow Charles

The blighting effects of slavery on black children is registered clearly by the frequency with which whites remarked that small black children were as quick to learn as whites, but that later on their relative abilities appeared to decline. Contemporary pro-slavery and anti-slavery writers differed sharply in their explanation of this situation, as one might expect. In any case numbers of black children managed, covertly, to learn how to read and write from white children, or from a sympathetic mistress. The laws against teaching slaves to read were not casually defied, however, because a slave-holding society understood that literacy made communications simpler, and thus facilitated potential insurrectionary movements.

On the other hand, in a Protestant society that believed that every Christian should interpret Scripture for his own soul's salvation, enforced ignorance was impossible to defend. Next to the omission of the law to protect slave marriages, the prohibition of instruction to slaves was the abuse most frequently attacked by Southerners who would like to have ameliorated the slave system. One of the best descriptions of the tragedy of enforced ignorance comes from the pen of Moncure Conway (1832–1907), an upper-class Virginian who grew up at Falmouth, near Fredericksburg. From his own experience he developed an early hostility to slavery that led him at length to the ranks of abolitionists. Conway was educated at Dickinson College and Harvard.

In the following account Conway describes the plight of his father's slave, Charles, who was assigned to accompany the white children to school. Conway is slightly wrong, but only slightly, in saying that the Virginia law proscribed the teaching of slaves to read. It forbade general meetings of classes and accepting *money* for teaching slaves to read. The Virginia law was widely interpreted as a complete prohibition, which was the legal situation in many Southern states during the last decades before the Civil War. The incidents described below must have occurred during the 1840s.

Source: M[oncure] D. Conway, *Testimonies Concerning Slavery* (London: Chapman & Hall, 1864), pp. 1–8.

The town of Falmouth, in Virginia, on the Rappahannock river, has been associated with important military events during the present war. Before the war, it was a village of about a thousand inhabitants, all of whom were very poor, with the exception of five or six families which were very rich. It is quite an ancient place, and was originally inhabited by some Scotchmen,—amongst others, an uncle of the poet Campbell,—who made it a centre of trade between the rich piedmont lands of Virginia and Baltimore. It was once the exact head of navigation on the Rappahannock; but afterwards the river was so filled with bars, that the trade fell to Fredericksburg, about two miles lower. As its name indicates, Falmouth has the advantage of being close to the falls which furnish the most magnificent water-power in Virginia; and if that State had been free, it must have been one of the chief manufacturing towns in America.

It was near this village that I was born, and in it that my parents resided during nearly all the early years that I can remember. There were a great many slaves and free Negroes in the neighbourhood. My father then owned fifty or sixty slaves, and many of my relatives a larger number. My parents were very kind to their slaves; and, indeed, I think that the marked contrast between the treatment of slaves to which I had been accustomed at home and that which I witnessed elsewhere, was the first occasion of my attention being drawn to what was going on around me. And yet no amount of benevolent intentions, or watchfulness, or religious observances on their part,

was adequate to secure a quiet or happy home. Not long ago, in conversation with a strong defender of Negro Slavery, I found that the corner-stone of his theory was an impression that there was in the homestead of the South a simplicity, a patriarchal relationship between the servants and superiors, which contrasted favourably with the corresponding conditions in other communities, where, he maintained, the relation between servant and master being purely and at each moment mercenary, the ties must be galling to both parties. I can well believe that a scholar who had never come into personal contact with Slavery, might think of that system as wearing in America the Oriental costume of customs and relations which it wore in the early days when slaves belonged to and loved men who had ransomed them from death as captives, or with races and ages under less pressure than our own to turn every thing to gold. In Brazil, where Slavery exists in connection with a race and government far behind any that it can find in the United States, it is less out of place, and need not use so much violence and coercion to exist at all; and hence there is much more simplicity and repose there with the institution. And so I was obliged to assure the gentleman alluded to that, however coarse and hard the relation between servants and employers in free communities might be, he was, in looking to the Southern States, appealing to an absolutely mythical Arcadia. Few are the really peaceful days that I remember as having smiled on my old Virginian home; the outbreaks of the Negroes among themselves, the disobediences which the necessary discipline can never suffer to be overlooked, the terrors of devoted parents at the opportunities for the display of evil tempers and the inception of nameless vices among their sons, I remember as the demons haunting those days. And for these most painful circumstances, giving to nearly every day its "scene," there is no compensation in the work accomplished. With two Irish girls for servants in Ohio, I am quite sure that I have had more work done, and infinitely better done, and with far less interruption of domestic quiet, than my father ever got from all his slaves. No doubt, if he had availed himself of the severe methods used by others around him, he might have got more work and money out of his slaves; for only perpetual violence and sleepless suspicion can really get any thing like the full amount of work out of men and women who know only the curse, and none of the rewards, of toil. I have often heard my parents say that the care of slaves had made them prematurely old.

The impression has gone around the world with ubiquitous sable minstrels that the slaves are a merry, singing, dancing population, far removed from the cares that gnaw the hearts of more civilised classes. In all the twenty-three years of my life in the land of Slavery, I never saw a Negro-dance, though in those years I have heard of a few in our neighborhood. The slaves of the Border States are almost invariably members of the Baptist and Methodist societies, which are particularly rigid in denying them such amusements. On the large plantations of the far South, dances are encouraged, and formerly were frequent; but of late years they have become infrequent, through the all-absorbing tendencies of the Negroes toward religious meetings. My observation confirms that of Dr. Russell when he visited the South as correspondent of the London *Times*, that the Negroes are a notably melancholy people. I have rarely known their enthusiasm enlisted in any thing except prayer-and-experience meetings and funerals. Our own kitchen-fireside was nightly the scene of religious exercises and conversations which were very fascinating to me, and from which I had to be dragged with each returning bed-time. The dreams, visions, and ecstasies there related were as gorgeous as those of the *Pilgrim's Progress;* for these humble and ignorant souls, denied the reading of the Bible, had conceived a symbolism of their own, and burdens of prophecy, and had changed the fields on which they toiled into the pavements of the New Jerusalem, glorified with spirits arrayed in white. The cant phrases of the white preachers whom they listened to had become alive to them, and mingled strangely in their speech and hymns; they had, too, their own rudimental Swedenborgianism and Transcendentalism.

A boy was born on my father's estate, who was named Charles. His obvious parents were servants, whom my father had long owned; but they were both quite black, and the boy was nearly white, besides being embarrassingly like a pious gentleman who now and then visited us. This lad at an early age indicated a remarkable intelligence, and was also of a remarkable beauty according to the European type. As he grew older, he increased in vivacity, wit, and amiability; and at his sixteenth year I remember him as one of the handsomest and noblest specimens of Humanity. Wherever he went in the village, a group of admiring white boys was around him, listening to his bewitching songs or romances or mimicries. He seemed to us all a hero of romance, and such a thing as remembering his colour never entered our heads.

His occupation at this age was to attend my brother and myself to and from our school, which was two miles distant. The monotony of this daily journey he varied by his songs and stories, and to him we both looked with implicit reverence. He was active and brave too, proud of being our protector, and eager to pounce upon the biggest snake in our path, or encounter and subdue the fiercest dog.

The day came to him, as it had to come to millions before him, when he desired to learn what we were learning in school. But the laws forbid the teaching of a Negro to read under severest penalties; and no law relating to Negroes is so carefully and strictly enforced in the South as that which forbids their being taught. The long imprisonment of Mrs. Douglas at Norfolk, a few years ago, for teaching a Negro child to read is a familiar case. In Falmouth, two or three ladies whom I knew met on Sunday afternoon to teach some Negro children; they had not so met three times, before they were dispersed by the authorities, although it appeared that they only gave the children oral and religious instruction. I do not believe that my father approved these laws; but being a jus-

tice of the county, he of course must take care that the laws were observed in his own house. So Charles's thirst must go unslaked.

There is a cruel pang that comes to nearly every slave's life, which has been very little considered. It is customary in nearly all households in the South for the white and black children connected with each to play together. The trial I have referred to comes when the young Negroes who have hitherto been on this democratic footing with the young whites are presently deserted by their more fortunate companions, who enter upon school-life and the acquaintance of white boys, and, ceasing to associate with their swarthy comrades any longer, meet them in future with the air of the master. This is the dawn of the first bitter consciousness of being a slave; and nothing can be sadder than to see the poor little things wandering about companionless and comfortless. It is doubtful whether either my brother or myself had natural gifts equal to the slaveboy Charles; nevertheless we were carried past him, and abandoned him. His knowledge, which once seemed to us unlimited, we gradually discovered to be inferior to our own. We gained new (white) companions, and should have been ashamed to be seen playing at any game with Charles.

But meanwhile the power of intellect and temperament which Nature had lodged in that youth increased. Had there been about him a society able to enclose that power in a fit engine, and set it upon true grooves, he might have borne the burdens which such souls are sent into the world to bear. But as it was, this power was as so much steam without a valve: it was a danger. His temper, from being mild, became bitter; his bravery became fierceness; and by his recklessness the whole family was kept in perpetual panic. Punishment only made him defiant. He was to be a noted personage in one way or another; his daring and ingenious tricks became at first the town's talk and then the town's alarm. He signalised his nineteenth year by setting fire to a house; whereupon my father was forced by public opinion, or perhaps by a legal order, to sell him to the far South. So Charles is now buried, alive or dead, among the cotton plantations.

Although I have dwelt upon this case because it is that which represents, in my own experience, one of the most tragical forms in which Slavery outrages human nature, yet let none think of this as an incident in any respect peculiar. On the contrary, I have myself known many cases where minds of high gifts have been thus waylaid and robbed of their God-given treasures by Slavery. It perhaps requires powers higher than any ordinarily vouchsafed to the Anglo-Saxon to discern the rare quality of the purely Negro spirit and mind; but, were we to grant all that Cant and Sophistry say about the inferiority of the Negro, what shall be said of those millions of the Southern slaves who have Anglo-Saxon blood in them? Not one-third of the Southern slaves are purely African; and in at least a third of them the white blood predominates. Certainly these are not under the curse of Ham. At least we can be certain that the pride, the curiosity, the thirst for knowledge, which are inherent in the

blood of the white race, must render Slavery to these a fearful crucifixion. Had Charles been born in the North, I know he would have been a noble and a distinguished man. And I have known at least ten others in Virginia who, I am persuaded, would, by a few years' tuition of freedom, have been equal in character and influence to Douglass, Charles Remond, and others.

I know that there is an impression abroad that the people of mixed blood in the Southern States are a very low and vicious class,—an impression which naturally originated with the slaveholders, to whom coloured people are always odious and evil in proportion as they are hard to keep enslaved. My observation leads me to believe that, so far from being a poor or inferior set, we might, under proper training, have had from just that mixture of the Saxon mind with the African temperament some of the first men of the world. They are said to have bad health: it proves only the greater chafing of the yoke, and the intentional severity with which it is made to weigh upon them. They are driven to the lowest occupations.

But the laws of God are inviolable. The South has by its own passions forged, and given a Saxon temper to, the sword which is now suspended over it, and which must soon fall. For these are not the men who run off at once to the Union lines; they remain to strike the blow for their race, and share the fate of comrades. They are such as Denmark Vesey, who travelled through the world with his master, and might have had freedom a thousand times; but returned to South Carolina, to set on foot a gigantic plot for insurrection. A group of such I met from the cotton plantations early in this war; they had made their way to Ohio to consult with Abolitionists; having done so, they abandoned the free soil upon which they stood and went back to the far South, to abide their time with the rest. And there are thousands of these who have long lived in the North, and whose motto is now SOUTHWARD: in them are the fiery hearts of crusaders who march to rescue the holy places of Humanity from the tread of the infidel. And for them wait the multitudes of starved intellects, beggared hearts, and famished souls, who have long lain under the altar, and cried day and night, "How long, O Lord; how long!"

81. Stolen Reading Lessons, Chimney Sweeps, and Dogs

For a touching domestic scene that illustrates the eagerness of slave children to read, and the cooperation they sometimes secured from slave-holders' children, we can turn again to the writing of Emily Burke, the New England governess who hated slavery but not slaveholders (see document 64). Few observers captured so well the happier aspects of relations between slaveholders and their favorite servants, and few captured so well the pathos of small black children put to such work as cleaning chimneys, and stealing, to make a living. The little sweeps, adrift in poverty and ignorance, will remind readers of Fagin's band of child-thieves in Charles Dickens's *Oliver Twist*.

Letter XIII.

Notwithstanding the great precaution which is used to prevent the mental improvement of the slaves, many of them steal knowledge enough to enable them to read and write with ease.

It is often the case, that the white children of a family impart much of that information they have acquired at school to those among the black children who happen to be their favorites; for it must be understood that not only every little boy and girl has each a fa-

Source: Emily P. Burke, *Reminiscences of Georgia* (n.p.: James M. Fitch, 1850), pp. 85–87, 89—91.

vorite slave, but also every young man and woman have their favorite servants, to whom they not only often impart much useful information, but confide in them more as companions than merely waiting men and women; and it is not uncommon to see the favorite slave nearly as wise as his master. A lad about eleven years of age, in the family where I once visited, made it his practice, unknown to the family, to spend an hour or two every day in teaching a black boy to read; an act exposing the father of the noble hearted boy to a heavy fine if found out. This fact come to my knowledge by a colored woman, who had sufficient confidence in me to believe I should not betray the child. Clerks often instruct the slaves who labor in the back stores, and many by this means acquire a decent education. I have often seen a young man belonging to one of the largest firms in Savannah, who could read, write, cipher, and transact business so correctly, that his masters often committed important trusts to his care. The firm valued him at fifteen hundred dollars. He read with great eagerness every northern paper that came within his reach, and had by this means gained a good knowledge of the political state of our country. At the time I was there, he was deeply interested in the election of President Harrison, as were the slaves generally in the Southern States, for they were all Harrison men, and they were bold enough to assert publicly that "when William Henry Harrison became President of the United States, they should have their freedom," and, believing as they did, who could lament the death of the worthy President more than the poor slaves?

I do not know that ever I was more deeply impressed with a sense of the cruelty of depriving the slaves of the means of instruction than one evening while on my way to my room I met two little colored children, apparently about eight years old, trying to find out between themselves some of the letters of the alphabet. It appeared that one of them had found an old, crumpled, soiled leaf torn from a toy-book, upon which a few of the large letters were still legible; and then they had seated themselves upon the stairs to study them out. One of the children was saying just as I reached them, that she heard somebody say that the round letter was O; the other replied that "she heard such a little girl say the straight letter was L," so alternately each was teacher and scholar. O, if the children at the North, who are almost compelled to go to school, could have witnessed that scene, it would I think have taught them a lesson not soon to be forgotten. I longed for an opportunity to give them that information they seemed so desirous to obtain; but I hastened up to my room, fearing to be found there, lest it might be thought I was attempting to instruct them. . . .

But those among this down-trodden race of people in our country, whom I commiserated as much as any while in Savannah, were the little chimney sweeps. These were the most forlorn, half-starved, emaciated looking beings I ever beheld. Their masters always accompanied them about the city, because they could not trust them to go to their labor alone; for they were invariably obliged to beat them before they would ascend a chimney, the task was so revolting even to those who are accustomed to this barbarous practice of using live flesh and blood for chimney brooms. But notwithstanding this task seemed so dreadful, extreme hunger often compelled them to climb upon the outside of the house in the night time, and then descend the chimney to steal something to eat. . . .

The slaves carry all their burdens upon their heads, and to me it is quite unaccountable how they can sustain such weights as they do in this manner. They will transport from one place to another, tubs of water, large, heavy, iron-bound trunks, or any other burden they can raise to their heads. I have seen the man who had the care of the city lamps going from one street to another, with a ladder in one hand, a large wooden box in the other, and a heavy can of oil on his head. Even the white children often learn from their nurses to carry things in this way. It is quite common to see a little group of school girls with all their books on their heads going to or returning from school, and almost the first thing the little child tries to do when it begins to walk is to balance its toys upon its head. I have often heard the old washerwomen complain of pain in their necks after supporting on their heads a large tub of water or basket of wet clothes.

The dog is the negro's favorite pet, and almost every man and woman owns one or two of these faithful animals; consequently they are exceedingly numerous in the city. Efforts are often made to diminish their numbers, but they seldom avail much, as their owners generally succeed in concealing them when their lives are threatened. For myself I was glad the poor slaves had something they could call their own, and think it extremely cruel in those who would take from the oppressed servant the only thing he might venture to set his heart upon. . . .

82. Slavery Develops Stealing in Blacks, Bad Temper and Fear in Whites

The impact of slavery on white children was often singled out for special censure, and even defenders of slavery admitted that bringing up their children posed peculiar problems. Judging from the following account, Emily Burke (see documents 64 and 81) would have agreed with Thomas Jefferson (see document 18) that slavery was a school for tyranny. She ob-

Source: Emily Burke, *Reminiscences of Georgia,* (n.p.: James M. Fitch, 1850), pp. 151–59.

served that slave-owners were constantly alert to pilfering, not only from their own possessions but among the slaves themselves.

Letter XXI.

Those who have never lived in the Southern States, can have but a faint conception of the evils that accrue to the master as well as slave, from their peculiar institutions. Incidents of such a nature have many times come under my own observation, as almost to cause me to feel that the master lived in the greatest bondage.

But it would be impossible for me to make you believe there is any truth in such an assertion, without something more tangible than the simple statement, therefore I will relate a few facts, not only to show that slaveholders live in constant fear for the safety of their lives and property, but also the corrupting and demoralizing influence such a system has upon every thing that comes in contact with it.

Of all the evils that a country under the dominion of slavery is heir to, I consider that the greatest which arises from the early training of its youth. Nothing in my opinion seems so calculated to sap the very foundation of all their institutions, both moral and religious, and even government itself, as this. Just think of the very individual who is destined to wield the scepter of government, receiving the first impress upon his mind from an ignorant, degraded, and perhaps profane nurse, to whose almost entire charge his mind as well as his body has been consigned ere his infant tongue has been taught to utter its first syllable. Yet such is the case in a thousand instances, and instead of all those holy influences that hover around the cradle in the Christian mother's nursery, the very atmosphere in which the slaveholder's son draws his first breath, is infected with that moral miasma which poisons the soul, and corrupts all the virtuous principles of the heart; and when the Christian mother would hush her little one to slumber with the sweet assurance that "holy angels will guard its bed," the untutored slave rocks the cradle of its infant master to the song of "Old Dan Tucker," or "Lucy Long." "The manner of training children at the South accounts for that pugilistic spirit and uncontrollable temper when excited we all know is characteristic of the Southerner. At that tender age when the heart is in its most plastic state, no attempts are made to subdue the will or control the passions, and the nurse, whether good or bad, often fosters in her bosom a little Nero, who is taught that it is manly to strike his nurse in the face in a fit of anger. I have seen a child plunge a fork into the face of its nurse, and no punishment was inflicted upon the little criminal. If the boy is allowed to make such free use of the fork, what could we expect to see in the hand of the man but the pistol and bowie knife, ready to be used upon the slightest provocation.

Another of the many evils of slavery and one which in its immediate influence is felt probably as much as any other, is that which arises from the universal want of confidence in the honesty of slaves. The fear of theft haunts the slaveholder at all times and in all places. In harvest time he is obliged to set a strict watch over his corn fields, orchards, and melon patches, when night comes every moveable article of property must be put under lock and key, even the fowls have to be all collected together every evening as soon as it is time for them to go to roost, and locked up in coops. It is really amusing to see kitchens, stables, cotton houses and graneries all fastened with great padlocks, and that too in the day time if not occupied. A slave can not be trusted for a moment with the key to the granary, if a peck of corn is to be measured, it must be done under the eye of a vigilant steward. It is just so too in the department that particularly belongs to the mistress of the family. She is obliged to weigh and measure every thing that passes into the hands of the cook. In a large family, this duty is so arduous that I have often thought the mistress was the greatest slave. Every cupboard, closet and drawer, in those apartments to which the slaves have access are kept constantly locked, and I myself found by experience that it was not safe to leave my work box in the drawing room unfastened. Then to sum up the whole, a family living on one of these isolated plantations must, when night comes, be all fastened up within windows and doors bolted and barred like a prison house.

In the city it is not unusual to hear of colored boys gaining admittance to a house by descending through the chimney. An instance of this kind came under my observation, while in Savannah. Two young men who boarded at one of the public houses, lodged in rooms over their office, one of which they had furnished for a parlor. It was their custom to send a servant into this room every evening to prepare a table of refreshments, which having done, he would lock the door and hand the key to his masters. At length they discovered that depredations were committed every evening upon their wines, cigars, etc., and notwithstanding they took great pains, they were not able to get the least clue to the source of this mischief, till one evening when going into the room as usual, they found the culprit lying upon the floor in a state of intoxication. When he recovered his senses sufficiently to give an account of himself, he confessed he had been in the practice of entering the room by the way of the chimney, and taking whatever he wanted, this time he had partaken to[o] freely of champaigne to escape detection.

The propensity for stealing among the slaves is so great that even the dead are often exhumed for the purpose of securing their grave clothes. In some parts of Georgia where I have been, it is customary to bury the dead in full dress. For example, a man is interred in every article of dress he would wear in life, even to a coat and boots. A female would be laid out in what would be called a full dress for church. When such is the custom, there is a strong temptation to disturb the grave for the wardrobe it contains. Such a violation, however, of the sacredness of the tomb, if found out, meets a penalty more cruel than death itself, though I could never see why such an act should be considered more criminal than it would be to steal the body and all, a theft that is committed as frequently by the medical student at the South as with us, and the student if detected is only sentenced a heavy fine.

But the fear the slaveholder often has for his life is much greater than that he suffers for his property. When I was living in the southern part of Georgia, a lady whose husband expected to be gone on a journey for several weeks sent for me to come and stay with her in his absence. While there she gave a particular account of her domestic trials. She said when her husband was not at home, there was not a person on her plantation she dared trust her life with, and as she could not defend herself with fire arms in case of an attack upon her life, she never retired at night without an axe so near her pillow she could lay her hand upon it instantly. In this instance, the fear of this lady had been greatly increased by an attempt a few years previous to an insurrection among her own slaves. This plantation was situated on the sea coast not far from Florida, in the immediate vicinity of the live oak timber. Here the slaves came in frequent contact with the lumber men from Maine, who go out there every winter in great numbers, to cut the live oak for ship building. Through the instigation of these men, every slave on this plantation united in a plot to rise on a certain night and massacre every member of their master's family. The plot was revealed however, just in time to prevent the execution of the dreadful deed, by one old servant, who felt she could not stand and see her master and mistress and all the children murdered.

In '35 deep measures for the same dreadful purpose were concerted in South Carolina, extending through that and several other contiguous States. The time then fixed upon was Christmas eve, in order to prevent any mistake. In this case, thousands were saved from a dreadful death by the warning one faithful slave gave to her master to take care of himself and family on Christmas night. Circumstances like these have excited so much fear among slaveholders, especially in the extreme South, where the plantations are large and slaves very numerous, they generally go armed with pistols or bowie knives. I have seen young men just on an equestrian excursion for an evening, conceal in their bosoms a brace of pistols loaded with balls, and others only going out a little distance in a gig, take with them their guns, and I had no reason to think that either had any other motive in doing so than self-defense. I must say, myself, if the use of carnal weapons could ever be justifiable, I should think it was in this, for the same season not far from the plantation where I was staying, three white men were murdered while passing from one plantation to another, by slaves who had secreted themselves for that purpose.

Ladies even, under certain circumstances, provide for their own defense in the use of firearms. I have known ladies that would not dare to go to sleep without one or two pistols under their pillows. A lady in Savannah came very near being the executioner of her own husband in consequence of such a custom. He had been from home on a journey, and wishing to give his wife an agreeable surprise, made his arrangements to return a few days sooner than she anticipated. Arriving at a late hour for retiring, he thought he would make her surprise to see him still greater by appearing without the least warning in her own room. Accordingly he succeeded in effecting an entrance into his house, by forcing a shutter in the basement, and with noiseless steps was making his way in the dark up to his wife's apartment. He had gone as far as the stairs, when that slight creaking which every one understands who has ever tried to walk stealthily in a noiseless house at night, reached her ears, and being prepared by every unusual sound to expect thieves and robbers, she sprang out of her bed, seized a pistol and commanding her chambermaid to follow, she stepped into the hall and then towards the stair case when she indistinctly saw the figure of a man cautiously approaching her. At the first sight she leveled her pistol, and the next instant would in all probability have fixed a bullet in his brain, had not one screech from the well known voice of her husband paralyzed her hand for the moment and caused the deadly weapon to fall harmless at her feet.

I think I have now said enough upon this subject to convince you that slaveholders are by no means, with all their possessions, the happiest people in the world. Sin and iniquity are often accompanied by their own reward, but in this case this truth is strikingly apparent. . . .

---

83. Treaty and Louisine Lose Their Babies

Although many examples of cruelty to children may be found in the record of slavery, most masters were alert to their own interests as well as to the call of humanity, and showed great interest in the proper care of mothers and infants. In an age of high infant mortality, slave children tended to die within the first year of life at a higher rate than white children, but slave mothers survived childbearing at approximately the same rate as white women. In their instructions to overseers, planters prescribed carefully and in some detail the term of confinement, lying-in, and the postnatal care of infants. The higher rate of infant mortality among slaves was

Source: Ulrich B. Phillips, ed., *Plantation and Frontier* (Cleveland: A. H. Clark, 1909), 1:312–13.

baffling to slave-masters, who often charged the mothers with neglect, or worse.

Sometimes an absentee owner found fault with overseers for working the mothers too long in the field. Such appears to have been the complaint of Col. John B. Lamar (see document 52) against Stancil Barwick, overseer of the Colonel's property near Americus, Georgia. In the following document Barwick replies to the charge. While Barwick's reply is subject to several interpretations, it is plain that he knows he has something to answer for in the cases of Treaty and Louisine.

Stancil Barwick to Col. John B. Lamar, July 15, 1855.

Dear Sir: I received your letter on yesterday ev'ng was vary sorry to hear that you had heard that I was treating your Negroes so cruely. Now sir I do say to you in truth that the report is false thear is no truth in it. No man nor set of men has ever seen me mistreat one of the Negroes on the Place. Now as regards the wimin loosing children, treaty lost one it is true. I never heard of her being in that way until she lost it. She was at the house all the time, I never made her do any work at all. She said to me in the last month that she did not know she was in that way her self untill she lost the child. As regards Louisine she was in the field it is true but she was workt as she please. I never said a word to her in any way at all untill she com to me in the field and said she was sick. I told her to go home. She started an on the way she miscarried. She was about five months gone. This is the true statement of case. Now sir a pon my word an honnor I have tride to carry out your wishes as near as I possibly could doo. Ever since I have been on the place I have not been to three neighbours houses since I have been hear I com hear to attend to my Businiss I have done it faithfully the reports that have been sent must have been carried from this Place by Negroes the fact is I have made the Negro men work an made them go strait that is what is the matter an is the reason why that my Place is [the] talk of the settlement. I have found among the Negro men two or three hard cases an I have had to deal rite Ruff but not cruly at all. Among them Abram has been as triflin as any man on the place. Now sir what I have wrote you is truth an it cant be disputed by no man on earth.

N.B. As regards my crop of corn I think I will make a plenty to doo the Place next year my cotton is injured by the wate weather an lice the weed is large enough but nothing on it. I will [be] done working it a week or ten days from this time.

84. A Visit to the Infirmary on Butler's Island

The hardships of the woman field-slave were nowhere more bitterly detailed than in the diary of Fanny (Frances Anne) Kemble, the famous English actress who married Pierce Butler, co-owner of a plantation off the coast of Georgia, and quintessential absentee-landlord. Butler lived in Philadelphia, and his estates were managed by Roswell King, who had been overseer for many years, succeeding his own father in that role. In 1838–39 Butler brought his wife to visit the plantation, and her letters from Georgia constitute a journal of her experiences and impressions. Miss Kemble was extremely hostile to slavery, and her record reveals her anger.

Mr. King and Mr. Butler inclined to the view that the servants complained to Miss Kemble unnecessarily, and because she encouraged them to do so by indulging them with excessive sympathy. It seemed to Miss Kemble that the slave women found it easier to tell her about "female" complaints than to tell the men. The plight of the woman field-slave who disliked telling the overseer or her master that she was pregnant (see document 83) or that she was having menstrual difficulties, or any other gynecological problem, has to be understood in the context of the Victorian world of women.

In any event, the facts as Miss Kemble presents them concerning slave women's complaints should not be too readily discounted, for other evidence from the same region indicates that the conditions she describes were by no means unique, and from time to time she registered favorable impressions that may also be verified. The task system, for instance, widely employed in the area, freed a majority of slaves to return from the field by mid-afternoon, from which time on they could work on their own gardens. On the whole, however, Miss Kemble showed no tendency to minimize the hardships of slavery. Her details concerning the health of slave women are particularly revealing, and probably accurate as well. Only a very sympathetic person could have found out so much as she did;

Source: Frances Anne Kemble, *Journal of a Residence on a Georgia Plantation*, ed. John A. Scott (New York: Alfred A. Knopf, 1961), pp. 75–79.

only an emancipated "lady" would have written about what she discovered so freely.

Miss Kemble's diary covering her visit to Butler's Island was not published until 1863, during the American Civil War. She was by that time divorced from Pierce Butler, and she hoped that her book might cast some light on the social problems associated with emancipation.

[January, 1839]

Dear E[lizabeth],

This morning I paid my second visit to the infirmary, and found there had been some faint attempt at sweeping and cleaning, in compliance with my entreaties. The poor woman Harriet, however, whose statement with regard to the impossibility of their attending properly to their children had been so vehemently denied by the overseer, was crying bitterly. I asked her what ailed her, when, more by signs and dumb show than words, she and old Rose informed me that Mr. O—— had flogged her that morning for having told me that the women had not time to keep their children clean. It is part of the regular duty of every overseer to visit the infirmary at least once a day, which he generally does in the morning, and Mr. O——'s visit had preceded mine but a short time only, or I might have been edified by seeing a man horsewhip a woman. I again and again made her repeat her story, and she again and again affirmed that she had been flogged for what she told me, none of the whole company in the room denying it or contradicting her. I left the room because I was so disgusted and indignant that I could hardly restrain my feelings, and to express them could have produced no single good result.

In the next ward, stretched upon the ground, apparently either asleep or so overcome with sickness as to be incapable of moving, lay an immense woman; her stature, as she cumbered the earth, must have been, I should think, five feet seven or eight, and her bulk enormous. She was wrapped in filthy rags, and lay with her face on the floor. As I approached, and stooped to see what ailed her, she suddenly threw out her arms, and, seized with violent convulsions, rolled over and over upon the floor, beating her head violently upon the ground, and throwing her enormous limbs about in a horrible manner. Immediately upon the occurrence of this fit, four or five women threw themselves literally upon her, and held her down by main force; they even proceeded to bind her legs and arms together, to prevent her dashing herself about; but this violent coercion and tight bandaging seemed to me, in my profound ignorance, more likely to increase her illness by impeding her breathing and the circulation of her blood, and I bade them desist, and unfasten all the strings and ligatures not only that they had put round her limbs, but which, by tightening her clothes round her body, caused any obstruction. How much I wished that, instead of music, and dancing, and such stuff, I had learned something of sickness and health, of the conditions and liabilities of the human body, that

I might have known how to assist this poor creature, and to direct her ignorant and helpless nurses! The fit presently subsided, and was succeeded by the most deplorable prostration and weakness of nerves, the tears streaming down the poor woman's cheeks in showers, without, however, her uttering a single word, though she moaned incessantly. After bathing her forehead, hands, and chest with vinegar, we raised her up, and I sent to the house for a chair with a back (there was no such thing in the hospital), and we contrived to place her in it. I have seldom seen finer women than this poor creature and her younger sister, an immense strapping lass called Chloe—tall, straight, and extremely well made—who was assisting her sister, and whom I had remarked, for the extreme delight and merriment which my cleansing propensities seemed to give her, on my last visit to the hospital. She was here taking care of a sick baby, and helping to nurse her sister Molly, who, it seems, is subject to those fits, about which I spoke to our physician here—an intelligent man residing in Darien, who visits the estate whenever medical assistance is required. He seemed to attribute them to nervous disorder, brought on by frequent childbearing. This woman is young, I suppose at the outside not thirty, and her sister informed me that she had had ten children—ten children, E[lizabeth]! Fits and hard labor in the fields, unpaid labor, labor exacted with stripes—how do you fancy that? I wonder if my mere narration can make your blood boil as the facts did mine?

Among the patients in this room was a young girl, apparently from fourteen to fifteen, whose hands and feet were literally rotting away piecemeal, from the effect of a horrible disease, to which the Negroes are subject here, and I believe in the West Indies, and when it attacks the joints of the toes and fingers, the pieces absolutely decay and come off, leaving the limb a maimed and horrible stump! I believe no cure is known for this disgusting malady, which seems confined to these poor creatures. Another disease, of which they complained much, and which, of course, I was utterly incapable of accounting for, was a species of lockjaw, to which their babies very frequently fall victims in the first or second week after their birth, refusing the breast, and the mouth gradually losing the power of opening itself. The horrible diseased state of the head, common among their babies, is a mere result of filth and confinement, and therefore, though I never anywhere saw such distressing and disgusting objects as some of these poor little woolly skulls presented, the cause was sufficiently obvious. Pleurisy, or a tendency to it, seems very common among them; also peripneumonia, or inflammation of the lungs, which is terribly prevalent, and generally fatal. Rheumatism is almost universal; and as it proceeds from exposure, and want of knowledge and care, attacks indiscriminately the young and old. A great number of the women are victims to falling of the womb and weakness in the spine; but these are necessary results of their laborious existence, and do not belong either to climate or constitution.

I have ingeniously contrived to introduce bribery, corruption, and pauperism, all in a breath, upon this island, which, until my advent, was as innocent of these pollutions, I suppose, as Prospero's isle of refuge. Wishing, however, to appeal to some perception, perhaps a little less dim in their minds than the abstract loveliness of cleanliness, I have proclaimed to all the little baby nurses that I will give a cent to every little boy or girl whose baby's face shall be clean, and one to every individual with clean face and hands of their own. My appeal was fully comprehended by the majority, it seems, for this morning I was surrounded, as soon as I came out, by a swarm of children carrying their little charges on their backs and in their arms, the shining, and, in many instances, wet faces and hands of the latter bearing ample testimony to the ablutions which had been inflicted upon them. How they will curse me and the copper cause of all their woes in their baby bosoms! Do you know that, little as grown Negroes are admirable for their personal beauty (in my opinion, at least), the black babies of a year or two old are very pretty; they have, for the most part, beautiful eyes and eyelashes, the pearly perfect teeth, which they retain after their other juvenile graces have left them; their skins are all (I mean of blacks generally) infinitely finer and softer than the skins of white people. Perhaps you are not aware that among the white race the *finest grained* skins generally belong to persons of dark complexion. This, as a characteristic of the black race, I think might be accepted as some compensation for the coarse woolly hair. The nose and mouth, which are so peculiarly displeasing in their conformation in the face of a Negro man or woman, being the features least developed in a baby's countenance, do not at first present the ugliness which they assume as they become more marked; and when the very unusual operation of washing has been performed, the blood shines through the fine texture of the skin, giving life and richness to the dingy color, and displaying a species of beauty which I think scarcely anybody who observed it would fail to acknowledge. I have seen many babies on this plantation who were quite as pretty as white children, and this very day stooped to kiss a little sleeping creature that lay on its mother's knees in the infirmary—as beautiful a specimen of a sleeping infant as I ever saw. The caress excited the irrepressible delight of all the women present—poor creatures! who seemed to forget that I was a woman, and had children myself, and bore a woman's and a mother's heart toward them and theirs; but, indeed, the Honorable Mr. Slumkey [1] could not have achieved more popularity by his performances in that line than I by this exhibition of feeling; and, had the question been my election, I am very sure nobody else would have had a chance of a vote through the island. But wisely is it said that use is second nature, and the contempt and neglect to which these poor people are used make the commonest expression of human sympathy appear a boon and gracious condescension.

While I am speaking of the Negro countenance, there is another beauty

1. The Dickensian prototype, from *The Pickwick Papers,* of the baby-kissing political campaigner. (*Scott note*)

which is not at all infrequent among those I see here—a finely-shaped oval face—and those who know (as all painters and sculptors, all who understand beauty do) how much expression there is in the outline of the head, and how very rare it is to see a well-formed face, will be apt to consider this a higher matter than any coloring, of which, indeed, the red and white one so often admired is by no means the most rich, picturesque, or expressive. At first the dark color confounded all features to my eye, and I could hardly tell one face from another. Becoming, however, accustomed to the complexion, I now perceive all the variety among these black countenances that there is among our own race, and as much difference in features and in expression as among the same number of whites. There is another peculiarity which I have remarked among the women here—very considerable beauty in the make of the hands; their feet are very generally ill-made, which must be a natural, and not an acquired defect, as they seldom injure their feet by wearing shoes. The figures of some of the women are handsome, and their carriage, from the absence of any confining or tightening clothing, and the habit they have of balancing great weights on their heads, erect and good. . . .

85.   Attending a Quadroon Ball

Nowhere else in the South was interracial sex formalized to the extent that it was in New Orleans, where French Creoles and blacks, slave and free, came close to regular marriage—as close as custom outside the law allowed. There was ritual, as evidenced by the famous Quadroon Balls, described in the following account by Karl Bernhard (see document 47), and there was also a demimonde with its own social rules that evolved to invest illegal unions with a pathetic and often evanescent dignity. Abandoned women knew in advance what to expect; and one asks about those who were not abandoned whether their "marriages" were not as authentic as those solemnized in the fashionable churches of the Crescent City. The

Source: Karl Bernhard, Duke of Saxe-Weimar Eisenach, *Travels through North America,* 2 vols. (Philadelphia: Carey, Lea & Carey, 1828), 2:61–63.

emotions of the male offspring of these unions, described by Prince Karl, and of the white women faced with such formidable competition, are more easily imagined than described.

At the masked balls, each paid a dollar for admission. As I visited it for the second time, I observed, however, many present by free tickets, and I was told that the company was very much mixed. The unmasked ladies belonging to good society, sat in the recesses of the windows, which were higher than the saloon, and furnished with galleries. There were some masks in character, but none worthy of remark. Two quarrels took place, which commenced in the ball-room with blows, and terminated in the vestibule, with pocket-pistols and kicking, without any interruption from the police.

On the same evening, what was called a quadroon ball took place. A quadroon is the child of a mestize mother and a white father, as a mestize is the child of a mulatto mother and a white father. The quadroons are almost entirely white: from their skin no one would detect their origin; nay many of them have as fair a complexion as many of the haughty creole females. Such of them as frequent these balls are free. Formerly they were known by their black hair and eyes, but at present there are completely fair quadroon males and females. Still, however, the strongest prejudice reigns against them on account of their black blood, and the white ladies maintain, or affect to maintain, the most violent aversion towards them. Marriage between the white and coloured population is forbidden by the law of the state. As the quadroons on their part regard the negroes and mulattoes with contempt, and will not mix with them, so nothing remains for them but to be the friends, as it is termed, of the white men. The female quadroon looks upon such an engagement as a matrimonial contract, though it goes no farther than a formal contract by which the "friend" engages to pay the father or mother of the quadroon a specified sum. The quadroons both assume the name of their friends, and as I am assured preserve this engagement with as much fidelity as ladies espoused at the altar. Several of these girls have inherited property from their fathers or friends, and possess handsome fortunes. Notwithstanding this, their situation is always very humiliating. They cannot drive through the streets in a carriage, and their "friends" are forced to bring them in their own conveyances after dark to the ball: they dare not sit in the presence of white ladies, and cannot enter their apartments without especial permission. The whites have the privilege to procure these unfortunate creatures a whipping like that inflicted on slaves, upon an accusation, proved by two witnesses. Several of these females have enjoyed the benefits of as careful an education as most of the whites; they conduct themselves ordinarily with more propriety and decorum, and confer more happiness on their "friends," than many of the white ladies to their married lords. Still, the white ladies constantly speak with the greatest contempt, and even with animosity, of these unhappy and oppressed beings. The strongest language of high nobility in the monarchies of the old world, cannot be more haughty, overweening or contemptuous towards their fellow creatures, than the expressions of the creole females with regard to the quadroons, in one of the much vaunted states of the free Union. In fact, such comparison strikes the mind of a thinking being very singularly! Many wealthy fathers, on account of the existing prejudices send daughters of this description to France, where these girls with a good education and property, find no difficulty in forming a legitimate establishment. At the quadroon ball, only coloured ladies are admitted, the men of that caste, be it understood, are shut out by the white gentlemen. To take away all semblance of vulgarity, the price of admission is fixed at two dollars, so that only persons of the better class can appear there.

As a stranger in my situation should see every thing, to acquire a knowledge of the habits, customs, opinions and prejudices of the people he is among, therefore I accepted the offer of some gentlemen who proposed to carry me to this quadroon ball. And I must avow I found it much more decent than the masked ball. The coloured ladies were under the eyes of their mothers, they were well and gracefully dressed, and conducted themselves with much propriety and modesty. Cotillions and waltzes were danced, and several of the ladies performed elegantly. I did not remain long there that I might not utterly destroy my standing in New Orleans, but returned to the masked ball and took grat care not to disclose to the white ladies where I had been. I could not however refrain from making comparisons, which in no wise redounded to the advantage of the white assembly.

86.   A Creole Father Counts His Children

New Orleans was undoubtedly the most cosmopolitan of Southern cities, one where Anglo-Saxon and Protestant ways were less apparent than the easy-going style of the French Creole population that predominated. There

Source: George Featherstonhaugh, *Excursion through the Slave States* . . . (New York: Harper & Bros., 1844), pp. 141–42.

alone was interracial sex ritualized to any extent. It followed, of course, that white women, however grudgingly, were forced to recognize a fundamental fact of life that their sisters in other regions were able to ignore, at least in public. The following excerpt from the writings of George Featherstonhaugh (see document 34) reveals this highly unusual circumstance in a highly explicit way.

The position of this unfortunate race of women is a very anomalous one; for Quadroons, who are the daughters of white men by half-blooded mothers, whatever be their private worth or personal charms, are forbidden by the laws to contract marriage with white men. A woman may be as fair as any European, and have no symptom of negro blood about her; she may have received a virtuous education, have been brought up with the greatest tenderness, may possess various accomplishments, and may be eminently calculated to act the part of a faithful wife and tender mother; but if it can be proved that she has one drop of negro blood in her veins, the laws do not permit her to contract a marriage with a white man; and as her children would be illegitimate, the men do not contract marriages with them. Such a woman being over-educated for the males of her own caste, is therefore destined from her birth to be a mistress, and great pains are lavished upon her education, not to enable her to aspire to be a wife, but to give her those attractions which a keeper requires.

The Quadroon balls are places to which these young creatures are taken as soon as they have reached womanhood, and there they show their accomplishments in dancing and conversation to the white men, who alone frequent these places. When one of them attracts the attention of an admirer, and he is desirous of forming a liaison with her, he makes a bargain with the mother, agrees to pay her a sum of money, perhaps 2000 dollars, or some sum in proportion to her merits, as a fund upon which she may retire when the liaison terminates. She is now called "une placée"; those of her caste who are her intimate friends give her fêtes, and the lover prepares "un joli appartement meuble." With the sole exception of "going to church," matters are conducted very much as if a marriage had been celebrated: the lady is removed to her establishment, has her little côteries of female friends, frequents their "Bals de Société," and brings up sons to be rejected by the society where the father finds his equals, with daughters to be educated for the Quadroon balls, and destined to pursue the same career which the mother has done. Of course it frequently happens that the men get tired of them and form new liaisons; when this happens they return to their mother or fall back upon the fund provided for them in that case; and in some instances I was informed that various families of daughters by the same father appear at the Quadroon ball on the very evenings when their *legitimate* brother is present for the purpose of following the example of his worthy Papa.

A very amusing anecdote, illustrative of this state of society, was related to me by a person who had been a resident here a great many years. On his first arrival in New Orleans, before it had become such a bustling place as it is now, and when the French population had rather the *dessus,* he presented a letter of introduction to a "habitant" of great respectability, by whom he was politely received, and invited to dine *en famille* the same day. Nobody was present at the dinner but the wife of Monsieur C——, an agreeable and well educated Creole lady, a native of the place, and three of their children. He found Monsieur C—— a lively agreeable Frenchman, full of *bonhommie,* and received a great deal of pleasant and useful information from him. Happening amongst other questions to ask him how many children he had,

Monsieur C—— gave him the following account of his domestic relations:—

"Combien d'enfants, Monsieur? Ah! voyons un peu, si on pourrait vous dire, Cela! Nous avons d'abord, oui, nous avons quatre nés à la Rue Royale, puis trois en haut là de la Rue de Chartres; il y a encore les deux Montbrillons, mon fils qui est au sucrier, et puis les trois petits que vous voyez. Voilà le bout du compte, à ce que je pense; n'est ce pas, ma chère?" patting the head of one of the children, and addressing himself in the most confiding, affectionate way to Madame. It is evident that the future population of New Orleans is likely to afford a rare specimen of the form society can be made to take in a semi-tropical climate, where the passions act unrestrainedly, and where money is the established religion of the country. . . .

87. Mrs. Hansley Sues for Divorce

The greatest problem of all in the study of slavery is determining what was typical behavior and what was exceptional behavior. With almost unlimited power assigned to them by law in the handling of slave property, the slaveholders gave evidence of every possible exercise of that power. Among their number were wise men and foolish, good managers and bad, the self-disciplined and the licentious. Certainly the proximity of exploit-

Source: James Iredell [ed.], *Reports of Cases at Law Argued and Determined in the Supreme Court of North Carolina from August Term, 1849, to December Term, 1849* . . . (Raleigh: Seaton Gales, 1850), 10:506–16.

able black women often created for the white mistress what Mary Boykin Chesnut (document 89) frankly named hell on earth.

Such seems to have been the case of Ruthey Ann Hansley of Hanover County, North Carolina, who in 1845 petitioned for a divorce from her husband Samuel because of his relations with his slave woman Lucy. The Superior Court of Hanover County granted the decree, but Samuel Hansley appealed the verdict against him, and in 1849 his case reached the Supreme Court of North Carolina. That he won his appeal is indicative of the great legal difficulties surrounding divorce in the nineteenth century.

Ruthey Ann Hansley vs. *Samuel G. Hansley.*

On the trial of issues directed by the Court, upon a petition for a divorce, the mere confession of the husband, that he was guilty of the adultery charged, is not admissible evidence.

A divorce *a vinculo matrimonii* will not be granted, unless it is alleged and shewn that the husband or wife lived in adultery, after the separation had taken place.

Appeal from the Superior Court of Law of New Hanover County, at the Spring Term 1848, his Honor Judge CALDWELL presiding.

This is a suit instituted by Ruth A. Hansley against her husband Samuel G. Hansley, for a divorce *a vinculo matrimonii,* and for alimony. The parties were married in 1836 and lived together until August 1844; when the wife left her husband and went to reside with her brother in the same neighborhood and has lived there ever since.

The petition was filed on the 25th day of March 1845. It states, that the "petitioner lived for many years the wife of the said Samuel, enjoying much happiness, and fondly hoped to do so for many years yet to come, as she cheerfully fulfilled all the duties of an affectionate wife, until the conduct of her husband became so intolerable that it could no longer be endured: that, without any cause known to her, her husband took to drink, and, while in that state, would commit so many outrages against the modesty and decency of the petitioner, that she refrains from repeating them: that the influence of his intoxication would last sometimes for a month; all of which time the conduct of the said Samuel G. towards the petitioner would be intolerable; and the petitioner was often cruelly beaten by him, and his whole course of conduct towards her would be so entirely different from what she might have reasonably anticipated, that he rendered her life burdensome and too intolerable to be borne, from a habit so well calculated to destroy the reason, the affections and all the social relations of life, and to which the petitioner must attribute this brutal conduct of her said husband: that for weeks the said Samuel G. would absent himself from the petitioner during the whole night, although during the day time residing on the same farm, while so absenting himself; that it has come to the knowledge of the petitioner, that her husband did habitually, while so absenting himself from the petitioner, bed and cohabit with a negro woman named Lucy, belonging to him: that for some time previous to this fact coming to her knowledge with that degree of certainty, upon which she could rely, her suspicions were aroused, that such must be the fact; but that, not being able to prove the charge, and not being satisfied to abandon her husband until the proof could be clearly satisfactory to her own mind, the petitioner tried to endure, as long as it was reasonable for any wife to endure, the conduct of her husband; and that, during all the said time, her husband not only abandoned her bed entirely, and bedded with the said negro Lucy, but he deprived the petitioner of the control of all those domestic duties and privileges connected with the house, which belong to a wife, and placed the said Lucy in the full possession and enjoyment of those privileges and duties, and insulted the petitioner by openly and repeatedly ordering her to give place to the said negro, and saying that the petitioner was an incumbrance, and encouraged the said Lucy to treat her also: that, when the petitioner would no longer endure these things, and became entirely satisfied of the cause of such treatment, and of the truth of her previous suspicions, the petitioner abandoned her said husband: that, besides all this, her said husband, not satisfied with the treatment as above set forth, would go from home and take with him the keys of the house, and deprive the petitioner of food for two or three days at a time, and of every comfort, to which, as a wife, she was entitled: that often he would, at night, compel the

petitioner to sleep in bed with said negro Lucy, when he would treat the said Lucy as his wife, he occupying the same bed with the petitioner and the negro Lucy: that from the cruel and severe treatment of her husband towards the petitioner, she was afraid to resist or to decline so occupying the same bed with her husband and the said negro woman: that, when it was not agreeable to her husband to permit the petitioner to occupy the house, he would often lock her out of doors and there compel her to remain, during the whole night, unprotected and exposed to all the trials incident to such a situation: that she, at length, abandoned the residence of her husband in August 1844, and has made her home with one of her brothers ever since: and that, since her knowledge of the adulterous conduct of her said husband with the said negro Lucy, the petitioner has not admitted him to conjugal embraces, and is resolved never again so to do."

The petition then sets out the husband's estate, with a view to alimony, and it prays for a divorce from the bonds of matrimony and for a suitable provision.

The answer admits, that, at one period the defendant was intemperate and in the habit of intoxication; but it states, that, for several years before his wife left him, he had been perfectly sober. The defendant also admits that he chastised his wife once: but he denies that he ever did so but at that time, or that that was a violent or severe beating: and he says, that he immediately regretted having done so, and acknowledged that he was wrong and made the most humble apologies to her therefor, which he thought reconciled her: but that on the same night she abandoned his house. The answer then denies all the other allegations of the libel specially.

Upon issues submitted to a jury, it was found, that the parties had been inhabitants of this State for three years immediately before the filing of the petition: that the defendant, by habits of adultery with his slave Lucy, by degrading his wife, the petitioner, by beating her, by insulting her, and by abandoning her bed for that of the slave Lucy, rendered the petitioner's life burthensome, and her condition intolerable, so as to compel her to leave his house, and seek an asylum elsewhere: that the defendant did separate himself from the petitioner and live in adultery with the slave Lucy: and that was known to the petitioner for six months previous to filing the petition: that the petitioner always conducted herself properly as a wife and a chaste woman: and that the petitioner had not admitted the defendant to conjugal embraces since her knowledge of his adulterous intercourse with the said slave Lucy.

Upon the trial, in order to prove that the defendant was living in adultery with his own slave named Lucy, the plaintiff offered evidence, that the defendant had a female slave, named Lucy, and that she had a child; and also of acts of familiarity on the part of the defendant with the said Lucy, and that she acted as a sort of manager of his house: and furthermore, that, in conversations respecting this suit, the defendant said, that he would spend every thing he had in defending it, except the said Lucy and his child; and

that, in a conversation between a brother of the petitioner and the defendant about a reconciliation between the parties, the former said to the latter, if he would sell Lucy he did not know what the petitioner might do as to living with him again, and that the defendant replied thereto, that he would part with all the property he had before he would with the said Lucy and his child, and that the petitioner might stay where she was. Objection was made to the admissibility of the defendant's declarations, but, as it was not suggested, that those declarations were made by collusion, the Court allowed them to go to the jury. There was a decree for a divorce *a vinculo matrimonii*, and for the costs against the defendant: and an enquiry was directed as to the settlement it would be proper to make on the petitioner; from all which the husband was allowed an appeal.

Strange, for the plaintiff, submitted the following authourities:

Greenleaf's Ev., Sec. 108. 2 *Phil. Ev.,* Hill & Cowan's notes 29, note 298 to page 156. *Loveden* v. *Loveden,* 2 Hagg. Con. Rep. 1.

W. H. Haywood, for the defendant.

RUFFIN, C.[hief] J.[ustice] The divorce act requires all the material facts charged to be submitted to a jury, upon whose verdict and not otherwise, the Court is to decree. It excludes, by necessary implication, from the consideration of the jury, admissions in the pleadings, and, consequently, any made orally on the trial. The purpose is to prevent collusion. That reason extends also to confessions in *pais*, when relied on to found a decree for divorce; for if they could be received, it would obviously defeat the requirement, that the facts shall be found by a jury, independent of their admission in the pleadings. It is not doubted, that, under circumstances, what a party says may, as well as his acts, be presumptive evidence of adultery. Thus letters written in the course of an intrigue, attentions paid and received, or terms of endearment used between the pair to whom guilt is imputed, assignations for private meetings, are admissible as being in their nature overt acts of criminal conversation. So, if a man and woman live together and act and speak upon the familiar terms of cohabitation, and, if the woman have a child, the man habitually treats and speaks of it as his child, that also would be evidence. But the acknowledging of the child is not received by itself as a confession merely, that he is the father, but as one incident among many connected with the intercourse of man and woman, and giving a criminal character to it, judging from the ordinary *indicia*, in the open conduct of men, of their secret acts. It is in the nature of an overt act, which tends to show the private habits of the man and woman. But that is very different from the mere declaration of this defendant to strangers on two different occasions, that the child was his, without connecting them with any conduct of the defendant towards the child. They seem to be nothing more than naked confessions of a fact, from which adultery is inferred, and, as such, were not competent. But it is said, there was no suggestion, that these declarations

were made collusively; and thence, that it is to be considered, the Court had no right to infer it. It is to be remembered, however, that supposing the collusion, it will certainly not be suggested by either party, and there is no one else to make the suggestion or establish the truth. The question, therefore, cannot turn on that, but it turns on this: that there is danger of collusion. Therefore, in order to guard against it, it is the office of the Judge himself to exclude such evidence, though neither party objects to it, but both should desire it to be received. The public is concerned, that divorces should not be improperly decreed; and this rule in particular is intended to protect the public morals, and promote the public policy, rather than to guard against the effects of perjury on the party. For this reason, a *venire de novo* would be awarded, if there were nothing more in the case.

The Court, however, is of opinion that a sufficient case does not appear in the record to authorize a divorce *a vinculo matrimonii*, which is that granted and the only one prayed for. The jury, indeed, found that the defendant separated himself from his wife and lived in adultery with his slave; and, if there were any corresponding allegation in the libel, there would be a case to render the decree right. But we think there is no such allegation. There is such a want of precision as to the dates and order of events charged, that one cannot say exactly, how far the allegations were meant to extend. The only periods given are those of 1836 for the marriage, and August 1844, for the separation of the petitioner from her husband and going to live with her brother. Everything, stated in the libel, is stated as having occurred between those periods. There is no separation of the parties alleged until that in 1844, when the petitioner left her husband's house, and there is no allegation of any adultery by him after that event. As far as we can understand the petition, it states that between the periods mentioned, the parties lived together on the husband's plantation, and for many years lived there happily: that he became, at some time, intemperate, and then was harsh, insulting and cruel to the wife—at times beating her: that occasionally, for a while, and, afterwards, for weeks, he absented himself from his wife's bed at night, and, as she suspected for some time, and afterwards ascertained, he spent those nights in bed with a negro woman he had on the same plantation: that he did himself, and allowed that woman to treat his wife with contempt, depriving her of all authority as mistress of the house, and conferring it on the negro: that, afterwards, instead of going to the house of the black woman, he brought her to his own house, and frequently made her and the wife sleep in the same bed with him, and in that situation he had carnal knowledge of the negro: that at other times the husband would not allow the wife to sleep in the house, but turned her out and locked the door against her and kept her out all night: that he at some times went away, carrying the keys and leaving her without food for several days together: and, finally, that she never admitted him to conjugal embraces after knowledge of his adultery, and abandoned his house in August 1844. Now, upon those

allegations, and upon such parts of the finding of the jury, as are consistent with them, the wife would be entitled to a decree for separation and alimony. The grossness of his debaucheries, and the cruelty and indignity, with which he treated his wife, made her condition with him intolerable and authorized her to escape from his society and control. In such cases the third section of the act allows a divorce a *mensa et thoro* to be granted, so as to protect the wife from the efforts of the husband to force her to return. But those are not sufficient causes for a divorce from the bonds of matrimony, under the second section. That does not authorize such a divorce for cruelty, nor for every act of adultery, nor even for habitual adultery, provided the parties continue to live together. On the contrary, the words are, that when "either party has separated him or herself from the other and is living in adultery," the injured person may be divorced a *vinculo*. In addition, the eighth section enacts, that if the party complaining admitted the other either to conjugal embraces or society, after knowledge of the criminal fact, it shall be a bar to a suit for divorce for cause of adultery. Now, in the first place, it is certain, upon the face of the libel, that the wife continued to live with the husband, not only after she knew such circumstances, as created the most violent presumption of his guilt, but after the actual knowledge of it by being present and in the same bed at the fact. There is no statement of any act of adultery, which we can say or suppose was posterior to those, to which the wife was thus privy. As they took place before the separation and she was privy to them, a divorce *a vinculo* cannot be founded on them by themselves. We are far, however, from thinking those defaults of the husband purged by the conduct of his wife. On the contrary she fully accounts for her finally leaving his house, and divested that act of the appearance of fault on her part. After such a separation, forced on her by the debasing depravity, violence and other outrages of the husband, she might well insist on any supervening criminality on his part. For, so far from being precluded from making complaint of the repetition of the fault, the guilt of the repetition, after such forbearance—not connivance—on the part of the wife, would be aggravated beyond that of the first fault. We shall hold, therefore, that she might insist on adultery with this slave, supervening the separation thus forced on her. From the evidence respecting the child, about whom the petition would hardly have been silent, if it had been born when it was filed, and from the findings of the jury, it may be presumed, that in fact the criminal and disgraceful connexion between this man and his negro woman did continue after the petitioner left him. If so, it is unfortunate that it should have been omitted in framing the petition. That it is omitted, is quite clear; for, the petition gives no account of the husband's life after the day the wife left him, excepting only that he had not subsequently been admitted by her into conjugal embraces. The finding of the jury, therefore, that the husband separated himself from his wife and is living or afterwards lived in adultery, and that she never admit-

ted him into conjugal embraces after her knowledge of that adultery, can have no influence on the decree, because it is incompatible with the petition, or, at least, is without any allegation in the petition of such supervening adultery, to authorize it. That the existence of such adultery in fact is indispensable, is clear from the words of the act "is living in adultery" after the separation. But it is equally clear from the reason of the thing. For, the law does not mean to dissolve the bonds of matrimony and exclude one of the parties from marriage, until there is no just ground to hope for a reconciliation. For that reason a divorce of that kind is denied, when the parties give such evidence of the probability of reconciliation, as to continue to live together. And even when there is a separation, if the offending party should reform forthwith and lead a pure life afterwards, the law does not look upon it as hopeless, that reconciliation may in time follow the reformation. It may not be a case, indeed, in which the law will permit the husband to insist on a restoration of the conjugal rights of society and cohabitation, by compelling the wife's return. But, on the other hand, it is not a case in which it is past hope, that the wife may not, upon the strength of ancient affections, and a sense of duty and interest, be willing of herself, at some time, to partake of the society and share in the fate of her reformed husband; and, until that be past hope, or, at least, a continuing impurity of life, after separation, so far impairs the hope of reformation as to leave no just expectation of it, the law will not cut off the parties from the liberty of uniting. In the present case, there is nothing in the petition to shew, that the husband and his former paramour have ever seen each other since the day the wife left the premises. Consequently, the decree was erroneous, and the petition ought to have been dismissed, notwithstanding the verdict; which will be certified accordingly.

Per Curiam. Ordered to be certified accordingly.

---

88. Rose Describes Being Forced To Live with Rufus

While planters of the Old South were often charged by abolitionists with being engaged in commercial breeding of slaves, evidence of this outrage is elusive and inconclusive. There were many economic and social forces at work in the great transfer of population, black and white, to the Southwest, and that planters offered young blacks for sale in the East who promptly turned up in the slave markets of the West does not of itself prove that the conception of those children was planned with their sale in mind. And yet a slave child assumed a commercial value early in life, and most planters were enthusiastic about "good breeders" among their slave women. They also took pains to see that the slave children of such women had a chance of growing up in health. Hence the only safe conclusion at this time is that most of the planters encouraged unions among their slaves. The extent of the "encouragement" was sometimes hard to measure, but in the following case of Rose, a slave woman born in Bell County, Texas, the master made his wish inescapably plain, not just through the reward system of clothing and favors of "time off," but by setting the intended couple to housekeeping in the same cabin.

What is especially interesting is that Rose was less hostile to her owner for his action than she might otherwise have been, for the reason that her master had bought her along with her two parents at a slave sale, at a moment when Rose had good reason to believe they might be separated forever. Although never able to forget what Master Hawkins did, Rose

Source: Manuscript Slave Narrative Collection, Federal Writers' Project (Washington, D.C.: Library of Congress, ca. 1930), Texas Narratives, pt. 4, pp. 174–78.

believed he did it from "no meanness." When Rose was ninety years old, she made her report to an interviewer from the Federal Writers' Project.

The value of such narratives to the historical researcher must be measured not only in terms of the age of the narrator, but by the skill of the interviewer as well. The authenticity of tone in the narratives is often closely related to the attitude of the person asking the questions; and those questioners, more often white than black, who received the plainest answers, were those who cultivated the trust of the narrator.

"What I say am de facts. If I's one day old, I's way over 90, and I's born in Bell County, right here in Texas, and am owned by Massa William Black. He owns mammy and pappy, too. Massa Black has a big plantation but he has more niggers dan he need for work on dat place, 'cause he am a nigger trader. He trade and buy and sell all de time.

"Massa Black am awful cruel and he whip de cullud folks and works 'em hard and feed dem poorly. We'uns have for rations de cornmeal and milk and 'lasses and some beans and peas and meat once a week. We'uns have to work in de field every day from daylight till dark and on Sunday we'uns do us washin'. Church? Shucks, we'uns don't know what dat mean.

"I has de correct mem'randum of when de war start. Massa Black sold we'uns right den. Mammy and pappy powerful glad to git sold, and dey and I is put on de block with 'bout ten other niggers. When we'uns gits te de tradin' block, dere lots of white folks dere what come to look us over. One man shows de intres' in pappy. Him named Hawkins. He talk to pappy and pappy talk to him and say, 'Dem my woman and chiles. Please buy all of us and have mercy on we'uns.' Massa Hawkins say, 'Dat gal am a likely look-in' nigger, she am portly and strong, but three am more dan I wants, I guesses.'

"De sale start and 'fore long pappy a put on de block. Massa Hawkins wins de bid for pappy and when mammy am put on de block, he wins de bid for her. Den dere am three or four other niggers sold befo' my time comes. Den massa Black calls me to de block and de auction man say, 'What am I offer for dis portly, strong young wench. She's never been 'bused and will make de good breeder.'

"I wants to hear Massa Hawkins bid, but him say nothin'. Two other men am biddin' 'gainst each other and I sho' has de worryment. Dere am tears comin' down my cheeks 'cause I's bein' sold to some man dat would make sep'ration from my mammy. One man bids $500 and de auction man ask, 'Do I hear more? She am gwine at $500.00.' Den someone say, $525.00 and de auction man say, 'She am sold for $525.00 to Massa Hawkins.' Am I glad and 'cited! Why, I's quiverin' all over.

"Massa Hawkins takes we'uns to his place and it am a nice plantation. Lots better am dat place dan Massa Black's. Dere is 'bout 50 niggers what is growed and lots of chillen. De first thing massa de when we'uns gits home am give we'uns rations and a cabin. You mus' believe dis nigger when I says dem rations a feast for us. Dere plenty meat and tea and coffee and white flour. I's never tasted white flour and coffee and mammy fix some biscuits and coffee. Well, de biscuits was yum, yum, yum to me, but de coffee I doesn't like.

"De quarters am purty good. Dere am twelve cabins all made from logs and a table and some benches and bunks for sleepin' and a fireplace for cookin' and de heat. Dere am no floor, jus' de ground.

"Massa Hawkins am good to he niggers and not force 'em work too hard. Dere am as much diff'ence 'tween him and old Massa Black in de way of treatment as 'twixt de Lawd and de devil. Massa Hawkins 'lows he niggers have reason'ble parties and go fishin', but we'uns am never tooken to church and has no books for larnin'. Dere am no edumcation for de niggers.

"Dere am one thing Massa Hawkins does to me what I can't shunt from my mind. I knows he don't do it for meanness, but I allus holds it 'gainst him. What he done am force me to live with dat nigger, Rufus, 'gainst my wants.

"After I been at he place 'bout a year, de massa come to me and say, 'You gwine live with Rufus in dat cabin over yonder. Go fix it for livin'.' I's 'bout sixteen year old and has no larnin', and I's jus' igno'mus chile. I's thought dat him mean for me to tend de cabin for Rufus and some other niggers. Well, dat am start de pestigation for me.

"I's took charge of de cabin after work am done and fixes supper. Now,

I don't like dat Rufus, 'cause he a bully. He am big and 'cause he so, he think everybody do what him say. We'uns has supper, den I goes here and dere talkin', till I's ready for sleep and den I gits in de bunk. After I's in, dat nigger come and crawl in de bunk with me 'fore I knows it. I says, 'What you means, you fool nigger?' He say for me to hush de mouth. 'Dis am my bunk, too,' he say.

" 'You's teched in de head. Git out,' I's told him, and I puts de feet 'gainst him and give him a shove and out he go on de floor 'fore he know what I's doin'. Dat nigger jump up and he mad. He look like de wild bear. He starts for de bunk and I jumps quick for de poker. It am 'bout three feet long and when he comes at me I lets him have it over de head. Did dat nigger stop in he tracks? I's say he did. He looks at me steady for a minute and you's could tell he thinkin' hard. Den he go and set on de bench and say, 'Jus wait. You thinks it am smart, but you's am foolish in de head. Dey's gwine larn you somethin'.'

" 'Hush yous big mouth and stay 'way from dis nigger, dat all I wants,' I say, and jus' sets and hold dat poker in de hand. He jus' sets, lookin' like de bull. Dere we'uns sets and sets for 'bout an hour and den he go out and I bars de door.

"De nex' day I goes to de missy and tells her what Rufus wants and missy say dat am de massa's wishes. She say, 'Yous am de portly gal and Rufus am de portly man. De massa wants you-uns fer to bring forth portly chillen.'

"I's thinkin' 'bout what de missy say, but say to myse'f, 'I's not gwine live with dat Rufus.' Dat night when him come in de cabin, I grabs de poker and sits on de bench and says, 'Git 'way from me, nigger, 'fore I busts yous brains out and stomp on dem.' He say nothin' and git out.

"De nex' day de massa call me and tell me, 'Woman, I's pay big money for you and I's done dat for de cause I wants yous to raise me chillens. I's put yous to live with Rufus for dat purpose. Now, if you doesn't want whippin' at de stake, yous do what I wants.'

"I thinks 'bout massa buyin' me offen de block and savin' me from bein' sep'rated from my folks and 'bout bein' whipped at de stake. Dere it am. What am I's to do? So I 'cides to do as de massa wish and so I yields.

"When we'uns am given freedom, Massa Hawkins tells us we can stay and work for wages or share crop de land. Some stays and some goes. My folks and me stays. We works de land on shares for three years, den moved to other land near by. I stays with my folks till they dies.

"If my mem'randum am correct, it am 'bout thirty year since I come to Fort Worth. Here I cooks for white folks till I goes blind 'bout ten year ago.

"I never marries, 'cause one 'sperience am 'nough for dis nigger. After what I does for de massa, I's never wants no truck with any man. De Lawd forgive dis cullud woman, but he have to 'scuse me and look for some others for to 'plenish de earth.

---

89. White Women Fear Violence from Slaves

Two important slavery-related anxieties of white women were seldom referred to candidly in print. The implicit competition of slave women for the love of the whites' sweethearts and husbands was one of them; the other was the ever-present possibility of personal violence to themselves or their children. Mary Boykin Chesnut, in her matchless diary covering the turbulent years of the Civil War, referred freely and with much bitterness to the first problem, and the murder of an aged relative by her slaves caused Mrs. Chesnut to explore in detail the effects of these fears on the women she knew well.

The significant point with Mary Boykin Chesnut is that "Cousin Mary

Source: Mary Boykin Chesnut, A Diary from Dixie, ed. Ben Ames Williams (Boston: Houghton Mifflin, 1949), pp. 138–51.

Witherspoon" was known far and wide as an indulgent and kind mistress, and this seemed to indicate that decent behavior toward one's chattels was no assurance of safety. Hence it is not by chance that it is at this point in her diary that Mary Chesnut falls into a superb character sketch of her own mother-in-law, the aging wife of Col. James Chesnut, and the very ideal of the competent plantation wife who kept her servants busy and happy—or tried to. The virtues of this great lady, who didn't believe in "fallen women" or concern herself overmuch about the sexual behavior of the slave women, are very sorely tried by the murder of Cousin Betsey, and her reaction bears a close examination.

[September 19, 1861]—A painful piece of news came to us yesterday. Our cousin, Mrs. Witherspoon of Society Hill, was found dead in her bed. She was quite well the night before. Killed, people say, by family troubles; by contentions, wrangling, ill blood among those nearest and dearest to her. She was a proud and high-strung woman, of a warm and tender heart, truth and uprightness itself. Few persons have ever been more loved and looked up to. A very handsome old lady, of fine presence, dignified and commanding. "Killed by family troubles!" . . .

September 21st.—Last night when the mail came in, I was seated near the lamp. Mr. Chesnut, lying on a sofa at a little distance, called out to me: "Look at my letters and tell me whom they are from?" I began to read one of them aloud. It was from Mary Witherspoon, and I broke down; horror and amazement was too much for me. Poor cousin Betsey Witherspoon was murdered! She did not die peacefully in her bed, as we supposed, but was murdered by her own people, her Negroes. I remember when Dr. Keith was

murdered by his Negroes, Mr. Miles met me and told me the dreadful story. "Very awkward indeed, this sort of thing. There goes Keith in the House always declaiming about the 'Benificent Institution'—How now?" Horrible beyond words! Her household Negroes were so insolent, so pampered, and insubordinate. She lived alone. She knew, she said, that none of her children would have the patience she had with these people who had been indulged and spoiled by her until they were like spoiled children, simply intolerable. Mr. Chesnut and David Williams have gone over at once. . . .

September 24th.—The men who went to Society Hill (the Witherspoon home) have come home again with nothing very definite. William and Cousin Betsey's old maid, Rhody, are in jail; strong suspicion but as yet no proof of their guilt. The neighborhood is in a ferment. Evans and Wallace say these Negroes ought to be burnt. Lynching proposed! But it is all idle talk. They will be tried as the law directs, and not otherwise. John Witherspoon will not allow anything wrong or violent to be done. He has a detective there from Charleston.

Hitherto I have never thought of being afraid of Negroes. I had never injured any of them; why should they want to hurt me? Two thirds of my religion consists in trying to be good to Negroes, because they are so in our power, and it would be so easy to be the other thing. Somehow today I feel that the ground is cut away from under my feet. Why should they treat me any better than they have done Cousin Betsey Witherspoon?

Kate and I sat up late and talked it all over. Mrs. Witherspoon was a saint on this earth, and this is her reward. Kate's maid Betsey came in—a strong-built, mulatto woman—dragging in a mattress. "Missis, I have brought my bed to sleep in your room while Mars' David is at Society Hill. You ought not to stay in a room by yourself these times." She went off for more bed gear. "For the life of me," said Kate gravely, "I cannot make up my mind. Does she mean to take care of me, or to murder me?" I do not think Betsey heard, but when she came back she said: "Missis, as I have a soul to be saved, I will keep you safe. I will guard you." We know Betsey well, but has she soul enough to swear by? She is a great stout, jolly, irresponsible, unreliable, pleasant-tempered, bad-behaved woman, with ever so many good points. Among others, she is so clever she can do anything, and she never loses her temper; but she has no moral sense whatever.

That night, Kate came into my room. She could not sleep. The thought of those black hands strangling and smothering Mrs. Witherspoon's grey head under the counterpane haunted her; we sat up and talked the long night through. . . .

Went over just now to have a talk with that optimist, my mother-in-law. Blessed are the pure in mind, for they shall see God. Her mind certainly is free from evil thoughts. Someone says, the most unhappy person is the one who has bad thoughts. She ought to be happy. She thinks no evil. And yet, she is the cleverest woman I know. She began to ask me something of Charlotte Temple (I call her this to keep back her true name). "Has she ever had any more children:" "She has one more." "Is she married?" "No." "Is she a bad girl, really?" "Yes." "Oh! Don't say that. Poor thing! Maybe after all she is not really bad, only to be pitied!" I gave it up. I felt like a fool. Here was one thing I had made sure of as a fixed fact. In this world, an unmarried girl with two children was, necessarily, not a good woman. If that can be waved aside, I give up, in utter confusion of mind. Ever since she came here sixty or seventy years ago, as a bride from Philadelphia, Mrs. Chesnut has been trying to make it up to the Negroes for being slaves. Seventeen ninety-six, I think, was the year of her marriage. Today someone asked her about it, when she was describing Mrs. Washington's drawing-room to us. Through her friendship for Nelly Custis, and living very near, and stiff, stern old Martha Washington not liking to have her coach horses taken out for trifles, and Mrs. Cox letting Nelly Custis and Mary Cox have the carriage at their pleasure, Mrs. Chesnut was a great deal thrown with the Washington household. Now she eloquently related for the hundredth time all this. "How came you to leave that pleasant Philadelphia and all its comforts for this half civilized Up-Country and all the horrors of slavery?" "Did you not know that my father owned slaves in Philadelphia? In his will he left me several of them." In the Quaker City, and in the lifetime of a living woman now present, there were slave holders. It is hard to believe. Time works its wonders like enchantment. So quickly we forget.

Grandma is so awfully clever, and you can't make her think any harm of anybody. She is a resolute optimist. A caller, speaking of "Charlotte Temple," said it was better for the world to call a fallen woman by her proper name. It might be unchristian and nasty; but it was better, just as it was better for the world to hang a murderer, however unpleasant for the individual. She said she did not believe in seduced women. They knew the consequences. To smile amiably, and with a lovely face and a sweet voice to call evil good, would hardly do for everybody to try, if there was to be any distinction made between right and wrong.

Mrs. Chesnut has a greediness of books such as I never saw in anyone else. Reading is the real occupation and solace of her life. In the soft luxurious life she leads, she denies herself nothing that she wants. In her well-regulated character she could not want anything that she ought not to have. Economy is one of her cherished virtues, and strange to say she never buys a book, or has been known to take a magazine or periodical; she has them all. They gravitate toward her, they

flow into her room. Everybody is proud to send, or lend, any book they have compassed by any means, fair or foul. Other members of the family who care nothing whatever for them buy the books and she reads them.

She spends hours every day cutting out baby clothes for the Negro babies. This department is under her supervision. She puts little bundles of things to be made in everybody's work basket and calls it her sewing society. She is always ready with an ample wardrobe for every newcomer. Then the mothers bring their children for her to prescribe and look after whenever they are ailing. She is not at all nervous. She takes a baby and lances its gums quite coolly and scientifically. She dresses all hurts, bandages all wounds. These people are simply devoted to her, proving they can be grateful enough when you give them anything to be grateful for. Two women always sleep in her room in case she should be ill, or need any attention during the night; and two others sleep in the next room—to relieve guard, so to speak. When it is cold, she changes her night clothes. Before these women give her the second dress, they iron every garment to make sure that it is warm and dry enough. For this purpose, smoothing irons are always before the fire, and the fire is never allowed to go down while it is cool enough for the family to remain at Mulberry. During the summer at Sandy Hill it is exactly the same, except that then she gets up and changes everything because it is so warm! It amounts to this, these old people find it hard to invent ways of passing the time, and they have such a quantity of idle Negroes about them that some occupation for them must be found. In the meantime, her standing employment is reading, and her husband is driving out with a pair of spanking thoroughbred bays, which have been trained to trot as slowly as a trot can be managed. . . .

[October 7] And now comes back on us that bloody story that haunts me night and day, Mrs. Witherspoon's murder. The man William, who was the master spirit of the gang, once ran away and was brought back from somewhere west; and then his master and himself had a reconciliation and the master henceforth made a pet of him. The night preceding the murder, John Witherspoon went over to his mother's to tell her of some of William's and Rhody's misdeeds. While their mistress was away from home, they had given a ball fifteen miles away from Society Hill. To that place they had taken their mistress's china, silver, house linen, etc. After his conversation with his mother, as he rode out of the gate, he shook his whip at William and said: "Tomorrow I mean to come here and give every one of you a thrashing." That night Mrs. Witherspoon was talking it all over with her grandson, a half-grown boy who lived with her and slept indeed in a room opening into hers. "I do not intend John to punish these Negroes. It is too late to begin discipline now. I have indulged them past bearing. They all say I ought to have tried to control them, that it is all my fault." Mrs. Edwards, who was a sister of Mrs. Witherspoon, sometime ago was found dead in her bed. It is thought this suggested their plan of action to the Negroes. What more

likely than she should die as her sister had done! When John went off, William said: "Listen to me and there will be no punishment here tomorrow." They made their plan, and then all of them went to sleep, William remaining awake to stir up the others at the proper hour.

What first attracted the attention of the family to the truth about her death was the appearance of black and blue spots about the face and neck of the body of their mother. Then someone, in moving the candle from the table at her bedside, found blood upon their fingers. Looking at the candlestick, they saw the print of a bloody hand which had held it. There was an empty bed in the entry, temporarily there for some purpose, and as they were preparing to lay her out, someone took up the counterpane from this bed to throw over her. On the under side of it, again, bloody fingers. Now they were fairly aroused. Rhody was helping Mary Witherspoon, a little apart from the rest. Mary cried: "I wish they would not say such horrid things. Poor soul, she died in peace with all the world. It is bad enough to find her dead, but nobody ever touched a hair of her head. To think any mortal could murder her. Never! I will not believe it!" To Mary's amazement, Rhody drew near her and, looking strangely in her eyes, she said: "Miss Mary, you stick to dat! You stick to dat!" Mary thrilled all over with suspicion nnd dread.

There was a trunk in Mrs. Witherspoon's closet where she kept money and a complete outfit ready for travelling at any moment; among other things, some new and very fine night gowns. One of her daughters noticed that her mother must have opened that trunk, for she was wearing one of those night gowns. They then looked into the closet and found the trunk unlocked and all the gold gone. The daughters knew the number of gold pieces she always kept under lock and key in that trunk. Now they began to scent mischief and foul play in earnest, and they sent for the detective.

The dectective dropped in from the skies quite unexpectedly. He saw that one of the young understrappers of the gang looked frightened and uncomfortable. This one he fastened upon, and got up quite an intimacy with him; and finally, he told this boy that he knew all about it, that William had confessed privately to him to save himself and hang the others. But he said he had taken a fancy to this boy, and if he would confess everything, he would take him as State's evidence instead of William. The young man fell in the trap laid for him and told every particular from beginning to end. Then they were all put in jail, the youth who had confessed among them, as he did not wish them to know of his treachery to them.

This was his story. After John went away that night, Rhody and William made a great fuss. They were furious at Mars' John threatening them after all these years. William said: "Mars' John more than apt to do what he say he will do, but you all follow what I say and he'll have something else to think of beside stealing and breaking glass and china. If old Marster was alive now, what would he say to talk of whipping us!" Rhody always kept the key to the house to let herself in every morning, so they arranged to go in at

twelve, and then William watched and the others slept the sleep of the righteous. Before that however, they had a "real fine supper and a heap of laughing at the way dey'd all look tomorrow." They smothered her with a counterpane from a bed in the entry. They had no trouble the first time, because they found her asleep and "done it all 'fore she waked." But after Rhody took her keys and went into the trunk and got a clean night gown—for they had spoiled the one she had on—and fixed everything, candle, medicine and all, she came to! Then she begged them hard for life. She asked them what she had ever done that they should want to kill her? She promised them before God never to tell on them. Nobody should ever know! But Rhody stopped her mouth with the counterpane, and William held her head and hands down, and the other two sat on her legs. Rhody had a thrifty mind and wished to save the sheets and night gown, so she did not destroy them. They were found behind her mantelpiece. There the money was also, all in a hole made among the bricks behind the wooden mantelpiece. A grandson of Rhody's slept in her house. Him she locked up in his room. She did not want him to know anything of this fearful night.

That innocent old lady and her grey hair moved them not a jot. Fancy how we feel. I am sure I will never sleep again without this nightmare of horror haunting me.

Mrs. Chesnut, who is their good angel, is and has always been afraid of Negroes. In her mind, the San Domingo stories were indelibly printed on her mind. She shows her dread now by treating every one as if they were a black Prince Albert or Queen Victoria. We were beginning to forget Mrs. Cunningham, the only other woman we ever heard of who was murdered by her Negroes. Poor cousin Betsey was goodness itself. After years of freedom and indulgence and tender kindness, it was an awful mistake to threaten them like children. It was only threats. Everybody knew she would never do anything. Mr. Cunningham had been an old bachelor, and the Negroes had it all their own way till he married. Then they hated her. They took her from her room, just over one in which her son-in-law and her daughter slept. They smothered her, dressed her, and carried her out—all without the slightest noise—and hung her by the neck to an apple tree, as if she had committed suicide. If they want to kill us, they can do it when they please, they are noiseless as panthers. They were discovered because, dressing her in the dark, her tippet was put on hindpart before, and she was supposed to have walked out and hung herself in a pair of brand new shoes whose soles obviously had never touched the ground.

We ought to be grateful that anyone of us is alive, but nobody is afraid of their own Negroes. I find everyone, like myself, ready to trust their own yard. I would go down on the plantation tomorrow and stay there even if there were no white person in twenty miles. My Molly and all the rest I believe would keep me as safe as I should be in the Tower of London.

Romeo was the Negro who first confessed to the detective; then Rhody, after she found they had discovered the money and sheets where she had hidden them. William and Silvie still deny all complicity in the plot or the execution of it.

John Williams has a bride! Has she not married South at a fine time? She is terrified, and who can blame her? It will be a miracle if she don't bolt altogether. The very name of Society Hill is enough to scare the life out of anyone. To expect the bride to come back, simply because her husband was here, and with details of that black tragedy ringing in her ears; indeed it was too much. I dare say she would as soon take up her abode in Sodom or Gomorrah.

It was Rhody who pointed out the blood on the counterpane. They suppose she saw it, knew they would see it, and did it to avert suspicion from herself. . . .

October 18th.—Mrs. Witherspoon's death has clearly driven us all wild. Mrs. Chesnut, although she talks admirably well and is a wonderfully clever woman, bored me by incessantly dwelling upon the transcendant virtues of her colored household, in full hearing of the innumerable Negro women who literally swarm over this house. She takes her meals in her own rooms, but today came in while we were at dinner. "I warn you, don't touch that soup! It is bitter. There is something wrong about it!" The family answered her pleasantly, but continued calmly to eat their soup. The men who waited at table looked on without change of face. Kate whispered: "It is cousin Betsey's fate. She is watching every trifle, and is terrified." My husband gave his mother his arm, and she went quietly back to her room. Afterwards Kate said to me: "She is afraid they will poison us. . . ."

90. A Scientist Assesses Miscegenation in the South

Defenders of Southern institutions in the ante-bellum period freely claimed a special purity in domestic relations, on grounds that the region was safely insulated from the waves of change that affected most of America in the 1830s. Hence it was with embarrassment that they considered the evidences of interracial sex revealed by the increase of the mulatto population. Interracial marriage was forbidden, and children of black mothers were slaves, after the condition of their mothers.

Sir Charles Lyell, who visited the South during the last decade of slavery, was a geologist of international renown, and something of a moralist as well. Although he knew that the availability of exploitable females in the enslaved population had an unhappy effect on the domestic life of whites, he found himself unable to empathize with the blacks victimized by the system. His estimation that interracial sex in rural districts was not widespread is substantiated by other witnesses, but if he had visited Southern cities with the same question in mind, he might have reached different conclusions. In any case, Lyell's comparison of sexual exploitation on the plantations with exploitation of the working poor women of England gives an advantage to the plantation South that many English visitors would not have accepted. It is safe to say that wherever a subordinate class or race exists, sexual exploitation exists as well. Sir Charles's comments in the following excerpt were based on a visit to a famous plantation in Glynn County, Georgia.

Some of the planters in Glynn County have of late permitted the distribution of Bibles among their slaves, and it was curious to remark that they who were unable to read were as anxious to possess them as those who could. Besides Christianizing the blacks, the clergy of all sects are doing them incalculable service, by preaching continually to both races that the matrimonial tie should be held sacred, without respect to color. To the dominant race one of the most serious evils of slavery is its tendency to blight domestic hap-

Source: Sir Charles Lyell, A Second Visit to the United States of North America, 2 vols. (New York: Harper & Bros., 1849), 1:271–73.

piness; and the anxiety of parents for their sons, and a constant fear of their licentious intercourse with slaves, is painfully great. We know but too much of this evil in free countries, wherever there is a vast distance between the rich and poor, giving a power to wealth which insures a frightful amount of prostitution. Here it is accompanied with a publicity which is keenly felt as a disgrace by the more refined of the white women. The female slave is proud of her connection with a white man, and thinks it an honor to have a mulatto child, hoping that it will be better provided for than a black child. Yet the mixed offspring is not very numerous. The mulattoes alone represent nearly all the illicit intercourse between the white man and negro of the living generation. I am told that they do not constitute more than two and a half per cent. of the whole population. If the statistics of the illegitimate children of the whites born here could be compared with those in Great Britain, it might lead to conclusions by no means favorable to the free country. Here there is no possibility of concealment, the color of the child stamps upon him the mark of bastardy, and transmits it to great-grand-children born in lawful wedlock; whereas if, in Europe, there was some mark or indelible stain betraying all the delinquencies and frailties, not only of parents, but of ancestors for three or four generations back, what unexpected disclosures should we not witness!

There are scarcely any instances of mulattoes born of a black father and a white mother. The colored women who become the mistresses of the white men are neither rendered miserable nor degraded, as are the white women who are seduced in Europe, and who are usually abandoned in the end, and left to be the victims of want and disease. In the northern states of America there is so little profligacy of this kind, that their philanthropists may perhaps be usefully occupied in considering how the mischief may be alleviated south of the Potomac; but in Great Britain there is so much need of reform at home, that the whole thoughts and energies of the rich ought to be concentrated in such schemes of improvement as may enable us to set an example of a higher moral standard to the slave-owning aristocracy of the Union.

On one of the estates in this part of Georgia, there is a mulatto mother who has nine children by a full black, and the difference of shade between them and herself is scarcely perceptible. If the white blood usually predominates in this way in the second generation, as I am told is the case, amalgamation would proceed very rapidly, if marriages between the races were once legalized; for we see in England that black men can persuade very respectable white women to marrry them, when all idea of the illegality and degradation of such unions is foreign to their thoughts.

Among the obstacles which the Christian missionaries encounter here when they teach the virtue of chastity, I must not omit to mention the loose code of morality which the Africans have inherited from their parents. My wife made the acquaintance of a lady in Alabama, who had brought up with great care a colored girl, who grew up modest and well-behaved, till at length she became the mother of a mulatto child. The mistress reproached her very severely for her misconduct, and the girl at first took the rebuke much to heart; but having gone home one day to visit her mother, a native African, she returned, saying, that her parent had assured her she had done nothing wrong, and had no reason to feel ashamed. When we are estimating, therefore, the amount of progress made by the American negroes since they left their native country, we ought always to bear in mind from how low a condition, both morally and intellectually considered, they have had to mount up.

91. General Cocke Enforces Matrimony

John Hartwell Cocke (1780–1866) was the master of Bremo Bluff plantation in central Virginia, on the banks of the James River. In many respects he was a late survivor of the Revolutionary generation. He detested slavery as an affront to natural law, and as inconsistent with the Declaration of Independence. But he was also a man much troubled by slavery, and much involved in a search for God's intention concerning the institution. He believed that blacks enslaved in America were destined to return to Africa to spread the Christian religion, and it followed that a good master would prepare his slaves for that fulfillment of God's purpose. A convinced colonizationist, Cocke spent money and sent emancipated slaves to Liberia to advance the cause, often supporting the freedmen until they were established in Africa.

In time Cocke also developed a new plantation in Alabama, where his slaves were to learn the arts of self-government by managing on their own. In fact Cocke liked to think of his Alabama plantation as a school for freedom. In the winter of 1848 he visited his faraway property, gave his slaves bad marks for poor performance, and provided vivid witness to his austere, unconscious paternalism; then he took the coach for home. Considering the pitiable vulnerability of slave marriage, it ought not to be surprising that occasional "free love" communities developed. Perhaps

Source: Manuscript Diary of John Hartwell Cocke, Alderman Library, University of Virginia, Charlottesville, Va.

General Cocke's shocked reaction to this "moral depravity" is actually an indication of the regularity that he had come to expect of the home life among slaves.

[January 26, 1848]—Separated from my traveling friends at Selma. and took the stage to Greensboro on 27 at night. The next morn[in]g reached John Cockes.

A few days looking into the state of my plantation while it discovered satisfactory improve[ment] of my agricultural prospects—Buildings—Stocks etc[,] disclosed a shocking state of moral depravity among the people of the place. Two of my Foremans Daughters had bastard White children. A state of almost indiscriminate sexual intercourse among them—not a marriage since I was last there—3 yrs. ago. The venereal disease had been prevalent—And to crown this mass of corruption—My Foreman with a wife and 10 living Children was keeping a young girl on the place. While his eldest daughters were the kept mistresses (there was strong reasons to believe by his consent) of two of the young Southern Gentlemen of the vicinity—Another man hitherto regarded as next in respectability to the Foreman also with a wife and 10 Children, had had the venereal—and these two both members of the Baptist Church. Finding things in this condition it may well be supposed my hopes of elevating the character of these people to the moral standard of the Community of Liberia were deeply depressed. It took me 8 or 10 days of carefully cross examination to ascertain the extent of the depravity—the result of which was that my School for ultimate Liberian freedom,

had become a plantation Brothel headed by my Foreman.

The Second Sabbath after my arrival—I reminded them, that I had enjoined upon them long ago—the propriety and advantages of marrying among themselves but as they had not only disregarded this advice and brought disgrace upon themselves and scandal upon my plantation—I now commanded, that which I had formerly requested and advised—"that they should be married forthwith or be punished and sold"—they chose the first alternative. I allowed one week for them to make matches among themselves—but what was not agreed upon, at the expiration of that time—I should finish by my own authority—until every single man and woman were disposed of and united in marriage. The consequence was nine couple reported themselves as willing to be married forthwith. And I commenced building 4 new Rooms required to accommodate the parties—which requiring two weeks aforded time to procure and make up a dress for each bride and some articles of simple furniture for the Chambers. To give solemnity to the matter—I engaged a respectable Baptist Clergyman on a given day—when all was ready to come to our little Chapel—to preach a Sermon upon the marriage relation—and unite the Nine Couple in the holy State of Wedlock. Having completed all arrangements on Saturday the 12th March the Ceremony was performed. Having preceded it with suitable corporal punishment inflicted upon the Foreman and his brother of the Baptist Church and having rec[eived] abundant promises of amendment and confessions—I left with the hope of doing better in future.

---

92. Master Jones Writes the Mother of His Little Slave

The following letter from a Maryland slave-owner to the mother of a little girl named Jenny, who is his property, illustrates how complicated personal attachments could become in a slaveholding family. The master is vacillating over whether to send Jenny to live with her mother, and in doing so reveals a fine mixture of personal attachment to Jenny, and a dash of self-interest as well. We only know of Jenny's attachment to her master through Master Jones, but if he is reporting to the mother honestly, we have a picture of how children became all the more confused in their loyalties when the master was benevolent.

Mr. Jones's reference to why he sold the mother and not the child leaves much unexplained, but the language of the letter is that of a paternalist who needs must scold a wayward child for her own good, make important decisions by himself, and suggest more gratitude on her part.

T. D. Jones to Eliza.

Princess Anne Somerset Co. Md
Septr 7th. 1860.

Eliza.

About two months ago Sandy handed me a letter directed to Mr. Levin Waters from you, requesting me to let you hear from your daughter, Jenny, and expressing the hope that I will let her go to live with you. I read your letter to her. She seemed glad to hear from you, & her countenance lightened up with smile at the names of Aunt Liza & Tillie Anne (as she calls you and her sister.) But she says she does not want to go away from her master. She is a sprightly lively active girl: & has enjoyed good health, except that she has suffered for some time from three very severe boils—one on the top of her head, one over her left ear & one on the side of her neck, the last just ruptured. She is very fond of

Source: Thomas Butler Papers, Louisiana State University, Baton Rouge, La.

me & is a considerable annoyance to me for I cannot keep her off my heels in the street. & viewing her in the light of a little orphan I cannot spurn her caresses. Sandy & Sally are as well as usual: Charlotte has had a severe and dangerous attack of brain fever, but is now able to perform her duties. her child Sarah is well. As to letting Jennie go to live with you I can hardly make up my mind what to say. I would be reluctant to part with her. She is petted as you used to be. She is a watchful little spy as you used to be. She has a good disposition, is neither cross obstinate nor mischievous: She is very useful for her services in the house, for going on errands, and for nursing: & I should miss her very much. Nevertheless I know how to estimate the claims of a Mother and to appreciate the affection of a Mother for her child. A request has been made of me thro' Mr. Henry Morris to let Jennie go to you, but I have not yet come to a decision.

However I profess to be a christian & have the happy and comforting assurance that I am, by the grace of God, what I profess to be. I am governed by christian principles which impose upon me the obligation to love mercy deal justly and walk humbly. Mercy will open a listening ear to your request. Justice will prompt me to do what is right and humility constrains me to condescend to answer the communication of her who, although formerly my servant, is not, on that account, excluded from the consideration of human sympathy, altho' you make no inquiry after my welfare, were you restrained by indignation or malice because I parted with you? I think you will acknowledge that I was to you a kind & forbearing master & that you were an ungrateful servant, & I think you feel assured that if you had conducted yourself faithfully, no offer would have tempted me to part with you. Your tender & affectionate services to your afflicted former mistress, created in me an attachment for you, that nothing but your ingratitude & faithlessness could have broken. But situated as I was after the death of [my] dear beloved and still lamented wife, the only alternative presented to me was to quit housekeeping or part with you—a painful one. Up to the period of this bad event you were as fine a servant as I ever knew. I wish you well. I am glad you have got a good home & hope you will try to deserve it. Let me advise you as your former Master—as one who takes an interest in your welbeing in this world, and still greater interest for welbeing in the eternal world & above as the one who stood sponsor for you in baptism, to repent of your misdeeds—to cease to do evil & learn to do well, to live up to the precepts of the gospel, & by the faith once delivered to the saints, & daily pray to God, thro' Jesus Christ, for his good spirit to help your infirmities & to lead you in the way everlasting. Serve your heavenly Master & your present owner faithfully, and be assured that I greatly regret the occasion that resulted in the separation of you from your child. Those to whom you sent your love return their's to you. With unfeigned benevolence & charity

I am
Your former owner
T. D. Jones

93. Nicey Kinney Fondly Remembers Her Owners on a Small Plantation

Life could be hard for slaves on big estates and on farms, for the slave's well-being depended first and last on the friendly disposition of a capable master and mistress. But on small properties the master and his wife were in closer contact with the slaves, and the work, though sometimes even harder than on great plantations, was apt to be more diverse, and often master and slave shared the effort. Under these conditions, provided the owners were reasonably humane, slaves could more readily accept their social and cultural values. Such appears to have been the case with Nicey Kinney, who remembered her owners with affection, even though the work was hard.

Mrs. Kinney was another of the aged survivors of slavery whose recollections were taken down during the 1930s by writers in the Works Progress Administration (WPA) (see document 88). Nicey Kinney called "Master Gerald's" place a plantation, but the description of his operations indicates a substantial diversified farm.

A narrow path under large water oaks led through a well-kept yard where a profusion of summer flowers surrounded Nicey Kinney's two-story frame house. The porch floor and a large portion of the roof had rotted down, and even the old stone chimney at one end of the structure seemed to sag. The middle-aged mulatto woman who answered the door shook her head when asked if she was Nicey Kinney. "No, mam," she protested, "but dat's my mother and she's sick in bed. She gits mighty lonesome lyin' dar in de bed and she sho does love to talk. Us would be mighty proud if you would come in and see her."

Nicey was propped up in bed and, although the heat of the September day was oppressive, the sick woman wore a black shoulder cape over her thick flannel nightgown; heavy quilts and blankets were piled close about her thin form, and the window at the side

Source: Manuscript Slave Narrative Collection, Federal Writers' Project (Washington, D.C.: Library of Congress, ca. 1930), Georgia Narratives, pt. 3 pp. 22–31.

of her bed was tightly closed. Not a lock of her hair escaped the nightcap that enveloped her head. The daughter removed an empty food tray and announced, "Mammy, dis lady's come to see you and I 'spects you is gwine to lak her fine 'cause she wants to hear 'bout dem old days dat you loves so good to tell about." Nicey smiled. "I'se so glad you come to see me," she said, " 'cause I gits so lonesome; jus' got to stay here in dis bed, day in and day out. I'se done wore out wid all de hard wuk I'se had to do, and now I'se a aged 'oman, done played out and sufferin' wid de high blood pressur'. But I kin talk and I does love to bring back dem good old days a-fore de war."

Newspapers had been pasted on the walls of Nicey's room. In one corner an enclosed staircase was cut off from the room by a door at the head of the third step; the space underneath the stair was in use as a closet. The marble topped bureau, two double beds, a couple of small tables, and some old chairs were all of a period prior to the current century. A pot of peas was perched on a pair of "firedogs" over the coals of a wood fire in the open fireplace. On a bed of red coals a thick iron pan held a large pone of cornbread, and the tantalizing aroma of coffee drew attention to a steaming coffeepot on a trivet in one corner of the hearth. Nicey's daughter turned the bread over and said, "Missy, I jus' bet you ain't never seed nobody cookin' dis way. Us is got a stove back in de kitchen, but our somepin t'eat seems to taste better fixed dis 'way; it brings back dem old days when us was chillun and all of us was at home wid mammy." Nicey grinned. "Missy,"

she said, "Annie—dat's dis gal of mine here—laughs at de way I laks dem old ways of livin', but she's jus' as bad 'bout 'em as I is, 'specially 'bout dat sort of cookin'; somepin t'eat cooked in dat old black pot is sho good.

"Marse Gerald Sharp and his wife, Miss Annie, owned us and, Child, dey was grand folks. Deir old home was 'way up in Jackson County 'twixt Athens and Jefferson. Dat big old plantation run plumb back down to de Oconee River. Yes, mam, all dem rich river bottoms was Marse Gerald's.

"Mammy's name was Ca'line and she b'longed to Marse Gerald, but Marse Hatton David owned my daddy—his name was Phineas. De David place warn't but 'bout a mile from our plantation and daddy was 'lowed to stay wid his fambly most evvy night; he was allus wid us on Sundays. Marse Gerald didn't have no slaves but my mammy and her chillun, and he was sho mighty good to us.

"Marse Gerald had a nice four-room house wid a hall all de way through it. It even had two big old fireplaces on one chimbly. No, mam, it warn't a rock chimbly; dat chimbly was made out of home-made bricks. Marster's fambly had deir cookin' done in a open fireplace lak evvybody else for a long time and den jus' 'fore de big war he bought a stove. Yes, mam, Marse Gerald bought a cook stove and us felt plumb rich 'cause dere warn't many folks dat had stoves back in dem days.

"Mammy lived in de old kitchen close by de big house 'til dere got to be too many of us; den Marse Gerald built us a house jus' a little piece off from de big house. It was jus' a log house, but Marster had all dem cracks chinked tight wid red mud, and he even had one of dem franklin-back chimblies built to keep our little cabin nice and warm. Why, Child, ain't you never seed none of dem old chimblies? Deir backs sloped out in de middle to throw out de heat into de room and keep too much of it from gwine straight up de flue. Our beds in our cabin was corded jus' lak dem up at de big house, but us slept on straw ticks and, let me tell you, dey sho slept good atter a hard days's wuk.

"De bestest water dat ever was come from a spring right nigh our cabin and us had long-handled gourds to drink it out of. Some of dem gourds hung by de spring all de time and dere was allus one or two of 'em hangin' by de side of our old cedar waterbucket. Sho', us had a cedar bucket and it had brass hoops on it; dat was some job to keep dem hoops scrubbed wid sand to make 'em bright and shiny, and dey had to be clean and pretty all de time or mammy would git right in behind us wid a switch. Marse Gerald raised all dem long-handled gourds dat us used 'stid of de tin dippers folks has now, but dem warn't de onliest kinds of gourds he growed on his place. Dere was gourds mos' as big as water-buckets, and dey had short handles dat was bent whilst de gourds was green, so us could hang 'em on a limb of a tree in de shade to keep water cool for us when us was wukin' in de field durin' hot weather.

"I never done much field wuk 'til de war come on, 'cause Mistess was larnin' me to be a housemaid. Marse Gerald and Miss Annie never had no chillun 'cause she warn't no bearin' 'oman, but dey was both mighty fond of little folks. On Sunday mornin's mammy used to fix us all up nice and clean and take us up to de big house for Marse Gerald to play wid. Dey was good christian folks and tuk de mostest pains to larn us chillun how to live right. Marster used to 'low as how he had done paid $500 for Ca'line but he sho wouldn't sell her for no price.

"Evvything us needed was raised on dat plantation 'cept cotton. Nary a stalk of cotton was growed dar, but jus' de same our clothes was made out of cloth dat Mistess and my mammy wove out of thread us chillun spun, and Mistess tuk a heap of pains makin' up our dresses. Durin' de war evvybody had to wear homespun, but dere didn't nobody have no better or prettier dresses dan ours, 'cause Mistess knowed more'n anybody 'bout dyein' cloth. When time come to make up a batch of clothes Mistess would say, 'Ca'line holp me git up my things for dyein', 'and us would fetch dogwood bark, sumach, poison ivy, and sweetgum bark. That poison ivy made the best black of anything us ever tried, and Mistess could dye the prettiest sort of purple wid sweetgum bark. Cop'ras was used to keep de colors from fadin', and she knowed so well how to handle it dat you could wash cloth what she had dyed all day long and it wouldn't fade a speck.

"Marster was too old to go to de war, so he had to stay home and he sho seed dat us done our wuk raisin' somepin t'eat. He had us plant all our cleared ground, and I sho has done some hard wuk down in dem old bottom lands, plowin', hoein', pullin' corn and fodder, and I'se even cut cordwood and split rails. Dem was hard times and evvybody had to wuk.

"Sometimes Marse Gerald would be

away a week at a time when he went to court at Jefferson, and de very last thing he said 'fore he driv off allus was, 'Ca'line, you and de chillun take good care of Mistess.' He most allus fetched us new shoes when he come back, 'cause he never kept no shoemaker man on our place, and all our shoes was store-bought. Dey was jus' brogans wid brass toes, but us felt powerful dressed up when us got 'em on, 'specially when dey was new and de brass was bright and shiny. Dere was nine of us chillun, four boys and five gals. Us gals had plain cotton dresses made wid long sleeves and us wore big sunbonnets. What would gals say now if dey had to wear dem sort of clothes and do wuk lak what us done? Little boys didn't wear nothin' but long shirts in summertime, but come winter evvybody had good warm clothes made out of wool off of Marse Gerald's own sheep, and boys, even little tiny boys, had britches in winter.

"Did you ever see folks shear sheep, Child? Well, it was a sight in dem days. Marster would tie a sheep on de scaffold, what he had done built for dat job, and den he would have me set on de sheep's head whilst he cut off de wool. He sont it to de factory to have it carded into bats and us chillun spun de thread at home and mammy and Mistess wove it into cloth for our winter clothes. Nobody warn't fixed up better on church days dan Marster's Niggers and he was sho proud of dat.

"Us went to church wid our white folks 'cause dere warn't no colored churches dem days. None of de churches 'round our part of de country had meetin' evvy Sunday, so us went to three diffunt meetin' houses. On de fust Sunday us went to Captain Crick

Baptist church, to Sandy Crick Presbyterian church on second Sundays, and on third Sundays meetin' was at Antioch Methodist church whar Marster and Mistess was members. Dey put me under de watchkeer of deir church when I was a mighty little gal, 'cause my white folks sho b'lieved in de church and in livin' for God; de larnin' dat dem two good old folks gimme is done stayed right wid me all through life, so far, and I aims to live by it to de end. I didn't sho 'nough jine up wid no church 'til I was done growed up and had left Marse Gerald; den I jined de Cedar Grove Baptist church and was baptized dar, and dar's whar I b'longs yit.

"Marster was too old to wuk when dey sot us free, so for a long time us jus' stayed dar and run his place for him. I never seed none of dem Yankee sojers but one time. Marster was off in Jefferson and while I was down at de washplace I seed 'bout 12 men come ridin' over de hill. I was sho skeered and when I run and told Mistess she made us all come inside her house and lock all de doors. Dem Yankee mens jus' rode on through our yard down to de river and stayed dar a little while; den dey turned around and rid back through our yard and on down de big road, and us never seed 'em no more.

"Soon atter dey was sot free Niggers started up churches of dey own and it was some sight to see and hear 'em on meetin' days. Dey would go in big crowds and sometimes dey would go to meetin's a fur piece off. Dey was all fixed up in deir Sunday clothes and dey walked barfoots wid deir shoes across deir shoulders to keep 'em from gittin' dirty. Jus' 'fore dey got to de church dey stopped and put on deir shoes and den dey was ready to git together to hear de preacher.

"Folks don't know nothin' 'bout hard times now, 'specially young folks; dey is on de gravy train and don't know it, but dey is headed straight for 'struction and perdition; dey's gwine to land in dat burnin' fire if dey don't mind what dey's about. Jus' trust in de Lord, Honey, and cast your troubles on Him and He'll stay wid you, but if you turns your back on Him, den you is lost, plumb gone, jus' as sho as shelled corn.

"When us left Marse Gerald and moved nigh Athens he got a old Nigger named Egypt, what had a big fambly, to live on his place and do all de wuk. Old Marster didn't last long atter us was gone. One night he had done let his farm hands have a big cornshuckin' and had seed dat dey had plenty of supper and liquor to go wid it and, as was custom dem days, some of dem Niggers got Old Marster up on deir shoulders and toted him up to de big house, singin' as dey went along. He was jus' as gay as dey was, and joked de boys. When dey put him down on de big house porch he told Old Mistess he didn't want no supper 'cept a little coffee and bread, and he strangled on de fust bite. Mistess sont for de doctor but he was too nigh gone, and it warn't long 'fore he had done gone into de glory of de next world. He was 'bout 95 years old when he died and he had sho been a good man. One of my nieces and her husband went dar atter Marse Gerald died and tuk keer of Mistess 'til she went home to glory too.

"Mammy followed Old Mistess to glory in 'bout 3 years. Us was livin' on de Johnson place den, and it warn't long 'fore me and George Kinney got married. A white preacher married us, but us didn't have no weddin' celebration. Us moved to de Joe Langford place in Oconee County, but didn't stay dar but one year; den us moved 'crost de crick into Clarke County and atter us farmed dar 9 years, us moved on to dis here place whar us has been ever since. Plain old farmin' is de most us is ever done, but George used to make some mighty nice cheers to sell to de white folks. He made 'em out of hick'ry what he seasoned jus' right and put rye split bottoms in 'em. Dem cheers lasted a lifetime; when dey got dirty you jus' washed 'em good and sot 'em in de sun to dry and dey was good as new. George made and sold a lot of rugs and mats dat he made out of plaited shucks. Most evvybody kep' a shuck footmat 'fore deir front doors. Dem sunhats made out of shucks and bulrushes was mighty fine to wear in de field when de sun was hot. Not long atter all ten of our chillun was borned, George died out and left me wid dem five boys and five gals.

TEN
After Hours...
Beliefs and Amusements

94. Henry Bibb Tries "Conjuration"

Throughout the eighteenth century, slaves from diverse tribes and geographical areas of Africa were making essential adaptations to the new world of the white people who had enslaved them, and to one another as well. In this process a distinctive culture emerged, a culture that blended elements of the African past with European beliefs and customs. Of these latter the Christian religion was surely the most significant for the blacks. But Africa retained a strong hold on her faraway children, and culture traits that survived in the black community contributed a unique character to the Old South, and ultimately to the nation. While this was particularly true of African music (see below, document 97), Africa's cultural influence on the new world was by no means limited to music.

It is not surprising to discover that the elements of African beliefs that stood the strongest chance of surviving were those most widely shared by the African tribes, and in communities where blacks constituted a large proportion of the population. In every region of Africa, animal stories, riddles, dances and songs accompanied by musical instruments capable of sophisticated patterns of rhythm were important. Important also were beliefs concerning the spirits of the dead, and ways of casting magical spells on the living. The practice of magic had different names in various parts of the New World, but its common elements stretch from Africa to the Caribbean, to coastal South Carolina, and demonstrate the tenacity of culture. The conjurer, or "doctor," was an important person, often to be feared, in the black community, though he sometimes put his "art" to a good cause.

In the following document Henry Bibb, formerly a Kentucky slave, describes what he remembered of a youthful attempt of his own at conjuring. Bibb was born in Shelby County, Kentucky, in 1815, the son of a slave mother; his father was probably white. Among the worst hardships of slavery, in Bibb's estimation, was the enforced ignorance of the slaves. Accordingly, Bibb does not romanticize the leisure-time amusements of his fellow sufferers, and he is not easy on "conjuration" or cock-fighting. For this cloud of ignorance that he so mercilessly indicts, Bibb makes it clear that he blames the masters. The special note of embitterment that marks Bibb's account of his marriage, and the foreboding that invests it,

Source: Henry Bibb, *Narrative of the Life and Adventures of Henry Bibb, An American Slave* (New York: Published by the Author, 1849), pp. 22–35.

result from the sad subsequent history of the pair. For a man of Bibb's light complexion, escape was a relatively easy matter. Bringing his wife Malinda and her child out of Kentucky proved impossible.

In 1833, I had some very serious religious impressions, and there was quite a number of slaves in that neighborhood, who felt very desirous to be taught to read the Bible. There was a Miss Davis, a poor white girl, who offered to teach a Sabbath School for the slaves, notwithstanding public opinion and the law was opposed to it. Books were furnished and she commenced the school; but the news soon got to our owners that she was teaching us to read. This caused quite an excitement in the neighborhood. Patrols were appointed to go and break it up the next Sabbath. They were determined that we should not have a Sabbath School in operation. For slaves this was called an incendiary movement.

The Sabbath is not regarded by a large number of the slaves as a day of rest. They have no schools to go to; no moral nor religious instruction at all in many localities where there are hundreds of slaves. Hence they resort to some kind of amusement. Those who make no profession of religion, resort to the woods in large numbers on that day to gamble, fight, get drunk, and break the Sabbath. This is often encouraged by slaveholders. When they wish to have a little sport of that kind, they go among the slaves and give them whiskey, to see them dance, "pat juber," sing and play on the banjo. Then get them to wrestling, fighting, jumping, running foot races, and butting each other like sheep. This

is urged on by giving them whiskey; making bets on them; laying chips on one slave's head, and daring another to tip it off with his hand; and if he tipped it off, it would be called an insult, and cause a fight. Before fighting, the parties choose their seconds to stand by them while fighting; a ring or a circle is formed to fight in, and no one is allowed to enter the ring while they are fighting, but their seconds, and the white gentlemen. They are not allowed to fight a duel, nor to use weapons of any kind. The blows are made by kicking, knocking, and butting with their heads; they grab each other by their ears, and jam their heads together like sheep. If they are likely to hurt each other very bad, their masters would rap them with their walking canes, and make them stop. After fighting, they make friends, shake hands, and take a dram together, and there is no more of it.

But this is all principally for want of moral instruction. This is where they have no Sabbath Schools; no one to read the Bible to them; no one to preach the gospel who is competent to expound the Scriptures, except slaveholders. And the slaves, with but few exceptions, have no confidence at all in their preaching, because they preach a pro-slavery doctrine. They say, "Servants be obedient to your masters;—and he that knoweth his master's will and doeth it not, shall be beaten with many stripes;—" means that God will send them to hell, if they disobey their masters. This kind of preaching has driven thousands into infidelity. They view themselves as suffering unjustly under the lash, without friends, without protection of law or gospel, and the green eyed monster tyranny staring them in the face. They know that they are destined to die in that wretched condition, unless they are delivered by the arm of Omnipotence. And they cannot believe or trust in such a religion, as above named. . . .

There is much superstition among the slaves. Many of them believe in what they call "conjuration," tricking, and witchcraft; and some of them pretend to understand the art, and say that by it they can prevent their masters from exercising their will over their slaves. Such are often applied to by others, to give them power to prevent their masters from flogging them. The remedy is most generally some kind of bitter root; they are directed to chew it and spit towards their masters when they are angry with their slaves. At other times they prepare certain kinds of powders, to sprinkle about their masters dwellings. This is all done for the purpose of defending themselves in some peaceable manner, although I am satisfied that there is no virtue at all in it. I have tried it to perfection when I was a slave at the South. I was then a young man, full of life and vigor, and was very fond of visiting our neighbors' slaves, but had no time to visit only Sundays, when I could get a permit to go, or after night, when I could slip off without being seen. If it was found out, the next morning I was called up to give an account of myself for going off without permission; and would very often get a flogging for it.

I got myself into a scrape at a certain time, by going off in this way, and I expected to be severely punished for it. I had a strong notion of running off, to escape being flogged, but was advised by a friend to go to one of those conjurers, who could prevent me from being flogged. I went and informed him of the difficulty. He said if I would pay him a small sum, he would prevent my being flogged. After I had paid him, he mixed up some alum, salt and other stuff into a powder, and said I must sprinkle it about my master, if he should offer to strike me; this would prevent him. He also gave me some kind of bitter root to chew, and spit towards him, which would certainly prevent my being flogged. According to order I used his remedy, and for some cause I was let pass without being flogged that time.

I had then great faith in conjuration and witchcraft. I was led to believe that I could do almost as I pleased, without being flogged. So on the next Sabbath my conjuration was fully tested by my going off, and staying away until Monday morning, without permission. When I returned home, my master declared that he would punish me for going off; but I did not believe that he could do it, while I had this root and dust; and as he approached me, I commenced talking saucy to him. But he soon convinced me that there was no virtue in them. He became so enraged at me for saucing him, that he grasped a handful of switches and punished me severely, in spite of all my roots and powders.

But there was another old slave in that neighborhood, who professed to understand all about conjuration, and I thought I would try his skill. He told me that the first one was only a quack, and if I would only pay him a certain amount in cash, that he would tell me how to prevent any person from striking me. After I had paid him his charge, he told me to go to the cow-pen after night, and get some fresh cow manure, and mix it with red pepper and white people's hair, all to be put into a pot over the fire, and scorched until it could be ground into snuff. I was then to sprinkle it about my master's bedroom, in his hat and boots, and it would prevent him from ever abusing me in any way. After I got it all ready prepared, the smallest pinch of it scattered over a room, was enough to make a horse sneeze from the strength of it; but it did no good. I tried it to my satisfaction. It was my business to make fires in my master's chamber, night and morning. Whenever I could get a chance, I sprinkled a little of this dust about the linen of the bed, where they would breathe it on retiring. This was to act upon them as what is called a kind of love powder, to change their sentiments of anger, to those of love, towards me, but this all proved to be vain imagination. The old man had my money, and I was treated no better for it.

One night when I went in to make a fire, I availed myself of the opportunity of sprinkling a very heavy charge of this powder about my master's bed. Soon after their going to bed, they began to cough and sneeze. Being close around the house, watching and listening, to know what the effect would be, I heard them ask each other what in the world it could be, that made them cough and sneeze so. All the while, I was trembling with fear, expecting every moment I should be called and asked if I knew any thing about it. After this, for fear they might find me out in my dangerous experiments upon them, I had to give them up, for the time being. I was then convinced that running away was the most effectual way by which a slave could escape cruel punishment.

But my attention was gradually turned in a measure from this subject, by being introduced into the society of young women. This for the time being took my attention from running away, as waiting on the girls appeared to be perfectly congenial to my nature. I wanted to be well thought of by them, and would go to great lengths to gain their affection. I had been taught by the old superstitious slaves, to believe in conjuration, and it was hard for me to give up the notion, for all I had been deceived by them. One of these conjurers, for a small sum agreed to teach me to make any girl love me that I wished. After I had paid him, he told me to get a bull frog, and take a certain bone out of the frog, dry it, and when I got a chance I must step up to any girl whom I wished to make love me, and scratch her somewhere on her naked skin with this bone, and she would be certain to love me, and would follow me in spite of herself; no matter who she might be engaged to, nor who she might be walking with.

So I got me a bone for a certain girl, whom I knew to be under the influence of another young man. I happened to meet her in the company of her lover, one Sunday evening, walking out; so when I got a chance, I fetched her a tremendous rasp across her neck with this bone, which made her jump. But in place of making her love me, it only made her angry with me. She felt more like running after me to retaliate on me for thus abusing her, than she felt like loving me. After I found there was no virtue in the bone of a frog, I thought I would try some other way to carry out my object. I then sought another counsellor among the old superstitious influential slaves; one who professed to be a great friend of mine, told me to get a lock of hair from the head of any girl, and wear it in my shoes: this would cause her to love me above all other persons. As there was another girl whose affections I was anxious to gain, but could not succeed, I thought, without trying the experiment of this hair. I slipped off one night to see the girl, and asked her for a lock of her hair; but she refused to give it. Believing that my success depended greatly upon this bunch of hair, I was bent on having a lock before I left that night let it cost what it might. As it was time for me to start home in order to get any sleep that night, I grasped hold of a lock of her hair, which caused her to screech, but I never let go until I had pulled it out. This of course made the girl mad with me, and I accomplished nothing but gained her displeasure.

Such are the superstitious notions of the great masses of southern slaves. It is given to them by tradition, and can never be erased, while the doors of education are bolted and barred against them. . . .

But when I had arrived at the age of eighteen, which was in the year of 1833, it was my lot to be introduced to the favor of a mulatto slave girl named Malinda, who lived in Oldham County, Kentucky, about four miles from the residence of my owner. Malinda was a medium sized girl, graceful in her walk, of an extraordinary make, and active in business. Her skin was of a smooth texture, red cheeks, with dark and penetrating eyes. She moved in the highest circle [1] of slaves, and free people of color. She was also one of the best singers I ever heard, and was much esteemed by all who knew her, for her benevolence, talent and industry. In fact, I considered Malinda to be equalled by few, and surpassed by none, for the above qualities, all things considered.

It is truly marvellous to see how sudden a man's mind can be changed by the charms and influence of a female. The first two or three visits that I paid this dear girl, I had no intention of courting or marrying her, for I was aware that such a step would greatly obstruct my way to the land of liberty. I only visited Malinda because I liked her company, as a highly interesting girl. But in spite of myself, before I was aware of it, I was deeply in love; and what made this passion so effectual and almost irresistable, I became satisfied that it was reciprocal. There was a union of feeling, and every visit

1. The distinction among slaves is as marked as the classes of society are in any aristocratic community, some refusing to associate with others whom they deem beneath them in point of character, color, condition, or the superior importance of their respective masters. (Bibb's note)

made the impression stronger and stronger. One or two other young men were paying attention to Malinda, at the same time; one of whom her mother was anxious to have her marry. This of course gave me a fair opportunity of testing Malinda's sincerity. I had just about opposition enough to make the subject interesting. That Malinda loved me above all others on earth, no one could deny. I could read it by the warm reception with which the dear girl always met me, and treated me in her mother's house. I could read it by the warm and affectionate shake.of the hand, and gentle smile upon her lovely cheek. I could read it by her always giving me the preference of her company; by her pressing invitations to visit even in opposition to her mother's will. I could read it in the language of her bright and sparkling eye, penciled by the unchangable finger of nature, that spake but could not lie. These strong temptations gradually diverted my attention from my acutal condition and from liberty, though not entirely.

But oh! that I had only then been enabled to have seen as I do now, or to have read the . . . slave code, which is but a stereotyped law of American slavery. It would have saved me I think from having to lament that I was a husband and am the father of slaves who are still left to linger out their days in hopeless bondage.

95. William Thomson Attends an "Imposing and Solemn" Baptism

Once the question of whether the slave was to be made a Christian had been settled affirmatively, religion became an increasingly important force in the lives of bondsmen. As the black spirituals so plainly show, faith in a heavenly future in which justice would prevail was a sustaining element for the oppressed, and in that sense was a support of the slave system itself. But some slaves reacted differently, and the basic value of the human personality so central to the faith caused them to reflect deeply on the wrong of their enslavement in a Christian land. In that sense religion brought forth both Nat Turners and Uncle Toms. But in either case it caused slaves to *think*, and was the only part of their education, aside from

Source: William Thomson, *A Tradesman's Travels, in the United States and Canada* . . . (Edinburgh: Oliver & Boyd, 1842), pp. 173–81.

work itself, that most planters encouraged. The practice of religion provided a means for the development of leadership among the slaves themselves, and many of those who emerged to prominence in the postwar period had once been slave preachers.

The slaves were more receptive to the Baptists and Methodists than to other denominations, perhaps because of the greater fervor of their evangelical efforts, but also because these sects adjusted to the understanding of an uneducated people more readily than did others. They were more willing to permit slave exhorters and preachers to carry on the work on the plantations. There were fewer official rituals that could be performed only by the officially ordained. The Baptists retained one such ritual—that of total immersion—and in the following selection, from his report of a visit to the United States in the 1840s, the Scottish weaver William Thomson describes how this took place on St. Helena Island in South Carolina (see document 72). As anthropologist Melville Herskovitz has explained in *The Myth of the Negro Past* (1941), the symbolism of water and its purifying effect was a powerful element in many African religions, and this may further explain the black preference for the Baptist denomination.

On my arrival in South Carolina, the first thing that particularly attracted my attention was negro slavery. Two days after my arrival in Beaufort, the quarterly meeting of the Baptist Church occurred, being Sunday the 11th October 1840; and, as I understood that some sixteen or eighteen negro slaves were to be baptized, I went to the river in the morning at seven o'clock, and found the banks crowded with some hundreds of black faces, and few white people.

It was a beautiful morning, with a clearer sky than is often seen in Scotland. I almost expected to see something ridiculous, but, in reality, the whole affair had rather an imposing and solemn effect. The black people behaved themselves decently, and with great propriety, much more so than a parcel of young gentlemen who were looking on, enjoying the scene in their own way, but not much to their credit, as men of sense or good feeling. The parson, who was dressed in a white gown, went into the river, till the water came up to his waist. A very large fat negro man, named Jacob, one of the deacons of the church, led the people into the river, and stood by, while the parson immersed them, I suppose, to see that none of them were carried off by the stream; and sure enough, it would have taken a pretty strong tide to carry *him* off. They went into the river one by one, the men first, and then the women. The effect was really solemn, as the clear voice of the pastor resounded through the crowd, and along the banks of the river, with the words—"I baptize thee in the name of the Father, and of the Son, and of the Holy Ghost—Amen;" and when all was done, they came up from the river, in a body, singing the beautiful hymn—

"I'm not ashamed to own my Lord,
Or to defend his cause:
Maintain the glory of his cross,
And honour all his laws."

At eleven o'clock we went to church, which was very crowded. I believe there are about twelve or fourteen hundred negro members belonging to it, partly house servants, but mostly slaves from the cotton plantations in the neighbourhood. In the church, the negroes (with the exception of those who were baptized in the morning), were seated in the gallery, the men on the one side, and the women on the other. They had a very strange appearance to me. It was a novel sight to see so many blacks. They appeared all very much alike, as much so as a flock of sheep does to a stranger. In their outward appearance, they were the most serious and attentive congregation I have seen. After prayer and praise, the negroes who were baptized in the morning, were requested by the pastor to stand up, when he addressed himself to them; telling them particularly their duty to God and to their master, and to hold fast by the profession of Christianity they had that day made. Then the pastor, the Rev. Mr. Fuller, who was standing, surrounded by his elders, immediately before the pulpit, told them to come forward, and receive the right hand of fellowship. As they came forward, he took them by the hand, and bade them welcome as

brethren in Christ. I took particular notice of the shaking of hands. It was a real transaction; and in the act, the women made a curtsey, and the men a bow, with a better grace than many of the servant lads and lasses in this country would have done. All, except one, were new members; and on this one they had been exercising church discipline; I believe, for incontinence; but, after a reprimand before the congregation, he was bid "Go in peace, and sin no more." All churches admit them members, after instructing them in the great features of Christianity and some of the most practical and useful dogmas. I frequently conversed with them on this subject, and they generally had a tolerable scriptural idea of Hell and the Devil, of God and Heaven, and of Jesus Christ, who died for their sins; or, with the ideas of a little schoolboy, they would tell me that Heaven is good and that Hell is bad,—that the wicked will be punished in the one, and the good enjoy the other. Yet some of them are learned in the Scriptures. I have heard them praying and exhorting in their own homely way; but, as with their white brethren, this does not appear to have any practical effect on their conduct.

In the afternoon the Sacrament of the Supper was administered. There were black deacons, who handed round the bread and wine to the negroes. They all used the same wine and bread. The white people did not use any of the cups that the slaves drank out of, but the cups that the whites had used were then used by some of the slaves. The negroes have generally fine voices, and they joined in the psalmody of the church. They, of course, do not use any books; for it is contrary to law to teach a negro to read or write; but the pastor gives out the hymn in two lines at a time. They appeared to pay great attention to the service; but I was sorry to observe that the minister never turned his eye to the galleries, nor addressed himself to the limited capacities of the slaves. Judging from the discourse, and the manner of the minister, one would not have known there was an ignorant negro in the house, although there were five or six times as many black skins as white.

It would be a hard task to describe the dress of the slaves. The men could not have presented a greater variety of dress if a cart-load of clothes, beggars' duds, gentlemen's dresscoats, with silk-velvet collars, good hats, shocking bad hats, the miserable remnants of black and white "castors" that had served a severe apprenticeship to their masters, and all sorts of inexpressibles,

had been all mixed together, and each one sent blindfolded to put on what first came to hand; and this would, indeed, convey some idea of their dress. About one-half of them had shoes on. I have often heard it said, it is the life of an old hat to cock it well, but never saw the thing so well illustrated as I did here. Their plantation dress, although coarse, is far more becoming; but they are so vain, and their taste is so little cultivated, that they prefer, when going to meeting, the very rags and tatters of an old dress coat to their own Osnaburg jacket. A few were as well dressed as many white men.

The dresses of the females were about as varied as those of the men. One uniform custom prevails of wearing gaudy-coloured handkerchiefs on the head, *à la turban*, many of them tartan, the bright and heart-warming colours of which seemed strangely out of place on the head of a slave.

96. The Reverend Jasper on Life, Death, and the Origin of Sin

The fact that many of the greatest black leaders in the Reconstruction period had once been preachers among slaves held little surprise for those who understood the unique influence exercised by religious leaders on the plantation. The mobility they enjoyed in preaching sermons in their communities, and sometimes well beyond its confines, gave them access to a

Source: William Eldridge Hatcher, *John Jasper: The Unmatched Negro Philosopher and Preacher* (Richmond: Fleming H. Revell Co., 1908), pp. 36–42, 47–57.

wider experience, and the exercise of their abilities trained them in the arts of persuasion. To the extent that the preachers emphasized the Christian virtue of submissiveness they were tolerated, encouraged, and often admired, by the white community. But when their ministrations served to create restlessness among the enslaved they were feared and distrusted by whites, and sometimes entirely suppressed. Virginia experienced a massive reaction against slave preachers in the aftermath of Nat Turner's insurrection, but it was never complete, and with the return of greater complacency the black preachers returned with vigor. The life of John Jasper illustrates the point.

Jasper's fame as a speaker was acknowledged in the Richmond-Petersburg vicinity from 1839 to the end of the century. It is doubtful that this would have been the case if Jasper had overtly challenged the slave system or the system of segregation that replaced it, but the simplest of his auditors saw in his personality and the force of his oratory an open contradiction of the arguments on which slavery and second-class citizenship were based. Jasper's biographer, Dr. William E. Hatcher, was a prominent white minister in Richmond, a man by no means free of the racial ideas of his time; yet his admiration of John Jasper was unstinted and surprisingly free of condescension. To Hatcher, Jasper was a man "of spotless and incorruptible honour," an "ascetic" and an "aristocrat," a being "as proud as Lucifer—too proud to be egotistical and too candid and self-assertive to affect a humility that he could not feel. He walked, Hatcher continues, "heights where company was scarce, and seemed to love his solitude." It is to Dr. Hatcher's credit that he stresses the difficulties Jasper overcame on his road to fame, and explains that it was a fellow black who taught Jasper to read.

Jasper was born of a field-hand mother, a woman who ultimately became a most important factotum, "the chief of a servant force in a rich family," and nurse to the plantation slaves. Jasper's father, who died some two months before his birth, had been a preacher, too. Though he began life as a field worker, Jasper came to Richmond as a young man to work in a tobacco factory, experienced a thrilling conversion, and began to preach. He read voraciously. Hatcher describes Jasper's countenance as "open, luminous, thoughtful," and expressive of "radiance and exultation" when animated by his subject.

Jasper never lost the accent and word patterns of his slave-bound youth, a fact that may have served to make his meaning plainer to those he served. Apparently it placed no barrier between him and his white listeners. They too were accustomed to expect a rich and concrete imagery in sermons, and they understood preaching as theater just as blacks did. Whatever may now be thought of Dr. Hatcher's effort to render Jasper's speech and style, or of Jasper's theological explanation of the origin of sin, the professional respect of Hatcher for Jasper is implicit in the conception and execution of this unique biography by a white minister who believed John Jasper to be "genuinely great among the sons of men."

It is as a preacher that John Jasper is most interesting. His personality was notable and full of force anywhere, but the pulpit was the stage of his chief performance. It is worth while to bear in mind that he began to preach in 1839 and that was twenty-five years before the coming of freedom. For a quarter of a century, therefore, he was a preacher while yet a slave. His time, of course, under the law belonged to his master, and under the laws of the period, he could preach only under very serious limitations. He could go only when his master said he might, and he could preach only when some white minister or committee was present to see that things were conducted in an orderly way. This is the hard way of stating the case, but there are many ways of getting around such regulations. The man who could preach, though a negro, rarely failed of an opportunity to preach. The man who was fit for the work had friends who enabled him to "shy around" his limitations.

There was one thing which the negro greatly insisted upon, and which not even the most hard-hearted masters were ever quite willing to deny them. They could never bear that their dead should be put away without a funeral. Not that they expected, at the time of the burial, to have the funeral service. Indeed, they did not desire it, and it was never according to their notions. A funeral to them was a pageant. It was a thing to be arranged for a long time ahead. It was to be marked by the gathering of the kindred and friends from far and wide. It was not satisfactory unless there was a vast and excitable crowd. It usually meant an all-day meeting, and often a meeting in a grove, and it drew white and black alike, sometimes almost in equal numbers. Another demand in the case,— for the slaves knew how to make their demands,—was that the negro preacher "should preach the funeral," as they called it. In things like this, the wishes of the slaves generally prevailed. "The funeral" loomed up weeks in advance, and although marked by sable garments, mournful manners and sorrowful outcries, it had about it hints of an elaborate social function with festive accompaniments. There was much staked on the fame of the officiating brother. He must be one of their own colour, and a man of reputation. They must have a man to plough up their emotional depths, and they must have freedom to indulge in the extravagancies of their sorrow. These demonstrations were their tribute to their dead and were expected to be fully adequate to do honour to the family.

It was in this way that Jasper's fame

began. At first, his temptestuous, un-grammatical eloquence was restricted to Richmond, and there it was hedged in with many humbling limitations. But gradually the news concerning this fiery and thrilling orator sifted itself into the country, and many invitations came for him to officiate at country funerals.

He was preëminently a funeral preacher. A negro funeral without an uproar, without shouts and groans, without fainting women and shouting men, without pictures of triumphant death-beds and the judgment day, and without the gates of heaven wide open and the subjects of the funeral dressed in white and rejoicing around the throne of the Lamb, was no funeral at all. Jasper was a master from the outset at this work. One of his favourite texts, as a young preacher, was that which was recorded in Revelations, sixth chapter, and second verse: "And I saw and beheld a white horse; and he that sat upon him had a bow, and a crown was given unto him, and he went forth conquering and to conquer." Before the torrent of his florid and spectacular eloquence the people were swept down to the ground, and sometimes for hours many seemed to be in trances, not a few lying as if they were dead.

Jasper's first visit to the country as a preacher of which we have any account was to Hanover County. A prominent and wealthy slaveholder had the custom of allowing his servants to have imposing funerals, when their kindred and friends died; but those services were always conducted by a white minister. In some way the fame of Jasper had penetrated that community,

and one of the slaves asked his master to let Jasper come and attend the funeral. But to this the master made an objection. He knew nothing about Jasper, and did not believe that any negro was capable of preaching the Gospel with good effect. This negro was not discouraged by the refusal of the proprietor of the great plantation to grant his request. He went out and collected a number of most trustworthy and influential negro men and they came in a body to his master and renewed the plea. They told him in their way about what a great man Jasper was, how anxious they were to hear him, what a comfort his presence would be to the afflicted family, and how thankful they would be to have their request honoured. They won their point in part. He said to them, as if yielding reluctantly, "very well, let him come." They however had something more to say. They knew Jasper would need to have a good reason in order to get his master's consent for him to come, and they knew that Jasper would not come unless he came under the invitation and protection of the white people, and therefore they asked the gentleman if he would not write a letter inviting him to come. Accordingly, in a spirit of compromise and courtesy very pleasing to the coloured people, the letter was written and Jasper came.

The news of his expected coming spread like a flame. Not only the country people in large numbers, but quite a few of the Richmond people, made ready to attend the great occasion. Jasper went out in a private conveyance, the distance not being great, and, in his kind wish to take along as many friends as possible, he overloaded the wagon and had a breakdown. The delay in his arrival was very long and unexplained; but still the people lingered and beguiled the time with informal religious services.

At length the Richmond celebrity appeared on the scene late in the day. The desire to hear him was imperative, and John Jasper was equal to the occasion. Late as the hour was, and wearied as were the people, he spoke with overmastering power. The owner of the great company of slaves on that plantation was among his hearers, and he could not resist the spell of devout eloquence which poured from the lips of the unscholared Jasper. It was a sermon from the heart, full of personal passion and hot with gospel fervour, and the heart of the lord of the plantation was powerfully moved. He undertook to engage Jasper to preach on the succeeding Sunday and handed the blushing preacher quite a substantial monetary token of his appreciation.

The day was accounted memorable by reason of the impression which Jasper made. Indeed, Jasper was a master of assemblies. No politician could handle a crowd with more consummate tact than he. He was the king of hearts and could sway throngs as the wind shakes the trees.

There is a facetious story abroad among the negroes that in those days Jasper went to Farmville to officiate on a funeral occasion where quite a number of the dead were to have their virtues commemorated and where their "mourning friends," as Jasper in time came to call them, were to be comforted. The news that Jasper was to be there went out on the wings of the wind and vast throngs attended. Of course, a white minister was present and understood that he was the master of ceremonies. The story is, that he felt that it would not be safe to entrust an occasion so vastly interesting to the hands of Jasper, and he decided that he would quiet Jasper and satisfy the public demands by calling on Jasper to pray. As a fact, Jasper was about as much of an orator in speaking to heaven as he was in speaking to mortal men. His prayer had such contagious and irresistible eloquence that whatever the Lord did about it, it surely brought quite a resistless response from the crowd. When the white preacher ended his tame and sapless address, the multitude cried out for Jasper. Inspired by the occasion and emboldened by the evident disposition to shut him out, Jasper took fire and on eagle wings he mounted into the heavens and gave such a brilliant and captivating address that he vast crowd went wild with joy and enthusiasm.

. . .

"WHAR SIN KUM FRUM?"

My first sight of Jasper must always remain in the chapter of unforgotten things. The occasion was Sunday afternoon, and the crowd was overflowing. Let me add that it was one of his days of spiritual intoxication, and he played on every key in the gamut of the human soul.

Two questions had been shot at him, and they both took effect. The first had to do with creation. For a half hour he pounded away on the creatorship of God. His address was very strong and had in it both argument and eloquence. He marshalled the Scriptures with consummate skill, and built an argument easily understood by the rudest of his hearers; and yet so compact and tactful was he, that his most cultured hearers bent beneath his force.

But the second question brought on the pyrotechnics. It had to do with the origin of sin,—"Whar sin kum frum?"—as he cogently put it. It was here that a riotous liberty possessed him, and he preached with every faculty of his mind, with every passion and sentiment of his soul, with every nerve, every muscle, and every feature of his body. For nearly an hour the air cracked with excitement and the crowd melted beneath his spell. It was my first experience of that unusual power of his to move people in all possible ways by a single effort.

Jasper knew the fundamental doctrines of the Bible admirably, and always lived in vital contact with their essence. There was a kinship between the Bible and himself, and, untaught of the schools, he studied himself in the light of the Bible and studied the Bible in the darkness of himself. This kept him in contact with people and whenever he preached he invaded their experience and made conscious their wants to themselves. And so it came to pass that questions which perplexed them they had the habit of bringing to him. This question as to the origin of sin had been spurring and nagging some of his speculative hearers. They had wrangled over it, and they unloaded their perplexity upon him. So it was with this burden heavy upon him that he came to the pulpit on this occasion.

It may have been a touch of his dramatic art, but at any rate he showed an amiable irritation, in view of his being under constant fire from his controversial church-members, and so he started in as if he had a grievance. It gave pith and excitement to his bearing, as he faced the issue thus thrust upon him. As a fact, he knew that many inquirers sought to entangle him by their questions and this opened the way for his saying, with cutting effect, that they would do better to inquire, "whar sin wuz gwine ter kerry 'em, instid uv whar it kum frum."

"An' yer wants ter know whar sin kum frum, yer say. Why shud yer be broozin' eroun' wid sich a questun as dat? Dar ain' but wun place in de univus uv Gord whar yer kin git any infermashun on dis pint, and dar, I am free ter tel yer, yer kin git all dat yer wish ter know, an' maybe a good deal mo'. De place whar de nollidge yer need kin be got iz in de Word uv Gord. I knows wat sum dat hav' bin talkin' 'bout dis thing iz arter. I know de side uv de questun dey iz struttin' up on. Dey say, or dey kinder hint, dat de Lord Gord iz de orthur uv sin. Dat's wat dey iz wispurrin' roun' dis town. Dey can't fool Jasper; but I tell you de debbul iz playin' pranks on um an' will drag um down ter de pit uv hell, ef dey doan luk out mity quick. De Lord Gord know'd frum de beginnin' dat sum uv dese debbullish people wud bring up dis very charge an' say dat He had tendid dat dar shud be sin frum de beginnin'. He done speak His mind 'bout dat thing, an' ef yer luk in de fust chaptur uv Jeems yer'll find de solum uttrunce on dis subjik an' it kleers Gord furevur frum dis base slandur. 'Let no man say,' says de Lord, 'wen he is temptid dat he is temptid uv Gord, fur Gord kin not be temptid uv any man, an' neethur tempts He any man.' Did yer hear dat? Dat's de Lord's own wurds. It spressly says dat people will be temptid,—everybody is temptid; I bin havin' my temptashuns all my life, an' I haz um yit, a heap uv um, an' sum uv um awful bad, but yer ain' ketchin' Jasper er sayin' dat Gord is at de bottum uv um. Ef I shud say it, it wud be a lie, an' all iz liars wen dey say dat Gord tempts um? De sinnur is gettin' towurds de wust wen he iz willin' ter lay de blame uv hiz sins on de Lord. Do it ef yer will, but de cuss uv Gord will be erpun yez wen yer try ter mek de Lord Gord sich es you iz; an' ter mek b'liev dat de Lord gits orf His throne an' kums down in ter mire an' clay uv your wicked life an' tries ter jog an' ter fool yer inter sin. I trimbul ter think uv sich a thing! I wonder dat de Lord duzn't forge new thunderbolts uv Hiz rath an' crush de heds uv dem dat charge 'im wid de folly uv human sin.

"Sum uv yer wud be mity glad ter git Gord mix'd up in yer sins an' ter feel dat He iz es bad es you iz. It jes' shows how base, how lost, how ded, you'se bekum. Wudn't we hev a pritty Gord ef He wuz willin' ter git out in de nite an' go plungin' down inter de horribul an' ruinus transgresshuns in wich sum men indulg'. Let me kleer dis thing up befo' I quit it. Bar in mind, dat Gord kin not be temptid uv any man. Try it ef yer chuze, an' He will fling yer in ter de lowes' hell, an' don't yer dar evur ter say, or ter think,

or ter hope, dat de temtashun ter du rong things kum ter yer from Gord. It do not kum frum erbuv, but it kum out uv your foul an' sinful hart. Dey iz born dar, born uv your bad thoughts, born uv your hell-born lusts, an' dey gits strong in yer' cause' yer don't strangul um at de start.

"But why shud dar be trubble 'bout dis subjic? Wat duz de Bibul say on dis here mattur 'bout whar sin kum frum? We kin git de troof out uv dat buk, fur it kuntains de Wurd uv Gord. Our Gord kin not lie; He nevur hav' lied frum de foundashun uv de wurl'. He iz de troof an' de life an' He nevur lies.

"Now, wat do He say kunsarnin' dis serus questun dat is plowin' de souls uv sum uv my brudderin. Ter de Bibul, ter de Bibul, we'll go an' wat do we git wen we git dar? De Bibul say dat Eve wuz obur dar in de gardin uv Edun one day an' dat she wuz dar by herself. De Lord med Eve, 'caus' it worn't gud fer Adum ter be erloan, an' it luks frum dis kase dat it wuz not quite safe fer Eve ter be lef' at home by herself. But Adum worn't wid her; doan know whar he wuz,—gorn bogin' orf sumwhars. He better bin at home tendin' ter his fambly. Dat ain' de only time, by a long shot, dat dar haz bin de debbul ter pay at home wen de man hev gorn gaddin' eroun', instid uv stayin' at home an' lookin' arter hiz fambly.

"While Eve wuz sauntrin' an' roamin' eroun' in de buterful gardin, de ole sarpint, dyked up ter kill, kum gallervantin' down de road an' he kotch'd site uv Eve an' luk lik he surpriz'd very much but not sorry in de leas'. Now yer mus' kno' dat ole sarpint wuz de trickies' an' de arties' uv all de beas' uv de feil',—de ole debbul, dat's wat he wuz. An' wat he do but go struttin' up ter Eve in a mity frien'ly way, scrapin' an' bowin' lik a fool ded in luv.

" 'How yer do?' He tries ter be perlite, an' puts on hiz sweetes' airs. Oh, dat wuz an orful momint in de life uv Eve an' in de histurry uv dis po' los' wurl uv ours. In dat momint de pizun eat thru her flesh, struck in her blud, an' went ter her hart. At fust she wuz kinder shame'; but she wuz kinder loansum, an' she wuz pleas'd an' tickl'd ter git notic'd in dat way an' so she stay'd dar instid uv runnin' fer her life.

" 'Ve'y wel, I thanks yer,' she say er-tremblin', 'how iz you dis mornin'?' De sarpint farly shouts wid joy. He dun got her tenshun an' she lek ter hear 'im, an' he feel he got hiz chanz an' so goes on:

" 'Nice gardin yer got dar,' he say in er admirin' way. 'Yer got heap uv nice appuls obur dar.'

" 'Oh, yes, indeed,' Eve replies. 'We got lots uv um.'

"Eve spoke dese wurds lik she wuz proud ter deth 'caus' de sarpint lik de gardin. Dar stood de sarpint ve'y quiut tel, suddin lek, he juk eroun' an' he says ter Eve:—

" 'Kin yet eat all de appuls yer got obur dar?'

" 'No, hindeed,' says Eve, 'we can't eat um all. We got moar'n we kin 'stroy save our lives. Dey gittin' ripe all de time; we hev jus' hogshids uv um.'

" 'Oh, I didn't mean dat,' spoke de sarpint, es ef shock'd by not bein' understud. 'My p'int iz, iz yer 'low'd ter eat um all? Dat's wat I want ter know.

As ter yer laws an' rites in de gardin, duz dey all sute yer?'

"Fer a minnit de 'oman jump'd same es if sumbudy struk her a blow. De col' chils run down her bak, an' she luk lik she wan ter run, but sumhow de eye uv de sarpint dun got a charm on her. Dar wuz a struggul, er reglur Bull Run battul, gwine on in her soul at dat momint.

" 'Wat yer ax me dat questun fur?' Eve axed, gaspin' w'ile she spoke. Den de debbul luk off. He tri ter be kam an' ter speak lo an' kine, but dar wuz a glar' in his eyes. 'I begs many parduns,' he says, 'skuse me, I did not mean ter meddul wid yer privit buzniz. I'd bettur skuse mysef, I reckin, and try an' git erlong.'

" 'No; doan go,' Eve sed. 'Yer havn't hurt my feelin's. Wat yer say jes' put new thoughts in my min' an' kinder shuk me up at fust. But I doan min' talkin'.'

" 'Ef dat be de kase,' speaks up de debbul, quite brave-lek, 'begs you skuse me ter ask agin ef de rules uv de gardin 'lows yer ter eat any uv dem appuls yer got in de gardin? I haz my reasuns fer axin' dis.'

"Eve stud dar shivurrin' like she freezin' an' pale es de marbul toomstoan. But arter a gud wile she pint her han obur to er tree, on de hill on de rite, an' she tel 'im, es ef she wuz mity 'fraid, dat dar wuz a tree obur dar uv de Nollidge an' uv de Deestinxshun, an' she say, 'De Lord Gord He tel us we mus' not eat dem appuls; dey pisun us, an' de day we eat um we got to die.'

"Oh, my brudderin, worn't times mity serus den? 'Twuz de hour wen de powurs uv darknis wuz gittin' in an' de foundashuns uv human hopes wuz givin' way. Den it wuz he git up close ter Eve an' wispur in her ear:—

" 'Did de Lord Gord tel yer dat? Doan tel nobody, but I wan' ter tel yer dat it ain't so. Doan yer b'liev it. Doan let 'im fool yer! He know dat's de bes' fruit in all de gardin,—de fruit uv de Nollidge an' de Deestinxshun, an' dat wen yer eats it yer will know es much es He do. Yes reckin He wants yer ter know es much es He do? Na-a-w; an' dat's why He say wat He do say. You go git um. Dey's de choysis' fruit in de gardin, an' wen yer eats um yer will be equ'ul ter Gord.'

"Erlas, erlas! po' deluded an' foolish Eve! It wuz de momint uv her evurlastin' downfall. Clouds uv darknis shrouds her min' an' de ebul sperrit leap inter her soul an' locks de do' behin' him. Dat dedly day she bruk 'way frum de Gord dat made her, Eve did, an' purtuk uv de fruit dat brought sin an' ruin an' hell inter de wurl'."

"Po' foolish Eve! In dat momunt darknis fils her min', evul leaps in ter er heart, an' she pluck de appul, bruk de kumman uv Gord, and ate de fatul fruit wat brought death ter all our race.

"Artur er wile, Adum kum walkin' up de gardin and Eve she runs out ter meet 'im. Wen he kum near she hol' up er appul in her han' and tell him it iz gud ter eat. Oh, blin' and silly womun! First deceived herself, she turn roun' and deceives Adum. Dat's de way; we gits wrong, an' den we pulls udder folks down wid us. We rarly goes down by oursefs.

"But whar wuz de rong? Whar, indeed? It wuz in Eve's believin' de deb-bul and not believin' Gord. It wuz doin' wat de debbul sed an' not doin' wat Gord sed. An' yer kum here and ax me whar sin kum frum! Yer see now, doan' sher? It kum out uv de pit uv hell whar it wuz hatched 'mong de ainjuls dat wuz flung out uv heav'n 'caus dey disurbeyd Gord. It kum from dat land whar de name uv our Gord is hated. It wuz brought by dat ole sarpint, de fathur uv lies, and he brung it dat he mite fool de woman, an' in dat way sot up on de urth de wurks uv de debbul. Sin iz de black chile uv de pit, it is. It kum frum de ole sarpint at fust, but it's here now, rite in po' Jasper's hart and in your hart; wharevur dar iz a man or a woman in dis dark wurl' in tears dar iz sin,—sin dat insults Gord, tars down His law, and brings woes ter evrybody.

"An' you, stung by de sarpint, wid Gord's rath on yer and yer feet in de paf uv deth, axin' whar sin kum frum? Yer bettur fly de rath uv de judgmint day.

"But dis iz ernuff. I jes' tuk time ter tell whar sin kum frum. But my tong carnt refuse ter stop ter tel yer dat de blud uv de Lam' slain frum de foundashun uve de wurl' is grettur dan sin and mitier dan hell. It kin wash erway our sins, mek us whitur dan de drivin snow, dress us in redemshun robes, bring us wid shouts and allerluejurs bak ter dat fellership wid our Fathur, dat kin nevur be brokin long ez 'ternity rolls."

This outbreak of fiery eloquence was not the event of the afternoon, but simply an incident. It came towards the end of the service, and its delivery took not much more time than is required to read this record of it. His language was perhaps never more broken; but what he said flamed with terrific light. While there were touches of humour in his description of the scene in the Garden, his message gathered a seriousness and solemnity which became simply overpowering. No words can describe the crushing and alarming effect which his weird story of the entrance of sin into the world had upon his audience. Men sobbed and fell to the floor in abject shame, and frightened cries for mercy rang wild through the church. Possibly never a sweeter gospel note sounded than that closing reference which he made to the cleansing power of the blood shed from the foundation of the world.

There were many white persons present, and they went away filled with a sense of the greatness and power of the Gospel.

97. Thomas Wentworth Higginson Describes "Negro Spirituals"

The most authentic and moving cultural expression of slaves was music. There were songs for every occasion, work, play, and worship, and such songs offered endless occasions for variety and improvisation. In the religious songs of the slave are found blendings of African rhythms and intervals with the imagery of the Old and New Testaments; and these songs may constitute the single truly original American contribution to the music of the world. It is fortunate that at least a few of the many fascinated listeners to the songs of the slaves took the time to write down what they heard. This was by no means easy to do, and the Northern teachers and army officers who undertook this task during the Civil War occasionally disagreed with one another about what they had heard.

A typical disagreement took place over whether most of the songs were written in keys on the major or the minor scale. Thomas Wentworth Higginson, in the selection offered below, comes out for the minor; others, including William Francis Allen, co-author, along with Charles Ware and Lucy McKim Garrison, of the first general work on the subject (see

Source: Atlantic Monthly, June 1867, pp. 685–94.

document 98), thought he heard the major keys most often. The mystery seems to reside in the appearance in slave music of a distinct African cultural survival: the striking of the musical intervals of the third and sixth degrees of the eight-tone scale somewhere between the major and minor degrees of the scale as conceived in European music and as most musical instruments are tuned.

Colonel Higginson, whose article on slave music for the *Atlantic Monthly* appears below in its entirety, was a militant abolitionist during the decades preceding the Civil War, and an open supporter of John Brown. During the war Higginson led a regiment of black troops, and it was during his service experience that he encountered the singers whose music he reports on in the article. Higginson wrote about his war experiences in *Army Life in a Black Regiment*, first published in 1869. He died in 1911 at the age of eighty-eight.

The war brought to some of us, besides its direct experiences, many a strange fulfilment of dreams of other days. For instance, the present writer had been a faithful student of the Scottish ballads, and had always envied Sir Walter the delight of tracing them out amid their own heather, and of writing them down piecemeal from the lips of aged crones. It was a strange enjoyment, therefore, to be suddenly brought into the midst of a kindred world of unwritten songs, as simple and indigenous as the Border Minstrelsy, more uniformly plaintive, almost always more quaint, and often as essentially poetic.

This interest was rather increased by the fact that I had for many years heard of this class of songs under the name of "Negro Spirituals," and had even heard some of them sung by friends from South Carolina. I could now gather on their own soil these strange plants, which I had before seen as in museums alone. True, the individual songs rarely coincided; there was a line here, a chorus there,—just enough to fix the class, but this was unmistakable. It was not strange that they differed, for the range seemed almost endless, and South Carolina, Georgia, and Florida seemed to have nothing but the generic character in common, until all were mingled in the united stock of camp-melodies.

Often in the starlit evening I have returned from some lonely ride by the swift river, or on the plover-haunted barrens, and, entering the camp, have silently approached some glimmering fire, round which the dusky figures moved in the rhythmical barbaric dance the negroes call a "shout," chanting, often harshly, but always in the most perfect time, some monotonous refrain. Writing down in the darkness, as I best could,—perhaps with my hand in the safe covert of my pocket,—the words of the song, I have afterwards carried it to my tent, like some captured bird or insect, and then, after examination, put it by. Or, summoning one of the men at some period of leisure,—Corporal Robert Sutton, for instance, whose iron memory held all the details of a song as if it were a ford or a forest,—I have completed the new specimen by supplying the absent parts. The music I could only retain by ear, and though the more common strains were repeated often enough to fix their impression, there were others that occurred only once or twice.

The words will be here given, as nearly as possible, in the original dialect; and if the spelling seems sometimes inconsistent, or the misspelling insufficient, it is because I could get no nearer. I wished to avoid what seems to me the only error of Lowell's "Biglow Papers" in respect to dialect,—the occasional use of an extreme misspelling, which merely confuses the eye, without taking us any closer to the peculiarity of sound.

The favorite song in camp was the following,—sung with no accompaniment but the measured clapping of hands and the clatter of many feet. It was sung perhaps twice as often as any other. This was partly due to the fact that it properly consisted of a chorus alone, with which the verses of other songs might be combined at random.

I. HOLD YOUR LIGHT.

"Hold your light, Brudder Robert,—
  Hold your light,
Hold your light on Canaan's shore.

"What make ole Satan for follow me so?
  Satan ain't got notin' for do wid me.
    Hold your light,
    Hold your light,
  Hold your light on Canaan's shore."

[476]

This would be sung for half an hour at a time, perhaps, each person present being named in turn. It seemed the simplest primitive type of "spiritual." The next in popularity was almost as elementary, and, like this, named successively each one of the circle. It was, however, much more resounding and convivial in its music.

II. BOUND TO GO.

"Jordan River, I'm bound to go,
  Bound to go, bound to go,—
Jordan River, I'm bound to go,
  And bid 'em fare ye well.

"My Brudder Robert, I'm bound to go,
  Bound to go, &c.

"My Sister Lucy, I'm bound to go,
  Bound to go," &c.

Sometimes it was "tink 'em" (think them) "fare ye well." The *ye* was so detached, that I thought at first it was "very" or "vary well."

Another picturesque song, which seemed immensely popular, was at first very bewildering to me. I could not make out the first words of the chorus, and called it the "Romandàr," being reminded of some Romaic song which I had formerly heard. That association quite fell in with the Orientalism of the new tent-life.

III. ROOM IN THERE.

"O, my mudder is gone! my mudder is gone!
  My mudder is gone into heaven, my Lord!
    I can't stay behind!
Dere's room in dar, room in dar,
Room in dar, in de heaven, my Lord!
    I can't stay behind,

Can't stay behind, my dear,
 I can't stay behind!

"O, my fader is gone!" &c.

"O, de angels are gone!" &c.

"O, I'se been on de road! I'se been on
    de road!
 I'se been on de road into heaven, my
    Lord!
  I can't stay behind!
O, room in dar, room in dar,
Room in dar, in de heaven, my Lord!
  I can't stay behind!"

By this time every man within hearing, from oldest to youngest, would be wriggling and shuffling, as if through some magic piper's bewitchment; for even those who at first affected contemptuous indifference would be drawn into the vortex erelong.

Next to these in popularity ranked a class of songs belonging emphatically to the Church Militant, and available for camp purposes with very little strain upon their symbolism. This, for instance, had a true companion-in-arms heartiness about it, not impaired by the feminine invocation at the end.

IV. HAIL MARY.

"One more valiant soldier here,
  One more valiant soldier here,
 One more valiant soldier here,
  To help me bear de cross.
 O hail, Mary, hail!
  Hail, Mary, hail!
 Hail, Mary, hail!
  To help me bear de cross."

I fancied that the original reading might have been "soul," instead of "soldier,"—with some other syllable inserted, to fill out the metre,—and

that the "Hail, Mary," might denote a Roman Catholic origin, as I had several men from St. Augustine who held in a dim way to that faith. It was a very ringing song, though not so grandly jubilant as the next, which was really impressive as the singers pealed it out, when marching or rowing or embarking.

V. MY ARMY CROSS OVER.

"My army cross over,
 My army cross over.
 O, Pharaoh's army drownded!
 My army cross over.

"We'll cross de mighty river,
  My army cross over;
 We'll cross de river Jordan,
  My army cross over;
 We'll cross de danger water,
  My army cross over;
 We'll cross de mighty Myo,
  My army cross over. (Thrice.)
 O, Pharaoh's army drownded!
 My army cross over."

I could get no explanation of the "mighty Myo," except that one of the old men thought it meant the river of death. Perhaps it is an African word. In the Cameroon dialect, "Mawa" signifies "to die."

The next also has a military ring about it, and the first line is well matched by the music. The rest is conglomerate, and one or two lines show a more Northern origin. "Done" is a Virginia shibboleth, quite distinct from the "been" which replaces it in South Carolina. Yet one of their best choruses, without any fixed words, was, "De bell done ringing," for which, in proper South Carolina dialect, would have been substituted, "De bell been a-ring." This refrain may have gone South with our army.

VI. RIDE IN, KIND SAVIOUR.

"Ride in, kind Saviour!
  No man can hinder me.
O, Jesus is a mighty man!
  No man, &c.
We're marching through Virginny
    fields.
  No man, &c.
O, Satan is a busy man,
  No man, &c.
And he has his sword and shield,
  No man, &c.
O, old Secesh done come and gone!
  No man can hinder me."

Sometimes they substituted "hinder *we*," which was more spicy to the ear, and more in keeping with the usual head-over-heels arrangement of their pronouns.

Almost all their songs were thoroughly religious in their tone, however quaint their expression, and were in a minor key, both as to words and music. The attitude is always the same, and, as a commentary on the life of the race, is infinitely pathetic. Nothing but patience for this life,—nothing but triumph in the next. Sometimes the present predominates, sometimes the future; but the combination is always implied. In the following, for instance, we hear simply the patience.

VII. THIS WORLD ALMOST DONE.

"Brudder, keep your lamp trimmin'
    and a-burnin',
  Keep your lamp trimmin' and
      a-burnin',
  Keep your lamp trimmin' and
      a-burnin',
    For dis world most done.

[478]

So keep your lamp, &c.
  Dis world most done."

But in the next, the final reward of patience is proclaimed as plaintively.

VIII. I WANT TO GO HOME.

"Dere's no rain to wet you,
  O, yes, I want to go home.
Dere's no sun to burn you,
  O, yes, I want to go home;
O, push along, believers,
  O, yes, &c.
Dere's no hard trials,
  O, yes, &c.
Dere's no whips-a-crackin',
  O, yes, &c.
My brudder on de wayside,
  O, yes, &c.
O, push along, my brudder,
  O, yes, &c.
Where dere's no stormy weather,
  O, yes, &c.
Dere's no tribulation,
  O, yes, &c."

This next was a boat-song, and timed well with the tug of the oar.

IX. THE COMING DAY.

"I want to go to Canaan,
  I want to go to Canaan,
  I want to go to Canaan,
    To meet 'em at de comin' day.
O, remember, let me go to Canaan,
      (*Thrice.*)
  To meet 'em, &c.
O brudder, let me go to Canaan,
      (*Thrice.*)
  To meet 'em, &c.
My brudder, you—of!—remember
      (*Thrice.*)
To meet 'em at de comin' day."

The following begins with a startling affirmation, yet the last line quite outdoes the first. This, too, was a capital boat-song.

X. ONE MORE RIVER.

"O, Jordan bank was a great old bank!
　Dere ain't but one more river to
　　cross.
We have some valiant soldier here,
　Dere ain't, &c.
O, Jordan stream will never run dry,
　Dere ain't, &c.
Dere's a hill on my leff, and he catch
　on my right,
Dere ain't but one more river to
　cross."

I could get no explanation of this last riddle, except, "Dat mean, if you go on de leff go to 'struction, and if you go on de right, go to God, for sure."

In others, more of spiritual conflict is implied, as in this next.

XI. O THE DYING LAMB!

"I wants to go where Moses trod,
　O de dying Lamb!
For Moses gone to de promised land,
　O de dying Lamb!
To drink from springs dat never run
　dry,
　O, &c.
Cry O my Lord!
　O, &c.
Before I'll stay in hell one day,
　O, &c.
I'm in hopes to pray my sins away,
　O, &c.
Cry O my Lord!
　O, &c.
Brudder Moses promised for be dar
　too,
　O, &c.
To drink from streams dat never run
　dry,
　O de dying Lamb!"

In the next, the conflict is at its height, and the lurid imagery of the Apocalypse is brought to bear. This book, with the books of Moses, constituted their Bible; all that lay between, even the narratives of the life of Jesus, they hardly cared to read or to hear.

XII. DOWN IN THE VALLEY.

"We'll run and never tire,
We'll run and never tire,
We'll run and never tire,
　Jesus set poor sinners free.
Way down in de valley,
　Who will rise and go with me?
You've heern talk of Jesus,
　Who set poor sinners free.

"De lightnin' and de flashin',
De lightnin' and de flashin',
De lightnin' and de flashin',
　Jesus set poor sinners free.
I can't stand de fire. (*Thrice.*)
　Jesus set poor sinners free,
De green trees a-flamin'. (*Thrice.*)
　Jesus set poor sinners free,
　Way down in de valley,
　　Who will rise and go with me?
　You've heern talk of Jesus
　　Who set poor sinners free."

"De valley" and "de lonesome valley" were familiar words in their religious experience. To descend into that region implied the same process with the "anxious-seat" of the camp-meeting. When a young girl was supposed to enter it, she bound a handkerchief by a peculiar knot over her head, and made it a point of honor not to change a single garment till the day of her baptism, so that she was sure of being in physical readiness for the cleansing rite, whatever her spiritual mood might be. More than once, in noticing a damsel thus mystically ker-chiefed, I have asked some dusky at-tendant its meaning, and have re-ceived the unfailing answer,—framed with their usual indifference to the genders of pronouns,—"He in de lone-some valley, sa."

The next gives the same dramatic conflict, while its detached and imper-sonal refrain gives it strikingly the character of the Scotch and Scan-dinavian ballads.

XIII. CRY HOLY.

"Cry holy, holy!
   Look at de people dat is born of
     God.
And I run down de valley, and I run
     down to pray,
   Says, look at de people dat is born
     of God.
When I get dar, Cappen Satan was dar
   Says, look at, &c.
Says, young man, young man, dere's
     no use for pray,
   Says, look at, &c.
For Jesus is dead, and God gone away,
   Says, look at, &c.
And I made him out a liar and I went
     my way,
   Says, look at, &c.
     Sing holy, holy!

"O, Mary was a woman, and he had a
     one Son,
   Says, look at, &c.
And de Jews and de Romans had him
     hung,
   Says, look at, &c.
     Cry holy, holy!

"And I tell you, sinner, you had better
     had pray,
   Says, look at, &c.
For hell is a dark and dismal place,
   Says, look at, &c.

And I tell you, sinner, and I wouldn't
     go dar!
   Says, look at, &c.
   Cry holy, holy!"

Here is an infinitely quaint descrip-tion of the length of the heavenly road:—

XIV. O'ER THE CROSSING.

"Yonder's my old mudder,
   Been a-waggin' at de hill so long.
It's about time she'll cross over;
   Get home bimeby.
Keep prayin', I do believe
   We're a long time waggin' o'er de
     crossin'.
Keep prayin', I do believe
   We'll get home to heaven bimeby.

"Hear dat mournful thunder
   Roll from door to door,
Calling home God's children;
   Get home bimeby.
Little chil'en, I do believe
   We're a long time, &c.
Little chil'en, I do believe
   We'll get home, &c.

"See dat forked lightnin'
   Flash from tree to tree,
Callin' home God's chil'en;
   Get home bimeby.
True believer, I do believe
   We're a long time, &c.
O brudders, I do believe,
   We'll get home to heaven bimeby."

One of the most singular pictures of future joys, and with a fine flavor of hospitality about it, was this:—

XV. WALK 'EM EASY.

"O, walk 'em easy round de heaven,
   Walk 'em easy round de heaven,

Walk 'em easy round de heaven,
   Dat all de people may join de band.
Walk 'em easy round de heaven.
   (*Thrice.*)
   O, shout glory till 'em join dat
   band!"

The chorus was usually the greater part of the song, and often came in paradoxically, thus:—

XVI. O YES, LORD.

"O, must I be like de foolish mans?
   O yes, Lord!
Will build de house on de sandy hill.
   O yes, Lord!
I'll build my house on Zion hill,
   O yes, Lord!
No wind nor rain can blow me down
   O yes, Lord!"

The next is very graceful and lyrical, and with more variety of rhythm than usual:—

XVII. BOW LOW, MARY.

"Bow low, Mary, bow low, Martha,
   For Jesus come and lock de door,
   And carry de keys away.
Sail, sail, over yonder,
And view de promised land.
   For Jesus come, &c.
Weep, O Mary, bow low, Martha,
   For Jesus come, &c.
Sail, sail, my true believer;
Sail, sail, over yonder;
Mary, bow low, Martha, bow low,
   For Jesus come and lock de door
   And carry de keys away."

But of all the "spirituals" that which surprised me the most, I think,— perhaps because it was that in which external nature furnished the images most directly,—was this. With all my experience of their ideal ways of speech, I was startled when first I came on such a flower of poetry in that dark soil.

XVIII. I KNOW MOON-RISE.

"I know moon-rise, I know star-rise,
   Lay dis body down.
I walk in de moonlight, I walk in de
   starlight,
   To lay dis body down.
I'll walk in de graveyard, I'll walk
   through de graveyard,
   To lay dis body down.
I'll lie in de grave and stretch out my
   arms;
   Lay dis body down.
I go to de judgment in de evenin' of
   de day,
   When I lay dis body down;
And my soul and your soul will meet
   in de day
   When I lay dis body down."

"I'll lie in de grave and stretch out my arms." Never, it seems to me, since man first lived and suffered, was his infinite longing for peace uttered more plaintively than in that line.

The next is one of the wildest and most striking of the whole series: there is a mystical effect and a passionate striving throughout the whole. The Scriptural struggle between Jacob and the angel, which is only dimly expressed in the words, seems all uttered in the music. I think it impressed by imagination more powerfully than any other of these songs.

XIX. WRESTLING JACOB.

"O wrestlin' Jacob, Jacob, day's
   a-breakin';
      I will not let thee go!

[481]

O wrestlin' Jacob, Jacob, day's
a-breakin';
    He will not let me go!
O, I hold my brudder wid a tremblin'
hand;
    I would not let him go!
I hold my sister wid a tremblin' hand;
    I would not let her go!

"O, Jacob do hang from a tremblin'
limb,
    He would not let him go!
O, Jacob do hang from a tremblin'
limb;
    De Lord will bless my soul.
O wrestlin' Jacob, Jacob," &c.

Of "occasional hymns," properly so called, I noticed but one, a funeral hymn for an infant, which is sung plaintively over and over, without variety of words.

XX. THE BABY GONE HOME.

"De little baby gone home,
De little baby gone home,
De little baby gone along,
    For to climb up Jacob's ladder.
And I wish I'd been dar,
I wish I'd been dar,
I wish I'd been dar, my Lord,
    For to climb up Jacob's ladder."

Still simpler is this, which is yet quite sweet and touching.

XXI. JESUS WITH US.

"He have been wid us, Jesus,
    He still wid us, Jesus,
He will be wid us, Jesus,
    Be wid us to the end."

The next seemed to be a favorite about Christmas time, when meditations on "de rollin' year" were frequent among them.

XXII. LORD, REMEMBER ME!

"O do, Lord, remember me!
    O do, Lord, remember me!
O, do remember me, until de year
    roll round!
Do, Lord, remember me!

"If you want to die like Jesus died,
    Lay in de grave.
You would fold your arms and close
    your eyes
And die wid a free good will.

"For Death is a simple ting,
    And he go from door to door,
And he knock down some, and he
    cripple up some,
And he leave some here to pray.

"O do, Lord, remember me!
    O do, Lord, remember me!
My old fader's gone till de year roll
    round;
Do, Lord, remember me!"

The next was sung in such an operatic and rollicking way that it was quite hard to fancy it a religious performance, which, however, it was. I heard it but once.

XXIII. EARLY IN THE MORNING.

"I meet little Rosa early in de mornin',
    O Jerusalem! early in de mornin';
And I ax her, How you do, my
    darter?
    O Jerusalem! early in de mornin'.

"I meet my mudder early in de
    mornin',
    O Jerusalem! &c.
And I ax her, How you do, my
    mudder?
    O Jerusalem! &c.

"I meet Budder Robert early in de
    mornin',
    O Jerusalem! &c.

And I ax him, How you do, my
    sonny?
  O Jerusalem! &c.

"I meet Tittawisa early in de mornin',
  O Jerusalem! &c.
And I ax her, How you do, my
    darter?
  O Jerusalem!" &c.

"Tittawisa" means "Sister Louisa."
In songs of this class the name of every
person present successively appears.

    Their best marching song, and one
which was invaluable to lift their feet
along, as they expressed it, was the following. There was a kind of spring and
lilt to it, quite indescribable by words.

XXIV. GO IN THE WILDERNESS.

"Jesus call you. Go in de wilderness,
  Go in de wilderness, go in de
    wilderness,
Jesus call you. Go in de wilderness
  To wait upon de Lord.
Go wait upon de Lord,
Go wait upon de Lord,
Go wait upon de Lord, my God,
  He take away de sins of de world.

"Jesus a-waitin'. Go in de wilderness,
  Go, &c.
All dem chil'en go in de wilderness
  To wait upon de Lord."

    The next was one of those which I
had heard in boyish days, brought
North from Charleston. But the chorus
alone was identical; the words were
mainly different, and those here given
are quaint enough.

XXV. BLOW YOUR TRUMPET, GABRIEL.

"O, blow your trumpet, Gabriel,
  Blow your trumpet louder;

And I want dat trumpet to blow me
  home
To my new Jerusalem.

"De prettiest ting dat ever I done
Was to serve de Lord when I was
    young.
  So blow your trumpet, Gabriel,
    &c.

"O, Satan is a liar, and he conjure too,
And if you don't mind, he'll conjure
    you.
  So blow your trumpet, Gabriel,
    &c.

"O, I was lost in de wilderness,
King Jesus hand me de candle down.
  So blow your trumpet, Gabriel,"
    &c.

    The following contains one of those
odd transformations of proper names
with which their Scriptural citations
were often enriched. It rivals their text,
"Paul may plant, and may polish wid
water," which I have elsewhere
quoted, and in which the sainted
Apollos would hardly have recognized
himself.

XXVI. IN THE MORNING.

"In de mornin',
  In de mornin',
  Chil'en? Yes, my Lord!
    Don't you hear de trumpet sound?
If I had a-died when I was young,
I never would had de race for run.
    Don't you hear de trumpet sound?

"O Sam and Peter was fishin' in de
    sea,
And dey drop de net and follow my
    Lord.
    Don't you hear de trumpet sound?

"Dere's a silver spade for to dig my
    grave
And a golden chain for to let me
    down.

Don't you hear de trumpet sound?
In de mornin',
In de mornin',
Chil'en? Yes, my Lord!
Don't you hear de trumpet sound?"

These golden and silver fancies remind one of the King of Spain's
daughter in "Mother Goose," and the
golden apple, and the silver pear,
which are doubtless themselves but
the vestiges of some simple early composition like this. The next has a
humbler and more domestic style of
fancy.

XXVII. FARE YE WELL.

"My true believers, fare ye well,
Fare ye well, fare ye well,
Fare ye well, by de grace of God,
For I'm going home.

Massa Jesus give me a little broom
For to sweep my heart clean,
And I will try, by de grace of God,
To win my way home."

Among the songs not available for
marching, but requiring the concentrated enthusiasm of the camp, was
"The Ship of Zion," of which they had
three wholly distinct versions, all quite
exuberant and tumultuous.

XXVIII. THE SHIP OF ZION.

"Come along, come along,
And let us go home,
O, glory, hallelujah!
Dis de ole ship o' Zion,
Halleloo! Halleloo!
Dis de ole ship o' Zion,
Hallelujah!

"She has landed many a tousand,
She can land as many more.
O, glory, hallelujah! &c.

"Do you tink she will be able
For to take us all home?
O, glory, hallelujah! &c.

"You can tell 'em I'm a comin',
Halleloo! Halleloo!
You can tell 'em I'm a comin',
Hallelujah!
Come along, come along," &c.

XXIX. THE SHIP OF ZION.
(Second version.)

"Dis de good ole ship o' Zion,
Dis de good ole ship o' Zion,
Dis de good ole ship o' Zion,
And she's makin' for de Promise
Land.
She hab angels for de sailors. (Thrice.)
And she's, &c.
And how you know dey's angels?
(Thrice.)
And she's, &c.
Good Lord, shall I be de one?
(Thrice.)
And she's, &c.

"Dat ship is out a-sailin', sailin',
sailin',
And she's, &c.
She's a-sailin' mighty steady,
steady, steady,
And she's, &c.
She'll neither reel nor totter, totter,
totter,
And she's, &c.
She's a-sailin' away cold Jordan,
Jordan, Jordan,
And she's, &c.
King Jesus is de captain, captain,
captain,
And she's makin' for de Promise
Land."

XXX. THE SHIP OF ZION.
(Third version.)

"De Gospel ship is sailin',
Hosann—sann.

O, Jesus is de captain,
  Hosann—sann.
De angels are de sailors,
  Hosann—sann.
O, is your bundle ready?
  Hosann—sann.
O, have you got your ticket?
  Hosann—sann."

This abbreviated chorus is given with unspeakable unction.

The three just given are modifications of an old camp-meeting melody; and the same may be true of the three following, although I cannot find them in the Methodist hymn-books. Each, however, has its characteristic modifications, which make it well worth giving. In the second verse of this next, for instance, "Saviour" evidently has become "soldier."

XXXI. SWEET MUSIC.

"Sweet music in heaven,
  Just beginning for to roll.
  Don't you love God?
  Glory, hallelujah!

"Yes, late I heard my soldier say,
Come, heavy soul, I am de way.
  Don't you love God?
  Glory, hallelujah!

"I'll go and tell to sinners round
What a kind Saviour I have found.
  Don't you love God?
  Glory, hallelujah!

"My grief my burden long has been,
Because I was not cease from sin.
  Don't you love God?
  Glory, hallelujah!"

XXXII. GOOD NEWS.

"O, good news! O, good news!
De angels brought de tidings down,
  Just comin' from de trone.

"As grief from out my soul shall fly,
  Just comin' from de trone;
I'll shout salvation when I die,
  Good news, O, good news!
  Just comin' from de trone.

"Lord, I want to go to heaven when I
  die,
  Good news, O, good news!&c.

"De white folks call us a noisy crew,
  Good news, O, good news!
But dis I know, we are happy too,
  Just comin' from de trone."

XXXIII. THE HEAVENLY ROAD.

"You may talk of my name as much as
  you please,
  And carry my name abroad,
But I really do believe I'm a child of
  God
  As I walk in de heavenly road.
O, won't you go wid me? (Thrice.)
  For to keep our garments clean.

"O, Satan is a mighty busy ole man,
  And roll rocks in my way;
But Jesus is my bosom friend,
  And roll 'em out of de way.
O, won't you go wid me? (Thrice.)
  For to keep our garments clean.

"Come, my brudder, if you never did
  pray,
  I hope you may pray to-night;
For I really believe I'm a child of God
  As I walk in de heavenly road.
O, won't you," &c.

Some of the songs had played an historic part during the war. For singing the next, for instance, the negroes had been put in jail in Georgetown, S.C., at the outbreak of the Rebellion. "We'll soon be free," was too dangerous an assertion; and though the chant was an old one, it was no doubt sung with redoubled emphasis during the new events. "De Lord will call us home," was evidently thought to be a symbolical verse; for, as a little drummer-boy explained to me, showing all his white teeth as he sat in the moonlight by the door of my tent, "Dey tink *de Lord* mean for say *de Yankees.*"

XXXIV. WE'LL SOON BE FREE.

"We'll soon be free,
  We'll soon be free,
  We'll soon be free,
    When de Lord will call us home.
  My brudder, how long,
  My brudder, how long,
  My brudder, how long,
    'Fore we done sufferin' here?
It won't be long (*Thrice.*)
    'Fore de Lord will call us home.
We'll walk de miry road (*Thrice.*)
    Where pleasure never dies.
We'll walk de golden street (*Thrice.*)
    Where pleasure never dies.
My brudder, how long (*Thrice.*)
    'Fore we done sufferin' here?
We'll soon be free (*Thrice.*)
    When Jesus sets me free.
We'll fight for liberty (*Thrice.*)
    When de Lord will call us home."

The suspicion in this case was unfounded, but they had another song to which the Rebellion had actually given rise. This was composed by nobody knew whom,—though it was the most recent, doubtless, of all these "spirituals,"—and had been sung in secret to avoid detection. It is certainly plaintive enough. The peck of corn and pint of salt were slavery's rations.

XXXV. MANY THOUSAND GO.

"No more peck o' corn for me,
  No more, no more,—
No more peck o' corn for me,
  Many tousand go.

"No more driver's lash for me, (*Twice.*)
  No more, &c.

"No more pint o' salt for me, (*Twice.*)
  No more, &c.

"No more hundred lash for me,
    (*Twice.*)
  No more, &c.

"No more mistress' call for me,
  No more, no more,—
No more mistress' call for me,
  Many tousand go."

Even of this last composition, however, we have only the approximate date, and know nothing of the mode of composition. Allan Ramsay says of the Scotch songs, that, no matter who made them, they were soon attributed to the minister of the parish whence they sprang. And I always wondered, about these, whether they had always a conscious and definite origin in some leading mind, or whether they grew by gradual accretion, in an almost unconscious way. On this point I could get no information, though I asked many questions, until at last, one day when I was being rowed across from Beaufort to Ladies' Island, I found myself, with delight, on the actual trail of a song. One of the oarsmen, a brisk young fellow, not a soldier, on being asked for his theory of the matter, dropped out a coy confession. "Some good sperituals," he said, "are start jess out o' curiosity. I been a-raise a sing, myself, once."

My dream was fulfilled, and I had traced out, not the poem alone, but the poet. I implored him to proceed.

"Once we boys," he said, "went for

tote some rice, and de nigger-driver, he keep a-callin' on us; and I say, 'O, de ole nigger-driver!' Den anudder said, 'Fust ting my mammy tole me was, notin' so bad as nigger-driver.' Den I made a sing, just puttin' a word, and den anudder word."

Then he began singing, and the men, after listening a moment, joined in the chorus as if it were an old acquaintance, though they evidently had never heard it before. I saw how easily a new "sing" took root among them.

XXXVI. THE DRIVER.

"O, de ole nigger-driver!
  O, gwine away!
Fust ting my mammy tell me,
  O, gwine away!
Tell me 'bout de nigger-driver,
  O, gwine away!
Nigger-driver second devil,
  O, gwine away!
Best ting for do he driver,
  O, gwine away!
Knock he down and spoil he labor,
  O, gwine away!"

It will be observed that, although this song is quite secular in its character, its author yet called it a "spiritual." I heard but two songs among them, at any time, to which they would not, perhaps, have given this generic name. One of these consisted simply in the endless repetition—after the manner of certain college songs—of the mysterious line,

"Rain fall and wet Becky Martin."

But who Becky Martin was, and why she should or should not be wet, and whether the dryness was a reward or a penalty, none could say. I got the impression that, in either case, the event was posthumous, and that there was some tradition of grass not growing over the grave of a sinner; but even this was vague, and all else vaguer.

The other song I heard but once, on a morning when a squad of men came in from picket duty, and chanted it in the most rousing way. It had been a stormy and comfortless night, and the picket station was very exposed. It still rained in the morning when I strolled to the edge of the camp, looking out for the men, and wondering how they had stood it. Presently they came striding along the road, at a great pace, with their shining rubber blankets worn as cloaks around them, the rain streaming from these and from their equally shining faces, which were almost all upon the broad grin, as they pealed out this remarkable ditty:—

HANGMAN JOHNNY.

"O, dey call me Hangman Johnny!
  O, ho! O, ho!
But I never hang nobody,
  O, hang, boys, hang!

"O, dey call me Hangman Johnny!
  O, ho! O, ho!
But we'll all hang togedder,
  O, hang, boys, hang!"

My presence apparently checked the performance of another verse, beginning, "De buckra 'list for money," apparently in reference to the controversy about the pay-question, then just beginning, and to the more mercenary aims they attributed to the white soldiers. But "Hangman Johnny" remained always a myth as inscrutable as "Becky Martin."

As they learned all their songs by ear, they often strayed into wholly new versions, which sometimes became popular, and entirely banished the others. This was amusingly the case, for instance, with one phrase in the popular camp-song of "Marching Along," which was entirely new to them until our quartermaster taught it to them, at my request. The words, "Gird on the armor," were to them a stumbling-block, and no wonder, until some ingenious ear substituted, "Guide on de army," which was at once accepted, and became universal.

"We'll guide on de army,
and be marching along,"

is now the established version on the Sea Islands.

These quaint religious songs were to the men more than a source of relaxation; they were a stimulus to courage and a tie to heaven. I never overheard in camp a profane or vulgar song. With the trifling exceptions given, all had a religious motive, while the most secular melody could not have been more exciting. A few youths from Savannah, who were comparatively men of the world, had learned some of the "Ethiopian Minstrel" ditties, imported from the North. These took no hold upon the mass; and, on the other hand, they sang reluctantly, even on Sunday, the long and short metres of the hymn-books, always gladly yielding to the more potent excitement of their own "spirituals." By these they could sing themselves, as had their fathers before them, out of the contemplation of their own low estate, into the sublime scenery of the Apocalypse. I remember that this minor-keyed pathos used to seem to me almost too sad to dwell upon, while slavery seemed destined to last for generations; but now that their patience has had its perfect work, history cannot afford to lose this portion of its record. There is no parallel instance of an oppressed race thus sustained by the religious sentiment alone. These songs are but the vocal expression of the simplicity of their faith and the sublimity of their long resignation.

98. Shout Songs, Work Songs, and Spirituals

Religion inspired many of the most beautiful slave songs. Death, heaven, and the love of Jesus for all men are the dominant motifs of the lyrics.

Source: William Francis Allen, Charles Pickard Ware, and Lucy McKim Garrison, *Slave Songs of the United States* (New York: A. Simpson & Co., 1867), pp. 6–7, 12–13, 15, 18–19, 23, 72–73.

Transcending the dialect, too often allowed to obscure the meaning, is the pervading sense of the immediacy of Christ, or "King Jesus." One could call it a kind of intimacy. The following songs illustrate this intimacy, and a beautiful blending of the secular language and spiritual themes. Important beyond all other themes is that the sufferings of the world, bravely borne, prepare the soul for heaven. Lucy McKim Garrison was a well-trained musicologist, and her collaboration with Charles Ware and William F. Allen was invaluable in setting down the music they heard while superintending labor on abandoned plantations during the Civil War.

The authors' notations indicate variations in the works sung to a given tune. "I Can't Stay Behind" is a "shout song," i.e., it was sung while the singers circled in a rhythmic dance expressing their religious enthusiasm but always taking care not to cross their feet, as this would have made the dances secular. See in document 97 the passage in which Colonel Higginson describes the "shout." "Poor Rosy," or "Heav'n Shall-a Be My Home," was a work song, as was "Michael Row the Boat Ashore"—as popular and moving today as it was a hundred years ago.

Variations on the wording of the songs were indicated in footnotes by the original editors, and I have kept these notes intact. The substantive notes of Allen, Ware, and Garrison are likewise included just as they appear in the 1867 edition.

8. I CAN'T STAY BEHIND.

Chor. I can't stay be-hind, my Lord, I can't stay be-hind!

1. Dere's room e-nough, Room e-nough, Room e-nough in de

Var.

heaven, my Lord;* Room enough, Room enough, I can't stay be-hind.

2 I been all around, I been all around,
  Been all around de Heaven, my Lord.

3 I've searched every room—in de Heaven, my Lord. †

4 De angels singin' ‡—all round de trone.

5 My Fader call—and I must go.

6 Sto-back, § member; sto-back, member.

* For you.   † And Heaven all around.   ‡ Crowned.   § "Sto-back" means "Shout backwards."

[This "shout" is very widely spread, and variously sung. In Charleston it is simpler in its movement, and the refrain is "I can't stay away." In Edgefield it is expostulating: "Don't stay away, my mudder." Col. Higginson gives the following version, as sung in his regiment:

"O, my mudder is gone! my mudder is gone!
My mudder is gone into heaven, my Lord!
  I can't stay behind!
Dere 's room in dar, room in dar.
Room in dar, in de heaven, my Lord!
  I can't stay behind.
Can't stay behind, my dear,
  I can't stay behind!

"O, my fader is gone! &c.

"O, de angels are gone! &c

"O, I 'se been on de road! I 'se been on de road!
I 'se been on de road into heaven, my Lord!
  I can't stay behind!
O, room in dar, room in dar,
Room in dar, in de heaven, my Lord!
  I can't stay behind!"

Lt. Col. Trowbridge is of opinion that it was brought from Florida, as he first heard it in Dec., 1862, from a boat-load of Florida soldiers brought up by Lt. Col. Billings. It was not heard by Mr. Ware at Coffin's Point until that winter. It seems hardly likely, however, that it could have made its way to Charleston and Edgefield since that time. The air became "immensely popular" in the regiment, and was soon adopted for military purposes, so that the class leaders indignantly complained of "the drum corps using de Lord's chune."]

9. POOR ROSY.

1. Poor Ro - sy, poor gal;* Poor Ro - sy, poor gal; Ro - sy break my poor heart, Heav'n shall-a be my home. I can - not stay in hell one day, Heav'n shall-a be my home; I'll sing and pray my soul a-way, Heav'n shall-a be my home.

2 Got hard trial in my way, *(ter)*
Heav'n shall-a be my home.
O when I talk, † I talk † wid God, } *(bis)*
Heav'n shall-a be my home. }

8 I dunno what de people ‡ want of me, *(ter)*
Heav'n shall-a be my home.

* Poor Cæsar, poor boy.   † Walk.   ‡ Massa.

[This song ranks with "Roll, Jordan," in dignity and favor. The following variation of the second part was heard at "The Oaks:"]

Be - fore I stay in hell one day, Heaven shall-a be my home;
I sing and pray my soul a - way, Heaven shall-a be my home.

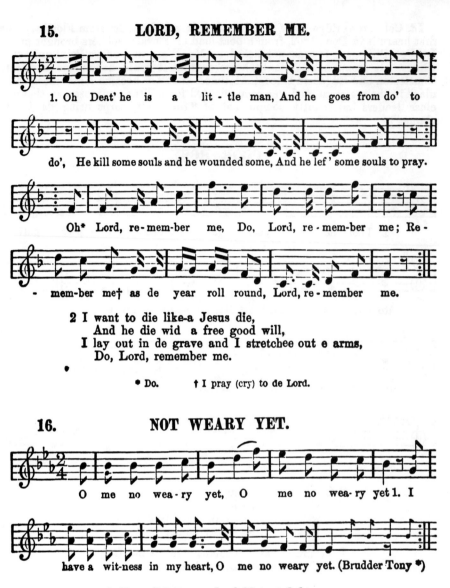

15. LORD, REMEMBER ME.

1. Oh Deat' he is a lit-tle man, And he goes from do' to do', He kill some souls and he wounded some, And he lef' some souls to pray.

Oh* Lord, re-mem-ber me, Do, Lord, re-mem-ber me; Re-mem-ber me† as de year roll round, Lord, re-mem-ber me.

2 I want to die like-a Jesus die,
  And he die wid a free good will,
I lay out in de grave and I stretchee out e arms,
  Do, Lord, remember me.

      * Do.   † I pray (cry) to de Lord.

16. NOT WEARY YET.

O me no wea-ry yet, O me no wea-ry yet 1. I have a wit-ness in my heart, O me no weary yet. (Brudder Tony *)

2 Since I been in de field to † fight.

3 I have a heaven to maintain.

4 De bond of faith are on my soul.

5 Ole Satan toss a ball at me.

6 Him tink de ball would hit my soul.

7 De ball for hell and I for heaven.

      * Sister Mary.   † Been-a.

17. RELIGION SO SWEET.

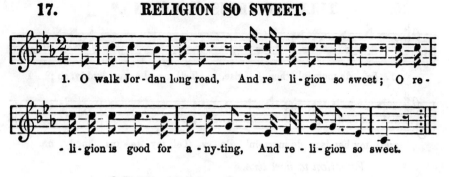

1. O walk Jor-dan long road, And re-li-gion so sweet; O re-
-li-gion is good for a-ny-ting, And re-li-gion so sweet.

3 Religion make you happy.*

4 Religion gib me patience.†

5 O member, get religion.

6 I long time been a-huntin'.

7 I seekin' for my fortune.

8 O I gwine to meet my Savior.

9 Gwine to tell him 'bout my trials.

10 Dey call me boastin' member.

11 Dey call me turnback‡ Christian.

12 Dey call me 'struction maker.

13 But I don't care what dey call me.

14 Lord, trial 'longs to a Christian.

15 O tell me 'bout religion.

16 I weep for Mary and Marta.

17 I seek my Lord and I find him

* Humble.　　　† Honor, Comfort.　　　‡ Lyin', 'ceitful.

18. HUNTING FOR THE LORD.

Hunt till you find him, Halle-lu-jah, And a-huntin' for de
Lord; Till you find him, Halle-lu-jah, And a-huntin' for de Lord.

20. TELL MY JESUS "MORNING."

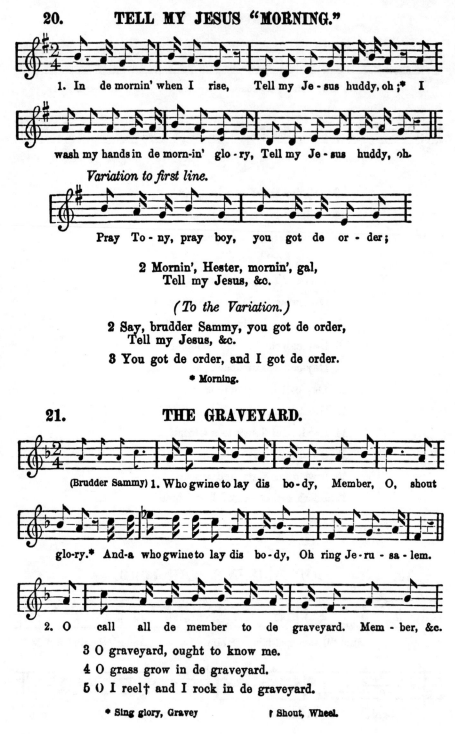

1. In de mornin' when I rise, Tell my Je-sus huddy, oh;* I wash my hands in de morn-in' glo-ry, Tell my Je-sus huddy, oh.

Variation to first line.

Pray To-ny, pray boy, you got de or-der;

2 Mornin', Hester, mornin', gal,
Tell my Jesus, &c.

(To the Variation.)

2 Say, brudder Sammy, you got de order,
Tell my Jesus, &c.

3 You got de order, and I got de order.

* Morning.

21. THE GRAVEYARD.

(Brudder Sammy) 1. Who gwine to lay dis bo-dy, Member, O, shout glo-ry.* And-a who gwine to lay dis bo-dy, Oh ring Je-ru-sa-lem.

2. O call all de member to de graveyard. Mem-ber, &c.

3 O graveyard, ought to know me.

4 O grass grow in de graveyard.

5 O I reel† and I rock in de graveyard.

* Sing glory, Gravey   † Shout, Wheel.

8 And blessèd me, and blessèd my,
   And blessèd all my soul;
  I didn't 'tend to lef' 'em go
   Till Jesus bless my soul.

[This tune appears to be borrowed from "And are ye sure the news is true?"
—but it is so much changed, and the words are so characteristic, that it seemed
undoubtedly best to retan it.]

24.   HUNTING FOR A CITY.

I am huntin' for a ci-ty, to stay a-while, I am

huntin' for a ci-ty, to stay awhile, I am huntin' for a ci-ty, to

stay a-while, O be-lie-ver got a home at las

25.   GWINE FOLLOW.

Tit-ty Ma-ry, you know I gwine fol low, I gwine fol-low, gwine

fol-low, Brudder William, you know I gwine to fol-low, For to

do my Fa-der will. 'Tis well and good I'm a-comin' here tonight, I'm a-

-com-in' here to-night, I'm a-com-in' here to-night, 'Tis

well and good, I'm a-comin' here tonight, For to do my Fader will.

[The second part of this tune is evidently "Buffalo" (variously known also as
"Charleston" or "Baltimore") "Gals;" the first part, however, is excellent and
characteristic.]

26. LAY THIS BODY DOWN.

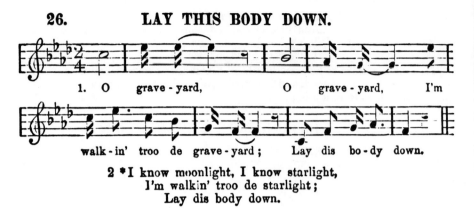

1. O grave-yard, O grave-yard, I'm
walk-in' troo de grave-yard; Lay dis bo-dy down.

2 *I know moonlight, I know starlight,
 I'm walkin' troo de starlight;
 Lay dis body down.

● O moonlight (*or* moonrise); O my soul, O your soul.

[This is probably the song heard by W. H. Russell, of the London *Times*, as described in chapter xviii. of "My Diary North and South" The writer was on his way from Pocotaligo to Mr. Trescot's estate on Barnwell Island, and of the midnight row thither he says:

"The oarsmen, as they bent to their task, beguiled the way by singing in unison a real negro melody, which was unlike the works of the Ethiopian Serenaders as anything in song could be unlike another. It was a barbaric sort of madrigal, in which one singer beginning was followed by the others in unison, repeating the refrain in chorus, and full of quaint expression and melancholy:—

'Oh your soul! oh my soul! I'm going to the churchyard
    To lay this body down;
Oh my soul! oh your soul! we're going to the churchyard
    To lay this nigger down.'

And then some appeal to the difficulty of passing the Jawdam' constituted the whole of the song, which continued with unabated energy during the whole of the little voyage. To me it was a strange scene. The stream, dark as Lethe, flowing between the silent, houseless, rugged banks, lighted up near the landing by the fire in the woods, which reddened the sky—the wild strain, and the unearthly adjurations to the singers' souls, as though they were palpable, put me in mind of the fancied voyage across the Styx."

We append with some hesitation the following as a variation; the words of which we borrow from Col. Higginson. Lt. Col. Trowbridge says of it that it was sung at funerals in the night time—one of the most solemn and character-istic of the customs of the negroes. He attributes its origin to St. Simon's Island, Georgia:]

I know moonlight, I know starlight; I lay dis bo-dy down.

2 I walk in de moonlight, I walk in de starlight;
 I lay dis body down.

3 I know de graveyard, I know de' graveyard,
 When I lay dis body down.

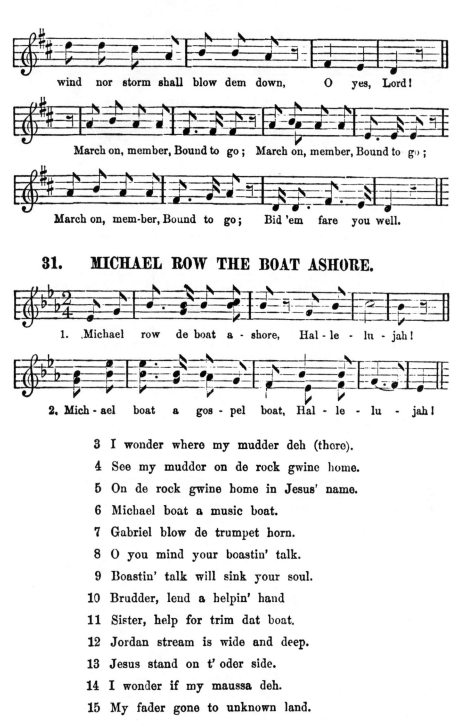

wind nor storm shall blow dem down, O yes, Lord!

March on, member, Bound to go; March on, member, Bound to go;

March on, mem-ber, Bound to go; Bid 'em fare you well.

31. MICHAEL ROW THE BOAT ASHORE.

1. .Michael row de boat a - shore, Hal - le - lu - jah!

2. Mich - ael boat a gos - pel boat, Hal - le - lu - jah!

3 I wonder where my mudder deh (there).

4 See my mudder on de rock gwine home.

5 On de rock gwine home in Jesus' name.

6 Michael boat a music boat.

7 Gabriel blow de trumpet horn.

8 O you mind your boastin' talk.

9 Boastin' talk will sink your soul.

10 Brudder, lend a helpin' hand

11 Sister, help for trim dat boat.

12 Jordan stream is wide and deep.

13 Jesus stand on t' oder side.

14 I wonder if my maussa deh.

15 My fader gone to unknown land.

16 O de Lord he plant his garden deh.

93. O'ER THE CROSSING.

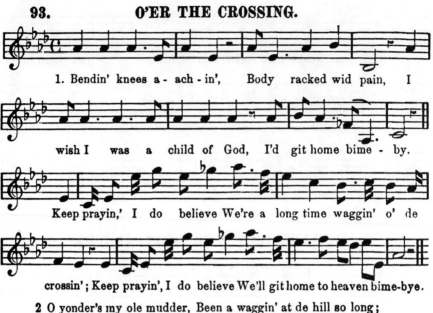

1. Bendin' knees a-ach-in', Body racked wid pain, I
wish I was a child of God, I'd git home bime-by.
Keep prayin,' I do believe We're a long time waggin' o' de
crossin'; Keep prayin', I do believe We'll git home to heaven bime-bye.

2 O yonder's my ole mudder, Been a waggin' at de hill so long;
It's about time she cross over, Git home bime-by.
   Keep prayin', I do believe, etc.

3 O hear dat lumberin' thunder A-roll from do' to do',
A-callin' de people home to God; Dey'll git home bime-by.
   Little chil'n, I do believe, etc.

4 O see dat forked lightnin' A-jump from cloud to cloud,
A-pickin' up God's chil'n; Dey'll git home bime-by.
   Pray mourner, I do believe, etc.

[This "infinitely quaint description of the length of the heavenly road," as Col. Higginson styles it, is one of the most peculiar and wide-spread of the spirituals. It was sung as given above in Caroline Co., Virginia, and probably spread southward from this State, variously modified in different localities. "My body rock 'long fever," (No. 45,) would hardly be recognised as the same, either by words or tune, and yet it is almost certainly the same, as is shown by the following, sung in Augusta, Georgia, which has some of the words of the present song, adapted to a tune which is unmistakably identical with No. 45.]

O yonder's my ole mother, Been a-waggin' at de hill so long; I
really do believe she's a child of God, She'll git home to heav'n bime-bye.

[We regret we have not the air of the Nashville variation, "My Lord called Daniel."]

94. **ROCK O' MY SOUL.**

1. Rock o' my soul in de bosom of Abraham, Rock o' my soul in de bo-som of A-braham, Rock o' my soul in de bosom of A-braham, Lord, Rock o' my soul. **(King Jesus)**

2 He toted the young lambs in his bosom, *(ter)*
  And leave the old sheep alone.

95. WE WILL MARCH THROUGH THE VALLEY.

1. We will march thro' the val-ley in peace, We will march thro' the val-ley in peace; If Je-sus himself be our lead-er, We will march thro' the val-ley in peace.

2 We will march, etc.
  Behold I give myself away, and
  We will march, etc.

3 We will march, etc.
  This track I'll see and I'll pursue;
  We will march, etc.

4 We will march, etc.
  When I'm dead and buried in the cold silent tomb,
  I don't want you to grieve for me.

99. Christmas . . . "the Carnival Season with the Children of Bondage"

Christmas was generally observed as an important holiday throughout the South. It was a time when planters (if they were generous) gave presents to their slaves, and for the slaves it was the one extended period during the year when they were free from labor. The number of days allowed for Christmas varied considerably from region to region, and over time, from as many as twelve days to as few as three. In the last decade before the Civil War three days is the number mentioned most frequently. Late in the slave regime there was a perceptible tendency to reduce the period of "frolic"—in part because the slave-owners feared mischief and bad effects from drunkenness, and in part (one assumes) because of the general pattern developing to regiment slave life more thoroughly.

In the following extract from his famous narrative, Solomon Northup described a hearty Christmas celebration in Louisiana. Northup was a talented free Negro from New York whose unhappy fate it was to be kidnapped and sold into slavery (see document 62). Northup's vantage point as a formerly free man alerted him to the special features of plantation slavery that were sometimes accepted as "given" by those who had been born in bondage. This account of the celebration on the Bayou Bœuf is a happy interlude in an otherwise depressing experience.

The only respite from constant labor the slave has through the whole year, is during the Christmas holidays. Epps allowed us three—others allow four, five and six days, according to the measure of their generosity. It is the only time to which they look forward with any interest or pleasure. They are glad when night comes, not only because it brings them a few hours repose, but because it brings them one day nearer Christmas. It is hailed with equal delight by the old and the young; even Uncle Abram ceases to glorify Andrew Jackson, and Patsey forgets her many sorrows, amid the general hilarity of the holidays. It is the time of feasting, and frolicking,

Source: Solomon Northup, *Twelve Years a Slave. Narrative of Solomon Northup, a Citizen of New-York* . . . (Auburn, N.Y.: Derby and Miller, 1853), pp. 213–22.

and fiddling—the carnival season with the children of bondage. They are the only days when they are allowed a little restricted liberty, and heartily indeed do they enjoy it.

It is the custom for one planter to give a "Christmas supper," inviting the slaves from neighboring plantations to join his own on the occasion; for instance, one year it is given by Epps, the next by Marshall, the next by Hawkins, and so on. Usually from three to five hundred are assembled, coming together on foot, in carts, on horseback, on mules, riding double and triple, sometimes a boy and girl, at others a girl and two boys, and at others again a boy, a girl and an old woman. Uncle Abram astride a mule, with Aunt Phebe and Patsey behind him, trotting towards a Christmas supper, would be no uncommon sight on Bayou Bœuf.

Then, too, "of all days i' the year," they array themselves in their best attire. The cotton coat has been washed clean, the stump of a tallow candle has been applied to the shoes, and if so fortunate as to possess a rimless or a crownless hat, it is placed jauntily on the head. They are welcomed with equal cordiality, however, if they come bare-headed and barefooted to the feast. As a general thing, the women wear handkerchiefs tied about their heads, but if chance has thrown in their way a fiery red ribbon, or a cast-off bonnet of their mistress' grandmother, it is sure to be worn on such occasions. Red—the deep blood red—is decidedly the favorite color among the enslaved damsels of my acquaintance. If a red ribbon does not encircle the neck, you will be certain to find all the hair of their woolly heads tied up with red strings of one sort or another.

The table is spread in the open air, and loaded with varieties of meat and piles of vegetables. Bacon and corn meal at such times are dispensed with. Sometimes the cooking is performed in the kitchen on the plantation, at others in the shade of wide branching trees. In the latter case, a ditch is dug in the ground, and wood laid in and burned until it is filled with glowing coals, over which chickens, ducks, turkeys, pigs, and not unfrequently the entire body of a wild ox, are roasted. They are furnished also with flour, of which biscuits are made, and often with peach and other preserves, with tarts, and every manner and description of pies, except the mince, that being an article of pastry as yet unknown among them. Only the slave who has lived all the year on his scanty allowance of meal and bacon can appreciate such suppers. White people in great numbers assemble to witness the gastronomical enjoyments.

They seat themselves at the rustic table—the males on one side, the females on the other. The two between whom there may have been an exchange of tenderness, invariably manage to sit opposite; for the omnipresent Cupid disdains not to hurl his arrows into the simple hearts of slaves. Unalloyed and exulting happiness lights up the dark faces of them all. The ivory teeth, contrasting with their black complexions, exhibit two long, white streaks the whole extent of the table. All round the bountiful board a multitude of eyes roll in ecstacy. Giggling and laughter and the clattering of cutlery and crockery succeed. Cuffee's elbow hunches his neighbor's side, impelled by an involuntary impulse of delight; Nelly shakes her finger at Sambo and laughs, she knows not why, and so the fun and merriment flows on.

When the viands have disappeared, and the hungry maws of the children of toil are satisfied, then, next in the order of amusement, is the Christmas dance. My business on these gala days always was to play on the violin. The African race is a music-loving one, proverbially; and many there were among my fellow-bondsmen whose organs of tune were strikingly developed, and who could thumb the banjo with dexterity; but at the expense of appearing egotistical, I must, nevertheless, declare, that I was considered the Ole Bull of Bayou Bœuf. My master often received letters, sometimes from a distance of ten miles, requesting him to send me to play at a ball or festival of the whites. He received his compensation, and usually I also returned with many picayunes jingling in my pockets—the extra contributions of those to whose delight I had administered. In this manner I became more acquainted than I otherwise would, up and down the bayou. The young men and maidens of Holmesville always knew there was to be a jollification somewhere, whenever Platt Epps was seen passing through the town with his fiddle in his hand. "Where are you going now, Platt?" and "What is coming off to-night, Platt?" would be interrogatories issuing from every door and window, and many a time when there was no special hurry, yielding to pressing importunities, Platt would

draw his bow, and sitting astride his mule, perhaps, discourse musically to a crowd of delighted children, gathered around him in the street.

Alas! had it not been for my beloved violin, I scarcely can conceive how I could have endured the long years of bondage. It introduced me to great houses—relieved me of many days' labor in the field—supplied me with conveniences for my cabin—with pipes and tobacco, and extra pairs of shoes, and oftentimes led me away from the presence of a hard master, to witness scenes of jollity and mirth. It was my companion—the friend of my bosom—triumphing loudly when I was joyful, and uttering its soft, melodious consolations when I was sad. Often, at midnight, when sleep had fled affrighted from the cabin, and my soul was disturbed and troubled with the contemplation of my fate, it would sing me a song of peace. On holy Sabbath days, when an hour or two of leisure was allowed, it would accompany me to some quiet place on the bayou bank, and, lifting up its voice, discourse kindly and pleasantly indeed. It heralded my name round the country—made me friends, who, otherwise would not have noticed me—gave me an honored seat at the yearly feasts, and secured the loudest and heartiest welcome of them all at the Christmas dance. The Christmas dance! Oh, ye pleasure-seeking sons and daughters of idleness, who move with measured step, listless and snail-like, through the slow-winding cotillon, if ye wish to look upon the celerity, if not the "poetry of motion"—upon genuine happiness, rampant and unrestrained—go down to Louisiana, and see the slaves dancing in the starlight of a Christmas night.

On that particular Christmas I have now in my mind, a description whereof will serve as a description of the day generally, Miss Lively and Mr. Sam, the first belonging to Stewart, the latter to Roberts, started the ball. It was well known that Sam cherished an ardent passion for Lively, as also did one of Marshall's and another of Carey's boys; for Lively was *lively* indeed, and a heart-breaking coquette withal. It was a victory for Sam Roberts, when, rising from the repast, she gave him her hand for the first "figure" in preference to either of his rivals. They were somewhat crest-fallen, and, shaking their heads angrily, rather intimated they would like to pitch into Mr. Sam and hurt him badly. But not an emotion of wrath ruffled the placid bosom of Samuel, as his legs flew like drum-sticks down the outside and up the middle, by the side of his bewitching partner. The whole company cheered them vociferously, and, excited with the applause, they continued "tearing down" after all the others had become exhausted and halted a moment to recover breath. But Sam's superhuman exertions overcame him finally, leaving Lively alone, yet whirling like a top. Thereupon one of Sam's rivals, Pete Marshall, dashed in, and, with might and main, leaped and shuffled and threw himself into every conceivable shape, as if determined to show Miss Lively and all the world that Sam Roberts was of no account.

Pete's affection, however, was greater than his discretion. Such violent exercise took the breath out of him directly, and he dropped like an empty bag. Then was the time for Harry Carey to try his hand; but Lively also soon out-winded him, amidst hurrahs and shouts, fully sustaining her well-earned reputation of being the "fastest gal" on the bayou.

One "set" off, another takes its place, he or she remaining longest on the floor receiving the most uproarious commendation, and so the dancing continues until broad daylight. It does not cease with the sound of the fiddle, but in that case they set up a music peculiar to themselves. This is called "patting," accompanied with one of those unmeaning songs, composed rather for its adaptation to a certain tune or measure, than for the purpose of expressing any distinct idea. The patting is performed by striking the hands on the knees, then striking the hands together, then striking the right shoulder with one hand, the left with the other—all the while keeping time with the feet, and singing, perhaps, this song:

"Harper's creek and roarin' ribber,
Thar, my dear, we'll live forebber;
Den we'll go to de Ingin nation,
All I want in dis creation,
Is pretty little wife and big plantation.

Chorus. Up dat oak and down dat ribber,
Two overseers and one little nigger"

Or, if these words are not adapted to the tune called for, it may be that "Old Hog Eye" *is*—a rather solemn and startling specimen of versification, not, however, to be appreciated unless heard at the South. It runneth as follows:

"Who's been here since I've been
  gone?
Pretty little gal wid a josey on.
                Hog Eye!
                Old Hog Eye,
                And Hosey too!

Never see de like since I was born,
Here come a little gal wid a josey on.
                Hog Eye!
                Old Hog Eye!
                And Hosey too!"

Or, maybe the following, perhaps,
equally nonsensical, but full of melody, nevertheless, as it flows from the
negro's mouth:

"Ebo Dick and Jurdan's Jo,
Them two niggers stole my yo'.
      Chorus. Hop Jim along,
                Walk Jim along,
                Talk Jim along," &c.
Old black Dan, as black as tar,
He dam glad he was not dar.
                Hop Jim along," &c.

During the remaining holidays succeeding Christmas, they are provided
with passes, and permitted to go
where they please within a limited distance, or they may remain and labor on
the plantation, in which case they are
paid for it. It is very rarely, however,
that the latter alternative is accepted.
They may be seen at these times hurrying in all directions, as happy looking
mortals as can be found on the face of
the earth. They are different beings
from what they are in the field; the
temporary relaxation, the brief deliverance from fear, and from the lash, producing an entire metamorphosis in
their appearance and demeanor. In
visiting, riding, renewing old friend-
ships, or, perchance, reviving some
old attachment, or pursuing whatever
pleasure may suggest itself, the time is
occupied. Such is "southern life as it
is," *three days in the year,* as I found
it—the other three hundred and sixty-
two being days of weariness, and fear,
and suffering, and unremitting labor.

Marriage is frequently contracted
during the holidays, if such an institution may be said to exist among them.
The only ceremony required before entering into that "holy estate," is to obtain the consent of the respective
owners. It is usually encouraged by the
masters of female slaves. Either party
can have as many husbands or wives
as the owner will permit, and either is
at liberty to discard the other at pleasure. The law in relation to divorce, or
to bigamy, and so forth, is not applicable to property, of course. If the wife
does not belong on the same plantation
with the husband, the latter is permitted to visit her on Saturday nights, if
the distance is not too far. Uncle
Abram's wife lived seven miles from
Epps', on Bayou Huff Power. He had
permission to visit her once a fortnight, but he was growing old, as has
been said, and truth to say, had latterly
well nigh forgotten her. Uncle Abram
had no time to spare from his meditations on General Jackson—connubial
dalliance being well enough for the
young and thoughtless, but unbecoming a grave and solemn philosopher
like himself.

100. "Levying Contributions" from Whites at Christmas

Planters of generous impulses undoubtedly enjoyed the relaxation the Christmas holiday brought to the plantation. Not only was the slave-owner relieved for a time from the task of driving his slaves to *their* tasks, but he also usually took this occasion to present his slaves with gifts, sometimes no more than the ration of blankets or clothing that the slaves had every right to expect in any case, but often some small items designed solely to give pleasure. Certainly evidences of gratitude from the slave were reassuring to the master.

Prominent visitors who came south at Christmas were, one supposes, most often the guests of open-handed squires, which probably explains why nearly all of their accounts give favorable assessments of the planters' part in the holiday cheer. Bishop Henry Benjamin Whipple (1822–1901), who visited Brig.-Gen. Duncan Clinch's plantation in Georgia, was pleased with the "scenes of joyous mirth" he witnessed, and there seems no reason to doubt his word. Bishop Whipple was an Episcopalian who interested himself particularly in the poor of Chicago as well as in the education of American Indians and the general improvement of their condition. The Indians called the Bishop by the complimentary name "Straight Tongue." It is clear from Bishop Whipple's account, however, that he belonged to the numerous throng who, disliking slavery in principle, saw no immediate means of doing anything to end it.

Dec 25. [1843]—Christmas day. At 12 o'clock we were all aroused from a sound sleep by the music of the negroes commencing the celebration of the Christmas holidays. A more motley group of dark skins I have never seen, all arrayed in their holiday dresses and full of joy and gladness at the return of their annual holidays. Their masters give them their time at this season of the year to celebrate the holidays and none can imagine the joy & enthusiasm with which a slave hails these seasons of festive enjoyment. As soon as we were up the servants were all waiting with laughing faces to wish us a

Source: Lester B. Shippee, ed., *Bishop Whipple's Southern Diary, 1843–44* (Minneapolis: University of Minnesota Press, 1937), pp. 48–52.

Merry Christmas, expecting to receive a bit or so as a contribution. I was truly gratified at the joyous faces of the negroes who met me in the street and their cheerful "happy Christmas, massa" made me feel a part of their happiness in hailing the Christmas holidays. In company with Mr. Hill & Griswold I left Saint Marys to visit the plantation of Gen¹ Clinch, who resides about 27 miles from here upon the Satilla River.¹ Our route lay through the pine barrens so common in the low country of Georgia. And we were astonished at the extreme sparseness of the population. We rode 23 miles only seeing 3 houses on our route and over as fine roads as I have ever seen. The road is dull and monotonous, as it is

1. Brigadier General Duncan L. Clinch (1787–1849) entered the regular army in 1808. He served through the War of 1812, in 1815 was assigned to the Fourth Infantry, and was made colonel in 1819. He probably acquired his property in Georgia during these years, for he was stationed in that state and in North Carolina much of the time. At about the same time he was promoted to a colonelcy he was put in command of the Eastern Division, Seventh Military District, with his headquarters first at Fernandino, Florida, and then at St. Marys, Georgia. Subsequently he was brevetted brigadier general and spent some time at Baton Rouge and at Jefferson Barracks, Missouri, as well as at Mobile. At the outbreak of the second Seminole War he was in command in Florida but resigned in 1836 on account of the attitude of the War Department. From then until the time of his death, he resided on his plantation near St. Marys, except for a short period in 1844–45, when he ran for Congress to fill an unexpired term, was elected, and served to the end of that Congress in March, 1845. See Fred. Cubberly, "Fort King," Florida Historical Society Quarterly, 5:139 ff., for several references to Clinch in the Seminole War. (Shippee note)

but one continual succession of pine trees thinly scattered over immense plains with no underbrush, and here and there we found small patches of swamp and hammock lands. We reached the residence of the Hero of Withlacochie [Gen. Clinch] just before dinner and were cordially welcomed. After partaking of an excellent Christmas dinner and enjoying a quiet siesta of an hour or so we took a walk out over his plantation. Gen¹ Clinch has one of the largest rice plantations in this section of country. He plants about 500 acres and has over one hundred field hands. The land is of the richest alluvial soil and owing to the deposits made upon it by the influx of the tide is inexhaustible. The land is surrounded by large embankments and laid out in squares of about 15 or 20 acres each, these intersected by ditches & embankments with flood gates to flow the land or to drain it so that one plot can be overflowed and another dry at the same time. The crop is planted in February and ripens about the last of August. After planting, the land is flowed until time for hoeing, then drained & hoed & then flowed again. The flowing of the land is beneficial in keeping down grass and weeds besides enriching the land. This land is worth from $100 to $200 per acre. It costs about 75 dollars to clear it and put into an excellent state of cultivation. After reaping it is threshed with a machine or flail, then winnowed and finally divested of the rough hull by means of mortars and pestles. Gen¹ Clinch raised this year about 25,000 bushels, which brings him about 60ᶜ per bushel. He raises about 70 bushels to the acre and its weight is about 46ˡᵇ to the bushel. Gen¹ Clinch is a good master and follows the task system. I found his daughters pleasant and agreeable as well as accomplished ladies. Here I found the negroes enjoying the holidays to the fill. Dancing was to be heard & seen from early dawn to 11 & 12 o'clock at night. The tamborine and fiddle were in constant use and the General's piazza in front of his house was used as the ball room. The negroes are good dancers and I laughed heartily at the quaint expressions & blunders of these negroes. They vie with each other in attentions to the fair sex and delight above all to ape the manners of the whites. I heard some fine negro songs a few lines of which I caught & insert. "Laugh you nigger, laugh away. Laugh, you chile 'tis holiday. Dance, you cuffy, dance away. Tis Christmas holiday. Sing, boys, sing sing away, sing for 'tis de holiday. Roll your eye, show your teeth, fiddle & dance away, 'tis holiday."

We spent the next day there and left after dinner & delighted with our visit. Long shall I remember the Christmas holidays in Georgia. I saw roses the 26ᵗʰ December in bloom in Gen¹ Clinch's garden. The weather is quite warm, almost sultry. We reached Saint Marys about 10½ P.M. fatigued with our long ride through the woods of Georgia.

Dec 27. [1843]—This is with the negroes the last day of the feast and with them the "great day." The negroes are out in great numbers arrayed in their best and their ebony faces shine with joy and happiness. Already have they paraded, with a corps of staff officers with red sashes, mock epaulettes &

goose quill feathers, and a band of music composed of 3 fiddles, 1 tenor & 1 bass drum, 2 triangles & 2 tamborines and they are marching up & down the streets in great style. They are followed by others, some dancing, some walking & some hopping, others singing, all as lively as lively can be. If any negro refuses to join them they seize him & have a mock trial & sentence him to a flogging which is well laid on. Already have they had several such court martials. Here they come again with flags flying and music enough to deafen one & they have now two fifes to increase their noise. Whatever others may think, I am satisfied that these seasons of joyous mirth have a happy effect upon the negro population. They levy contributions on all the whites they see & thus find themselves in pocket money. I am really sore I have laughed so long and so heartily. Every negro's face is wreathed in smiles & never have I seen such a display of ebony & ivory in my life and never expect to again. Mr. Sadler gave me an interesting account today of the proceedings of the blacks on his plantation during the holidays and of the way in which he cured his negroes of fighting. These scenes of joyous mirth are like manna to a hungry soul to these fun loving Africans and the effect must be good. It would make a northern abolitionist change his sentiments in reference to slavery could he see as I have seen the jollity & mirth of the black population during the Christmas holidays. Never have I seen any class of people who appeared to enjoy more than do these negroes. And during my visit to the plantation of Gen¹ C I was gratified by the kind feeling which seemed to exist between the master and his slave. On the breaking up of the dance each slave came in and bade his "massa good night" and all seemed to feel as if he were their dearest and best friend. There was none of that fear, that servile fear, that is the offspring of tyranny and cruelty. I know there are men who do not treat their slaves kindly, men whose slaves bear the looks of abject sorrow but these are the exceptions not the general rule.

101. Singing and Dancing Secular Music in Louisiana

Although religious songs were far more numerous, the secular songs are especially interesting from the standpoint of regional distinctions and possible African provenance. When the three young people who compiled the materials of document 98 were at work on their volume, they solicited songs from people they knew in regions less familiar to them than the Carolinas and Georgia. A group of secular songs came from an acquaintance who heard them on the "Good Hope" plantation in St. Charles Parish, Louisiana. "Remon," "Aurore Bradaire," and "Caroline" were sung to a dance called the "Coonjai," evidently a simple dance that the correspondent described as being much like the more familiar minuet. She believed the dance and its name to be African in origin.

As the editors write, "When the *Coonjai* is danced, the music is furnished by an orchestra of singers, the leader of whom—a man selected both for the quality of his voice and for his skill in improvising—sustains the solo part, while the others afford him an opportunity, as they shout in chorus, for inventing some neat verse to compliment some lovely *danseuse*, or celebrate the deeds of some plantation hero." The dancers themselves did not sing, in contrast to the combined singing and dancing of the "shout." Musical instruments used to accompany the singers and dancers were the barrel-head drum, or the jaw-bone and key. The "Calinda" was another dance, but by 1867 no longer in use, according to the contributor

Source: William Francis Allen, Charles Pickard Ware, and Lucy McKim Garrison, *Slave Songs of the United States* (New York: A. Simpson & Co., 1867), pp. 110–13.

of these songs. It was supposed to have been a "very lascivious" dance, with two lines of dancers approaching and retreating from each other, making "very singular"—and, one assumes, suggestive—gestures.

If the reader knows a little French, and pronounces the words aloud, most of them will explain themselves; but for the aid of the reader, the editors offered the following translation of the words most frequently employed. In the left column are the words as they appear in the French songs of the Louisiana blacks; on the right are their French equivalents.

mo	me, mon, je
li	lui, le, la, il, elle
mouin	moi
yé	ils, leur
ainé	un, une
dé	deux
té	été, était
ya, yavé	il y a
ouar	vouloir
pancor	pas encore
michié	monsieur
tépé	un peu

131.   **RÉMON.**

SOLO.

Mo par - lé Ré - mon, Ré - mon, Li par - lé Si - mon, Si-

- mon, Li par - lé Ti - tine, Ti - tine, Li tom - bé dans chagrin.

CHORUS.

O femme Rom - u - lus, oh!   Belle femme Romu - lus, oh!   O

femme Rom - u - lus, oh!   Belle femme qui ça vou - lé mo fai.

132.   **AURORE BRADAIRE.**

CHORUS.

Au - rore Bradaire, belle ti fille, Au - rore Bradaire, belle ti fille, Au-

- rore Bradaire,   belle ti fille, C'est li   mo ou - lé, c'est

FINE.   SOLO.

li ma pren.   Li pas man - dé robe mous-se - line,   Li

pas man - dé   dé - ba bro - dé,   Li   pas   man - dé sou-

D. C.

- lier prinelle, C'est li   mo ou - lé, c'est li ma pren.

[510]

133. **CAROLINE.**

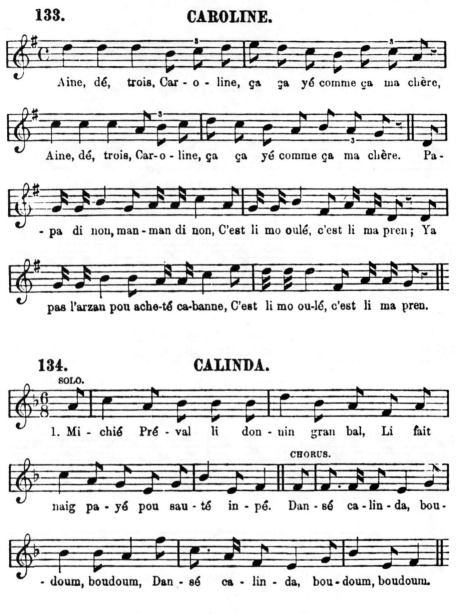

Aine, dé, trois, Car-o-line, ça ça yé comme ça ma chère,

Aine, dé, trois, Car-o-line, ça ça yé comme ça ma chère. Pa-

-pa di non, man-man di non, C'est li mo oulé, c'est li ma pren; Ya

pas l'arzan pou ache-té ca-banne, C'est li mo ou-lé, c'est li ma pren.

134. **CALINDA.**

SOLO.

1. Mi-chié Pré-val li don-nin gran bal, Li fait

CHORUS.

naig pa-yé pou sau-té in-pé. Dan-sé ca-lin-da, bou-

-doum, boudoum, Dan-sé ca-lin-da, bou-doum, boudoum.

2 Michié Préval li té capitaine bal,
  So cocher Louis té maite cérémonie.

3 Dans lequirie la yavé gran gala,
  Mo cré choual layé té bien étonné.

4 Yavé des négresse belle passé maitresse,
  Yé volé bébelle dans l'ormoire mamzelle.

LOLOTTE.

Pauve pi - ti Lolotte a mouin, Pauve pi - ti Lolotte a mouin,

Pauve pi - ti Lolotte a mouin, Li gaignin doulair. Ca - la -

- lou por - té madrasse, li por - té ji - pon gar - ni, Ca - la -

- lou por - té madrasse, li por - té ji - pon gar - ni.

Pauve pi - ti Lolotte a mouin, Pauve pi - ti Lolotte a mouin,

Pauve pi - ti Lo - lotte a mouin, Li gai - gnin

doulair, doulair, doulair, Li gaignin doulair dans cœur à li.

Voyez ce mu-let là, Musieu Bainjo, Comme il est in - so-

FINE.   D. C.

- lent.   { Chapeau sur cô - té, Musieu Bain - jo, }
           { La canne à la main, Musieu Bain - jo, }
           { Botte qui fait crin, crin, Musieu Bain - jo, }

[The seven foregoing songs were obtained from a lady who heard them sung, before the war, on the "Good Hope" plantation, St. Charles Parish, Louisiana. The language, evidently a rude corruption of French, is that spoken by the negroes in that part of the State; and it is said that it is more difficult for persons who speak French to interpret this dialect, than for those who speak English to understand the most corrupt of the ordinary negro-talk. The pronunciation of this negro-French is indicated, as accurately as possible, in the versions given here, which furnish, also, many interesting examples of the peculiar phrases and idioms employed by this people. The frequent omission of prepositions, articles, and auxiliary verbs, as well as of single letters, and the contractions constantly occurring, are among the most noticeable peculiarities. Some of the most difficult words are: *mo* for *me, mon, je; li* for *lui, le, la, il, elle; mouin* for *moi; yé* for *ils, leur; aine, dé,* for *un, deux; té* for *été, était; ya, yavé* for *il y a,* etc.; *ouar* for *voir* and its inflections; *oulé* for *vouloir,* etc.; *pancor* for *pas encore; michié* for *monsieur; inpé* for *un peu.* The words are, of course, to be pronounced as if they were pure French.

Four of these songs, Nos. 130, 131, 132 and 133, were sung to a simple dance, a sort of minuet, called the *Coonjai;* the name and the dance are probably both of African origin. When the *Coonjai* is danced, the music is furnished by an orchestra of singers, the leader of whom—a man selected both for the quality of his voice and for his skill in improvising—sustains the solo part, while the others afford him an opportunity, as they shout in chorus, for inventing some neat verse to compliment some lovely *danseuse,* or celebrate the deeds of some plantation hero. The dancers themselves never sing, as in the case of the religious "shout" of the Port Royal negroes; and the usual musical accompaniment, besides that of the singers, is that furnished by a skilful performer on the barrel-head-drum, the jaw-bone and key, or some other rude instrument.

No. 134. The "calinda" was a sort of contra-dance, which has now passed entirely out of use. Bescherelle describes the two lines as "avançant et reculant en cadence, et faisant des contorsions fort singulières et des gestes fort lascifs."

The first movement of No. 135, "Lolotte," has furnished M. Gottschalk with the theme of his "Ballade Créole," "La Savane," op. 3 de la Louisiane.

In 136, we have the attempt of some enterprising negro to write a French song; he is certainly to be congratulated on his success.

It will be noticed that all these songs are "seculars"; and that while the words of most of them are of very little account, the music is as peculiar, as interesting, and, in the case of two or three of them, as difficult to write down, or to sing correctly, as any that have preceded them.]

102. Drums and Drumming in Congo Square

Complex African rhythms were a special feature of the music of slaves. Fortunately, the architect Benjamin Henry Latrobe described and sketched the percussion and stringed instruments in use in New Orleans around 1820. The African ancestry of these musical instruments may be seen by comparing the sketches with African instruments still in use. The banjo is recognized as a more or less direct African import.

Latrobe was born in England of American parentage in 1764, and came to the United States in 1796. It was here that he earned fame as architect of many important buildings of the Federal and early Republican periods. In 1803 he was appointed Surveyor of Public Buildings by President Thomas Jefferson, who charged him with completion of the U.S. Capitol. He also rebuilt the White House after the British burned it in the War of 1812. One of his most distinguished designs was that of the (old) Baltimore Cathedral, first Roman Catholic cathedral to be built in the United States. Latrobe's death in 1820 was a great loss to the profession of architecture in the young republic.

Latrobe's thoroughly classical training clearly limited his appreciation of the singing he heard in New Orleans, and he was equally disdainful of the dancing. Yet his descriptions are rendered with accuracy of detail. It is possible, since Latrobe was traveling in 1818, that the dancing he saw was the "Coonjai" described in the headnote of document 101. There is no way of being sure. The "long dissertation" alluded to in the first sentence is a section of his diary explaining why he believes that Sunday "blue laws" are ridiculous. The events he described took place while Latrobe was walking near what became known later as "Congo Square," in company with Andrew S. Coulter, the collaborating engineer on the New Orleans waterworks, a project that Latrobe was designing.

Source: Benjamin Henry Boneval Latrobe, *Impressions Respecting New Orleans,* ed. Samuel Wilson, Jr. (New York: Columbia University Press, 1951), pp. 49–51. The papers of Latrobe are currently being edited at the Maryland Historical Society, Baltimore.

This long dissertation has been suggested by my accidentally stumbling upon the assembly of negroes which I am told every Sunday afternoon meets on the Common in the rear of the city. My object was to take a walk with Mr. Coulter on the bank of the Canal Carondelet as far as the Bayou St. John. In going up St. Peters Street & approaching the common I heard a most extraordinary noise, which I supposed to proceed from some horse mill, the horses trampling on a wooden floor. I found, however, on emerging from the houses onto the Common, that it proceeded from a crowd of 5 or 600 persons assembled in an open space or public square. I went to the spot & crowded near enough to see the performance. All those who were engaged in the business seemed to be *blacks*. I did not observe a dozen yellow faces. They were formed into circular groupes [sic] in the midst of four of which, which I examined (but there were more of them), was a ring, the largest not 10 feet in diameter. In the first were two women dancing. They held each a coarse handkerchief extended by the corners in their hands, & *set* to each other in a miserably dull & slow figure, hardly moving their feet or bodies. The music consisted of two drums and a stringed instrument. An old man sat astride of a cylindrical drum about a foot in diameter, & beat it with incredible quickness with the edge of his hand & fingers. The other drum was an open staved thing held between the knees & beaten in the same manner. They made an incredible noise. The most curious instrument, however, was a stringed instrument which no doubt was imported from Africa. On

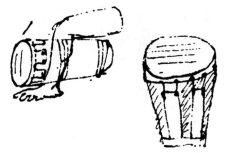

the top of the finger board was the rude figure of a man in a sitting posture, & two pegs behind him to which the strings were fastened. The body was a calabash. It was played upon by a very little old man, apparently 80 or 90 years old.

The women squalled out a burthen to the playing at intervals, consisting of two notes, as the negroes, working in our cities, respond to the song of their leader. Most of the circles contained the same sort of dancers. One was larger, in which a ring of a dozen women walked, by way of dancing, round the music in the center. But the instruments were of a different construction. One, which from the color of the wood seemed new, consisted of a block cut into something of the form of a cricket bat with a long & deep mortice down the center. This thing made a considerable noise, being beaten lustily on the side by a short stick. In the same orchestra was a square drum, looking like a stool, which made an abominably loud noise; also a calabash with a round hole in it, the hole studded with brass nails, which was beaten by a woman with two short sticks.

A man sung an uncouth song to the

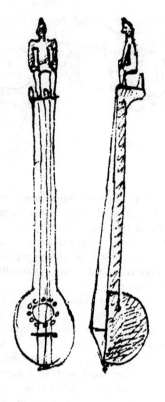

dancing which I suppose was in some African language, for it was not French, & the women screamed a detestable burthen on one single note. The allowed amusements of Sunday have, it seems, perpetuated here those of Africa among its inhabitants. I have never seen anything more brutally savage, and at the same time dull & stupid, than this whole exhibition. Continuing my walk about a mile along the canal, & returning after Sunset near the same spot, the noise was still heard. There was not the least disorder among the crowd, nor do I learn on enquiry, that these weekly meetings of the negroes have ever produced any mischief.

103. "Brer Rabbit" Plays Tricks in South Carolina

Storytelling is an ancient form of human amusement, and undoubtedly among the most revealing of all from the standpoint of social psychology. Tales a people enjoys tell very much about them. It seems safe to say also that the stories that survive the test of time are those most often repeated and the best loved. Many of the stories that survived from slavery cast animals in the roles of speaking human beings, with all their virtues and foibles. The key animal figures in American slave stories apparently had their beginnings in Africa, but they soon became acclimatized here.

Brer Rabbit himself, in most of the stories, speaks the part of the slave. The slave, like Brer Rabbit, had to live by his wits, not his strength, and it gratified the powerless slave to follow the clever little animal's cheerfully devious expertise in manipulating his enemies. In the low country of the Carolinas and Georgia, African traditions were refreshed by many late importations of slaves, and by their high concentration along the coast. Below are several animal stories that were told in this region from the slave era until relatively recent times. The first is the classic story of Brer Rabbit and the Tar Baby.

Tar Baby: Mock Plea (in the Brier-Patch).

Ber Wolf had a pease-patch. An' every night somebody go in de pease-patch an' eat de pease. So Ber Wolf made a tar baby an' set him up in de yard. So Ber Rabbit went in de patch, an' he meet de tar baby standin' up. So Ber Rabbit said, "Good-mornin', gal!" Tar Baby ain't got no manners, say nothin'. Say, "Man, I slap you." His hand fasten. Ber Rabbit say, "I got anoder han'." So he hit him wid dat han'. Dat one fasten. Ber Rabbit said, "I got a head." Said he butt him wid de head. De head fasten. "Gal, you don't see I got a foot?" So he kick him wid de foot. De foot fasten. "I kick him wid de oder foot." Dat one fasten. Ber Rabbit said, "I got a mout'." De mout' fasten. Den Rabbit say, "Tu'n me loose!"

Next t'ing come along Wolf. Wolf

Source: Elsie Clews Parsons, *Folk-Lore of the Sea Islands of South Carolina*, Memoirs of the American Folk-Lore Society, vol. 16 (Cambridge, Mass., 1923), pp. 26–27, 66–67.

say, "I ketch yer, t'ief! you eat all my pease. I putshyer head down on de choppin'-block an' chop em off."—"Oh, don't duh dat! Dat will kill me." Say, "I want ter kill you." Say, "I'll t'row you in de creek, drown you."—"Ah, don't duh dat!" he say. "I'll t'row you in de briar-patch," he say. "Yes, Ber Wolf, t'row me in de briar-patch! Den you'll kill me." When Ber Wolf t'row him in de briar-patch, Rabbit say, "Ping! Ping! Dat's de place my mammy done born me!" So dat ol' rabbit git away.

Tie Me Tight!

I.

Oncet Rabbit an' Wolf go out; an' Rabbit tol' Wolf dat ef he would le' him tie um to a tree, he would get um two fat hen. So he tie um to a tree wid wine [vine], tie um fas'. An' Wolf say, "Don' tie me too tight, Ber Rabbit!" Ber Rabbit say couldn' get de hen ef he don' tie um tight. So Wolf say, "Tie me tight, Ber Rabbit! Tie me tight!" So Ber Rabbit wen' to de barnyard an' call two houn'. An' dey chase um. An' he run back to de tree whey he tie Ber Wolf. Ber Wolf see de houn' comin', an' cry out, "Go 'roun', Ber Rabbit, go 'roun'!" But Rabbit keep straight on. An' de houn' get Ber Wolf; an' he call out, "I tol' you to go 'roun'! I tol' you to go 'roun'! Dat wasn' right.'

II.

De fox had a way goin' to de man hawg-pen an' eatin' up all his hawg. So de people didn' know how to ketch de fox. An' so de rabbit was goin' along one Sunday mornin'. Say was

goin' to church. Ber Fox singin', "Good-mornin', Ber Rabbit!" Ber Rabbit singin', "Good-mornin', Ber Fox!" Say, "Whey you goin'?" Say, "I'm goin' to church." Ber Fox say, "Dis is my time. I'm hungry dis mornin'. I'm goin' to ketch you."—"O Ber Fox! leave me off dis mornin'! I will sen' you to a man house where he got a penful of pretty little pig, an' you will get yer brakefus' fill. Ef you don' believe me, you can tie me here, an' you can go down to de house, an' I'll stay here until you come back." So Ber Fox tie him. When he wen' down to de house, de man had about fifty head of houn'-dawg. An' de man tu'n de houn'-dawg loose on him. An' de fox made de long run right by Ber Rabbit. Ber Fox say, "O Ber Rabbit! dose is no brakefus', dose is a pile of houn'-dawg."—"Yes, you was goin' to eat me, but dey will eat you for your brakefus' and supper to-night." An' so dey did. Dey cut [caught] de fox. An' Ber Rabbit give to de dawgs, "Gawd bless yer soul! dat what enemy get for meddlin' Gawd's people when dey goin' to church." Said, "I was goin' to school all my life an' learn every letter in de book but *d*, an' D was death, an' death was de en' of Ber Fox."

III.

One day the wolf said, "Brother Rabbit, I am going to eat you up."—"No," said Brother Rabbit, "don't eat me! I know where some fine geese is. If you let me tie you here, I will go and get them for you."—"All right," said the wolf. So the rabbit tied the wolf. Then the rabbit went on his way until he came to a farmyard. Then he said,

"Farmer, give me trouble." So the farmer went into the yard and get a hound-dog and two hound-puppies and put them in a bag, and said, "When you get out in the field, you must open the bag, and you will have all the trouble you want."—"All right," said the rabbit. So the rabbit went back to the wolf. He waited until he came near the wolf, then he loose the bag and ran the dogs behind him. He ran right straight for the wolf. Wolf said, "Bear off, Rabbit, bear off!" So he saw the rabbit was close upon him, he called out harder, "Bear off, Rabbit, bear off!" The rabbit said, "Not a bit. I am running in straight deal this morning." So the dogs killed the wolf and eat him up. The story is end.

104. "Compair Lapin" and Other Louisiana Tricksters

Brer Rabbit was universally familiar among slaves, but in Creole country he was called, properly enough, "Compair Lapin" (*Confrère* Lapin). Here, as elsewhere, the cunning rabbit is forgiven all manner of deceit in the superb cause of confounding more powerful creatures and bringing ridicule upon them.

The first of the following tales told among the slaves in Louisiana is a classic of the genre, ranking with the Tar Baby story in popularity. The "Compair Lapin" of "N'elephant avec Baleine" is clearly the same trickster who got his friend into such deep trouble in document 103. The rabbit's closing announcement to Compair Bouki is actually an assertion of the slave's daily retribution upon his master. Compair Bouki, apparently an African survival, plays a much larger part in many of the stories than he does here. Bouki possesses some of the traits of Brer Fox, but in some of the Louisiana stories he is described as having feathers, and he is not always a real enemy of the rabbit—and seldom a worthy foeman either. He is often a straight-man of sorts, as in the elephant story. He is always a sycophant, and foolish.

The second story, concerning the destruction of the owl by the mockingbirds, is susceptible to an interpretation showing resentment of interracial

Source: Alcée Fortier, *Louisiana Folk-Tales in French Dialect and English Translation* (Boston and New York: Houghton Mifflin, 1895), pp. 3–7, 35–37, 75–81.

sexual adventures; but if so it is quite restrained, and probably unconscious. It is suggestive of the fables of Aesop. The third story, one that purports to come from Manga's Africa, has some of the grisly qualities of the fairy tales from Grimm's and Andersen's. If it is not a true story about an actual event, it is a fascinating literary invention.

[I]

The Elephant and the Whale.

One day Compair Lapin and Compair Bouki were going on a journey together. Compair Lapin often took Bouki with him to make fun of him, and to hear all the news which Bouki knew. When they reached the seashore, they saw something which was very strange, and which astonished them so much that they stopped to watch and listen. It was an elephant and a whale which were conversing together.

"You see," said Bouki, "they are the two largest beasts in the world, and the strongest of all animals."

"Hush up," said Lapin, "let us go nearer and listen. I want to hear what they are saying."

The elephant said to the whale: "Commère Baleine, as you are the largest and strongest in the sea, and I am the largest and strongest on land, we must rule over all beasts; and all those who will revolt against us we shall kill them, you hear, commère."

"Yes, compair; keep the land and I shall keep the sea."

"You hear," said Bouki, "let us go, because it will be bad for us if they hear that we are listening to their conversation."

"Oh! I don't care," said Lapin; "I am more cunning than they; you will see how I am going to fix them."

"No," said Bouki, "I am afraid, I must go."

"Well, go, if you are so good for nothing and cowardly; go quickly, I am tired of you; you are too foolish."

Compair Lapin went to get a very long and strong rope, then he got his drum and hid it in the grass. He took one end of the rope, and went to the elephant: "Mister, you who are so good and so strong. I wish you would render me a service; you would relieve me of a great trouble and prevent me from losing my money."

The elephant was glad to hear such a fine compliment, and he said: "Compair, I shall do for you everything you want. I am always ready to help my friends."

"Well," said Lapin, "I have a cow which is stuck in the mud on the coast; you know that I am not strong enough to pull her out; I come for you to help me. Take this rope in your trunk. I shall tie it to the cow, and when you hear me beat the drum, pull hard on the rope. I tell you that because the cow is stuck deep in the mud."

"That is all right," said the elephant. "I guarantee you I shall pull the cow out, or the rope will break."

Compair Lapin took the other end of the rope and ran towards the sea. He paid a pretty compliment to the whale, and asked her to render him the same service about the cow, which was stuck in a bayou in the woods. Compair Lapin's mouth was so honeyed that no one could refuse him anything. The whale took hold of the rope and said: "When I shall hear the drum beat I shall pull."

"Yes," said Lapin, "begin pulling gently, and then more and more."

"You need not be afraid," said the whale; "I shall pull out the cow, even if the Devil were holding her."

"That is good," said Lapin; "we are going to laugh." And he beat his drum.

The elephant began to pull so hard that the rope was like a bar of iron. The whale, on her side, was pulling and pulling, and yet she was coming nearer to the land, as she was not so well situated to pull as the elephant. When she saw that she was mounting on land, she beat her tail furiously and plunged headlong into the sea. The shock was so great that the elephant was dragged to the sea. "What, said he, what is the matter? that cow must be wonderfully strong to drag me so. Let me kneel with my front feet in the mud." Then he twisted the rope round his trunk in such a manner that he pulled the whale again to the shore. He was very much astonished to see his friend the whale. "What is the matter," said he. "I thought it was Compair Lapin's cow I was pulling."

"Lapin told me the same thing. I believe he is making fun of us."

"He must pay for that," said the elephant. "I forbid him to eat a blade of grass on land because he laughed at us."

"And I will not allow him to drink a drop of water in the sea. We must watch for him, and the first one that sees him must not miss him."

Compair Lapin said to Bouki: "It is growing hot for us; it is time to leave."

"You see," said Bouki, "you are always bringing us into trouble."

"Oh! hush up, I am not through with them yet; you will see how I shall fix them."

They went on their way and after a while they separated. When Compair Lapin arrived in the wood, he found a little dead deer. The dogs had bitten him so that the hair had fallen off his skin in many places. Lapin took off the deer's skin and put it on his back. He looked exactly like a wounded deer. He passed limping by the elephant, who said to him: "Poor little deer, how sick you look."

"Oh! yes, I am suffering very much; you see it is Compair Lapin who poisoned me and put his curse on me, because I wanted to prevent him from eating grass, as you had ordered me. Take care, Mr. Elephant, Compair Lapin has made a bargain with the Devil; he will be hard on you, if you don't take care."

The elephant was very much frightened. He said, "Little deer, you will tell Compair Lapin that I am his best friend; let him eat as much grass as he wants and present my compliments to him."

The deer met a little later the whale in the sea. "But poor little deer, why are you limping so; you seem to be very sick."

"Oh! yes, it is Compair Lapin who did that. Take care, Commère Baleine." The whale also was frightenèd, and said: "I want to have nothing to do with the Devil; please tell Compair Lapin to drink as much water as he wants."

The deer went on his way, and when he met Compair Bouki he took off the deer's skin and said: "You see that I am more cunning than all of them, and that I can make fun of them all the time. Where I shall pass another will be caught."

"You are right indeed" said Compair Bouki.

[II]

Miss Mockingbird, Mr. Mockingbird, and Mr. Owl.

Once upon a time the Mockingbird and the Owl were courting Miss Mockingbird. She said to them: "Well, I shall marry the one who will remain the longer without eating. I shall remain under the tree and you upon it."

Now, the mockingbird looked at his lady-love and flew down to her, singing:

> Chivi! Chivi! Ta la la!
> Chivi! Chivi! Ta la la!
> Hévé! Ta la la!

When he reached Miss Mockingbird, he did as if he wanted to kiss her, and she gave him some food which she had in her beak. Mr. Mockingbird flew back to his tree.

The Owl in his turn flew towards his lady love, and he sang:

> Coucou! Ta la la!
> Coucou! Ta la la!
> Hévé! Ta la la!

He wished to kiss Miss Mockingbird, but she turned her head aside, and said: "Go away; your wings hurt me." The poor Owl had nothing to eat, while every day the mockingbird flew down, and, kissing the young lady, got something to eat. The Owl came down also from the tree, but he was beginning to be very hungry, and his voice was very weak when he sang:

> Coucou! Ta la la la!
> Coucou! Ta la la la!
> Hévé! Ta la la la!

Miss Mockingbird did not want to look at him or to give him anything to eat, and he had to go back to his tree with an empty stomach. Mr. Mockingbird, on the contrary, grew more boastful every day, and sang in a loud voice:

> Chivi! Chivi! Ta la la!
> Chivi! Chivi! Ta la la!
> Hévé! Ta la la!

The poor Owl was dying of hunger, and one could hardly hear his song:

> Coucou! Ta la!
> Coucou! Ta la!
> Hévé! Ta la!

He tried to kiss Miss Mockingbird, but she said to him: "Go away; your large wings hurt me," and she gave him a slap which threw him down. He was so weak from hunger that he died, and Mr. Mockingbird flew away with his bride.

[III]
The Little Finger.

Before we came here, poor devils, we were all free, we were not obliged to work for any master. It is the whites who came into our country, Africa, to get us. They stole some of us; they bought some of us from our fathers for a red handkerchief, for a bottle of tafia, or an old gun. When we went to war those who were caught were sold to the whites who came to trade on the seacoast. We were led away, tied together, tied two by two; and when we reached the seacoast like a herd of cattle, men, women, and children, we were exchanged, not for money, but for any kind of merchandise, and the whites put us into ships and brought us here. This is how we became slaves in America.

When Manga, my grandmother, arrived at the seacoast, she saw a pretty little town with small houses. There were many ships, and they seemed to be dancing on the sea; some were going up, others down. It was the wind, you know, that was blowing and shaking up the sea. My poor grandmother, who was young then, was afraid when she saw they were putting all the Negroes on board the ships. She thought they were going to drown them in the sea. A white man came to her and bought her from her master. He took her to his house and told her in her own language: "I bought you to take care of my little boy." He had a pretty house with a store in it, and a pretty garden. Behind the house was an orange grove, and the trees were so large that there was a fine shade underneath. To show you how my grandmother's country was a good one, I will tell you that the orange-trees were in bloom the whole year; there were flowers and little oranges and ripe oranges all the time. The house was near the sea, and every morning Manga took little Florimond to take a bath. The little boy was so pretty, and his father and mother were so good, that Manga would not have left them for anything in the world. She loved little Florimond so much; his hair was curly, his eyes were blue, his skin was white and rosy. Everybody adored the poor little boy, he was so pretty and smart. He could sing so well and imitate all birds so admirably that often they thought it was the Nita that was singing in the trees. Nita is a little bird in Africa which sings at night when the moon is shining. It perches on the top of the tallest tree; and if there is a light breeze it sings better, for the swinging of the branch helps the little bird to sing, as the rocking of the hammock helps a man's lullaby. Florimond imitated the Nita so well that everybody was mistaken, and it amused the boy very much.

Florimond's father used to trade with the Negroes that lived far in the woods, so one day he started to get gold dust and elephants' teeth. On leaving he said to Manga: "Take good care of my wife and my little boy. You know I gave you already a pair of shoes; I will give you, on my return, a fine dress and a necklace." The first time Manga put on her shoes they hurt her so much that she could hardly walk. She took them off on arriving at the house, and sat on the steps looking at her toes: "Wiggle, wiggle, poor things," she said, "you were in prison just now: you are free now, you are glad, is it not? Oh! I shall never shut you up again. I don't understand how white folks can put their toes in such things!" From that time Manga never put shoes on.

Well, the master went into the big woods, and three days afterwards the lady said to Manga to take Florimond to the sea and give him a bath. While the little boy was playing with the shells and the white sand, they saw a skiff with several persons come ashore. A white man disembarked, and passed by Manga, and she felt a peculiar sensation, as if some misfortune was to happen. The eyes of the man shone like those of a cat in the dark. As he passed, he said: "Good morning, Florimond," but the little boy did not reply anything. When they arrived home the lady sent them to play in the yard, and everytime the master was away the strange man would come to the house. Florimond did not want to see him, and he said one day he would tell his father about the stranger. The latter said to Manga: "You little black imp, if ever you open your mouth about what you see here, I will cut your tongue with my big knife; then I will carry you to my ship, sew you up in a sack, and throw you into the sea for the fish to eat you." Manga was so frightened that she would not have said a word even if they had whipped her for a whole day. In the evening Florimond cried so much that it was with great difficulty that Manga succeeded in putting him to sleep. Her cot was near the bed of the little boy, and during the night she saw the pirate enter the room with a big stick. He struck the little boy on the head and said: "He is dead. I will put him in the hole which I dug in the yard. Now I must attend to the black girl."

Manga, however, had already run away into the yard; but the man, thinking that she was in the road, ran out to catch her. Florimond's mother came into the room, took the little boy's body in her arms, and buried him in a hole near the place where Manga was. She was not quite through with her ugly work when she heard a noise and ran away. She met the man, who said: "I believe the girl has gone to the woods; we need not trouble about her any more; the lions and tigers will soon eat her up. Now I must go on board my ship, and when I come back I will take you with me."

The lady went into the house, and Manga came out of her hiding-place. She felt so weak that she could hardly stand, but before she left she kissed the ground where her dear little master was buried. She said: "Farewell, little angel," and ran into the woods. She preferred to stay with the wild animals than with the cruel mother.

After walking for some time as fast as she could, she stopped by a bayou in the wood, drank some water, and sat down to rest. She fell asleep, but soon she was awakened by loud talking. She saw some men standing around her, and among them was her master, who seemed to be very angry: "What are you doing here so far from my house? I left you to take care of my little boy. I suppose you did something wrong and ran away." Manga did not reply anything, because she remembered the threats of the pirate. The master ordered his men to bring her back to his house, and he hastened to go home. He found his wife, who was weeping bitterly, and she said to him: "Oh! what a dreadful misfortune! Manga let Florimond fall on his head, and our poor little boy is dead. I wanted to kill the Negress, but she ran away, and I don't know where she is. If ever I catch her I will strangle her with my own hands."

When the poor man heard that his dear boy was dead, he fell in a swoon. They put him in bed, and he remained fifteen days delirious. During that time the lady said to Manga that she would kill her if she opened her mouth. She shut the girl in a cabin, and gave her nothing but bread and water.

At last Florimond's father got out of bed, but he would not be consoled, and he wept all day for his little boy. As Manga was still in her prison, her master did not see her, and did not think of her. One day as he was walking about in the yard, he looked from time to time at his dear boy's grave, and tears flowed from his eyes. In the mean time the Nita was singing on a tree near by, and its song was so sad that the poor man felt more sad than ever. It seemed to him it was his Florimond who was singing, and he came to the grave and looked at it a long time. All at once the poor father thought he was dreaming. He saw something that was so strange that many people will not believe it; but so many people told me the same story, that I believe it is as sure as the sun is

shining. When the lady had buried the little boy, she had not had time to cover the body completely, and one little hand was out of the grave, and it was the pretty little finger which was moving as if it was making a sign to call some one. The little finger moved on one side and then on the other, and never stopped beckoning, so to say. The poor father dug up the earth with his hand and uncovered the body. He found it as fresh as if it had just been buried, and he took it in his arms and carried it to the house. He put the boy on a bed and rubbed him so long that the child came back to consciousness. The father sent for a surgeon, who began to attend to the boy, and said that he would revive. There was no danger for his life, as the skull was not broken; the child was only in a state of lethargy, and would soon be well again. Indeed, in a few days Florimond was running about as if nothing had happened, but he never said anything about his mother and the stranger, and the lady at last allowed Manga to leave her prison. Remorse had taken hold of Florimond's mother; she grew thinner every day, and one evening, in spite of the most tender care, she died. Her last words were, "Oh! my God, forgive me!" She was buried in the grave where her little boy had been; and as to the pirate, he never came back. They say that he was hanged.

After his wife's death Florimond's father left Africa, and sold poor Manga. She was put upon a ship, and this is how she became a slave in Louisiana, and related to me the story of the little finger.

105. Asking Riddles about Who Gets the Lady

Riddles have universal appeal, and they were a popular form of social amusement among slaves. Elsie Clews Parsons, the folklorist who collected the following slightly varying riddles from informants on the Sea Islands of South Carolina, identified tales comparable to the "Trackwell, Divewell, Breathewell" riddles in the work of anthropologists who studied the Ewe people and Sierra Leone. Miss Parsons reported that after the first version of the riddle, which is presented here in the form of a story, the listeners fell into a discussion as to whether "Breavewell" in fact deserved to win the lady.

[I]

Trackwell, Divewell, Breathewell.

De man had one daughter. An' dere was t'ree men comin' to see her. Dey was Trackwell, Divewell, an' Breavewell. Dey said de man dat had de best right could marry to de daughter. De daughter went an' got lost. After de woman leave de house, she went down to de river. Trackwell track her f'om de house to de aidge of de water. Dat was all Trackwell could do. She went into de river. Divewell went, an' dive until he fin' her. An' after Divewell foun' her, he brought her up on de sho'. An' Breavewell breave his breat' back into her. An' it come a-disputin'. The father said to de t'ree mens, "Which one of

you is entitled to the daughter?" Trackwell said, "I am entitled to the woman, because she was los', an' I track her out." Divewell says, "Your track didn' done no good, because you couldn' fin' her. You track her to the aidge of the water. I had to dive out in dat ocean, take chance of my life, an' hunt until I foun' her." Breavewell said, "All for that what you folk have done, the woman is mine, because she was dead, an' I brought life into her again." So the fader give her to Breavewell.

[II]

Smellwell, Di'well, Trackwell, an Breat'well,—dey was fo'. De moder had a daughter. Dey was fo' boys what

Source: Elsie Clews Parsons, *Folk-Lore of the Sea Islands of South Carolina*, Memoirs of the American Folk-Lore Society, 16:75–76.

love dis girl. Dis girl went down to de riber an' drown. Now, after de fo' boys went down to de riber, dey foun' de girl, an' de argymen' come about which boy would have de mos' right to de girl. An' Trackwell said, "I have a right to de girl, because I tracked her to de river." An' Smellwell said, "I have a right to de girl, because I smell her down in de water." An' Di'well said, "I have a right to de girl, 'cause I di' fo' her." An' Breat'well said, "I have a right to de girl, because I blow breat' in her." An' durin' de time dey got fo' judges to judge de cause. An' de judges say, "Not any one have a right to de girl," dat de girl moder have mo' right to her. An' dat was de en' of de riddle. What did you think have mos' right to de girl,—de boys, or de moder?

[III]

Dere was a lady had a girl name Lilly. An' she went down to de riber, go across. An' she get drownded. An' a man come in de house name Trackum. She leave de house, an' nobody know she gone. An' Trackum track um by de house down to de riber. Den Trackum couldn' go no mo'. Dis time didn' know wheder she gone across or was drownded or what. Nex' man come, name was Diveum. Now Diveum dive down, an' he brought her up on de hill. Now Blowbreat' come. Now Blowbreat' blow breat', an' bring um back alive like how he [she] was. Now each one of dem men wan' ter marry to her fo' deir po'tion. Now, who have de bes' right to de girl? Who de girl fall to?

A Bibliographical Introduction
to the Sources

A complete bibliography of slavery in the United States would require far more space than is available in this volume. The following pages attempt much less, aspiring only to provide practical suggestions to the student engaged in building a bibliography on a topic in this field for the first time. The suggestions will, I hope, afford constructive leads to more specific items in other books, and in the libraries.

The largest single body of manuscript material originating with those who were once slaves is the collection of narratives made by the Federal Writers Project in the 1920s and 1930s, based on interviews with aging survivors of the slave system. The originals are in the Library of Congress; fortunately, however, these recollections have been reprinted in their entirety, without editorial corrections or changes of any sort, as volumes 2–17 of *The American Slave: A Composite Autobiography* (Westport, Conn.: Greenwood, 1972); volume 1 of the series is *From Sundown to Sunup: The Making of the Black Community*, by George P. Rawick, a work that makes extensive, though not exclusive, use of the slave narratives to recreate the cultural life of the slaves in their life beyond the field. Volumes 18 and 19 include similar matter drawn up at Fisk University. Many of the most fascinating of the WPA narratives were collected and edited in B. A. Botkin, ed., *Lay My Burden Down: A Folk History of Slavery* (Chicago: University of Chicago Press, 1945.)

The best evaluation of the advantages and limitations of these narratives, which were taken down in response to questions of interviewers of varied abilities, perceptions, and prejudices, is found in C. Vann Woodward, "History from Slave Sources," *American Historical Review* 79.2 (1974):470–81. Norman Yetman's *Voices from Slavery* (New York: Holt, Rinehart and Winston, 1970) includes a hundred of these narratives, edited heavily, and providing an analysis of their utility to the scholar. A much shorter collection of autobiographical material based on similar interviews in John B. Cade's "Out of the Mouths of Slaves," in *The Journal of Negro History* 20 (1935):294–337.

A second general category of primary source material revealing the slave's view of his condition consists of narratives of fugitives and those survivors of slavery who bought their freedom, or were manumitted by act of their masters, or by the Civil War. These works, somewhat inade-quately categorized as "fugitive narratives," found their way into print before, during, and after the Civil War, and were sometimes written by blacks directly involved, and sometimes by friendly amanuenses—usually white abolitionists though not exclusively so. While the accuracy of these narratives has been freely challenged by historians of slavery, the ten-dency in recent years has been to employ them, exercising caution and commonsense, subjecting them to the same standards of credibility a thoughtful historian would apply to other sources. John W. Blassingame, in *The Slave Community: Plantation Life in the Ante-Bellum South* (New York: Oxford University Press, 1972), pp. 227–38, offers a very useful ap-praisal of this material, listing (on p. 235) those he believes to be the most informative and accurate. His bibliography includes most of the best works in this category. The most extensive single listing of this large liter-ature—which became very popular reading matter in the ante-bellum North and in England—is found in the bibliography of Charles H. Nichols's *Many Thousand Gone* (Leiden, 1963). This listing is not annota-ted, and the reader must be discriminating in using the titles.

A third category of primary material arising from the slaves themselves reflects indirectly the emotions and attitudes of slaves to their condition. These are the songs, riddles, and stories that survived long enough after slavery to be recorded. Most of this material was published after the Civil War, but it is nonetheless valid for that circumstance. The publications of the American Folk-Lore Society reveal clearly that stories taken down late in the nineteenth century, and early in the twentieth century, are really stories originating in slavery; and these provide a significant insight into the interpersonal relations of the slave system as perceived and subli-mated by slaves themselves. Documents 48, 49, 101–5 in the present book come from the volumes Elsie Clews Parsons and Alcée Fortier contributed to the series. The most complete and valuable collection of slave songs was made during the Civil War by a group of young people involved in the ed-ucation of the freedmen, William F. Allen, Charles P. Ware, and Lucy McKim Garrison. The songs of documents 98 and 101 come from their book, *Slave Songs of the United States* (New York: A. Simpson & Co., 1867).

The legal specifics of the Southern slave codes may be followed in their development over time in the two-volume treatise of a Northerner, James Codman Hurd, *The Law of Freedom and Bondage in the United States* (Bos-ton: Little, Brown, 1858). Another important work on the state laws and their interpretation by Southern jurists is Thomas R. R. Cobb's *An Inquiry into the Law of Negro Slavery* (Philadelphia: T. & J. W. Johnson, 1858).

These learned works are not only valuable in themselves but also provide the best approach to the state reports, which reveal specifically and by example how the laws were interpreted in individual instances in the high courts of the Southern states. Because the background of the cases is included in the report of a case on appeal, these state reports provide vivid, if often clinical, views of the day-to-day activities of slaves and masters, overseers, and others involved in the system and its enforcement. By learning just what becomes a judiciable point, we can often determine what was usual or unusual in a given jurisdiction. The thousands of cases included in brief summary in Helen Tunnicliff Catterall's *Judicial Cases Concerning American Slavery and the Negro,* published in five volumes by the Carnegie Institution (Washington, 1926–27) are indispensible as leads into the legal aspects of slavery.

The records of lower courts are not so complete, nor so well-preserved, as those of the high courts of appeal, especially before the nineteenth century. The Virginia State Library is exceptional in having numerous local court records, and legislative petitions, for the eighteenth and nineteenth centuries. In other states many local records are now available, or are shortly to become so, on microfilm. The Church of Christ of the Latter-Day Saints has microfilmed many such records, and exchanged for cooperation from the localities copies of the records for each state. A short bibliography of published works on the law of slavery, based on legal compilations, is to be found in Stanley Elkins's *Slavery: A Problem in American Institution and Intellectual Life* (Chicago: University of Chicago Press, 1959) in an extended footnote on page 3.

Travelers' accounts are of mixed value for slavery studies, some being very useful, and others impressionistic and biased. A listing of the most reliable and best-known of this category may be found in Elkins, *Slavery,* in an extended footnote on pages 3 and 4. By general consent, scholars denominate the works of Frederick Law Olmsted outstanding in this genre for their readability, balance, and comprehensiveness: *A Journey in the Seaboard Slave States* (New York: Mason, 1856), *A Journey through Texas* (New York: Edwards, 1857), and *A Journey in the Back Country* (New York: Mason, 1860). In *The Cotton Kingdom* (New York: Mason, 1861), Olmsted made his culminating contribution to the subject. While no other traveler left so extensive and valuable a record, one so free of bias, even Olmsted's work must be evaluated with a view to his orientation as a classical liberal in economics, and some of his views on the productivity of slave labor may well have been affected by these convictions.

The memoirs, letters, and autobiographies of the slaveholding class also contribute to the historian's understanding of the slave system. The inquiring historian will find listings of the most valuable of these in Blassingame, *The Slave Community*, pp. 242–44. Although no more concerned with slavery than with other dominant aspects of Southern life, the recently published letters of the Charles Colcock Jones family, because of their sheer volume, contribute much to our knowledge of the relations between slaves and masters in the best educated and most humane circles of Southern society. These letters were edited by Robert M. Myers as *The Children of Pride* (New Haven: Yale University Press, 1972), and, while good as representative of a genre of material, have appeared too recently to be in the better-known bibliographies.

Among the most illuminating half-dozen or so such works, are Susan Dabney Smedes, *Memorials of a Southern Planter* (Baltimore: Cushings & Bailey, 1887), and Mary Boykin Chesnut's *A Diary from Dixie*, edited by Ben Ames Williams (Boston: Houghton Mifflin, Sentry ed., 1949). Sharply critical of the entire slave system, Frances Anne Kemble, then the wife of the large slaveholder Pierce Butler, also left an important record of her impressions of life on her husband's Georgia estate in her *Journal of a Residence on a Georgia Plantation in 1838–39* (London: Longman, Green, Longman, Roberts & Green, 1863). For eighteenth-century slavery *The Diary of Colonel Landon Carter of Sabine Hall, 1752–1778,* edited by Jack P. Greene in two volumes (Charlottesville: University of Virginia Press, 1965), is the best single printed source deriving from the planter class in its period.

Newspapers are very important for the study of slavery, not only for what they reveal about prices and markets and the general economy of the plantation South, but also because runaways were often advertised. Gerald L. Mullin, in his *Flight and Rebellion: Slave Resistance in Eighteenth Century Virginia* (New York: Oxford University Press, 1972), made good use of such advertisements to determine the characteristics of eighteenth-century fugitives. Important publications available for this kind of work in the Colonial era are the *Maryland Gazette,* the *South Carolina Gazette,* the (Williamsburg) *Virginia Gazette,* and the (Richmond) *Virginia Argus.* For the nineteenth century the indispensable source is the New Orleans publication, *DeBow's Review,* edited by James B. Dunwoody DeBow, which carried many articles relating to the management of slave labor, the health of slaves, their nutrition and housing. *Niles Weekly Register* also reported on topics relating to slavery—often very critically. Agricultural journals concentrate on the same subjects. General information on the newspapers and agricultural magazines most useful for the various regions of the South may be found in the bibliographies of the state monographs named in the final section of this bibliographical note.

The United States Census Reports for 1820, 1830, 1840, 1850, and 1860 offer a wealth of demographic and social data, showing changes over time in the concentration of slave population, conditions of life, and the plantation economy. Easy access to some of these statistics is afforded by *Historical Statistics of the United States, Colonial Times to 1957*, prepared by the Bureau of the Census and the Social Science Research Council, and published by the U.S. Government Printing Office in 1960.

The larger manuscript libraries, especially in the Southern states, offer vast treasures of letters, documents, and rare books bearing on the slave system. The most famous of such resources are the Southern Historical Collection at the University of North Carolina in Chapel Hill and the Library of Congress in Washington, D.C.; other less thoroughly worked libraries are equally significant for the researcher, especially if he has a particular aspect of slavery in mind. The Alderman Library at the University of Virginia is richly endowed with materials from the eighteenth century, and in the industrial use of slaves. The South Caroliniana Collection in the University of South Carolina (Columbia, S.C.), the Department of Archives at Louisiana State University (Baton Rouge, La.), the Duke University Library (Durham, N.C.) are notable collections. To name all would be futile, and the inquiring student could hardly do better at the beginning than to consult the list of libraries visited by Kenneth M. Stampp in *The Peculiar Institution*, pages 431–36. But he should consult also the best index to manuscript collections, the *National Union Catalogue of Manuscript Collections* (Ann Arbor, Mich.: J. W. Edwards, 1962—), remembering always that, in manuscript work, patience pays. Many libraries have vaster holdings than their economic substance permits them to catalogue thoroughly, and in most instances the librarians and archivists are able, and more than willing, to assist the scholar who can describe with some accuracy the kind of material he wants to see. Archives present a problem for students accustomed to manuscript libraries, for in such libraries, materials are organized under the names of persons who wrote, received, made, or donated the letters, whereas in archives materials and documents are usually organized under the institution, department, bureau, or branch of government that accumulated the materials in the course of business. Many materials are overlooked because the researcher fails to trace clues through their probable course into some archival repository. These repositories are often rich in the substance of social history; thus, in studying slavery the state and federal archives should be consulted, as well as the historical society collections and university libraries.

Several manuscript and document collections have been assembled, edited, and published, and for students unable to travel extensively on a research project, these are especially important. Ulrich B. Phillips's *Planta-tion and Frontier, 1649–1863* (Cleveland: A. H. Clark, 1909), vols. 1 and 2 of John R. Commons and others, eds., *A Documentary History of American In-dustrial Society*, in eleven volumes, is rich and varied. James M. McPher-son and others, eds., *Blacks in America: Bibliographical Essays* (Garden City, N.Y.: Doubleday, Anchor Books, 1972), on pages 12–13, offers a list-ing of original documents reproduced in collected anthologies, and Wil-liam K. Scarborough in the bibliography of his *The Overseer: Plantation Management in the Old South* (Baton Rouge: Louisiana State University Press, 1966) pp. 236–37, offers an excellent list specifically relating to the slave system.

The natural way to begin the serious study of slavery is through the out-standing general works and monographs on individual states, localities, or specific aspects of the slave system. Not only does the reader discover in such books the areas of scholarly contention, he also finds the footnotes and bibliographical matter valuable leads to sources that could be of even greater value to a researcher who checks them again for a use other than that of the original researcher. Success would depend on the question asked of the material, and the intervening progress of scholarship. For in-stance, in Albert Bushnell Hart's *Slavery and Aboliton, 1831–1841* (New York: Harper, 1906) will be found an excellent basic bibliography. Hart's work reflected a New England and anti-slavery background, a view quickly challenged by the Georgian Ulrich Bonnell Phillips, in his monu-mental *American Negro Slavery: A Survey of the Supply, Employment and Control of Negro Labor* . . . (New York: Appleton, 1918). His *Life and Labor in the Old South* (Boston: Little, Brown, 1929) represented a consider-able modification of views expressed or implicit in the earlier work, and suggests that if Phillips had lived longer he might well have eliminated the flaw that has opened his work to so much criticism in recent years.

Although Phillips's work was flawed by his assumption of black racial inferiority—a prejudice shared by most white writers of the period—he is nevertheless essential reading because of the broad knowledge of South-ern agriculture he displayed, the developmental and evolutionary frame-work of the special topics covered, and his footnote references to a wide range of sources. In time Kenneth M. Stampp wrote a work of transcen-dent importance on a scale comparable to Phillips's *American Negro Slav-ery*, but free of Phillips's racial assumptions. *The Peculiar Institution* (New York: Knopf, 1956) contains in its footnotes numerous helpful leads, and in its bibliography a listing of the important manuscript collections in Southern libraries.

Also basic as an introduction to the study of slavery is Stanley Elkins's

Slavery. The bibliographical footnotes cover a great variety of topics, and the evaluation of the importance of the works he mentions is not the smallest part of their value to the inquiring scholar. Although Elkins's view that blacks were to a large extent shattered by their experience in bondage (with serious and perduring effects on personality and family life) has been challenged by many scholars, his work opened many fruitful areas of investigation, and remains a most important book for the study of slavery. A recent and comprehensive study of slavery is Eugene D. Genovese's *Roll, Jordan, Roll* (New York, Harper & Row, 1974), especially important for its coverage of the slave's ideas about time, religion, his life. Another new work providing interesting contrasts is Stanley Engerman and Robert Fogel, *Time on the Cross,* in two volumes (Boston: Little, Brown, 1974), a work that relies on a computerized analysis of available statistical data to reach favorable conclusions about the physical care of slave property at a variance with much that has been written since Phillips's volumes appeared. Their conclusions about the profitability of slavery, on the other hand, would have surprised Phillips, while most subsequent writers would question only the extent of the profitability and efficiency Fogel and Engerman have described. Though the bibliographical matter may not be of immediate use to scholars, especially those trained as traditional historians, the work is mentioned because it is too new to be listed in the standard bibliographies, and because of its unique character.

Since the appearance in 1955 of Elkins's *Slavery,* scholars have become increasingly involved in the comparison of slavery in North America with slavery in other parts of the Western Hemisphere. In a general collection of essays on this topic, edited by Laura Foner and Eugene D. Genovese as *Slavery in the New World* (Englewood Cliffs, N.J.: Prentice-Hall, 1969), reference is made to most of the best work done before its publication. The towering work of David Brion Davis, *The Problem of Slavery in Western Culture* (Ithaca: Cornell University Press, 1966), deserves special mention in this category, for its breadth and erudition. The author's concern with the response of institutions to the problem of slavery is carried forward in the more recent work, *The Problem of Slavery in the Age of Revolution, 1770–1823* (idem, 1974).

Many important general books on slavery have been omitted from the preceding paragraphs, but those noted seem essential, and useful especially for the initial development of a working bibliography. Further aid will be found on special topics in James M. McPherson and others, *Blacks in America,* mentioned above. On pages 4–7 are listed dozens of further bibliographical books and articles. A work not listed in that section of

Blacks in America but of special value in the bibliography of slavery is Bennett H. Wall's "African Slavery" in Arthur S. Link and Rembert W. Patrick, eds., *Writing Southern History: Essays in Historiography in Honor of Fletcher M. Green* (Baton Rouge: Louisiana State University Press, 1965), pp. 175–97.

For the convenience of the general reader, or the purposes of a person working up a bibliography for a particular period, state, region, or topic, the following titles are suggested as being interesting in themselves, and suggestive in their bibliographical references. For the seventeenth and eighteenth centuries see Winthrop D. Jordan, *White over Black; American Attitudes toward the Negro, 1550–1812* (Chapel Hill: University of North Carolina Press, 1968) with its superb "Essay on Sources"; the above-mentioned Gerald W. Mullin, *Flight and Rebellion; Slave Resistance in Eighteenth Century Virginia;* Wesley Frank Craven, *White, Red, and Black; The Seventeenth Century Virginian* (Charlottesville; University Press of Virginia, 1971); Thad W. Tate, Jr., *The Negro in Eighteenth Century Williamsburg* (ibid. 1965); Edmund P. Morgan, "Slavery and Freedom," in *Journal of American History,* vol. 59 (January 1973). For comparable work on South Carolina consult Peter H. Wood, *Black Majority: Negroes in Colonial South Carolina from 1670 through the Stono Rebellion* (New York: Knopf, 1974), and Eugene Sirmans, "The Legal Status of Slaves in South Carolina 1670–1740," in *Journal of Southern History,* vol. 28 (November 1962). Other works in the area are John Spencer Bassett, *Slavery and Servitude in the Colony of North Carolina* (Baltimore: Johns Hopkins Press, 1896); and Lorenzo Greene, *The Negro in Colonial New England* (New York: Columbia University Press, 1942).

The following state studies are valuable for differing reasons: some because they are the only books readily available for their states, some because of their intrinsic merits or readability, some because they have good footnotes and bibliography. James C. Ballagh's *History of Slavery in Virginia* (Baltimore: Johns Hopkins Press, 1902), though quite old, is the only effort to date to comprehend the entire slave period in Virginia. Jeffrey C. Brackett's *The Negro in Maryland: A Study of the Institution of Slavery* (Baltimore: Johns Hopkins Press, 1889) belongs to the same period. Howell M. Henry's *Police Control of the Slave in South Carolina* (Emory, Va., 1914) is similar to the other two works in time of writing, in its emphasis on the entire period of slaveholding, and on the legal aspects of its development. Harrison A. Trexler's *Slavery in Missouri* (Baltimore: Johns Hopkins Press, 1914) is another book from the same era of writing, with a political emphasis.

Ralph B. Flanders's *Plantation Slavery in Georgia* (Chapel Hill: University of North Carolina Press, 1933) and J. Winston Coleman, Jr., *Slave Times in Kentucky* (Chapel Hill: University of North Carolina Press, 1940) are from a more recent period, and standard for their states. More recent studies include Chase C. Mooney, *Slavery in Tennessee* (Bloomington: University of Indiana Press, 1957), Charles Sackett Sydnor, *Slavery in Mississippi* (New York: Appleton, 1933); Joe Gray Taylor, *Negro Slavery in Louisiana* (Baton Rouge: Louisiana State University Press, 1963); James B. Sellers, *Slavery in Alabama* (University: Alabama University Press, 1950), and Orville W. Taylor, *Negro Slavery in Arkansas* (Durham, N.C.: Duke University Press, 1958).

The standard work on the internal slave trade is Frederic Bancroft's *Slave-Trading in the Old South* (Baltimore: J. H. Furst, 1931), but Wendell H. Stephenson's *Isaac Franklin, Slave Trader and Planter of the Old South* (University: University of Alabama Press, 1938) provides a fascinating account of an individual trader. The footnotes and bibliographies of both books afford numerous leads into the original sources of this subject. For further suggestions consult McPherson and others, *Blacks in America*, pp. 58–59. Lewis C. Gray, *History of Agriculture in the Southern United States to 1860*, 2 vols., (Washington, D.C.: Carnegie Institution, 1933), has long been the standard reference for its topic, but a recent book affording more up-to-date references to sources and other books is Harold D. Woodman's *Slavery and the Southern Economy: Sources and Readings* (New York: Harcourt, Brace & World, 1966).

Slavery in the Cities, the South, 1820–1860, by Richard C. Wade (New York, Oxford University Press, 1964), includes no bibliography, but the explicit and valuable footnotes, which may be reached through imaginative use of the index, will lead the reader directly to the sources. Robert Starobin's *Industrial Slavery in the Old South* (New York: Oxford University Press, 1970) includes useful footnotes and a bibliographical essay. For further suggestions on this area of investigation consult the essays of Charles B. Dew, especially "Disciplining Slave Iron Workers in the Antebellum South: Coercion, Conciliation, and Accommodation," in *American Historical Review* 79 (April 1974). Finally, a listing of bibliographies on slavery may be found in McPherson, and others, pp. 4–7. In the newly revised *Harvard Guide to American History* in two volumes (Cambridge: Harvard Unitversity Press, Belknap Press, 1974) drawn up under the direction of Frank Freidel, all the better bibliographies will be found under subject entries.